Grade 5, Unit 1

Meeting Challenges

scottforesman.com

Editorial Offices: Glenview, Illinois • Parsippany, New Jersey • New York, New York
Sales Offices: Boston, Massachusetts • Duluth, Georgia • Glenview, Illinois
Coppell, Texas • Sacramento, California • Mesa, Arizona

We dedicate Reading Street to
Peter Jovanovich.

His wisdom, courage,
and passion for education
are an inspiration to us all.

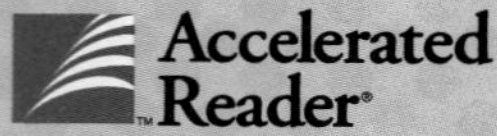

Cover Greg Newbold

About the Cover Artist
Award-winning artist Greg Newbold began drawing and painting at age three—and never stopped. His illustrated books for children include *Spring Song* and *Winter Lullaby*. Mr. Newbold also does illustrations for magazines, motion pictures, and food products, such as catsup and jelly. He creates his illustrations in a studio next to his house, snuggled in the Rocky Mountains of Utah.

ISBN-13: 978-0-328-24385-3

ISBN-10: 0-328-24385-X

6 7 8 9 10 11 V063 16 15 14 13 12 11 10 09
CC:N1

Reading STREET

Where the Love of Reading Begins

There's a moose on the loose.

Where can I go to find just what I need?

You don't have to go far to find the big, lovable, moose-spectacular reading program you crave. You're on *Reading Street,* where the love of reading begins. *Reading Street* provides research-based reading instruction that meets the needs of teachers, students, and administrators. It works perfectly with *Scott Foresman My Sidewalks* and *Reading Street for the Guided Reading Teacher* to answer all your reading needs.

Where the Love of Reading Begins

Literature for Learning and Thinking

Deepen students' understanding with literature that's organized around themes.

Priority Skills and Success Predictors

Teach the right skills at the right time and monitor students' progress.

Differentiated Instruction for Group Time

Ensure success for students of varying ability levels and experiences.

More Reading Support

Reinforce instruction with intensive reading intervention and leveled text.

When I was little, I'd curl up in bed and wait for a sssssssssstory.

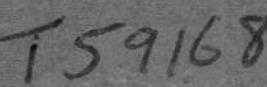

In ancient Greece there was a golden fleece.

How do I help every child love to read?

It all starts with a "golden" collection of literature. *Reading Street* has funny stories, scary stories, real-life adventures! One story perfectly leads to the next—one concept is explored from many sides. Children have enough time to think about a big idea, learn, and enjoy.

Reading Street
is a solid gold hit.
Be-bop-a-loopa.
PRE-K/KINDERGARTEN
60% Fiction • 40% Nonfiction
GRADES 1–3
50% Fiction • 50% Nonfiction
GRADES 4–6
40% Fiction • 60% Nonfiction

My class needs more nonfiction.

Reading Street is nicely balanced and geared to introduce more and more nonfiction.

How do I get children to think about what they read?

The literature in *Reading Street* is organized around unit themes. Each selection connects and expands the concept to build deeper understanding.

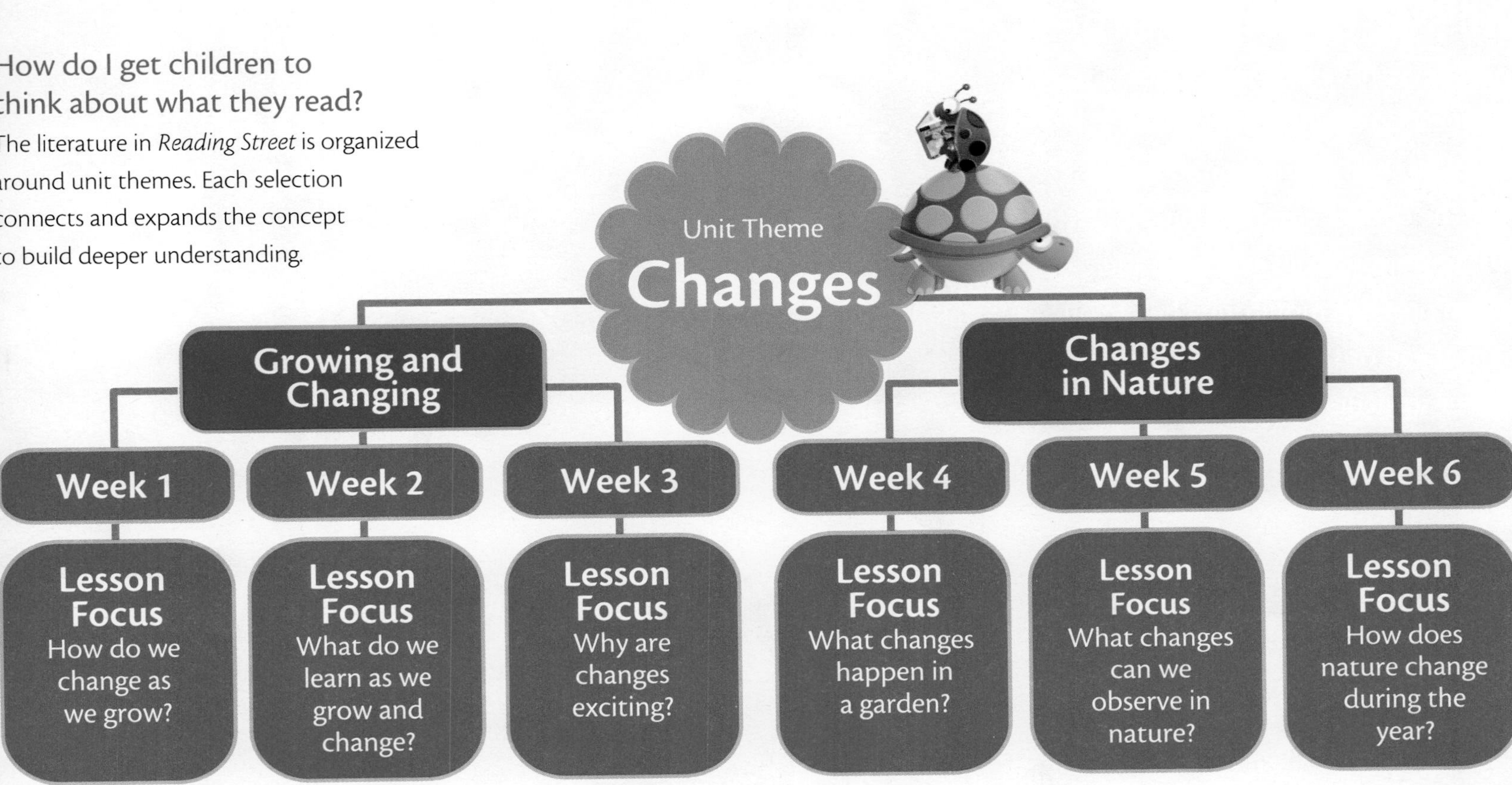

Grade 1, Unit 3 Organization

There's never enough time to cover content areas.

Every selection in *Reading Street* emphasizes a science or social studies concept. Your reading lessons become the tools to meet content-area standards.

Don't lose sleep! You're on Reading Street.

Am I teaching the right skills at the right time?

You'll never have to worry about this question again. *Reading Street* prioritizes skills instruction so you place the correct emphasis on the most important skills at your grade. Built-in progress monitoring helps you zoom ahead or slow down, depending on your students' needs.

Help me prioritize my day!
Reading Street prioritizes the five core areas of reading instruction across the grades, so you know where to place your instructional emphasis. By assessing key predictors, you can ensure student success. (See below.)

PRIORITY SKILL	SUCCESS PREDICTOR
PHONEMIC AWARENESS	Blending and Segmenting
PHONICS	Word Reading
FLUENCY	Words Correct per Minute
VOCABULARY	Word Knowledge
COMPREHENSION	Retelling

Can I predict reading success?
The research says "YES!" Only *Reading Street* helps you monitor students' progress by assessing the research-based predictors of reading success.

Monitor Progress

Check Retelling Rubric 4 3 2 1

If... students have difficulty retelling the story, **then...** use the Scoring Rubric for Retelling below to help move them toward fluent retelling.

SUCCESS PREDICTOR

I need a data management system.
Success Tracker is an online assessment and data management system that prescribes remediation, helps with grouping, and disaggregates and aggregates data.
Learn more at www.scottforesman.com/tours.

Hey, the people who created this worked hard. Please, no ZZZs.

One size never fits all.

How can I make sure every child reads?

One of the most important lessons our teachers taught us was that everyone is unique *and* the same. *Reading Street* provides a daily plan for whole-group teaching and for meeting with small groups to attend to specific needs. Don't you just love it?

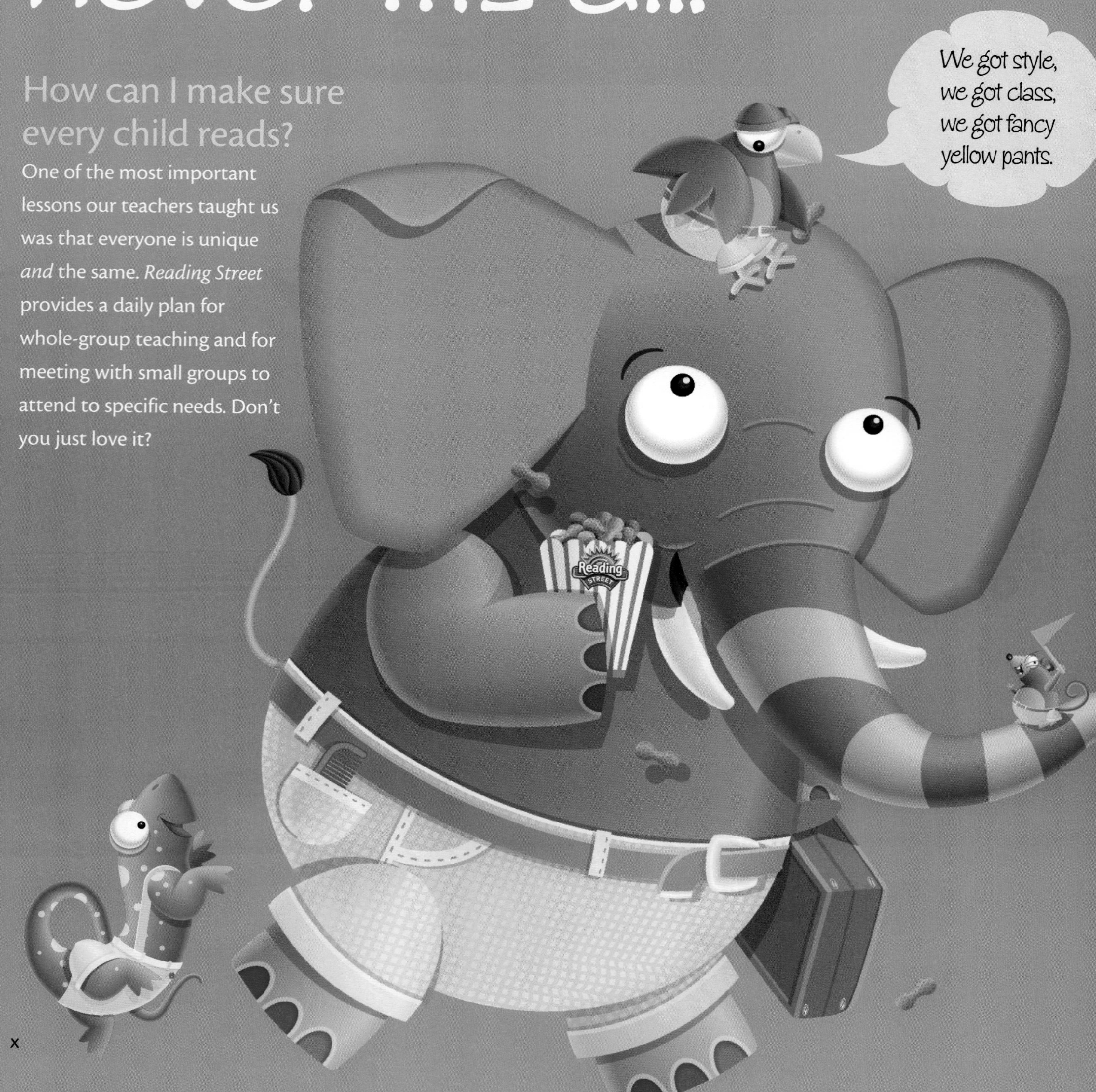

We got style, we got class, we got fancy yellow pants.
Reading
STREET

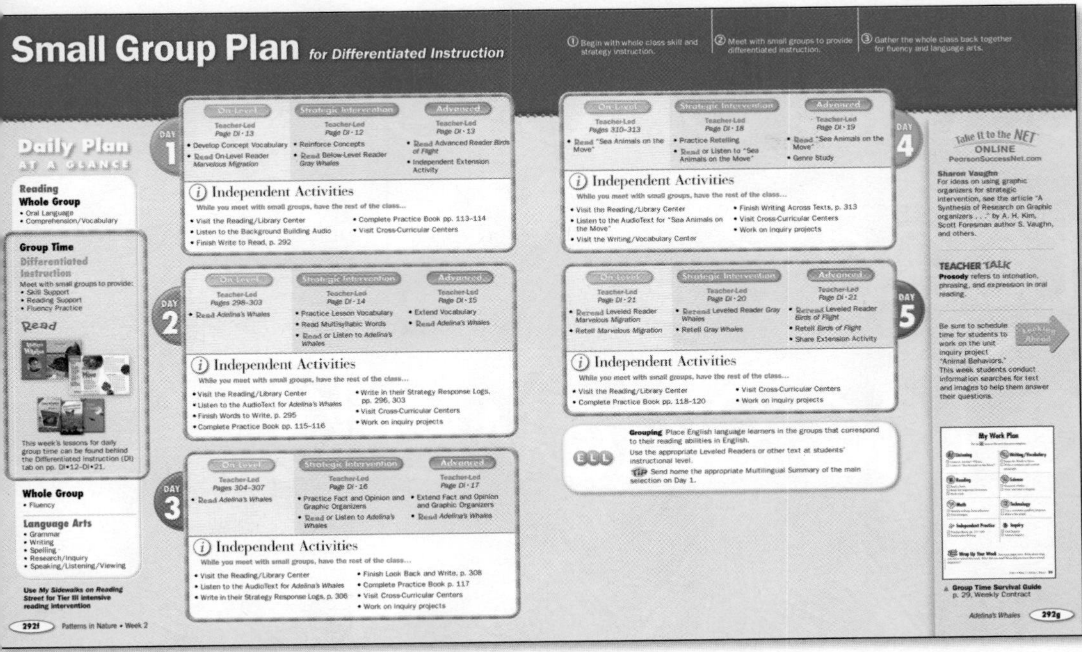

Teacher's Edition Grade 4 Unit 3

Give me a plan for group time. *Reading Street* provides a daily plan for whole-group and small-group instruction. Assign the Independent Activities to the rest of the class when you meet with your small groups.

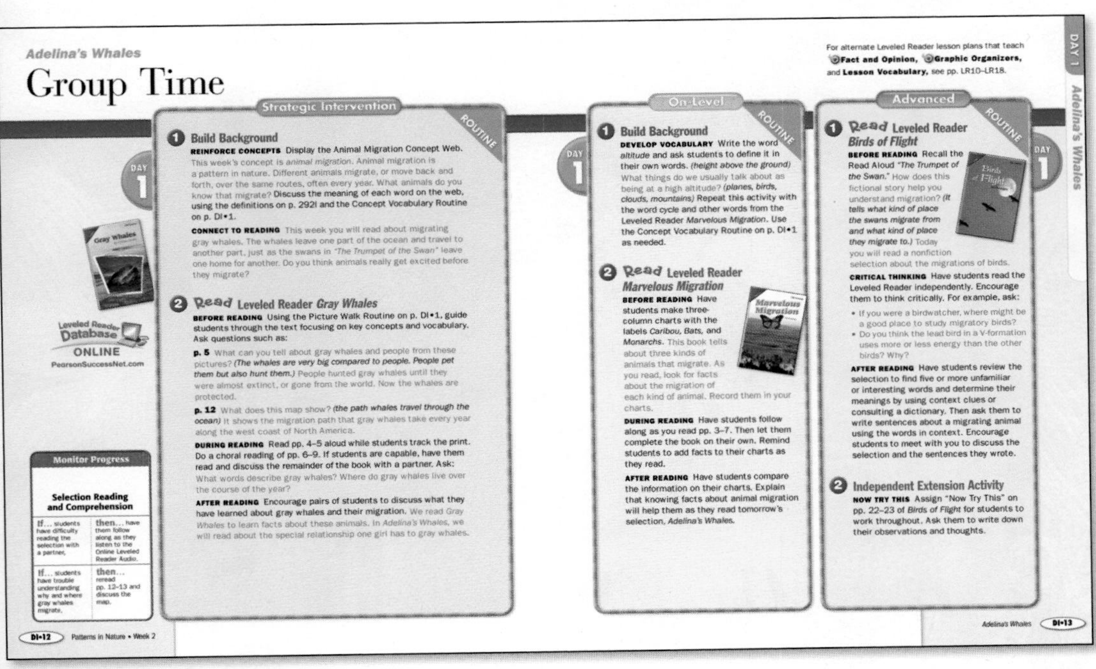

Teacher's Edition Grade 4 Unit 3

Help me teach my struggling and advanced readers. *Reading Street* has daily instructional routines for both your Strategic Intervention and Advanced groups. See the Differentiated Instruction section at the back of the Teacher's Edition.

ELL

How can I support my English language learners? Look for ELL instructional strategies, alternate comprehension lessons, and grade-level readers to build vocabulary and key concepts each week.

Q: Why did the chicken cross the road? A: To get to the sidewalk!

What do I do when *Reading Street* isn't enough?

Every teacher knows that some students need more support. For those children, Scott Foresman provides *My Sidewalks*—an intensive reading intervention program that aligns perfectly with *Reading Street. My Sidewalks* accelerates reading development for children at risk.

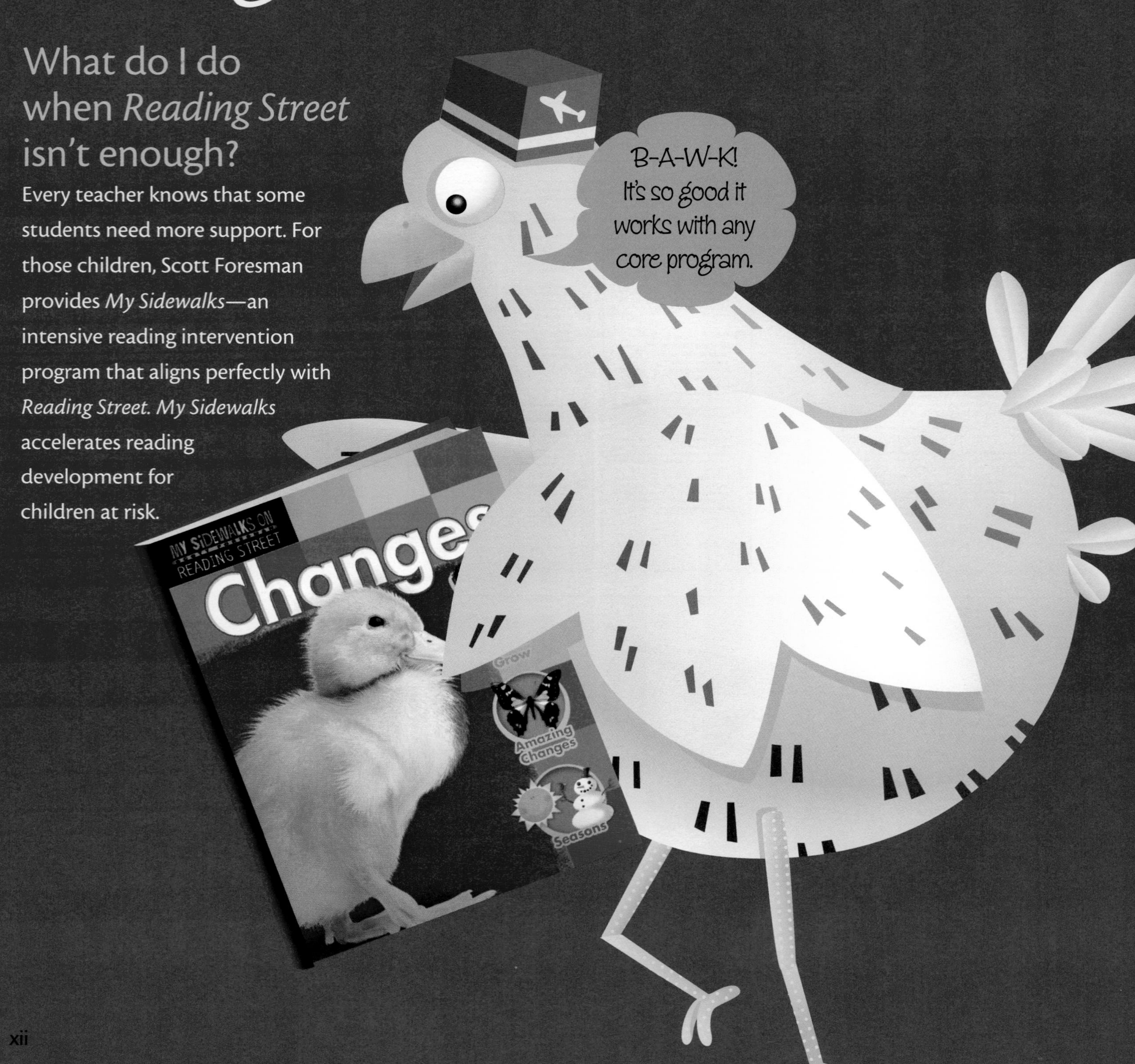

What is Tier III Instruction?

Tier III instruction is for students with low reading skills and a lack of adequate progress. *My Sidewalks* provides sustained instruction, intensive language and concept development, and more focus on critical comprehension skills and strategies for Tier III students.

TIER I PRIMARY
Comprehensive Core Program

TIER II SECONDARY
Core Program Plus Strategic Intervention

TIER III TERTIARY
Intensive Reading Intervention

MY SIDEWALKS ON
SCOTT FORESMAN
READING STREET
Intensive Reading Intervention

How does *My Sidewalks* support *Reading Street?*

My Sidewalks provides daily lessons for 30 weeks—for a minimum of 30 minutes a day. The oral language, vocabulary, and concepts developed in *My Sidewalks* parallel those in *Reading Street.*

Reading Street Student Edition

My Sidewalks Student Reader

When do I teach *My Sidewalks?*

Use *My Sidewalks* during group time, as a pull-out intervention program, or as a before- or after-school program. The *My Sidewalks* acceleration plan prioritizes skills so you teach less, more thoroughly.

Are you an
adventurous
reading
teacher?

Do you love teaching with leveled text?

Reading Street for the Guided Reading Teacher will support you in organizing research-based reading instruction. It features the *Guide on the Side* to implement instruction around leveled text. All the resources are derived from *Reading Street* and its proven teaching methods.

I want to match my students to leveled text.

Reading Street for the Guided Reading Teacher organizes instruction around leveled text and helps you differentiate instruction. It's a complete guided reading program with leveled readers, lessons plans, practice, and assessment.

Does the program support *Reading Street*?

The scope and sequence, instructional routines, and teacher resources all align with *Reading Street.* Use the *Guide on the Side* as your main Teacher's Edition or to supplement your *Reading Street* Teacher's Edition.

READING

Pace Yourself

How do I know I am covering all the skills before the test?

This chart shows the instructional sequence from Scott Foresman Reading Street. *You can use this pacing guide as is to ensure you're following a comprehensive scope and sequence, or you can adjust it to match your school/district focus calendar, curriculum map, or testing schedule.*

BACK TO SCHOOL!

	Unit 1					Unit 2	
	WEEK 1	WEEK 2	WEEK 3	WEEK 4	WEEK 5	WEEK 6	WEEK 7
Comprehension Skill	Realism and Fantasy	Sequence of Events	Sequence of Events	Realism and Fantasy	Character and Setting	Main Idea and Details	Character
Comprehension Strategy	Activate/ Use Prior Knowledge	Summarize	Visualize	Monitor and Fix Up	Story Structure	Graphic Organizers	Visualize
Vocabulary Strategy/Skill	Context Clues/ Homonyms	Word Structure/ Compound Words	Reference Sources/ Unfamiliar Words	Context Clues/ Multiple-Meaning Words	Word Structure/ Prefixes and Suffixes	Context Clues/ Synonyms	Context Clues/ Unfamiliar Words
Fluency	Accuracy	Appropriate Pace/Rate	Express Character-ization	Expression/ Intonation	Appropriate Phrasing	Accuracy and Appropriate Pace/Rate	Express Character-ization
Spelling/ Word Work	Short Vowels VCCV	Plurals *-s, -es*	Adding *-ed, -ing, -er, -est*	Long Vowel Digraphs	Vowel Sounds in *out* and *toy*	Syllable Patterns V/CV, VC/V	Words Ending in *-le*

				Unit 3				
	WEEK 8	WEEK 9	WEEK 10	WEEK 11	WEEK 12	WEEK 13	WEEK 14	WEEK 15
Comprehension Skill	Main Idea and Details	Author's Purpose	Draw Conclusions	Cause and Effect	Author's Purpose	Draw Conclusions	Generalize	Compare/ Contrast
Comprehension Strategy	Monitor and Fix Up	Predict	Ask Questions	Story Structure	Summarize	Ask Questions	Answer Questions	Monitor and Fix Up
Vocabulary Strategy/Skill	Dictionary/ Unfamiliar Words	Context Clues/ Antonyms	Context Clues/ Unfamiliar Words	Word Structure/ Endings	Glossary/ Unfamiliar Words	Word Structure/ Compound Words	Context Clues/ Unfamiliar Words	Dictionary/ Unfamiliar Words
Fluency	Expression/ Intonation	Appropriate Phrasing	Read Silently with Fluency	Expression/ Intonation	Express Character-ization	Appropriate Phrasing	Accuracy and Appropriate Pace/Rate	Read Silently with Fluency and Accuracy
Spelling/ Word Work	Compound Words	Words with *spl, thr, squ, str*	Digraphs *sh, th, ph, ch, tch*	Contractions	Prefixes *un-, re-, mis-, dis-*	Consonant Sounds /j/ and /k/	Suffixes *-ly, -ful, -ness, -less*	Words with *wr, kn, mb, gn*

	Unit 4					Unit 5	
	WEEK 16	WEEK 17	WEEK 18	WEEK 19	WEEK 20	WEEK 21	WEEK 22
Comprehension Skill	Cause and Effect	Compare and Contrast	Generalize	Fact and Opinion	Plot and Theme	Compare and Contrast	Fact and Opinion
Comprehension Strategy	Answer Questions	Ask Questions	Activate and Use Prior Knowledge	Monitor and Fix Up	Graphic Organizers	Predict	Text Structure
Vocabulary Strategy/Skill	Word Structure/ Endings	Word Structure/ Compound Words	Context Clues/ Multiple-Meaning Words	Context Clues/ Multiple-Meaning Words	Word Structure/ Endings	Context Clues/ Synonyms	Context Clues/ Antonyms
Fluency	Accuracy and Appropriate Pace/Rate	Read Silently with Fluency and Accuracy	Character-ization	Appropriate Phrasing	Expression/ Intonation	Accuracy and Appropriate Pace/Rate	Read Silently with Fluency and Accuracy
Spelling/ Word Work	Plurals	Vowels with *r*	Prefixes *pre-, mid-, over-, out-*	Suffixes *-er, -or, -ess, -ist*	Syllable Pattern VCCCV	Syllable Patterns CVVC, CVV	Homo-phones

				Unit 6				
	WEEK 23	WEEK 24	WEEK 25	WEEK 26	WEEK 27	WEEK 28	WEEK 29	WEEK 30
Comprehension Skill	Sequence	Draw Conclusions	Author's Purpose	Main Idea	Cause and Effect	Fact and Opinion	Plot and Theme	Generalize
Comprehension Strategy	Monitor and Fix Up	Summarize	Prior Knowledge	Text Structure	Graphic Organizers	Answer Questions	Visualize	Predict
Vocabulary Strategy/Skill	Word Structure/ Compound Words	Context Clues/ Unfamiliar Words	Context Clues/ Homonyms	Word Structure/ Prefixes	Context Clues/ Antonyms	Glossary/ Unfamiliar Words	Word Structure/ Prefixes and Suffixes	Context Clues/ Synonyms
Fluency	Expression/ Intonation	Express Character-ization	Appropriate Phrasing	Accuracy and Appropriate Pace/Rate	Appropriate Phrasing	Read Silently with Fluency and Accuracy	Accuracy and Appropriate Pace/Rate	Express Character-ization
Spelling/ Word Work	Vowel Sound in *ball*	More Vowel Sound in *ball*	Suffixes *-y, -ish, -hood, -ment*	Vowels in *tooth, cook*	Schwa	Words with *-tion, -sion, -ture*	Multisyllabic Words	Related Words

4 IT'S TEST TIME! WHEN IS YOUR STATE TEST? 5

Will I teach the skills my students need?

Reading Street for the Guided Reading Teacher provides a comprehensive scope and sequence that helps you pace instruction and prepare students for your state test.

Welcome to Reading Street!

Hip, hip, hooray! We're on the way.

PRE-KINDERGARTEN

KINDERGARTEN

GRADE 1

Student Edition (Unit 1)

Student Edition (Unit 2)

Student Edition (Unit 3)

Student Edition (Unit 4)

Student Edition (Unit 5)

5 Teacher's Editions
(1 per unit)

GRADE 2

Student Edition
(Units 1–3)

Student Edition
(Units 4–6)

6 Teacher's Editions
(1 per unit)

GRADE 3

Student Edition
(Units 1–3)

Student Edition
(Units 4–6)

6 Teacher's Editions
(1 per unit)

GRADE 4

Student Edition

6 Teacher's Editions
(1 per unit)

GRADE 5

Student Edition

6 Teacher's Editions
(1 per unit)

GRADE 6

Student Edition

6 Teacher's Editions
(1 per unit)

MORE READING SUPPORT

My Sidewalks Intensive
Reading Intervention (Levels A–E)

Reading Street for the Guided
Reading Teacher (Grades 1–6)

Ready, Teddy?

(On Reading Street, you're ready for everything and anything!)

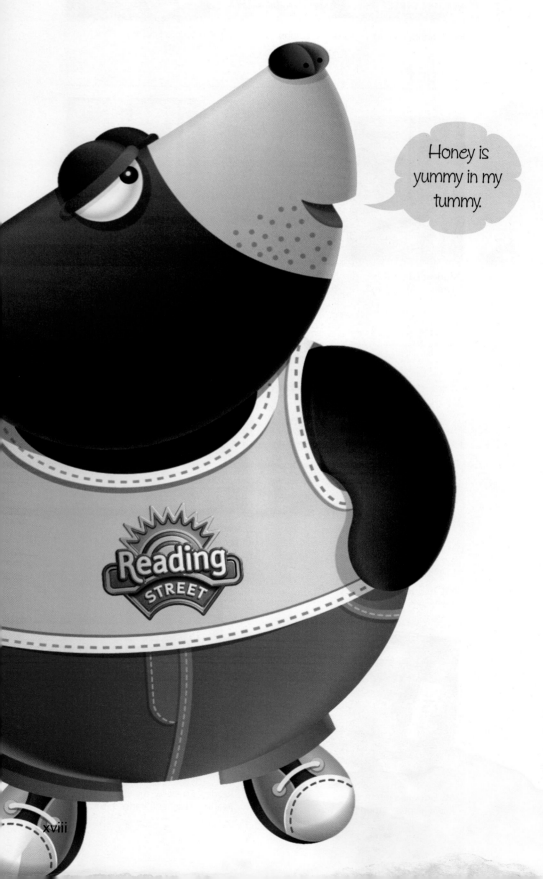

Honey is yummy in my tummy.

Reading Street

Student Editions (1–6)

Teacher's Editions (PreK–6)

Assessment

Assessment Handbook (K–6)

Baseline Group Tests (K–6)

DIBELS™ Assessments (K–6)

Examview® Test Generator CD-ROM (2–6)

Fresh Reads for Differentiated Test Practice (1–6)

Online Success Tracker™ (K–6)*

Selection Tests Teacher's Manual (1–6)

Unit and End-of-Year Benchmark Tests (K–6)

Leveled Readers

Concept Literacy Leveled Readers (K–1)

Independent Leveled Readers (K)

Kindergarten Student Readers (K)

Leveled Reader Teaching Guides (K–6)

Leveled Readers (1–6)

Listen to Me Readers (K)

Online Leveled Readers Database (K–6)*

Take-Home Leveled Readers (K–6)

Trade Books and Big Books

Big Books (PreK–2)

Read Aloud Trade Books (PreK–K)

Sing with Me Big Book (1–2)

Trade Book Library (1–6)

* 

)ecodable Readers

)ecodable Readers (K–3)

ɛtrategic Intervention
)ecodable Readers (1–2)

'ake-Home Decodable Readers (K–3)

'honics and Word Study

ılphabet Cards in English and Spanish
'reK–K)

ılphabet Chart in English and Spanish
'reK–K)

ınimal ABCs Activity Guide (K)

inger Tracing Cards (PreK–K)

atterns Books (PreK–K)

honics Activities CD-ROM (PreK–2)*

'honics Activities Mats (K)

'honics and Spelling Practice Book (1–3)

'honics and Word-Building Board and Letters
PreK–3)

'honics Songs and Rhymes Audio CD (K–2)

'honics Songs and Rhymes Flip Chart (K–2)

'icture Word Cards (PreK–K)

'lastic Letter Tiles (K)

ound-Spelling Cards and Wall Charts (1–2)

trategies for Word Analysis (4–6)

Vord Study and Spelling Practice Book (4–6)

.anguage Arts

)aily Fix-It Transparencies (K–6)

Grammar & Writing Book and
'eacher's Annotated Edition, The (1–6)

Grammar and Writing Practice Book
ınd Teacher's Manual (1–6)

Grammar Transparencies (1–6)

ɩix-Trait Writing Posters (1–6)

Vriting Kit (1–6)

Vriting Rubrics and Anchor Papers (1–6)

Vriting Transparencies (1–6)

Practice and Additional Resources

AlphaBuddy Bear Puppet (K)

Alphasaurus Annie Puppet (PreK)

Amazing Words Posters (K–2)

Centers Survival Kit (PreK–6)

Graphic Organizer Book (2–6)

Graphic Organizer Flip Chart (K–1)

High-Frequency Word Cards (K)

Kindergarten Review (1)

Practice Book and Teacher's Manual (K–6)

Read Aloud Anthology (PreK–2)

Readers' Theater Anthology (K–6)

Research into Practice (K–6)

Retelling Cards (K–6)

Scott Foresman Research Base (K–6)

Skill Transparencies (2–6)

Songs and Rhymes Flip Chart (PreK)

Talk with Me, Sing with Me Chart (PreK–K)

Tested Vocabulary Cards (1–6)

Vocabulary Transparencies (1–2)

Welcome to Reading Street (PreK–1)

ELL

ELL and Transition Handbook (PreK–6)

ELL Comprehensive Kit (1–6)

ELL Posters (K–6)

ELL Readers (1–6)

ELL Teaching Guides (1–6)

Ten Important Sentences (1–6)

Digital Components

AudioText CDs (PreK–6)

Background Building Audio CDs (3–6)

ExamView® Test Generator
CD-ROM (2–6)

Online Lesson Planner (K–6)

Online New Literacies Activities (1–6)*

Online Professional Development (1–6)

Online Story Sort (K–6)*

Online Student Editions (1–6)*

Online Success Tracker™ (K–6)*

Online Teacher's Editions (PreK–6)

Phonics Activities CD-ROM (PreK–2)*

Phonics Songs and Rhymes
Audio CD (K–2)

Sing with Me/Background Building
Audio CDs (PreK–2)

Songs and Rhymes Audio CD (PreK)

My Sidewalks Early Reading Intervention (K)

My Sidewalks Intensive Reading Intervention (Levels A–E)

Reading Street for the Guided Reading Teacher (1–6)

* 

We told you a moose was on the loose.

Reading Street Program Authors

Peter Afflerbach, Ph.D.
Professor, Department of Curriculum and Instruction
University of Maryland at College Park

Camille L.Z. Blachowicz, Ph.D.
Professor of Education
National-Louis University

Candy Dawson Boyd, Ph.D.
Professor, School of Education
Saint Mary's College of California

Wendy Cheyney, Ed.D.
Professor of Special Education and Literacy, Florida International University

Connie Juel, Ph.D.
Professor of Education, School of Education, Stanford University

Edward J. Kame'enui, Ph.D.
Professor and Director, Institute for the Development of Educational Achievement, University of Oregon

Donald J. Leu, Ph.D.
John and Maria Neag Endowed Chair in Literacy and Technology
University of Connecticut

Marvin D. Moose, Ph.D.
Reading Street University
(Hee-hee)

Jeanne R. Paratore, Ed.D.
Associate Professor of Education
Department of Literacy and Language Development
Boston University

P. David Pearson, Ph.D.
Professor and Dean,
Graduate School of Education
University of California, Berkeley

Sam L. Sebesta, Ed.D.
Professor Emeritus,
College of Education,
University of Washington, Seattle

Deborah Simmons, Ph.D.
Professor, College of Education and Human Development
Texas A&M University
(Not pictured)

Sharon Vaughn, Ph.D.
H.E. Hartfelder/Southland Corporation Regents Professor
University of Texas

Susan Watts-Taffe, Ph.D.
Independent Literacy Researcher
Cincinnati, Ohio

Karen Kring Wixson, Ph.D.
Professor of Education
University of Michigan

Consulting Authors

m Cummins, Ph.D.
rofessor
epartment of Curriculum, Teaching
nd Learning, University of Toronto
oronto, Ontario, Canada
nglish Language Learners

ily Wong Fillmore, Ph.D.
rofessor Emerita
raduate School of Education
niversity of California, Berkeley
nglish Language Learners

arbara Kay Foots, M.Ed.
cience Education Consultant
ouston, Texas
cience Integration

eorgia Earnest García, Ph.D.
rofessor
anguage and Literacy Division,
niversity of Illinois at Urbana-
hampaign
nglish Language Learners

eorge González, Ph.D.
rofessor (Retired)
chool of Education, University of Texas
an-American, Edinburg
nglish Language Learners,
ilingual Education

alerie Ooka Pang, Ph.D.
rofessor
chool of Teacher Education
an Diego State University
ocial Studies Integration

ally M. Reis, Ph.D.
rofessor and Department Head
ducational Psychology
niversity of Connecticut
ifted and Talented

Consultants

. Karen Hatfield, Ed.D.
arrodsburg, Kentucky
ssessment

ynn F. Howard, M.Ed.
untersville, North Carolina
ssessment

tudent Edition Reviewers

ahna Anhalt
eading Coordinator
eForest Area School District
eForest, Wisconsin

eresa M. Beard
ary Elementary School
ary, North Carolina

Ebony Cross
Glassmanor Elementary School
Oxon Hill, Maryland

Melisa G. Figurelli
Fourth and Fifth Grade Teacher
Hans Herr Elementary School
Lampeter, Pennsylvania

Jennifer Flynn
Second Grade Teacher
Weatherstone Elementary School
Cary, North Carolina

Linda Halbert
Centennial Elementary School
Springfield, Oregon

Angela Hartman
Hutto Elementary School
Hutto, Texas

Judy Holiday
Program Coordinator for
Special Education
Woodmen Center, Academy SD #20
Colorado Springs, Colorado

Victoria Holman
Third Grade Teacher
Mount Pleasant Elementary School
San Jose, California

Harriett Horton
Barnwell Elementary School
Alpharetta, Georgia

Mary Beth Huber
Elementary Curriculum Specialist
Calcasieu Parish School System
Lake Charles, Louisiana

Jeff James
Fay Wright Elementary School
Salem, Oregon

Debbie Jessen
Learning Strategist
Clifford J. Lawrence Jr. High School
Las Vegas, Nevada

Sherry Johnston
Literacy Coach
Bruce Elementary School
Milwaukee, Wisconsin

Carol Kelly
Hudson School
Union City, New Jersey

Linda Lindley
Fort Hall Elementary School
Pocatello, Idaho

Karen McCarthy
Goddard School
Brockton, Massachusetts

Patsy Mogush
Educational Coordinator
Central Kindergarten Center
Eden Prairie, Minnesota

Stacie Moncrief
Ventura Park Elementary School
Portland, Oregon

Nancy Novickis
Support Services
Douglass Valley Elementary School
United States Air Force Academy,
Colorado

Betty Parsons
Past President
Santa Clara Reading Council
San Jose, California

Greta Peay
Clark County School District
North Las Vegas, Nevada

Leslie Potter
Blackwood Elementary School
Blackwood, New Jersey

Cyndy Reynolds
Williams Elementary School
Georgetown, Texas

Sharyle Shaffer
Fourth Grade Teacher
Summit Elementary School
Smithfield, Utah

Barbara Smith
Goddard School
Brockton, Massachusetts

Jane Stewart
Lakeshore Elementary School
Monroe, Louisiana

Nancey Volenstine
Chinle Elementary School
Chinle, Arizona

Teacher's Edition Reviewers

Alyssa E. Agoston
First Grade Teacher
Elms Elementary School
Jackson, New Jersey

Laura Beltchenko
Wauconda CUSD #118
Wauconda, Illinois

Lisa Bostick
NSU Elementary Lab School
Natchitoches, Louisiana

Debra O. Brown
First Grade Teacher
McFadden School
Murfreesboro, Tennessee

Cheri S. DeLaune
Paulina Elementary School
Paulina, Louisiana

Dr. Susan B. Dold
Elementary English/Language Arts Staff
Development Coordinator
Memphis City Schools
Memphis, Tennessee

Amy Francis
Montview Elementary School
Aurora, Colorado

Dawn Julian
First Grade Teacher
Elms Elementary School
Jackson, New Jersey

Suzette Kelly
Woodmen-Roberts
Elementary School
Colorado Springs, Colorado

Suzanne Lank
Primary Teacher
Maury Elementary School
Alexandria, Virginia

Sharon Loos
Foothills Elementary School
Colorado Springs, Colorado

R. Franklin Mace
Title I Teacher
Bridgeview Elementary Center
South Charleston, West Virginia

Carol Masur
Second Grade Teacher
Elms Elementary School
Jackson, New Jersey

Jennifer D. Montgomery
Houston, Texas

Diana B. Nicholson
Cynthia Mann Elementary School
Boise, Idaho

Richard Potts
Memphis, Tennessee

Antonia Rogers
Richardson Independent
School District
Richardson, Texas

Audrey Sander
Brooklyn, New York

Dr. Johnny Warrick
Gaston County Schools
Gastonia, North Carolina

Diane Weatherstone
Second Grade Teacher
Elms Elementary School
Jackson, New Jersey

Becky Worlds
Charlotte, North Carolina

UNIT
1

Unit 1

Meeting Challenges

Unit 2

Doing the Right Thing

Unit 3

Inventors and Artists

Unit 4

Adapting

nit 5

dventurers

Unit 6

The Unexpected

UNIT 1

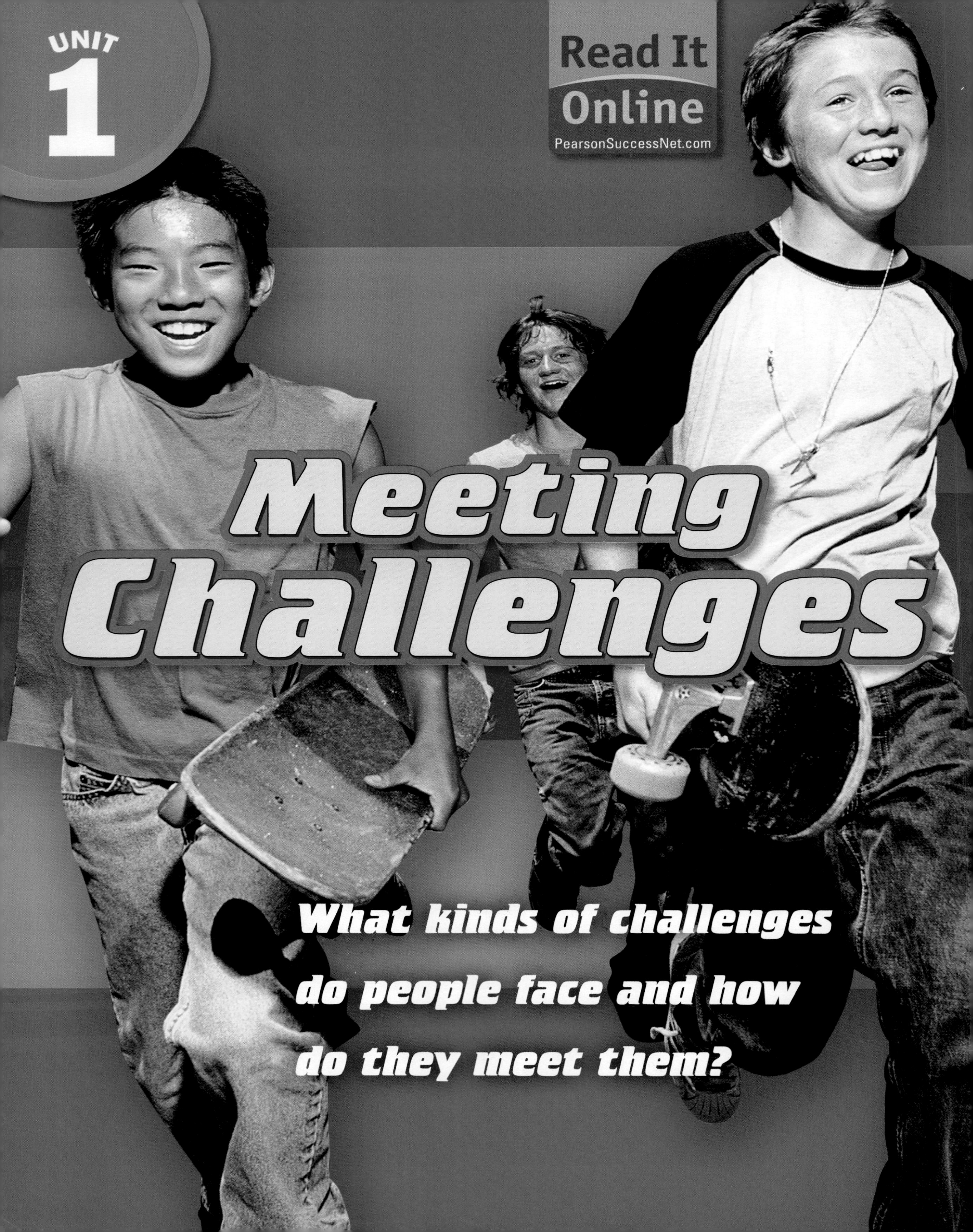

Read It Online
PearsonSuccessNet.com

Meeting Challenges

What kinds of challenges do people face and how do they meet them?

Frindle

A boy must get to know his teacher.

HUMOROUS FICTION

connect to SOCIAL STUDIES

Paired Selection

Punctuation Takes a Vacation

FANTASY

Thunder Rose

A cowgirl faces challenges on the range.

TALL TALE

connect to SCIENCE

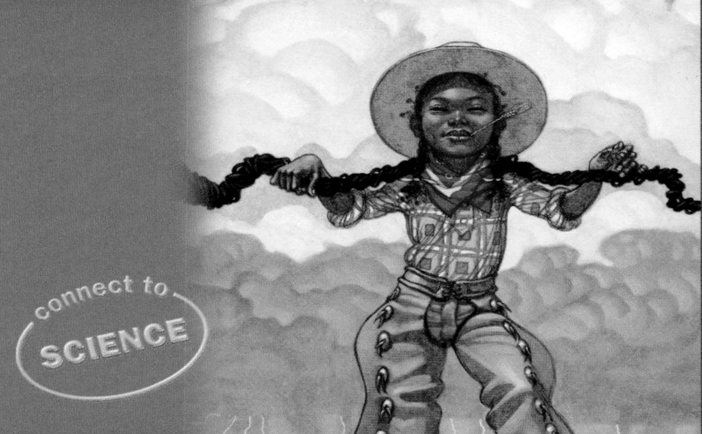

Paired Selection

Measuring Tornadoes

EXPOSITORY NONFICTION

Island of the Blue Dolphins

A young girl must survive on an island alone.

HISTORICAL FICTION

connect to SOCIAL STUDIES

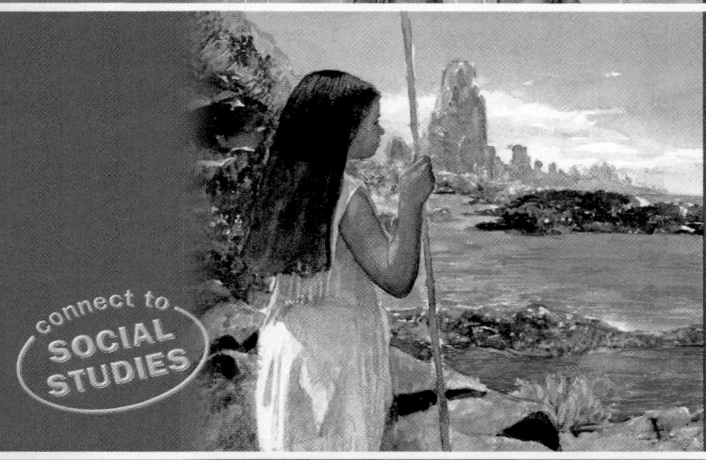

Paired Selection

Seven Survival Questions

INTERVIEW

Satchel Paige

A player meets the challenges of the game.

BIOGRAPHY

connect to SOCIAL STUDIES

Paired Selection

The Girls of Summer

EXPOSITORY NONFICTION

Shutting Out the Sky

Immigrants must find new homes in America.

EXPOSITORY NONFICTION

connect to SOCIAL STUDIES

Paired Selection

The Immigrant Experience

E-MAIL

Unit 1

Skills Overview

		WEEK 1	WEEK 2
		22–41 **Frindle/ Punctuation Takes a Vacation** HUMOROUS FICTION *How do we meet the challenges of learning?*	46–67 **Thunder Rose/ Measuring Tornadoes** TALL TAI *How can nature challenge us?*
Reading	Comprehension	T ◎ **Skill** Character and Plot ◎ **Strategy** Prior Knowledge T REVIEW **Skill** Cause and Effect	T ◎ **Skill** Cause and Effect ◎ **Strategy** Monitor and Fix Up T REVIEW **Skill** Character and Plot
	Vocabulary	T ◎ **Strategy** Word Structure	T ◎ **Strategy** Context Clues
	Fluency	Tone of Voice	Tone of Voice
Word Work	Spelling and Phonics	Short Vowel VCCV, VCV	Long Vowel VCV
Oral Language	Speaking/Listening/ Viewing	Dramatization Listen to Dramatization	Storytelling Analyze an Illustration
Language Arts	Grammar, Usage, and Mechanics	T Four Kinds of Sentences	T Subjects and Predicates
	Weekly Writing	Character Sketch Writing Trait: Voice	Tall Tale Writing Trait: Word Choice
	Unit Process Writing	Personal Narrative	Personal Narrative
	Research and Study Skills	Dictionary/Glossary	Almanac
	Integrate Science and Social Studies Standards	Time for Social Studies: Education, Communication	Time for Science: Weather, Atmosphere

◎ Target Skill T Tested Skill

Big Idea What kinds of challenges do people face and how do they meet them?

EEK 3	WEEK 4	WEEK 5

72–89 **Island of the Blue Dolphins/ Seven Survival Questions** HISTORICAL FICTION *How do people survive in the wilderness?*	94–111 **Satchel Paige/ The Girls of Summer** BIOGRAPHY *How do we face personal challenges?*	116–133 **Shutting Out the Sky/The Immigrant Experience** EXPOSITORY NONFICTION *What challenges do immigrants encounter?*
T **Skill** Theme and Setting **Strategy** Visualize T REVIEW **Skill** Character and Plot	T **Skill** Sequence **Strategy** Ask Questions T REVIEW **Skill** Compare and Contrast	T **Skill** Cause and Effect **Strategy** Summarize T REVIEW **Skill** Sequence
T **Strategy** Dictionary/Glossary	T **Strategy** Context Clues	T **Strategy** Context Clues
Pitch	Phrasing	Pauses
Long Vowel Digraphs	Adding *-ed, -ing*	Contractions
Group Review Analyze Film Media	Sportscast Listen to Audio CD	Interview Analyze a Photo
T Independent and Dependent Clauses	T Compound and Complex Sentences	T Common and Proper Nouns
Friendly or Thank You Letter Writing Trait: Organization/Paragraphs	Feature Article Writing Trait: Word Choice	Narrative Writing Writing Trait: Word Choice
Personal Narrative	Personal Narrative	Personal Narrative
SPQ3R	Newspaper/Newsletter	Electronic Encyclopedia
Time for SOCIAL STUDIES Map and Globe Skills, Geography, Native Americans	Time for SOCIAL STUDIES Sports, Contributions of Women, Segregation	Time for SOCIAL STUDIES Ethnic Groups, Cultures, Immigration, Customs, U.S. History

Unit 1

Monitor Progress

Predictors of Reading Success	WEEK 1	WEEK 2	WEEK 3	WEEK 4
WCPM **Fluency**	Tone of Voice 105–110 WCPM	Tone of Voice 105–110 WCPM	Pitch 105–110 WCPM	Phrasing 105–110 WCPM
Vocabulary **Vocabulary/ Concept Development** (assessed informally)	examinations mistakes superintendent	meteorologist roaring severe terror tornado	flint green gutted quartz	courage hardships taunts
Lesson Vocabulary	**Strategy** Word Structure acquainted assignment essential expanded guaranteed procedures reputation worshiped	**Strategy** Context Clues branded constructed daintily devastation lullaby pitch resourceful thieving veins	**Strategy** Dictionary/ Glossary gnawed headland kelp lair ravine shellfish sinew	**Strategy** Context Clues confidence fastball mocking outfield unique weakness windup
Retelling **Text Comprehension**	**Skill** Character and Plot **Strategy** Prior Knowledge	**Skill** Cause and Effect **Strategy** Monitor and Fix Up	**Skill** Setting and Theme **Strategy** Visualize	**Skill** Sequence **Strategy** Ask Questions

Target Skill   SuccessTracker/Unit 1 Benchmark Tested Skills

Make Data–Driven Decisions

Data Management
- Assess
- Diagnose
- Prescribe
- Disaggregate

Classroom Management
- Monitor Progress
- Group
- Differentiate Instruction
- Inform Parents

WEEK 5

Pauses

105–110 WCPM

Ellis Island immigration Registry Room

Strategy Context Clues

advice
advised
circumstances
elbow
hustled
immigrants
luxury
newcomer
peddler

Skill Cause and Effect

Strategy Summarize

ONLINE CLASSROOM

Manage Data

- Assign the Unit 1 Benchmark Test for students to take online.
- SuccessTracker records results and generates reports by school, grade, classroom, or student.
- Use reports to disaggregate and aggregate Unit 1 skills and standards data to monitor progress.
- Based on class lists created to support the categories important for AYP (gender, ethnicity, migrant education, English proficiency, disabilities, economic status), reports let you track adequate yearly progress every six weeks.

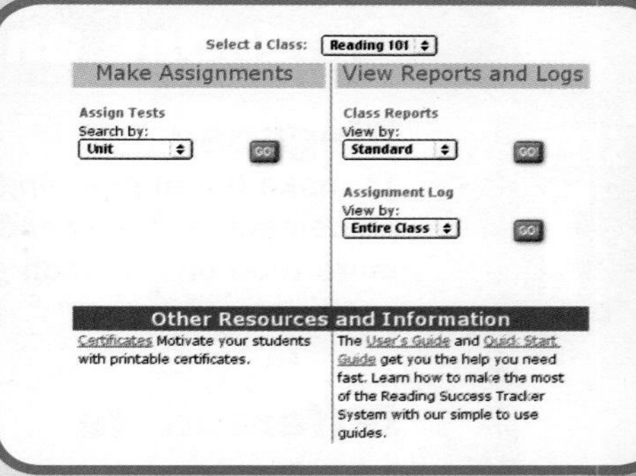

Group

- Use results from Unit 1 Benchmark Tests taken online through SuccessTracker to regroup students.
- Reports in SuccessTracker suggest appropriate groups for students based on test results.

Individualize Instruction

- Tests are correlated to Unit 1 tested skills and standards so that prescriptions for individual teaching and learning plans can be created.
- Individualized prescriptions target instruction and accelerate student progress toward learning outcome goals.
- Prescriptions include resources to reteach Unit 1 skills and standards.

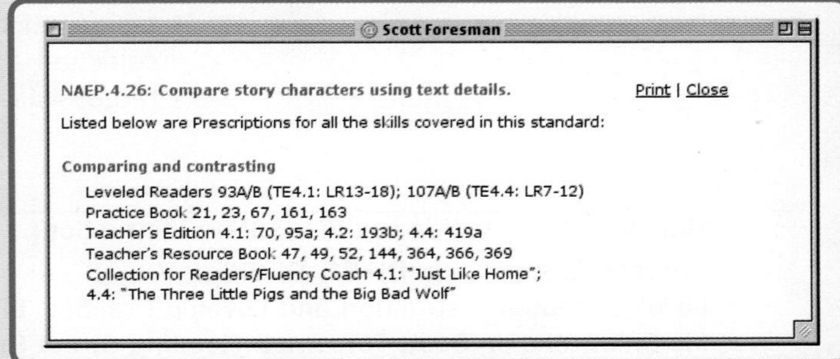

Scott Foresman
NAEP.4.26: Compare story characters using text details.
Print | Close
Listed below are Prescriptions for all the skills covered in this standard:
Comparing and contrasting
Leveled Readers 93A/B (TE4.1: LR13-18); 107A/B (TE4.4: LR7-12)
Practice Book 21, 23, 67, 161, 163
Teacher's Edition 4.1: 70, 95a; 4.2: 193b; 4.4: 419a
Teacher's Resource Book 47, 49, 52, 144, 364, 366, 369
Collection for Readers/Fluency Coach 4.1: "Just Like Home";
4.4: "The Three Little Pigs and the Big Bad Wolf"

Unit 1

Grouping for AYP

Diagnose and Differentiate

STEP 1

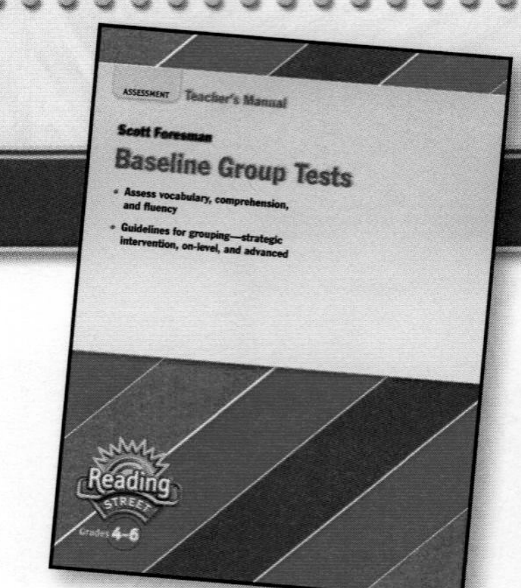

Diagnose

To make initial grouping decisions, use the Baseline Group Test or another initial placement test. Depending on students' ability levels, you may have more than one of each group.

Differentiate

If... student performance is	Below-Level	**then...** use the regular instruction and the daily Strategic Intervention lessons, pp. DI•2–DI•50.
If... student performance is	On-Level	**then...** use the regular instruction for On-Level learners throughout each selection.
If... student performance is	Advanced	**then...** use the regular instruction and the daily instruction for Advanced learners, pp. DI•3–DI•51.

Group Time

On-Level

- Explicit instructional routines teach core skills and strategies.
- Independent activities provide practice for core skills and extension and enrichment options.
- Leveled readers (LR1–45) provide additional reading and practice with core skills and vocabulary.

Strategic Intervention

- Daily Strategic Intervention lessons provide more intensive instruction, more scaffolding, more practice with critical skills, and more opportunities to respond.
- Reteach lessons (DI•52–DI•56) provide additional instructional opportunities with target skills.
- Leveled readers instruction (LR1–45) builds background for the main selection and provides practice with target skills and vocabulary.

Advanced

- Daily Advanced Lessons provide compacted instruction for accelerated learning, options for investigative work, and challenging reading content.
- Leveled readers (LR1–45) provide additional reading tied to lesson concepts.

Additional opportunities to differentiate instruction:

- Reteach Lessons, pp. DI•52–DI•56
- Leveled Reader Instruction and Leveled Practice, LR1–45
- My Sidewalks on Scott Foresman Reading Street Street Intensive Reading Intervention Program

4–Step Plan for Assessment

1. Diagnose and Differentiate
2. Monitor Progress
3. Assess and Regroup
4. Summative Assessment

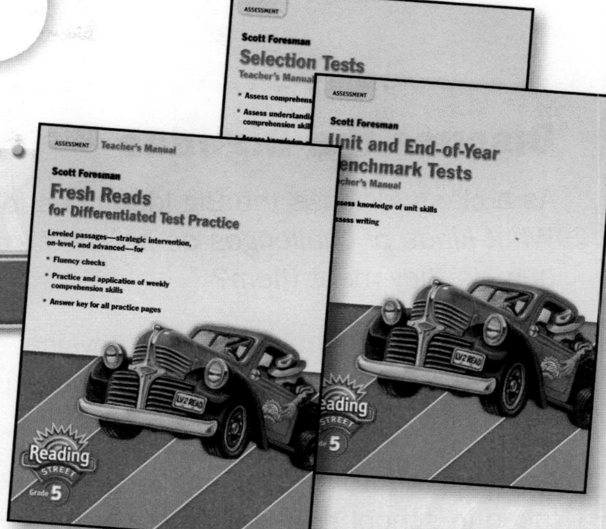

STEP 2 Monitor Progress

- **Guiding comprehension questions** and skill and strategy instruction during reading
- **Monitor Progress boxes** to check comprehension and vocabulary
- **Weekly Assessments** on Day 3 for comprehension, Day 4 for fluency, and Day 5 for vocabulary
- **Practice Book** pages at point of use
- **Weekly Selection Tests** or **Fresh Reads for Differentiated Test Practice**

STEP 3 Assess and Regroup

- **Days 3, 4, and 5 Assessments** Record results of weekly Days 3, 4, and 5 assessments in retelling, fluency, and vocabulary (WA16–WA17) to track student progress.
- **Unit 1 Benchmark Test** Administer this test to check mastery of unit skills.
- The first opportunity for regrouping occurs at the end of Unit 2. Use weekly assessment information, Unit Benchmark Test performance, and the Unit 1 Assess and Regroup (WA18) to make regrouping decisions at the end of Unit 2. See the time line below.

YOU ARE HERE
Begin Unit 1

SCOTT FORESMAN ASSESSMENT: Group Baseline Group Test → Assess → Regroup Units 1 & 2 (p. WA18) → Regroup Unit 3 → Regroup Unit 4 → Regroup Unit 5 → Assess

Week 1 | 5 | 10 | 15 | 20 | 25 | 30 END OF YEAR

OUTSIDE ASSESSMENT: Initial placement → Outside assessment for regrouping → Outside assessment for regrouping

Outside assessments (e.g., DIBELS) may recommend regrouping at other times during the year.

STEP 4 Summative Assessment

- **Benchmark Assessment** Use to measure a student's mastery of each unit's skills.
- **End-of-Year Benchmark Assessment** Use to measure a student's mastery of program skills covered in all six units.

Unit 1

Theme Launch

Discuss the Big Idea

As a class, discuss the Big Idea question, *What kinds of challenges do people face and how do they meet them?*

Explain that challenges can be physical or mental and that facing them can make people stronger.

Ask students to think of challenges they have faced in school or at home. Have them discuss ways they met those challenges.

A good example of a mental challenge students face is studying for tests. Physical challenges may occur in sports or overcoming a limitation. Some physical challenges may be short-term, such as a broken arm. Others may be permanent disabilities, such as blindness.

Theme and Concept Connections

Weekly lesson concepts help students connect the reading selections and the unit theme. Theme-related activities throughout the week provide opportunities to explore the relationships among the selections, the lesson concepts, and the unit theme.

UNIT 1
Read It Online
PearsonSuccessNet.com
Meeting Challenges
What kinds of challenges do people face and how do they meet them?
16

CONNECTING CULTURES

Use the following selections to help students learn more about how people face the challenge of living without their families and solving problems on their own.

Island of the Blue Dolphins Have students discuss how Karana survives on her own. They can also share their feelings about living alone on an island.

Shutting Out the Sky Have students discuss the things Marcus learned from Mrs. Segal and the man from Romania. Ask: *How did they help Marcus succeed? What would it be like to move to a new place without your family?*

rindle
boy must get to know
s teacher.
MOROUS FICTION

connect to SOCIAL STUDIES

Paired Selection
Punctuation Takes a Vacation
FANTASY

hunder Rose
cowgirl faces challenges
the range.
L TALE

connect to SCIENCE

Paired Selection
Measuring Tornadoes
EXPOSITORY NONFICTION

sland of the
lue Dolphins
young girl must survive
an island alone.
STORICAL FICTION

connect to SOCIAL STUDIES

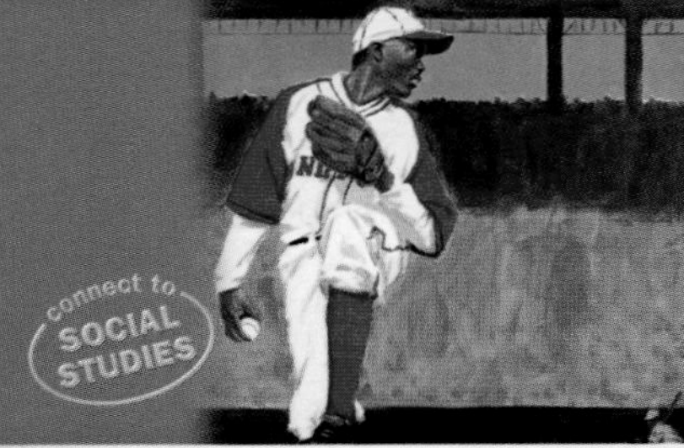

Paired Selection
Seven Survival Questions
INTERVIEW

atchel Paige
player meets the
allenges of the game.
GRAPHY

connect to SOCIAL STUDIES

Paired Selection
The Girls of Summer
EXPOSITORY NONFICTION

hutting Out
ne Sky
migrants must find new
mes in America.
POSITORY NONFICTION

connect to SOCIAL STUDIES

Paired Selection
The Immigrant Experience
E-MAIL

17

Unit Inquiry Project

Facing Challenges

In the unit inquiry project, students each choose an event in the Special Olympics and research the challenges competitors face. They may use print or online resources as available.

The project assessment rubric can be found on p. 134a. Discuss the rubric's expectations before students begin the project. Rubric 4 3 2 1

PROJECT TIMETABLE

WEEK	ACTIVITY/SKILL CONNECTION
1	**IDENTIFY QUESTIONS** Each student chooses an event in the Special Olympics and browses a few Web sites or print reference materials to develop an inquiry question about the challenges competitors face in this event.
2	**NAVIGATE/SEARCH** Students conduct effective information searches and look for text and images that can help them answer their questions.
3	**ANALYZE** Students explore Web sites or print materials. They analyze the information they have found to determine whether or not it will be useful to them. Students print or take notes on valid information.
4	**SYNTHESIZE** Students combine relevant information they've collected from different sources to develop answers to their inquiry questions from Week 1.
5	**ASSESSMENT OPTIONS** **COMMUNICATE** Students prepare posters advertising their Special Olympic events. Students may also create newspaper articles about their events.

CONCEPT DEVELOPMENT

Unit 1
Meeting Challenges

CONCEPT QUESTION

What kinds of challenges do people face and how do they meet them?

Week 1

Expand the Concept
How do we meet the challenges of learning?

Time for SOCIAL STUDIES

Connect the Concept

Literature

Develop Language
examinations, mistakes, superintendent

Teach Content
Dictionaries
Lexicography
Punctuation

Writing
Character Sketch

Internet Inquiry
Famous Educators

Week 2

Expand the Concept
How can nature challenge use?

Time for Science

Connect the Concept

Literature

Develop Language
meteorologist, roaring, severe, terror, tornado

Teach Content
Lightning
Myths and Nature
Tornadoes
Storm Warnings

Writing
Tall Tale

Internet Inquiry
Nature's Challenges

Week 3

Expand the Concept
How do people survive in the wilderness?

Time for SOCIAL STUDIES

Connect the Concept

Literature

Develop Language
flint, green, gutted, quartz

Teach Content
Map and Globe Skills
Channel Islands
Native Americans

Writing
Friendly or Thank you Letter

Internet Inquiry
Wilderness Survival

Week 4

Expand the Concept
How do we face personal challenges?

Time for SOCIAL STUDIES

Connect the Concept

Literature

Develop Language
courage, hardships, taunts

Teach Content
History of Baseball
Segregation
Women in Sports

Writing
Feature Article

Internet Inquiry
Athletes Meeting Challenges

Week 5

Expand the Concept
What challenges do immigrants encounter?

Time for SOCIAL STUDIES

Connect the Concept

Literature

Develop Language
Ellis Island, immigration, Registry Room

Teach Content
Tenement Museum
Ellis Island

Writing
Narrative Writing

Internet Inquiry
The Immigrant Experience

Unit 1

Meeting Challenges

CONCEPT QUESTION

What kinds of challenges do people face and how do they meet them?

Week 1

How do we meet the challenges of learning?

Week 2

How can nature challenge us?

Week 3

How do people survive in the wilderness?

Week 4

How do we face personal challenges?

Week 5

What challenges do immigrants encounter?

Week 1

EXPAND THE CONCEPT

How do we meet the challenges of learning?

Frindle

by Andrew Clements
illustrated by James Bernardin

How do Nick and Mrs. Granger meet the challenge of getting to know each other?

Genre **Humorous fiction** has characters and action that make you laugh. As you read, notice how the author makes you wonder how things will turn out in the end.

2

Fantasy

Genre

- A fantasy is a make-believe story that could never happen in the real world.
- Some characters and plot situations may be realistic, while others are exaggerated and even silly.
- The author uses a realistic classroom setting but then introduces fantastic characters who do impossible things.
- Preview the story. What is it about the title and art that make you think, "This is a fantasy"?

Link to Writing

Write another postcard to the vacationing punctuation marks. Try to convince them to return to the classroom. This time, use correct punctuation marks.

36

Punctuation Takes a Vacation

by Robin Pulver

Day after day, the punctuation marks showed up in Mr. Wright's classroom. Day after day, they did their jobs. They put up with being erased and replaced and corrected and ignored and moved around.

Then on the hottest, stickiest day the class had ever seen, right in the middle of a lesson about commas, Mr. Wright mopped his forehead and said, "Let's give punctuation a vacation."

As the kids cheered and headed for the playground to cool off, the punctuation marks stared at one another in disbelief.

"Is this the thanks we get?" asked a question mark.

"Well!" huffed an exclamation point.

"Now, now," said a comma.

"We *should* take a vacation," said a period. "They'll soon learn how much they need us."

Character What is bothering Mr. Wright? Why?

37

CONNECT THE CONCEPT

▶ **Build Background**

examinations, mistakes, superintendent

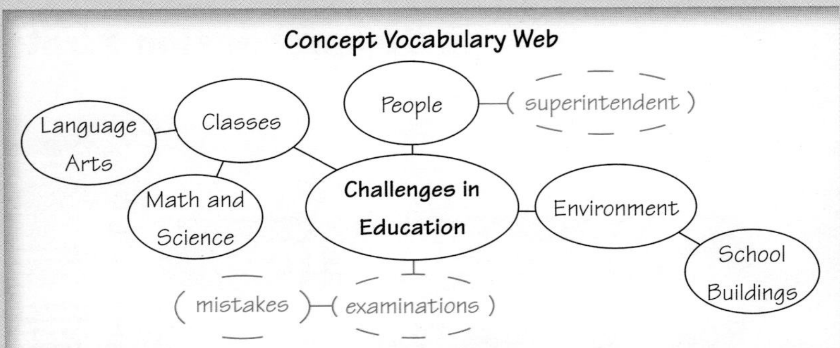

▶ **Social Studies Content**

Dictionaries, Lexicography, Punctuation

▶ **Writing**

Character Sketch

▶ **Internet Inquiry**

Famous Educators

Preview Your Week

How do we meet the challenges of learning?

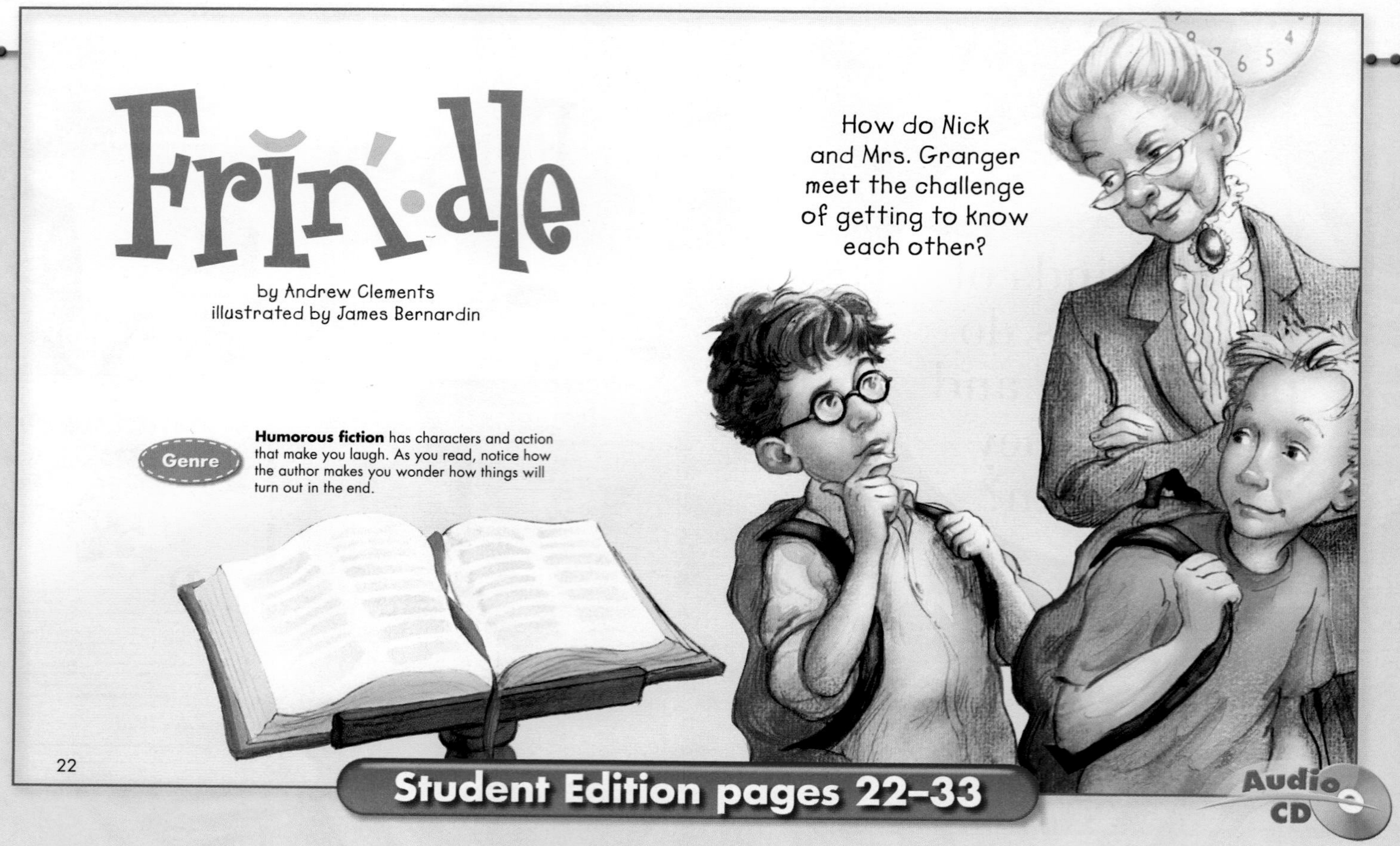

Genre Humorous Fiction

Vocabulary Strategy Word Structure

Comprehension Skill Character and Plot

Comprehension Strategy Prior Knowledge

Paired Selection

Reading Across Texts

Compare Character Qualities

Genre

Fantasy

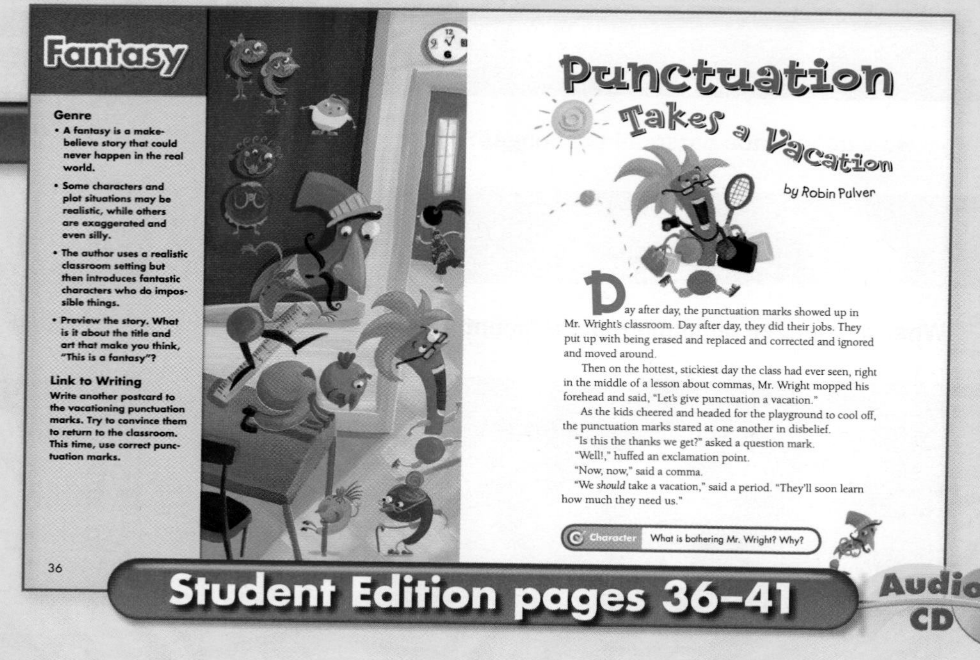

- Student Edition
- Leveled Readers

Leveled Readers

Skill Character and Plot

Strategy Prior Knowledge

Lesson Vocabulary

Below-Level

On-Level

Advanced

ELL Reader

- Concept Vocabulary
- Text Support
- Language Enrichment

Time for SOCIAL STUDIES

Integrate Social Studies Standards

- Education
- Communication

Frindle, pp. 22–33

"Punctuation Takes a Vacation," pp. 36–41

Leveled Readers

Below-Level

- **Support Concepts**

On-Level

- **Develop Concepts**

Advanced

- **Extend Concepts**

ELL Reader

Build **Concept Vocabulary**
Challenges in Education, pp. 18l–18m

Teach **Social Studies Concepts**
Dictionaries, p. 27
Lexicography, p. 31
Punctuation, p. 37

Explore **Social Studies Center**
Research Education, p. 18k

Weekly Plan

PearsonSuccessNet.com

READING

45–90 minutes

TARGET SKILLS OF THE WEEK

Comprehension Skill Character and Plot

Comprehension Strategy Prior Knowledge

Vocabulary Strategy Word Structure

DAY 1

PAGES 18l–20b, 41a, 41e–41k

Oral Language

QUESTION OF THE WEEK *How do we meet the challenges of learning?*

Read Aloud: "Understood Betsy," 18m

Build Concepts, 18l

Comprehension/Vocabulary

Comprehension Skill/Strategy Lesson, 18–19

Character and Plot **T**

Prior Knowledge

Build Background, 20a

Introduce Lesson Vocabulary, 20b

acquainted, assignment, essential, expanded, guaranteed, procedures, reputation, worshipped **T**

Read Leveled Readers

Grouping Options 18f–18g

Fluency

Model Tone of Voice, 18l–18m, 41a

DAY 2

PAGES 20–29, 41a, 41e–41k

Oral Language

QUESTION OF THE DAY *Many of the descriptions of Mrs. Granger make her seem larger than life. Why do you think this is?*

Comprehension/Vocabulary

Vocabulary Strategy Lesson, 20–21

Word Structure **T**

Read *Frindle,* 22–29

Grouping Options 18f–18g

Character and Plot **T**

Prior Knowledge

REVIEW Cause and Effect **T**

Develop Vocabulary

Fluency

Choral Reading, 41a

LANGUAGE ARTS

30–60 minutes

Trait of the Week

Voice

	DAY 1	DAY 2
Language Arts	**Grammar,** 41e Introduce Four Kinds of Sentences **T** **Writing Workshop,** 41g Introduce Character Sketch Model the Trait of the Week: Voice **Spelling,** 41i Pretest for Short Vowel VCCV, VCV **Internet Inquiry,** 41k Identify Questions	**Grammar,** 41e Develop Four Kinds of Sentences **T** **Writing Workshop,** 41g Improve Writing with Voice **Spelling,** 41i Teach the Generalization **Internet Inquiry,** 41k Navigate/Search
DAILY WRITING ACTIVITIES	**Day 1** Write to Read, 18	**Day 2** Words to Write, 21 Strategy Response Log, 22, 29
DAILY SOCIAL STUDIES CONNECTIONS	**Day 1** Challenges in Education Concept Web, 18l	**Day 2** Time for Social Studies: Dictionaries, 27 Revisit the Challenges in Education Concept Web, 29

DAILY SUCCESS PREDICTORS for Adequate Yearly Progress

Monitor Progress and Corrective Feedback

Vocabulary	Check Vocabulary, *18l*	

RESOURCES FOR THE WEEK

- Practice Book, *pp. 1–10*
- Word Study and Spelling Practice Book, *pp. 1–4*
- Grammar and Writing Practice Book, *pp. 1–4*
- Selection Test, *pp. 1–4*
- Fresh Reads for Differentiated Test Practice, *pp. 1–6*
- The Grammar and Writing Book, *pp. 50–55*

Grouping Options for Differentiated Instruction

Turn the page for the small group lesson plan.

DAY 3 PAGES 30–35, 41a, 41e–41k

Oral Language

QUESTION OF THE DAY *How do you think Nick will describe his first class with Mrs. Granger to his friends or family?*

Comprehension/Vocabulary

Read *Frindle*, 30–34

Grouping Options 18f–18g

Prior Knowledge

Word Structure **T**

Develop Vocabulary

Reader Response

Selection Test

Fluency

Model Tone of Voice, 41a

Grammar, 41f
Apply Four Kinds of Sentences in Writing **T**

Writing Workshop, 35, 41h
Write Now
Prewrite and Draft

Spelling, 41j
Connect Spelling to Writing

Internet Inquiry, 41k
Analyze Sources

Day 3 Strategy Response Log, 32
Look Back and Write, 34

Day 3 Time for Social Studies: Lexicography, 31
Revisit the Challenges in Education Concept Web, 33

DAY 4 PAGES 36–41a, 41e–41k

Oral Language

QUESTION OF THE DAY *What qualities or abilities do good teachers have to help their students overcome challenges?*

Comprehension/Vocabulary

Read "Punctuation Takes a Vacation," 36–41

Grouping Options 18f–18g

Fantasy

Reading Across Texts

Fluency

Partner Reading, 41a

Grammar, 41f
Practice Four Kinds of Sentences for Standardized Tests **T**

Writing Workshop, 41h
Draft, Revise, and Publish

Spelling, 41j
Provide a Strategy

Internet Inquiry, 41k
Synthesize Information

Day 4 Writing Across Texts, 41

Day 4 Time for Social Studies: Punctuation, 37

DAY 5 PAGES 41a–41l

Oral Language

QUESTION OF THE WEEK *To wrap up the week, revisit the Day 1 question.*

Build Concept Vocabulary, 41c

Fluency

Read Leveled Readers

Grouping Options 18f–18g

Assess Reading Rate, 41a

Comprehension/Vocabulary

Reteach Character and Plot, 41b **T**

Point of View, 41b

Review Word Structure, 41c **T**

Speaking and Listening, 41d
Dramatization
Listen to Dramatization

Grammar, 41f
Cumulative Review

Writing Workshop, 41h
Connect to Unit Writing

Spelling, 41j
Posttest for Short Vowel VCCV, VCV

Internet Inquiry, 41k
Communicate Results

Research/Study Skills, 41l
Dictionary/Glossary

Day 5 Point of View, 41b

Day 5 Revisit the Challenges in Education Concept Web, 41c

KEY ◉ = Target Skill **T** = Tested Skill

Comprehension	Fluency	Vocabulary
Check Retelling, *34*	Check Fluency WCPM, *41a*	Check Vocabulary, *41c*

SUCCESS PREDICTO

Small Group Plan *for Differentiated Instructio*

Daily Plan AT A GLANCE

Reading

Whole Group
- Oral Language
- Comprehension/Vocabulary

Group Time

Differentiated Instruction

Meet with small groups to provide:
- Skill Support
- Reading Support
- Fluency Practice

Read

This week's lessons for daily group time can be found behind the Differentiated Instruction (DI) tab on pp. DI • 2–DI • 11.

Whole Group
- Fluency

Language Arts
- Grammar
- Writing
- Spelling
- Research/Inquiry
- Speaking/Listening/Viewing

Use *My Sidewalks on Reading Street* for Tier III intensive reading intervention.

DAY 1

On-Level

Teacher-Led
Page DI • 3
- Develop Concept Vocabulary
- **Read** On-Level Reader *Learning from Ms. Liang*

Strategic Intervention

Teacher-Led
Page DI • 2
- Reinforce Concepts
- **Read** Below-Level Reader *The Spelling Bee*

Advanced

Teacher-Led
Page DI • 3
- **Read** Advanced Reader *This Is the Way We Go to School*
- Independent Extension Acti

i Independent Activities

While you meet with small groups, have the rest of the class...

- Visit the Reading/Library Center
- Listen to the Background Building Audio
- Finish Write to Read, p. 18
- Complete Practice Book pp. 3–4
- Visit Cross-Curricular Centers

DAY 2

On-Level

Teacher-Led
Pages 24-29
- **Read** *Frindle*

Strategic Intervention

Teacher-Led
Page DI • 4
- Practice Lesson Vocabulary
- Read Multisyllabic Words
- **Read** or Listen to *Frindle*

Advanced

Teacher-Led
Page DI • 5
- Extend Vocabulary
- **Read** *Frindle*

i Independent Activities

While you meet with small groups, have the rest of the class...

- Visit the Reading/Library Center
- Listen to the AudioText for *Frindle*
- Finish Words to Write, p. 21
- Complete Practice Book pp. 5–6
- Write in their Strategy Response Logs, pp. 22, 29
- Visit Cross-Curricular Centers
- Work on inquiry projects

DAY 3

On-Level

Teacher-Led
Pages 30-33
- **Read** *Frindle*

Strategic Intervention

Teacher-Led
Page DI • 6
- Practice Character and Plot and Prior Knowledge
- **Read** or Listen to *Frindle*

Advanced

Teacher-Led
Page DI • 7
- Extend Character and Plot and Prior Knowledge
- **Read** *Frindle*

i Independent Activities

While you meet with small groups, have the rest of the class...

- Visit the Reading/Library Center
- Listen to the AudioText for *Frindle*
- Write in their Strategy Response Logs, p. 32
- Finish Look Back and Write, p. 34
- Complete Practice Book p. 7
- Visit Cross-Curricular Centers
- Work on inquiry projects

1 Begin with whole class skill and strategy instruction.

2 Meet with small groups to provide differentiated instruction.

3 Gather the whole class back together for fluency and language arts.

DAY 4

On-Level	Strategic Intervention	Advanced
Teacher-Led *Pages 36–41*	**Teacher-Led** *Page DI • 8*	**Teacher-Led** *Page DI • 9*
Read "Punctuation Takes a Vacation"	• Practice Retelling • **Read** or Listen to "Punctuation Takes a Vacation"	• **Read** "Punctuation Takes a Vacation" • Genre Study

Independent Activities

While you meet with small groups, have the rest of the class...

- Visit the Reading/Library Center
- Listen to the AudioText for "Punctuation Takes a Vacation"
- Visit the Writing/Vocabulary Center
- Finish Writing Across Texts, p. 41
- Visit Cross-Curricular Centers
- Work on inquiry projects

DAY 5

On-Level	Strategic Intervention	Advanced
Teacher-Led *Page DI • 11*	**Teacher-Led** *Page DI • 10*	**Teacher-Led** *Page DI • 11*
Reread Leveled Reader *Learning from Ms. Liang* Retell *Learning from Ms. Liang*	• **Reread** Leveled Reader *The Spelling Bee* • Retell *The Spelling Bee*	• **Reread** Leveled Reader *This Is the Way We Go to School* • Share Extension Activity

Independent Activities

While you meet with small groups, have the rest of the class...

- Visit the Reading/Library Center
- Complete Practice Book pp. 8–10
- Visit Cross-Curricular Centers
- Work on inquiry projects

Grouping Place English language learners in the groups that correspond to their reading abilities in English.

Use the appropriate Leveled Reader or other text at students' instructional level.

Tip Send home the appropriate Multilingual Summary of the main selection on Day 1.

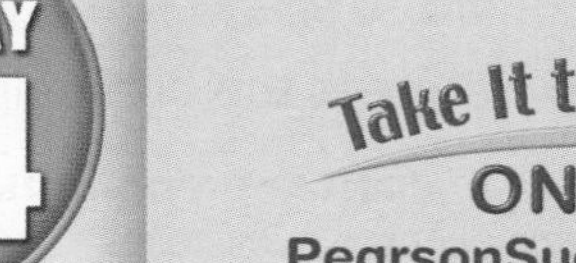

PearsonSuccessNet.com

P. David Pearson
For research on comprehension instruction, see the article "An Instructional Study" by J. Hansen and Scott Foresman author P. D. Pearson.

TEACHER TALK

Comprehension strategies are steps a reader takes to make sense of text. Strategies include monitoring comprehension, using graphic organizers, answering and generating questions, summarizing, and so on.

Looking Ahead

Be sure to schedule time for students to work on the unit inquiry project "Facing Challenges." This week students choose events in the Special Olympics and develop inquiry questions about the challenges competitors face.

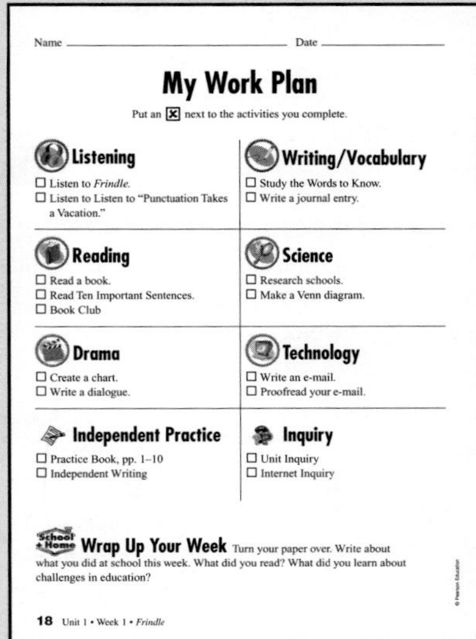
Name ______ Date ______

My Work Plan

Put an ☒ next to the activities you complete.

Listening
☐ Listen to *Frindle*.
☐ Listen to Listen to "Punctuation Takes a Vacation."

Writing/Vocabulary
☐ Study the Words to Know.
☐ Write a journal entry.

Reading
☐ Read a book.
☐ Read Ten Important Sentences.
☐ Book Club

Science
☐ Research schools.
☐ Make a Venn diagram.

Drama
☐ Create a chart.
☐ Write a dialogue.

Technology
☐ Write an e-mail.
☐ Proofread your e-mail.

Independent Practice
☐ Practice Book, pp. 1–10
☐ Independent Writing

Inquiry
☐ Unit Inquiry
☐ Internet Inquiry

Wrap Up Your Week Turn your paper over. Write about what you did at school this week. What did you read? What did you learn about challenges in education?

18 Unit 1 • Week 1 • *Frindle*

▲ **Group-Time Survival Guide** p. 18, Weekly Contract

Customize Your Plan by Stran

ORAL LANGUAGE

SOCIAL STUDIES

Concept Development

How do we meet the challenges of learning?

CONCEPT VOCABULARY

examinations *mistakes* *superintendent*

BUILD

- ❑ **Question of the Week** Introduce and discuss the question of the week. This week students will read a variety of texts and work on projects related to the concept *challenges in education*. Post the question for students to refer to throughout the week. DAY 1 *18d*

- ❑ **Read Aloud** Read aloud "Understood Betsy." Then begin a web to build concepts and concept vocabulary related to this week's lesson and the unit theme, Meeting Challenges. Introduce the concept words *examinations, mistakes,* and *superintendent* and have students place them on the web. Display the web for use throughout the week. DAY 1 *18l–18m*

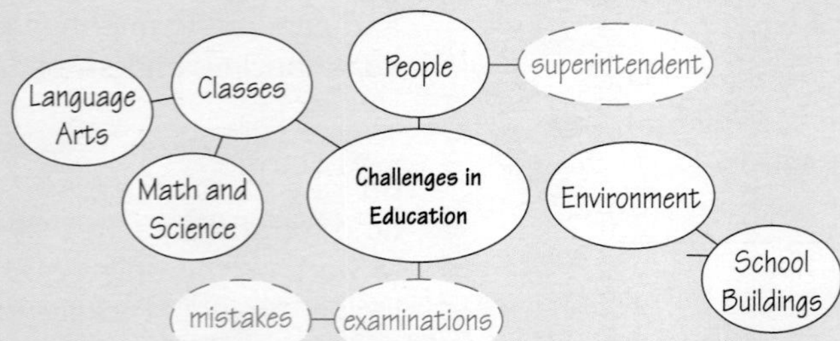

DEVELOP

- ❑ **Question of the Day** Use the prompts from the Weekly Plan to engage students in conversations related to this week's reading and the unit theme. EVERY DAY *18d–18e*

- ❑ **Concept Vocabulary Web** Revisit the Challenges in Education Concept Web and encourage students to add concept words from their reading and life experiences. DAY 2 *29*, DAY 3 *33*

CONNECT

- ❑ **Looking Back/Moving Forward** Revisit the Challenges in Education Concept Web and discuss how it relates to this week's lesson and the unit theme. Then make connections to next week's lesson. DAY 5 *41c*

CHECK

- ❑ **Concept Vocabulary Web** Use the Challenges in Education Concept Web to check students' understanding of the concept vocabulary words *examinations, mistakes,* and *superintendent*. DAY 1 *18l*, DAY 5 *41c*

VOCABULARY

STRATEGY WORD STRUCTURE
When you are reading and you come to a longer word that is unfamiliar, you can use what you know about suffixes to help figure out the word's meaning. The meanings for suffixes can be found in a dictionary.

LESSON VOCABULARY

acquainted *guaranteed*
assignment *procedures*
essential *reputation*
expanded *worshipped*

TEACH

- ❑ **Words to Know** Give students the opportunity to tell what they already know about this week's lesson vocabulary words. Then discuss word meaning. DAY 1 *20b*

- ❑ **Vocabulary Strategy Lesson** Use the vocabulary strategy lesson in the Student Edition to introduce and model this week's strategy, *word structure*. DAY 2 *20–21*

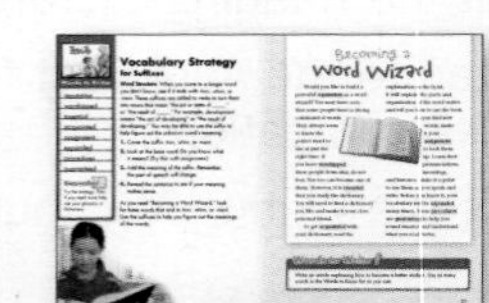

Vocabulary Strategy Lesson

PRACTICE/APPLY

- ❑ **Leveled Text** Read the lesson vocabulary in the context of leveled text. DAY 1 *LR1–LR9*

Leveled Readers

- ❑ **Words in Context** Read the lesson vocabulary and apply *word structure* in the context of *Frindle*. DAY 2 *22–29*, DAY 3 *30–34*

Main Selection—Fiction

- ❑ **Writing/Vocabulary Center** Write a journal entry on "My Most Memorable First Day of School." ANY DAY *18k*

- ❑ **Homework** Practice Book pp. 4–5. DAY 1 *20b*, DAY 2 *21*

- ❑ **Word Play** Have students work in small groups to identify and compile a list of antonyms from *Frindle*. ANY DAY *41c*

ASSESS

- ❑ **Selection Test** Use the Selection Test to determine students' understanding of the lesson vocabulary words. DAY 3

RETEACH/REVIEW

- ❑ **Reteach Lesson** If necessary, use this lesson to reteach and review *word structure*. DAY 5 *41c*

1 Use assessment data to determine your instructional focus.

2 Preview this week's instruction by strand.

3 Choose instructional activities that meet the needs of your classroom.

COMPREHENSION

SKILL CHARACTER AND PLOT Characters are people or animals in a story. The plot is the pattern of events in a story.

STRATEGY PRIOR KNOWLEDGE Prior knowledge is what the reader already knows. Good readers use their prior knowledge to help them understand what they read and then take the new information and connect it to something they already know.

TEACH

- ❑ **Skill/Strategy Lesson** Use the skill/strategy lesson in the Student Edition to introduce and model *character and plot* and *prior knowledge*. DAY 1 *18-19*
- ❑ **Extend Skills** Teach point of view. **ANY DAY** *41b*

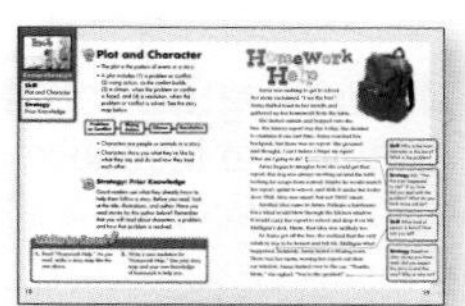

Skill/Strategy Lesson

PRACTICE/APPLY

- ❑ **Leveled Text** Apply *character and plot* and *prior knowledge* to read leveled text. DAY 1 *LR1-LR9*
- ❑ **Skills and Strategies in Context** Read *Frindle,* using the Guiding Comprehension questions to apply *character and plot* and *prior knowledge*. DAY 2 *22-29,* DAY 3 *30-34*
- ❑ **Skills and Strategies in Context** Read "Punctuation Takes a Vacation," guiding students as they apply *character and plot* and *prior knowledge*. Then have students discuss and write across texts. DAY 4 *36-41*
- ❑ **Homework** Practice Book pp. 3, 7, 8. DAY 1 *19,* DAY 3 *33,* DAY 5 *41b*
- ❑ **Fresh Reads for Differentiated Test Practice** Have students practice *character and plot* with a new passage. DAY 3

Leveled Readers

Main Selection—Fiction

Paired Selection—Fiction

ASSESS

- ❑ **Selection Test** Determine students' understanding of the selection and their use of *character and plot*. DAY 3
- ❑ **Retell** Have students retell *Frindle.* DAY 3 *34-35*

RETEACH/REVIEW

- ❑ **Reteach Lesson** If necessary, reteach and review *character and plot*. DAY 5 *41b*

FLUENCY

SKILL TONE OF VOICE Tone of voice is the ability to add emotion to words. By changing your tone you can bring the words to life, create the mood, and make the reading lively.

TEACH

- ❑ **Read Aloud** Model fluent reading by rereading "Understood Betsy." Focus on this week's fluency skill, tone of voice. DAY 1 *18l-18m, 41a*

PRACTICE/APPLY

- ❑ **Choral Reading** Read aloud selected paragraphs from *Frindle,* emphasizing the inflections in your voice. Then practice as a class, doing three choral readings of the selected paragraphs. DAY 2 *41a,* DAY 3 *41a*
- ❑ **Partner Reading** Have partners practice reading aloud, reading with changing inflection to reflect different characters' voices and offering each other feedback. As students reread, monitor their progress toward their individual fluency goals. DAY 4 *41a*
- ❑ **Listening Center** Have students follow along with the AudioText for this week's selections. **ANY DAY** *18j*
- ❑ **Reading/Library Center** Have students reread a selection of their choice. **ANY DAY** *18j*
- ❑ **Fluency Coach** Have students use Fluency Coach to listen to fluent readings or practice reading on their own. **ANY DAY**

ASSESS

- ❑ **Check Fluency** WCPM Do a one-minute timed reading, paying special attention to this week's skill—tone of voice. Provide feedback for each student. DAY 5 *41a*

Customize Your Plan by Stran

GRAMMAR

SKILL FOUR KINDS OF SENTENCES There are four kinds of sentences. Declarative sentences make a statement and end with a period. Interrogative sentences ask a question and end with a question mark. Imperative sentences command or request and end with a period. Exclamatory sentences show strong feelings, end with an exclamation mark, and often have an interjection.

TEACH

- ❑ **Grammar Transparency 1** Use Grammar Transparency 1 to teach conjunctions. DAY 1 *41e*

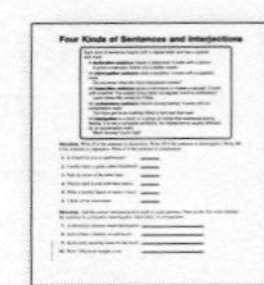

Grammar Transparency 1

PRACTICE/APPLY

- ❑ **Develop the Concept** Review the concept of four kinds of sentences and provide guided practice. DAY 2 *41e*
- ❑ **Apply to Writing** Have students review something they have written and apply four kinds of sentences. DAY 3 *41f*
- ❑ **Test Preparation** Examine common errors in four kinds of sentences to prepare for standardized tests. DAY 4 *41f*
- ❑ **Homework** Grammar and Writing Practice Book pp. 1–3. DAY 2 *41e*, DAY 3 *41f*, DAY 4 *41f*

ASSESS

- ❑ **Cumulative Review** Use Grammar and Writing Practice Book p. 4. DAY 5 *41f*

RETEACH/REVIEW

- ❑ **Daily Fix-It** Have students find and correct errors in grammar, spelling, and punctuation. EVERY DAY *41e–41f*
- ❑ **The Grammar and Writing Book** Use pp. 50–53 of The Grammar and Writing Book to extend instruction for four kinds of sentences. ANY DAY

The Grammar and Writing Book

WRITING

Trait of the Week

VOICE Good writers have a strong voice—an attitude and a personality that comes through in the tone and style of their writing. Voice shows that a writer knows and cares about a topic. A strong voice speaks directly to readers and keeps their attention.

TEACH

- ❑ **Writing Transparency 1A** Use the model to introduce and discuss the Trait of the Week. DAY 1 *41g*
- ❑ **Writing Transparency 1B** Use the transparency to show students how voice can improve their writing. DAY 2 *41g*

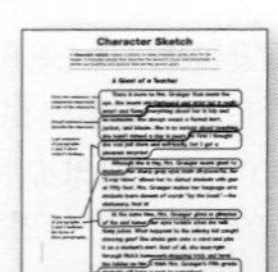

Writing Transparency 1A

Writing Transparency 1B

PRACTICE/APPLY

- ❑ **Write Now** Examine the model on Student Edition p. 35. Then have students write their own character sketch. DAY 3 *35, 41h*, DAY 4 *41h*

  Prompt *Frindle* tells about a teacher with an unusual reputation. Think about a character or person who has an interesting trait. Now write a character sketch about that character or person.

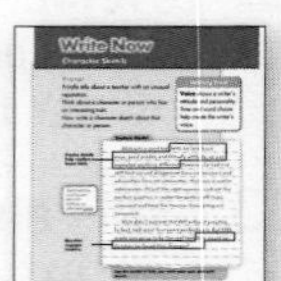

Write Now p. 35

- ❑ **Writing/Vocabulary Center** Write a journal entry on "My Most Memorable First Day of School." ANY DAY *18k*

ASSESS

- ❑ **Writing Trait Rubric** Use the rubric to evaluate students' writing. DAY 4 *41h*

RETEACH/REVIEW

- ❑ **The Grammar and Writing Book** Use pp. 50–55 of The Grammar and Writing Book to extend instruction for four kinds of sentences, voice, and character sketches. ANY DAY

The Grammar and Writing Book

1 Use assessment data to determine your instructional focus.

2 Preview this week's instruction by strand.

3 Choose instructional activities that meet the needs of your classroom.

SPELLING

GENERALIZATION SHORT VOWELS VCCV, VCV Short vowels are often spelled *a: channel, e: method, i: distance, o: problem, u: butter*. When a syllable ends with a single vowel and a single consonant, the vowel stands for its short sound.

TEACH

- ☐ **Pretest** Give the pretest for words with short vowels VCCV, VCV patterns. Guide students in self-correcting their pretests and correcting any misspellings. DAY 1 *41i*
- ☐ **Think and Practice** Connect spelling to the phonics generalization for short vowels VCCV, VCV. DAY 2 *41i*

PRACTICE/APPLY

- ☐ **Connect to Writing** Have students use spelling words to write about a person they admire. Then review frequently misspelled words: *and, to, too.* DAY 3 *41j*
- ☐ **Homework** Word Study and Spelling Practice Book pp. 1-4. EVERY DAY

RETEACH/REVIEW

- ☐ **Review** Review spelling words to prepare for the posttest. Then provide students with a spelling strategy—steps for spelling new words. DAY 4 *41j*

ASSESS

- ☐ **Posttest** Use dictation sentences to give the posttest for words with short vowels VCCV, VCV. DAY 5 *41j*

Spelling Words

1. distance	8. perhaps	15. mustard
2. method	9. figure*	16. shuttle
3. anger	10. channel	17. advance
4. problem	11. admire	18. drummer
5. butter	12. comedy	19. regular
6. petals	13. husband	20. denim
7. enjoy*	14. tissue	

Challenge Words

21. avalanche	23. reluctant	25. tangerine
22. monopoly	24. adequate	

*Word from the selection

RESEARCH AND INQUIRY

- ☐ **Internet Inquiry** Have students conduct an Internet inquiry on famous educators from the past. EVERY DAY *41k*
- ☐ **Dictionary/Glossary** Review the parts of a dictionary and glossary and discuss how students can use dictionaries and glossaries to find the meanings of unfamiliar words. DAY 5 *41l*
- ☐ **Unit Inquiry** Allow time for students to choose events in the Special Olympics and develop inquiry questions about the challenges competitors face. ANY DAY *17*

SPEAKING AND LISTENING

- ☐ **Dramatization** Have students work in small groups to dramatize a scene from *Frindle*. DAY 5 *41d*
- ☐ **Listen to Dramatization** Have students listen to their classmates' dramatizations and answer questions. DAY 5 *41d*

Resources for

Differentiated Instruction

LEVELED READERS

- **Comprehension**
  - **Skill** Character and Plot
  - **Strategy** Prior Knowledge
- **Lesson Vocabulary**
  - Word Structure

- **Social Studies Standards**
  - Education
  - Communication

Pearsonsuccessnet.com

Use the Online Database of over 600 books to

- Download and print additional copies of this week's leveled readers.
- Listen to the readers being read online.
- Search for more titles focused on this week's skills, topic, and content.

On-Level

On-Level Reader

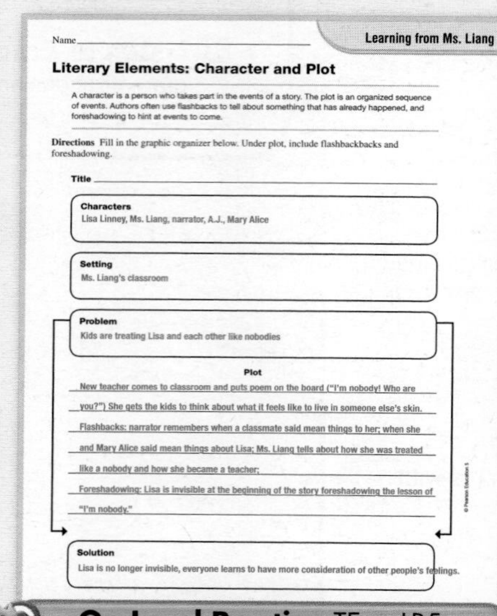

Name________ Learning from Ms. Liang

Literary Elements: Character and Plot

A character is a person who takes part in the events of a story. The plot is an organized sequence of events. Authors often use flashbacks to tell about something that has already happened, and foreshadowing to hint at events to come.

Directions Fill in the graphic organizer below. Under plot, include flashbackbacks and foreshadowing.

Title ________

Characters
Lisa Linney, Ms. Liang, narrator, A.J., Mary Alice

Setting
Ms. Liang's classroom

Problem
Kids are treating Lisa and each other like nobodies

Plot
New teacher comes to classroom and puts poem on the board ("I'm nobody! Who are you?") She gets the kids to think about what it feels like to live in someone else's skin.
Flashbacks: narrator remembers when a classmate said mean things to her; when she and Mary Alice said mean things about Lisa; Ms. Liang tells about how she was treated like a nobody and how she became a teacher;
Foreshadowing: Lisa is invisible at the beginning of the story foreshadowing the lesson of "I'm nobody."

Solution
Lisa is no longer invisible, everyone learns to have more consideration of other people's feelings.

On-Level Practice TE p. LR5

Name________ Learning from Ms. Liang

Vocabulary

Directions Read each sentence. Write the word from the Word Box that has the same meaning as the underlined word or phrase. Some words may be used more than once.

Check the Words You Know

__acquainted	__guaranteed
__assignment	__procedures
__essential	__reputation
__expanded	__worshipped

1. It wasn't long before Lisa adored Ms. Liang. worshipped
2. Ms. Liang told the class that it was extremely important for them to get inside someone else's skin. esssential
3. She also established certain rules and regulations for participating in class. procedures
4. Slowly, the class's understanding of other people's feelings grew. expanded
5. By the end, even A.J. was ready to "get to know each other better." acquainted
6. The narrator had trouble doing her writing homework. assignment
7. Ms. Liang assured her students that she had once been a nobody herself. guaranteed
8. Are you familiar with the poetry of Emily Dickinson? acquainted
9. By the end of the story, Lisa's standing in the class had grown. reputation
10. The narrator promised she would not make mean remarks about Lisa again. guaranteed

On-Level Practice TE p. LR6

Strategic Intervention

Below-Level Reader

Name________ The Spelling Bee

Literary Elements: Plot Structure

1. How does *The Spelling Bee* **begin**?
   We meet Kate who is a chatterbox.
2. What is the **problem** in the story?
   Kate is nervous and excited about the spelling bee.
3. What do we learn in **flashback**?
   Kate has dyslexia and has to work hard to improve her reading.
4. What is the **climax**?
   Kate isn't sure she can spell the first spelling word.
5. What is the **resolution**?
   Kate successfully spells the word and feels she can conquer any challenge.

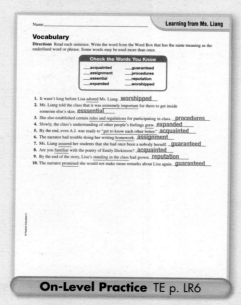

Below-Level Practice TE p. LR2

Name________ The Spelling Bee

Vocabulary

Directions In each of the following sentences, underline the synonyms for the vocabulary words. Then write the vocabulary word above the synonym. Note: Some synonyms may include more than one word.

Check the Words You Know

__acquainted	__guaranteed
__assignment	__procedures
__essential	__reputation
__expanded	__worshipped

essential for necessary
1. Our teacher said it was necessary to bring our coats on the hike.

acquainted for friendly
2. Paulo was friendly with all his neighbors.

worshipped for adored
3. Alice adored her new puppy.

assignment for project
4. "The project our teacher gave out yesterday was easy!" exclaimed Jasper.

"had a reputation" for "was known"
5. He was known as a good ball player.

procedures for processes
6. The two recipes showed different processes for making the same cookies.

guaranteed for made sure
7. I made sure I had a chance for a good grade by studying hard.

expanded for stretched
8. Reading that book stretched my horizons.

Below-Level Practice TE p. LR3

Advanced

This Is the Way We Go to School

by Colin Kong
illustrated by Burgandy Beam

Advanced Reader

Name ______ The Way We Go To School

Literary Elements: Character and Plot

A **character** is a person who takes part in the events of a story. The **plot** is an organized sequence of events. Authors often use flashbacks to tell about something that has already happened, and foreshadowing to hint at events to come.

Directions Fill in the graphic organizer below. Under plot, include flashbacks and foreshadowing.

Title ______

Characters
Miss Jacobson, Ben, Lizzie, Haley, Greg, Jamie, Ben, Sofia; Katie, Tim, and Jeffrey

Setting
Miss Jacobson's classroom, a colonial New England schoolhouse, a 19th century one-room schoolhouse in Massachusetts, a classroom in Mississippi in 1925.

Problem
The class must take over and give three presentations on the history of education in America.

Plot
Ms. Jacobson tells class they will take over and make 3 presentations on the history of education in America. Lizzie and Haley tell about Katie, a girl who lives on a farm in Connecticut in 1725 and goes to dame school while her brothers go to primary school. Greg and Jamie tell about Tim, a boy who goes to public school in Massachusetts in 1830. Ben and Sofia tell about Jeffrey, an African-American boy who goes to school in Mississippi in 1925.
The presentations are flashbacks.

Foreshadowing: On page 17, Ben announces the Mississippi presentation very dramatically, foreshadowing the fact that Jeffrey is none other than Sofia's great-grandfather.

Solution

Advanced Practice TE p. LR8

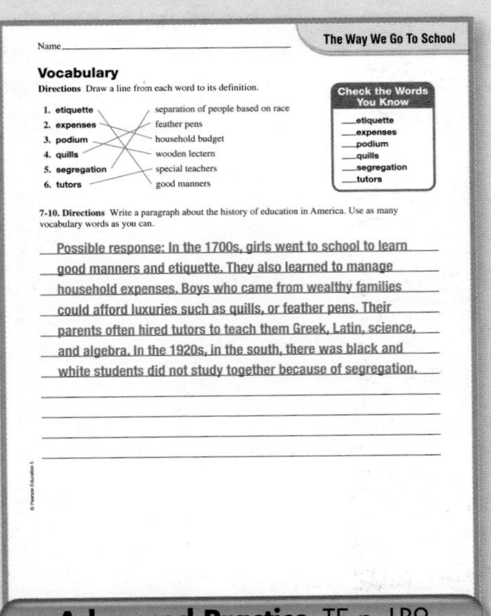
Name ______ The Way We Go To School

Vocabulary
Directions Draw a line from each word to its definition.

1. etiquette — separation of people based on race
2. expenses — feather pens
3. podium — household budget
4. quills — wooden lectern
5. segregation — special teachers
6. tutors — good manners

Check the Words You Know
__etiquette
__expenses
__podium
__quills
__segregation
__tutors

7–10. Directions Write a paragraph about the history of education in America. Use as many vocabulary words as you can.

Possible response: In the 1700s, girls went to school to learn good manners and etiquette. They also learned to manage household expenses. Boys who came from wealthy families could afford luxuries such as quills, or feather pens. Their parents often hired tutors to teach them Greek, Latin, science, and algebra. In the 1920s, in the south, there was black and white students did not study together because of segregation.

Advanced Practice TE p. LR9

ELL

ELL Reader

ELL Poster 1

Teacher's Edition Notes

ELL notes throughout this lesson support instruction and reference additional resources at point of use.

Teaching Guide
pp. 1–7, 212–213

- Multilingual summaries of the main selection
- Comprehension lesson
- Vocabulary strategies and word cards
- ELL Reader 5.1.1 lesson

ELL and Transition Handbook

Ten Important Sentences

- Key ideas from every selection in the Student Edition
- Activities to build sentence power

More Reading

Readers' Theater Anthology

- Fluency practice
- Five scripts to build fluency
- Poetry for oral interpretation

Leveled Trade Books

- Extended reading tied to the unit concept
- Lessons in the Trade Book Library Teaching Guide

Homework

- Family Times Newsletter
- ELL Multilingual Selection Summaries

Take-Home Books

- Leveled Readers

Cross-Curricular Centers

Listening

Listen to the Selections

MATERIALS
CD player, headphones, AudioText CD, student book

SINGLES

LISTEN TO LITERATURE Listen to *Frindle* and "Punctuation Takes a Vacation" as you follow or read along in your book. Listen for details about the characters and plot in both stories.

If there is anything you don't understand, you can listen again to any section.

Audio CD

Reading/ Library

Read It Again!

MATERIALS
Collection of books for self-selected reading, reading logs, student book

SINGLES
PAIRS
GROUPS

Select a book you have already read. Record the title of the book in your reading log. You may want to read with a partner.

Choose from the following:

- **Leveled Readers**
- **ELL Readers**
- **Stories Written by Classmates**
- **Books from the Library**
- ***Frindle***

TEN IMPORTANT SENTENCES Read the Ten Important Sentences for the story. Then locate the sentences in *Frindle*.

BOOK CLUB Identify and discuss some of the humorous details from *Frindle* to help you set up a genre study of humorous fiction. Read other books from this genre and get together with a group to share your favorites.

Drama

Write a Dialogue

MATERIALS
Paper, pencil, two-column chart

PAIRS
GROUPS

Find words describing Nick and Mrs. Granger.

1. **Complete a two-column chart with words from the story or your own words that describe Nick and Mrs. Granger.**
2. **Based on these words, write a dialogue that seems to fit their characters.**

EARLY FINISHERS Add stage directions for both characters to the dialogue. Remember that stage directions belong in parentheses.

"Mrs. Granger, how were all those words chosen for the dictionary?"

"Nick, that's an interesting question. Perhaps you could do some research tonight and find out."

Nick	Mrs. Granger
Class clown	strict
mischievous	stern

Scott Foresman Reading Street Centers Survival Kit

Use the *Frindle* materials from the Reading Street Centers Survival Kit to organize this week's centers.

Writing/ Vocabulary

Write a Narrative

MATERIALS Writing and art materials, journal

SINGLES

In *Frindle*, Nick was anxious about his first day as a fifth grader. Think about your own experiences on the first day of school.

1. **Write a journal entry using the following topic: "My Most Memorable First Day of School."**
2. **Be sure to include details that explain why that particular day was so memorable.**

EARLY FINISHERS Draw an illustration for your journal entry.

Social Studies

Research Education

MATERIALS Books on education in other countries, Internet access, writing and art materials, Venn diagram

SINGLES

PAIRS

Work alone or with a partner to research schools in another country.

1. **Find ways that the schools in that country are like schools in the United States, and ways they are different.**
2. **Organize your findings in a Venn diagram comparing and contrasting education in the two countries.**
3. **Share your results by displaying your finished chart in the classroom.**

EARLY FINISHERS Use a Venn diagram to design a pamphlet showing how education in the two countries is alike and how it is different.

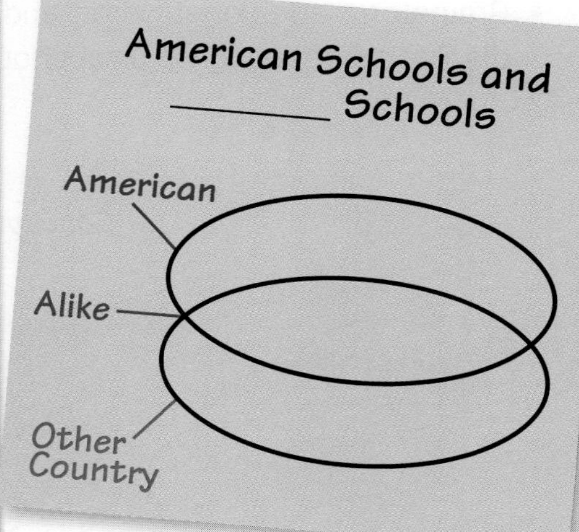

Technology

Compose an E-Mail

MATERIALS E-mail program, printer

SINGLES

Use e-mail to compose a new message to an older friend or relative.

1. **In your e-mail, explain why you are interested in learning about education in earlier times. Ask three questions about what school was like when that person was a student.**
2. **Type a topic into the subject line to let the person know what your message is about.**
3. **Proofread your message before printing it out.**

EARLY FINISHERS Imagine how different today's schools are from schools fifty or more years ago. Use your word processing program to write a short journal entry describing some of the ways you think things have changed.

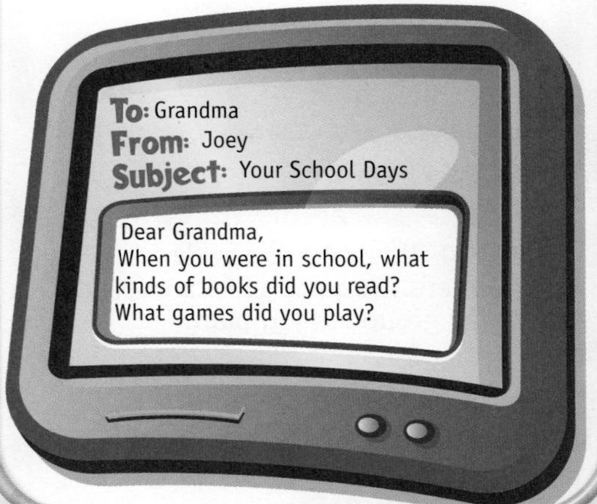

To: Grandma
From: Joey
Subject: Your School Days
Dear Grandma,
When you were in school, what kinds of books did you read? What games did you play?

Build Concepts

FLUENCY

MODEL TONE OF VOICE As you read "Understood Betsy," use your tone of voice to model reading with expression. You can use a nervous or anxious tone of voice for Betsy and a more confident tone for Cousin Ann's reactions to Betsy.

LISTENING COMPREHENSION

After reading "Understood Betsy," use the following questions to assess listening comprehension.

1. **How would you describe Betsy?** *(Possible answers: eager to please, nervous, anxious)* ***Character***
2. **What is the problem in this story?** *(Betsy made some mistakes in school in front of the superintendent and is upset about it.)* ***Plot***

BUILD CONCEPT VOCABULARY

Start a web to build concepts and vocabulary related to this week's lesson and the unit theme.

- Draw the Challenges in Education Concept Web.
- Read the sentence with the word *superintendent* again. Ask students to pronounce *superintendent* and discuss its meaning.
- Place *superintendent* in an oval attached to *People*. Explain that *superintendent* is related to this concept. Read the sentences in which *examinations* and *mistakes* appear. Have students pronounce the words, place them on the web, and provide reasons.
- Brainstorm additional words and categories for the web. Keep the web on display and add words throughout the week.

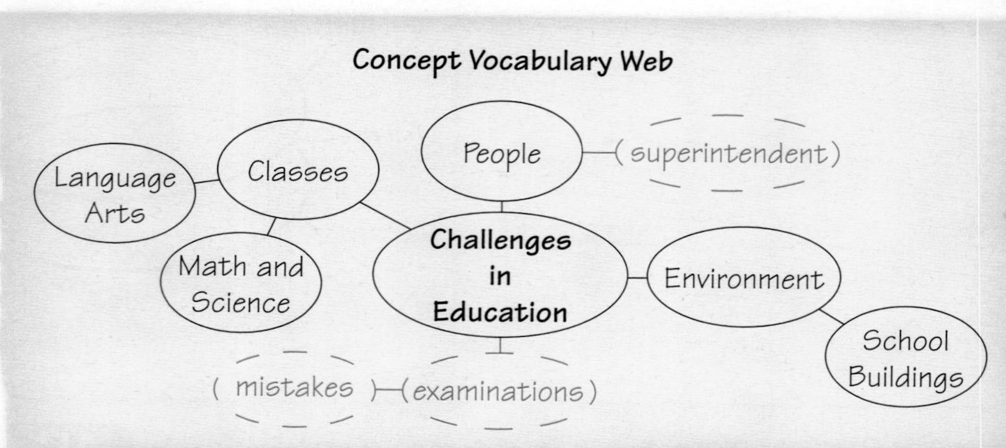

OBJECTIVES

- Build vocabulary by finding words related to the lesson concept.
- Listen for details about character and plot.

Concept Vocabulary

examinations tests of knowledge
mistakes errors or blunders
superintendent person who oversees or directs schools

Monitor Progress

Check Word Use

If...	then...
students are unable to place words on the web,	review the lesson concept. Place the words on the web and provide additional words for practice, such as *curriculum* and *anxiety.*

SUCCESS PREDICTOR

DAY 1 Grouping Options

Reading

Whole Group
Introduce and discuss the Question of the Week. Then use pp. 18l–20b.

Group Time
Differentiated Instruction
Read this week's Leveled Readers. See pp. 18h–18i for the small group lesson plan.

Whole Group
Use p. 41a.

Language Arts
Use pp. 41e–41k.

Understood Betsy

by Dorothy Canfield Fisher

Betsy is upset because she had a hard day at school. Her cousin, Ann, tries to make her feel better over a special taffy-like treat called "waxed syrup."

"Hello, Betsy, you're just in time. I've saved a cupful of hot syrup for you, all ready to wax."

Betsy hardly heard this, although she had been wild about waxed sugar on snow ever since her very first taste of it. "Cousin Ann," she said unhappily, "the Superintendent visited our school this afternoon."

"Did he?" said Cousin Ann, dipping a thermometer into the boiling syrup.

"Yes, and we had examinations!" said Betsy.

"Did you?" said Cousin Ann, holding the thermometer up to the light and looking at it.

"And you know how perfectly awful examinations make you feel," said Betsy, very near to tears again.

"Why, no," said Cousin Ann, sorting over syrup tins. "They never made me feel awful. I thought they were sort of fun."

"Fun!" Betsy cried indignantly, staring through the beginnings of her tears.

"Why, yes. Like taking a dare, don't you know. Somebody stumps you to jump off the hitching-post, and you do it to show 'em. I always used to think examinations were like that. Somebody stumps you to spell 'pneumonia,' and you do it to show 'em. Here's your cup of syrup. You'd better go right out and wax it while it's hot."

Elizabeth Ann automatically took the cup in her hand, but she did not look at it. "But supposing you get so scared you can't spell 'pneumonia' or anything else!" She stopped. Cousin Ann had said she did *not* know all those things. "Well, anyhow, I got so scared I could hardly stand up! And I made the most awful mistakes—things I know just as *well*! I spelled 'doubt' without any *b* and 'separate' with an *e*, and I said Iowa was bounded on the north by *Wisconsin*, and I..."

"Oh, well," said Cousin Ann, "it doesn't matter if you really know the right answers, does it? That's the important thing."

This was an idea which had never in all her life entered Betsy's brain and she did not take it in at all now. She only shook her head miserably and went on in a doleful tone. "And I said 13 and 8 are 22! and I wrote March without any capital *M*, and I..."

"Look here, Betsy, do you *want* to tell me all this?" Cousin Ann spoke in the quick, ringing voice she used every once in a while...Betsy gathered [her thoughts]; and she came to an unexpected conclusion. No, she didn't really want to tell Cousin Ann all about it. Why was she doing it? Because she thought that was the thing to do. "Because if you don't really want to," went on Cousin Ann, "I don't see that it's doing anybody any good. I guess Hemlock Mountain will stand right there just the same even if you did forget to put a *b* in 'doubt.' And your syrup will be too cool to wax right if you don't take it out pretty soon."

BEFORE READING

Activate Prior Knowledge

Before students listen to the Read Aloud, ask them what they know about the challenges of taking tests.

Set Purpose

Read the title aloud and have students predict what the selection will be about.

Read the introduction aloud. Have students listen for details about Betsy and events related to the plot of the story, for example, the problem, rising actions, climax, and resolution.

Creative Response

Have students work in pairs to improvise a conversation in which Betsy tells another family member about her day at school. Remind students that Betsy may view the day differently after her conversation with Cousin Ann. ***Drama***

Access Content Before reading, share this summary: Betsy tells Cousin Ann how badly she did on her test, and Cousin Ann tries to make her feel better.

Homework Send home this week's Family Times newsletter.

SUCCES PREDICTO

SKILLS ↔ STRATEGIES IN CONTEXT

Character and Plot Prior Knowledge

OBJECTIVES

- Identify the main character and plot of the story.
- Use prior knowledge to understand story characters and events.

Skills Trace

Character and Plot

Introduce/Teach	**TE: 5.1 18–19, 68–69; 5.5 512–513**
Practice	Practice Book: 3, 7, 8, 16, 23, 26, 27, 28, 96, 203, 207, 208
Reteach/Review	TE: 5.1 41b, 49, 61, 77, 89b, DI•52, DI•54; 5.2 237; 5.5 535b, DI•52
Test	Selection Test: 1–4, 9–12, 81–84; Benchmark Test: Unit 1

INTRODUCE

Name and briefly summarize a book that will be familiar to students; for example, a *Harry Potter* book. Ask students to identify the main character and tell about some of the key events in the story's plot. *(Responses will vary.)*

Have students read the information on p. 18. Explain the following:

- Most stories have one or more characters, a problem or conflict, and actions leading to a climax and resolution of the problem.
- Thinking about what you already know about the story's author, main characters, and plot can help you follow story events and figure out what might happen next.

Use Skill Transparency 1 to teach literary elements and prior knowledge.

Comprehension

Skill
Plot and Character

Strategy
Prior Knowledge

Plot and Character

Skill

- The plot is the pattern of events in a story.
- A plot includes (1) a problem or conflict, (2) rising action, as the conflict builds, (3) a climax, when the problem or conflict is faced, and (4) a resolution, when the problem or conflict is solved. See the story map below.

- Characters are people or animals in a story.
- Characters show you what they're like by what they say and do and how they treat each other.

Strategy: Prior Knowledge

Good readers use what they already know to help them follow a story. Before you read, look at the title, illustrations, and author. Have you read stories by this author before? Remember that you will read about characters, a problem, and how that problem is resolved.

Write to Read

1. Read "Homework Help." As you read, make a story map like the one above.
2. Write a new resolution for "Homework Help." Use your story map and your own knowledge of homework to help you.

18

Strategic Intervention

Character and Plot Remind students they can learn about characters and story events by paying attention to what the characters say and do. Have pairs reread the story, one paragraph at a time, stopping and making notes about Anna's problem, her ideas for solving the problem, the climax of the story, and the way in which the problem is resolved.

ELL

Access Content

Beginning/Intermediate For a Picture It! lesson on plot and character, see the ELL Teaching Guide, pp. 1–2.

Advanced Have students preview "Homework Help" by identifying the names of the characters they will read about. After reading, ask them to tell something about each character they identified.

Homework Help

Anna was rushing to get to school. r mom exclaimed, "I see the bus!" na stuffed toast in her mouth and thered up her homework from the table.

She darted outside and hopped onto the s. Her history report was due today. She decided examine it one last time. Anna searched her ckpack, but there was no report. She groaned d thought, *I can't believe I forgot my report! hat am I going to do?*

Anna began to imagine how she could get that port. Her dog was always snorting around the table oking for scraps from a meal. Maybe he would snatch r report, sprint to school, and slide it under her locker or. Well, Max was smart, but not THAT smart.

Another idea came to Anna. Perhaps a hurricane-ce wind would blow through the kitchen window. would carry her report to school and drop it on Mr. ulligan's desk. Hmm, that idea was unlikely too.

As Anna got off the bus, she realized that the only ution was to be honest and tell Mr. Mulligan what ppened. Suddenly, Anna heard a blaring horn. ere was her mom, waving her report out their r window. Anna dashed over to the car. "Thanks, m," she sighed. "You're the greatest!"

1 **Skill** Who is the main character in this story? What is the problem?

2 **Strategy** Ask: "Has this ever happened to me?" If so, how did you deal with the problem? What do you think Anna will do?

3 **Skill** What kind of person is Anna? How can you tell?

4 **Strategy** Based on other stories you have read, did you expect this story to end this way? Why or why not?

19

Available as **Skill Transparency** 1

t and Character

- The **plot** is the pattern of events in a story.
- A plot includes (1) a problem or **conflict,** (2) **rising action,** as the conflict builds, (3) a **climax,** when the problem or conflict is faced, and (4) a **resolution,** when the problem or conflict is solved.

ctions Read the following passage. Then complete the diagram by filling in the elements of ory.

Julia was worried about the school fundraiser. She was one of the organizers, but it didn't seem that much had been organized. She spent Saturday afternoon helping the other volunteers make signs, set up tables in the gym, and hang decorations. Suddenly, she realized that they had forgotten an important part of the fundraiser: the bake sale! Nobody had baked anything yet. Julia called seven of her friends and got them to agree to bake things for the sale. She took a deep breath. Maybe the fundraiser would be a success, after all.

oblem or Conflict
Julia is worried about the school fundraiser.

sing Action
The volunteers make signs.

sing Action
e volunteers set up tables

sing Action
The volunteers hang decorations.

imax
Julia realizes that nobody has baked for the bake sale.

solution
Possible answer: Julia calls her friends and they agree to help.

ool ome **Home Activity** Your child analyzed the plot of a short passage. Discuss a story with your child and identify its problem or conflict, rising action, climax, and resolution.

Practice Book p. 3

BEFORE READING

TEACH

1 **SKILL** Use paragraphs 1 and 2 to model how to identify the main character and problem in the story.

MODEL As I read the first paragraph, I meet a girl named Anna, who is rushing to get to the school bus. By the end of the second paragraph, I learn that, in her rush, Anna has forgotten her report at home. This must be the problem.

2 **STRATEGY** Use prior knowledge to predict what might happen next.

MODEL If I think back to similar situations I've been in, I can figure out what Anna might do. For example, let's say I forgot something important for school. I could make up an excuse, or admit that I forgot it. If Anna is anything like me, I think she is likely to do one of these things.

PRACTICE AND ASSESS

3 **SKILL** Anna is honest and responsible. She did her assignment, but forgot it. She decides to tell her teacher the truth.

4 **STRATEGY** Answers will vary, but should reflect events in other stories they have read.

WRITE Have students complete steps 1 and 2 of the Write to Read activity. Remind students that the resolution is the solution to the problem; in this case, Anna's mother brings her homework to school. You might consider using this as a whole-class activity.

Monitor Progress

Character and Plot

If... students are unable to complete **Write to Read** on p. 18,	then... use Practice Book p. 3 to provide additional practice.

Build Background

ACTIVATE PRIOR KNOWLEDGE

BEGIN A T-CHART about the challenges that accompany the start of a new school year.

- Give students two to three minutes to write about the challenges of starting a new school year. Prompt them with examples provided on the T-chart.
- Give students two minutes to write some things they can do to meet those challenges and ensure that the new school year gets off to a good start. Encourage them to think back to the start of school in years past.
- Tell students that, as they read, they should add information to the chart.

Challenges of a New School Year	Ways to Meet Challenges
1. New teacher	1. Understand his or her expectations
2. New classroom rules	
3. New school	
4. More homework	
5. New students	

▲ **Graphic Organizer** 25

BACKGROUND BUILDING AUDIO This week's audio explores funny characters and stories in the classroom. After students listen, discuss what they found out and how it relates to any funny experiences they may have had in the classroom.

Background Building Audio

Students can use the keywords *school rules* or *back to school* in a student-friendly search engine for information about how to start off the school year on the right foot. Be sure to follow classroom guidelines for Internet use.

ELL

Build Background Use ELL Poster 1 to build background and vocabulary for the lesson concept of education.

▲ **ELL Poster** 1

Introduce Vocabulary

PREDICT DEFINITIONS

Have students predict a definition and write a sample sentence for each word. Direct them to underline the word in each sentence, then verify its meaning in the dictionary. Check all sentences to be sure that words are used correctly. Have students rewrite any sentences that are incorrect. You may wish to continue this activity with the More Words to Know. ***Activate Prior Knowledge***

Ask students to share if they have seen some of these words before. Tell them that they may be familiar with synonyms and/or antonyms for some of this week's more difficult words like *essential*, *acquainted*, and *expanded*. ***Synonyms • Antonyms***

Have students return to their synonym/antonym list at the end of the week and expand it to include other vocabulary words.

Also, if students have difficulty decoding multisyllabic words, have them use these steps for reading them. (See the Multisyllabic Word Routine on p. DI·1.)

1. **Look for Meaningful Word Parts** (base words, endings, prefixes, suffixes, roots) Think about the meaning of each part. Use the parts to read the word. Model: I see *–ed* at the end of *acquainted. Acquaint* means "to make aware" or "to inform; let know," and *–ed* means it happened in the past. Therefore, *acquainted* means "made aware" or "informed."
2. **Chunk Words with No Recognizable Parts** Say each chunk slowly. Then say the chunks fast to make a word. Model: *cam, e, o—cameo.*

Lesson Vocabulary

WORDS TO KNOW

T acquainted made aware; informed

T assignment something assigned, especially a piece of work to be done

T essential absolutely necessary; very important

T expanded made larger; increased in size; enlarged

T guaranteed made certain that something would happen as a result

T procedures ways of proceeding; methods of doing things

T reputation what people think and say the character of someone or something is

T worshipped paid great honor and reverence to

MORE WORDS TO KNOW

cameo a semiprecious stone carved so that there is a raised design on a background, usually of a different color

shutdown a stopping; a checking of

sidetrack to draw someone's attention away from something

T = Tested Word

Vocabulary

Directions Choose the word from the box that best matches each definition. Write the word on the line shown to the left.

worshipped	1.	paid great honor or reverence to
procedures	2.	methods of doing things
expanded	3.	made larger
essential	4.	absolutely necessary
reputation	5.	what people think or say the character of someone is

Check the Words You Know

___acquainted
___assignment
___essential
___expanded
___guaranteed
___procedures
___reputation
___worshipped

Directions Choose the word from the box that best completes the sentences below. Write the word on the line shown to the left.

guaranteed	6.	He ____ that his plan would be a success.
reputation	7.	Her excellent ____ was the main reason her teachers trusted her.
assignment	8.	He had a million excuses for why he didn't turn in the ____.
essential	9.	Good music is an ____ part of any dance party.
acquainted	10.	I got ____ with my new teammates while we waited for practice to start.

Write an Advertisement

Pretend you own a company. On a separate sheet of paper, write a script for a radio advertisement about your company's new product or service. Use as many vocabulary words from this week as you can.

Advertisements should include vocabulary words from the list and provide some detail about the product or service.

School + Home **Home Activity** Your child identified and used vocabulary words from the story *Frindle*. Review the definitions of each of the vocabulary words with your child and work together to use the words in sentences.

▲ **Practice Book** p. 4

DAY 2

Vocabulary Strategy

OBJECTIVE

Use word structure to determine word meaning.

INTRODUCE

Discuss the strategy for word structure using the steps on p. 20.

TEACH

- Have students read "Becoming a Word Wizard," paying attention to how vocabulary is used.
- Model using word structure to determine the meaning of *reputation*.

MODEL The word *reputation* ends with the suffix *-tion,* which means "the result of." The base word *repute* means "to be considered in a certain way." If I put the meanings of the base word and the suffix together, I can figure out the meaning of the word. *Reputation* means "the way in which others consider or think about you."

Frindle

Words to Know

reputation
worshipped
essential
acquainted
assignment
expanded
procedures
guaranteed

Remember

Try the strategy. Then, if you need more help, use your glossary or dictionary.

Vocabulary Strategy for Suffixes

Word Structure When you come to a longer word you don't know, see if it ends with *-tion, -ation,* or *-ment.* These suffixes are added to verbs to turn them into nouns that mean "the act or state of _____" or "the result of _____." For example, *development* means "the act of developing" or "the result of developing." You may be able to use the suffix to help figure out the unknown word's meaning.

1. Cover the suffix *-tion, -ation,* or *-ment.*
2. Look at the base word. Do you know what it means? (Try this with *assignment.*)
3. Add the meaning of the suffix. Remember, the part of speech will change.
4. Reread the sentence to see if your meaning makes sense.

As you read "Becoming a Word Wizard," look for base words that end in *-tion, -ation,* or *-ment.* Use the suffixes to help you figure out the meanings of the words.

20

DAY 2 Grouping Options

Reading

Whole Group Discuss the Question of the Day. Then use pp. 20–23.

Group Time Differentiated Instruction

Read *Frindle.* See pp. 18h–18i for the small group lesson plan.

Whole Group Use p. 41a.

Language Arts

Use pp. 41e–41k.

Strategic Intervention

Word Structure Have students work in pairs to write meanings for *explanation* and *organization.* Remind them to follow the steps on p. 20. They can use a dictionary to check meanings.

Access Content Use ELL Poster 1 to preteach vocabulary. Choose from the following to meet language proficiency levels.

Beginning In Spanish, *-mente* changes an adjective to an adverb, like adding *-ly* on English. In English, *-ment* creates a noun.

Intermediate Have students use a three-column chart labeled *base, suffix,* and *vocabulary word* to organize vocabulary. Show them how the base and the suffix can help them understand the vocabulary word.

Advanced Teach the lesson on pp. 20–21. Students can report on popular suffixes in their home languages.

Resources for home-language words may include parents, bilingual staff members, bilingual dictionaries, or online translation sources.

Becoming a Word Wizard

Would you like to build a powerful reputation as a word wizard? You may have seen that some people have a strong command of words. They always seem to know the perfect word to use at just the right time. If you have worshipped these people from afar, do not fear. You too can become one of them. However, it is essential that you study the dictionary. You will need to find a dictionary you like and make it your close personal friend.

To get acquainted with your dictionary, read the explanation in the front. It will explain the parts and organization of the word entries and tell you how to use the book.

As you find new words, make it your assignment to look them up. Learn their pronunciations, meanings, and histories. Make it a point to use them as you speak and write. Before you know it, your vocabulary will be expanded many times. These procedures are guaranteed to help you sound smarter and understand what you read better.

Words to Write

Write an article explaining how to become a better student. Use as many words in the Words to Know list as you can.

21

Connect to Phonics

Word Study/Decoding Point out that a suffix changes the meaning of the base word. Model identifying the suffix and base word using *assignment* on p. 21, paragraph 3. Have students suggest other words they know with *-tion, -ation,* and *-ment.* Have students identify the suffix and base in each word. Then have them identify the meaning of each word with and without the suffix.

PRACTICE AND ASSESS

- Have students use word structure to figure out the meanings of other unfamiliar words they come across in the selection.
- Point out that word structure doesn't work with every word. Students may have to use context clues, the glossary or a dictionary to find the exact meaning of some words.
- Invite students to look back at their predicted definitions (p. 20b), and tell what more they learned about each word. Have them use each word in a sentence.
- Have students complete Practice Book p. 5.

WRITE Writing should include vocabulary words that are related to the development of good study skills and becoming a better student.

Monitor Progress

 **Context Clues**

If... students need more practice with the lesson vocabulary,	**then...** use Tested Vocabulary Cards.

Vocabulary • Word Structure

- A **suffix** is added to the end of a word to change its meaning or the type of word it is. Recognizing suffixes will help you figure out a word's meaning.
- The suffixes *–tion, –ation,* and *–ment* all make a word mean "the act or state of ____" or "the result of ____," as in the words *development* or *sensation.* They all turn verbs into nouns.

Directions Read the following passage about meeting new people. Then answer the questions below.

One of my assignments was to try to interview a well-known figure in our town. My teacher told us to always keep an open mind when meeting new people. She said that this was the most important instruction she could give us. Sometimes, she said, a person's reputation will come before them. Other times, a popular person who appears to be worshipped by others simply rubs you the wrong way. I looked forward to the enjoyment I would get from this assignment, so I started on it right away.

1. What part of speech is *reputation?* How do you know?
   It is a noun; *–ation* turns a verb into a noun.
2. What does *assignment* mean? What is the suffix?
   Something that is assigned like homework; *–ment*
3. How does the suffix change the meaning of the base word in *instruction?*
   It turns "instruct" into "the result of instructing."
4. What suffix is added to the word *enjoy?* What does *enjoyment* mean?
   –ment; act of enjoying
5. Write a sentence using the words *reputation* and *assignment.*
   Possible answer: The teacher had a reputation for giving very difficult assignments to her students.

School + Home **Home Activity** Your child identified and answered questions about suffixes in a passage. Have your child add different suffixes to words and define the new words.

▲ **Practice Book** p. 5

BEFORE READING

Prereading Strategies

OBJECTIVES

- Activate and use prior knowledge to improve comprehension.
- Use prior knowledge to help recognize character and plot.

GENRE STUDY

Humorous Fiction

Frindle is humorous fiction. Explain that humorous fiction tells the story of imaginary people who seem real. Story events are true-to-life and often funny.

PREVIEW AND PREDICT

Have students preview the selection title and illustrations and discuss the topics or ideas they think this selection will cover. Have students use selection vocabulary words as they talk about what they expect to learn.

Strategy Response Log

Predict Have students write their predictions in their strategy response logs. Students will check their predictions in the Strategy Response Log activity on p. 29.

Frĭn′·dle

by Andrew Clements
illustrated by James Bernardin

Humorous fiction has characters and action that make you laugh. As you read, notice how the author makes you wonder how things will turn out in the end.

22

ELL

Activate Prior Knowledge Have students talk about qualities of helpful teachers. Provide vocabulary as needed.

Consider having students read the selection summary in English or in students' home languages. See the Multilingual Summaries in the ELL Teaching Guide, pp. 5–7.

How do Nick and Mrs. Granger meet the challenge of getting to know each other?
23

SET PURPOSE

Discuss the illustration on the first page of the selection. Have students read to find out what happens as the two main characters get to know each other.

Remind students to use their prior knowledge as they read.

STRATEGY RECALL

Students have now used these before-reading strategies:

- preview the selection to be aware of its genre, features, and possible content;
- activate prior knowledge about that content and what to expect of that genre;
- make predictions;
- set a purpose for reading.

Remind students to be aware of and flexibly use the during-reading strategies they have learned:

- link prior knowledge to new information;
- summarize text they have read so far;
- ask clarifying questions;
- answer questions they or others pose;
- check their predictions and either refine them or make new predictions;
- recognize the text structure the author is using, and use that knowledge to make predictions and increase comprehension;
- visualize what the author is describing;
- monitor their comprehension and use fix-up strategies.

After reading, students will use these strategies:

- summarize or retell the text;
- answer questions they or others pose;
- reflect to make new information become part of their prior knowledge.

AudioText

Guiding Comprehension

1 Vocabulary • Context Clues
Use context clues to determine the meaning of *monopoly* on p. 25, paragraph 2, sentence 3.
Clues: There were seven fifth-grade teachers but only one language arts teacher for all 150 kids in fifth grade. Meaning: complete control of something.

2 Character • Inferential
What kind of teacher is Mrs. Granger?
Possible response: She is a dedicated teacher who is set in her ways.

Monitor Progress	
Character and Plot	
If... students are unable to infer character traits,	**then...** use the skill and strategy instruction on p. 25.

Access Content Tell students that the words *monopoly* and *reputation* have Spanish cognates (*monopolio* and *reputación*). Explain that to have a *monopoly* means to have total control over something. A *reputation* is what people think or say the character of another person is. Ask students to use these words to describe Mrs. Granger.

Fifth grade was different. That was the year to get ready for middle school. Fifth grade meant passing classes. It meant no morning recess. It meant real letter grades on your report cards. But most of all, it meant Mrs. Granger.

There were about one hundred fifty kids in fifth grade. And there were seven fifth-grade teachers: two math, two science, two social studies, but only one language arts teacher. In language arts, Mrs. Granger had a monopoly—and a reputation. 1

Mrs. Granger lived alone in a tidy little house in the older part of town. She drove an old, pale blue car to school every morning, rain or shine, snow or sleet, hail or wind. She had 2 a perfect attendance record that stretched back farther than anyone could remember.

Her hair was almost white, swept away from her face and up into something like a nest on the back of her head. Unlike some of the younger women teachers, she never wore pants to school. She had two skirt-and-jacket outfits, her gray uniform and her blue uniform, which she always wore over a white shirt with a little cameo pin at the neck. And Mrs. Granger was one of those people who never sweats. It had to be over ninety degrees before she even took off her jacket.

SKILLS ↔ STRATEGIES IN CONTEXT

Character and Plot

TEACH

- Explain that character and plot are essential elements of a fictional story. Note that the characterization in this story is especially rich.
- To learn what a character is like we can look at the words the author uses to describe the character, how the character interacts with others, and what the other characters say about that character. Understanding characters help readers predict events in the story.
- Use p. 25, paragraph 3 to model how to find out about a character.

MODEL First I'll read the sentences in the paragraph to see what they tell me about Mrs. Granger. I learn that Mrs. Granger lives in a small, tidy house; drives an older car to school every day no matter what the weather; and that she has never missed a day of school. If I put this information together, I can infer that she is a serious person who is dedicated to her profession.

PRACTICE AND ASSESS

Have students reread p. 25, paragraph 4. Ask them to use the information in the paragraph to decide which of the following statements best describes Mrs. Granger. *(Choice b)*

a) She is popular.

b) She is old-fashioned.

c) She is trendy.

Guiding Comprehension

3 Simile • Inferential

What do you learn about Mrs. Granger from the simile "Mrs. Granger seemed like a giant"?

Mrs. Granger had power over her students.

4 Cause and Effect • Literal

What happened to the students that Mrs. Granger caught chewing gum?

She made them stick the gum onto index cards, which were then safety-pinned onto their shirts and worn for the rest of the day. They also had to bring the card home for their parent to sign.

Monitor Progress

REVIEW Cause and Effect

If... students have difficulty identifying cause and effect,	**then...** use the skill and strategy instruction on p. 27.

She was small, as teachers go. There were even some fifth graders who were taller. But Mrs. Granger seemed like a giant.
3 It was her eyes that did it. They were dark gray, and if she turned them on full power, they could make you feel like a speck of dust. Her eyes could twinkle and laugh, too, and kids said she could crack really funny jokes. But it wasn't the jokes that made her famous.

Everyone was sure that Mrs. Granger had X-ray vision. Don't even think about chewing a piece of gum within fifty feet
4 of her. If you did, Mrs. Granger would see you and catch you and make you stick the gum onto a bright yellow index card. Then she would safety-pin the card to the front of your shirt, and you'd have to wear it for the rest of the school day. After that, you had to take it home and have your mom or dad sign the card, and bring it back to Mrs. Granger the next day. And it didn't matter to Mrs. Granger if you weren't in fifth grade, because the way she saw it, sooner or later, you would be.

All the kids at Lincoln Elementary School knew that at the end of the line—fifth grade—Mrs. Granger would be the one grading their spelling tests and their reading tests, and worst of all, their vocabulary tests—week after week, month after month.

Every language arts teacher in the world enjoys making kids use the dictionary: "Check your spelling. Check that definition. Check those syllable breaks."

But Mrs. Granger didn't just enjoy the dictionary. She *loved* the dictionary—almost worshipped it. Her weekly vocabulary list was thirty-five words long, sometimes longer.

26

Understanding Idioms Read aloud p. 26, paragraph 2, sentence 1, "Everyone was sure that Mrs. Granger had X-ray vision." Explain that an *X-ray* is an electromagnetic ray that sees through things and is often used by doctors to see inside bodies. *X-ray vision*, then, means "eyesight so strong it practically sees through things." In this case, the author was exaggerating how powerful Mrs. Granger's eyes were.

As if that wasn't bad enough, there was a "Word for the Day" on the blackboard every morning. If you gave yourself a day off and didn't write one down and look it up and learn the definition—sooner or later Mrs. Granger would find out, and then, just for you, there would be two Words for the Day for a whole week.

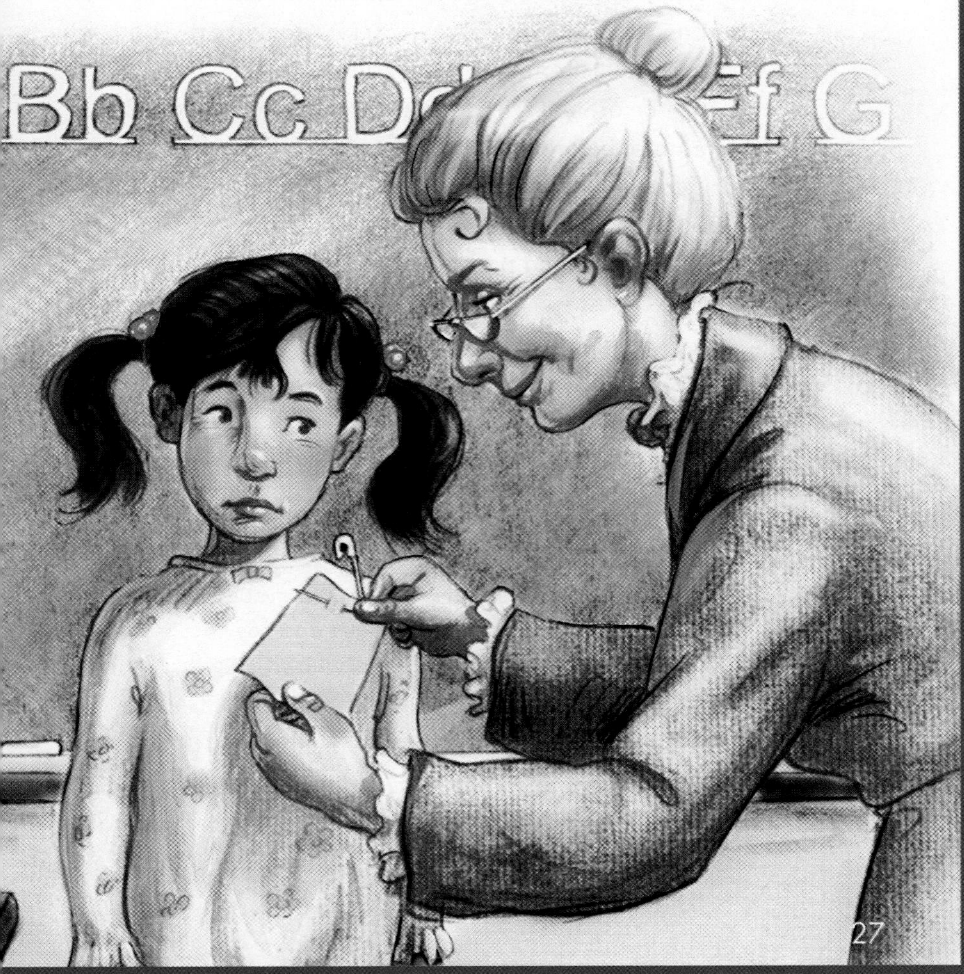

Time for SOCIAL STUDIES

)ictionaries

efore the widespread availability and use of dic- onaries, there was no consistent style or spelling f words. People spelled words the way they sounded, hich meant that the same word could be spelled several differ- nt ways, making communication more difficult. In the United States, ictionaries came into wider use in schools during the 18th century. oah Webster, who grew up during the American Revolution, believed an independent United States. He thought that America should reate a unique language with its own style, pronunciation, and spell- ıgs. Distinctly American words, spellings, and phrases were known as Americanisms." In 1806, Webster published the first American diction- ry called *A Compendious Dictionary of the English Language.*

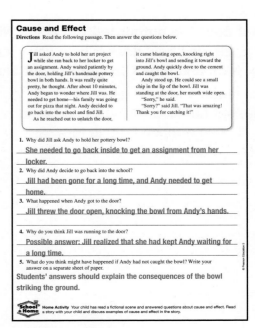

SKILLS ↔ STRATEGIES IN CONTEXT

Cause and Effect REVIEW

TEACH

- An effect is what happens and a cause is why it happens.
- Clue words such as *if* and *then* sometimes signal causes and effects.
- An effect may have more than one cause and a cause may have more than one effect.

Think Aloud **MODEL** The second sentence of the second paragraph, p. 26 says that students should not chew gum near Mrs. Granger. The words "If you did" in the next sentence signal multiple effects: students have to stick the gum onto an index card, wear the card pinned to their shirts, and bring it home to be signed.

PRACTICE AND ASSESS

- Have students identify a cause-and-effect relationship. *(If you didn't know the definition of the "Word for the Day" and Mrs. Granger caught you, you would get two Words for the Day for a week.)*
- To assess, use Practice Book p. 6.

Cause and Effect

Directions Read the following passage. Then answer the questions below.

Jill asked Andy to hold her art project while she ran back to her locker to get an assignment. Andy waited patiently by the door, holding Jill's handmade pottery bowl in both hands. It was really quite pretty, he thought. After about 10 minutes, Andy began to wonder where Jill was. He needed to get home—his family was going out for pizza that night. Andy decided to go back into the school and find Jill.

As he reached out to unlatch the door, it came blasting open, knocking right into Jill's bowl and sending it toward the ground. Andy quickly dove to the cement and caught the bowl.

Andy stood up. He could see a small chip in the lip of the bowl. Jill was standing at the door, her mouth wide open.

"Sorry," he said.

"Sorry?" said Jill. "That was amazing! Thank you for catching it!"

1. Why did Jill ask Andy to hold her pottery bowl?
   She needed to go back inside to get an assignment from her locker.
2. Why did Andy decide to go back into the school?
   Jill had been gone for a long time, and Andy needed to get home.
3. What happened when Andy got to the door?
   Jill threw the door open, knocking the bowl from Andy's hands.
4. Why do you think Jill was running to the door?
   Possible answer: Jill realized that she had kept Andy waiting for a long time.
5. What do you think might have happened if Andy had not caught the bowl? Write your answer on a separate sheet of paper.

Students' answers should explain the consequences of the bowl striking the ground.

School + Home **Home Activity** Your child has read a fictional scene and answered questions about cause and effect. Read a story with your child and discuss examples of cause and effect in the story.

▲ **Practice Book** p. 6

DURING READING

Guiding Comprehension

5 Prior Knowledge • Critical

Nick receives a letter from school before school starts. Has this ever happened to you? How did this make you feel?

Answers will vary, but some students will identify with Nick's dread, while others will recall curiosity or excitement.

Monitor Progress

Prior Knowledge

If... students have difficulty activating and using prior knowledge,	**then...** use the skill and strategy instruction on p. 29.

6 Compare and Contrast • Inferential

How does Mrs. Allen's reaction to Mrs. Granger's letter compare to Nick's reaction?

Mrs. Allen thinks Mrs. Granger takes her work seriously. Nick becomes anxious about school.

7 Predict • Inferential

What does the author tell you about Nick on p. 29, and how does it help you predict how Nick and Mrs. Granger will get along?

Nick reads a lot and uses words all the time, but he doesn't use the dictionary. He might have a tough time in Mrs. Granger's class.

Mrs. Granger kept a full set of thirty dictionaries on a shelf at the back of the room. But her pride and joy was one of those huge dictionaries with every word in the universe in it, the kind of book it takes two kids to carry. It sat on its own little table at the front of her classroom, sort of like the altar at the front of a church.

Every graduate of Lincoln Elementary School for the past thirty-five years could remember standing at that table listening to Mrs. Granger's battle cry: "Look it up! That's why we have the dictionary."

Even before the school year started, when it was still the summer before fifth grade for Nick and his friends, Mrs. Granger was already busy. Every parent of every new fifth grader got a letter from her.

5 Nick's mom read part of it out loud during dinner one night in August.

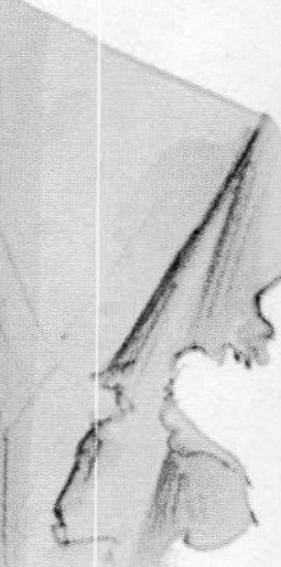

Every home is expected to have a good dictionary in it so that each student can do his or her homework properly. Good spelling and good grammar and good word skills are essential for every student. Clear thinking requires a command of the English language, and fifth grade is the ideal time for every girl and boy to acquire an expanded vocabulary.

And then there was a list of the dictionaries that Mrs. Granger thought would be "acceptable for home study."

Mrs. Allen said, "It's so nice to have a teacher who takes her work this seriously."

28

Understanding Idioms Read the sentence that begins, "When Nick ran into a word he didn't know..." Explain that the phrase *ran into* usually means "met or found by chance." For example, I ran into my teacher at the movies. Ask students what Nick usually did when he ran into a word he didn't know.

Nick groaned and tried to enjoy the rest of his hamburger. But even watermelon for dessert didn't cheer him up much. 6

Nick had no particular use for the dictionary. He liked words a lot, and he was good at using them. But he figured that he got all the words he needed just by reading, and he read all the time.

When Nick ran into a word he didn't know, he asked his brother or his dad or whoever was handy what it meant, and if they knew, they'd tell him. But not Mrs. Granger. He had heard all about her, and he had seen fifth graders in the library last year, noses stuck in their dictionaries, frantically trying to finish their vocabulary sheets before English class. 7

It was still a week before school and Nick already felt like fifth grade was going to be a very long year.

29

SKILLS ↔ STRATEGIES IN CONTEXT

Character/Plot Prior Knowledge

TEACH

Ask students to explain how using prior knowledge helps them better understand the characters and the plot of a story. (Possible responses: *When I think about meeting a new coach or teacher, it helps me understand Nick and the things that happened to him.*) Use this exercise to model how activating prior knowledge helps improve understanding of characters and plot.

MODEL The first sentence on p. 29 says "Nick groaned" after his mother finished reading the letter from Mrs. Granger. I can think back to a time when a teacher sent a letter home to my parents and how it made me feel. I can use my own experience to better understand how Nick feels.

PRACTICE AND ASSESS

Have students activate prior knowledge and use personal experiences to understand Nick's feelings and actions as they read the rest of the story.

Strategy Response Log

Confirm Predictions Provide the following prompt: Were your predictions accurate? Revise your old predictions. (See p. 22.) Then write new ones about the rest of the story.

Develop Vocabulary

PRACTICE LESSON VOCABULARY

Students respond *yes* or *no* orally to each question and give a reason.

1. Is it *guaranteed* that every student will love a new challenge? *(No, it is not certain. Some may be nervous at first.)*
2. Are students *acquainted* with other students in class? *(Yes, because students usually know each other from the previous grade.)*
3. Have students *expanded* their vocabulary if they have learned and use new words? *(Yes, they have increased their vocabulary.)*

BUILD CONCEPT VOCABULARY

Review previous concept words with students. Ask if students have come across any words today in their reading that they would like to add to the Challenges in Education Concept Web, such as *graduate* and *essential.*

If you want to teach this selection in two sessions, stop here.

DAY 3

Guiding Comprehension

If you are teaching the selection in two days, discuss the characters and plot so far and review the vocabulary.

8 **Vocabulary • Word Structure**

Have students use their knowledge of the suffix *-ment* to figure out the meaning of *assignment* on p. 31, paragraph 3.

The suffix *-ment* turns the verb *assign* into the noun *assignment,* which means "a task that is given to be done."

Monitor Progress

Word Structure

If... students are unable to use word structure to figure out the meaning of *assignment,*	**then...** use the vocabulary strategy instruction on p. 31.

9 **Author's Purpose • Critical**

Why did the author tell us about Nick's success with delaying questions?

Possible responses: To give us a glimpse into Nick's character, to set up a possible conflict, to foreshadow a story event.

DAY 3 Grouping Options

Reading

Whole Group Discuss the Question of the Day.

Group Time Differentiated Instruction

Read *Frindle.* See pp. 18h–18i for the small group lesson plan.

Whole Group Discuss the Reader Response questions on p. 34. Then use p. 41a.

Language Arts

Use pp. 41e–41k.

The first day of school was always a get-acquainted day. Books were passed out, and there was a lot of chatter. Everyone asked, "What did *you* do over the summer?"

Periods one through six went by very smoothly for Nick.

But then came period seven. Mrs. Granger's class was all business.

The first thing they did was take a vocabulary pretest to see how many of the thirty-five words for the week the kids already knew. *Tremble, circular, orchestra*—the list went on and on. Nick knew most of them.

Then there was a handout about class procedures. After that there was a review paper about cursive writing, and then there was a sample sheet showing how the heading should look on every assignment. No letup for thirty-seven minutes straight. 8

30

ELL

Access Content Explain to students that *sidetrack* means "to turn attention away from the main issue or course." Ask students to tell what Nick did to sidetrack his teacher. Challenge them to tell why he did it.

Nick was an expert at asking the delaying question—also known as the teacher-stopper, or the guaranteed-time-waster. At three minutes before the bell, in that split second between the end of today's class work and the announcement of tomorrow's homework, Nick could launch a question guaranteed to sidetrack the teacher long enough to delay or even wipe out the homework assignment. 9

Timing was important, but asking the right question—that was the hard part. Questions about stuff in the news, questions about the college the teacher went to, questions about the teacher's favorite book or sport or hobby—Nick knew all the tricks, and he had been very successful in the past.

Here he was in fifth grade, near the end of his very first language arts class with Mrs. Granger, and Nick could feel a homework assignment coming the way a farmer can feel a rainstorm.

31

Time for SOCIAL STUDIES

.exicography

ɜxicography is the writing and compilation of dic-ɔnaries. A lexicographer is one who writes or edits ctionaries. Lexicography is a specialized branch of ɪe study of linguistics, or language. Words are compiled from ʋery available source, from existing word lists to works of obscure lit-ˀature, to create the most complete list of words found in the English nguage. Lexicographers research and analyze the origin, history, ɜvelopment, uses, spellings, pronunciation, and grammatical forms of ɪese thousands of words. Lexicographers also make important judg-ɪents as to which words and meanings not to include because they ɜve fallen into disuse and which new words or phrases have become ɔpular enough to add.

VOCABULARY STRATEGY

Word Structure

TEACH

- Remind students that they can figure out the meanings of some words by breaking them into parts. Some words contain a base word that might be familiar if the suffix is not (e.g., *punishment*).
- When added to a word, the suffix *-ment* turns a verb into a noun.
- Model using word structure to determine the meaning of *assignment* on p. 31, paragraph 3.

MODEL When I see the word *assignment,* I stop and break the word into its two parts: the base word *assign* and the suffix *-ment.* I know that the verb *assign* means to give someone work to do. If I add the suffix *-ment* to the base word, I can figure out the meaning of *assignment. Assignment* is a noun that means "a piece of work to be done."

PRACTICE AND ASSESS

Have students reread the second sentence on p. 31, paragraph 1. Ask them to explain how they can use the base word *announce* and the suffix *-ment* to determine the meaning of *announcement.*

(Announce *means "to give formal notice of something." Adding the suffix* -ment *changes the word into a noun that means "the act of giving formal notice about something."*)

Guiding Comprehension

10 **Character • Critical**
Use what you know about Mrs. Granger's character to tell whether Nick's question will prevent her from giving a homework assignment. Explain your answer.
No, because Mrs. Granger is very focused and experienced.

11 **Character, Plot • Inferential**
Text to Self **The characters in this story learned to overcome their problems with each other. Does this remind you of an experience you've had with someone you did not get along with at first? Explain.**
Answers may vary, but should include discussion of a time the student learned to get along with someone.

Strategy Response Log

Summarize When students finish reading the selection, provide this prompt: Imagine that a friend has asked you what *Frindle* is about. In four or five sentences, tell about the story's main characters and events.

Mrs. Granger paused to catch her breath, and Nick's hand shot up. She glanced down at her seating chart and then up at him. Her sharp gray eyes were not even turned up to half power.

"Yes, Nicholas?"

"Mrs. Granger, you have so many dictionaries in this room, and that huge one especially . . . where did all those words come from? Did they just get copied from other dictionaries?
10 It sure is a big book."

It was a perfect thought-grenade—KaPow!

Several kids smiled, and a few peeked at the clock. Nick was famous for this, and the whole class knew what he was doing.

Unfortunately, so did Mrs. Granger. She hesitated a moment and gave Nick a smile that was just a little too sweet to be real. Her eyes were the color of a thundercloud.

"Why, what an interesting question, Nicholas. I could talk about it for hours, I bet." She glanced around the classroom.

"Do the rest of you want to know too?" Everyone nodded yes. "Very well then. Nicholas, will you do some research on that

32

ELL

Build Background Tell students that the statement, "Don't mess around with the Lone Granger" is a play on words. Explain that the Lone Ranger was a character in an early TV Western. Ask students to guess why kids referred to Mrs. Granger as "The Lone Granger."

subject and give a little oral report to the class? If you find out the answer yourself, it will mean so much more than if I just told you. Please have your report ready for our next class."

Mrs. Granger smiled at him again. Very sweetly. Then it was back to business. "Now, the homework for tomorrow can be found on page twelve of your *Words Alive* book. . . ."

Nick barely heard the assignment. His heart was pounding, and he felt small, very small. He could feel the tops of his ears glowing red. A complete shutdown. An extra assignment. And probably a little black mark next to his name on the seating chart.

Everything he had heard about this teacher was true—don't mess around with The Lone Granger.

11

33

Develop Vocabulary

PRACTICE LESSON VOCABULARY

As a class, complete the following sentences orally.

1. Mrs. Granger has a _____ as a strict teacher. *(reputation)*
2. One thing that is _____ for success in school is good study skills. *(essential)*
3. The class received a homework _____ in spite of Nick's delaying question about dictionaries. *(assignment)*
4. Classroom _____ are important for keeping order. *(procedures)*

BUILD CONCEPT VOCABULARY

Review previous concept words with students. Ask if students have come across any words today in their reading that they would like to add to the Challenges in Education Concept Web such as *cursive* and *hesitated.*

STRATEGY SELF-CHECK

Prior Knowledge

Have students tell how they used prior knowledge to gain insight into the characters of Nick and Mrs. Granger. Ask them to explain how this helped them predict how the characters would interact and what would happen in the story. Use Practice Book p. 7.

SELF-CHECK

Students can ask themselves these questions to assess their ability to use the skill and strategy.

- Did I use my prior knowledge as I read *Frindle*?
- Did it help me better understand the characters and the plot?

Monitor Progress

Character and Plot

If... students are unable to infer from character traits and the plot,	**then...** use the Reteach lesson on p. 41b.

Character and Plot

- A **character** is a person or animal that takes part in the events of a story.
- The **plot** is the pattern of events in a story, and includes (1) a problem or **conflict,** (2) **rising action,** as the conflict builds, (3) a **climax,** when the problem or conflict is faced, and (4) a **resolution,** when the problem or conflict is solved.

Directions Read the following passage. Then answer the questions below.

Larry was excited about lunch. For the first time, he had made his own triple-decker sandwich, just the way he liked it. Plus, his mom had added one of his favorite snacks to the bag. Usually Larry just gobbled up his sandwich at lunch and ran out to the playground. But not today—he was going to take his time.

When the lunch bell rang, he grabbed his bag and rushed to the cafeteria. He was so excited he didn't see the backpack someone had left on the floor. SPLAT! Larry tumbled to the floor, landing flat on his lunch bag. When he took his prized sandwich out, it was flat. But Larry didn't mind—he knew it would still be delicious!

Possible answers given for 2–4.

1. Why was Larry excited about lunch?
   Larry had made his own sandwich for the first time.
2. How do you think Larry felt about making his own sandwich?
   He probably felt proud and excited.
3. Why was Larry in such a hurry to get to the cafeteria?
   He was looking forward to eating the sandwich, which he had made just how he liked it.
4. What about Larry's character makes you think Larry didn't mind what happened to his sandwich?
   Larry was still proud, and knew that the sandwich would still taste good.
5. On a separate sheet of paper, describe something that you did for yourself for the first time. How was that experience similar to Larry's?
   Students' responses should compare their own experiences with Larry's sense of pride and accomplishment.

School + Home **Home Activity** Your child analyzed character elements in a passage and answered questions about them. Tell your child a few things that have happened to you recently. Have your child explain how you probably felt about these events.

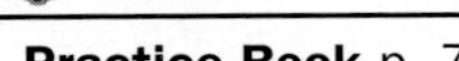

▲ **Practice Book** p. 7

Reader Response

Open for Discussion **Personal Response**

MODEL I'd start by thinking about a plan I've had that backfired on me. One time I saw a watch I really wanted, but I decided not to buy it in case it went on sale. When I went back to the store, someone else had bought it.

Comprehension Check **Critical Response**

1. Possible response: The author wants the story to sound realistic. ***Author's Purpose***
2. Possible response: rigid, consistent, old-fashioned. ***Literary Elements***
3. Responses will vary but should point out how Nick's fifth grade experience is alike or different from the students'. ***Prior Knowledge***
4. Students should include *loved*, *worshipped*, and additional words to their webs to show how Mrs. Granger feels about the dictionary. ***Vocabulary***

Look Back and Write For test practice, assign a 10–15 minute time limit. For assessment, see the Scoring Rubric at the right.

Retell

Have students retell *Frindle*.

Monitor Progress

Check Retelling Rubric 4 3 2 1

If...	then...
If... students have difficulty retelling the story,	**then...** use the Retelling Cards and the Scoring Rubric for Retelling on p. 35 to assist fluent retelling.

SUCCESS PREDICTOR

Check Retelling Have students use the illustrations to guide their retellings of the story. For more ideas on assessing students' retellings, see the ELL and Transition Handbook.

Reader Response

Open for Discussion Nick's plan to sidetrack Mrs. Granger backfires. Have you or someone you know ever had a plan that didn't work out as planned? Tell what happened and why.

1. The author uses many details about school life. Give some examples of these details. Why do you think he has included those details in this story? **Think Like an Author**
2. Reread the author's description of his character, Mrs. Granger, on pages 25–26. What three adjectives would you use to describe her? Explain your choices. **Plot and Character**
3. Think about what you know about fifth grade. Does Nick's description of fifth grade match your prior knowledge? Explain why or why not. **Prior Knowledge**
4. The story says that "Mrs. Granger loved the dictionary—almost worshipped it." Make a web with *dictionary* at the center. Add to the web with words from the Words to Know list and from the story. **Vocabulary**

TEST PRACTICE

Look Back and Write How does Mrs. Granger meet Nick's challenge at the end of the story? Use details from the story to support your answer.

Meet author **Andrew Clements on page 769.**

34

Scoring Rubric **Look Back and Write**

Top-Score Response A top-score response will describe how Mrs. Granger turns Nick's attempt to waste class time into an assignment that will use up Nick's time.

Example of a Top-Score Response Nick knows Mrs. Granger loves words and dictionaries. He has had success in distracting teachers by asking questions the teacher likes to answer. Nick tries to distract Mrs. Granger by asking how all the words got into the dictionary. However, she knows he just wants to waste class time. She tells him to research the question and give an oral report. This causes him to use his own time, not the class's time.

For additional rubrics, see p. WA10.

Write Now

Character Sketch

Prompt

Frindle tells about a teacher with an unusual reputation.

Think about a character or person who has an interesting trait.

Now write a character sketch about that character or person.

Writing Trait

Voice shows a writer's attitude and personality. Tone and word choice help create the writer's voice.

Student Model

Nick was a good kid. With his laid-back ways, good grades, and friendly attitude, no one expected anything different. However, he had one skill that earned disapproval from his teachers and admiration from his classmates. Nick was a master sidetracker. At just the right moment, he'd ask the perfect question or make the perfect off-topic comment and keep the teacher from giving out homework.

Nick didn't achieve this skill without practice. In fact, he'd spent four years perfecting it. But fifth grade was going to be the real test. How would he do when he faced Mrs. Granger?

Precise details help readers know Nick.

Contractions and humor give the writing an informal voice.

Question engages readers.

Use the model to help you write your own character sketch.

Write Now

Look at the Prompt Have students identify and discuss key words and phrases in the prompt. *(character or person, interesting trait, character sketch)*

Strategies to Develop Voice

Have students

- use figurative language to give a picture.

NO: He's a good pitcher.

YES: His arm is a deadly weapon.

- think how they feel about the person and try to get readers to feel the same way.
- choose a tone that matches the personality of their subject.

For additional suggestions and rubric, see pp. 41g–41h.

Hints for Better Writing

- Carefully read the prompt.
- Use a graphic organizer to plan your writing.
- Support your ideas with information and details.
- Use words that help readers understand.
- Proofread and edit your work.

Scoring Rubric Narrative Retelling

Rubric 4 3 2 1	4	3	2	1
Connections	Makes connections and generalizes beyond the text	Makes connections to other events, stories, or experiences	Makes a limited connection to another event, story, or experience	Makes no connection to another event, story, or experience
Author's Purpose	Elaborates on author's purpose	Tells author's purpose with some clarity	Makes some connection to author's purpose	Makes no connection to author's purpose
Characters	Describes the main character(s) and any character development	Identifies the main character(s) and gives some information about them	Inaccurately identifies some characters or gives little information about them	Inaccurately identifies the characters or gives no information about them
Setting	Describes the time and location	Identifies the time and location	Omits details of time or location	Is unable to identify time or location
Plot	Describes the problem, goal, events, and ending using rich detail	Tells the problem, goal, events, and ending with some errors that do not affect meaning	Tells parts of the problem, goal, events, and ending with gaps that affect meaning	Retelling has no sense of story

Retelling Plan

- ☑ **This week assess Strategic Intervention students.**
- ☐ **Week 2** Assess Advanced students.
- ☐ **Week 3** Assess Strategic Intervention students.
- ☐ **Week 4** Assess On-Level students.
- ☐ **Week 5** Assess any students you have not yet checked during this unit.

Use the Retelling Chart on p. TR16 to record retelling.

Selection Test To assess with *Frindle*, use Selection Tests, pp. 1–4.

Fresh Reads for Differentiated Test Practice For weekly leveled practice, use pp. 1–6.

Fantasy

OBJECTIVES

- Examine features of fantasy.
- Practice a test-taking strategy.
- Compare and contrast across texts.

PREVIEW

As students preview "Punctuation Takes a Vacation," have them look at the story's illustrations. After they preview ask:

- **What do you think this story is about?** *(Possible response: Punctuation marks go on vacation, and the students are having trouble reading and writing without the punctuation marks.)*

Link to Writing

Have students look at the letter on p. 40. Review the parts of a friendly letter and work together to correct the punctuation. Then have students write a letter, using correct punctuation, providing a convincing reason for the punctuation to return.

Fantasy

Genre

- **A fantasy is a make-believe story that could never happen in the real world.**
- **Some characters and plot situations may be realistic, while others are exaggerated and even silly.**
- **The author uses a realistic classroom setting but then introduces fantastic characters who do impossible things.**
- **Preview the story. What is it about the title and art that make you think, "This is a fantasy"?**

Link to Writing

Write another postcard to the vacationing punctuation marks. Try to convince them to return to the classroom. This time, use correct punctuation marks.

36

Grouping Options

Reading

Whole Group Discuss the Question of the Day.

Group Time Differentiated Instruction

Read "Punctuation Takes a Vacation." See pp. 18h–18i for the small group lesson plan.

Whole Group Use p. 41a.

Language Arts

Use pp. 41e–41k.

Access Content Preview the text by reviewing punctuation. Write the following marks on the board and help students name them: *question mark, exclamation point, period, comma, apostrophe, colon, semi-colon, quotation marks*. Point to each mark on the board and challenge students to find the picture of the character on p. 36. Then invite partners to take turns pointing to the punctuation marks on p. 36 and naming them.

Punctuation Takes a Vacation

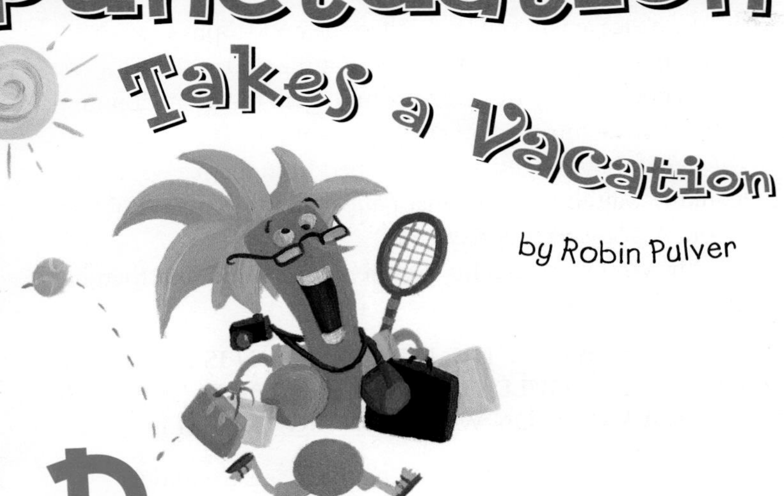

by Robin Pulver

Day after day, the punctuation marks showed up in Mr. Wright's classroom. Day after day, they did their jobs. They put up with being erased and replaced and corrected and ignored and moved around.

Then on the hottest, stickiest day the class had ever seen, right in the middle of a lesson about commas, Mr. Wright mopped his forehead and said, "Let's give punctuation a vacation."

As the kids cheered and headed for the playground to cool off, the punctuation marks stared at one another in disbelief.

"Is this the thanks we get?" asked a question mark.

"Well!" huffed an exclamation point.

"Now, now," said a comma.

"We *should* take a vacation," said a period. "They'll soon learn how much they need us."

Character What is bothering Mr. Wright? Why?

37

Punctuation

Time for SOCIAL STUDIES

Punctuation plays a very important role in written language. Proper punctuation helps readers know how to break up long sentences. For example, a comma signals a pause in a sentence. Punctuation also helps readers know the proper tone of voice to use when reading. A sentence that ends with an exclamation point should be read excitedly or even angrily, while a sentence ending with a question mark should be read with a questioning tone, or a rise in the voice.

FANTASY

Use the sidebar on p. 36 to guide discussion.

- Explain to students that a fantasy is a type of fiction and is usually written to entertain. Point out that a fantasy can be set in any time period and may include characters with special powers.
- Tell students that successful fantasies cause readers to forget for a time their disbelief and accept the characters or actions as reasonable even though they are not possible in real life.
- Discuss with students how the actions of the characters in this fantasy seem real even though they are not possible.

AudioText

Character

Possible response: He is hot and tired of teaching his students about punctuation. His students do not seem to care about or use punctuation correctly.

Strategies for Fiction

USE DIALOGUE Explain that students will be asked to read fictional stories and answer questions about these stories on standardized tests. When a story such as "Punctuation Takes a Vacation" has dialogue, students should pay attention to what the characters are saying to one another, as it will help them understand the story. Provide the following strategy.

Use the Strategy

1. Read the test question slowly and carefully. Be sure you understand it.
2. Ask yourself who or what the question is about.
3. Scan the dialogue in the story, looking for answers to the question.

GUIDED PRACTICE Have students discuss how they would use the strategy to answer the following question.

How should you read what question mark says on p. 37, paragraph 4? Why?

INDEPENDENT PRACTICE After students answer the following test question, discuss the process they used.

How do you think the exclamation point is feeling at the beginning of the story on p. 37, paragraph 5? Why do you think that way?

"It's 11:00 now," said a colon. "Let's leave at 11:02."

"Great!" said an exclamation point.

"Don't leave without us!" yelled the apostrophes.

Whoosh! Punctuation rushed out the door.

Whoosh! They rushed back in to grab the quotation marks, who were too busy talking to pay attention.

When Mr. Wright's class returned from the playground, they couldn't wait to find out what happened in Chapter 4 of their book, *Ace Scooper, Dog Detective.*

Mr. Wright opened his mouth to read aloud, but then he stopped and stared.

THIS IS WEIRD THE PUNCTUATION IS MISSING UH OH WHERE COULD IT BE YIKES MAYBE PUNCTUATION TOOK A VACATION WE ARE IN BIG TROUBLE NOW

Mr. Wright was right. Nothing made sense without punctuation.

38

Test Practice Remind students that what a character says and how it is spoken can reveal how the character is feeling. Have students read aloud what the exclamation point says at the beginning of the story. Encourage them to read with correct intonation. Then discuss how they think the exclamation point is feeling.

A couple days later, the school secretary delivered a small bundle of postcards to Mr. Wright's class. They were postmarked "Take-a-Break Lake."

The kids guessed who wrote the postcards, and they wanted to write back. But they couldn't write without punctuation. The best they could do was borrow some from Mr. Rongo's class next door, where punctuation seemed to be running wild.

Wow! What a ride!
You should try
tubing! Scary! Fun!
Yikes! Hold on!
We want
Mommmmmeeeeeeee!

Emotional Us

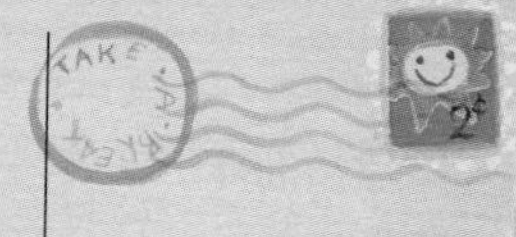

Do you miss us?
How much?
Why couldn't we
take a vacation
sooner?

Guess who?

Dear Friends,
Swimming, sailing,
sunning, soaring,
waterskiing. Next time
we must remember
bug spray, toothpaste,
flashlight, water shoes.

Mr. Wright's
class
Hometown

We flop. We plop.
We stop. We stay
put in our lounge
chairs. We are happy
thinking our
complete thoughts.

Thoughtfully yours,
Sentence Stoppers

A big "hello" from vacation
paradise, "where the water
is as clear as a
well-punctuated sentence."
We talk all day. We talk all
night. Too busy talking to
write any more.

The Yackity Yaks

Mr. Wright's
class
Hometown
USA 46738

Plot Who is upset and why?

39

DURING READING

Plot

Possible response: The students are upset because they can't write without punctuation.

Access Content Read aloud the following phrase from the last postcard: "where the water is as clear as a well-punctuated sentence." Explain that the punctuation marks are comparing the clean lake water to a sentence with correct punctuation. Challenge students to make a sentence comparing something to a poorly punctuated sentence.

DURING READING

USE TEXT FEATURES

Have students try to read the letter on p. 40. Ask:

- **How does the letter reinforce the concept that punctuation is important?** *(It shows how difficult it is to read and write without proper punctuation.)*
- **How should the quote from Mr. Wright be punctuated?** *(Mr. Wright says, "Punctuation, please come home.")*
- **Which punctuation symbol should be used to properly show 10 o'clock?** *(Colon, 10:00)*

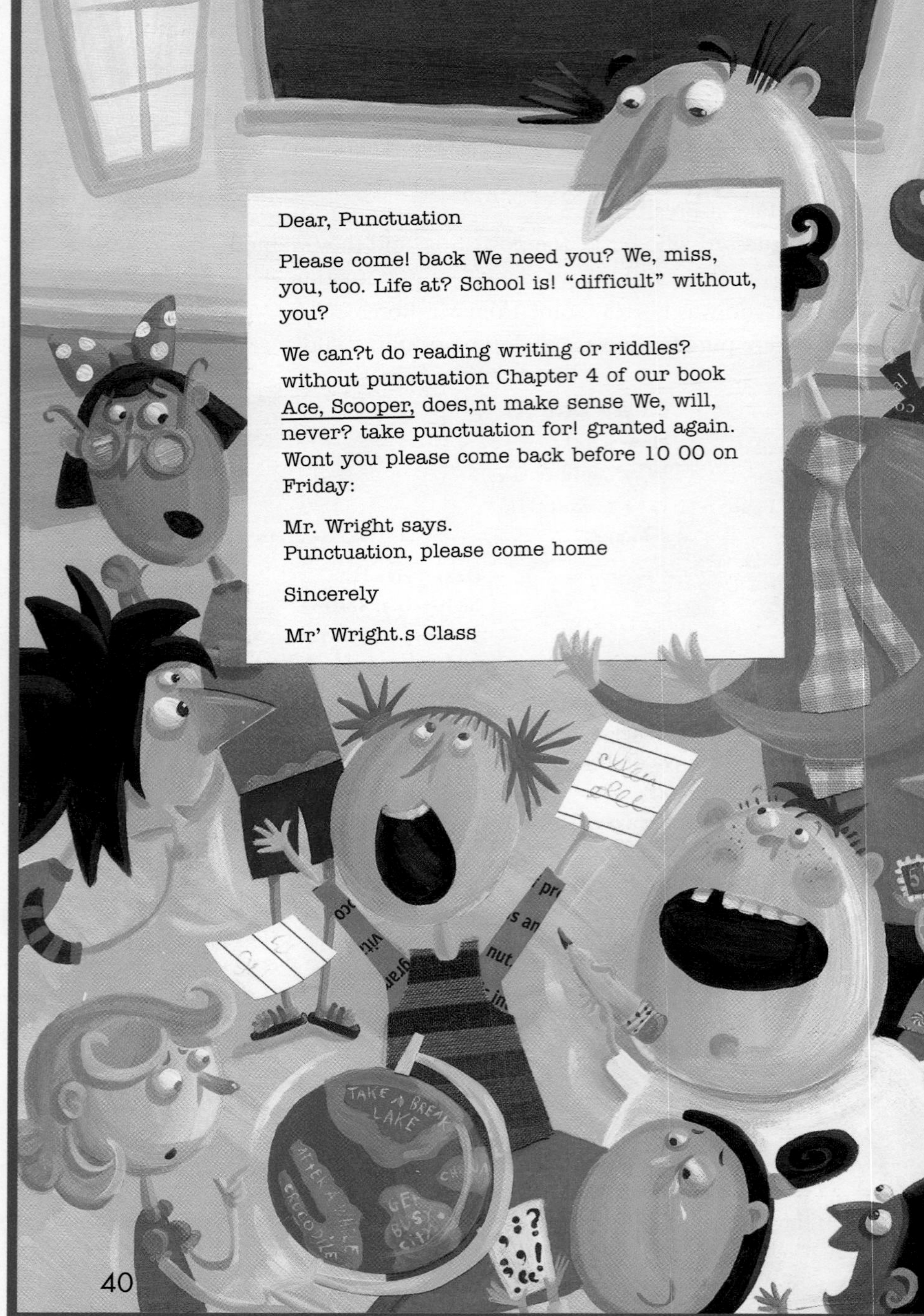

Dear, Punctuation

Please come! back We need you? We, miss, you, too. Life at? School is! "difficult" without, you?

We can?t do reading writing or riddles? without punctuation Chapter 4 of our book Ace, Scooper, does,nt make sense We, will, never? take punctuation for! granted again. Wont you please come back before 10 00 on Friday:

Mr. Wright says.
Punctuation, please come home

Sincerely

Mr' Wright.s Class

Understanding Idioms Restate the idea "We will never take punctuation for granted again": We will never underestimate the value of punctuation. Ask students why the students in Mr. Wright's class will never take punctuation for granted again.

So the punctuation marks returned to Mr. Wright's classroom to do the jobs only they could do. Mr. Rongo's unruly punctuation scrambled back to their own classroom.

We have so much to tell you.

Who did you miss the most?

It's good to be back in Mr. Wright's class!

COMMAS, PERIODS, EXCLAMATION POINTS,
QUESTION MARKS, COLONS, APOSTROPHES,
QUOTATION MARKS: TAKE YOUR PLACES
10:00 A.M. TIME TO STUDY US.

Reading Across Texts

Which character do you think is a stronger, more confident person, Mrs. Granger in *Frindle* or Mr. Wright in *Puctuation Takes a Vacation?*

Writing Across Texts Draw pictures of the two characters and write your answer below them.

Prior Knowledge What makes this a happy ending?

41

DURING READING

CONNECT TEXT TO TEXT

Reading Across Texts

Discuss similarities and differences between the two teachers and how they interact with the students. Have students use this information to decide which character is the stronger person.

Writing Across Texts Students can use information from their discussion to determine the characteristics they wish to convey in their drawings.

Prior Knowledge

Possible response: The students in Mr. Wright's class welcome back the punctuation marks after realizing how important proper punctuation is to writing.

DAY 5

Fluency Assessment Plan

- ☑ **This week assess Advanced students.**
- ☐ **Week 2** Assess Strategic Intervention students.
- ☐ **Week 3** Assess On-Level students.
- ☐ **Week 4** Assess Strategic Intervention students.
- ☐ **Week 5** Assess any students you have not yet checked during this unit.

Set individual goals for students to enable them to reach the year-end goal.

- Current Goal: 105–110 wcpm
- Year-End Goal: 140 wcpm

For English language learners, emphasize repeated readings to build fluency with enjoyable passages in English, with as much teacher guidance as feasible.

To develop fluent readers, use Fluency Coach.

DAY 5 Grouping Options

Reading

Whole Group
Revisit the Question of the Week.

Group Time
Differentiated Instruction
Reread this week's Leveled Readers. See pp. 18h–18i for the small group lesson plan.

Whole Group
Use p. 41b–41c.

Language Arts
Use pp. 41d–41l.

TONE OF VOICE

Fluency

DAY 1

Model Reread "Understood Betsy" on p. 18m. Explain that you will use different tones of voice to show sadness, anxiety, or other emotions as you read the selection. Model for students as you read.

DAY 2

Choral Reading Read aloud the last paragraph on p. 26 and the paragraph on p. 27. These paragraphs describe Mrs. Granger's love of the dictionary. Have students notice voice changes for quotations and italicized words. Have students practice as a class doing three choral readings of these paragraphs.

DAY 3

Model Read aloud the conversation between Nick and Mrs. Granger on p. 32. Have students notice how you adjust your voice to reflect the change in character. Practice as a class by doing three choral readings.

DAY 4

Partner Reading Partners practice reading aloud the conversation between Nick and Mrs. Granger on p. 32, three times. Students should read with proper inflection and offer each other feedback.

Monitor Progress — Check Fluency WCPM

As students reread, monitor their progress toward their individual fluency goals Current Goal: 105–110 words correct per minute. End-of-Year Goal: 140 words correct per minute.

If... students cannot read fluently at a rate of 105–110 words correct per minute,
then... make sure students practice with text at their independent level. Provide additional fluency practice, pairing nonfluent readers with fluent readers.

If... students already read at 140 words correct per minute,
then... they do not need to reread three to four times.

SUCCESS PREDICTOR

DAY 5

Assessment
Individual Reading Rate Use the Fluency Assessment Plan and do a one-minute timed reading of either selection from this week to assess students in Week 1. Pay special attention to this week's skill, tone of voice. Provide corrective feedback for each student.

RETEACH

Character and Plot

TEACH

Remind students that plot refers to the important events in a story, and that characters are the people in the story. Students can complete Practice Book p. 8 on their own, or you can complete it as a class. Point out that they must complete the sentences in each box and that one answer is provided for them.

ASSESS

Have partners read pp. 32–33 in their books and identify the climax, resolution, and how the characters react to each other. *(Climax: Mrs. Granger responds to Nick's question by having him do a research project; Resolution: Nick learns everything he heard about Mrs. Granger is true.)*

For additional instruction on character and plot, see DI • 52.

EXTEND SKILLS

Point of View

TEACH

The perspective from which an author tells a story is called point of view. Who the author chooses to tell the story determines what we learn about the characters and their actions.

- In first-person point of view, a character tells a story and uses the pronoun *I* or *we*.
- In third-person point of view, the narrator tells the story and descibes the events. The narrator uses the pronouns *he, she, they,* or *it*.

Authors sometimes mix points of view within a story.

Read p. 25, paragraph 3. Point out the use of Mrs. Granger's name and the pronoun *she*. Explain to students that this tells you that the story is told from a third-person point of view.

ASSESS

Have students reread p. 29. Have students write responses to these questions:

1. Who is the narrator of the story?

2. How would the story be different if it were told from Nick's point of view?

OBJECTIVES

- Identify the important events that occur in a story.
- Identify the point of view of the story.

Skills Trace	
Character and Plot	
Introduce/Teach	TE: 5.1 18–19, 68–69; 5.5 512–513
Practice	Practice Book: 3, 7, 8, 16, 23, 26, 27, 28, 96, 203, 207, 208
Reteach/Review	**TE: 5.1 41b, 49, 61, 77, 89b, DI•52, DI•54; 5.2 237; 5.5 535b, DI•52**
Test	Selection Test: 1–4, 9–12, 81–84; Benchmark Test: Unit 1

Access Content Reteach the skill by reviewing the Picture It! lesson on character and plot in the ELL Teaching Guide, pp. 1–2.

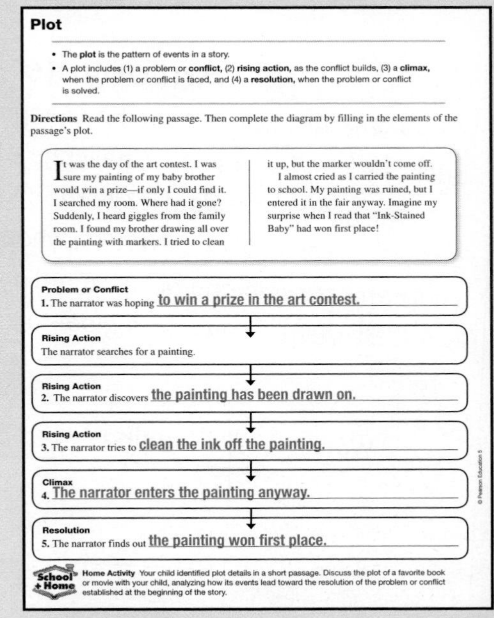

Plot

- The **plot** is the pattern of events in a story.
- A plot includes (1) a problem or **conflict,** (2) **rising action,** as the conflict builds, (3) a **climax,** when the problem or conflict is faced, and (4) a **resolution,** when the problem or conflict is solved.

Directions Read the following passage. Then complete the diagram by filling in the elements of the passage's plot.

It was the day of the art contest. I was sure my painting of my baby brother would win a prize—if only I could find it. I searched my room. Where had it gone? Suddenly, I heard giggles from the family room. I found my brother drawing all over the painting with markers. I tried to clean it up, but the marker wouldn't come off.

I almost cried as I carried the painting to school. My painting was ruined, but I entered it in the fair anyway. Imagine my surprise when I read that "Ink-Stained Baby" had won first place!

Problem or Conflict
1. The narrator was hoping to win a prize in the art contest.

Rising Action
The narrator searches for a painting.

Rising Action
2. The narrator discovers the painting has been drawn on.

Rising Action
3. The narrator tries to clean the ink off the painting.

Climax
4. The narrator enters the painting anyway.

Resolution
5. The narrator finds out the painting won first place.

Home Activity Your child identified plot details in a short passage. Discuss the plot of a favorite book or movie with your child, analyzing how its events lead toward the resolution of the problem or conflict established at the beginning of the story.

▲ **Practice Book** p. 8

Vocabulary and Word Study

VOCABULARY STRATEGY

Word Structure

SUFFIXES Tell students that they can use their knowledge of suffixes to determine the meanings of longer words. Remind them that the suffixes *-tion, -ation,* and *-ment* turn verbs into nouns. Then have students apply this understanding to complete the chart below. Challenge them to add to the chart other words they know that fit this pattern.

Verb	+	Suffix	=	Noun	New Meaning
define	+	-tion		definition	the act of making clear the meaning of a word
punctuate		-ation			
announce		-ment			

Antonyms

Antonyms are words that have opposite meanings, such as *liquid* and *solid*. Challenge students to work in small groups to identify words from the story, such as *essential* or *different*, whose meanings they know and provide one or more antonyms for each word. Students can use a glossary or thesaurus as needed.

Word	Meaning	Antonym
essential	necessary	unimportant insignificant
different	not alike	alike similar

BUILD CONCEPT VOCABULARY

Challenges in Education

LOOKING BACK Remind students of the question of the week: *How do we meet the challenges of learning?* Discuss how this week's Concept Web of vocabulary words relates to the theme of challenges in education. Ask students if they have any words or categories to add. Discuss whether the words and categories are appropriately related to the concept.

MOVING FORWARD Preview the title of the next selection, *Thunder Rose.* Ask students which Concept Web words might apply to the new selection based on the title alone.

Put a star next to these words on the web.

Display the Concept Web and revisit the vocabulary words as you read the next selection to check predictions.

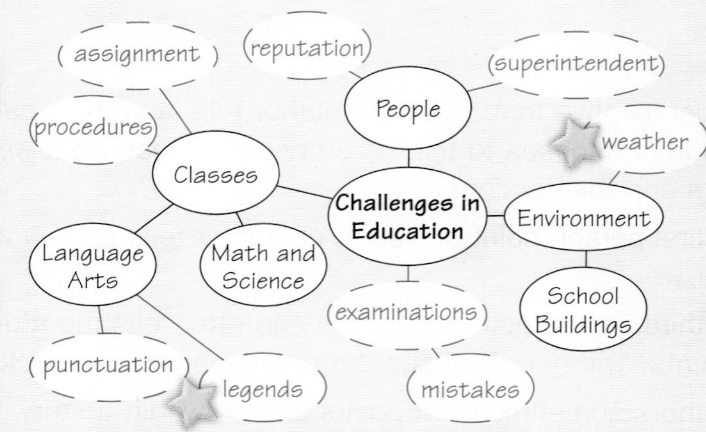

Monitor Progress

Check Vocabulary

If... students suggest words or categories that are not related to the concept,	**then...** review the words and categories on the Concept Web and discuss how they relate to the lesson concept.

Speaking and Listening

SPEAKING

Dramatization

SET-UP Divide students into groups and have them choose a scene from *Frindle* to dramatize for the class.

PLANNING Have students create a script based on the dialogue and descriptions in the scene they choose. They should assign each member of the group a role to play, including a narrator, if they wish. Suggest that each student have a copy of the script and highlight his or her speeches.

WRITING Provide these suggestions:

- If you use a narrator, you must decide how much description to include.
- Don't keep phrases like "she said" or "he replied" in your dramatization.
- Show, don't tell. Don't have a narrator describe actions that actors should act out.

REHEARSAL Allow students time to rehearse their dramatizations. Provide the following suggestions:

- Practice your lines so you become comfortable with them and they sound natural.
- Use expression, body language, and gestures to capture the emotions of the characters.
- Use simple props, if appropriate, and practice so that you are comfortable with them.

LISTENING

Listen to Dramatization

Have students listen to their classmates' dramatizations. As a class, discuss these questions.

1. **Describe how your classmates depicted characters in their scenes.** *(Responses will vary but should describe how students portrayed characters—voice, tone, etc.)*
2. **How were your classmates' portrayals of Nick and Mrs. Granger different from what you expected? How were they similar?** *(Students should compare their interpretations of characters from reading the story to their classmates' interpretations in the dramatizations.)*
3. **Did hearing dramatizations enhance your enjoyment of the story?** *(Possible response: Yes, it's fun to see and hear the story acted out instead of just reading the words to myself.)*

Support Vocabulary Use the following to review and extend vocabulary and to explore lesson concepts further:
- ELL Poster 1, Days 3–5 instruction
- Vocabulary Activities and Word Cards in ELL Teaching Guide, pp. 3–4

Assessment For information on assessing students' speaking and listening, see the ELL and Transition Handbook.

AFTER READING

Grammar Four Kinds of Sentences

OBJECTIVES

- Define and identify four kinds of sentences.
- Use end punctuation correctly.
- Use four kinds of sentences in writing.
- Become familiar with sentence assessment on high-stakes tests.

Monitor Progress

Grammar

If... students have difficulty distinguishing kinds of sentences,	**then...** provide additional instruction and practice in The Grammar and Writing Book pp. 50–53.

DAILY FIX-IT

This week use Daily Fix-It Transparency 1.

Support Grammar See the Grammar Transition lessons in the ELL and Transition Handbook.

▲ **The Grammar and Writing Book** For more instruction and practice, use pp. 50–53.

DAY 1 Teach and Model

DAILY FIX-IT

1. Do you no how to use the dictionary. *(know; dictionary?)*
2. We use *Webster's School dictionary* in are class. (Dictionary; *our*)

READING-GRAMMAR CONNECTION

Write this sentence from *Frindle* on the board:

What did you do over the summer?

Explain that this is an **interrogative sentence.** It asks a question and ends with a question mark. It is one of the four kinds of sentences.

Display Grammar Transparency 1. Read aloud the definitions and sample sentences. Work through the items.

Four Kinds of Sentences and Interjections

Each kind of sentence begins with a capital letter and has a special end mark.

A **declarative sentence** makes a statement. It ends with a period.
A good vocabulary makes you a better reader.

An **interrogative sentence** asks a question. It ends with a question mark.
Do you know what the word *loquacious* means?

An **imperative sentence** gives a command or makes a request. It ends with a period. The subject *(you)* does not appear, but it is understood.
Learn these fifty words by Friday.

An **exclamatory sentence** shows strong feeling. It ends with an exclamation mark.
You have got to be kidding! What a hard test that was!

An **interjection** is a word or a group of words that expresses strong feeling. It is not a complete sentence. An interjection is usually followed by an exclamation mark.
Wow! Hooray! Ouch! Ugh!

Directions Write *D* if the sentence is declarative. Write *IN* if the sentence is interrogative. Write *IM* if the sentence is imperative. Write *E* if the sentence is exclamatory.

1. Is it hard for you to spell words? IN
2. I really enjoy a game called Scrabble®. D
3. Pick up seven of the letter tiles. IM
4. Players spell words with their letters. D
5. What a terrible bunch of letters I have! E
6. I drew seven consonants. D

Directions Add the correct end punctuation mark to each sentence. Then on the line write whether the sentence is *declarative, interrogative, imperative,* or *exclamatory.*

7. A dictionary contains much information . declarative
8. Does it have a history of each word ? interrogative
9. Read every meaning listed for the word . imperative
10. Wow! This book weighs a ton ! exclamatory

Unit 1 Frindle Grammar 1

▲ **Grammar Transparency** 1

DAY 2 Develop the Concept

DAILY FIX-IT

3. some teacher's are amazing characters. *(Some teachers)*
4. They can be funny they can also give a ton of homework? *(funny. They [or funny, but they]; homework.)*

GUIDED PRACTICE

Review kinds of sentences.

- **Declarative sentences** make a statement and end with a period.
- **Interrogative sentences** ask a question and end with a question mark.
- **Imperative sentences** command or request, and end with a period. *You* is the understood subject.
- **Exclamatory sentences** show strong feelings, end with an exclamation mark, and often have an interjection.

HOMEWORK Grammar and Writing Practice Book p. 1.

Four Kinds of Sentences and Interjections

Each kind of sentence begins with a capital letter and has a special end mark.

A **declarative sentence** makes a statement. It ends with a period.
A teacher needs a sense of humor.

An **interrogative sentence** asks a question. It ends with a question mark.
Have you read this joke book?

An **imperative sentence** gives a command or makes a request. It ends with a period. The subject (*you*) does not appear, but it is understood.
Tell us a joke, please.

An **exclamatory sentence** shows strong feeling. It ends with an exclamation mark.
What a hilarious punch line that was!
I can't believe you said that!

An **interjection** is a word or a group of words that expresses strong feeling. It is not a complete sentence.
Ha, ha! What a funny joke!

Directions Rewrite each sentence. Make any needed corrections in capitalization and punctuation.

1. darius played jokes on people?
Darius played jokes on people.
2. that rubber snake scared me to death.
That rubber snake scared me to death!
3. would he play a joke on the teacher.
Would he play a joke on the teacher?

Directions Complete each sentence with words from the box. Then write whether the sentence is *declarative, interrogative, imperative,* or *exclamatory.*

at the size of that book!	is an interesting subject.
the assignment for me.	need a class in reading?

4. Language arts is an interesting subject. declarative
5. Do we really need a class in reading? interrogative
6. Wow, look at the size of that book! exclamatory
7. Copy down the assignment for me. imperative

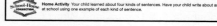

School-Home CONNECTION **Home Activity** Your child learned about four kinds of sentences. Have your child write about an event at school using one example of each kind of sentence.

▲ **Grammar and Writing Practice Book** p. 1

DAY 3 Apply to Writing

DAILY FIX-IT

5. Mr. williams showed us how to solve the problim. *(Williams; problem.)*
6. Reglar practice will help your math skills? *(Regular; skills.)*

WRITE A VARIETY OF SENTENCES

Explain that using several different kinds of sentences when writing makes the writing more interesting to read.

- Have students review something they have written to see if sentences could be more varied.
- Have students revise their sample to include a variety of simple and complex sentences.

HOMEWORK Grammar and Writing Practice Book p. 2.

Four Kinds of Sentences and Interjections

Directions Complete each sentence by adding your own words and the correct end punctuation. The label tells what kind of sentence each should be. Possible answers:

1. A big pile of homework ________ (declarative)
   A big pile of homework sits on the table.
2. Did Mrs. Granger ________ (interrogative)
   Did Mrs. Granger give Nick an extra assignment?
3. Wow! This test ________ (exclamatory)
   Wow! This test is a tough one!
4. This report ________ (declarative)
   This report on the history of the word *sinister* is very interesting.
5. Please buy me ________ (imperative)
   Please buy me some note cards for research.

Directions What is the most unusual homework assignment you ever had? Write three sentences describing the assignment. Make each sentence a different kind.

Possible answer: I was told to dress as my favorite person in history. What items would best show Benjamin Franklin's personality? Help me find bifocals, a kite, and a skeleton key.

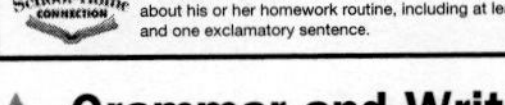
Home Activity Your child learned how to use four kinds of sentences in writing. Have your child write about his or her homework routine, including at least one declarative, one interrogative, one imperative, and one exclamatory sentence.

▲ **Grammar and Writing Practice Book** p. 2

DAY 4 Test Preparation

DAILY FIX-IT

7. Bill love mayonnaise, but i prefer mustard. *(loves; I)*
8. The best meal at the Cafeteria is, pizza. *(cafeteria; is pizza)*

STANDARDIZED TEST PREP

Test Tip

Watch out for commands that are expressed with excitement. They can be classified as either imperative or exclamatory sentences.

Imperative: Please calm down.

Exclamatory: What a glorious day this is!

Both Imperative and Exclamatory: Stop that car!

HOMEWORK Grammar and Writing Practice Book p. 3.

Four Kinds of Sentences and Interjections

Directions Read the paragraph. Mark the letter that identifies what kind of sentence each is.

(1) Middle school is a challenge for many students. (2) Are you moving from classroom to classroom this school year? (3) What a zoo the hallways are between classes! (4) The lock on my locker never opens properly. (5) Please be on time for class. (6) All the teachers make this request. (7) How can I make it on time? (8) I can barely get my locker open in four minutes.

1. (A) Declarative B Interrogative C Imperative D Exclamatory
2. A Declarative (B) Interrogative C Imperative D Exclamatory
3. A Declarative B Interrogative C Imperative (D) Exclamatory
4. (A) Declarative B Interrogative C Imperative D Exclamatory
5. A Declarative B Interrogative (C) Imperative D Exclamatory
6. (A) Declarative B Interrogative C Imperative D Exclamatory
7. A Declarative (B) Interrogative C Imperative D Exclamatory
8. (A) Declarative B Interrogative C Imperative D Exclamatory

Directions Circle the letter of the sentence that has correct end punctuation.

9. A Mr. Smith teaches science? B What is your favorite subject. C Fifth graders take several classes! (D) They also have music and gym class.
10. A Jim is good in language arts! B He has a huge vocabulary? (C) Didn't he win the spelling bee? D Hurray, he won again.

Home Activity Your child prepared for taking tests on kinds of sentences. Have your child read part of a story to you and identify each sentence as declarative, interrogative, imperative, or exclamatory.

▲ **Grammar and Writing Practice Book** p. 3

DAY 5 Cumulative Review

DAILY FIX-IT

9. Yesterday I gived my report on tooths. *(gave; teeth)*
10. Gum with sugar are badder for teeth than sugarless gum. *(is worse)*

ADDITIONAL PRACTICE

Assign pp. 50–53 in The Grammar and Writing Book.

EXTRA PRACTICE Grammar and Writing Practice Book p. 122.

ASSESSMENT

CUMULATIVE REVIEW Grammar and Writing Practice Book p. 4.

Four Kinds of Sentences and Interjections

Directions Add the correct end punctuation to each sentence. Then on the line write whether the sentence is *declarative, interrogative, imperative,* or *exclamatory.*

1. Do you like chewing gum ? interrogative
2. Lucy stuck a wad of gum in her mouth . declarative
3. Please spit that out . imperative
4. Oh, no! I swallowed it ! exclamatory
5. Gum leaves a sticky mess on shoes . declarative

Directions Underline the mistakes in each sentence. Write the correct letter or punctuation mark above each underline.

6. once I got gum stuck in my hair? (O .)
7. what an awful mess that was (W !)
8. rub this ice cube on the gum! (R .)
9. mom had to cut it out with scissors? (M .)
10. how do you like my new haircut (H ?)
11. i think it looks great? (I !)

Directions Add your own words to complete each sentence. Write the new sentences. Be sure you use end punctuation correctly. Possible answers:

12. The rules for every class ______
    The rules for every class are a little different.
13. The rule about gum ______
    The rule about gum always seems the same.
14. Don't ______
    Don't bring it to class.
15. Do you think ______
    Do you think that is a good rule?

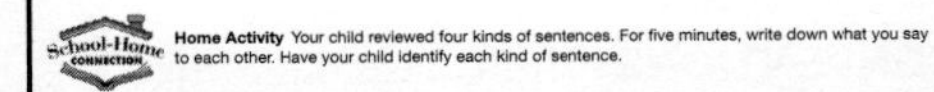
Home Activity Your child reviewed four kinds of sentences. For five minutes, write down what you say to each other. Have your child identify each kind of sentence.

▲ **Grammar and Writing Practice Book** p. 4

Writing Workshop Character Sketch

OBJECTIVES

- Identify qualities of a character sketch.
- Write a character sketch with a strong voice.
- Focus on voice.
- Use a rubric.

Genre Character Sketch
Writer's Craft Voice
Writing Trait Voice

Voice Encourage English learners to use a bilingual dictionary if available, to find powerful verbs to express feelings. For example, *tremble* or *faint* could express nervousness. See more writing support in the ELL and Transition Handbook.

Writing Traits

FOCUS/IDEAS Strong supporting details make the person or character come alive.

ORGANIZATION/PARAGRAPHS The character sketch reports actions and gives descriptions that reveal character traits and builds to the most important one.

VOICE Writing is engaging and lively. The writer's view of the subject is clear.

WORD CHOICE The writer uses vivid adjectives to describe character traits *(tidy, no-nonsense)* and strong verbs *(detect, twinkle)* to describe actions.

SENTENCES Uses questions and exclamations in addition to statements to create variety. *(What happens to the unlucky kid caught chewing gum?).*

CONVENTIONS There is excellent control and accuracy. Sentences are complete and correctly punctuated.

DAY 1 Model the Trait

READING-WRITING CONNECTION

- *Frindle* gives a humorous account of a fifth grader's conflict with a veteran teacher.
- Students will refer to the text to identify author's use of voice.
- Students will write a **character sketch** using word choice and tone to create a unique voice.

MODEL VOICE Discuss Writing Transparency 1A. Then discuss the model and the writing trait of voice.

Think Aloud I see that the writer includes sentences that show her feelings about the character. The last sentence in paragraph 1 shows that the writer at first felt negative toward Mrs. Granger, but wound up being pleasantly surprised. Words like *old-fashioned, strict, smart,* and *funny* make the voice lively and show that a complex, interesting person is being described.

Character Sketch

A **character sketch** makes a person or story character come alive for the reader. It includes details that describe the person's looks and personality. It points out qualities and actions that set the person apart.

A Giant of a Teacher

First two sentences summarize important traits of the character.

Detail sentences describe the character.

Last sentences of paragraphs 1 and 3 show writer's feelings.

Topic sentences of paragraphs 2 and 3 indicate the focus of these paragraphs.

There is more to Mrs. Granger than meets the eye. She seems old-fashioned and strict but is really smart and funny. Everything about her is tidy and no-nonsense. She always wears a formal skirt, jacket, and blouse. She is so serious about teaching, she hasn't missed a day in years. At first I thought she was just stern and unfriendly, but I got a pleasant surprise!

Although she is tiny, Mrs. Granger seems giant to students. Her sharp gray eyes seem all-powerful. Her "X-ray vision" allows her to detect students with gum at fifty feet. Mrs. Granger makes her language arts students learn dozens of words "by the book"—the dictionary, that is!

At the same time, Mrs. Granger gives us glimpses of fun and humor. Her eyes twinkle when she tells funny jokes. What happens to the unlucky kid caught chewing gum? She sticks gum onto a card and pins it on a student's shirt. Best of all, she sees right through Nick's homework-stopping trick and turns the tables on him. I think Mrs. Granger's fifth grade students will have a year to remember!

Unit 1 Frindle — Writing Model **1A**

▲ **Writing Transparency** 1A

DAY 2 Improve Writing

WRITER'S CRAFT
Voice

Display Writing Transparency 1B.

Work together with students to analyze passages to identify use of voice.

Think Aloud **DEVELOP AN APPROPRIATE VOICE** Tomorrow we will write a **character sketch.** I could write about my friend Ruby who wants to be a stand-up comic. How could I use a humorous tone and show how I feel about Ruby? I could write, "Ruby keeps up a steady stream of jokes during lunch. She cracks up the whole table. Once, I laughed so hard milk shot out my nose." These sentences have a comic tone and show I think Ruby is funny.

GUIDED WRITING Some students may need more help with voice. Work with them to identify the voice of the narrator in the reading selection.

Voice

Your tone and choice of words create the **voice** of your writing. Choose a voice that is appropriate to your purpose. Use words that show your personality and your feelings on the topic.

Directions Circle the word that best describes the voice of each writer.

1. Do you like Mr. Cole as much as I do? He is an awesome teacher to me because he makes learning fun. He can always think of a way to make me understand science, and he never makes me feel like a dork for asking questions. His way of reviewing for tests rocks! We play games using the facts and ideas we have learned.

   formal (informal)

2. Members of the Awards Committee:
   I would like to nominate Ms. Mason for the Smithfield Teacher of the Year Award. She works very hard to teach us to read and write. She is always helpful and friendly. Her students respect her because she respects them.

   (serious) funny

Directions Each underlined part has a problem that weakens the voice. Write the letter of the correct problem in the box.

A. too formal **B.** too informal

3. The problem with chewing gum in school is what students do when they are through with it. It is like totally gross and icky to feel a sticky wad of gum under your desk or—worse—on your shoe!
   B

4. On the other hand, it seems unfair to say students cannot chew gum in school at all. After all, most youngsters are fine, upstanding citizens who understand about wastepaper baskets.
   A

Directions Write two or three sentences describing a gum-chewing experience. Choose words and a style that create a humorous voice. Possible answer:

Once I was determined to blow a bubble as big as my head. With ten pieces of bubble gum in my mouth, I looked like a chipmunk. The bubble was magnificent—until it burst on my face and hair!

Unit 1 Frindle — Writer's Craft **1B**

▲ **Writing Transparency** 1B

Trait of the Week

Voice

DAY 3 Prewrite and Draft

READ THE WRITING PROMPT on page 35 in the Student Edition.

Frindle *tells about a teacher with an unusual reputation.*

Think about a character or person who has an interesting trait.

Now write a character sketch about that character or person.

Writing Test Tips

- Write details about the person's looks and actions.
- Explain how these details show what kind of person he or she is.
- Use specific adjectives and lively verbs to make the person come alive.

GETTING STARTED Students can do any of the following:

- Make a word web about the person listing descriptive words and actions in outer circles.
- Brainstorm specific adjectives and strong action words that fit the character's personality.
- List the character's traits. Beneath each one, list example actions showing the trait.

DAY 4 Draft and Revise

EDITING/REVISING CHECKLIST

☑ Do the voice and tone of the writing fit the subject?

☑ Do my word choices show my personality and feelings?

☑ Have I used different kinds of sentences?

☑ Are words with short vowels spelled correctly?

See *The Grammar and Writing Book*, pp. 50–55.

Revising Tips

Voice

- Support descriptions of traits with exact, vivid adjectives and verbs.
- Include details about the person that touch your feelings.
- Choose a tone that matches the personality of the subject.

PUBLISHING Students can attach their writing to construction paper and add a portrait or illustration that suggests the character's personality.

ASSESSMENT Use the scoring rubric to evaluate students' work.

DAY 5 Connect to Unit Writing

Personal Narrative

Week 1	Character Sketch 41g–41h
Week 2	Tall Tale 67g–67h
Week 3	Friendly or Thank-You Letter 89g–89h
Week 4	Feature Article 111g–111h
Week 5	Narrative Writing 133g–133h

PREVIEW THE UNIT PROMPT

Write a personal narrative about a challenge or difficult problem. Describe what the challenge was and tell how you met it. Use details that make the events clear and interesting.

APPLY

- A personal narrative is a story about an interesting experience or event in the storyteller's life.

Writing Trait Rubric

	4	3	2	1
Voice	Excellent sense of writer's attitude toward topic; strongly engages audience and speaks directly to them	Clear sense of how writer feels and thinks; engages audience	Some sense of how writer feels and thinks; weak attempt to engage audience	No sense of how writer feels and thinks about topic; no attempt to engage audience
	Uses well-chosen words in character sketch to clearly show feelings toward topic	Uses words in character sketch that show some feelings about topic	Needs to use more words in character sketch that show feelings about topic	Uses no words in character sketch that show feelings about topic

AFTER READING

Spelling & Phonics Short Vowel VCCV, VCV

OBJECTIVE

- Spell short vowel words with the VCCV and VCV syllable patterns.

Generalization

Connect to Phonics Short vowels are often spelled *a: channel, e: method, i: distance, o: problem, u: butter.* When a syllable ends with a single vowel and a single consonant, the vowel stands for its short sound.

Spelling Words

1. distance	11. admire
2. method	12. comedy
3. anger	13. husband
4. problem	14. tissue
5. butter	15. mustard
6. petals	16. shuttle
7. enjoy*	17. advance
8. perhaps	18. drummer
9. figure*	19. regular
10. channel	20. denim

Challenge Words

21. avalanche	24. adequate
22. monopoly	25. tangerine
23. reluctant	

*Words from the selection

Spelling/Phonics Support See the ELL and Transition Handbook for spelling support.

DAY 1 Pretest and Sort

PRETEST

Use the Dictation Sentences from Day 5 to administer the pretest. Read the word, read the sentence, and then read the word again. Guide students in self-correcting their pretests and correcting any misspellings.

Monitor Progress

Spelling

If... students misspell more than 5 pretest words,	**then...** use words 1–10 for Strategic Intervention.
If... students misspell 1–5 pretest words,	**then...** use words 1–20 for On-Level practice.
If... students correctly spell all pretest words,	**then...** use words 1–25 for Advanced Learners.

HOMEWORK Spelling Practice Book, p. 1.

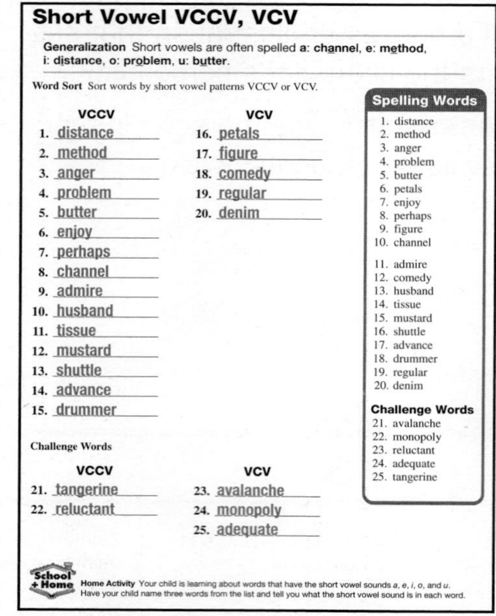

Short Vowel VCCV, VCV

Generalization Short vowels are often spelled **a: channel, e: method, i: distance, o: problem, u: butter.**

Word Sort Sort words by short vowel patterns VCCV or VCV.

VCCV	VCV
1. distance	16. petals
2. method	17. figure
3. anger	18. comedy
4. problem	19. regular
5. butter	20. denim
6. enjoy	
7. perhaps	
8. channel	
9. admire	
10. husband	
11. tissue	
12. mustard	
13. shuttle	
14. advance	
15. drummer	

Challenge Words

VCCV	VCV
21. tangerine	23. avalanche
22. reluctant	24. monopoly
	25. adequate

Spelling Words
1. distance
2. method
3. anger
4. problem
5. butter
6. petals
7. enjoy
8. perhaps
9. figure
10. channel
11. admire
12. comedy
13. husband
14. tissue
15. mustard
16. shuttle
17. advance
18. drummer
19. regular
20. denim

Challenge Words
21. avalanche
22. monopoly
23. reluctant
24. adequate
25. tangerine

School + Home **Home Activity** Your child is learning about words that have the short vowel sounds *a, e, i, o,* and *u*. Have your child name three words from the list and tell you what the short vowel sound is in each word.

▲ **Spelling Practice Book** p. 1

DAY 2 Think and Practice

TEACH

When a syllable ends with a single vowel and a single consonant, the vowel has its short sound. Write *husband* on the board and draw a line to divide the word into syllables between *s* and *b*. Underline *u* and identify *u* as a short vowel. Model dividing the short vowel words *denim* and *figure* after the consonant. Help students understand that the words are divided after the consonant because the first vowel is short.

hus|band

DIVIDE THE WORDS Have students read the list words, tell how to divide them, and say the vowel sound in the first syllable of each word.

HOMEWORK Spelling Practice Book, p. 2.

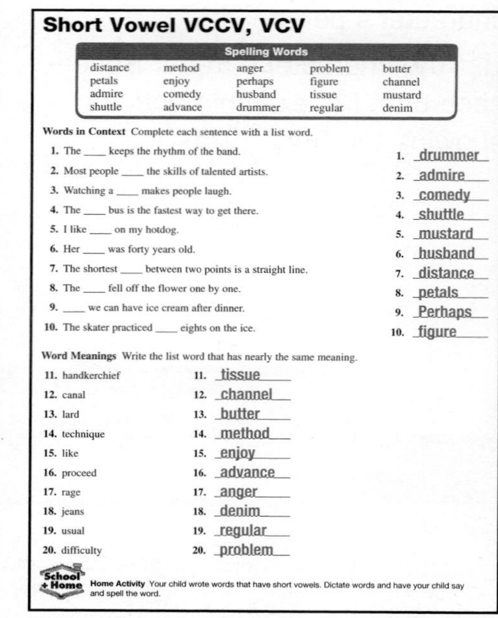

Short Vowel VCCV, VCV

Spelling Words				
distance	method	anger	problem	butter
petals	enjoy	perhaps	figure	channel
admire	comedy	husband	tissue	mustard
shuttle	advance	drummer	regular	denim

Words in Context Complete each sentence with a list word.

1. The ____ keeps the rhythm of the band. — 1. drummer
2. Most people ____ the skills of talented artists. — 2. admire
3. Watching a ____ makes people laugh. — 3. comedy
4. The ____ bus is the fastest way to get there. — 4. shuttle
5. I like ____ on my hotdog. — 5. mustard
6. Her ____ was forty years old. — 6. husband
7. The shortest ____ between two points is a straight line. — 7. distance
8. The ____ fell off the flower one by one. — 8. petals
9. ____ we can have ice cream after dinner. — 9. Perhaps
10. The skater practiced ____ eights on the ice. — 10. figure

Word Meanings Write the list word that has nearly the same meaning.

11. handkerchief	11. tissue
12. canal	12. channel
13. lard	13. butter
14. technique	14. method
15. like	15. enjoy
16. proceed	16. advance
17. rage	17. anger
18. jeans	18. denim
19. usual	19. regular
20. difficulty	20. problem

School + Home **Home Activity** Your child wrote words that have short vowels. Dictate words and have your child say and spell the word.

▲ **Spelling Practice Book** p. 2

DAY 3 Connect to Writing

WRITE ABOUT A PERSON

Ask students to use at least four spelling words to write about a person they admire.

Frequently Misspelled Words

and *to*
too

These words may seem easy to spell, but they are often misspelled by fifth-graders. Alert students to these frequently misspelled words. Tell students to be sure to add the final *d* when writing *and.* Discuss the correct usage of *to* and *too.*

HOMEWORK Spelling Practice Book, p. 3.

Short Vowel VCCV, VCV

Proofread a Poster Sarah made a poster for the school fair. Circle seven spelling errors. Find one capitalization error. Write the corrections on the lines.

Come too the village fair!
See the funny comady team show.
Milk a cow and churn some buttar at the farm exhibit.
Sample hot dogs with twenty choices of musterd.
Make tisseu flower bouquets.
Decorate your denim jeans with a special new art method.
Enjoy fifty booths of crafts, fun, and games.
park at the Town Hall parking lot.
Ride the special shuttal bus to fair grounds.
Discount tickets are on sale in advanse.

1. to
2. comedy
3. butter
4. mustard
5. tissue
6. shuttle
7. advance
8. Park at the Town Hall parking lot.

Spelling Words: distance, method, anger, problem, butter, petals, enjoy, perhaps, figure, channel, admire, comedy, husband, tissue, mustard, shuttle, advance, drummer, regular, denim

Frequently Misspelled Words: and, to, too

Proofread Words Circle the correct spelling of the word.

9.	channal	chanel	(channel)
10.	(drummer)	drumer	drummor
11.	metod	methid	(method)
12.	parhaps	(perhaps)	pirhaps
13.	(figure)	figger	figour
14.	petles	petels	(petals)
15.	problam	(problem)	problim

School + Home **Home Activity** Your child found misspelled list words with VCCV and VCV patterns. Select a list word and ask your child to spell it.

▲ **Spelling Practice Book** p. 3

DAY 4 Review

REVIEW SHORT VOWEL VCCV AND VCV WORDS

Have students write the list words on cards and divide the words into syllables by cutting apart the cards. Tell students to exchange cards and reassemble each other's words.

Spelling Strategy
Steps for Spelling New Words

Step 1: Look at the word. Say it and listen to the sounds.

Step 2: Spell the word aloud.

Step 3: Think about its spelling. Is there anything special to remember?

Step 4: Picture the word with your eyes shut.

Step 5: Look at the word and write it.

Step 6: Cover the word. Picture it and write it again. Check its spelling.

HOMEWORK Spelling Practice Book, p. 4.

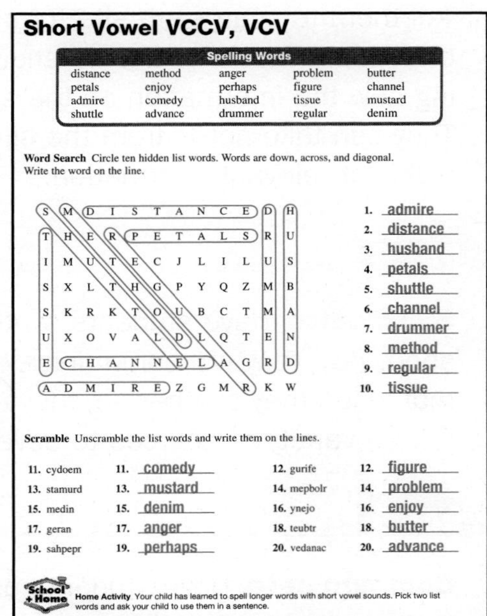

Short Vowel VCCV, VCV

Spelling Words

distance	method	anger	problem	butter
petals	enjoy	perhaps	figure	channel
admire	comedy	husband	tissue	mustard
shuttle	advance	drummer	regular	denim

Word Search Circle ten hidden list words. Words are down, across, and diagonal. Write the word on the line.

S	M	D	I	S	T	A	N	C	E	D	H
T	H	E	R	P	E	T	A	L	S	R	U
I	M	U	T	E	C	J	L	I	L	U	S
S	X	L	T	H	G	P	Y	Q	Z	M	B
S	K	R	K	T	O	U	B	C	T	M	A
U	X	O	V	A	L	D	L	Q	T	E	N
E	C	H	A	N	N	E	L	A	G	R	D
A	D	M	I	R	E	Z	G	M	R	K	W

1. admire
2. distance
3. husband
4. petals
5. shuttle
6. channel
7. drummer
8. method
9. regular
10. tissue

Scramble Unscramble the list words and write them on the lines.

11. cydoem	11. comedy	12. gurife	12. figure
13. stamurd	13. mustard	14. mepbolr	14. problem
15. medin	15. denim	16. ynejo	16. enjoy
17. geran	17. anger	18. teubtr	18. butter
19. sahpepr	19. perhaps	20. vedanac	20. advance

School + Home **Home Activity** Your child has learned to spell longer words with short vowel sounds. Pick two list words and ask your child to use them in a sentence.

▲ **Spelling Practice Book** p. 4

DAY 5 Posttest

DICTATION SENTENCES

1. I saw a train in the distance.
2. What is the best method for learning spelling words?
3. Teasing may cause anger.
4. How can we solve the problem?
5. Mom spread butter on the bread.
6. The rose petals are pink.
7. Do you enjoy hiking?
8. Perhaps she will go to the party.
9. That figure has six sides.
10. The boat sailed up the channel.
11. Whom do you admire most?
12. I always laugh at a good comedy.
13. My uncle is my aunt's husband.
14. Use a tissue when you sneeze.
15. Do you like mustard on your pretzel?
16. The space shuttle landed safely.
17. We bought the tickets in advance.
18. My sister is the band's drummer.
19. We will follow our regular plan.
20. Jake got a new pair of denim jeans.

CHALLENGE

21. The avalanche missed the skier.
22. The cable company has a monopoly in our town.
23. We were reluctant to leave.
24. School lunches give us an adequate amount of food.
25. A tangerine is easy to peel.

OBJECTIVES

- Formulate an inquiry question that is connected to this week's lesson focus.
- Effectively and efficiently find, evaluate, and communicate information related to an inquiry question using electronic sources.

New Literacies	
Day 1	**Identify Questions**
Day 2	**Navigate/Search**
Day 3	**Analyze**
Day 4	**Synthesize**
Day 5	**Communicate**

NEW LITERACIES

Internet Inquiry Activity

EXPLORE FAMOUS EDUCATORS

Use the following 5-day plan to help students conduct this week's Internet inquiry activity about famous educators from the past. Remind students to follow classroom rules when using the Internet.

DAY 1

Identify Questions Discuss the lesson focus question: *How do we meet the challenges of learning?* Brainstorm ideas for specific inquiry questions about famous educators. For example, students might want to find out about Anne Sullivan, Helen Keller's teacher. Have students work individually, in pairs, or in small groups to write inquiry questions they want to answer.

DAY 2

Navigate/Search Explain how to begin a simple Internet search using a student-friendly search engine. Have students determine keywords, such as *teachers* or *history of education,* related to their inquiry questions. Point out that using too many keywords may not provide the best search results. Discuss how to use search engine results to identify a few helpful Web sites.

DAY 3

Analyze Have students explore the Web sites they identified on Day 2. Tell them to scan each site for information that helps answer their inquiry questions. Students should analyze information for usefulness, determining how the information on the site relates to their inquiry questions. They can take notes from the site, or if appropriate, they can print out and highlight relevant information.

DAY 4

Synthesize Have students synthesize information from Day 3 and think about how they will communicate it to the rest of the class. Remind them that when they synthesize, they combine relevant ideas and information from a variety of sources to develop answers to their inquiry questions.

DAY 5

Communicate Have students use presentation software to create multimedia presentations showing some of the things they learned about famous educators.

RESEARCH/STUDY SKILLS

Dictionary/Glossary

TEACH

Ask students where they would look to find the meaning of a word they didn't know. Show a dictionary and glossary to students. Define the features of each, with emphasis on the difference between the two tools.

- A **dictionary** lists all words in alphabetical order.
- A **specialized dictionary** lists words in a particular field or language in alphabetical order.
- A **dictionary entry** includes the word, its pronunciation, parts of speech, and meaning. If a word has more than one meaning, the dictionary entry will include all meanings.
- An **online dictionary** is an electronic resource found on the Internet.
- A book may include a **glossary** at the back of it with important words used in the book.
- A **glossary entry** gives the word and its meaning as it is used in the book.

Have students work in pairs, using the glossaries at the back of their books and classroom dictionaries to identify each of the features discussed above. Then, have them answer the following questions:

1. **Is the word *essential* found in the glossary at the back of your book? Explain why.** *(Yes; it is important to the story.)*
2. **What meaning is given for the word *essential* in the glossary? What part of speech is it?** *(absolutely necessary; very important; adjective)*
3. **How is the glossary different from a dictionary?** *(Possible response: A dictionary includes all words; a glossary only includes words used in a story selection, or book.)*

es • sen • tial (əsen ʹshəl)
1. *adj.* absolutely necessary; very important: *Good food and enough rest are essential to good health.* **2. essentials,** *n. pl.* absolutely necessary elements or qualities: *Learn the essentials first, then learn the details.*

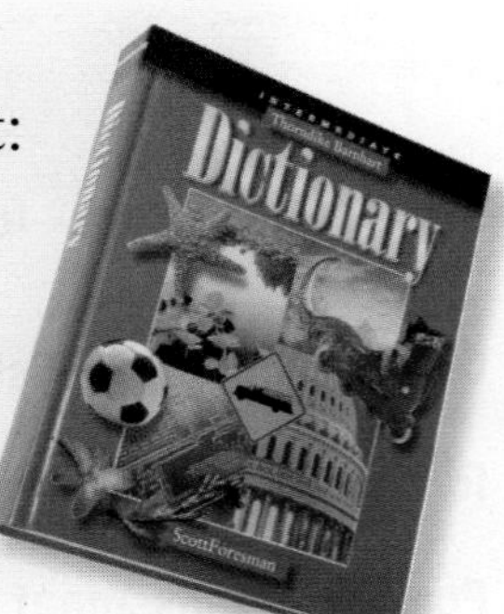

ASSESS

As students work with glossaries and dictionaries, check that they can distinguish between the two reference tools and understand the information in the entries, such as parts of speech and word meanings.

For more practice or to assess students, use Practice Book pp. 9–10.

OBJECTIVES

- Review the parts of a dictionary and glossary.
- Use dictionaries and glossaries to find the meanings of unfamiliar words.

Dictionary/Glossary

- A **dictionary** lists words in alphabetical order and gives their meanings, pronunciations, and other helpful information.
- A **glossary** is a list of important words and their meanings that are used in a book. Glossaries are located at the back of a book.
- When you see an unfamiliar word, and context clues do not help you figure out its meaning, you can use a dictionary or glossary to learn what it means.

Directions Read the dictionary and glossary entries.

Dictionary Entry

rep•u•ta•tion (rep' ye ta' shen) **1.** *n.* what people think and say the character of someone or something is; character in the opinion of others; name; repute: *This store has an excellent reputation for fair dealing.* **2.** good name; good reputation: *Cheating ruined his reputation.* **3.** fame: *an international reputation.*

Glossary Entry

Ice Age *n.* a cold period in which huge ice sheets spread outward from the polar regions, the last one of which lasted from about 1,600,000 to 10,000 B.C. (p. 107)

▲ **Practice Book** p. 9

Directions Answer the questions below.

1. In the dictionary entry, what does the initial bold entry for the word *reputation* tell you?
   It tells you how the word is broken down into syllables.
2. In the dictionary entry, what does the representation of the word in parenthesis tell you?
   It tells you how to pronounce the word.
3. Why do you think the dictionary provides sentence examples in the definition of the word?
   The examples show how to use the word properly in a sentence.
4. How many definitions does this dictionary list for *reputation*? Which is the most commonly used definition?
   There are three; The first one is the most commonly used.
5. What does the italicized *n.* stand for in both entries?
   It stands for *noun.*
6. What two things do you notice are missing from a glossary entry that you find in the dictionary entry?
   The syllable and pronunciation guides are missing.
7. What is the page number listed at the end of the glossary entry for?
   It tells you on which page the glossary word is first used.
8. What information do you get in both a dictionary and glossary entry?
   Both give you a definition of the word.
9. If you were reading a book about life in the desert, would you expect to find *Ice Age* in the glossary? Why or why not?
   No; Glossaries only define the words in the book, and a book about desert life is unlikely to talk about an ice age.
10. If you were reading a story and came across a word you did not know, where would be the first place you would look for a definition—a glossary or a dictionary?
    Possible answer: I would look to see if the book had a glossary in the back first.

School + Home **Home Activity** Your child learned how to use a dictionary and a glossary. Make a list of all the possible times you might use a dictionary or glossary.

▲ **Practice Book** p. 10

AFTER READING

Assessment Checkpoints for the Week

Selection Assessment

Use pp. 1–4 of Selection Tests to check:

 **Selection Understanding**

 **Comprehension Skill** *Plot and Character*

 **Selection Vocabulary**

acquainted	*gauranteed*
assignment	*procedures*
essential	*reputation*
expanded	*worshipped*

Leveled Assessment

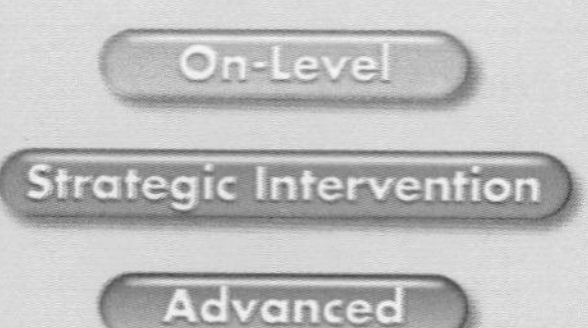

Use pp. 1–6 of Fresh Reads for Differentiated Test Practice to check:

 **Comprehension Skill** *Plot and Character*

 REVIEW **Comprehension Skill** *Cause and Effect*

 **Fluency** *Words Correct Per Minute*

Managing Assessment

Use Assessment Handbook for:

 **Observation Checklists**

 **Record-Keeping Forms**

 **Portfolio Assessment**

Unit 1

Meeting Challenges

CONCEPT QUESTION

What kinds of challenges do people face and how do they meet them?

Week 1

How do we meet the challenges of learning?

Week 2

How can nature challenge us?

Week 3

How do people survive in the wilderness?

Week 4

How do we face personal challenges?

Week 5

What challenges do immigrants encounter?

Week 2

EXPAND THE CONCEPT

How can nature challenge us?

CONNECT THE CONCEPT

▶ **Build Background**

meteorologist, roaring, severe, terror, tornado

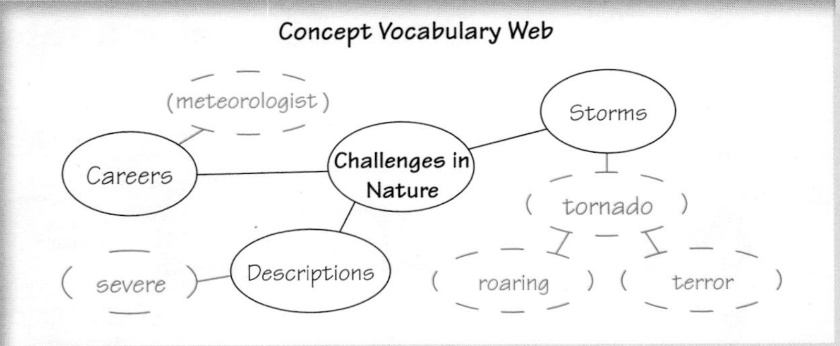

▶ **Science Content**

Lightning, Myths and Nature, Tornadoes, Storm Warnings

▶ **Writing**

Tall Tale

▶ **Internet Inquiry**

Nature's Challenges

Preview Your Week

How can nature challenge us?

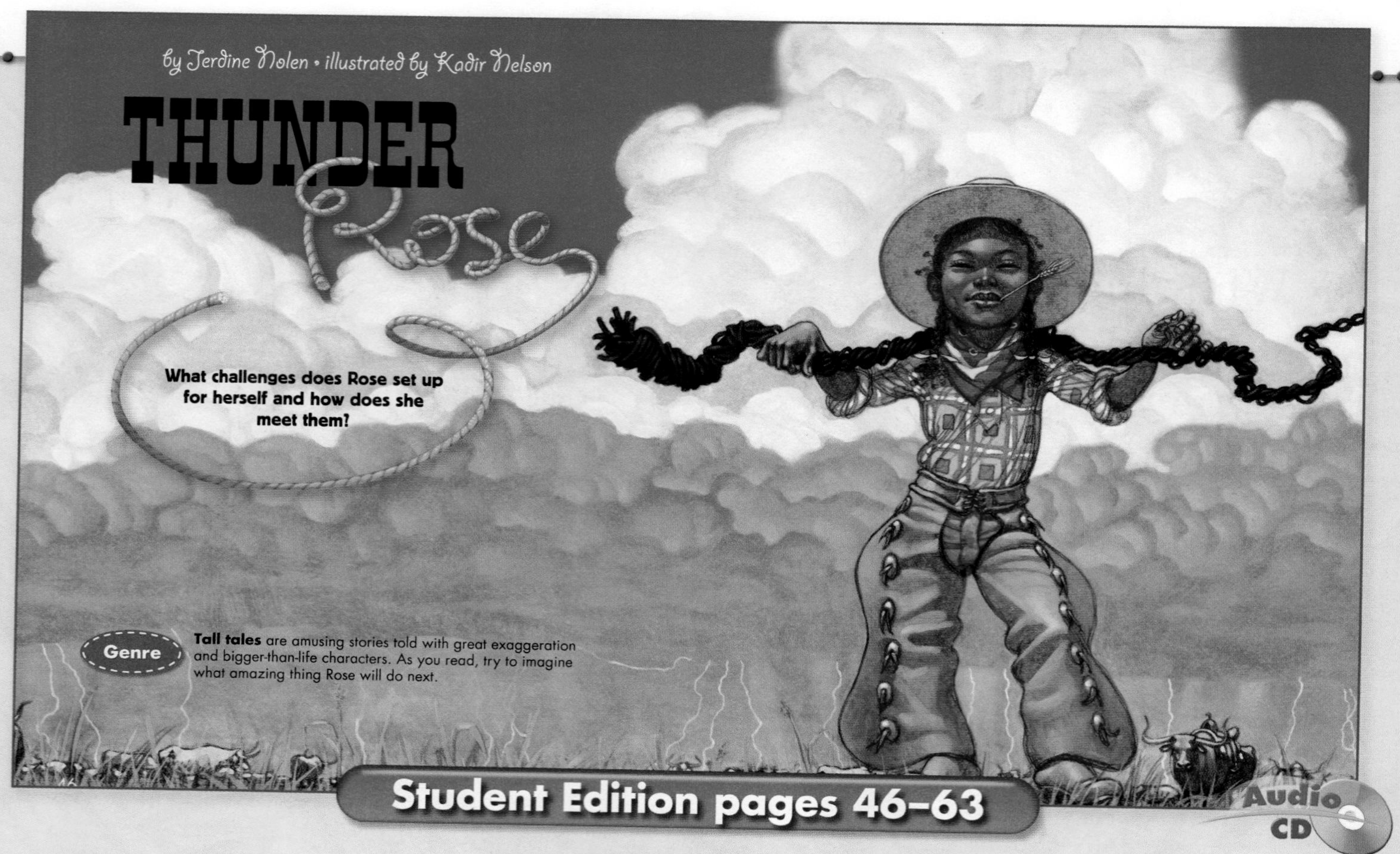

by Jerdine Nolen • illustrated by Kadir Nelson
THUNDER Rose
What challenges does Rose set up for herself and how does she meet them?
Genre
Tall tales are amusing stories told with great exaggeration and bigger-than-life characters. As you read, try to imagine what amazing thing Rose will do next.

Student Edition pages 46–63

Audio CD

Genre Tall Tale

Vocabulary Strategy Context Clues

Comprehension Skill Cause and Effect

Comprehension Strategy Monitor and Fix Up

Paired Selection

Reading Across Texts
Use Scale to Classify Tornadoes in *Thunder Rose*

Genre
Expository Nonfiction

Text Features
Charts

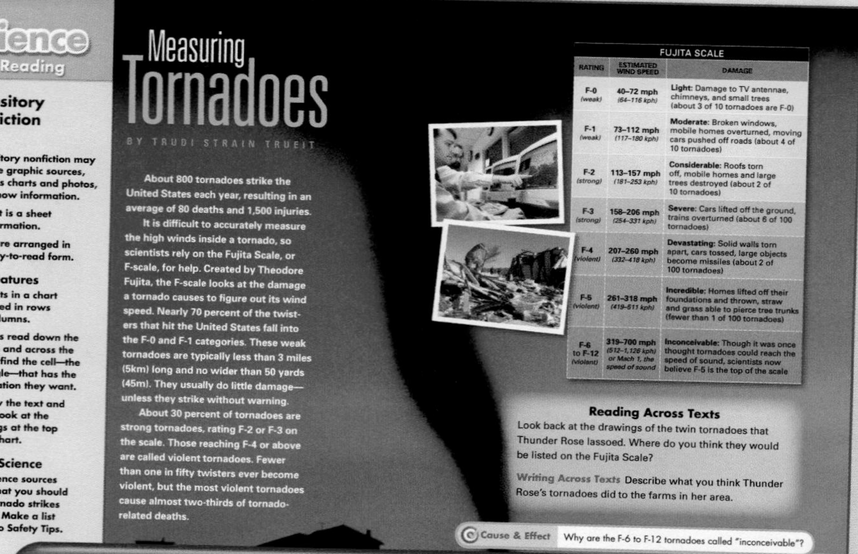

Science in Reading

Expository Nonfiction

Genre
- Expository nonfiction may include graphic sources, such as charts and photos, that show information.
- A chart is a sheet of information.
- Facts are arranged in an easy-to-read form.

Text Features
- The facts in a chart are listed in rows and columns.
- Readers read down the column and across the row to find the cell—the rectangle—that has the information they want.
- Preview the text and chart. Look at the headings at the top of the chart.

Link to Science
Use reference sources to find what you should do if a tornado strikes near you. Make a list of Tornado Safety Tips.

66

Measuring Tornadoes

BY TRUDI STRAIN TRUEIT

About 800 tornadoes strike the United States each year, resulting in an average of 80 deaths and 1,500 injuries.

It is difficult to accurately measure the high winds inside a tornado, so scientists rely on the Fujita Scale, or F-scale, for help. Created by Theodore Fujita, the F-scale looks at the damage a tornado causes to figure out its wind speed. Nearly 70 percent of the twisters that hit the United States fall into the F-0 and F-1 categories. These weak tornadoes are typically less than 3 miles (5km) long and no wider than 50 yards (45m). They usually do little damage—unless they strike without warning.

About 30 percent of tornadoes are strong tornadoes, rating F-2 or F-3 on the scale. Those reaching F-4 or above are called violent tornadoes. Fewer than one in fifty twisters ever become violent, but the most violent tornadoes cause almost two-thirds of tornado-related deaths.

FUJITA SCALE

RATING	ESTIMATED WIND SPEED	DAMAGE
F-0 *(weak)*	40–72 mph *(64–116 kph)*	**Light:** Damage to TV antennae, chimneys, and small trees (about 3 of 10 tornadoes are F-0)
F-1 *(weak)*	73–112 mph *(117–180 kph)*	**Moderate:** Broken windows, mobile homes overturned, moving cars pushed off roads (about 4 of 10 tornadoes)
F-2 *(strong)*	113–157 mph *(181–253 kph)*	**Considerable:** Roofs torn off, mobile homes and large trees destroyed (about 2 of 10 tornadoes)
F-3 *(strong)*	158–206 mph *(254–331 kph)*	**Severe:** Cars lifted off the ground, trains overturned (about 6 of 100 tornadoes)
F-4 *(violent)*	207–260 mph *(332–418 kph)*	**Devastating:** Solid walls torn apart, cars tossed, large objects become missiles (about 2 of 100 tornadoes)
F-5 *(violent)*	261–318 mph *(419–511 kph)*	**Incredible:** Homes lifted off their foundations and thrown, straw and grass able to pierce tree trunks (fewer than 1 of 100 tornadoes)
F-6 to F-12 *(violent)*	319–700 mph *(512–1,126 kph) or Mach 1, the speed of sound*	**Inconceivable:** Though it was once thought tornadoes could reach the speed of sound, scientists now believe F-5 is the top of the scale

Reading Across Texts

Look back at the drawings of the twin tornadoes that Thunder Rose lassoed. Where do you think they would be listed on the Fujita Scale?

Writing Across Texts Describe what you think Thunder Rose's tornadoes did to the farms in her area.

Cause & Effect Why are the F-6 to F-12 tornadoes called "inconceivable"?

Student Edition pages 66–67

Audio CD

- Student Edition
- Leveled Readers

Leveled Readers

Skill Cause and Effect

Strategy Monitor and Fix Up

Lesson Vocabulary

Earth Science
Storm Danger!
by Kristin Cashore
Below-Level
Earth Science
The Challenges of Storm Chasing
by Chris Downey
On-Level
Earth Science
Forecasting the Weather
by Donna Latham
Advanced

ELL Reader

- Concept Vocabulary
- Text Support
- Language Enrichment

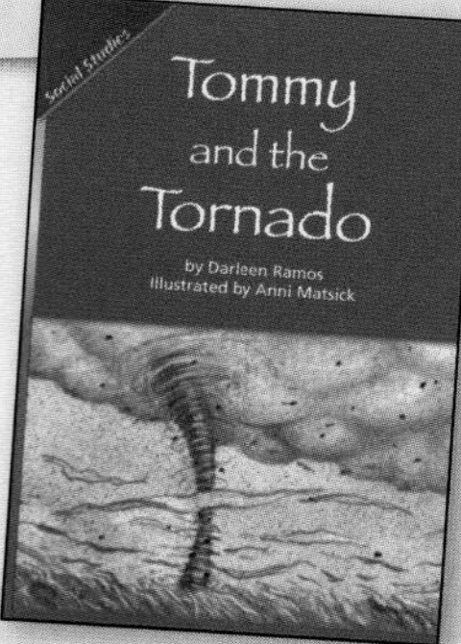

TIME FOR Science

Integrate Science Standards

- Weather
- Atmosphere

Thunder Rose,
pp. 46–63

"Measuring Tornadoes,"
pp. 66–67

Leveled Readers

Below-Level

- Support Concepts

On-Level

- Develop Concepts

Advanced

- Extend Concepts
- Science Extension Activity

ELL Reader

Build **Concept Vocabulary**
Challenges in Nature,
pp. 42l–42m

Teach **Science Concepts**
Lightning, p. 49
Myths and Nature, p. 53
Tornadoes, p. 59
Storm Warnings, p. 67

Explore **Science Center**
Research Tornadoes, p. 42k

Weekly Plan

READING

45–90 minutes

TARGET SKILLS OF THE WEEK

Comprehension Skill
Cause and Effect

Comprehension Strategy
Monitor and Fix Up

Vocabulary Strategy
Context Clues

DAY 1

PAGES 42l–44b, 67a, 67e–67k

Oral Language

QUESTION OF THE WEEK *How can nature challenge us?*

Read Aloud: "Night of the Twisters," 42m
Build Concepts, 42l

Comprehension/Vocabulary

Comprehension Skill/Strategy Lesson, 42–43
Cause and Effect **T**
Monitor and Fix Up

Build Background, 44a

Introduce Lesson Vocabulary, 44b
branded, constructed, daintily, devastation, lullaby, pitch, resourceful, thieving, veins **T**

Read Leveled Readers

Grouping Options 42f–42g

Fluency

Model Tone of Voice, 42l–42m, 67a

DAY 2

PAGES 44–55, 67a, 67e–67k

Oral Language

QUESTION OF THE DAY *Why do you think Rose likes to take on challenges?*

Comprehension/Vocabulary

Vocabulary Strategy Lesson, 44–45
Context Clues **T**

Read *Thunder Rose,* 46–55

Grouping Options 42f–42g

Cause and Effect **T**
Monitor and Fix Up
Context Clues **T**
REVIEW Character and Plot **T**
Develop Vocabulary

Fluency

Echo Reading, 67a

LANGUAGE ARTS

30–60 minutes

Trait of the Week

Word Choice

Day 1

Grammar, 67e
Introduce Subjects and Predicates **T**

Writing Workshop, 67g
Introduce Tall Tale
Model the Trait of the Week: Word Choice

Spelling, 67i
Pretest for Long Vowel VCV

Internet Inquiry, 67k
Identify Questions

Day 2

Grammar, 67e
Develop Subjects and Predicates **T**

Writing Workshop, 67g
Improve Writing with Creating Mood

Spelling, 67i
Teach the Generalization

Internet Inquiry, 67k
Navigate/Search

DAILY WRITING ACTIVITIES

Day 1 Write to Read, 42

Day 2 Words to Write, 45
Strategy Response Log, 46, 55

DAILY SCIENCE CONNECTIONS

Day 1 Challenges in Nature Concept Web, 42l

Day 2 Time for Science: Lightning, 49; Myths and Nature, 53; Revisit the Challenges in Nature Concept Web, 55

DAILY SUCCESS PREDICTORS
for Adequate Yearly Progress

Monitor Progress and Corrective Feedback

Vocabulary: Check Vocabulary, *42l*

RESOURCES FOR THE WEEK

- Practice Book, *pp. 11–20*
- Word Study and Spelling Practice Book, *pp. 5–8*
- Grammar and Writing Practice Book, *pp. 5–8*
- Selection Test, *pp. 5–8*
- Fresh Reads for Differentiated Test Practice, *pp. 7–12*
- The Grammar and Writing Book, *pp. 56–61*

Grouping Options for Differentiated Instruction

Turn the page for the small group lesson plan.

DAY 3 PAGES 56–65, 67a, 67e–67k

Oral Language

QUESTION OF THE DAY *What kind of force does Rose use to overpower the tornadoes?*

Comprehension/Vocabulary

Read *Thunder Rose,* 56–64

Grouping Options 42f–42g

Cause and Effect T

Monitor and Fix Up

REVIEW Plot T

Develop Vocabulary

Reader Response

Selection Test

Fluency

Model Tone of Voice, 67a

Grammar, 67f
Apply Subjects and Predicates in Writing T

Writing Workshop, 65, 67h
Write Now
Prewrite and Draft

Spelling, 67j
Connect Spelling to Writing

Internet Inquiry, 67k
Analyze Sources

Day 3 Strategy Response Log, 62
Look Back and Write, 64

Day 3 Time for Science: Tornadoes, 59
Revisit the Challenges in Nature Concept Web, 63

DAY 4 PAGES 66–67a, 67e–67k

Oral Language

QUESTION OF THE DAY *Why do you think people often tell tall tales about destructive forces of nature?*

Comprehension/Vocabulary

Read "Measuring Tornadoes," 66–67

Grouping Options 42f–42g

Expository Nonfiction

Reading Across Texts

Content-Area Vocabulary

Fluency

Partner Reading, 67a

Grammar, 67f
Practice Subjects and Predicates for Standardized Tests T

Writing Workshop, 67h
Draft, Revise, and Publish

Spelling, 67j
Provide a Strategy

Internet Inquiry, 67k
Synthesize Information

Day 4 Writing Across Texts, 67

Day 4 Time for Science: Storm Warnings, 67

DAY 5 PAGES 67a–67l

Oral Language

QUESTION OF THE WEEK *To wrap up the week, revisit the Day 1 question.*

Build Concept Vocabulary, 67c

Fluency

Read Leveled Readers

Grouping Options 42f–42g

Assess Reading Rate, 67a

Comprehension/Vocabulary

Reteach Cause and Effect, 67b T

Author's Craft, 67b

Review Context Clues, 67c T

Speaking and Viewing, 67d
Storytelling
Analyze an Illustration

Grammar, 67f
Cumulative Review

Writing Workshop, 67h
Connect to Unit Writing

Spelling, 67j
Posttest for Long Vowel VCV

Internet Inquiry, 67k
Communicate Results

Research/Study Skills, 67l
Almanac

Day 5 Author's Craft, 67b

Day 5 Revisit the Challenges in Nature Concept Web, 67c

KEY ◎ = Target Skill T = Tested Skill

Comprehension	Fluency	Vocabulary
Check Retelling, *64*	Check Fluency WCPM, *67a*	Check Vocabulary, *67c*

SUCCESS PREDICTOR

Small Group Plan *for Differentiated Instruction*

Daily Plan AT A GLANCE

Reading

Whole Group
- Oral Language
- Comprehension/Vocabulary

Group Time

Differentiated Instruction

Meet with small groups to provide:
- Skill Support
- Reading Support
- Fluency Practice

Read

This week's lessons for daily group time can be found behind the Differentiated Instruction (DI) tab on pp. DI • 12–DI • 21.

Whole Group
- Fluency

Language Arts
- Grammar
- Writing
- Spelling
- Research/Inquiry
- Speaking/Listening/Viewing

Use *My Sidewalks on Reading Street* for Tier III intensive reading intervention.

DAY 1

On-Level	Strategic Intervention	Advanced
Teacher-Led *Page DI • 13*	**Teacher-Led** *Page DI • 12*	**Teacher-Led** *Page DI • 13*
• Develop Concept Vocabulary • **Read** On-Level Reader *The Challenges of Storm Chasing*	• Reinforce Concepts • **Read** Below-Level Reader *Storm Danger*	• **Read** Advanced Reader *Forecasting the Weather* • Independent Extension Activity

Independent Activities

While you meet with small groups, have the rest of the class...

- Visit the Reading/Library Center
- Listen to the Background Building Audio
- Finish Write to Read, p. 42
- Complete Practice Book pp. 13–14
- Visit Cross-Curricular Centers

DAY 2

On-Level	Strategic Intervention	Advanced
Teacher-Led *Pages 48–55*	**Teacher-Led** *Page DI • 14*	**Teacher-Led** *Page DI • 15*
• **Read** *Thunder Rose*	• Practice Lesson Vocabulary • Read Multisyllabic Words • **Read** or Listen to *Thunder Rose*	• Extend Vocabulary • **Read** *Thunder Rose*

Independent Activities

While you meet with small groups, have the rest of the class...

- Visit the Reading/Library Center
- Listen to the AudioText for *Thunder Rose*
- Finish Words to Write, p. 45
- Complete Practice Book pp. 15–16
- Write in their Strategy Response Logs, pp. 46, 55
- Visit Cross-Curricular Centers
- Work on inquiry projects

DAY 3

On-Level	Strategic Intervention	Advanced
Teacher-Led *Pages 56–63*	**Teacher-Led** *Page DI • 16*	**Teacher-Led** *Page DI • 17*
• **Read** *Thunder Rose*	• Practice Cause and Effect and Monitor and Fix Up • **Read** or Listen to *Thunder Rose*	• Extend Cause and Effect ar Monitor and Fix Up • **Read** *Thunder Rose*

Independent Activities

While you meet with small groups, have the rest of the class...

- Visit the Reading/Library Center
- Listen to the AudioText for *Thunder Rose*
- Write in their Strategy Response Logs, p. 62
- Finish Look Back and Write, p. 64
- Complete Practice Book p. 17
- Visit Cross-Curricular Centers
- Work on inquiry projects

1 Begin with whole class skill and strategy instruction.

2 Meet with small groups to provide differentiated instruction.

3 Gather the whole class back together for fluency and language arts.

DAY 4

On-Level	Strategic Intervention	Advanced
Teacher-Led *Pages 66–67*	**Teacher-Led** *Page DI • 18*	**Teacher-Led** *Page DI • 19*
Read "Measuring Tornadoes"	• Practice Retelling • **Read** or Listen to "Measuring Tornadoes"	• **Read** "Measuring Tornadoes" • Genre Study

i Independent Activities

While you meet with small groups, have the rest of the class...

- Visit the Reading/Library Center
- Listen to the AudioText for "Measuring Tornadoes"
- Visit the Writing/Vocabulary Center
- Finish Writing Across Texts, p. 67
- Visit Cross-Curricular Centers
- Work on inquiry projects

DAY 5

On-Level	Strategic Intervention	Advanced
Teacher-Led *Page DI • 21*	**Teacher-Led** *Page DI • 20*	**Teacher-Led** *Page DI • 21*
• **Reread** Leveled Reader *The Challenges of Storm Chasing* • Retell *The Challenges of Storm Chasing*	• **Reread** Leveled Reader *Storm Danger* • Retell *Storm Danger*	• **Reread** Leveled Reader *Forecasting the Weather* • Share Extension Activity

i Independent Activities

While you meet with small groups, have the rest of the class...

- Visit the Reading/Library Center
- Complete Practice Book pp. 18–20
- Visit Cross-Curricular Centers
- Work on inquiry projects

Grouping Place English language learners in the groups that correspond to their reading abilities in English.

Use the appropriate Leveled Reader or other text at students' instructional level.

TIP Send home the appropriate Multilingual Summary of the main selection on Day 1.

PearsonSuccessNet.com

Peter Afflerbach
For ideas on implementing ongoing assessment, see the article "STAIR" by Scott Foresman author Peter Afflerbach.

TEACHER TALK

Scaffolding is temporary support given as students learn a new skill. Scaffolded instruction includes direct explanations, crutches, and other support which is gradually removed as skills are mastered.

Looking Ahead

Be sure to schedule time for students to work on the unit inquiry project "Facing Challenges." This week students conduct searches that can help them find information about their Special Olympics events and the challenges the competitors face.

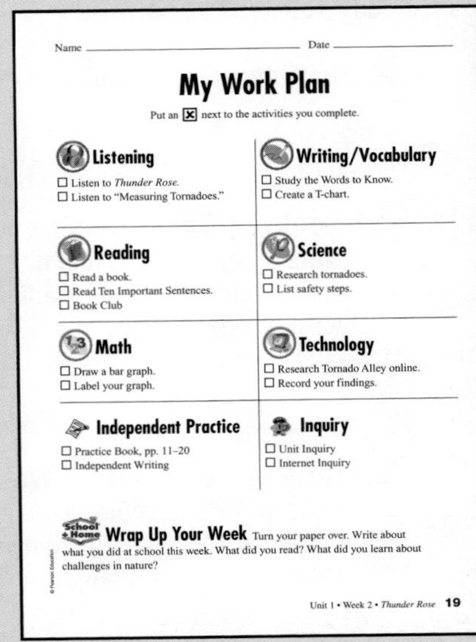

Name ______________ Date ______________

My Work Plan

Put an ☒ next to the activities you complete.

Listening
- ☐ Listen to *Thunder Rose*.
- ☐ Listen to "Measuring Tornadoes."

Writing/Vocabulary
- ☐ Study the Words to Know.
- ☐ Create a T-chart.

Reading
- ☐ Read a book.
- ☐ Read Ten Important Sentences.
- ☐ Book Club

Science
- ☐ Research tornadoes.
- ☐ List safety steps.

Math
- ☐ Draw a bar graph.
- ☐ Label your graph.

Technology
- ☐ Research Tornado Alley online.
- ☐ Record your findings.

Independent Practice
- ☐ Practice Book, pp. 11–20
- ☐ Independent Writing

Inquiry
- ☐ Unit Inquiry
- ☐ Internet Inquiry

School + Home Wrap Up Your Week Turn your paper over. Write about what you did at school this week. What did you read? What did you learn about challenges in nature?

© Pearson Education

Unit 1 • Week 2 • *Thunder Rose* 19

▲ **Group-Time Survival Guide** p. 19, Weekly Contract

Customize Your Plan by Stran

ORAL LANGUAGE

Concept Development

How can nature challenge us?

CONCEPT VOCABULARY

meteorologist *roaring* *severe* *terror* *tornado*

BUILD

- ❑ **Question of the Week** Introduce and discuss the question of the week. This week students will read a variety of texts and work on projects related to the concept *challenges in nature.* Post the question for students to refer to throughout the week DAY 1 *42d*
- ❑ **Read Aloud** Read aloud "Night of the Twisters." Then begin a web to build concepts and concept vocabulary related to this week's lesson and the unit theme, Meeting Challenges. Introduce the concept words *meteorologist, roaring, severe, terror,* and *tornado* and have students place them on the web. Display the web for use throughout the week. DAY 1 *42l–42m*

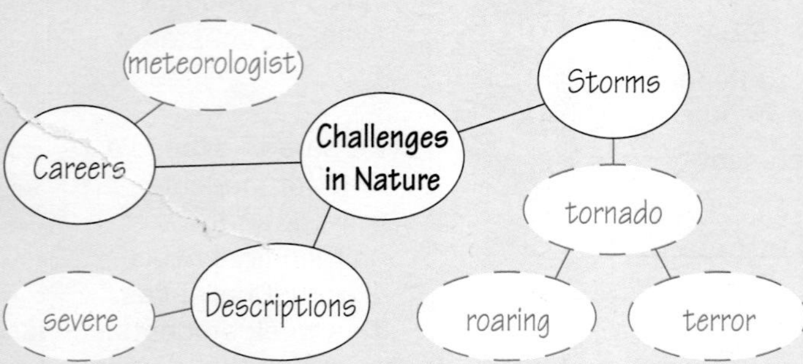

DEVELOP

- ❑ **Question of the Day** Use the prompts from the Weekly Plan to engage students in conversations related to this week's reading and the unit theme. **EVERY DAY** *42d–42e*
- ❑ **Concept Vocabulary Web** Revisit the Challenges in Nature Concept Web and encourage students to add concept words from their reading and life experiences. DAY 2 *55,* DAY 3 *63*

CONNECT

- ❑ **Looking Back/Moving Forward** Revisit the Challenges in Nature Concept Web and discuss how it relates to this week's lesson and the unit theme. Then make connections to next week's lesson. DAY 5 *67c*

CHECK

- ❑ **Concept Vocabulary Web** Use the Challenges in Nature Concept Web to check students' understanding of the concept vocabulary words *meteorologist, roaring, severe, terror,* and *tornado.* DAY 1 *42l,* DAY 5 *67c*

VOCABULARY

STRATEGY CONTEXT CLUES
When you are reading, you may come to a familiar word used in an unfamiliar way. The word may be a homonym. Homonyms are words that are spelled the same, but have different meanings. You can use the context—the words and sentences around the word—to figure out which meaning is being used.

LESSON VOCABULARY

branded *constructed* *daintily* *devastation* *lullaby* *pitch* *resourceful* *thieving* *veins*

TEACH

- ❑ **Words to Know** Give students the opportunity to tell what they already know about this week's lesson vocabulary words. Then discuss word meaning. DAY 1 *44b*
- ❑ **Vocabulary Strategy Lesson** Use the vocabulary strategy lesson in the Student Edition to introduce and model this week's strategy, *context clues.* DAY 2 *44–45*

Vocabulary Strategy Lesson

PRACTICE/APPLY

- ❑ **Leveled Text** Read the lesson vocabulary in the context of leveled text. DAY 1 *LR10–LR18*

Leveled Readers

- ❑ **Words in Context** Read the lesson vocabulary and apply *context clues* in the context of *Thunder Rose.* DAY 2 *46–55,* DAY 3 *56–64*
- ❑ **Writing/Vocabulary Center** Make a T-chart of some of the words and phrases in *Thunder Rose* that help make it a tall tale. **ANY DAY** *42k*

Main Selection—Fiction

- ❑ **Homework** Practice Book pp. 14–15. DAY 1 *44b,* DAY 2 *45*
- ❑ **Word Play** Have partners select words from *Thunder Rose* and see how many new words they can make by adding suffixes. **ANY DAY** *67c*

ASSESS

- ❑ **Selection Test** Use the Selection Test to determine students' understanding of the lesson vocabulary words. DAY 3

RETEACH/REVIEW

- ❑ **Reteach Lesson** If necessary, use this lesson to reteach and review *context clues.* DAY 5 *67c*

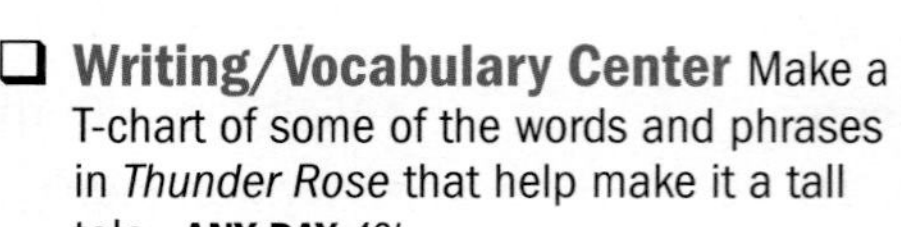

1 Use assessment data to determine your instructional focus.

2 Preview this week's instruction by strand.

3 Choose instructional activities that meet the needs of your classroom.

COMPREHENSION

SKILL CAUSE AND EFFECT A cause is what made something happen. An effect is what happened as the result of a cause.

STRATEGY MONITOR AND FIX UP At times when reading, you may realize that you did not understand what you just read and do not understand how causes produce certain effects. When this happens, you should reread the text slowly and ask yourself guiding questions.

TEACH

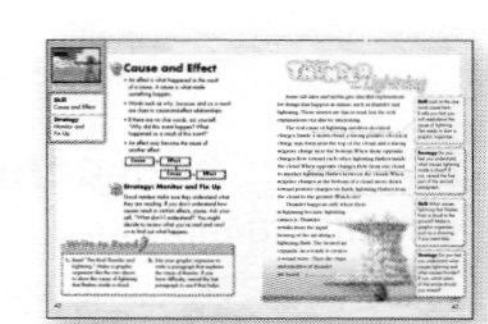

Skill/Strategy Lesson

- ❑ **Skill/Strategy Lesson** Use the skill/strategy lesson in the Student Edition to introduce and model *cause and effect* and *monitor and fix up*. DAY 1 *42-43*
- ❑ **Extend Skills** Teach author's craft. **ANY DAY** *67b*

PRACTICE/APPLY

Leveled Readers

Main Selection—Fiction

Paired Selection—NonFiction

- ❑ **Leveled Text** Apply *cause and effect* and *monitor and fix up* to read leveled text. DAY 1 *LR10-LR18*
- ❑ **Skills and Strategies in Context** Read *Thunder Rose,* using the Guiding Comprehension questions to apply *cause and effect* and *monitor and fix up*. DAY 2 *46-55,* DAY 3 *56-64*

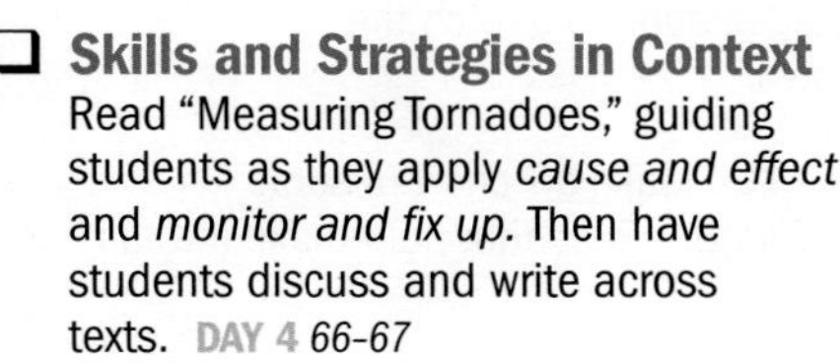

- ❑ **Skills and Strategies in Context** Read "Measuring Tornadoes," guiding students as they apply *cause and effect* and *monitor and fix up.* Then have students discuss and write across texts. DAY 4 *66-67*

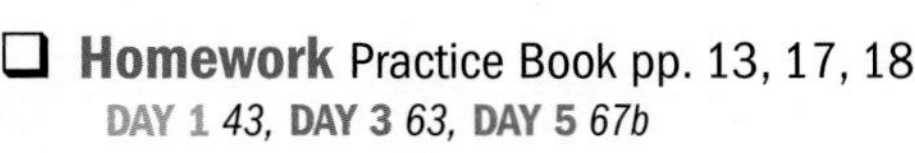

- ❑ **Homework** Practice Book pp. 13, 17, 18. DAY 1 *43,* DAY 3 *63,* DAY 5 *67b*
- ❑ **Fresh Reads for Differentiated Test Practice** Have students practice *cause and effect* with a new passage. DAY 3

ASSESS

- ❑ **Selection Test** Determine students' understanding of the selection and their use of *cause and effect.* DAY 3
- ❑ **Retell** Have students retell *Thunder Rose.* DAY 3 *64-65*

RETEACH/REVIEW

- ❑ **Reteach Lesson** If necessary, reteach and review *cause and effect.* DAY 5 *67b*

FLUENCY

SKILL TONE OF VOICE Tone of voice is the ability to add emotion to words. By changing your tone you can bring words to life, create the mood, and make the reading lively.

TEACH

- ❑ **Read Aloud** Model fluent reading by rereading "Night of the Twisters." Focus on this week's fluency skill, tone of voice. DAY 1 *42l-42m, 67a*

PRACTICE/APPLY

- ❑ **Echo Reading** Read aloud selected paragraphs from *Thunder Rose,* emphasizing the inflections in your voice. Then practice as a class, doing three echo readings of the selected paragraphs. DAY 2 *67a,* DAY 3 *67a*
- ❑ **Partner Reading** Have partners practice reading aloud, reading with changing inflection to reflect different characters' voices and offering each other feedback. As students reread, monitor their progress toward their individual fluency goals. DAY 4 *67a*
- ❑ **Listening Center** Have students follow along with the AudioText for this week's selections. **ANY DAY** *42j*
- ❑ **Reading/Library Center** Have students reread a selection of their choice. **ANY DAY** *42j*
- ❑ **Fluency Coach** Have students use Fluency Coach to listen to fluent readings or practice reading on their own. **ANY DAY**

ASSESS

- ❑ **Check Fluency** WCPM Do a one-minute timed reading, paying special attention to this week's skill—tone of voice. Provide feedback for each student. DAY 5 *67a*

Customize Your Plan by Stran

GRAMMAR

SKILL SUBJECTS AND PREDICATES Every sentence has a subject and a predicate. The words that tell whom or what the sentence is about are the *complete subject*. The most important word in the complete subject is the *simple subject,* or the noun or pronoun. The words that tell what the subject is or does are the *complete predicate.* The most important word in the complete predicate is the *simple predicate,* or the verb.

TEACH

- ❑ **Grammar Transparency 2** Use Grammar Transparency 2 to teach subjects and predicates. DAY 1 *67e*

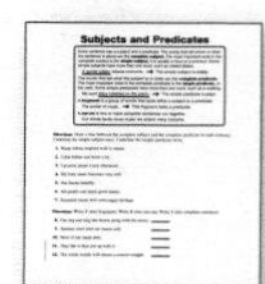

Grammar Transparency 2

PRACTICE/APPLY

- ❑ **Develop the Concept** Review the concept of subjects and predicates and provide guided practice. DAY 2 *67e*
- ❑ **Apply to Writing** Have students review something they have written and apply subjects and predicates. DAY 3 *67f*
- ❑ **Test Preparation** Examine common errors in subjects and predicates to prepare for standardized tests. DAY 4 *67f*
- ❑ **Homework** Grammar and Writing Practice Book pp. 5–7. DAY 2 *67e*, DAY 3 *67f*, DAY 4 *67f*

ASSESS

- ❑ **Cumulative Review** Use Grammar and Writing Practice Book p. 8. DAY 5 *67f*

RETEACH/REVIEW

- ❑ **Daily Fix-It** Have students find and correct errors in grammar, spelling, and punctuation. EVERY DAY *67e–67f*
- ❑ **The Grammar and Writing Book** Use pp. 56–59 of The Grammar and Writing Book to extend instruction for subjects and predicates. ANY DAY

The Grammar and Writing Book

WRITING

Trait of the Week

WORD CHOICE Good writers choose their words carefully. Strong verbs, specific nouns, and vivid adjectives help writers elaborate on their ideas. Well-chosen words make writing clear and lively, and help readers "see" the action.

TEACH

- ❑ **Writing Transparency 2A** Use the model to introduce and discuss the Trait of the Week. DAY 1 *67g*
- ❑ **Writing Transparency 2B** Use the transparency to show students how creating mood can improve their writing. DAY 2 *67g*

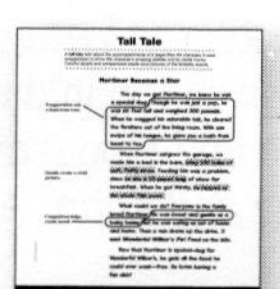

Writing Transparency 2A

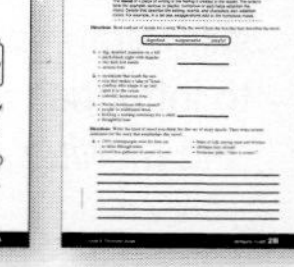

Writing Transparency 2B

PRACTICE/APPLY

- ❑ **Write Now** Examine the model on Student Edition p. 65. Then have students write their own tall tale. DAY 3 *65, 67h*, DAY 4 *67h*

  Prompt *Thunder Rose* is a tall tale about a girl with out-of-this world-skills. Think about another character or a person who is larger than life. Now write a tall tale, using exaggeration to stretch the truth in an entertaining way.

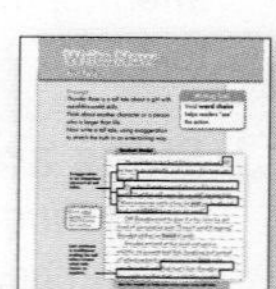

Write Now p. 65

- ❑ **Writing/Vocabulary Center** Make a T-chart of some of the words and phrases in *Thunder Rose* that help make it a tall tale. ANY DAY *42k*

ASSESS

- ❑ **Writing Trait Rubric** Use the rubric to evaluate students' writing. DAY 4 *67h*

RETEACH/REVIEW

- ❑ **The Grammar and Writing Book** Use pp. 56–61 of The Grammar and Writing Book to extend instruction for subjects and predicates, creating mood, and tall tales. ANY DAY

The Grammar and Writing Book

1 Use assessment data to determine your instructional focus.

2 Preview this week's instruction by strand.

3 Choose instructional activities that meet the needs of your classroom.

SPELLING

GENERALIZATION LONG VOWEL VCV Long vowels can be spelled *a: basic, e: fever, i: climate, o: hotel.* When a single vowel appears at the end of a word or syllable, the vowel usually stands for its long sound.

TEACH

- ❑ **Pretest** Give the pretest for words with long vowel VCV patterns. Guide students in self-correcting their pretests and correcting any misspellings. DAY 1 *67i*
- ❑ **Think and Practice** Connect spelling to the phonics generalization for long vowel VCV. DAY 2 *67i*

PRACTICE/APPLY

- ❑ **Connect to Writing** Have students use spelling words to write exaggerations. Then review frequently misspelled words: *favorite, buy*. DAY 3 *67j*
- ❑ **Homework** Word Study and Spelling Practice Book pp. 5–8. **EVERY DAY**

RETEACH/REVIEW

- ❑ **Review** Review spelling words to prepare for the posttest. Then provide students with a spelling strategy—dividing long words. DAY 4 *67j*

ASSESS

- ❑ **Posttest** Use dictation sentences to give the posttest for words with long vowel VCV. DAY 5 *67j*

Spelling Words

1. fever	8. silent	15. vital
2. broken	9. labor	16. acorn
3. climate	10. spider	17. item
4. hotel	11. label	18. aroma
5. basic	12. icon	19. legal
6. vocal	13. agent	20. solo
7. native	14. motive	

Challenge Words

21. society	23. notation	25. equation
22. rhinoceros	24. idealistic	

*Word from the selection

RESEARCH AND INQUIRY

- ❑ **Internet Inquiry** Have students conduct an Internet inquiry on nature's challenges. **EVERY DAY** *67k*
- ❑ **Almanac** Review what types of information can be found in an almanac and discuss how students can use an almanac to locate information. DAY 5 *67l*
- ❑ **Unit Inquiry** Allow time for students to conduct searches that can help them find information about their Special Olympics events and the challenges the competitors face. **ANY DAY** *17*

SPEAKING AND VIEWING

- ❑ **Storytelling** Have students select a scene from *Thunder Rose* to retell to the class. DAY 5 *67d*
- ❑ **Analyze an Illustration** Have students study the illustration of the tornado coming toward Thunder Rose on p. 60 and answer questions. DAY 5 *67d*

Resources for

Differentiated Instruction

LEVELED READERS

- **Comprehension**
  - **Skill** Cause/Effect
  - **Strategy** Monitor/Fix Up
- **Lesson Vocabulary**
  - Context Clues

- **Science Standards**
  - Weather
  - Atmosphere

PearsonSuccessNet.com

Use the Online Database of over 600 books to

- Download and print additional copies of this week's leveled readers.
- Listen to the readers being read online.
- Search for more titles focused on this week's skills, topic, and content.

On-Level

On-Level Reader

Name__________ **Storm Chasing**

Cause and Effect

- A **cause** is the reason something happens. The **effect** is what happens.
- A cause may have more than one effect, and an effect may have more than one cause.
- Sometimes a cause is not directly stated, and you need to think about why something happened.

Directions Read the following passage. Then answer the questions that follow.

> Tornadoes form when a layer of cold air moves over a layer of warm air. The lighter air rises up through the cold air. This makes the funnel cloud rotate as the air changes places. A tornado can do amazing damage to buildings, property, and land. Tornado winds, rising to a furious pitch, will rip through a town, and destroy everything in their path. Houses and mobile homes may be flattened, ripped apart, or carried away completely. A tornado can even peel the bark off trees!
>
> But as dangerous as they are, tornadoes are a great source of delight for storm chasers. They love to seek out, or chase, tornadoes. Their task is a dangerous one. High winds can flip the chaser's vehicle or blow out car windows. Heavy rain and hail can make it hard to see. Flooding and fog can make traveling harder and might strand a chaser in the path of a storm. Lightning, a release of electricity in the atmosphere, is another danger for storm chasers. It can strike without warning!

Possible responses given.

1. Describe the cause of tornadoes.
   When a layer of cold air moves over a layer of warm air, the lighter air rises up through the cold air and makes the funnel cloud rotate.
2. What are two effects of tornadoes?
   Houses and mobile homes may be flattened, ripped apart, or carried away. A tornado can even peel the bark off trees.
3. What is the cause for lightning, as stated in the passage?
   Lightning is a release of electricity in the atmosphere.
4. What are two effects of tornadoes on storm chasers?
   High winds can flip the chaser's vehicle or blow out car windows. Heavy rain and hail can make it hard to see.
5. Would you like to be a storm chaser? Why or why not? Give examples from the reader to support your choice.
   Yes, because storms are amazing to look at and you can learn a lot about them. I would like to work in a truck with tracking equipment.

On-Level Practice TE p. LR14

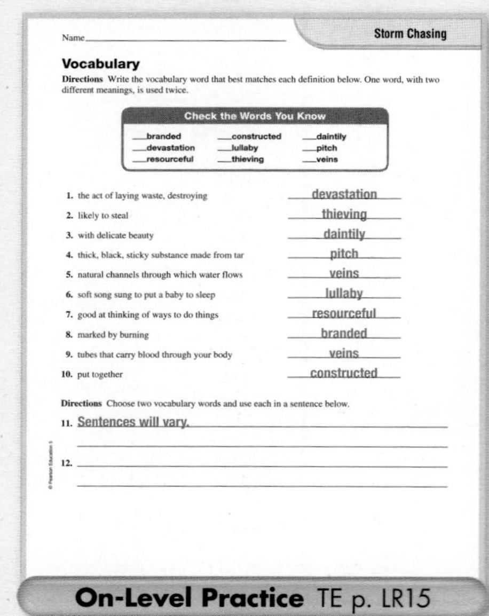
Name__________ **Storm Chasing**

Vocabulary

Directions Write the vocabulary word that best matches each definition below. One word, with two different meanings, is used twice.

Check the Words You Know		
__branded	__constructed	__daintily
__devastation	__lullaby	__pitch
__resourceful	__thieving	__veins

1. the act of laying waste, destroying — devastation
2. likely to steal — thieving
3. with delicate beauty — daintily
4. thick, black, sticky substance made from tar — pitch
5. natural channels through which water flows — veins
6. soft song sung to put a baby to sleep — lullaby
7. good at thinking of ways to do things — resourceful
8. marked by burning — branded
9. tubes that carry blood through your body — veins
10. put together — constructed

Directions Choose two vocabulary words and use each in a sentence below.

11. Sentences will vary.
12. __________

On-Level Practice TE p. LR15

Strategic Intervention

Science
Earth Science
Storm Danger!
by Kristin Cashore

Below-Level Reader

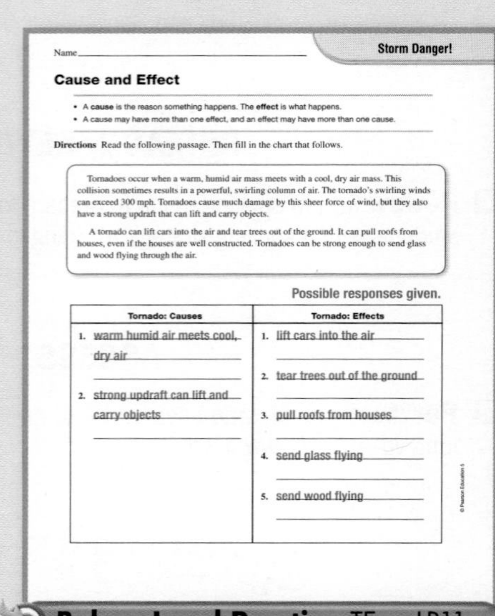
Name__________ **Storm Danger!**

Cause and Effect

- A **cause** is the reason something happens. The **effect** is what happens.
- A cause may have more than one effect, and an effect may have more than one cause.

Directions Read the following passage. Then fill in the chart that follows.

> Tornadoes occur when a warm, humid air mass meets with a cool, dry air mass. This collision sometimes results in a powerful, swirling column of air. The tornado's swirling winds can exceed 300 mph. Tornadoes cause much damage by this sheer force of wind, but they also have a strong updraft that can lift and carry objects.
>
> A tornado can lift cars into the air and tear trees out of the ground. It can pull roofs from houses, even if the houses are well constructed. Tornadoes can be strong enough to send glass and wood flying through the air.

Possible responses given.

Tornado: Causes	Tornado: Effects
1. warm humid air meets cool, dry air	1. lift cars into the air
2. strong updraft can lift and carry objects	2. tear trees out of the ground
	3. pull roofs from houses
	4. send glass flying
	5. send wood flying

Below-Level Practice TE p. LR11

Name__________ **Storm Danger!**

Vocabulary

Directions Complete each sentence with a vocabulary word from the box. One word with two different meanings is used twice.

Check the Words You Know		
__branded	__constructed	__daintily
__devastation	__lullaby	__pitch
__resourceful	__thieving	__veins

1. The resourceful mother found a new safe spot for her son to wait out the storm.
2. As the baby cried, her mother sang her a lullaby to help her sleep.
3. Blood flows through your veins.
4. The tornado caused a massive amount of devastation.
5. The men used pitch to repair the loose tiles on the roof.
6. The thieving teenagers began to hatch their plot to grab jewelry from the store.
7. The tree was branded black after it was struck by lightning.
8. The veins in the leaf helped distribute water.
9. Jenny's home is constructed of stucco, with a tile roof.
10. The ballerinas moved daintily across the stage.

Directions Write a paragraph about storms, using as many vocabulary words as you can.

Paragraphs will vary.

Below-Level Practice TE p. LR12

Advanced

Advanced Reader

Name________________ **Forecasting the Weather**

Cause and Effect

- A **cause** is the reason something happens. The **effect** is what happens.
- A cause may have more than one effect, and an effect may have more than one cause.
- Sometimes a cause is not directly stated, and you need to think about why something happened.

Directions Read the following passage. Then answer the questions that follow.

> Hurricanes are huge tropical storms. The warm humid air of the tropics rises. As the air rises, it cools, and the moisture condenses to cloud and rain drops. Heat energy is released in this condensation process. In addition, winds collide and push warm, moist air upward. This rising air reinforces the air that is already rising from the surface, so the circulation and wind speeds of the storm increase. A tropical storm with a wind speed of 74 miles per hour is classified as a hurricane. When a hurricane makes landfall it loses the tropical moisture and weakens rapidly. But it can cause massive damage before it does.
>
> High winds are a primary cause of the loss of life and home destruction that can result from hurricanes. Winds create airborne projectiles out of trees and sharp objects that hurl through the air and then bang into homes, businesses and even people. In addition, flooding caused by the coastal storm surge of the ocean and the massive rains that come with hurricanes create damage. Hurricanes have destroyed fishing piers and other businesses, too.

Possible responses given.

1. What are two major causes of hurricanes?
   Warm humid air rises and then cools. Winds collide and push warm, moist air upward.
2. Name two major causes of hurricane damage.
   high winds; flooding caused by coastal storm surge
3. What is one major effect of hurricanes?
   loss of life
4. What is another major effect of hurricanes?
   damages to residences and businesses
5. What might you do to prepare for a hurricane?
   temporarily move inland; board up doors and windows of home and businesses

Advanced Practice TE p. LR17

Name________________ **Forecasting the Weather**

Vocabulary

Directions Write the vocabulary word that best matches each definition below. One word is used twice.

Check the Words You Know		
___anemometer	___atmosphere	___barometer
___Doppler radar	___hygrometer	___meteorologists
___radiosondes	___troposphere	___weather forecasts

1. devices carried into the atmosphere by a balloon that use radio to gather and send data — radiosondes
2. method of tracking the movement of weather systems — Doppler radar
3. device for measuring air pressure — barometer
4. device for measuring the speed of wind — anemometer
5. device for measuring humidity — hygrometer
6. predictions about weather in the near future — weather forecasts
7. the layer of atmosphere where weather occurs — troposphere
8. scientists who study and predict the weather — meteorologists
9. the lowest, most dense layer of atmosphere — troposphere
10. air that surrounds Earth — atmosphere

Directions Select two vocabulary words and use each in a sentence below.

11. Sentences will vary.
12. ____________

Advanced Practice TE p. LR18

ELL

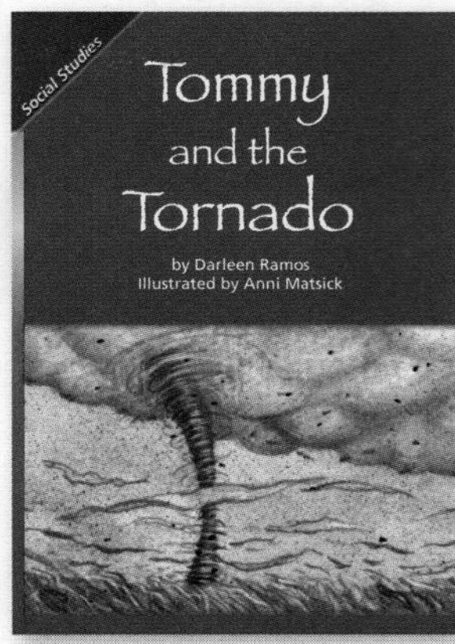

ELL Reader

ELL Poster 2

Teacher's Edition Notes

ELL notes throughout this lesson support instruction and reference additional resources at point of use.

Teaching Guide pp. 8–14, 214–215

- Multilingual summaries of the main selection
- Comprehension lesson
- Vocabulary strategies and word cards
- ELL Reader 5.1.2 lesson

ELL and Transition Handbook

Ten Important Sentences

- Key ideas from every selection in the Student Edition
- Activities to build sentence power

More Reading

Readers' Theater Anthology

- Fluency practice
- Five scripts to build fluency
- Poetry for oral interpretation

Leveled Trade Books

- Extended reading tied to the unit concept
- Lessons in the Trade Book Library Teaching Guide

Homework

- Family Times Newsletter
- ELL Multilingual Selection Summaries

Take-Home Books

- Leveled Readers

Cross-Curricular Centers

Listening

Listen to the Selections

MATERIALS
CD player, headphones, AudioText CD, student book

SINGLES

LISTEN TO LITERATURE Listen to *Thunder Rose* and "Measuring Tornadoes" as you follow or read along in your book. Listen for examples of cause and effect that occur in *Thunder Rose*.

If there is anything you don't understand, you can listen again to any section.

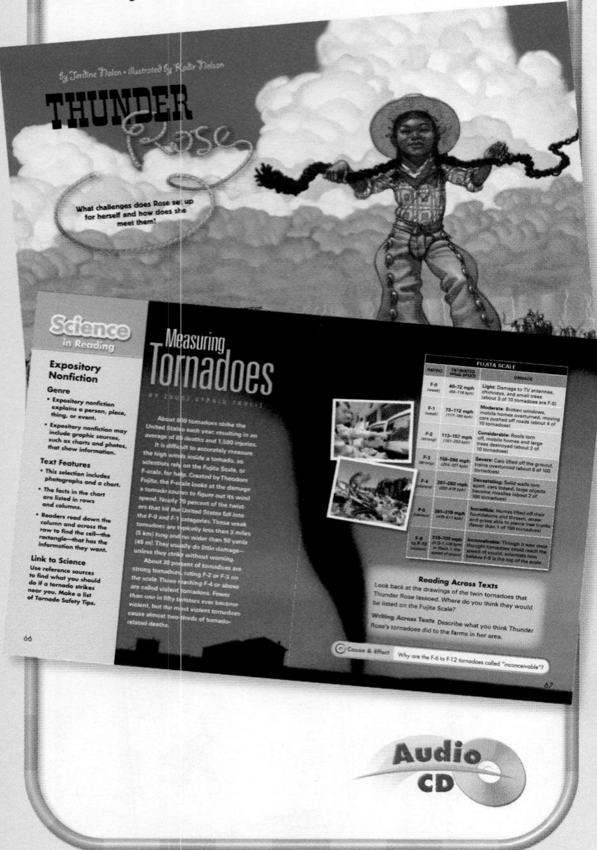

Reading/ Library

Read It Again!

MATERIALS
Collection of books for self-selected reading, reading logs, student book

SINGLES
PAIRS
GROUPS

REREAD BOOKS Select a book you have already read. Record the title of the book in your reading log. You may want to read with a partner.

Choose from the following:

- **Leveled Readers**
- **ELL Readers**
- **Stories Written by Classmates**
- **Books from the Library**
- ***Thunder Rose***

TEN IMPORTANT SENTENCES Read the Ten Important Sentences for *Thunder Rose*. Then locate the sentences in the student book.

BOOK CLUB Look at "Meet Authors" on p. 764 of the student book. Read other books by Jerdine Nolen and get together with a group to share your favorites.

Math

Make a Bar Graph

MATERIALS
Paper, pencil, copy of chart below, graph paper

SINGLES
PAIRS
GROUPS

Use the chart below to create a bar graph showing the number of tornadoes for each rating category on the Fujita scale. The chart shows how many tornadoes out of 100 receive each type of rating.

1. **Draw and label a horizontal bar graph to show the ratings for categories F-0 through F-4 and the corresponding number of tornadoes for each.**
2. **Be sure to line up the end of each bar that you draw with the correct number on the graph's horizontal axis.**

EARLY FINISHERS Write a paragraph summarizing the information that appears in the chart and on the bar graph.

Fujita Scale	
Rating	Number of Tornadoes (out of 100)
F-0	30
F-1	40
F-2	20
F-3	6
F-4	2

Writing/Vocabulary

Find the Right Words

MATERIALS
Writing and art materials

SINGLES

Find some of the words in *Thunder Rose* that help make it a tall tale.

1. **Choose words and phrases that describe both Thunder Rose and her adventures.**
2. **Organize your words and phrases into a T-chart with the headings "Thunder Rose" and "Adventures."**

EARLY FINISHERS Draw an illustration of one of the best examples of exaggeration from the story.

Thunder Rose	Adventures
booming thunder	paper-bag brown
hungry as a bear	

Science

Research Tornadoes

MATERIALS
Books on tornadoes, Internet access, index cards, writing and art materials

SINGLES
PAIRS

Work alone or with a partner to gather information on what to do to prepare for a tornado if you are indoors.

1. **List your findings on index cards.**
2. **Share your findings with the rest of the class and compile a single class list of steps for tornado safety using the information gathered.**

EARLY FINISHERS Design a poster that shows steps to follow if you are caught outside during a tornado.

Class List
1.
2.
3.
4.
5.

What to Do in Case of a Tornado
1. Head for the lowest part of the building
2.
3.

Technology

Use a Search Engine

MATERIALS
Internet access, writing materials

SINGLES

Choose a student-friendly search engine to help you learn more about Tornado Alley.

1. **Follow classroom Internet rules. Find an Internet resource that tells you where Tornado Alley is located and about the characteristics of the area.**
2. **Record your findings.**

EARLY FINISHERS Locate information on other regions of the world where tornadoes occur.

ALL CENTERS

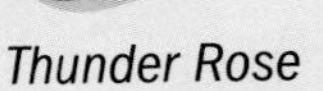

DAY 1

Build Concepts

FLUENCY

MODEL TONE OF VOICE As you read "Night of the Twisters," vary your voice to reflect what is happening in the story. For example, you can lower your voice as you read the first paragraph describing the quiet before the storm.

LISTENING COMPREHENSION

After reading "Night of the Twisters," use the following questions to assess listening comprehension.

1. **What caused the boys to seek shelter in the basement?** *(They heard warnings on the television; basements are the safest places to be during tornadoes.)* ***Cause and Effect***
2. **Describe the damage caused by the tornado.** *(Possible responses: Pieces of furniture smashed into each other; chunks of the ceiling started falling down; the house was ripped apart)* ***Cause and Effect***

BUILD CONCEPT VOCABULARY

Start a web to build concepts and vocabulary related to this week's lesson and the unit theme.

- Draw the Challenges in Nature Concept Web.
- Read the sentence with the word *meteorologist* again. Ask students to pronounce *meteorologist* and discuss its meaning.
- Place *severe* in an oval attached to *Descriptions.* Explain that *severe* is related to this concept. Read the sentences in which *tornado, terror,* and *roaring* appear. Have students pronounce the words, place them on the web, and provide reasons.
- Brainstorm additional words and categories for the web. Keep the web on display and add words throughout the week.

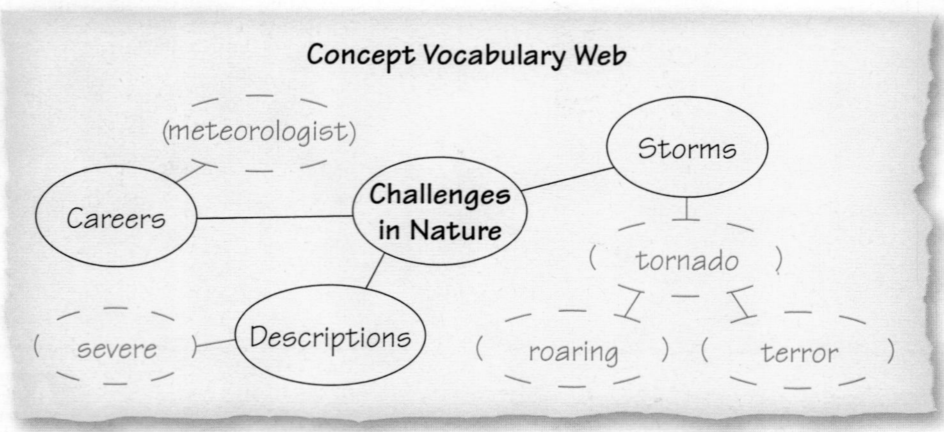

OBJECTIVES

- Build vocabulary by finding words related to the lesson concept.
- Listen for causes and effects.

Concept Vocabulary

meteorologist a scientist who studies the atmosphere and weather

roaring making a loud, deep sound or noise

severe serious or harsh

terror great fear

tornado an extremely violent and destructive funnel-shaped windstorm

Monitor Progress

Check Vocabulary

If...	**then...**
students are unable to place words on the web,	review the lesson concept. Put the words on the web and give more words for practice, such as *shattered* and *howling.*

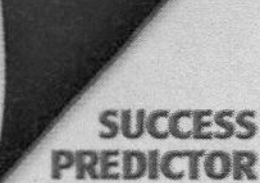

DAY 1 Grouping Options

Reading

Whole Group
Introduce and discuss the Question of the Week. Then use pp. 42l–42b.

Group Time
Differentiated Instruction

Read this week's Leveled Readers. See pp. 42h–42i for the small group lesson plan.

Whole Group
Use p. 67a.

Language Arts
Use pp. 67e–67k.

Night of the Twisters

by Ivy Ruckman

BEFORE READING

Tornadoes have been spotted near Dan's hometown! His mother ecides to check on an elderly neighbor, Mrs. Smiley, leaving Dan and his riend Arthur to protect Dan's baby brother, Ryan. They seek shelter in ne basement's bathroom.

We heard it next. The lull. The deadliest quiet ever, one that nakes you think you might explode. The heat in the room built until couldn't get my breath.

Then I began to hear noises. A chair scraping across the kitchen oor upstairs.

"Your mom's back!" Arthur said, pushing at my leg.

I knew it wasn't my mother moving the chair.

The noises got worse. It seemed as if every piece of furniture was noving around up there...big, heavy things, smashing into each other.

A window popped.

Crash! Another.

Glass, shattered everywhere.

Ten seconds more and that howling, shrieking **tornado** was upon us.

"The blanket!" I screamed at Arthur's ear.

We covered ourselves, hands shaking wildly. I wasn't worrying bout my mom then or my dad or Mrs. Smiley. Just us. Ryan and rthur and me, huddled together there on the shower floor.

The **roaring** had started somewhere to the east, then came earing down on us like a hundred freight trains. Only that twister idn't move on. It stationed itself right overhead, making the loudest oise I'd ever heard, whining worse than any jet. There was a remendous crack, and I felt the wall shudder behind us. I new then our house was being ripped apart. Suddenly hunks of ceiling were falling on our heads. We'll be buried! vas all I could think.

There was nothing but **terror** as the roar of that tornado went on nd on. I thought the world was coming to an end. And so would we, ny minute.

Then I felt Ryan's fat fingers close around one of mine. He pulled ny hand to his mouth and started sucking on my finger. It made ne cry. The tears ran down my cheeks and onto his head. With the vhole world blowing to pieces around us, Ryan took my hand and nade me feel better.

"A tornado's forward speed is generally thirty to fifty miles an our," a **meteorologist** had told us.

Our tornado's forward speed was zero. Five minutes or ten, ve couldn't tell, but it seemed like an hour. Roaring and humming nd shrieking, that twister was right on top of us. I'll never be that cared again as long as I live. Neither will Arthur.

Activate Prior Knowledge

Before students listen to the Read Aloud, ask them what they know about the challenges of test taking.

Set Purpose

Read aloud the title and have students predict what the selection will be about.

Read the introduction aloud. Have students listen to how the threat of a dangerous storm causes two friends to fear for their lives.

Creative Response

Have students work in small groups to improvise on-the-spot interviews with the boys after the tornado. Interviews should focus on the boys' description of the storm and the feelings they experienced while in the basement. ***Drama***

Access Content Before reading, share this summary: Dan, Arthur, and Dan's baby brother, Ryan, are home alone when a tornado hits the house. They seek shelter in the basement. They hear the tornado as it destroys the house above them.

Homework Send home this week's Family Times newsletter.

Vocabulary

SUCCESS PREDICTOR

SKILLS ↔ STRATEGIES IN CONTEXT

Cause and Effect Monitor/Fix Up

OBJECTIVES

- Identify causes and effects.
- Monitor comprehension to understand causes and effects.

Skills Trace

Cause and Effect

Introduce/Teach	**TE: 5.1 42–43, 112–113; 5.5 582–583**
Practice	Practice Book: 6, 13, 17, 18, 43, 47, 48, 106, 233, 237, 238
Reteach/Review	TE: 5.1 27, 67b, 133b; 5.3 267, DI·53, DI·56, TR16; 5.5 603b, DI·55
Test	Selection Test: 5–8, 17–20, 93–96; Benchmark Test: Unit 1

INTRODUCE

Write the heading *Cause* and add: *The baseball flew off Maria's bat toward her house.* Ask what might be an effect in a story with this cause. *(Possible response: The baseball breaks a window.)*

Have students read the information on p. 42. Explain the following:

- In a cause-effect relationship, one thing makes another happen.
- Asking questions and rereading can help you identify causes and effects and better understand a selection.

Use Skill Transparency 2 to teach cause and effect and monitor and fix up.

Comprehension

Skill
Cause and Effect

Strategy
Monitor and Fix Up

Cause and Effect

- An effect is what happened as the result of a cause. A cause is what made something happen.
- Words such as *why, because,* and *as a resu*[lt] are clues to cause-and-effect relationships.
- If there are no clue words, ask yourself, "Why did this event happen? What happened as a result of this event?"
- An effect may become the cause of another effect.

Cause → Effect

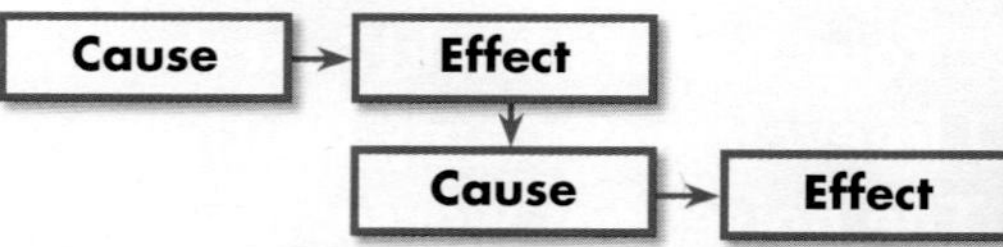

Strategy: Monitor and Fix Up

Good readers make sure they understand wha[t] they are reading. If you don't understand how causes result in certain effects, pause. Ask your self, "What don't I understand?" You might decide to review what you've read and *read on* to find out what happens.

Write to Read

1. Read "The Real Thunder and Lightning." Make a graphic organizer like the one above to show the cause of lightning that flashes inside a cloud.
2. Use your graphic organizer to write a paragraph that explains the cause of thunder. If you have difficulty, reread the last paragraph to see if that helps.

42

Strategic Intervention

Cause and Effect Read the first sentence of paragraph 2 on p. 43, and ask: *Why does lightning happen? What is the cause? (electrical charges).* Then read the next two sentences and ask: *Why does lightning flash inside a cloud? What is the cause? (opposite charges)* Repeat this procedure with the rest of the paragraph.

Access Content

Beginning/Intermediate For a Picture It! lesson on cause and effect, see the ELL Teaching Guide, pp. 8–9.

Advanced Before students read "The Real Thunder and Lightning," explain that lightning causes thunder. Help students understand that lightning is the cause and thunder is the effect.

The Real

THUNDER and Lightning

Some tall tales and myths give fanciful explanations things that happen in nature, such as thunder and ıtning. These stories are fun to read, but the real ›lanations can also be interesting.

The real cause of lightning involves electrical ırges. Inside a storm cloud, a strong positive electrical ırge may form near the top of the cloud, and a strong ›ative charge near the bottom. When these opposite ırges flow toward each other, lightning flashes inside : cloud. When opposite charges flow from one cloud another, lightning flashes between the clouds. When ›ative charges at the bottom of a cloud move down vard positive charges on Earth, lightning flashes from : cloud to the ground. Watch out!

Thunder happens only when there ightning because lightning ıses it. Thunder ults from the rapid ıting of the air along a ntning flash. The heated air pands. As a result, it creates ound wave. Then the claps d rumbles of thunder : heard.

1 Skill Look at the clue word *cause* here. It tells you that you will read about the cause of lightning. Get ready to start a graphic organizer.

2 Strategy Do you feel you understand what causes lightning inside a cloud? If not, reread the first part of the second paragraph.

3 Skill What causes lightning that flashes from a cloud to the ground? Make a graphic organizer, such as a drawing, if you need help.

4 Strategy Do you feel you understand what causes lightning and what causes thunder? If not, which parts of the article should you reread?

43

Available as **Skill Transparency** 2

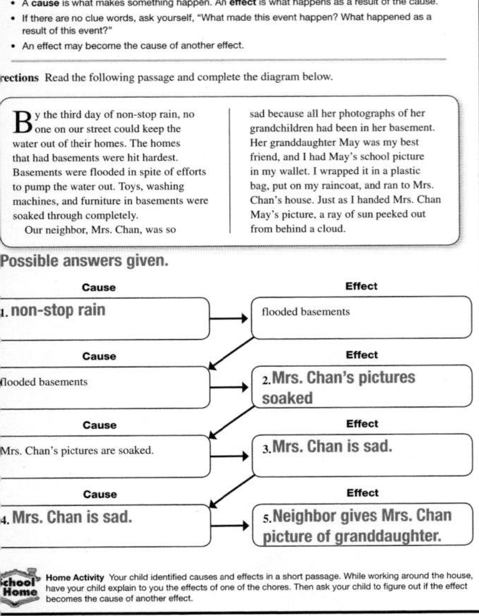

ause and Effect

- A **cause** is what makes something happen. An **effect** is what happens as a result of the cause.
- If there are no clue words, ask yourself, "What made this event happen? What happened as a result of this event?"
- An effect may become the cause of another effect.

rections Read the following passage and complete the diagram below.

By the third day of non-stop rain, no one on our street could keep the water out of their homes. The homes that had basements were hit hardest. Basements were flooded in spite of efforts to pump the water out. Toys, washing machines, and furniture in basements were soaked through completely.

Our neighbor, Mrs. Chan, was so sad because all her photographs of her grandchildren had been in her basement. Her granddaughter May was my best friend, and I had May's school picture in my wallet. I wrapped it in a plastic bag, put on my raincoat, and ran to Mrs. Chan's house. Just as I handed Mrs. Chan May's picture, a ray of sun peeked out from behind a cloud.

Possible answers given.

Cause	Effect
1. non-stop rain	flooded basements
flooded basements	2. Mrs. Chan's pictures soaked
Mrs. Chan's pictures are soaked.	3. Mrs. Chan is sad.
4. Mrs. Chan is sad.	5. Neighbor gives Mrs. Chan picture of granddaughter.

School+Home **Home Activity** Your child identified causes and effects in a short passage. While working around the house, have your child explain to you the effects of one of the chores. Then ask your child to figure out if the effect becomes the cause of another effect.

Practice Book p. 13

BEFORE READING

TEACH

1 SKILL Use paragraph 2 to model how to identify the cause of lightning.

Think Aloud **MODEL** The word *cause* in the first sentence of paragraph 2 signals a cause-effect relationship. The sentence tells me that electrical charges cause lightning. When opposite charges flow toward each other, the effect is lightning. I can record this information in a graphic organizer.

2 STRATEGY Model how to monitor understanding of causes and effects.

Think Aloud **MODEL** I'm not sure I understand what causes lightning inside a cloud. I think I'd better reread the second and third sentences in paragraph 2 again.

PRACTICE AND ASSESS

3 SKILL Negative charges at the bottom of a cloud moving down toward positive charges on Earth cause lightning that flashes from a cloud to the ground.

4 STRATEGY Students should reread the second paragraph if they are confused about the causes of lightning and the last paragraph if they are confused about the causes of thunder.

WRITE Have students complete steps 1 and 2 of the Write to Read activity. You might consider using this as a whole-class activity.

Monitor Progress	
Cause and Effect	
If... students are unable to complete **Write to Read** on p. 42,	**then...** use Practice Book p. 13 to provide additional practice.

Build Background

ACTIVATE PRIOR KNOWLEDGE

BEGIN A WEB DIAGRAM about tall tales.

- Ask students to think about tall tales they have read or heard of, such as *Paul Bunyan* or *Johnny Appleseed.* Remind them that tall tales are humorous stories about exaggerated, or impossible, events.
- Complete a web diagram with students. Fill in the center oval with *Tall Tales.* Ask students to brainstorm characteristics of tall tales *(humorous, exaggerated, superhuman qualities)* and write them in the small ovals. Add more ovals if necessary.
- After they read, invite them to think about other characteristics of the genre and add them to their diagrams.

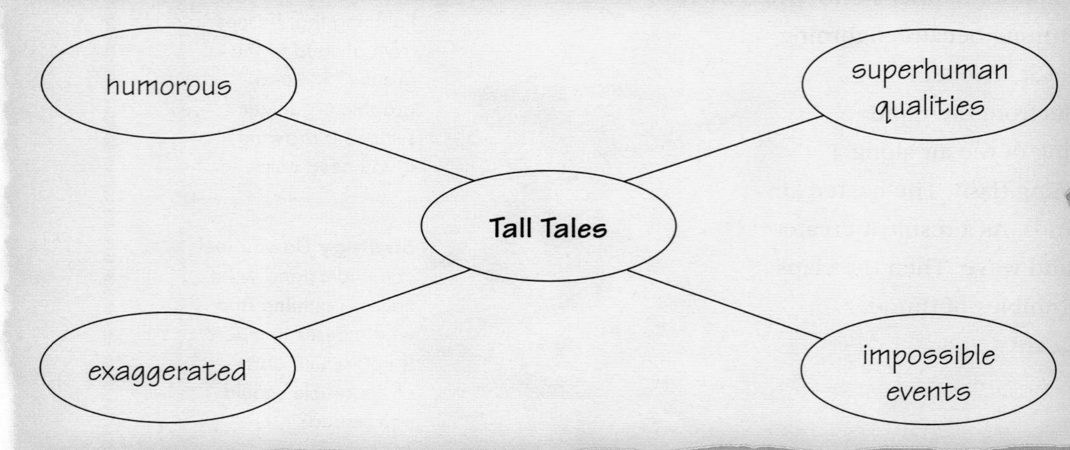

▲ **Graphic Organizer** 15

BACKGROUND BUILDING AUDIO This week's audio explores tall tales and where they originated. After students listen, discuss what they found out and what surprised them most about the origins of tall tales.

Background Building Audio

Students can find out more about storms by searching the Internet. Have them use a student-friendly search engine and the keyword *storms.* Be sure to follow classroom guidelines for Internet use.

ELL

Build Background Use ELL Poster 2 to build background and vocabulary for the lesson concept of the power of nature.

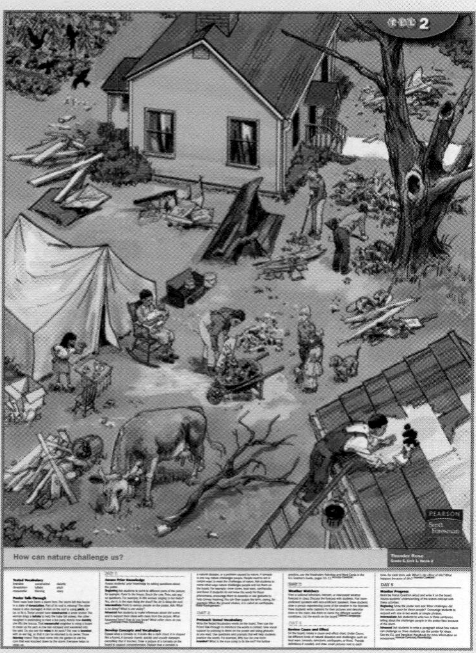

▲ **ELL Poster** 2

Introduce Vocabulary

WORD RATING CHART

Create word rating charts using the categories *Know*, *Have Seen*, and *Don't Know*.

Word	Know	Have Seen	Don't Know
branded			
constructed			
daintily			
devastation			
lullaby			
pitch			
resourceful			
thieving			
veins			

▲ **Graphic Organizer** 5

Read each word to students and have them place it in one of the three columns: *Know* (know and can use); *Have Seen* (have seen or heard the word; don't know meaning); *Don't Know* (don't know the word). ***Activate Prior Knowledge***

Have students share where they may have seen some of these words. Point out that some of this week's words may be unfamiliar to them and one is a homonym *(pitch)*. Students may learn other words and new definitions for words they recognize. ***Homonyms • Unfamiliar Words***

Check charts with students at the end of the week and have them make changes to their ratings.

Use the Multisyllabic Word Routine on p. DI • 1 to help students read multisyllabic words.

Lesson Vocabulary

WORDS TO KNOW

T branded marked by burning the skin with a hot iron

T constructed put together; fitted together; built

T daintily with delicate beauty; freshly and prettily

T devastation the act of laying waste; destruction

T lullaby song for singing to a child; soft song

T pitch a thick, black, sticky substance made from tar or turpentine

T resourceful good at thinking of ways to do things; quick witted

T thieving stealing

T veins membranous tubes forming part of the system of vessels that carry blood to the heart

MORE WORDS TO KNOW

cantankerous ready to make trouble; ill-natured

irascible easily made angry

varmint an objectionable animal or person *(DIALECT)*

T = Tested Word

Vocabulary

Directions Choose the word from the box that best matches each definition. Write the word on the line.

veins 1. blood vessels that carry blood to the heart from all parts of the body

lullaby 2. song for singing to a child

thieving 3. stealing

pitch 4. a thick, black, sticky substance made from tar or turpentine

constructed 5. fitted together; built

Check the Words You Know

___branded
___constructed
___daintily
___devastation
___lullaby
___pitch
___resourceful
___thieving
___veins

Directions Choose the word from the box that best completes the sentences below. Write the word on the line shown to the left.

branded 6. The rancher ________ his cattle with the symbol from his ranch so nobody else could claim them.

pitch 7. The cracks in the roof were sealed with ________ .

daintily 8. Grandma and Grandpa danced ________ in time with the music's gentle beat.

resourceful 9. When no one else could think of how to solve the school's litter problem, Marisa impressed the principal with her________ idea.

devastation 10. The tornado caused a lot of ________ when it whipped through town and ripped several homes from their foundations.

Write a Friendly Letter

On a separate sheet of paper, write a friendly letter to someone living out of town about an event that happened where you live. Use as many vocabulary words as you can.

Letter should include words from the vocabulary list and details about an event that happened.

School + Home **Home Activity** Your child identified and used vocabulary words from *Thunder Rose*. Work with your child to learn the words and their definitions. Have your child create colorful flash cards to do so.

▲ **Practice Book** p. 14

DAY 2

Vocabulary Strategy

OBJECTIVE

Use context clues to determine the meanings of homonyms.

INTRODUCE

Discuss the strategy for context clues to understand homonyms using the steps on p. 44.

TEACH

- Have students read "The Tale of Carrie the Calf," paying attention to how vocabulary is used.
- Model using context clues to determine the meaning of *pitch*.

Think Aloud **MODEL** The homonym *pitch* can mean "to throw or fling" or "black, sticky substance made from tar." The author uses the word *pitch* to describe Carrie's eyes. Therefore in this sentence, *pitch* must mean "black, sticky substance made from tar."

Words to Know

- pitch
- veins
- daintily
- thieving
- devastation
- branded
- constructed
- resourceful
- lullaby

Remember

Try the strategy. Then, if you need more help, use your glossary or dictionary.

Vocabulary Strategy for Homonyms

Context Clues When you are reading, you may come across a familiar word used in an unfamiliar way. The word may be a homonym. Homonyms are spelled the same, but they have different meanings. For example, *feet* can be units of measurement or the end parts of the legs. You can use the context—the words and sentences around the word—to figure out which meaning is being used.

1. Reread the sentence in which the homonym appears.
2. Look for clues to the homonym's meaning.
3. If you need more help, read the sentences around the sentence with the homonym. Look for clues or additional information that suggests the homonym's meaning.
4. Try the meaning in the sentence. Does it make sense?

As you read "The Tale of Carrie the Calf," look for homonyms. Use the context to determine the meanings of the homonyms.

44

DAY 2 Grouping Options

Reading

Whole Group Discuss the Question of the Day. Then use pp. 44–47.

Group Time Differentiated Instruction

 *Thunder Rose.* See pp. 42h–42i for the small group lesson plan.

Whole Group Use p. 67a.

Language Arts

Use pp. 67e–67k.

Strategic Intervention

Context Clues Have students work in pairs to identify homonyms they find in "The Tale of Carrie the Calf." Then, have them use story clues to figure out the best meaning of each homonym.

ELL

Access Content Use ELL Poster 2 to preteach vocabulary. Choose from the following to meet language proficiency levels.

Beginning Point out clues on p. 45 that show that pitch is a dark, sticky substance made from tar and used to waterproof roofs.

Intermediate Point out that the words *veins* and *devastation* have Spanish cognates: *venas* and *devastación*.

Advanced Teach the lesson on pp. 44–45. Have students find home-language terms for some of the new vocabulary.

Resources for home-language words may include parents, bilingual staff members, bilingual dictionaries, or online translation sources.

The Tale of Carrie the Calf

From the moment she was born, we knew Carrie the calf was different. Her eyes were black as pitch, and she was strong as a bull. Instead of blood, she seemed to have a magic potion in her veins. Overnight, she grew fifty feet tall. Morning found her daintily eating the tops of trees.

It was hard finding enough for her to eat! We would give her a hundred bales of hay for breakfast, but by lunch she would be over at the next ranch, happily eating its trees and anything else in sight. This thieving did not make her too popular. It also caused considerable devastation around the country.

Then the time came to brand the calves! How could a hundred-and-fifty-foot-tall calf be branded? We quickly constructed a two-hundred-foot-tall fence to hold her in. She just smiled and hopped over it, and then ambled off to find another forest to eat. To catch Carrie, we were going to have to be more resourceful.

Next, we made a set of speakers big as a house. We broadcast a soothing lullaby that could be heard over three states. Soon Carrie was sleeping without a care.

Words to Write

Look at the pictures in the story. Choose one to write about. Use as many words in the Words to Know list as you can.

45

PRACTICE AND ASSESS

- Encourage students to use context clues to determine the meanings of other lesson vocabulary words.
- Explain that context clues do not always work for determining the meanings of homonyms. Suggest that sometimes students should use a dictionary to figure out which meaning makes the most sense in the text.
- If you began a Word Rating Chart (p. 44b), have students reassess their ratings.
- Have students complete Practice Book p. 15.

WRITE Writing should include vocabulary words that describe and explain the actions, setting, and/or character(s) depicted in the illustration.

Monitor Progress

Context Clues

If... students need more practice with the lesson vocabulary,	**then...** use Tested Vocabulary Cards.

Vocabulary • Context Clues

- **Homonyms** are words that are spelled the same but have different meanings.
- Look for **context clues**—words and sentences around a word—to figure out which meaning is being used in the sentence.

Directions Read the following passage about a hurricane. Then answer the questions below. Look for homonyms as you read.

As Pedro scaled the ladder to the roof, he felt the blood in his veins pumping through his body. He was the first person to get a look at the destruction the hurricane had created. He looked at the roof and reminded himself to bring up a bucket of pitch next time to repair the new cracks. Looking out over the countryside, he saw that many buildings would need to be constructed again. He started gathering broken branches to pitch down to the ground below. Then he paused and took a deep breath, thinking about what this disaster had done to his community. He knew that none of his neighbors would have to pitch tents and live in their yards while repairs were made to their homes. The people of his town would help each other find shelter, and everyone would be fine.

1. *Vein* can mean "a blood vessel" or "a crack in a rock filled with a mineral deposit." How is it used in the passage? How can you tell?
   a blood vessel; The sentence talks about blood.
2. What does *pitch* mean in the third sentence of this passage? What clues help you understand the meaning used in this sentence?
   It means a dark, sticky substance; bucket, repair, cracks
3. What does *pitch* mean in the fifth sentence of this passage? What clues help you understand the meaning used in this sentence?
   It means to throw; down to the ground below
4. To *scale* something can mean "to climb up something" or "to measure something." How is it used in this passage? How can you tell?
   to climb up; Pedro goes to the roof using a ladder.
5. What does *pitch* mean in the second-to-last sentence of this passage? What clues help you understand the meaning used in this sentence?
   To put up; tents

Home Activity Your child read a short passage and used context clues to understand homonyms, words that are spelled the same but have different meanings. With your child, make a list of homonyms. Challenge your child to make up a sentence using each meaning.

▲ **Practice Book** p. 15

BEFORE READING

Prereading Strategies

OBJECTIVES

- Identify causes and effects to improve comprehension.
- Monitor comprehension to understand cause-and-effect relationships.

GENRE STUDY

Tall Tale

Thunder Rose is a tall tale. Explain that a tall tale is a humorous story that tells about exaggerated or impossible events.

PREVIEW AND PREDICT

Have students preview the story title and illustrations and discuss the topics or ideas they think it will cover. Have students use lesson vocabulary as they talk about what they expect to learn.

Strategy Response Log

Activate Prior Knowledge Have students record what they know about tall tales in their strategy response logs. Students will monitor their comprehension in the Strategy Response Log activity on p. 55.

by Jerdine Nolen • illustrated by Kadir Nelson
THUNDER Rose
What challenges does Rose set up for herself and how does she meet them?
46

Genre

Tall tales are amusing stories told with great exaggeration and bigger-than-life characters. As you read, try to imagine what amazing thing Rose will do next.

ELL

Build Background Use pictures and gestures to preview ranching vocabulary, such as *branding iron, longhorn steer, stampeding* (p. 53), *head of cattle, herd* (p. 55), *lassoed* (p. 56), and *roundup* (p. 61).

Consider having students read the story summary in English or in students' home languages. See the Multilingual Summaries in the ELL Teaching Guide, pp. 12–14.

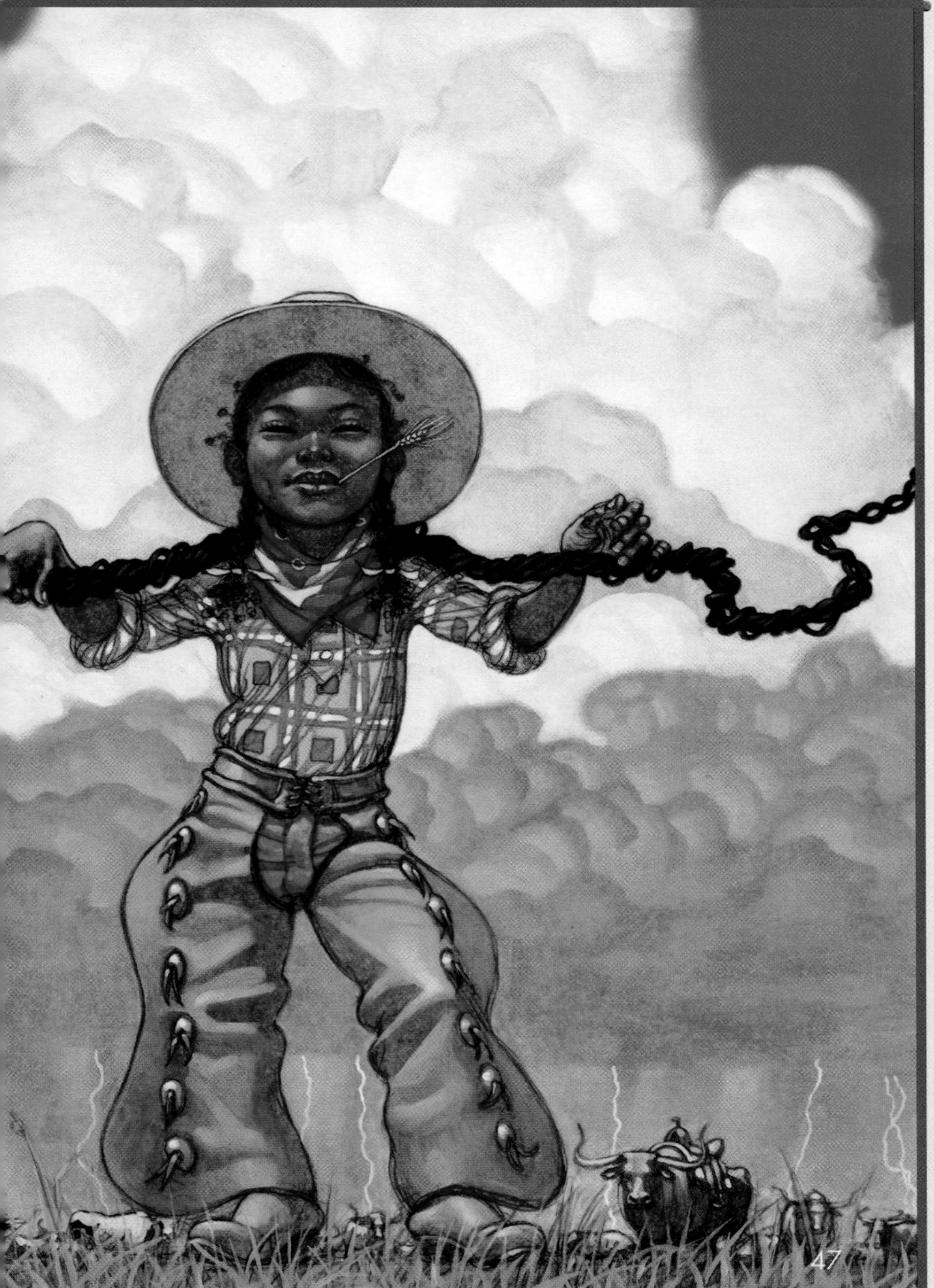

SET PURPOSE

After reviewing the illustrations and considering their preview discussion, ask students to make predictions about the main character and the kinds of experiences she might have.

Remind students to look for causes and effects as they read.

STRATEGY RECALL

Students have now used these before-reading strategies:

- preview the selection to be aware of its genre, features, and possible content;
- activate prior knowledge about that content and what to expect of that genre;
- make predictions;
- set a purpose for reading.

Remind students that, as they read, they should monitor their own comprehension. If they realize something does not make sense, they can regain their comprehension by using fix-up strategies they have learned, such as:

- use phonics and word structure to decode new words;
- use context clues or a dictionary to figure out meanings of new words;
- adjust their reading rate—slow down for difficult text, speed up for easy or familiar text, or skim and scan just for specific information;
- reread parts of the text;
- read on (continue to read for clarification);
- use text features such as headings, subheadings, charts, illustrations, and so on as visual aids to comprehension;
- make a graphic organizer or a semantic organizer to aid comprehension;
- use reference sources, such as an encyclopedia, dictionary, thesaurus, or synonym finder;
- use another person, such as a teacher, a peer, a librarian, or an outside expert, as a resource.

After reading, students will use these strategies:

- summarize or retell the text;
- answer questions they or others pose;
- reflect to make new information become part of their prior knowledge.

AudioText

DURING READING

Guiding Comprehension

1 Character • Inferential

Reread p. 48, paragraph 2. What do you learn about Rose?

Possible response: She is not an ordinary baby. She has superhuman strength and power.

Monitor Progress

REVIEW Character and Plot

If... students are unable to describe Rose's character,	**then...** use the skill and strategy instruction on p. 49.

2 Author's Craft • Critical

Question the Author **Why does the author use slang, or informal language, in the dialogue?**

Possible response: Common, informal language is often used in tall tales. The informal language makes the character sound realistic. The dialect also suggests a rural setting.

If students have access to the Internet, they can search for information by using a student-friendly search engine and the keywords *tall tales*. Be sure to follow classroom guidelines for Internet use.

Rose was the first child born free and easy to Jackson and Millicent MacGruder. I recall most vividly the night she came into this world. Hailing rain, flashing lightning, and booming thunder pounded the door, inviting themselves in for the blessed event.

Taking in her first breath of life, the infant did not cry out. Rather, she sat up and looked around. She took ahold of that
1 lightning, rolled it into a ball, and set it above her shoulder, while the thunder echoed out over the other. They say this just accentuated the fact that the child had the power of thunder and lightning coursing through her veins.

"She's going to grow up to be good and strong, all right," Doc Hollerday said.

The child turned to the good doctor with a thoughtful glance and replied, "I reckon I will want to do more than that. Thank you very kindly!"

2 Shifting her gaze to the two loving lights shining on her, which were her ma and pa, she remarked, "Much obliged to you both for this chance to make my way in the world!" Then she announced to no one in particular, "I am right partial to the name Rose."

So much in love with this gift of their lives, her ma and pa hovered over her in watchful splendor. Overcome with that love, they lifted their voices in song, an old song and a melody so sweet and true—a lullaby passed down from the ages, echoing since the beginning of time.

48

Access Content Read the phrase "the child had the power of thunder and lightning coursing through her veins." Explain that *coursing* means "moving quickly."

SKILLS ↔ STRATEGIES IN CONTEXT

Character and Plot REVIEW

TEACH

- Characters are the people or animals in stories and the plot is the series of events that show the characters in action.
- Analyzing a character's words and actions helps the reader better understand the plot.
- Model analyzing a character's actions on p. 48, paragraph 2.

MODEL It says that Rose sat up, took hold of the lightning, rolled it into a ball, and set it above her shoulder. This tells me Rose is not an ordinary baby. She has extraordinary abilities and strength.

PRACTICE AND ASSESS

- Have students reread p. 48. Ask them to identify another clue that shows Rose is no ordinary baby. *(She speaks to the doctor and her parents.)*

TIME FOR Science

Lightning

ghtning is formed inside thunderclouds. ıunderclouds are created when hot, moist air rises nd condenses. The hot air combines with cold air to eate water or ice particles. Inside the thundercloud, the parti- es bump into each other, eventually creating electric charges. Usually ıe top part of the thundercloud becomes positively charged and the ottom part becomes negatively charged. The positive and negative ıarges are pulled toward each other, and electricity is released as ghtning. Lightning contains millions of volts of electricity and the sur- ounding air heats up to about 54,000°F, or about five times the tem- erature of the sun's surface. This increase in air temperature around ıe lightning causes shock waves, which we hear as thunder.

Guiding Comprehension

3 **Cause and Effect • Inferential**

Why did Rose's parents call her Thunder Rose?

Thunder and lightning kept watch over her the first night and her snoring was as loud as the thunderstorm outside.

Monitor Progress

Cause and Effect

If... students have difficulty identifying why Rose is called Thunder Rose,	**then...** use the skill and strategy instruction on p. 51.

4 **Genre • Inferential**

Find an example of exaggeration on p. 51.

Possible responses: Rose woke up hungry as a bear. Rose could lift a whole cow over her head and almost drink it dry.

50

ELL

Extend Language Reread aloud the phrase "as hungry as a bear in spring." Explain that when the word *as* is used to compare two unlike things, the comparison is called a simile. Help students understand that bears are very hungry in spring because they spend the whole winter hibernating. Ask students to find another simile on p. 51 and explain what it means ("as pretty as a picture" means beautiful, like a painting or photograph).

"There is a music ringing so sweetly in my ears," the newborn exclaimed. "It's giving me a fortunate feeling rumbling deep in the pit of me. I'll register it here at the bull's-eye set in the center of my heart, and see what I can do with it one day!"

Rose snored up plenty that first night breathing on her own, rattling the rafters on the roof right along with the booming thunder. There was nothing quiet about her slumber. She seemed determined to be just as forceful as that storm. With the thunder and lightning keeping watch over her the rest of the night, her ma and pa just took to calling her 3 Thunder Rose.

The next morning, when the sun was high yellow in that billowy blue sky, Rose woke up hungry as a bear in spring, 4 but not the least bit ornery. Minding her manners, she politely thanked her ma for the milk, but it was not enough to quench her hungry thirst. Rose preferred, instead to drink her milk straight from the cow.

Her ma was right grateful to have such a resourceful child. No other newborn had the utter strength to lift a whole cow clear over her head and almost drink it dry. In a moment's time, Rose did, and quite daintily so. She was as pretty as a picture, had the sweetest disposition, but don't let yourself be misled, that child was full of lightning *and* thunder.

Out on that paper-bag brown, dusty dry, wide-open space, Rose often was found humming a sweet little tune as she did her chores. And true to her word, Rose did *more* than grow good and strong.

The two-year-old became quite curious about the pile of scrap iron lying next to the barn. Rose took a good-sized

51

SKILLS ↔ STRATEGIES IN CONTEXT

Cause and Effect

TEACH

- Remind students that a cause is why something happened and an effect is what happened.
- Sometimes clue words such as *because* and *since* signal a cause and effect. Sometimes there are no clue words and the reader has to detect them.
- Model finding the cause and effect on p. 51, paragraph 2.

MODEL In paragraph 2 it says Rose snored right along with the booming thunder. Then it says, "with the thunder and lightning keeping watch over her the rest of the night, her ma and pa just took to calling her Thunder Rose." This tells me that her parents called her Thunder Rose because of her loud snoring during the thunderstorm. So the cause was the snoring and the storm. The effect was her nickname.

PRACTICE AND ASSESS

Have students reread paragraph 3. Ask them to identify the effect of Rose's "hungry thirst." *(Choice b)*

a) She was hungry as a bear.

b) She preferred to drink her milk straight from the cow rather than from a glass.

c) She was ornery.

EXTEND SKILLS

Foreshadowing

Foreshadowing is the technique used in literature and drama that gives the reader, listener, or viewer hints of what is to come. Have students reread the third sentence in the first paragraph. Tell them to keep this idea in mind as they read the second half of the selection. Tomorrow, students will make connections in the last sentence of selection.

Guiding Comprehension

5 **Vocabulary • Context Clues**

Use context clues to determine the meaning of *punctuate* on p. 52, line 2.

Clues: She constructed a thunderbolt called Cole that was always by her side. Meaning: to emphasize or draw attention to something.

Monitor Progress

Context Clues

If... students have difficulty using context clues to determine the meaning of *punctuate*,	**then...** use vocabulary strategy instruction on p. 53.

6 **Character • Inferential**

Reread paragraph 1 on p. 52 and paragraph 1 on p. 53. Based on these actions, how would you describe Rose?

Possible responses: She is strong, helpful, giving, thoughtful, smart.

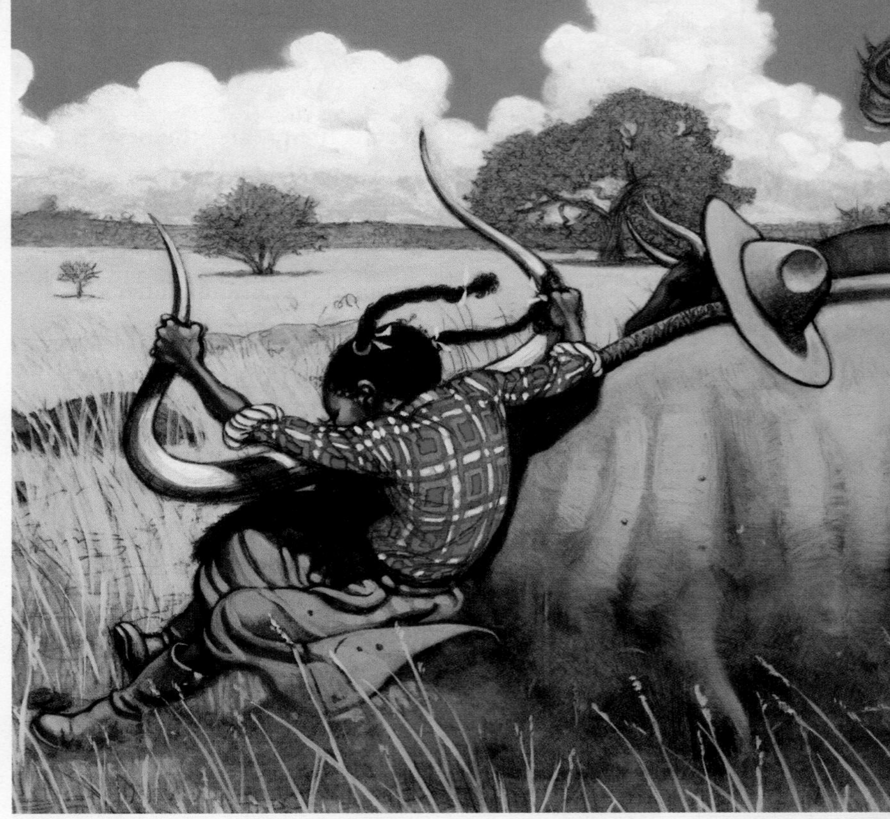

piece, stretched it here, bent and twisted it there. She constructed
5 a thunderbolt as black as pitch to punctuate her name. She called it Cole. Wherever she went, Cole was always by her side. Noticing how skilled Rose was with the metal, her pa made sure there was an extra supply of it always around.

At the age of five, Rose did a commendable job of staking the fence without a bit of help. During her eighth and ninth years, Rose
6 assembled some iron beams together with the wood blocks she used to play with and constructed a building tall enough to scrape the sky, always humming as she worked.

52

Access Content Tell students that *commendable* means worthy of praise. Ask them to name other commendable things Rose did.

By the time she turned twelve, Rose had perfected her metal-bending practices. She formed delicately shaped alphabet letters to help the young ones learn to read. For his birthday, Rose presented her pa with a branding iron, a circle with a big *M-A-C* for MacGruder in the middle, just in time, too, because a herd of quick-tempered longhorn steer was stampeding its way up from the Rio Grande. They were plowing a path straight toward her front door.

Rose performed an eye-catching wonder, the likes of which was something to see. Running lightning-fast toward the herd, using Cole for support, Rose vaulted into the air and landed on the back of the

53

TIME FOR Science

Myths and Nature

Myths explain how things in the natural world came to be, such as rivers, lakes, and mountains; the creation of seasons; and explanations for droughts, thunder, and lightning. For instance, one myth told by the Miwok Indians describes how two fawns, wearing the skin of the bear that killed their mother, make thunder and rain when they run around in the sky.

DURING READING

VOCABULARY STRATEGY

Context Clues

TEACH

Homonyms are words that are spelled and pronounced the same but have different meanings. In text, clues from surrounding words can help the reader decide the correct meaning of the homonym. Model using context clues to determine the meaning of *pitch* on p. 52.

Think Aloud **MODEL** It says she constructed a thunderbolt as black as pitch. I know that one meaning of *pitch* is to throw a baseball, but that doesn't make sense in this sentence. In this case *pitch* means a black, tarry substance.

PRACTICE AND ASSESS

Have students use context clues to determine the meaning of the homonym *rose,* part of Thunder Rose's name. *(Clues: a baby girl's name Meaning: a flower)* The other meaning of rose is the past tense of the verb *rise.*

EXTEND SKILLS

Exaggeration/Hyperbole

Explain that exaggeration, or hyperbole, is something overstated or made greater than it really is. In tall tales, exaggeration is often used for comic effect. Have students find more examples of exaggeration or hyperbole in *Thunder Rose* as they read on.

Guiding Comprehension

7 **Cause and Effect • Literal**
What effect did Rose's lullaby have on Tater, the bull?
It calmed the bull and put him to sleep.

8 **Character • Inferential**
Reread paragraph 5 on p. 55. Why do you think Rose blushed when her ma praised her for being clever?
Possible response: Rose was embarrassed. She didn't like to make a big deal about her talents.

9 **Monitor and Fix-Up • Inferential**
Think about what has happened so far in the story. What are some of Rose's accomplishments? If you have trouble recalling, review the story.
Rose has become skilled at metal-bending, staked a fence without help, built a skyscraper, helped young ones to read, stopped a herd of cattle, and invented barbed wire.

ELL

Access Content Point to the words *varmint* (line 2) and *critter* (line 5) on p. 55. Explain that *varmint* is a variation of *vermin*, meaning "an animal that is thought to be undesirable or troublesome." *Critter* is a variation of *creature*. Explain that these informal terms are part of an English dialect common to certain rural areas of the United States.

biggest lead steer like he was a merry-go-round pony. Grabbing a horn in each hand, Rose twisted that varmint to a complete halt. It was just enough to restrain that top bull and the rest of the herd.

But I believe what touched that critter's heart was when Rose began humming her little tune. That cantankerous ton of beef was restless no more. He became as playful as a kitten and even tried to purr. Rose named him Tater on account of that was his favorite vegetable. Hearing Rose's lullaby put that considerable creature to sleep was the sweetest thing I had witnessed in a long, long time. 7

After the dust had settled, Ma and Pa counted twenty-seven hundred head of cattle, after they added in the five hundred they already had. Using the scrap iron, Rose had to add a new section to the bull pen to hold them all.

"What did you do to the wire, Rose?" Ma asked, surprised and pleased at her daughter's latest creation.

"Oh, that," she said. "While I was staking the fence, Pa asked me to keep little Barbara Jay company. That little twisty pattern seemed to make the baby laugh. So I like to think of it as a Barbara's Wire."

"That was right clever of you to be so entertaining to the little one like that!" her ma said. Rose just blushed. Over the years, that twisty wire caught on, and folks just called it barbed wire. 8

Rose and her pa spent the whole next day sorting the animals that had not been branded. "One day soon, before the cold weather gets in," she told her pa, "I'll have to get this herd up the Chisholm Trail and to market in Abilene. I suspect Tater is the right kind of horse for the long drive northward." 9

55

Develop Vocabulary

PRACTICE LESSON VOCABULARY

Students orally respond *yes* or *no* to each question and provide a reason for each answer.

1. Does *lullaby* have a restatement in the context that tells its meaning? *(Yes, an old song and a melody.)*

2. Can a herd of cattle *daintily* stampede? *(No, cattle use great force when they run.)*

3. Is the sunrise the color of *pitch*? *(No, the sunrise is not dark or black like pitch.)*

BUILD CONCEPT VOCABULARY

Review previous concept words with students. Ask if students have come across any words today in their reading that they would like to add to the Challenges in Nature Concept Web, such as *thunderbolt* and *lightning*.

STRATEGY SELF-CHECK

Monitor and Fix-Up

Ask students to think about what has happened in the story so far. Have them identify causes and effects. Remind them they can review and reread the story to help them recall. (Possible response: *Cause: Rose was skilled at metal-bending. Effect: She staked fences, built a sky-scraper, made metal letters to help teach young ones to read.*)

Students can use causes and effects to help them understand story events.

SELF-CHECK

Students can ask themselves these questions to assess their ability to use the skill and strategy.

- Did I identify causes and effects when I reviewed or reread *Thunder Rose*?
- Did the causes and effects better help me understand the character and plot?
- If I didn't understand something the first time, did rereading help me understand?

Monitor Progress

Cause and Effect

If... students have difficulty recognizing causes and effects,	**then...** revisit the skill lesson on p. 42. Reteach as necessary.

Monitor Comprehension Ask students to review what they wrote earlier about tall tales. (See p. 46.) Ask, "What makes *Thunder Rose* a tall tale? How does it compare to what you wrote about tall tales?"

If you want to teach this selection in two sessions, stop here.

DAY 3

Guiding Comprehension

If you are teaching the selection in two days, discuss the causes and effects so far and review the vocabulary.

10 Vocabulary • Homonyms

What does *steer* mean in paragraph 4? What clues helped you figure this out?

Clue: those bulls. Meaning: bull or cattle

11 Cause and Effect • Literal

What problems did the lack of rain cause?

There was no water. The cattle were thirsty and angry and wouldn't move.

Monitor Progress

Cause and Effect

If... students are unable to determine the causes and effects,	**then...** use the skill and strategy instruction on p. 57.

12 Character • Inferential

"I've got to do something about this," Rose declared. What does this tell you about Rose?

She doesn't back down from a challenge; she is determined.

DAY 3 Grouping Options

Reading

Whole Group Discuss the Question of the Day.

Group Time Differentiated Instruction

Read *Thunder Rose.* See pp. 42h–42i for the small group lesson plan.

Whole Group Discuss the Reader Response questions on p. 64. Then use p. 67a.

Language Arts

Use pp. 67e–67k.

On Rose's first trip to Abilene, while right outside of Caldwell, that irascible, full-of-outrage-and-ire outlaw Jesse Baines and his gang of desperadoes tried to rustle that herd away from Rose.

Using the spare metal rods she always carried with her, Rose lassoed those hot-tempered hooligans up good and tight. She dropped them all off to jail, tied up in a nice neat iron bow. "It wasn't any trouble at all," she told Sheriff Weaver. "Somebody had to put a stop to their thieving ways."

But that wasn't the only thieving going on. The mighty sun was draining the moisture out of every living thing it touched. Even the rocks were crying out. Those clouds stood by and watched it all happen. They weren't even trying to be helpful.

Why, the air had turned so dry and sour, time seemed to all
10 but stand still. And there was not a drop of water in sight. Steer will not move without water. And that was making those bulls mad, real mad. And when a bull gets angry, it's like a disease that's catching, making the rest of the herd mad, too. Tater was looking
11 parched and mighty thirsty.

12 "I've got to do something about this!" Rose declared.

Stretching out several iron rods lasso-fashion, then launching Cole high in the air, Rose hoped she could get the heavens to yield forth. She caught hold of a mass of clouds and squeezed them hard, real hard, all the while humming her song. Gentle rain began to fall. But anyone looking could see there was not enough moisture to refresh two ants, let alone a herd of wild cows.

56

Extend Language Explain that *steer* is both the singular and the plural form of the word. Introduce the words *deer* and *sheep*. Tell students that these words are also both singular and plural.

SKILLS ↔ STRATEGIES IN CONTEXT

Cause and Effect Monitor/Fix Up

TEACH

Reread p. 56. After reading, have students ask themselves, “Do I understand what happened?” and “Do I understand why?” Ask students to identify one cause and its effects. (Possible response: *Cause: drought; Effects: no water, bulls were angry, Rose couldn’t move the herd*) Use this exercise to model how looking for causes and effects can help you monitor your comprehension.

Think Aloud **MODEL** I’ll reread p. 56. At the end of the page, I ask myself “What’s happening on this page?” One thing that happens is the cattle won’t move. Then I ask, “Why won’t the cattle move?” I reread and see that because there is no rain, the cattle are thirsty and angry. Asking questions and rereading to identify causes and effects helps me better understand what I read.

PRACTICE AND ASSESS

As students continue reading the story, encourage them to stop at the end of each page and ask, “What happened?” and “Why?” If they are not sure, remind them to reread. If they still don’t understand, have them write questions and see if their questions are answered as they read on.

DURING READING

Guiding Comprehension

13 **Cause and Effect • Literal**
What caused the storm? Why?

The clouds caused the storm because they didn't like someone telling them what to do.

Monitor Progress	
Cause and Effect	
If... students have difficulty identifying cause and effect,	**then...** use the skill and strategy instruction on p. 59.

14 **Author's Craft • Inferential**
Question the Author **Why does the author use hyperbole by saying, "Her eyes flashed lightning. She bit down and gnashed thunder from her teeth," instead of just saying she was angry?**

Possible response: Exaggeration helps show how really angry she was and how powerful her anger was. It also reminds us of her name, Thunder Rose, and of the thunder and lightning she had in her veins.

Students can use a student-friendly search engine and the keywords *severe weather* to find photos, information, and safety tips on tornadoes and thunderstorms. Be sure to follow classroom guidelines for Internet use.

Suddenly a rotating column of air came whirling and swirling around, picking up everything in its path. It sneaked up on Rose. "Whoa, there, now just hold on a minute," Rose called out to the storm. Tater was helpless to do anything about that sort of wind. **13** Those meddlesome clouds caused it. They didn't take kindly to someone telling them what to do. And they were set on creating a riotous rampage all on their own.

Oh, this riled Rose so much, she became the only two-legged

58

ELL

Context Clues Reread aloud the first sentence on p. 58, paragraph 1. Ask students to use context clues to help them determine the meaning of a "rotating column" of air. *(The clues "whirling and swirling around" suggest* rotating *means the air was turning fast. A column is a slender upright structure, so the air must have looked like a spinning column.)*

ıpest to walk the western plains. "You don't know who you're
ling with," Rose called out to the storm. Her eyes flashed light-
g. She bit down and gnashed thunder from her teeth. I don't
ɔw why anyone would want to mess with a pretty young
man who had the power of thunder and lightning coursing
ɔugh her veins. But, pity for them, the clouds did! 14

Rose reached for her iron rod. But there was only one piece
. She did not know which way to turn. She knew Cole alone

59

Tornadoes

A tornado is a column of swirling air that extends from a thundercloud down to the ground. Tornadoes are formed from very strong thunderstorms. In order for a tornado to form, warm, moist air has to move upward, and cold, dry air has to move downward. The air masses combine with winds to develop into a tornado. An area known as "Tornado Alley" in the Midwestern part of the United States experiences more tornadoes than any other region in the world. "Tornado Alley" extends from the Gulf Coast of Texas north through eastern South Dakota. Because this region is so flat, cold, dry air from the north and warm, moist air from the south can move towards each other with nothing to block their paths. Where the air masses meet is where tornadoes are most likely to develop.

SKILLS ↔ STRATEGIES IN CONTEXT

Cause and Effect

TEACH

- Remind students that clue words like *cause* or *because* sometimes signal cause and effect.
- Model using clue words to identify the cause of the storm on p. 58, paragraph 1.

MODEL When I read paragraph 1, I notice the word *caused* in the sentence *"Those meddlesome clouds caused it."* So the clouds caused something. I go back and reread the sentences before to find out what "it" refers to. The sentences describe a storm, so the clouds caused a storm.

PRACTICE AND ASSESS

Ask students why Rose became riled. *(Choice c)*

a) She became the only two-legged tempest on the western plains.

b) Tater was helpless against the swirling air.

c) The storm was set on creating a riotous rampage.

Guiding Comprehension

15 Plot • Inferential

What problem did Rose face on p. 61?

Two tornadoes are coming at her from opposite directions.

Monitor Progress

REVIEW **Plot**	
If... students have difficulty understanding plot,	**then...** use the skill instruction on p. 61.

16 Drawing Conclusions • Inferential

How do you think Rose felt as she faced her challenge? Why?

Possible response: She felt determined because she never backed down from a challenge. Her courage made her strong. She was scared because it was a strong storm that didn't back down. She didn't know how it would turn out.

17 Compare and Contrast • Critical

How was this challenge different from the other challenges Rose faced? How was it the same?

Possible response: The tornadoes were stronger and more powerful than the other challenges. She quieted the tornadoes with her singing, just as she did with the bull.

60

Extend Language Reread aloud the phrase "a windstorm bent on her disaster." Point to the word *bent.* Explain that this word has two meanings. Help students name the more common meaning (*curved* or *crooked*). Tell them that *bent* can also mean "determined."

was not enough to do the job right. Unarmed against her own growing thirst and the might of the elements, Rose felt weighted down. Then that churning column split, and now there were two. They were coming at her from opposite directions. Rose had some fast thinking to do. Never being one to bow down under pressure, she considered her options, for she was not sure how this would all come out in the end. 15

"Is this the fork in the road with which I have my final supper? Will this be my first and my last ride of the roundup?" she queried herself in the depths of her heart. Her contemplations brought her little relief as she witnessed the merciless, the cataclysmic efforts of a windstorm bent on her disaster. Then the winds joined hands and cranked and churned a path heading straight toward her! Calmly Rose spoke out loud to the storm as she stood alone to face the wrack and ruin, the multiplying devastation. "I *could* ride at least *one* of you out to the end of time! But I've got this fortunate feeling rumbling deep in the pit of me, and I see what I am to do with it this day!" Rose said, smiling. 16

The winds belted at a rumbling pitch. Rose squarely faced that storm. "Come and join me, winds!" She opened her arms wide as if to embrace the torrent. She opened her mouth as if she were planning to take a good long drink. But from deep inside her, she heard a melody so real and sweet and true. And when she lifted her heart, she unleashed *her* song of thunder. It was a sight to see: Rose making thunder and lightning rise and fall to the ground at her command, at the sound of *her song*. Oh, how her voice rang out so clear and real and true. It rang from the mountaintops. It filled up the valleys. It flowed like a healing river in the breathing air around her. 17

61

SKILLS ↔ STRATEGIES IN CONTEXT

DURING READING

Plot REVIEW

TEACH

- Remind students that plot is the organization of story events.
- The plot usually includes a problem or conflict, rising action, climax, and resolution.
- Often the author also gives background information at the beginning of the story that helps the reader better understand the action to come.
- In addition, the author may add a segment on falling action after the climax that eventually leads to the resolution.

PRACTICE AND ASSESS

- Have students identify the climax and explain what makes it the climax. *(Climax: Rose sang and her voice controlled the thunder and lightning. This is the climax because it is a turning point in the action and comes just before we learn the resolution, or how the story ends).*
- To assess, use Practice Book p. 16.

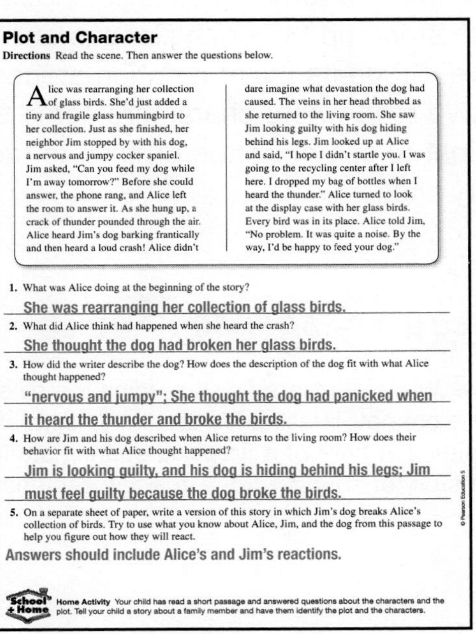

Plot and Character

Directions Read the scene. Then answer the questions below.

Alice was rearranging her collection of glass birds. She'd just added a tiny and fragile glass hummingbird to her collection. Just as she finished, her neighbor Jim stopped by with his dog, a nervous and jumpy cocker spaniel. Jim asked, "Can you feed my dog while I'm away tomorrow?" Before she could answer, the phone rang, and Alice left the room to answer it. As she hung up, a crack of thunder pounded through the air. Alice heard Jim's dog barking frantically and then heard a loud crash! Alice didn't dare imagine what devastation the dog had caused. The veins in her head throbbed as she returned to the living room. She saw Jim looking guilty with his dog hiding behind his legs. Jim looked up at Alice and said, "I hope I didn't startle you. I was going to the recycling center after I left here. I dropped my bag of bottles when I heard the thunder." Alice turned to look at the display case with her glass birds. Every bird was in its place. Alice told Jim, "No problem. It was quite a noise. By the way, I'd be happy to feed your dog."

1. What was Alice doing at the beginning of the story?
   She was rearranging her collection of glass birds.
2. What did Alice think had happened when she heard the crash?
   She thought the dog had broken her glass birds.
3. How did the writer describe the dog? How does the description of the dog fit with what Alice thought happened?
   "nervous and jumpy"; She thought the dog had panicked when it heard the thunder and broke the birds.
4. How are Jim and his dog described when Alice returns to the living room? How does their behavior fit with what Alice thought happened?
   Jim is looking guilty, and his dog is hiding behind his legs; Jim must feel guilty because the dog broke the birds.
5. On a separate sheet of paper, write a version of this story in which Jim's dog breaks Alice's collection of birds. Try to use what you know about Alice, Jim, and the dog from this passage to help you figure out how they will react.

Answers should include Alice's and Jim's reactions.

School + Home **Home Activity** Your child has read a short passage and answered questions about the characters and the plot. Tell your child a story about a family member and have them identify the plot and the characters.

▲ **Practice Book** p. 16

DURING READING

Guiding Comprehension

18 **Cause and Effect • Critical**
Why do you think Rose's voice had the effect it did on the tornadoes?

Possible response: She sang with the thunder and lightning that was in her veins and it was very powerful. The storm was wild and angry and her voice was calming.

19 **Figurative Language • Critical**
What do you think the author means by the "bull's-eye that was set at the center of her heart" in the last sentence?

Possible response: A bull's-eye is a target. Challenges seem to head straight for Rose, as though she's a target for them. It could also refer to the bull she rides and has come to love.

20 **Monitor and Fix-Up • Critical**
Text To Text **Think about the challenges Rose faced. Did Rose's challenges remind you of challenges faced by characters in other stories you've read?**

Responses should include the cattle stampede and the tornadoes and the idea that Rose stood up to her challenges and was brave. Students might mention stories they've read where characters come up against forces of nature or have to face a scary challenge.

Strategy Response Log

Summarize When students finish reading the selection, provide this prompt: Imagine it's a stormy night, and your family is sitting in front of a fireplace sharing stories. Share the story of *Thunder Rose* in a few sentences.

Those tornadoes, calmed by her song, stopped their churning masses and raged no more. And, gentle as a baby's bath, a soft, drenching-and-soaking rain fell. **18**

And Rose realized that by reaching into her own heart to bring forth the music that was there, she had even touched the hearts of the clouds.

62

The stories of Rose's amazing abilities spread like wildfire, far and wide. And as sure as thunder follows lightning, and sun follows rain, whenever you see a spark of light flash across a heavy steel gray sky, listen to the sound of the thunder and think of Thunder Rose and *her* song. That mighty, mighty song pressing on the bull's-eye that was set at the center of her heart.  

63

STRATEGY SELF-CHECK

Monitor and Fix Up

As students think about the challenges Rose faced, have them use a T-chart to record causes and effects related to her challenges. Encourage them to review the story if necessary. Students can use their charts to write a brief summary of what happened and why. Use Practice Book p. 17.

SELF-CHECK

Students can ask themselves these questions to assess their ability to use the skill and strategy.

- Did I look for causes and effects to help me identify Rose's challenges?
- If I didn't understand something, did I reread?
- How did rereading help me understand the story?

Monitor Progress

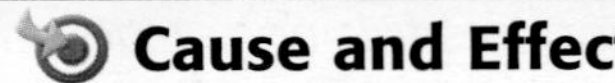

Cause and Effect

If... students have difficulty recognizing causes and effects and monitoring their comprehension,	**then...** use the Reteach lesson on p. 67b.

Cause and Effect

- A **cause** is what makes something happen. An **effect** is what happens as a result of the cause.
- If there are no clue words, ask yourself, "What made this event happen? What happened as a result of this event?"
- An effect may become the cause of another effect.

Directions Read the following passage. Then answer the questions below.

Walking home, Arthur could hardly see where he was going. The fierce wind whipped the snow around. At least a foot of snow covered the sidewalks. His socks, shoes, and pant legs were soaked, and his hands felt like ice. He knew his dad would be home from work when he got there. He just hoped that there would be some warm cocoa and popcorn waiting.

Finally, he reached his door. As he hurried inside, he could smell cocoa and popcorn. Arthur changed out of his wet clothes and sat down to enjoy his snack with his dad. But the best part of all was the news on television. Because of the bad storm that Arthur had walked through, there would be no school the next day!

Possible answers given for 2–5.

1. Why was Arthur unable to see where he was going?
   The wind was blowing the snow around.
2. What were some of the effects of the snowstorm in the neighborhood?
   At least a foot of snow covered the sidewalks.
3. What was an effect of the snowstorm that pleased Arthur?
   School was cancelled for the following day.
4. If you had a day off from school because of bad weather, what would you do with it?
   I would stay inside and play a game with my family.
5. What was the cause of the last day you had off from school, other than a weekend?
   I had a doctor's appointment.

School + Home **Home Activity** Your child read a short passage and answered questions about cause and effect. With your child, write a short story about a hero. Include what caused the person to act heroically and the effects of his or her heroism.

▲ **Practice Book** p. 17

Develop Vocabulary

PRACTICE LESSON VOCABULARY

As a class, complete the following sentences orally.

1. Tornadoes can cause *devastation* to *(buildings).*
2. *Veins* run through our *(bodies).*
3. A *thieving* bunch spends their time *(stealing).*
4. A new calf is *branded* with the *(mark or letters)* of its owner.

BUILD CONCEPT VOCABULARY

Review previous concept words with students. Ask if students have come across any words today in their reading that they would like to add to the Challenges in Nature Concept Web, such as *tornadoes* and *drenching.*

Reader Response

Open for Discussion **Personal Response**

MODEL To tell the story of *Thunder Rose,* I would use some of the biggest exaggerations to get my audience's attention.

Comprehension Check **Critical Response**

1. Possible response: Rose sang to quiet the tornadoes. Knowing what happened the day she was born makes the ending more believable.
   Author's Purpose
2. Possible response: Thunder Rose was nearly out of iron, thirsty, and facing a mighty storm. Her song calmed the storm.
   Cause and Effect
3. Possible response: The thunderstorms I've seen and heard were really loud but not quite as exciting as the ones in this story.
   Monitor and Fix Up
4. *Lullaby; resourceful; constructed; thieving; devastation; pitch* ***Vocabulary***

Look Back and Write For test practice, assign a 10–15 minute time limit. For assessment, see the Scoring Rubric at the right.

Retell

Have students retell *Thunder Rose.*

Monitor Progress

Check Retelling Rubric 4 3 2 1

If... students have difficulty retelling the story,	**then...** use the Retelling Cards and the Scoring Rubric for Retelling on p. 65 to assist fluent retelling.

SUCCESS PREDICTOR

Check Retelling Encourage students to use the illustrations to help them recall and retell important story events. For more ideas on assessing students' retellings, see the ELL and Transition Handbook.

Reader Response

Open for Discussion An old-timer says, "What? You've never heard of Thunder Rose? Didn't you see her TV interview last night?" Now you take the old-timer's role. Tell the tall tale of Thunder Rose, based on what you've just read, as the old-timer would tell it.

1. Thunder Rose meets the challenge of the twin tornadoes. How? Her solution may seem unusual, but the author has prepared you for it. You got a preview of Rose's unusual talent early in the story. How does this preview make the ending more believable? **Think Like an Author**
2. What caused Rose to question her survival? What effect did her *song* have on the storm? **Cause and Effect**
3. Think about the thunder and lightning storms you have been in or watched outside. Compare what you have heard and seen to the storms in "Thunder Rose." **Monitor and Fix Up**
4. The author uses colorful vocabulary to describe objects and events in the story. Which words from the Words to Know list did he use instead of *song, clever, built, stealing, mess,* and *tar?* **Vocabulary**

Look Back and Write Rose loves to make puns—word plays with words that have two meanings. Look back at page 61 and find Rose's pun. Write the sentence in which the pun appears and explain it.

Meet author **Jerdine Nolen on page 764** and illustrator **Kadir Nelson on page 775.**

64

Scoring Rubric **Look Back and Write**

Top-Score Response A top-score response will quote the pu on p. 61 of the selection and explain two meanings that *fork* can have in the context of the storms Rose is facing.

Example of a Top-Score Response "Is this the fork in the roa with which I have my final supper?" A *fork* is an eating tool. It also a place where a tree, road, or stream divides. Rose is say ing that the tornadoes represent a new challenge that she cou face in different ways. The way she tackles them may cause h death, her "final supper."

For additional rubrics, see p. WA10.

Write Now

Tall Tale

Prompt

Thunder Rose is a tall tale about a girl with out-of-this-world skills.
Think about another character or a person who is larger than life.
Now write a tall tale, using exaggeration to stretch the truth in an entertaining way.

Writing Trait

Vivid **word choice** helps readers "see" the action.

Student Model

My grandpa is the best fisherman around. All he has to do is whistle, and a dozen fish leap into his net.

One day, Grandpa heard about a fish as big as a boat. "That fish will never be caught," he was told. "When someone casts a line, he pops up, laughs out loud, and splashes back into his pond."

Off Grandpa went to give it a try. Soon he got tired of carrying his pole. "I won't need it anyway," Grandpa said as he tossed it aside.

Grandpa arrived at the pond and gave a whistle. Up jumped that fish, laughing, but instead of splashing back into the pond, he leapt right into Grandpa's net. And that's how Grandpa came home with the fish that couldn't be caught.

Exaggeration is an important element of tall tales.

Vivid word choice creates clear pictures for readers.

Last sentence is traditional ending for tall tales—states what tale claims to explain.

Use the model to help you write your own tall tale.

65

Write Now

Look at the Prompt Explain that each sentence in the prompt has a purpose.

- Sentence 1 presents a topic.
- Sentence 2 suggests students think about the topic.
- Sentence 3 tells what to write—a tall tale.

Strategies to Develop Word Choice

Have students

- record colorful words from *Thunder Rose.*
- check a thesaurus for strong verbs.

NO: made, pulled, walked

YES: crafted, yanked, sauntered

- choose words that appeal to the senses.

NO: a hot day

YES: a muggy, sticky day

For additional suggestions or rubric, see pp. 67g–67h.

Writer's Checklist

- ☑ **Focus** Is every sentence necessary to the story?
- ☑ **Organization** Do transitions show sequence clearly?
- ☑ **Support** Are voice and word choice suitable?
- ☑ **Conventions** Are grammar and spelling correct?

Scoring Rubric Narrative Retelling

Rubric 4 3 2 1	4	3	2	1
Connections	Makes connections and generalizes beyond the text	Makes connections to other events, stories, or experiences	Makes a limited connection to another event, story, or experience	Makes no connection to another event, story, or experience
Author's Purpose	Elaborates on author's purpose	Tells author's purpose with some clarity	Makes some connection to author's purpose	Makes no connection to author's purpose
Characters	Describes the main character(s) and any character development	Identifies the main character(s) and gives some information about them	Inaccurately identifies some characters or gives little information about them	Inaccurately identifies the characters or gives no information about them
Setting	Describes the time and location	Identifies the time and location	Omits details of time or location	Is unable to identify time or location
Plot	Describes the problem, goal, events, and ending using rich detail	Tells the problem, goal, events, and ending with some errors that do not affect meaning	Tells parts of the problem, goal, events, and ending with gaps that affect meaning	Retelling has no sense of story

Retelling Plan

- ☑ **Week 1** Assess Strategic Intervention students.
- ☑ **This week assess Advanced students.**
- ☐ **Week 3** Assess Strategic Intervention students.
- ☐ **Week 4** Assess On-Level students.
- ☐ **Week 5** Assess any students you have not yet checked during this unit.

Use the Retelling Chart on p. TR16 to record retelling.

Selection Test To assess with *Thunder Rose*, use Selection Tests, pp. 5–8.

Fresh Reads for Differentiated Test Practice For weekly leveled practice, use pp. 7–12.

DAY 4

Science in Reading

OBJECTIVES

- Examine features of expository nonfiction.
- Practice a test-taking strategy.
- Compare and contrast across texts.

PREVIEW/USE TEXT FEATURES

As students preview "Measuring Tornadoes," have them look at the chart. Then ask:

- **What do you think the graphic source will be about?** *(Possible response: The damage done by tornadoes of different wind speeds.)*

Link to Science

Help students brainstorm federal and state agencies and other sources of information.

EXPOSITORY NONFICTION

Use the sidebar on p. 66 to guide discussion.

- Explain that expository nonfiction gives information about real events. Often graphic sources, such as charts, show information.
- Discuss how the chart on p. 67 helps students understand the information on p. 66.

DAY 4 Grouping Options

Reading

Whole Group Discuss the Question of the Day.

Group Time Differentiated Instruction

Read "Measuring Tornadoes." See pp. 42h–42i for the small group lesson plan.

Whole Group Use p. 67a.

Language Arts

Use pp. 67e–67k.

Science in Reading

Expository Nonfiction

Genre

- **Expository nonfiction explains a person, place, thing, or event.**
- **Expository nonfiction may include graphic sources, such as charts and photos, that show information.**

Text Features

- **This selection includes photographs and a chart.**
- **The facts in the chart are listed in rows and columns.**
- **Readers read down the column and across the row to find the cell—the rectangle—that has the information they want.**

Link to Science

Use reference sources to find what you should do if a tornado strikes near you. Make a list of Tornado Safety Tips.

Measuring Tornadoes

BY TRUDI STRAIN TRUEIT

About 800 tornadoes strike the United States each year, resulting in an average of 80 deaths and 1,500 injuries.

It is difficult to accurately measure the high winds inside a tornado, so scientists rely on the Fujita Scale, or F-scale, for help. Created by Theodore Fujita, the F-scale looks at the damage a tornado causes to figure out its wind speed. Nearly 70 percent of the twisters that hit the United States fall into the F-0 and F-1 categories. These weak tornadoes are typically less than 3 miles (5 km) long and no wider than 50 yards (45 m). They usually do little damage—unless they strike without warning.

About 30 percent of tornadoes are strong tornadoes, rating F-2 or F-3 on the scale. Those reaching F-4 or above are called violent tornadoes. Fewer than one in fifty twisters ever become violent, but the most violent tornadoes cause almost two-thirds of tornado-related deaths.

66

Content-Area Vocabulary Science

accurately	without errors or mistakes; exactly
foundations	parts on which the other parts rest for support

AudioText

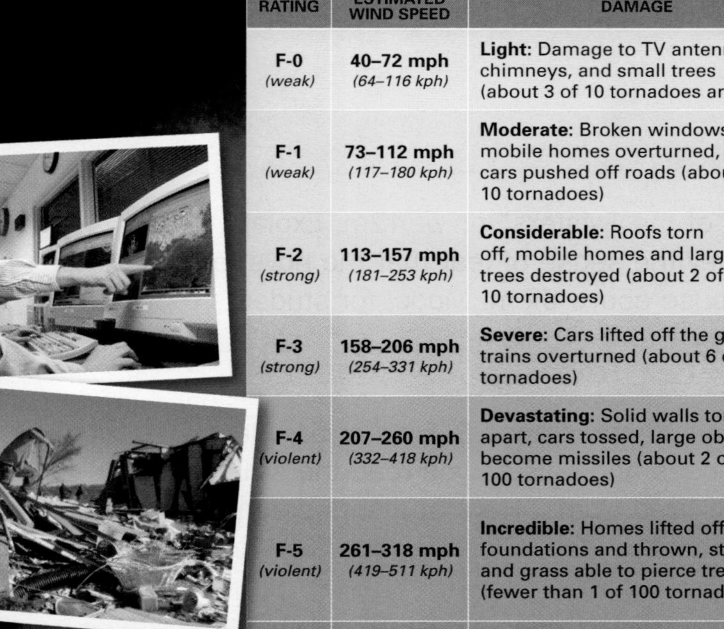

FUJITA SCALE		
RATING	ESTIMATED WIND SPEED	DAMAGE
F-0 *(weak)*	**40–72 mph** *(64–116 kph)*	**Light:** Damage to TV antennae, chimneys, and small trees (about 3 of 10 tornadoes are F-0)
F-1 *(weak)*	**73–112 mph** *(117–180 kph)*	**Moderate:** Broken windows, mobile homes overturned, moving cars pushed off roads (about 4 of 10 tornadoes)
F-2 *(strong)*	**113–157 mph** *(181–253 kph)*	**Considerable:** Roofs torn off, mobile homes and large trees destroyed (about 2 of 10 tornadoes)
F-3 *(strong)*	**158–206 mph** *(254–331 kph)*	**Severe:** Cars lifted off the ground, trains overturned (about 6 of 100 tornadoes)
F-4 *(violent)*	**207–260 mph** *(332–418 kph)*	**Devastating:** Solid walls torn apart, cars tossed, large objects become missiles (about 2 of 100 tornadoes)
F-5 *(violent)*	**261–318 mph** *(419–511 kph)*	**Incredible:** Homes lifted off their foundations and thrown, straw and grass able to pierce tree trunks (fewer than 1 of 100 tornadoes)
F-6 to **F-12** *(violent)*	**319–700 mph** *(512–1,126 kph) or Mach 1, the speed of sound*	**Inconceivable:** Though it was once thought tornadoes could reach the speed of sound, scientists now believe F-5 is the top of the scale

Reading Across Texts

Look back at the drawings of the twin tornadoes that Thunder Rose lassoed. Where do you think they would be listed on the Fujita Scale?

Writing Across Texts Describe what you think Thunder Rose's tornadoes did to the farms in her area.

Cause & Effect Why are the F-6 to F-12 tornadoes called "inconceivable"?

67

TIME FOR Science

Storm Warnings

you live in a certain part of Alaska and hear siren wail for several seconds, you know that a sunami (soo NAH mee) is approaching. But, there re other ways to learn about approaching severe weather. The ational Weather Service (NWS) maintains a Web site on the Internet hat people can use to determine if any significant storms are headed heir way. Radio and television are also good sources of information for torm watches and warnings. Watches are usually issued when severe eather is possible. A watch may be in effect for several hours, and hay cover a large geographic area. Warnings are issued when severe eather is about to occur. Warnings usually last for a shorter period of me (i.e., an hour) and cover sometimes a smaller area. The goal of atches and warnings is to give people a chance to get to safety.

Strategies for Nonfiction

USE CHARTS A chart provides information in an organized, concise form. Students can use charts to help answer test questions. Provide the following strategy.

Use the Strategy

1. Read the test question and locate one or two key words.
2. Scan the chart, looking for key words.
3. Read the information to find an answer to the test question.

GUIDED PRACTICE How would students use the strategy to answer the following question?

Which tornado category produces "severe" damage?

INDEPENDENT PRACTICE After students answer the following test question, discuss the process they used to find information.

What is the estimated wind speed of a F-4 tornado?

Cause and Effect

Scientists no longer believe that tornadoes can have speeds higher than category F-5.

CONNECT TEXT TO TEXT

Reading Across Texts

Have students identify some of the things shown flying in the air and then locate those things, or similarly heavy things, in the chart.

Writing Across Texts Once students decide what type of tornadoes Thunder Rose lassoes, have them use the information in the *Damage* column of the chart.

DAY 5

Fluency Assessment Plan

- ☑ **Week 1** Assess Advanced students.
- ☑ **This week assess Strategic Intervention students.**
- ☐ **Week 3** Assess On-Level students.
- ☐ **Week 4** Assess Strategic Intervention students.
- ☐ **Week 5** Assess any students you have not yet checked during this unit.

Set individual goals for students to enable them to reach the year-end goal.

- Current Goal: 105–110 wcpm
- Year-End Goal: 140 wcpm

Oral fluency depends not only on reading without halting but also on word recognition. After students read passages aloud for assessment, help them recognize unfamiliar English words and their meanings. Focus on each student's progress.

To develop fluent readers, use Fluency Coach.

DAY 5 Grouping Options

Reading

Whole Group
Revisit the Question of the Week.

Group Time
Differentiated Instruction
Reread this week's Leveled Readers. See pp. 42h–42i for the small group lesson plan.

Whole Group
Use p. 67b–67c.

Language Arts
Use pp. 67d–67l.

TONE OF VOICE

Fluency

DAY 1

Model Reread "Night of the Twisters" on p. 42m. Explain that you will use your voice to convey the sense of fear that the boys felt as the tornado tore apart the house above them. Model for students as you read.

DAY 2

Echo Reading Read aloud paragraphs 3–5 on p. 51. Have students notice how your voice rises and falls as you read the strings of phrases and emphasize the italicized words. Have students practice as a class reading after you three times.

DAY 3

Model Read aloud the first two paragraphs on p. 56. Have students notice how you pause at the commas to emphasize the beginnings and endings of phrases. Practice as a class by doing three echo readings.

DAY 4

Partner Reading Partners practice reading the first two paragraphs on p. 56, three times. Students should raise and lower their voices to show groups of words and offer each other feedback.

Monitor Progress — Check Fluency WCPM

As students reread, monitor their progress toward their individual fluency goals Current Goal: 105–110 words correct per minute. End-of-Year Goal: 140 words correct per minute.

If... students cannot read fluently at a rate of 105–110 words correct per minute,
then... make sure students practice with text at their independent level. Provide additional fluency practice, pairing nonfluent readers with fluent readers.

If... students already read at 140 words correct per minute,
then... they do not need to reread three to four times.

SUCCES PREDICTOR

DAY 5

Assessment
Individual Reading Rate Use the Fluency Assessment Plan and do a one-minute timed reading of either selection from this week to assess students in Week 2. Pay special attention to this week's skill, tone of voice. Provide corrective feedback for each student.

RETEACH

Cause and Effect

TEACH

Review the definitions of *cause* and *effect* on p. 42. Students can complete Practice Book p. 18 on their own, or you can complete it as a class. Explain that they need to complete the sentences in the graphic organizers based on the passage provided. Point out that three boxes are already completed for them.

ASSESS

Have students reread pp. 53–54 to find the cause of Rose forming delicately shaped alphabet letters *(to help young ones learn to read);* and the effect of Rose landing on the back of a stampeding longhorn *(She stopped it).*

For additional instruction on cause and effect, see DI • 53.

EXTEND SKILLS

Author's Craft

TEACH

When an author goes about creating a piece of writing, he or she makes choices about the genre, or kind of writing, it will be; who the characters are; what the setting and plot will be; the point of view from which it will be written; and what type of language and style he or she will use.

Review with students a few of the choices the author made in *Thunder Rose* about genre *(tall tale)*, point of view *(third person)*, and language and style *(exaggeration, humor).*

ASSESS

Have small groups discuss and write about other choices Jerdine Nolen made when writing *Thunder Rose.*

1. Who are the characters she chose to write about?

2. What was the setting she chose for the story?

AFTER READING

OBJECTIVES

- Recognize causes and effects.
- Identify examples of author's craft.

Skills Trace	
Cause and Effect	
Introduce/Teach	TE: 5.1 42–43, 112–113; 5.5 582–583
Practice	Practice Book: 6, 13, 17, 18, 43, 47, 48, 106, 233, 237, 238
Reteach/Review	**TE: 5.1 27, 67b, 133b; 5.3 267, DI•53, DI•56; 5.5 603b, DI•55**
Test	Selection Test: 5–8, 17–20, 93–96; Benchmark Test: Unit 1

Access Content Reteach the skill by reviewing the Picture It! lesson on cause and effect in the ELL Teaching Guide, pp. 8–9.

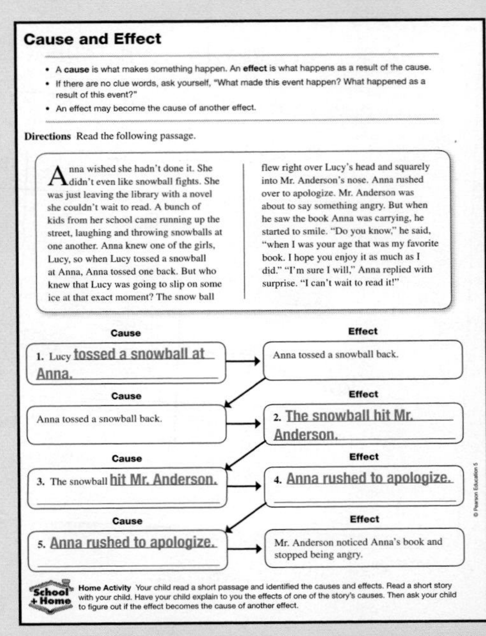

Cause and Effect

- A **cause** is what makes something happen. An **effect** is what happens as a result of the cause.
- If there are no clue words, ask yourself, "What made this event happen? What happened as a result of this event?"
- An effect may become the cause of another effect.

Directions Read the following passage.

Anna wished she hadn't done it. She didn't even like snowball fights. She was just leaving the library with a novel she couldn't wait to read. A bunch of kids from her school came running up the street, laughing and throwing snowballs at one another. Anna knew one of the girls, Lucy, so when Lucy tossed a snowball at Anna, Anna tossed one back. But who knew that Lucy was going to slip on some ice at that exact moment? The snow ball flew right over Lucy's head and squarely into Mr. Anderson's nose. Anna rushed over to apologize. Mr. Anderson was about to say something angry. But when he saw the book Anna was carrying, he started to smile. "Do you know," he said, "when I was your age that was my favorite book. I hope you enjoy it as much as I did." "I'm sure I will," Anna replied with surprise. "I can't wait to read it!"

Cause	Effect
1. Lucy tossed a snowball at Anna.	Anna tossed a snowball back.
Anna tossed a snowball back.	2. The snowball hit Mr. Anderson.
3. The snowball hit Mr. Anderson.	4. Anna rushed to apologize.
5. Anna rushed to apologize.	Mr. Anderson noticed Anna's book and stopped being angry.

School + Home **Home Activity** Your child read a short passage and identified the causes and effects. Read a short story with your child. Have your child explain to you the effects of one of the story's causes. Then ask your child to figure out if the effect becomes the cause of another effect.

▲ **Practice Book** p. 18

Words Correct Per Minute

SUCCESS PREDICTOR

AFTER READING

Vocabulary and Word Study

VOCABULARY STRATEGY

Context Clues

HOMONYMS Remind students that homonyms are spelled and pronounced the same but have different meanings. If they come across a homonym in their reading, they should look for context clues that can help them figure out the word's meaning. Have students write homonyms from *Thunder Rose* and a sentence for each meaning of the word.

Homonym	Sentences
horn	The goat scratched its horn on the ground. The driver honked his horn to prevent an accident.
pen	

Suffixes

Remind students that a suffix is a syllable added to the end of a base word to change its meaning or the way it is used in a sentence. Challenge pairs of students to take words from *Thunder Rose* and see how many new words they can make by adding suffixes.

Word	Suffix	New Word
child	-like	childlike
	-ish	childish
	-less	childless
love	-ly	lovely
music		

BUILD CONCEPT VOCABULARY

Challenges in Nature

LOOKING BACK Remind students of the question of the week: How can nature challenge us? Discuss how this week's Concept Web of vocabulary words relates to the theme of the power of nature. Ask students if they have any words or categories to add. Discuss if words and categories are appropriately related to the concept.

MOVING FORWARD Preview the title of the next selection, *Island of the Blue Dolphins.* Ask students which Concept Web words might apply to the new selection based on the title alone.

Put a star next to these words on the web.

Display the Concept Web and revisit the vocabulary words as you read the next selection to check predictions.

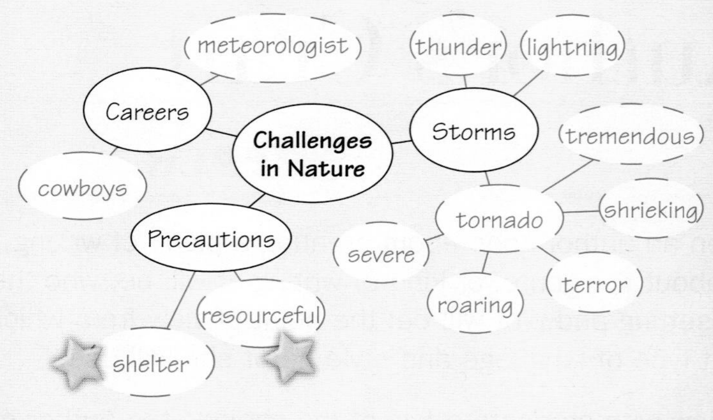

Monitor Progress

Check Vocabulary

If... students suggest words or categories that are not related to the concept,	**then...** review the words and categories on the Concept Web and discuss how they relate to the lesson concept.

Speaking and Viewing

SPEAKING

Storytelling

SET-UP Explain that storytelling is how many traditional stories, such as tall tales, fables, and fairy tales, have been passed down for many years. Have students use the tall tales they wrote in Writing Workshop or a scene from *Thunder Rose* to retell a tall tale. Emphasize that students are not to *read* their tall tales, but to *tell* them.

REHEARSAL After students have chosen one scene from a tall tale they'd like to retell, provide them with time to rehearse. Share these ideas:

- Practice with a family member or friend. Ask for helpful feedback.
- Rehearse in front of a mirror. Check your posture. Make sure you don't fidget or move around.
- Practice your lines so they sound natural.

Delivery Tips

- *Use vivid language and expressive body movement to create a mood.*
- *Vary your inflection and your tone.*
- *Keep your voice natural.*
- *Maintain eye contact with your audience—first one audience member, then another, and so on.*

VIEWING

Analyze an Illustration

Have students study the illustration of the tornado coming toward Thunder Rose on p. 60. They can answer these questions in writing.

1. **What is happening in this illustration?** *(Rose is facing a large tornado.)*
2. **What words would you use to describe the tornado? What details in the illustration support your description?** *(Possible responses: It is powerful, fierce, gigantic, and destructive. It lifts up a wagon and a horse. It appears very large compared to Rose.)*
3. **What kind of movement does the picture suggest?** *(Possible response: fast, violent, uncontrollable.)*

Have students look again at the illustration for details. Discuss how viewing the illustration gives a better understanding of the reading.

ELL

Support Vocabulary Use the following to review and extend vocabulary and to explore lesson concepts further:

- ELL Poster 2, Days 3–5 instruction
- Vocabulary Activities and Word Cards in ELL Teaching Guide, pp. 10–11

Assessment For information on assessing students' speaking, listening, and viewing, see the ELL and Transition Handbook.

Grammar Subjects and Predicates

OBJECTIVES

- Define and identify subjects and predicates.
- Identify and correct fragments and run-ons.
- Use subjects and predicates correctly in writing.
- Become familiar with subject and predicate assessment on high-stakes tests.

Monitor Progress

Grammar

If... students have difficulty identifying subjects and predicates,	**then...** provide additional instruction and practice in The Grammar and Writing Book pp. 56–59.

DAILY FIX-IT

This week use Daily Fix-It Transparency 2.

Grammar Support See the Grammar Transition lessons in the ELL and Transition Handbook.

▲ **The Grammar and Writing Book** For more instruction and practice, use pp. 56–59.

DAY 1 Teach and Model

DAILY FIX-IT

1. Do you know eny lullabys? *(any; lullabies)*
2. These songs puts babies to sleep? *(put; sleep.)*

READING-GRAMMAR CONNECTION

Write this sentence from *Thunder Rose* on the board:

> *Her voice rang out so clear and real and true.*

Explain that the complete subject of this sentence is *Her voice,* and the complete predicate is *rang out so clear and real and true.*

Display Grammar Transparency 2. Read aloud the definitions and sample sentences. Work through the items.

Subjects and Predicates

Every sentence has a subject and a predicate. The words that tell whom or what the sentence is about are the **complete subject.** The most important word in the complete subject is the **simple subject.** It is usually a noun or a pronoun. Some simple subjects have more than one word, such as *United States.*

A gentle lullaby relaxes everyone. → The simple subject is *lullaby.*

The words that tell what the subject is or does are the **complete predicate.** The most important word in the complete predicate is the **simple predicate,** or the verb. Some simple predicates have more than one word, such as *is walking.*

My aunt plays lullabies on the piano. → The simple predicate is *plays.*

A **fragment** is a group of words that lacks either a subject or a predicate.

The power of music. → This fragment lacks a predicate.

A **run-on** is two or more complete sentences run together.

Our whole family loves music we attend many concerts.

Directions Draw a line between the complete subject and the complete predicate in each sentence. Underline the simple subject once. Underline the simple predicate twice.

1. Many babies/respond well to music.
2. Little babies/can learn a lot.
3. I/practice piano every afternoon.
4. My baby sister/becomes very still.
5. She/listens intently.
6. All people/can enjoy good music.
7. Beautiful music/will calm angry feelings.

Directions Write *F* after fragments. Write *R* after run-ons. Write *S* after complete sentences.

8. Our dog can sing she howls along with the piano. R
9. Animals must find our music odd. S
10. Most of our many pets. F
11. They like it they put up with it. R
12. The whole family will attend a concert tonight. S

Unit 1 Thunder Rose Grammar 2

▲ **Grammar Transparency** 2

DAY 2 Develop the Concept

DAILY FIX-IT

3. Whats the climet like where you live? *(What's; climate)*
4. In Spring, we sometimes has tornadoes here. *(spring; have)*

GUIDED PRACTICE

Review the concept of subjects and predicates.

- A **complete subject** is the part of a sentence that tells whom or what the sentence is about.
- A **complete predicate** is the part of a sentence that tells what the subject is or does.
- A **fragment** is a group of words that lacks a subject or predicate.
- A **run-on** is two or more complete sentences run together.

HOMEWORK Grammar and Writing Practice Book p. 5. Work through the first two items with the class.

Simple and Complete Subjects and Predicates

Every sentence has a subject and a predicate. The words that tell whom or what the sentence is about are the **complete subject.** The most important word in the complete subject is the **simple subject.** It is usually a noun or a pronoun. Some simple subjects have more than one word, such as *Kansas City.*

Many families moved west in the 1840s. The simple subject is *families.*

The words that tell what the subject is or does are the **complete predicate.** The most important word in the complete predicate is the **simple predicate,** or the verb. Some simple predicates have more than one word, such as *is walking.*

The trip could take up to six months. The simple predicate is *could take.*

A **fragment** is a group of words that lacks a subject or a predicate.

Had to carry everything with them. This fragment lacks a subject.

A **run-on** is two or more complete sentences run together.

The settlers needed food they needed tools.

Directions Underline each simple subject once. Underline each simple predicate twice.

1. A tornado's shape is like a funnel.
2. The deadly funnel measures up to a mile wide.
3. They are unpredictable in their movements.
4. Settlers feared the awful twister.

Directions Write *F* after a fragment. Write *R* after a run-on. Then correct the sentence errors. Write a complete sentence or two complete sentences on the lines. Possible answers:

5. The wind inside a tornado F
   The wind inside a tornado can spin at up to 300 miles per hour.
6. A tornado can be called a twister it is also sometimes called a cyclone. R
   A tornado can be called a twister. It is also sometimes called a cyclone.

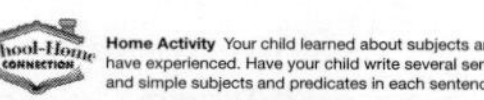

Home Activity Your child learned about subjects and predicates. Talk about a storm you and your child have experienced. Have your child write several sentences about the storm and identify the complete and simple subjects and predicates in each sentence.

▲ **Grammar and Writing Practice Book** p. 5

DAY 3 Apply to Writing

DAILY FIX-IT

5. My sister write funny tall tails. *(writes; tales)*
6. They are a laber of love for she. *(labor; her)*

WRITE COMPLETE SENTENCES

Explain that making sure every sentence has a subject and a predicate will ensure that complete thoughts are written.

- Have students review something they have written to see if there are any fragments or run-ons they need to correct.

HOMEWORK Grammar and Writing Practice Book p. 6.

Simple and Complete Subjects and Predicates

Directions Use each noun and verb pair as the simple subject and simple predicate. Add words to make a complete sentence. Underline the complete subject once and the complete predicate twice.

1. tall tales include Possible answers:
Tall tales include funny exaggerations and amazing characters.
2. hero is
The hero is always very big and powerful.
3. stories make
These silly stories make me laugh.
4. Pecos Bill lassoed
Pecos Bill lassoed a cyclone for the rain.
5. Paul Bunyan rode
Paul Bunyan rode an enormous blue ox.

Directions This paragraph contains fragments and a run-on. Rewrite the paragraph. Add words and punctuation to make sure every sentence has a subject and a predicate.

Davy Crockett was a real person he was also the hero of many tall tales. A good frontiersman and hunter. Killed a bear when he was only three. This "king of the wild frontier."

Possible answer: Davy Crockett was a real person. He was also the hero of many tall tales. Crockett was a good frontiersman and hunter. Tales claim that he killed a bear when he was only three. This "king of the wild frontier" probably did no such thing.

School-Home CONNECTION **Home Activity** Your child learned how to write sentences that have subjects and predicates. Name a familiar person. Have your child write three sentences about the person and underline the subject and circle the predicate in each sentence.

▲ **Grammar and Writing Practice Book** p. 6

DAY 4 Test Preparation

DAILY FIX-IT

7. Alice is a storyteller she makes stories come to life. *(storyteller. She)*
8. The children were silint when she telled a ghost story. *(silent; told)*

STANDARDIZED TEST PREP

Test Tip

A run-on can be corrected in different ways. You can write it as two separate sentences, or you can add a comma and a conjunction to make a compound sentence.

Run-on: I love short stories I am also fond of poems.

Two Sentences: I love short stories. I am also fond of poems.

Compound Sentence: I love short stories, but I am also fond of poems.

HOMEWORK Grammar and Writing Practice Book p. 7.

Simple and Complete Subjects and Predicates

Directions Mark the letter of the sentence in which the simple subject and simple predicate are correctly underlined.

1. A Cowboys of Texas herded cattle to Kansas on the Abilene Trail.
   B Cowboys of Texas herded cattle to Kansas on the Abilene Trail.
   C Cowboys of Texas herded cattle to Kansas on the Abilene Trail.
   (D) Cowboys of Texas herded cattle to Kansas on the Abilene Trail.
2. A The great herds moved along slowly.
   B The great herds moved along slowly.
   (C) The great herds moved along slowly.
   D The great herds moved along slowly.
3. (A) These large animals must graze for hours each day.
   B These large animals must graze for hours each day.
   C These large animals must graze for hours each day.
   D These large animals must graze for hours each day.
4. A They needed a vast supply of water.
   (B) They needed a vast supply of water.
   C They needed a vast supply of water.
   D They needed a vast supply of water.
5. (A) Lean, tanned cowboys urged the cattle forward.
   B Lean, tanned cowboys urged the cattle forward.
   C Lean, tanned cowboys urged the cattle forward.
   D Lean, tanned cowboys urged the cattle forward.

Directions Mark the letter of the group of words that has a subject and a predicate.

6. A Crossed dangerously swift rivers.
   B In the dark of night under the light of the moon.
   (C) The cowboys also protected the cattle from predators.
   D Sleeping in shifts on the hard ground.
7. A A cowboy's horse.
   B For miles in the hot, dusty country.
   (C) They shared water and companionship.
   D Became a best friend and a well-loved co-worker.
8. (A) A well-made hat was a prized possession.
   B Also a sturdy saddle and bridle.
   C Tough leather chaps for the legs.
   D Protected the cowboy's face from heat and dust.

School-Home CONNECTION **Home Activity** Your child prepared for taking tests on subjects, predicates, fragments, and run-ons. Circle a paragraph in the newspaper. Have your child identify the subject and predicate of each sentence in the paragraph.

▲ **Grammar and Writing Practice Book** p. 7

DAY 5 Cumulative Review

DAILY FIX-IT

9. A horses hoofbeates sound like drumming. *(horse's hoofbeats)*
10. A stampeding, herd of cattel must sound like thunder. *(stampeding herd; cattle)*

ADDITIONAL PRACTICE

Assign pp. 56–59 in The Grammar and Writing Book.

EXTRA PRACTICE Grammar and Writing Practice Book p. 123.

ASSESSMENT

CUMULATIVE REVIEW Grammar and Writing Practice Book p. 8.

Simple and Complete Subjects and Predicates

Directions Draw a line between the complete subject and the complete predicate in each sentence. Circle the simple subject and the simple predicate.

1. A blacksmith / was important to the pioneer community.
2. People / called this metal worker a smithy.
3. He / could mend a plow or tools.
4. The powerful man / pounded steel on his anvil.
5. Fascinated children / watched the smithy at work.

Directions Identify the part of the sentence that is underlined. Write *complete subject, simple subject, complete predicate,* or *simple predicate.*

6. Patient oxen were once beasts of burden. complete predicate
7. A pair of oxen might pull a wagon. complete subject
8. These big animals could plow all day. simple predicate
9. The farmer walked along behind. simple subject

Directions: Write *F* if a group of words is a fragment. Write *R* if it is a run-on sentence. Rewrite each one to make a complete sentence or a compound sentence. Possible answers:

10. Barbed wire was invented in Illinois it quickly became popular all over the United States. R
Barbed wire was invented in Illinois, and it quickly became popular all over the United States.
11. Fenced in their cattle. F
Ranchers eagerly fenced in their cattle.
12. These fences kept cattle in and rustlers out cattle injured themselves on the fences at first. R
These fences kept cattle in and rustlers out, but cattle injured themselves on the fences at first.

School-Home CONNECTION **Home Activity** Your child reviewed subjects, predicates, fragments, and run-ons. Ask your child to make a note card for each term with the definition on one side and an example on the other.

▲ **Grammar and Writing Practice Book** p. 8

Writing Workshop Tall Tale

OBJECTIVES

- Identify qualities of a tall tale.
- Write a tall tale using humor and exaggeration to create a mood.
- Focus on word choice.
- Use a rubric.

Genre Tall Tale
Writer's Craft Creating Mood
Writing Trait Word Choice

Word Choice Work with students to use vivid words that appeal to readers' senses. A bilingual dictionary, picture dictionary, or thesaurus, as well as other home-language speakers, may help provide words that create pictures for readers.

Writing Traits

FOCUS/IDEAS Strong supporting details make character come alive.

ORGANIZATION/PARAGRAPHS An amazing pup is described *(six feet tall, weighed 300 pounds).* Larger-than-life actions then develop problem.

VOICE Writing is humorous. Writer clearly enjoys telling the story.

WORD CHOICE The writer uses humorous exaggerations and figurative language to describe actions *(lapped up the whole fish pond)* and comparisons to create mood *(sweet and gentle as a baby bunny).*

SENTENCES Sentences of varied length and kind add interest and clarity.

CONVENTIONS There is excellent control and accuracy.

DAY 1 Model the Trait

READING-WRITING CONNECTION

- *Thunder Rose* is a tall tale.
- The story uses outrageous exaggerations and figurative language to create a fantastic mood.
- Students will write a **tall tale** using word choice to create a humorous mood.

MODEL WORD CHOICE Discuss Writing Transparency 2A. Then discuss the model and the writing trait of word choice.

The writer uses exaggeration to describe Mortimer colorfully. For example, "one swipe of his tongue" covers a person "from head to toe." These words create an image of a huge but friendly puppy energetically licking its soggy owner. This exaggeration is both funny and vivid.

Tall Tale

A **tall tale** tells about the accomplishments of a larger-than-life character. It uses exaggeration to show the character's amazing abilities and to create humor. Colorful details and comparisons create vivid pictures of the fantastic events.

Mortimer Becomes a Star

Exaggeration sets a humorous tone.

Details create a vivid picture.

Comparison helps create mood.

The day we got Mortimer, we knew he was a special dog. Though he was just a pup, he was six feet tall and weighed 300 pounds. When he wagged his adorable tail, he cleared the furniture out of the living room. With one swipe of his tongue, he gave you a bath from head to toe.

When Mortimer outgrew the garage, we made him a bed in the barn, using 100 bales of soft, fluffy straw. Feeding him was a problem, since he ate a 50-pound bag of chow for breakfast. When he got thirsty, he lapped up the whole fish pond.

What could we do? Everyone in the family loved Mortimer. He was sweet and gentle as a baby bunny. But he was eating us out of house and home. Then a van drove up the drive. It said *Wonderful Wilbur's Pet Food* on the side.

Now that Mortimer is spokes-dog for Wonderful Wilbur's, he gets all the food he could ever want—free. He loves having a fan club!

Unit 1 Thunder Rose — Writing Model **2A**

▲ **Writing Transparency** 2A

DAY 2 Improve Writing

WRITER'S CRAFT
Creating Mood

Display Writing Transparency 2B. Read the directions and work together to identify mood and write details to create a specific mood.

CREATE MOOD WITH WORD CHOICES Tomorrow we will write a **tall tale.** I could write about my neighbor Annie Pickens who loves to bake. I might write, "she bakes 2,000 cookies before breakfast" or "her ten-story-high angel food cake was so light it floated right into the clouds." These details establish a funny, silly mood about this larger-than-life character with exaggeration and vivid, specific words.

GUIDED WRITING Some students may need more help with creating mood. Work with them to identify the mood of the reading selection and the details that help create that mood.

Creating Mood

The **mood** of a piece of writing is the feeling it creates in the reader. The writer's tone (for example, serious or playful, humorous or sad) helps establish the mood. Details that describe the setting, events, and characters also establish mood. For example, in a tall tale, exaggerations add to the humorous mood.

Directions Read each set of details for a story. Write the word from the box that best describes the mood.

dignified suspenseful playful

1. • big, deserted mansion on a hill
   • pitch-black night with thunder
   • two kids lost inside
   • serious tone
   suspenseful
2. • mountains that reach the sun
   • rain that makes a lake of Texas
   • cowboy who slurps it up and spits it in the ocean
   • colorful, humorous tone
   playful
3. • Native American tribal council
   • people in traditional dress
   • holding a naming ceremony for a child
   • thoughtful tone
   dignified

Directions Write the kind of mood you think fits this set of story details. Then write several sentences for the story that establishes this mood.

4. • 1900: townspeople wait for first car to drive through town
   • crowd has gathered in center of town
   • buzz of talk among men and women
   • children race around
   • Someone yells, "Here it comes!"

Possible answers: anticipation

Men and women stood on the village green, talking in low voices. Children raced down the road every few seconds to try to be first to see it—the first horseless carriage ever to come to Farmington. A loud voice announced like a trumpet, "Here it comes!"

Unit 1 Thunder Rose — Writer's Craft **2B**

▲ **Writing Transparency** 2B

DAY 3 Prewrite and Draft

READ THE WRITING PROMPT on page 65 in the Student Edition.

Thunder Rose *is a tall tale about a girl with out-of-this-world skills.*

Think about another character or a person who is larger than life.

Now write a tall tale, using exaggeration to stretch the truth in an entertaining way.

Writing Test Tips

- Write an outline of events, saving the most incredible feat for last.
- Use comparisons to make events and descriptions more colorful.
- Use exaggeration and a humorous tone in describing the character and his or her actions to create a lighthearted mood.

GETTING STARTED Students can do any of the following:

- Use a graphic organizer such as a sequence ladder to organize the hero's feats in order of importance.
- Brainstorm colorful figures of speech or comparisons, such as similes and metaphors, to describe the hero.
- Write exaggerated descriptions of things, actions, and people.

DAY 4 Draft and Revise

EDITING/REVISING CHECKLIST

☑ Do the mood and tone of the writing fit the genre?

☑ Have I used exaggerations to create humor and set the tone?

☑ Does every sentence include a subject and predicate?

☑ Are words with long vowel sounds spelled correctly?

See *The Grammar and Writing Book*, pp. 56–61.

Revising Tips

Word Choice

- Support descriptions of larger-than-life actions with colorful words.
- Use comparisons to add to the mood and the vivid picture of the hero or event.
- Use specific adjectives and verbs to create exact images.

PUBLISHING Create a tall-tale bulletin-board display of student writing. Ask them to add illustrations.

ASSESSMENT Use the scoring rubric to evaluate students' work.

DAY 5 Connect to Unit Writing

Personal Narrative

Week 1	Character Sketch 41g–41h
Week 2	Tall Tale 67g–67h
Week 3	Friendly or Thank-You Letter 89g–89h
Week 4	Feature Article 111g–111h
Week 5	Narrative Writing 133g–133h

PREVIEW THE UNIT PROMPT

Write a personal narrative about a challenge or difficult problem. Describe what the challenge was and tell how you met it. Use details that make the events clear and interesting.

APPLY

- A personal narrative is a story about an interesting experience or event in the storyteller's life.
- Students may use descriptions or ideas from their tall tales in a personal narrative.

Writing Trait Rubric

	4	3	2	1
Word Choice	Vivid style created by use of exact nouns, strong verbs, exciting adjectives, and clear figurative language	Some style created by strong and precise words	Little style created by strong, precise words; some lack of clarity	Word choice vague or incorrect
	Uses strong, specific words that make tall tale clear, lively, and energetic	Uses some specific words that make tall tale clear and vivid at times	Needs more precise word choice to create style and clarity in tall tale	Tall tale made dull or unclear by vague, repetitive, and word choice

Spelling & Phonics Long Vowel VCV

OBJECTIVE

- Spell long vowel words with the VCV syllable pattern.

Generalization

Connect to Phonics Long vowels can be spelled *a: basic, e: fever, i: climate, o: hotel.* When a single vowel appears at the end of a word or syllable, the vowel usually stands for its long sound.

Spelling Words

1. fever	11. label
2. broken	12. icon
3. climate	13. agent
4. hotel	14. motive
5. basic	15. vital
6. vocal	16. acorn
7. native	17. item
8. silent	18. aroma
9. labor	19. legal
10. spider	20. solo

Challenge Words

21. society	24. idealistic
22. rhinoceros	25. equation
23. notation	

ELL

Spelling/Phonics Support See the ELL and Transition Handbook for spelling support.

DAY 1 Pretest and Sort

PRETEST

Use the Dictation Sentences from Day 5 to administer the pretest. Read the word, read the sentence, and then read the word again. Guide students in self-correcting their pretests and correcting any misspellings.

Monitor Progress

Spelling

If... students misspell more than 5 pretest words,	**then...** use words 1–10 for Strategic Intervention.
If... students misspell 1–5 pretest words,	**then...** use words 1–20 for On-Level practice.
If... students correctly spell all pretest words,	**then...** use words 1–25 for Advanced Learners.

HOMEWORK Spelling Practice Book, p. 5.

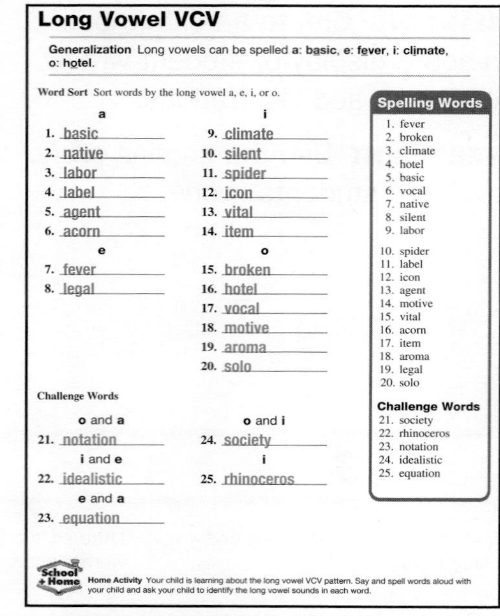

Long Vowel VCV

Generalization Long vowels can be spelled **a: basic, e: fever, i: climate, o: hotel**.

Word Sort Sort words by the long vowel a, e, i, or o.

a
1. basic
2. native
3. labor
4. label
5. agent
6. acorn

e
7. fever
8. legal

i
9. climate
10. silent
11. spider
12. icon
13. vital
14. item

o
15. broken
16. hotel
17. vocal
18. motive
19. aroma
20. solo

Challenge Words

o and a
21. notation

i and e
22. idealistic

e and a
23. equation

o and i
24. society

i
25. rhinoceros

Spelling Words
1. fever 2. broken 3. climate 4. hotel 5. basic 6. vocal 7. native 8. silent 9. labor 10. spider 11. label 12. icon 13. agent 14. motive 15. vital 16. acorn 17. item 18. aroma 19. legal 20. solo

Challenge Words
21. society 22. rhinoceros 23. notation 24. idealistic 25. equation

School + Home **Home Activity** Your child is learning about the long vowel VCV pattern. Say and spell words aloud with your child and ask your child to identify the long vowel sounds in each word.

▲ **Spelling Practice Book** p. 5

DAY 2 Think and Practice

TEACH

Remind students that VCV words are divided after the consonant if the first vowel has its short sound. Then write *spider* on the board and write VCV over *ide.* Say *spider* and point out that the first vowel stands for the long *i* sound. Draw a line to divide *spi-der* after the *i.* Help students discover how to divide long vowel VCV words by dividing *item* and *broken.*

VCV
spi|der

DIVIDE THE WORDS Have students read the list words, tell how to divide them, and say the vowel sound in the first syllable of each word.

HOMEWORK Spelling Practice Book, p. 6.

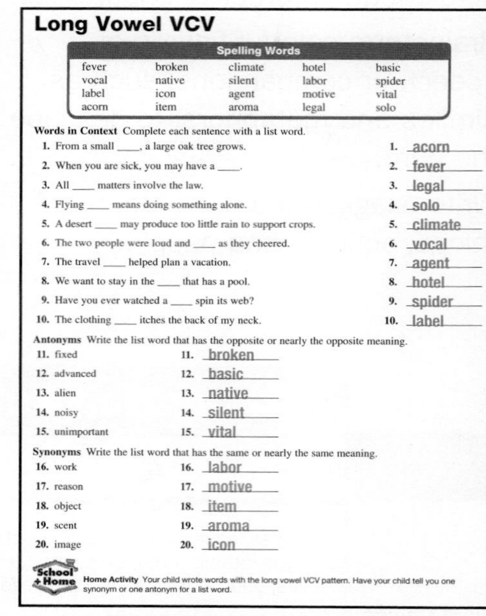

Long Vowel VCV

Spelling Words

fever	broken	climate	hotel	basic
vocal	native	silent	labor	spider
label	icon	agent	motive	vital
acorn	item	aroma	legal	solo

Words in Context Complete each sentence with a list word.

1. From a small ____, a large oak tree grows. — 1. acorn
2. When you are sick, you may have a ____. — 2. fever
3. All ____ matters involve the law. — 3. legal
4. Flying ____ means doing something alone. — 4. solo
5. A desert ____ may produce too little rain to support crops. — 5. climate
6. The two people were loud and ____ as they cheered. — 6. vocal
7. The travel ____ helped plan a vacation. — 7. agent
8. We want to stay in the ____ that has a pool. — 8. hotel
9. Have you ever watched a ____ spin its web? — 9. spider
10. The clothing ____ itches the back of my neck. — 10. label

Antonyms Write the list word that has the opposite or nearly the opposite meaning.

11. fixed — 11. broken
12. advanced — 12. basic
13. alien — 13. native
14. noisy — 14. silent
15. unimportant — 15. vital

Synonyms Write the list word that has the same or nearly the same meaning.

16. work — 16. labor
17. reason — 17. motive
18. object — 18. item
19. scent — 19. aroma
20. image — 20. icon

School + Home **Home Activity** Your child wrote words with the long vowel VCV pattern. Have your child tell you one synonym or one antonym for a list word.

▲ **Spelling Practice Book** p. 6

DAY 3 Connect to Writing

WRITE EXAGGERATIONS

Ask students to use at least four spelling words to write exaggerations such as *The climate was so hot that we had to wear potholders on our feet.*

Frequently Misspelled Words

favorite *buy*

These words may seem easy to spell, but they are often misspelled by fifth-graders. Alert students to these frequently misspelled words. Model how to pronounce all three syllables in *favorite.* Suggest that students use a phrase such as *buy us something* to remember to write the *u* in *buy.*

HOMEWORK Spelling Practice Book, p. 7.

Long Vowel VCV

Proofread a Postcard Yolanda wrote a postcard to her friend. Circle six spelling errors and one capitalization error. Write the corrections on the lines.

dear Margaret,
I'm having a great time at the hotle. There are lemon trees everywhere and the eroma from the blossoms is awesome. Today, I'm going to by some gifts. There are many nateve crafts to choose from. It's very quiet and silant here. The only noise comes from the wind and the ocean. Thank your travel agant for suggesting this place. It's now a family favorite!
Your friend,
Yolanda

1. Dear 2. hotel
3. aroma 4. buy
5. native 6. silent
7. agent

Proofread Words Circle the correct spelling of the word.

8. vocle	vocal	vocel
9. label	laebel	labal
10. brokin	brokan	broken
11. basec	basic	basuc
12. ikon	icon	ican
13. motive	motife	motove
14. akorn	acern	acorn
15. fever	fevar	feaver
16. legle	legal	leagle

Spelling Words
fever, broken, climate, hotel, basic, vocal, native, silent, labor, spider, label, icon, agent, motive, vital, acorn, item, aroma, legal, solo

Frequently Misspelled Words
favorite, buy

School + Home **Home Activity** Your child identified misspelled list words in a paragraph. Ask your child to name one list word with a long *a* sound and one with a long *o* sound.

▲ **Spelling Practice Book** p. 7

DAY 4 Review

REVIEW LONG VOWEL VCV WORDS

Have pairs of students take turns saying the first syllable of a list word and challenging their partner to finish the word. Tell students they may give a meaning clue if necessary.

Spelling Strategy

Dividing Long Words

Use syllables to make long words easier to study.

Step 1: Say the word slowly and listen for the syllables.

Step 2: Write the word and draw lines between the syllables.

Step 3: Study the word syllable by syllable.

HOMEWORK Spelling Practice Book, p. 8.

Long Vowel VCV

Spelling Words				
fever	broken	climate	hotel	basic
vocal	native	silent	labor	spider
label	icon	agent	motive	vital
acorn	item	aroma	legal	solo

Scrambled Words Unscramble the list words and write them on the line.

1. oslo	1. solo
2. calvo	2. vocal
3. marao	3. aroma
4. coin	4. icon
5. racon	5. acorn
6. ernkbo	6. broken
7. vietom	7. motive
8. vainte	8. native
9. tinsel	9. silent
10. livat	10. vital
11. baell	11. label
12. cabsi	12. basic
13. geant	13. agent
14. dresip	14. spider
15. rabol	15. labor
16. mite	16. item

Hidden Words Each of these small words can be found inside one of the list words. Write the list word that contains the small words.

17. mate	17. climate	18. ever	18. fever
19. hot	19. hotel	20. leg	20. legal

School + Home **Home Activity** Your child has unscrambled words with long vowel sounds. Ask your child to scramble two list words and see if you can unscramble them.

▲ **Spelling Practice Book** p. 8

DAY 5 Posttest

DICTATION SENTENCES

1. Stay in bed if you have a fever.
2. The old sports record has been broken.
3. People who live in a cold climate need warm clothes.
4. The hotel has a swimming pool.
5. Food is one of our basic needs.
6. Dad is vocal about his ideas.
7. Palm trees are native plants in Florida.
8. Everyone grew silent when the play began.
9. Some workers join labor unions.
10. A spider catches bugs in its web.
11. You'll find the size on the label.
12. Just click on the icon on the screen.
13. The story is about a secret agent.
14. What was the motive for the crime?
15. The heart is a vital organ.
16. The squirrel hid the acorn.
17. Which item is on sale?
18. The aroma of baking led us to the kitchen.
19. Stealing is never legal.
20. Jane played a solo at the concert.

CHALLENGE

21. The club is a secret society.
22. A rhinoceros has one big horn.
23. The actor wrote a notation on the script.
24. The plan is idealistic.
25. Can you solve the equation?

OBJECTIVES

- Formulate an inquiry question that is connected to this week's lesson focus.
- Effectively and efficiently find, evaluate, and communicate information related to an inquiry question using electronic sources.

New Literacies	
Day 1	Identify Questions
Day 2	Navigate/Search
Day 3	Analyze
Day 4	Synthesize
Day 5	Communicate

NEW LITERACIES

Internet Inquiry Activity

EXPLORE NATURE'S CHALLENGES

Use the following 5-day plan to help students conduct this week's Internet inquiry activity on nature's challenges. Remind students to follow classroom rules when using the Internet.

DAY 1

Identify Questions Discuss the lesson focus question: *How can nature challenge us?* Point out that Thunder Rose faces a powerful challenge from nature—tornadoes. Ask students to name other challenging forces of nature, such as earthquakes, and hurricanes. Brainstorm ideas for specific inquiry questions. For example: How do people prepare for earthquakes? Students can work individually, in pairs, or in small groups.

DAY 2

Navigate/Search Encourage students to use a student-friendly search engine as a research tool for their inquiries. Have them identify keywords or phrases related to the topics to help narrow their searches. Read the descriptions of the Web sites that the search engine provides with students and, if appropriate, have students bookmark the ones they think will be the most useful.

DAY 3

Analyze Have students skim and scan the Web sites they identified on Day 2. Point out that URLs are Web addresses with a dot ending. Addresses with *.gov* (government sites) or *.edu* (educational institutions) suffixes are generally reliable. After narrowing their choices of sites, students can take notes on their contents or print out the relevant pages with a teacher's permission. If possible, students can bookmark Web addresses that are frequently accessed.

DAY 4

Synthesize To synthesize information have students pull together facts and ideas from the sources they've reviewed to answer their inquiry questions. Remind students that if they lift text word-for-word from a site they must put it in quotation marks and provide a citation that gives credit to the author, publisher, and Web site.

DAY 5

Communicate Have students report to the class on their inquiry results. They can use a word processing program to create numbered lists or outlines for fact sheets on the specific natural challenges they investigated.

RESEARCH/STUDY SKILLS

Almanac

TEACH

Ask students to name a single book that can identify their state's governor, its tallest building, and its hottest day last year—a dictionary, one volume of an encyclopedia, or an almanac. Display an almanac and explain the following.

- An **almanac** is a book published yearly containing calendars, weather information, dates of holidays, and charts of current information.
- Almanacs include addresses, telephone numbers, and e-mail addresses of many agencies and organizations.
- Almanacs contain basic information about population, climate, and geography of many cities, states, and countries.
- Almanacs list well-known people and prize winners in science, sports, and the arts.
- Almanacs can be a valuable research tool.

Have students work in small groups and provide each with an almanac. Invite students to find the following information about their state: population, state motto, largest city, and names of elected officials. Then, discuss these questions:

1. What groups of people might use an almanac? *(Possible responses: Students could use an almanac to find statistics or information for a report. Farmers might use it to learn about weather patterns and predictions.)*

2. If you wanted to find out causes for the change in the unemployment rate in the U.S., would an almanac be a good source? *(No, an almanac only gives statistics; it wouldn't explain why the unemployment rate has increased or decreased.)*

3. Which city in the U.S. has the greatest population? *(New York City)*

The United States of America

President: George W. Bush (2001)
Vice President: Richard B. Cheney (2001)
Area (2003): 3,717,792 sq mi
Population (2004 est.): 293,027,571
Capital (2003 est.): Washington, DC, 570,898
Largest Cities: New York, 8,085,742 (city proper); Los Angeles, 3,819,951; Chicago, 2,869,121; Houston, 2,009,960
Monetary Unit: dollar
Languages: English, sizable Spanish speaking population

World Almanac

ASSESS

As students work with an almanac, check that they understand its purpose and are able to use the almanac to locate information.

For more practice or to assess students, use Practice Book pp. 19–20.

OBJECTIVES

- Understand types of information found in an almanac.
- Use an almanac to locate information.

Almanac

An **almanac** is a yearly book that contains calendars, weather information, and dates of holidays. Almanacs also contain charts and tables of current information in subject areas such as populations of cities and nations, and lists of recent prize winners in science, literature, and sports.

Directions Read this almanac entry about the United States Census. Use the information to answer the questions on the next page.

United States Census

Every ten years, the federal government conducts a census, or count, of the number of people who live in the United States. According to the federal Constitution, a census must be completed every ten years to determine the number of representatives each state may send to the U.S. House of Representatives.

The census shows how the populations of cities, regions, and states compare. This data helps government officials decide how and where to spend federal money. Traditionally, a census not only counts the number of citizens, but it also gathers other information, such as:

- the ethnic background of citizens
- the number of adults and children
- the number of employed people and unemployed people
- the income level of citizens and their type of housing

For many decades, the three largest cities have remained New York City, Los Angeles, and Chicago. However, other cities are growing more quickly than any of these three. Many sociologists, economists, and government officials find the growth rates of cities the most interesting information in the census. In recent years, the trend has been for great numbers of people to move from the North to the South—especially to states in the Southwest.

The federal government collects data every year, not just every decade. For instance, the chart below shows data from the 2000 census in one column, but it also includes data collected by the government in 2002. This chart shows the ten fastest growing cities of 100,000 people or more in the United States.

CITY	2000 Population	2002 Population	Numerical Change	Percentage Change
Gilbert, AZ	109,920	135,005	25,085	22.8
North Las Vegas, NV	115,488	135,902	20,414	17.7
Henderson, NV	175,750	206,153	30,403	17.3
Chandler, AZ	176,652	202,016	25,364	14.4
Peoria, AZ	108,685	123,239	14,554	13.4
Irvine, CA	143,072	162,122	19,050	13.3
Rancho Cucamonga, CA	127,743	143,711	15,968	12.5
Chula Vista, CA	173,566	193,919	20,353	11.7
Fontana, CA	128,938	143,607	14,669	11.4
Joliet, IL	106,334	118,423	12,089	11.4

▲ **Practice Book** p. 19

1. According to the U.S. Constitution, what is the maximum number of years that can pass between federal censuses?
   A census must be conducted every ten years.
2. What is the purpose of conducting a federal census, according to the U.S. Constitution?
   The purpose is to determine the number of representatives each state will send to the U.S. House of Representatives.
3. In addition to population, what are two examples of other data a census provides?
   the number of adults and children; the number of employed people and unemployed people
4. What types of people consult the federal census?
   Among others, sociologists, economists, government officials, and ordinary citizens consult the federal census.
5. What are the three largest cities in the United States?
   New York City, Los Angeles, and Chicago
6. Which state has the most listings among the fastest-growing cities on the 2002 census?
   California has the most, with four cities listed.
7. Would an almanac be a good place to find information on why nine of ten fastest-growing U.S. cities are located in the Southwest or West? Why or why not?
   Almanacs only provide statistics, so they are probably not the best resource for learning the reasons for the growth of cities.
8. Which city had the highest numerical increase in population between 2000 and 2002?
   Henderson, Nevada, had the highest increase.
9. Why is the city with the highest numerical increase in population not listed first in the chart?
   This chart is arranged by percentage change in population. Henderson, Nevada, ranks third—not first—in percentage change.
10. Between 2000 and 2002, Los Angeles (population 3,503,532) saw a numerical increase in population of 104,239. Why do you think Los Angeles isn't listed on this chart?
   Despite the high numerical increase, Los Angeles was already a big city, so this is a low percentage change.

School + Home **Home Activity** Your child learned about the contents of almanacs and analyzed data from an almanac. Together, look up information about your town or area of the country in an almanac. Read about population, weather forecast, historical sites, and so on. Discuss how the information in the almanac helps you better understand your own geographical area.

▲ **Practice Book** p. 20

Unit 1

Meeting Challenges

CONCEPT QUESTION

What kinds of challenges do people face and how do they meet them?

Week 1

How do we meet the challenges of learning?

Week 2

How can nature challenge us?

Week 3

How do people survive in the wilderness?

Week 4

How do we face personal challenges?

Week 5

What challenges do immigrants encounter?

Week 3

EXPAND THE CONCEPT

How do people survive in the wilderness?

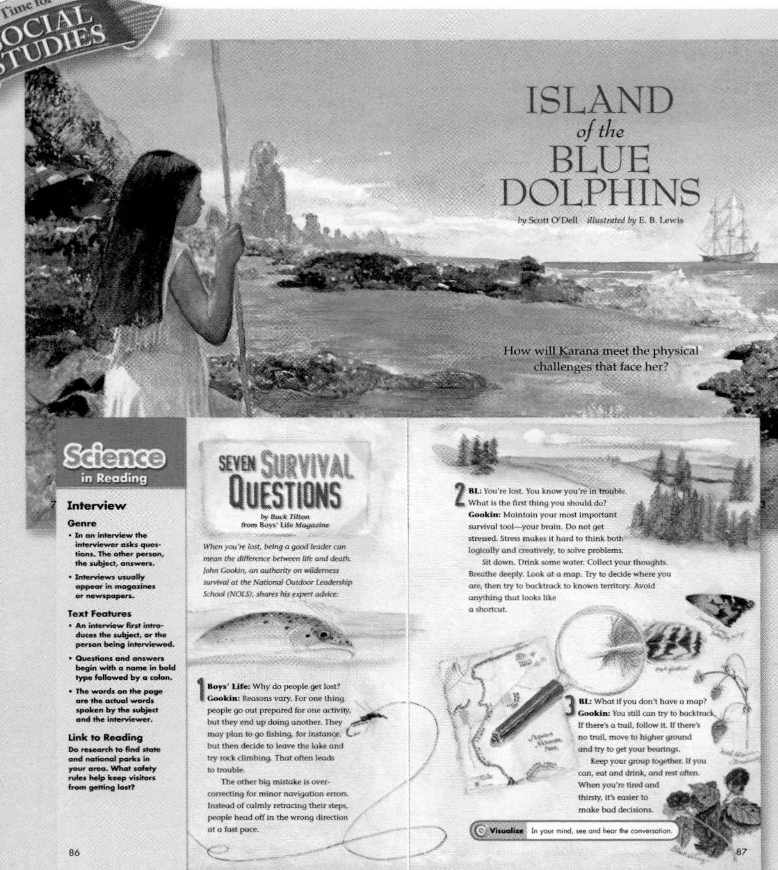

Time for SOCIAL STUDIES

ISLAND of the BLUE DOLPHINS

by Scott O'Dell illustrated by E. B. Lewis

How will Karana meet the physical challenges that face her?

Science in Reading

Interview

Genre

- In an interview the interviewer asks questions. The other person, the subject, answers.
- Interviews usually appear in magazines or newspapers.

Text Features

- An interview first introduces the subject, or the person being interviewed.
- Questions and answers begin with a name in bold type followed by a colon.
- The words on the page are the actual words spoken by the subject and the interviewer.

Link to Reading

Do research to find state and national parks in your area. What safety rules help keep visitors from getting lost?

86

SEVEN SURVIVAL QUESTIONS

by Buck Tilton from Boys' Life Magazine

When you're lost, being a good leader can mean the difference between life and death. John Gookin, an authority on wilderness survival at the National Outdoor Leadership School (NOLS), shares his expert advice:

1 **Boys' Life:** Why do people get lost?
Gookin: Reasons vary. For one thing, people go out prepared for one activity, but they end up doing another. They may plan to go fishing, for instance, but then decide to leave the lake and try rock climbing. That often leads to trouble.

The other big mistake is overcorrecting for minor navigation errors. Instead of calmly retracing their steps, people head off in the wrong direction at a fast pace.

2 **BL:** You're lost. You know you're in trouble. What is the first thing you should do?
Gookin: Maintain your most important survival tool—your brain. Do not get stressed. Stress makes it hard to think both logically and creatively, to solve problems.

Sit down. Drink some water. Collect your thoughts. Breathe deeply. Look at a map. Try to decide where you are, then try to backtrack to known territory. Avoid anything that looks like a shortcut.

3 **BL:** What if you don't have a map?
Gookin: You still can try to backtrack. If there's a trail, follow it. If there's no trail, move to higher ground and try to get your bearings.

Keep your group together. If you can, eat and drink, and rest often. When you're tired and thirsty, it's easier to make bad decisions.

Visualize In your mind, see and hear the conversation.

87

CONNECT THE CONCEPT

▶ **Build Background**

flint, gutted, quartz

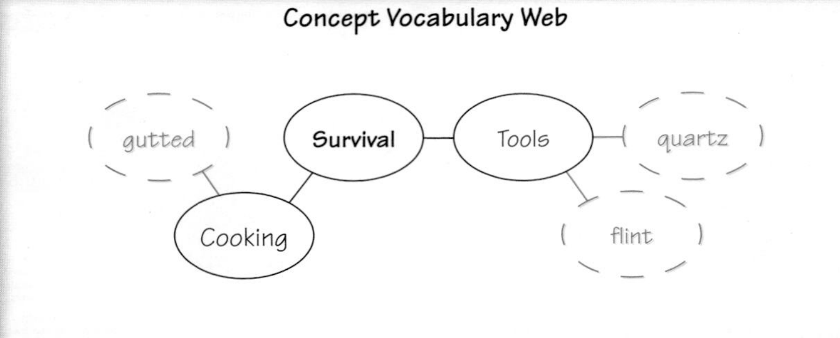

▶ **Social Studies Content**

Map and Globe Skills, Channel Islands, Native Americans

▶ **Writing**

Friendly or Thank-You Letter

▶ **Internet Inquiry**

Wilderness Survival

Preview Your Week

How do people survive in the wilderness?

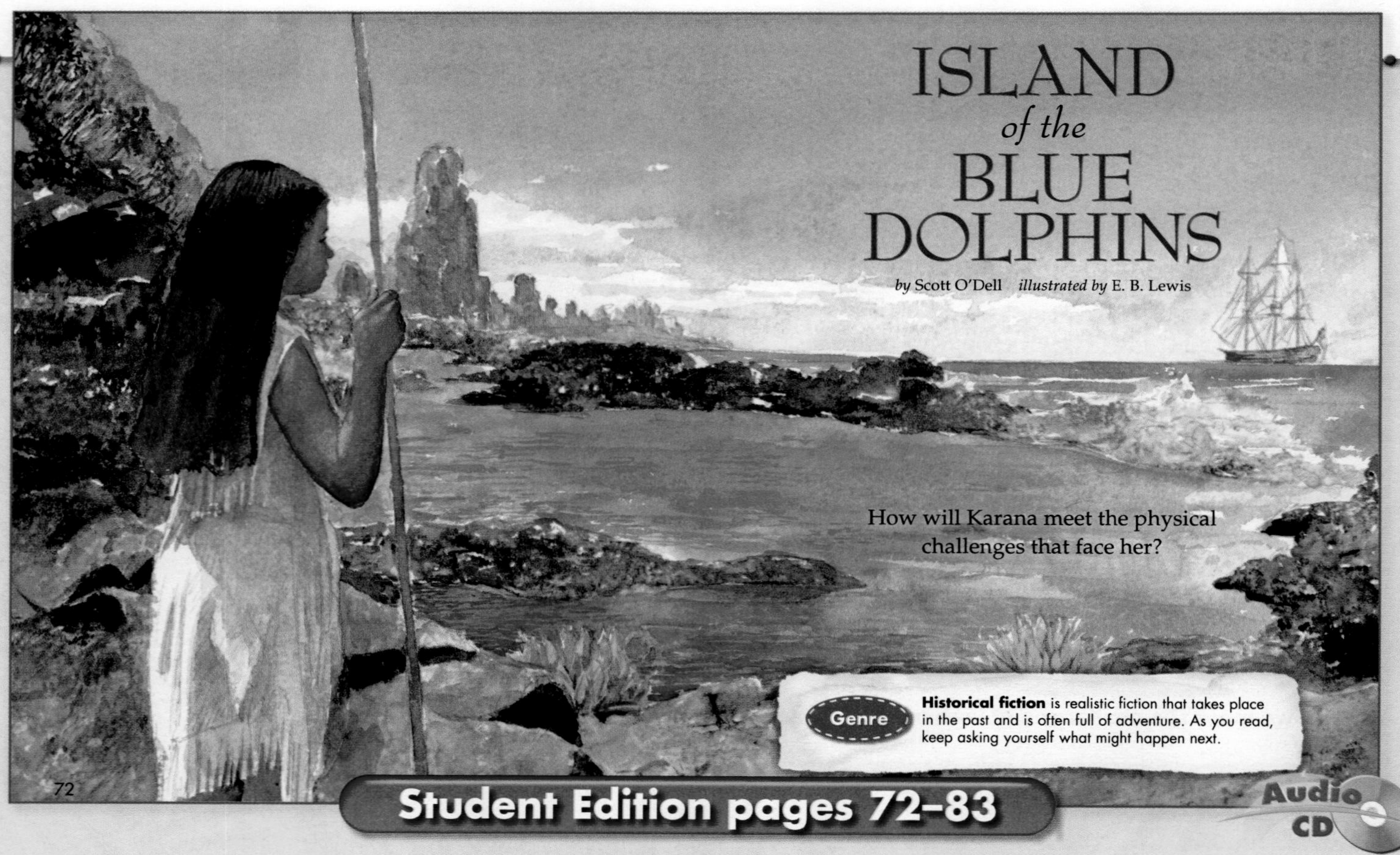

ISLAND of the BLUE DOLPHINS
by Scott O'Dell illustrated by E. B. Lewis
How will Karana meet the physical challenges that face her?
Genre
Historical fiction is realistic fiction that takes place in the past and is often full of adventure. As you read, keep asking yourself what might happen next.
72

Student Edition pages 72–83

Audio CD

Genre Historical Fiction

Vocabulary Strategy Dictionary/Glossary

Comprehension Skill Theme and Setting

Comprehension Strategy Visualize

Science

Paired Selection

Reading Across Texts

Compare Survival Tips

Genre

Interview

Text Features

Introductory Paragraph

Question-and-Answer Format

Science in Reading

Interview

Genre

- In an interview the interviewer asks questions. The other person, the subject, answers.
- Interviews usually appear in magazines or newspapers.

Text Features

- An interview first introduces the subject, or the person being interviewed.
- Questions and answers begin with a name in bold type followed by a colon.
- The words on the page are the actual words spoken by the subject and the interviewer.
- Preview the interview. How do you think reading it might help you out some day?

Link to Reading

Do research to find state and national parks in your area. What safety rules help keep visitors from getting lost?

86

SEVEN SURVIVAL QUESTIONS

by Buck Tilton from Boys' Life Magazine

When you're lost, being a good leader can mean the difference between life and death. John Gookin, an authority on wilderness survival at the National Outdoor Leadership School (NOLS), shares his expert advice:

1 **Boys' Life:** Why do people get lost?
Gookin: Reasons vary. For one thing, people go out prepared for one activity, but they end up doing another. They may plan to go fishing, for instance, but then decide to leave the lake and try rock climbing. That often leads to trouble.

The other big mistake is overcorrecting for minor navigation errors. Instead of calmly retracing their steps, people head off in the wrong direction at a fast pace.

2 **BL:** You're lost. You know you're in trouble. What is the first thing you should do?
Gookin: Maintain your most important survival tool—your brain. Do not get stressed. Stress makes it hard to think both logically and creatively, to solve problems.

Sit down. Drink some water. Collect your thoughts. Breathe deeply. Look at a map. Try to decide where you are, then try to backtrack to known territory. Avoid anything that looks like a shortcut.

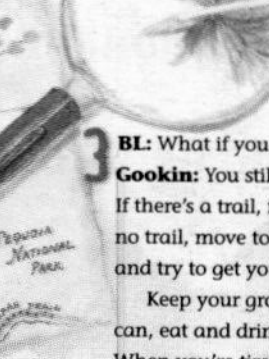

3 **BL:** What if you don't have a map?
Gookin: You still can try to backtrack. If there's a trail, follow it. If there's no trail, move to higher ground and try to get your bearings.

Keep your group together. If you can, eat and drink, and rest often. When you're tired and thirsty, it's easier to make bad decisions.

Visualize In your mind, see and hear the conversation.

Student Edition pages 86–89

Audio CD

- Student Edition
- Leveled Readers

Leveled Readers

Skill Theme and Setting

Strategy Visualize

Lesson Vocabulary

Below-Level

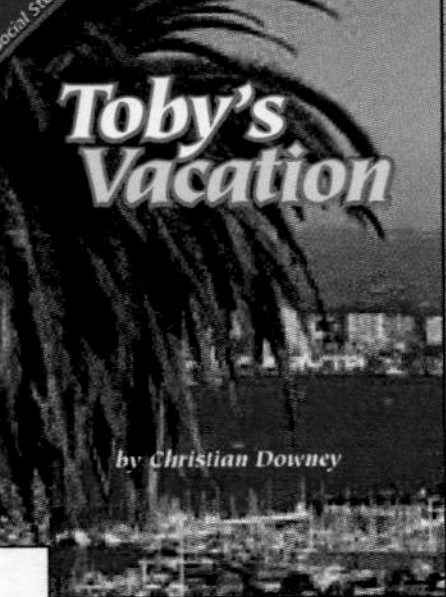

On-Level

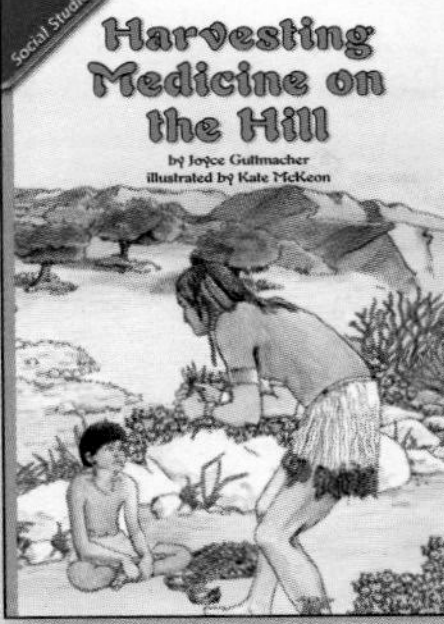

Advanced

- Concept Vocabulary
- Text Support
- Language Enrichment

Time for SOCIAL STUDIES

Integrate Social Studies Standards

- Map and Globe Skills
- Geography
- Native Americans

Island of the Blue Dolphins, pp. 72–83

"Seven Survival Questions," pp. 86–89

Leveled Readers

- Support Concepts

On-Level

- Develop Concepts

Advanced

- Extend Concepts

ELL Reader

Build **Concept Vocabulary**
Survival, pp. 68l–68m

Teach **Social Studies Concepts**
Map and Globe Skills, pp. 75, 87
Channel Islands, p. 77
Native Americans, p. 81

Explore **Social Studies Center**
Be Prepared!, p. 68k

Weekly Plan

PearsonSuccessNet.com

<table>
<tr><th></th><th>DAY 1 PAGES 68l–70b, 89a, 89e–89k</th><th>DAY 2 PAGES 70–79, 89a, 89e–89k</th></tr>
<tr><td>READING
45–90 minutes

TARGET SKILLS OF THE WEEK
Comprehension Skill
Theme and Setting
Comprehension Strategy
Visualize
Vocabulary Strategy
Dictionary/Glossary</td><td>Oral Language
QUESTION OF THE WEEK How do people survive in the wilderness?
Read Aloud: "Jenks and the Fire," 68m
Build Concepts, 68l

Comprehension/Vocabulary
Comprehension Skill/Strategy Lesson, 68–69
Theme and Setting T
Visualize
Build Background, 70a
Introduce Lesson Vocabulary, 70b
gnawed, headland, kelp, lair, ravine, shellfish, sinew T
Read Leveled Readers
Grouping Options 68f–68g

Fluency
Model Pitch, 68l–68m, 89a</td><td>Oral Language
QUESTION OF THE DAY What challenges does the setting present for Karana?

Comprehension/Vocabulary
Vocabulary Strategy Lesson, 70–71
Dictionary/Glossary T
Read Island of the Blue Dolphins, 72–79
Grouping Options 68f–68g

Theme and Setting T
Dictionary/Glossary T
REVIEW Character and Plot T
Develop Vocabulary

Fluency
Choral Reading, 89a</td></tr>
<tr><td>LANGUAGE ARTS
30–60 minutes

Trait of the Week
Organization/Paragraphs</td><td>Grammar, 89e
Introduce Independent and Dependent Clauses T
Writing Workshop, 89g
Introduce Friendly or Thank-You Letter
Model the Trait of the Week: Organization/Paragraphs
Spelling, 89i
Pretest for Long Vowel Digraphs
Internet Inquiry, 89k
Identify Questions</td><td>Grammar, 89e
Develop Independent and Dependent Clauses T
Writing Workshop, 89g
Improve Writing with Transitions
Spelling, 89i
Teach the Generalization
Internet Inquiry, 89k
Navigate/Search</td></tr>
<tr><td>DAILY WRITING ACTIVITIES</td><td>Day 1 Write to Read, 68</td><td>Day 2 Words to Write, 71
Strategy Response Log, 72, 79</td></tr>
<tr><td>DAILY SOCIAL STUDIES CONNECTIONS</td><td>Day 1 Survival Concept Web, 68l</td><td>Day 2 Time for Social Studies: Map and Globe Skills, 75; Channel Islands, 77
Revisit the Survival Concept Web, 79</td></tr>
</table>

DAILY SUCCESS PREDICTORS for Adequate Yearly Progress

Monitor Progress and Corrective Feedback

	Day 1	Day 2
Vocabulary	Check Vocabulary, *68l*	

RESOURCES FOR THE WEEK

- Practice Book, *pp. 21–30*
- Word Study and Spelling Practice Book, *pp. 9–12*
- Grammar and Writing Practice Book, *pp. 9–12*
- Selection Test, *pp. 9–12*
- Fresh Reads for Differentiated Test Practice, *pp. 13–18*
- The Grammar and Writing Book, *pp. 62–67*

Grouping Options for Differentiated Instruction

Turn the page for the small group lesson plan.

DAY 3 PAGES 80–85, 89a, 89e–89k

Oral Language

QUESTION OF THE DAY *How does Karana's personality help her survive on the isolated island?*

Comprehension/Vocabulary

Read *Island of the Blue Dolphins,* 80–84

Grouping Options 68f–68g

Theme and Setting T

Visualize

Develop Vocabulary

Reader Response

Selection Test

Fluency

Model Pitch, 89a

Grammar, 89f
Apply Independent and Dependent Clauses in Writing T

Writing Workshop, 85, 89h
Write Now
Prewrite and Draft

Spelling, 89j
Connect Spelling to Writing

Internet Inquiry, 89k
Analyze Sources

Day 3 Strategy Response Log, 82
Look Back and Write, 84

Day 3 Time for Social Studies: Native Americans, 81
Revisit the Survival Concept Web, 83

DAY 4 PAGES 86–89a, 89e–89k

Oral Language

QUESTION OF THE DAY *What physical abilities and personal qualities do you think are important in order to survive a wilderness crisis?*

Comprehension/Vocabulary

Read "Seven Survival Questions," 86–89

Grouping Options 68f–68g

Interview

Reading Across Texts

Content-Area Vocabulary

Fluency

Partner Reading, 89a

Grammar, 89f
Practice Independent and Dependent Clauses for Standardized Tests T

Writing Workshop, 89h
Draft, Revise, and Publish

Spelling, 89j
Provide a Strategy

Internet Inquiry, 89k
Synthesize Information

Day 4 Writing Across Texts, 89

Day 4 Time for Social Studies: Map and Globe Skills, 87

DAY 5 PAGES 89a–89l

Oral Language

QUESTION OF THE WEEK *To wrap up the week, revisit the Day 1 question.*

Build Concept Vocabulary, 89c

Fluency

Read Leveled Readers

Grouping Options 68f–68g

Assess Reading Rate, 89a

Comprehension/Vocabulary

Reteach Theme and Setting, 89b T

Imagery, 89b

Review Dictionary/Glossary, 89c T

Speaking and Viewing, 89d
Group Review
Analyze Media

Grammar, 89f
Cumulative Review

Writing Workshop, 89h
Connect to Unit Writing

Spelling, 89j
Posttest for Long Vowel Digraphs

Internet Inquiry, 89k
Communicate Results

Research/Study Skills, 89l
SPQ3R

Day 5 Imagery, 89b

Day 5 Revisit the Survival Concept Web, 89c

KEY ◎ = Target Skill T = Tested Skill

Comprehension	Fluency	Vocabulary
Check Retelling, *84*	Check Fluency WCPM, *89a*	Check Vocabulary, *89c*

SUCCESS PREDICTOR

Small Group Plan *for Differentiated Instruction*

Daily Plan AT A GLANCE

Reading

Whole Group
- Oral Language
- Comprehension/Vocabulary

Group Time

Differentiated Instruction

Meet with small groups to provide:
- Skill Support
- Reading Support
- Fluency Practice

Read

This week's lessons for daily group time can be found behind the Differentiated Instruction (DI) tab on pp. DI • 22–DI • 31.

Whole Group
- Fluency

Language Arts
- Grammar
- Writing
- Spelling
- Research/Inquiry
- Speaking/Listening/Viewing

Use *My Sidewalks on Reading Street* for Tier III intensive reading intervention.

DAY 1

On-Level	Strategic Intervention	Advanced
Teacher-Led *Page DI • 23* • Develop Concept Vocabulary • **Read** On-Level Reader *Toby's Vacation*	**Teacher-Led** *Page DI • 22* • Reinforce Concepts • **Read** Below-Level Reader *Stuk's Village*	**Teacher-Led** *Page DI • 23* • **Read** Advanced Reader *Harvesting Medicine on the Hill* • Independent Extension Activity

Independent Activities

While you meet with small groups, have the rest of the class...

- Visit the Reading/Library Center
- Listen to the Background Building Audio
- Finish Write to Read, p. 68
- Complete Practice Book pp. 23–24
- Visit Cross-Curricular Centers

DAY 2

On-Level	Strategic Intervention	Advanced
Teacher-Led *Pages 74–79* • **Read** *Island of the Blue Dolphins*	**Teacher-Led** *Page DI • 24* • Practice Lesson Vocabulary • Read Multisyllabic Words • **Read** or Listen to *Island of the Blue Dolphins*	**Teacher-Led** *Page DI • 25* • Extend Vocabulary • **Read** *Island of the Blue Dolphins*

Independent Activities

While you meet with small groups, have the rest of the class...

- Visit the Reading/Library Center
- Listen to the AudioText for *Island of the Blue Dolphins*
- Finish Words to Write, p. 71
- Complete Practice Book pp. 25–26
- Write in their Strategy Response Logs, pp. 72, 79
- Visit Cross-Curricular Centers
- Work on inquiry projects

DAY 3

On-Level	Strategic Intervention	Advanced
Teacher-Led *Pages 80–83* • **Read** *Island of the Blue Dolphins*	**Teacher-Led** *Page DI • 26* • Practice Theme and Setting and Visualize • **Read** or Listen to *Island of the Blue Dolphins*	**Teacher-Led** *Page DI • 27* • Extend Theme and Setting and Visualize • **Read** *Island of the Blue Dolphins*

Independent Activities

While you meet with small groups, have the rest of the class...

- Visit the Reading/Library Center
- Listen to the AudioText for *Island of the Blue Dolphins*
- Write in their Strategy Response Logs, p. 82
- Finish Look Back and Write, p. 84
- Complete Practice Book p. 27
- Visit Cross-Curricular Centers
- Work on inquiry projects

1 Begin with whole class skill and strategy instruction.

2 Meet with small groups to provide differentiated instruction.

3 Gather the whole class back together for fluency and language arts.

DAY 4

On-Level	Strategic Intervention	Advanced
Teacher-Led *Pages 86–89* **Read** "Seven Survival Questions"	**Teacher-Led** *Page DI • 28* • Practice Retelling • **Read** or Listen to "Seven Survival Questions"	**Teacher-Led** *Page DI • 29* • **Read** "Seven Survival Questions" • Genre Study

Independent Activities

While you meet with small groups, have the rest of the class...

- Visit the Reading/Library Center
- Listen to the AudioText for "Seven Survival Questions"
- Visit the Writing/Vocabulary Center
- Finish Writing Across Texts, p. 89
- Visit Cross-Curricular Centers
- Work on inquiry projects

DAY 5

On-Level	Strategic Intervention	Advanced
Teacher-Led *Page DI • 31* **Reread** Leveled Reader *Toby's Vacation* Retell *Toby's Vacation*	**Teacher-Led** *Page DI • 30* • **Reread** Leveled Reader *Stuk's Village* • Retell *Stuk's Village*	**Teacher-Led** *Page DI • 31* • **Reread** Leveled Reader *Harvesting Medicine on the Hill* • Share Extension Activity

Independent Activities

While you meet with small groups, have the rest of the class...

- Visit the Reading/Library Center
- Complete Practice Book pp. 28–30
- Visit Cross-Curricular Centers
- Work on inquiry projects

ELL

Grouping Place English language learners in the groups that correspond to their reading abilities in English.

Use the appropriate Leveled Reader or other text at students' instructional level.

TIP Send home the appropriate Multilingual Summary of the main selection on Day 1.

Take It to the NET™ ONLINE
PearsonSuccessNet.com

Camille Blachowicz
For ideas and activities to develop vocabulary, see a summary of the book *Teaching Vocabulary in All Classrooms* by Scott Foresman author Camille Blachowicz and Peter Fisher.

TEACHER TALK

Rich instruction is a technique for teaching vocabulary. Students encounter a set of words in multiple contexts and manipulate the words in varied ways for deep processing.

Be sure to schedule time for students to work on the unit inquiry project "Facing Challenges." This week students analyze their information.

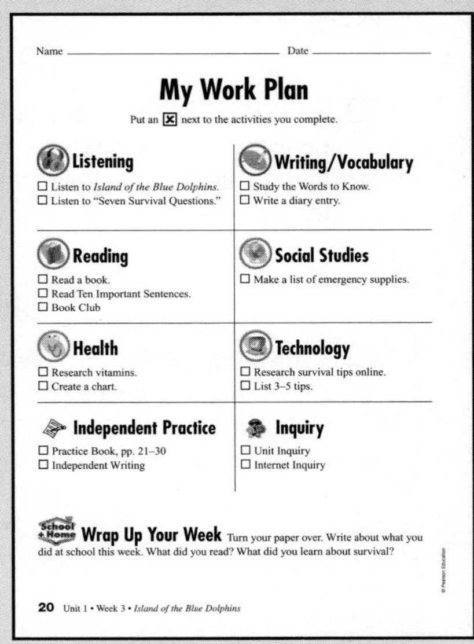

Name ____ Date ____

My Work Plan

Put an ☒ next to the activities you complete.

Listening
☐ Listen to *Island of the Blue Dolphins*.
☐ Listen to "Seven Survival Questions."

Writing/Vocabulary
☐ Study the Words to Know.
☐ Write a diary entry.

Reading
☐ Read a book.
☐ Read Ten Important Sentences.
☐ Book Club

Social Studies
☐ Make a list of emergency supplies.

Health
☐ Research vitamins.
☐ Create a chart.

Technology
☐ Research survival tips online.
☐ List 3–5 tips.

Independent Practice
☐ Practice Book, pp. 21–30
☐ Independent Writing

Inquiry
☐ Unit Inquiry
☐ Internet Inquiry

Wrap Up Your Week Turn your paper over. Write about what you did at school this week. What did you read? What did you learn about survival?

20 Unit 1 • Week 3 • *Island of the Blue Dolphins*

▲ **Group-Time Survival Guide** p. 20, Weekly Contract

Customize Your Plan by Stran

ORAL LANGUAGE

Concept Development

How do people survive in the wilderness?

CONCEPT VOCABULARY
flint *gutted* *quartz*

BUILD

❑ **Question of the Week** Introduce and discuss the question of the week. This week students will read a variety of texts and work on projects related to the concept *survival*. Post the question for students to refer to throughout the week. DAY 1 *68d*

❑ **Read Aloud** Read aloud "Jenks and the Fire." Then begin a web to build concepts and concept vocabulary related to this week's lesson and the unit theme, Meeting Challenges. Introduce the concept words *flint, gutted,* and *quartz* and have students place them on the web. Display the web for use throughout the week. DAY 1 *68l–68m*

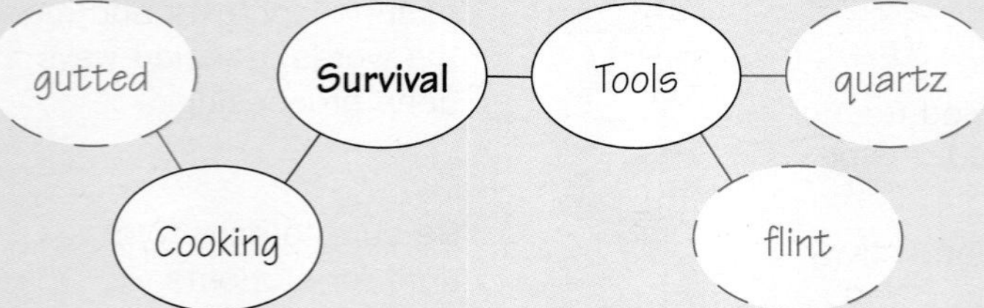

DEVELOP

❑ **Question of the Day** Use the prompts from the Weekly Plan to engage students in conversations related to this week's reading and the unit theme. EVERY DAY *68d–68e*

❑ **Concept Vocabulary Web** Revisit the Survival Concept Web and encourage students to add concept words from their reading and life experiences. DAY 2 *79*, DAY 3 *83*

CONNECT

❑ **Looking Back/Moving Forward** Revisit the Survival Concept Web and discuss how it relates to this week's lesson and the unit theme. Then make connections to next week's lesson. DAY 5 *89c*

CHECK

❑ **Concept Vocabulary Web** Use the Survival Concept Web to check students' understanding of the concept vocabulary words *flint, gutted,* and *quartz*. DAY 1 *68l*, DAY 5 *89c*

VOCABULARY

STRATEGY DICTIONARY/GLOSSARY When reading you may come across a word you do not know. Using a glossary or dictionary will help find the meaning of the word. A glossary is a list of important words in a book and their meanings. A dictionary lists all words, in alphabetical order, and gives their meanings, pronunciations, and other helpful information.

LESSON VOCABULARY
gnawed *ravine*
headland *shellfish*
kelp *sinew*
lair

TEACH

❑ **Words to Know** Give students the opportunity to tell what they already know about this week's lesson vocabulary words. Then discuss word meaning. DAY 1 *70b*

❑ **Vocabulary Strategy Lesson** Use the vocabulary strategy lesson in the Student Edition to introduce and model this week's strategy, *dictionary/glossary*. DAY 2 *70–71*

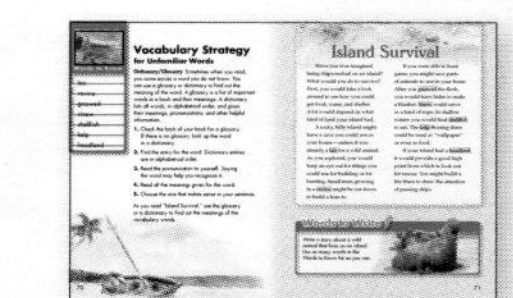

Vocabulary Strategy Lesson

PRACTICE/APPLY

❑ **Leveled Text** Read the lesson vocabulary in the context of leveled text. DAY 1 *LR19–LR27*

Leveled Readers

❑ **Words in Context** Read the lesson vocabulary and apply *dictionary/glossary* in the context of *Island of the Blue Dolphins*. DAY 2 *72–79*, DAY 3 *80–84*

Main Selection—Fiction

❑ **Writing/Vocabulary Center** Write a diary entry imagining you were surviving alone outdoors for several days. ANY DAY *68k*

❑ **Homework** Practice Book pp. 24–25. DAY 1 *70b*, DAY 2 *71*

❑ **Word Play** Have students work in small groups to brainstorm lists of ocean-related compound words. ANY DAY *89c*

ASSESS

❑ **Selection Test** Use the Selection Test to determine students' understanding of the lesson vocabulary words. DAY 3

RETEACH/REVIEW

❑ **Reteach Lesson** If necessary, use this lesson to reteach and review *dictionary/glossary*. DAY 5 *89c*

1 Use assessment data to determine your instructional focus.

2 Preview this week's instruction by strand.

3 Choose instructional activities that meet the needs of your classroom.

COMPREHENSION

SKILL THEME AND SETTING The theme is the underlying meaning of a story and is often not stated. The setting is where and when the story takes place.

STRATEGY VISUALIZE Visualizing, or creating pictures of the story in your mind using sights, smells, sounds, tastes, and feelings, can help you understand the setting, the characters, and the events better.

TEACH

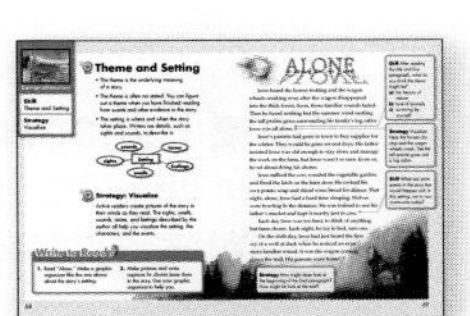
Skill/Strategy Lesson

- ❑ **Skill/Strategy Lesson** Use the skill/strategy lesson in the Student Edition to introduce and model *theme and setting* and *visualize*. DAY 1 *68-69*
- ❑ **Extend Skills** Teach imagery. **ANY DAY** *89b*

PRACTICE/APPLY

Leveled Readers

Main Selection—Fiction

Paired Selection—Nonfiction

- ❑ **Leveled Text** Apply *theme and setting* and *visualize* to read leveled text. DAY 1 *LR19-LR27*
- ❑ **Skills and Strategies in Context** Read *Island of the Blue Dolphins,* using the Guiding Comprehension questions to apply *theme and setting* and *visualize*. DAY 2 *72-79,* DAY 3 *80-84*
- ❑ **Skills and Strategies in Context** Read "Seven Survival Questions," guiding students as they apply *theme and setting* and *visualize*. Then have students discuss and write across texts. DAY 4 *86-89*
- ❑ **Homework** Practice Book pp. 23, 27, 28. DAY 1 *69,* DAY 3 *83,* DAY 5 *89b*
- ❑ **Fresh Reads for Differentiated Test Practice** Have students practice *theme and setting* with a new passage. DAY 3

ASSESS

- ❑ **Selection Test** Determine students' understanding of the selection and their use of *theme and setting*. DAY 3
- ❑ **Retell** Have students retell *Island of the Blue Dolphins*. DAY 3 *84-85*

RETEACH/REVIEW

- ❑ **Reteach Lesson** If necessary, reteach and review *theme and setting*. DAY 5 *89b*

FLUENCY

SKILL PITCH Pitch is the ability to add expression to your voice. By changing your pitch, a drop in pitch at periods and a rise in pitch at question marks, you will help listeners understand dialogue and important moments in the text.

TEACH

- ❑ **Read Aloud** Model fluent reading by rereading "Jenks and the Fire." Focus on this week's fluency skill, pitch. DAY 1 *68l-68m, 89a*

PRACTICE/APPLY

- ❑ **Choral Reading** Read aloud selected paragraphs from *Island of the Blue Dolphins,* emphasizing the change in pitch. Then practice as a class, doing three choral readings of the selected paragraphs. DAY 2 *89a,* DAY 3 *89a*
- ❑ **Partner Reading** Have partners practice reading aloud, reading with varying pitch and offering each other feedback. As students reread, monitor their progress toward their individual fluency goals. DAY 4 *89a*
- ❑ **Listening Center** Have students follow along with the AudioText for this week's selections. **ANY DAY** *68j*
- ❑ **Reading/Library Center** Have students reread a selection of their choice. **ANY DAY** *68j*
- ❑ **Fluency Coach** Have students use Fluency Coach to listen to fluent readings or practice reading on their own. **ANY DAY**

ASSESS

- ❑ **Check Fluency WCPM** Do a one-minute timed reading, paying special attention to this week's skill—pitch. Provide feedback for each student. DAY 5 *89a*

Customize Your Plan by Strand

GRAMMAR

SKILL INDEPENDENT AND DEPENDENT CLAUSES A related group of words with a subject and a predicate is called a *clause*. A clause that makes sense by itself is an *independent clause*. A clause that does not make sense by itself is a *dependent clause*.

TEACH

- ❑ **Grammar Transparency 3** Use Grammar Transparency 3 to teach independent and dependent clauses. DAY 1 *89e*

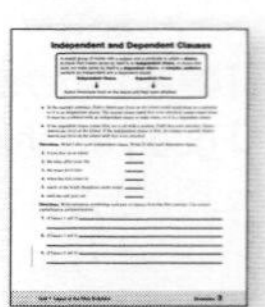

Grammar Transparency 3

PRACTICE/APPLY

- ❑ **Develop the Concept** Review the concept of independent and dependent clauses and provide guided practice. DAY 2 *89e*
- ❑ **Apply to Writing** Have students review something they have written and apply independent and dependent clauses. DAY 3 *89f*
- ❑ **Test Preparation** Examine common errors in independent and dependent clauses to prepare for standardized tests. DAY 4 *89f*
- ❑ **Homework** Grammar and Writing Practice Book pp. 9–11. DAY 2 *89e*, DAY 3 *89f*, DAY 4 *89f*

ASSESS

- ❑ **Cumulative Review** Use Grammar and Writing Practice Book p. 12. DAY 5 *89f*

RETEACH/REVIEW

- ❑ **Daily Fix-It** Have students find and correct errors in grammar, spelling, and punctuation. **EVERY DAY** *89e–89f*
- ❑ **The Grammar and Writing Book** Use pp. 62–65 of The Grammar and Writing Book to extend instruction for independent and dependent clauses. **ANY DAY**

The Grammar and Writing Book

WRITING

Trait of the Week

ORGANIZATION/PARAGRAPHS Good writers have organization to their writing. Their ideas are written in an order that helps readers understand and that shows logical connections among those ideas.

TEACH

- ❑ **Writing Transparency 3A** Use the model to introduce and discuss the Trait of the Week. DAY 1 *89g*
- ❑ **Writing Transparency 3B** Use the transparency to show students how transitions can improve their writing. DAY 2 *89g*

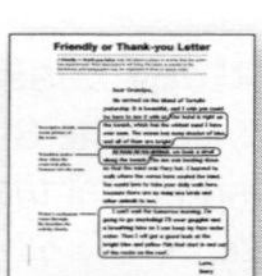

Writing Transparency 3A

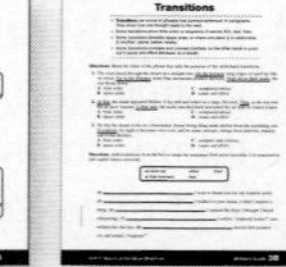

Writing Transparency 3B

PRACTICE/APPLY

- ❑ **Write Now** Examine the model on Student Edition p. 85. Then have students write their own friendly or thank-you letter. DAY 3 *85, 89h*, DAY 4 *89h*

  Prompt In *Island of the Blue Dolphins,* the narrator describes a place as she might in a letter to a friend. Think about a place you could describe. Now write a friendly or thank-you letter about the place.

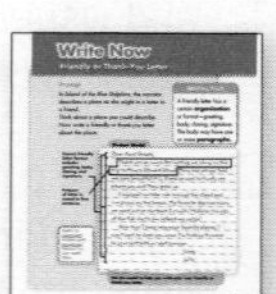

Write Now p. 85

- ❑ **Writing/Vocabulary Center** Write a diary entry imagining you were surviving alone outdoors for several days. **ANY DAY** *68k*

ASSESS

- ❑ **Writing Trait Rubric** Use the rubric to evaluate students' writing. DAY 4 *89h*

RETEACH/REVIEW

- ❑ **The Grammar and Writing Book** Use pp. 62–67 of The Grammar and Writing Book to extend instruction for independent and dependent clauses, transitions, and friendly or thank-you letters. **ANY DAY**

The Grammar and Writing Book

❶ Use assessment data to determine your instructional focus.

❷ Preview this week's instruction by strand.

❸ Choose instructional activities that meet the needs of your classroom.

SPELLING

GENERALIZATION LONG VOWEL DIGRAPHS Long *a* is sometimes spelled *ai*: *paint*. Long *e* is sometimes spelled *ee* or *ea*: *speech, feast*. Long *o* is sometimes spelled *oa* or *ow*: *coast, arrow*. If a word has two vowels in a row, the first vowel is usually long, and the second vowel is silent.

TEACH

- ❑ **Pretest** Give the pretest for words with long vowel digraphs. Guide students in self-correcting their pretests and correcting any misspellings. **DAY 1** *89i*
- ❑ **Think and Practice** Connect spelling to the phonics generalization for long vowel digraphs. **DAY 2** *89i*

PRACTICE/APPLY

- ❑ **Connect to Writing** Have students use spelling words to write about famous people. Then review frequently misspelled words: *Halloween, really*. **DAY 3** *89j*
- ❑ **Homework** Word Study and Spelling Practice Book pp. 9–12. **EVERY DAY**

RETEACH/REVIEW

- ❑ **Review** Review spelling words to prepare for the posttest. Then provide students with a spelling strategy—rhyming helpers. **DAY 4** *89j*

ASSESS

- ❑ **Posttest** Use dictation sentences to give the posttest for words with long vowel digraphs. **DAY 5** *89j*

Spelling Words

1. coast*	8. needle	15. breeze
2. feast	9. charcoal	16. willow
3. speech	10. praise	17. appeal
4. wheat	11. faint	18. bowling
5. Spain	12. maintain	19. complain
6. paint	13. crease	20. sneeze
7. arrow*	14. groan	

Challenge Words

21. dungarees	23. campaign	25. referee
22. bungalow	24. speedometer	

*Word from the selection

RESEARCH AND INQUIRY

- ❑ **Internet Inquiry** Have students conduct an Internet inquiry on wilderness survival. **EVERY DAY** *89k*
- ❑ **SPQ3R** Review the meaning and steps in **SPQ3R** (**S**urvey, **P**redict, **Q**uestion, **R**ead, **R**ecite, and **R**eview) and discuss how students can use this strategy to help understand nonfiction text. **DAY 5** *89l*
- ❑ **Unit Inquiry** Allow time for students to analyze the information they have gathered for their "Facing Challenges" project. **ANY DAY** *17*

SPEAKING AND VIEWING

- ❑ **Group Review** Have students work in small groups to reread *Island of the Blue Dolphins* and discuss the literary features of the story. **DAY 5** *89d*
- ❑ **Analyze Media** Have students discuss part of a TV show or movie that has a focus on surviving outdoors, on land or water. Follow up with a class discussion. **DAY 5** *89d*

Resources for

Differentiated Instruction

LEVELED READERS

- **Comprehension**
  - **Skill** Setting/Theme
  - **Strategy** Visualize
- **Lesson Vocabulary**
  - Dictionary/Glossary

- **Social Studies Standards**
  - Map and Globe Skills
  - Geography
  - Native Americans

PearsonSuccessNet.com

Use the Online Database of over 600 books to

- Download and print additional copies of this week's leveled readers.
- Listen to the readers being read online.
- Search for more titles focused on this week's skills, topic, and content.

On-Level

On-Level Reader

Name________ Toby's Vacation

Setting and Theme

- **Setting** is the time and place in which the story occurs.
- **Theme** is the subject or idea of a story.

Directions Based on your understanding of *Toby's Vacation*, answer the questions below.
Possible responses given.

1. What is the setting of the story?
   the Channel Islands
2. What is the story's theme?
   If everybody respects nature, plants and animals can be saved from extinction.
3. Does the theme depend on the setting of the story? Why or why not?
   Responses will vary. Yes. The setting is a place where animals live undisturbed.
4. What is another setting where the theme of the story would still be the same? Why?
   a forest Responses will vary.

© Pearson Education 5

On-Level Practice TE p. LR23

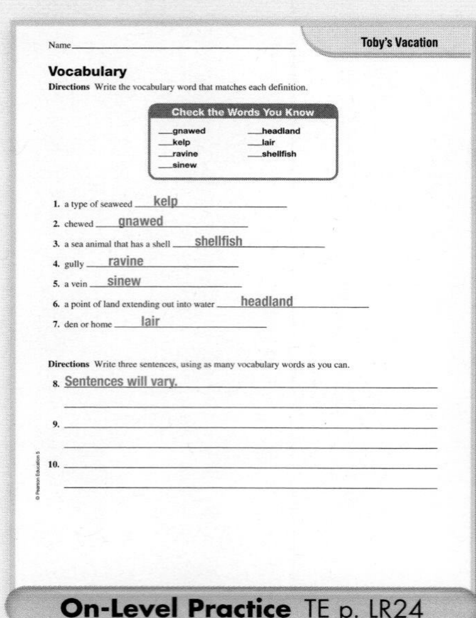
Name________ Toby's Vacation

Vocabulary

Directions Write the vocabulary word that matches each definition.

Check the Words You Know
___gnawed ___headland
___kelp ___lair
___ravine ___shellfish
___sinew

1. a type of seaweed kelp
2. chewed gnawed
3. a sea animal that has a shell shellfish
4. gully ravine
5. a vein sinew
6. a point of land extending out into water headland
7. den or home lair

Directions Write three sentences, using as many vocabulary words as you can.

8. Sentences will vary.
9. ________
10. ________

© Pearson Education 5

On-Level Practice TE p. LR24

Strategic Intervention

Below-Level Reader

Name________ Stuk's Village

Setting and Theme

Setting is the time and place in which the story occurs.
Theme is the subject or idea that a story is about.

Directions Based on your understanding of *Stuk's Village*, answer the questions below.
Possible responses given.

1. What is the setting of the story?
   The village of Shisholop.
2. How would the story be different if it were set in a different time?
   There would be easier, more modern ways to make crafts and get food.
3. What is the story's theme?
   The canoes that Stuk's family builds are very important to the whole village.
4. Does the theme depend on the setting of the story?
   Yes. The setting is at a time and place where Native Americans didn't have modern conveniences, so they had to trade to survive.

© Pearson Education 5

Below-Level Practice TE p. LR20

Name________ Stuk's Village

Vocabulary

Directions Use the vocabulary words in the box to fill in the blanks in the sentences below.

1. The fish hide in the kelp.
2. The dog gnawed on the bone.
3. My family eats shellfish on Fridays.
4. The ravine flooded when it rained a lot.
5. We made rope from the animal's sinew.
6. She stood on the headland to see the boats coming.

Check the Words You Know
___gnawed
___headland
___kelp
___ravine
___shellfish
___sinew

Directions For each group of words below, write the vocabulary word that belongs with the group.

7. gully, valley, ravine
8. tendon, vein, sinew
9. den, home, lair
10. chewed, nibbled, gnawed

© Pearson Education 5

Below-Level Practice TE p. LR21

Advanced

Advanced Reader

Name ____________ Harvesting Medicine

Setting and Theme

- **Setting** is the time and place in which a story occurs.
- **Theme** is the subject or idea that a story is about.

Directions Based on your understanding of *Harvesting Medicine on the Hill*, answer the questions below.

Possible responses given.

1. What is the setting of the story?
nature's pharmacy of flowers, roots, and leaves

2. What is the story's theme?
Red Hawk is learning from his grandfather about the different healing plants.

3. Does the theme depend on the setting of the story? Why or why not?
Yes. The setting is a place where Native Americans lived and where there were many plants.

Advanced Practice TE p. LR26

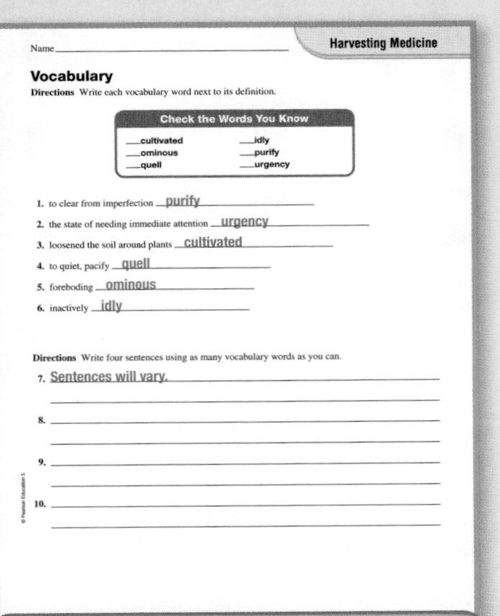

Name ____________ Harvesting Medicine

Vocabulary

Directions Write each vocabulary word next to its definition.

Check the Words You Know	
___cultivated	___idly
___ominous	___purify
___quell	___urgency

1. to clear from imperfection purify
2. the state of needing immediate attention urgency
3. loosened the soil around plants cultivated
4. to quiet, pacify quell
5. foreboding ominous
6. inactively idly

Directions Write four sentences using as many vocabulary words as you can.

7. Sentences will vary.
8.
9.
10.

Advanced Practice TE p. LR27

ELL

ELL Reader

ELL Poster 3

Teacher's Edition Notes

ELL notes throughout this lesson support instruction and reference additional resources at point of use.

Teaching Guide pp. 15–21, 216–217

- Multilingual summaries of the main selection
- Comprehension lesson
- Vocabulary strategies and word cards
- ELL Reader 5.1.3 lesson

ELL and Transition Handbook

Ten Important Sentences

- Key ideas from every selection in the Student Edition
- Activities to build sentence power

More Reading

Readers' Theater Anthology

- Fluency practice
- Five scripts to build fluency
- Poetry for oral interpretation

Leveled Trade Books

- Extended reading tied to the unit concept
- Lessons in the Trade Book Library Teaching Guide

Homework

- Family Times Newsletter
- ELL Multilingual Selection Summaries

Take-Home Books

- Leveled Readers

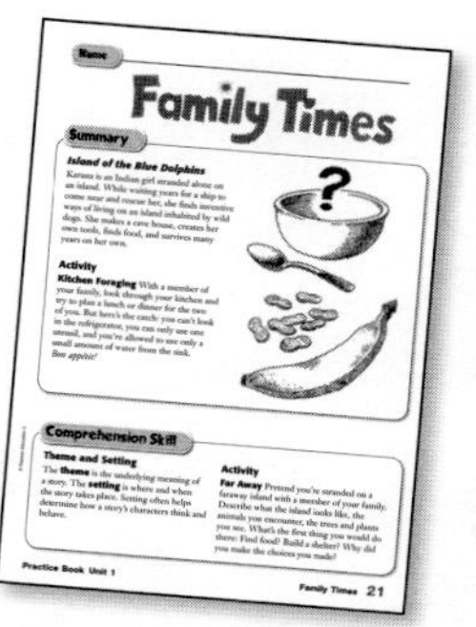

Cross-Curricular Centers

Listening

Listen to the *Selections*

MATERIALS
CD player, headphones, AudioText CD, student book

SINGLES

LISTEN TO LITERATURE Listen to *Island of the Blue Dolphins* and "Seven Survival Questions" as you follow or read along in your book. Listen for details about the setting and theme of the story.

If there is anything you don't understand, you can listen again to any section.

ISLAND of the BLUE DOLPHINS

by Scott O'Dell illustrated by E. B. Lewis

How will Karana meet the physical challenges that face her?

Science in Reading

SEVEN SURVIVAL QUESTIONS

Audio CD

Reading/ Library

Read It Again!

MATERIALS
Collection of books for self-selected reading, reading logs, student book

SINGLES
PAIRS
GROUPS

Select a book you have already read. Record the title of the book in your reading log. You may want to read with a partner.

Choose from the following:

- **Leveled Readers**
- **ELL Readers**
- **Stories Written by Classmates**
- **Books from the Library**
- ***Island of the Blue Dolphins***

TEN IMPORTANT SENTENCES Read the Ten Important Sentences for *Island of the Blue Dolphins*. Then locate the sentences in the student book.

BOOK CLUB Organize a book discussion on *Island of the Blue Dolphins*. Discuss the challenges Karana faced and how you might deal with similar situations.

Health

Research Nutrition

MATERIALS
Research materials, Internet access, writing materials

SINGLES

In *Island of the Blue Dolphins*, Karana was able to find food and water to survive. Find out about three kinds of vitamins you need in order to survive and be healthy.

1. **Use the Internet and other research materials to gather information on vitamins important for your health.**
2. **Create a chart showing at least three different types of vitamins. Under each type, list some of the foods that are good sources of the vitamin.**

EARLY FINISHERS Create a lunch menu that contains foods with all three vitamins.

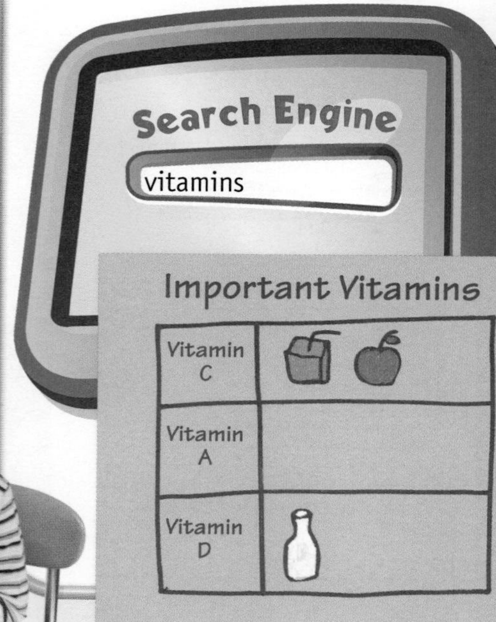

Scott Foresman Reading Street Centers Survival Kit

Use the *Island of the Blue Dolphins* materials from the Reading Street Centers Survival Kit to organize this week's centers.

Writing/ Vocabulary

Write a Diary Entry

MATERIALS
Writing materials

SINGLES

Imagine that you were faced with the challenge of surviving alone outdoors for several days.

1. **Write a diary entry describing the imaginary situation.**
2. **Include some of the things you thought about, imagined, or felt while you were alone.**

EARLY FINISHERS Make a list of ten items that you would pack if you had to survive alone outdoors for several days.

Today was my first full day alone on the mountain.

Social Studies

Be Prepared!

MATERIALS
Writing and art materials

SINGLES

Prepare an emergency kit for your home.

1. **Think about the types of emergencies your family might face and the supplies and phone numbers you would need.**
2. **Make a list of the supplies and phone numbers.**

EARLY FINISHERS Draw and label the supplies in your home emergency kit.

Technology

Research Survival Tips

MATERIALS
Internet access, writing materials

SINGLES

Use a student-friendly search engine to conduct an Internet search to find survival tips.

1. **Focus on tips for surviving severe weather such as a flood, hurricane, or blizzard.**
2. **List 3–5 survival tips.**

EARLY FINISHERS Use the information you gathered to write a mini-handbook of survival tips.

Weather Survival Tips
1. Keep a positive attitude and remain calm.
2.
3.

DAY 1

Build Concepts

FLUENCY

MODEL PITCH As you read "Jenks and the Fire," use your tone of voice to model the correct pitch for reading fiction. Lower your voice to indicate straight narration and raise it to indicate dialogue or an important moment, such as when Jenks learns how to start a fire.

LISTENING COMPREHENSION

After reading "Jenks and the Fire," use the following questions to assess listening comprehension.

1. **Describe the time and place for this story.** *(Possible responses: Evening outside in a clearing of a thick forest with a stream nearby; by a small campfire with sticks and rocks)* ***Setting***
2. **What lesson does Jenks learn?** *(Possible response: He teaches himself how to build a fire without matches, how to roast a fish, and how to be respectful of nature.)* ***Theme***

BUILD CONCEPT VOCABULARY

Start a web to build concepts and vocabulary related to this week's lesson and the unit theme.

- Draw the Survival Concept Web.
- Read the sentence with the word *quartz* again. Ask students to pronounce *quartz* and discuss its meaning.
- Place *quartz* in an oval attached to *Tools.* Explain that *quartz* is related to the concept of tools found in nature. Read the sentences in which *flint* and *gutted* appear. Have students pronounce the words, place them on the web, and provide reasons.
- Brainstorm additional words and categories for the web. Keep the web on display and add words throughout the week.

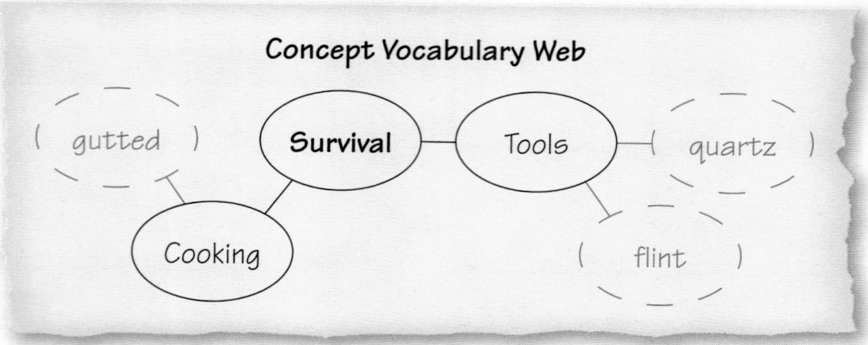

OBJECTIVES

- Build vocabulary by finding words related to the lesson concept.
- Listen for clues about setting and theme.

Concept Vocabulary

flint hard, gray or brown stone that makes a spark when struck against steel

gutted removed the intestines of

quartz hard mineral made of silicon and oxygen found in many different kinds of rocks

Monitor Progress

Check Vocabulary

If...	then...
students are unable to place words on the web,	review the lesson concept. Place the words on the web and provide additional words for practice, such as *blazing* and *squatted.*

SUCCESS PREDICTOR

DAY 1 Grouping Options

Reading

Whole Group
Introduce and discuss the Question of the Week. Then use pp. 68l–70b.

Group Time
Differentiated Instruction
Read this week's Leveled Readers. See pp. 68h–68i for the small group lesson plan.

Whole Group
Use p. 89a.

Language Arts
Use pp. 89e–89k.

JENKS AND THE FIRE

BY DONNA LATHAM

Jenks hadn't planned on laboring so long to prepare the trout. Washed, scaled, nd gutted it was ready to roast. Yet, he suddenly realized, there was no fire. He adn't even located a fire area. Sunshine faded along with Jenks' spirits.

"I should've built the fire first," Jenks moaned. "Before the sun started to set." is heart thumped wildly in his chest. Blood roared in his ears, and he gulped air ith ragged gasps.

"Don't panic," he ordered himself. "That's the first rule of survival."

Fear rooted him in place. The longer he delayed, the darker the sky grew.

"What'll happen to me if I can't build the fire?" he wondered. "I'll freeze to eath, all alone. Or ravenous animals—bears, panthers—will surround me."

Surrounding him now, the sky turned steely gray. Its dreariness smothered the last its of the sun's gold.

"Snap out of it," Jenks said. "Hurry."

He rapidly selected a fire area and hunched over it. With the calloused tips of his ngers, he clawed away prickly weeds and revealed bare earth.

Next, Jenks built a miniature mound of dry grass and parched pine needles. ristles bit his palms. Stacking dry twigs, he constructed a tiny teepee around it.

"Perfect," he cried with soaring confidence. "Almost finished."

The fire would start instantly. Jenks was certain. All he had to do now was plunk lit match into the gaps between the twigs. The grasses heaped beneath them ould burst into flames.

Jenks yanked a box of matches from his pocket and fumbled to open it. He gawked t its contents. His heart stampeded into his throat. A single match remained.

"Hey, no pressure." Jenks chuckled despite himself.

He firmly brushed the match against the scratch pad. *Pfft!* With a sizzle, the flame ared. It glowed blue and yellow on the wooden match. Jenks sighed in relief.

Whoosh! A sudden gust of wind blasted over Jenks. It knocked the cap from his ead and extinguished his flame.

"No, no! I don't believe this," Jenks cried. He rocked forward, clunking his head on scratchy rock. He quickly grasped the rock to toss it aside, but stopped. He lifted it to is eyes and peered closely. Quartz, clear and smooth, peeked from its tip.

In a flash, Jenks ripped a pocketknife from his belt hook. He huddled over his eepee and smacked the quartz against the knife like a flint. A spark flashed, and he tinder ignited. He fueled the flames with knobby branches.

With his fire blazing, Jenks realized he was starving.

"Cooking time—finally," he said.

BEFORE READING

Read ALOUD

Activate Prior Knowledge

Before students listen to the Read Aloud, ask them what they know about surviving in the wild.

Set Purpose

Read aloud the title and have students predict what the selection will be about.

Read the introduction aloud. Have students listen for clues to the setting.

Creative Response

Have partners create a scene depicting Jenks cleaning up after his dinner of trout and extinguishing the fire. Invite volunteers to read their scenes in front of the class. ***Drama***

Access Content Before reading, share this summary: Jenks is alone in the wilderness. He has a fish to cook, but he waits until after dark to start a fire. He makes a fire using a rock and a knife, and then he cooks the fish.

Homework Send home this week's Family Times newsletter.

SUCCESS PREDICTOR

BEFORE READING

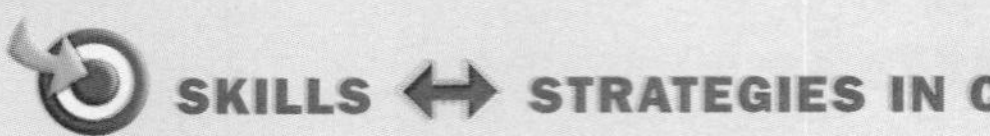

Theme and Setting Visualize

OBJECTIVES

- Identify theme and setting.
- Use visualizing to better understand the theme and setting.

Skills Trace

Theme and Setting

Introduce/Teach	**TE: 5.1 18–19, 68–69; 5.5 512–513**
Practice	Practice Book: 3, 7, 8, 16, 23, 26, 27, 28, 96, 203, 207, 208
Reteach/Review	TE: 5.1 41b, 49, 61, 77, 89b, DI•52, DI•54; 5.2 237; 5.5 535b, DI•52
Test	Selection Test: 1–4, 9–12, 81–84; Benchmark Test: Unit 1

INTRODUCE

Read the following: *I love to visit my grandmother. The air in her house is always filled with soft, soothing music and the smell of hot, sweet desserts. My feet feel so good when they sink into her thick, warm carpet.* Have students name the place you are describing. *(grandmother's house)* Ask them to tell what you are trying to say about your grandmother's house. *(It is a nice place to visit.)*

Have students read the information on p. 68. Explain the following:

- *Setting* is where and when a story happens.
- *Theme* is the idea that holds a story together.
- *Visualizing* what happens in a story can help you understand the theme and setting.

Use Skill Transparency 3 to teach theme and setting and visualize.

Comprehension

Skill
Theme and Setting

Strategy
Visualize

- The theme is the underlying meaning of a story.
- The theme is often not stated. You can figure out a theme when you have finished reading from events and other evidence in the story.
- The setting is where and when the story takes place. Writers use details, such as sights and sounds, to describe it.

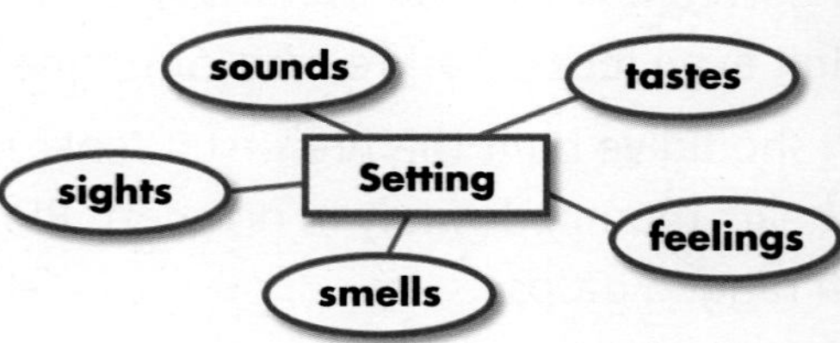

Strategy: Visualize

Active readers create pictures of the story in their minds as they read. The sights, smells, sounds, tastes, and feelings described by the author all help you visualize the setting, the characters, and the events.

Write to Read

1. Read "Alone." Make a graphic organizer like the one above about the story's setting.
2. Make pictures and write captions for chores Jesse does in the story. Use your graphic organizer to help you.

68

Strategic Intervention

Theme and Setting Reread the information about theme. Have a volunteer paraphrase the definition of this term. Then draw an organizer like the one shown on page 68. Ask a volunteer to name a place to write in the middle, and then brainstorm as a group the sensory details that relate to the place.

Access Content

Beginning/Intermediate For a Picture It! lesson on theme and setting, see ELL Teaching Guide, pp. 15–16.

Advanced Before students read "Alone," ask them to look carefully at the picture and talk about the setting. Provide language as needed.

ALONE

Jesse heard the horses trotting and the wagon heels creaking even after the wagon disappeared to the thick forest. Soon, those familiar sounds faded. hen he heard nothing but the summer wind rustling e tall prairie grass surrounding his family's log cabin. sse was all alone.

Jesse's parents had gone to town to buy supplies for e winter. They would be gone several days. His father sisted Jesse was old enough to stay alone and manage e work on the farm, but Jesse wasn't so sure. Even so, set about doing his chores.

Jesse milked the cow, weeded the vegetable garden, nd fixed the latch on the barn door. He cooked his wn potato soup and sliced some bread for dinner. That ght, alone, Jesse had a hard time sleeping. Wolves ere howling in the distance. He was trained to use his ther's musket and kept it nearby just in case.

Each day Jesse was too busy to think of anything ut farm chores. Each night, he lay in bed, nervous.

On the sixth day, Jesse had just heard the first y of a wolf at dusk when he noticed an even ore familiar sound. It was the wagon coming own the trail. His parents were home!

1 Skill After reading the title and first paragraph, what do you think the theme might be?
a) the beauty of nature
b) love of animals
c) surviving by yourself

2 Strategy Visualize: Hear the horses clip-clop and the wagon wheels creak. See the tall prairie grass and a log cabin.

3 Skill What are some events in the story that would happen only in this setting, not in your community today?

4 Strategy How might Jesse look at the beginning of the final paragraph? How might he look at the end?

69

Available as **Skill Transparency** 3

TEACH

1 SKILL Model how to consider the theme of a story.

Think Aloud **MODEL** I know that theme usually has something to do with characters and events. I see that Jesse watches the wagon pull away. He is alone. This tells me that *c* must be the correct answer. I'll read on to confirm that this is the theme.

2 STRATEGY Use paragraph 1 to model how to visualize.

Think Aloud **MODEL** Details like "horses trotting," "wheels creaking," and "rustling the tall prairie grass" help me see and hear the setting of this story in my mind. These details also help me understand how alone Jesse is.

PRACTICE AND ASSESS

3 SKILL Possible responses: people traveling by horse and wagon; taking several days to go to town and back; wolves howling

4 STRATEGY Possible response: He might look scared at the beginning of the paragraph and then really relieved and happy at the end.

WRITE Have students complete steps 1 and 2 of the Write to Read activity. You might consider using this as a whole-class activity.

Monitor Progress

Theme and Setting

If... students are unable to complete **Write to Read** on p. 68,	**then...** use Practice Book p. 23 to provide additional practice.

eme and Setting

- The **theme** is the underlying meaning of a story. It is often not stated. You can figure out a theme from events and other evidence in the story.
- The **setting** is where and when the story takes place. Writers use details, such as sights and sounds, to describe it.

ctions Read the following passage. Then complete the diagram with the sights, sounds, ls, or feelings expressed in the passage.

I love to go to the beach in the summer, because a beach can excite the senses. I might hear the roaring waves or the squawk of seagulls. I might feel the gritty warmth of the sand underfoot. Even the mix of odors on the breeze—an airy freshness with a hint of rotting fish—can stay with me long after I've left the water's edge. When I look out toward the vast horizon over the water, I feel as free as the birds darting and diving above my head, and as small as the grains of sand blowing across my toes.

Possible answers given for 1, 3–5.

roaring waves
Setting
2. a beach in summer
3. gritty warmth of sand
smell of fish
seagulls' cries

What is the theme of the passage?

A person's senses are awakened at the beach.

Visualize that you are on a beach. On a separate piece of paper, list a few of the sights, sounds, smells, or feelings you included in your scene.

I imagined the sound of people laughing, the smell of sunscreen, the coolness of the water, and the sight of children.

ool ome **Home Activity** Your child identified the setting and theme in a fictional passage. Sit with your child in a familiar place and identify its sights, sounds, and smells.

Practice Book p. 23

Build Background

ACTIVATE PRIOR KNOWLEDGE

CREATE A CONCEPT WEB about the Pacific coast.

- Give students ten minutes to fill in a concept web.
- Have them start by writing *Pacific coast* in the center oval. Ask them to brainstorm things they know about the Pacific coast in the outer ovals.
- Encourage students to fill in as many ovals as they can and to add more if needed.

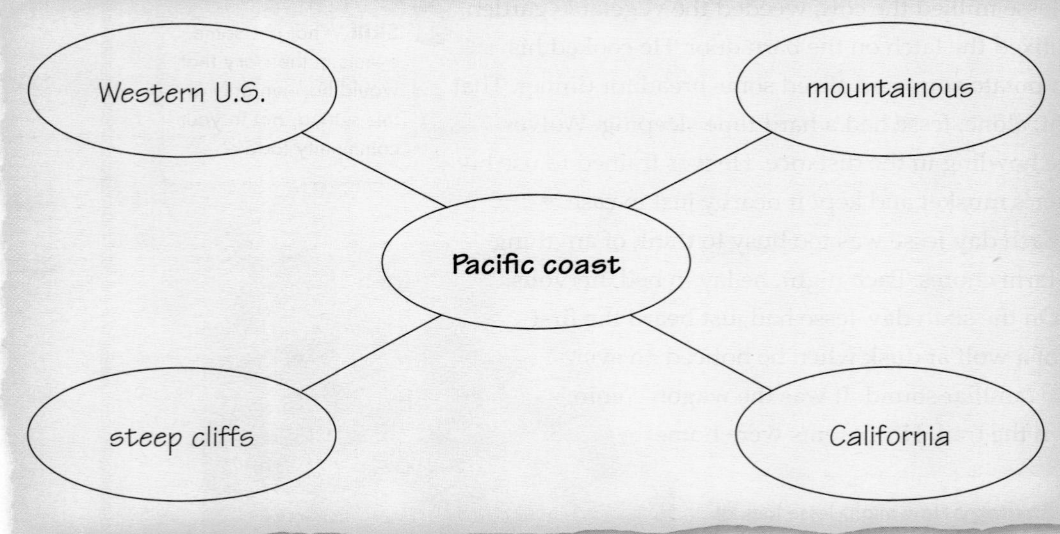

▲ **Graphic Organizer** 15

BACKGROUND BUILDING AUDIO This week's audio explores challenges of surviving in the wilderness and information about the basic necessities of life. After students listen, discuss what they learned and what surprised them the most about the challenges.

Background Building Audio

Tech Files ONLINE

Students can use the keyword *wilderness survival* to search the Internet for more information about this subject. Be sure to follow classroom guidelines for Internet use.

ELL

Build Background Use ELL Poster 3 to build background and vocabulary for the lesson concept of surviving in the wild.

▲ **ELL Poster** 3

Introduce Vocabulary

FOUR-COLUMN CHART

Make a four-column chart for the vocabulary words. Use the titles *Word, Synonym, Antonym,* and *Sentence.*

Word	Synonym	Antonym	Sentence
1. headland	highland	lowland	I could see the ocean from the edge of the headland.
2.			
3.			
4.			

▲ **Graphic Organizer** 27

Read each word and have students place the words in the first column. Have students share where they may have seen some of these words.

Activate Prior Knowledge

Point out that some of this week's words are environmental words *(lair, ravine, headland, cove)* and students may learn new definitions for these words.

Environmental Words

Have students work with a partner and choose four words from the list and fill in the chart with a synonym, antonym, and a sentence example. Have students leave columns for any words they don't know blank. Students can fill them in later in the week.

Use the Multisyllabic Word Routine on p. DI·1 to help students read multisyllabic words.

Lesson Vocabulary

WORDS TO KNOW

T gnawed bitten at or worn away
T headland a narrow ridge of high land jutting out into the water
T kelp any of various large, tough, brown seaweeds
T lair den or resting place of a wild animal
T ravine a long, deep, narrow, valley eroded by running water
T shellfish a water animal with a shell
T sinew tendon

MORE WORDS TO KNOW

brackish slightly salty
cove a small, sheltered bay; inlet on a shore
deafening very loud; amazingly noisy

T = Tested Word

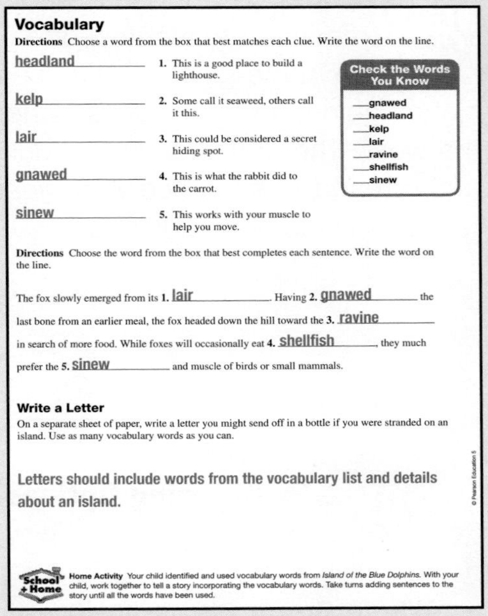

Vocabulary

Directions Choose a word from the box that best matches each clue. Write the word on the line.

headland 1. This is a good place to build a lighthouse.
kelp 2. Some call it seaweed, others call it this.
lair 3. This could be considered a secret hiding spot.
gnawed 4. This is what the rabbit did to the carrot.
sinew 5. This works with your muscle to help you move.

Check the Words You Know
___gnawed
___headland
___kelp
___lair
___ravine
___shellfish
___sinew

Directions Choose the word from the box that best completes each sentence. Write the word on the line.

The fox slowly emerged from its **1.** lair. Having **2.** gnawed the last bone from an earlier meal, the fox headed down the hill toward the **3.** ravine in search of more food. While foxes will occasionally eat **4.** shellfish, they much prefer the **5.** sinew and muscle of birds or small mammals.

Write a Letter

On a separate sheet of paper, write a letter you might send off in a bottle if you were stranded on an island. Use as many vocabulary words as you can.

Letters should include words from the vocabulary list and details about an island.

School + Home **Home Activity** Your child identified and used vocabulary words from *Island of the Blue Dolphins.* With your child, work together to tell a story incorporating the vocabulary words. Take turns adding sentences to the story until all the words have been used.

▲ **Practice Book** p. 24

DAY 2

Vocabulary Strategy

OBJECTIVE

Use a dictionary or glossary to determine word meaning.

INTRODUCE

Discuss the strategy for using a dictionary or glossary by following the steps on p. 70.

TEACH

- Have students read "Island Survival," paying attention to how vocabulary is used.
- Model using a glossary to find the meaning of *sinew*.

Think Aloud **MODEL** I'm not sure what *sinew* means in this selection so I'll look it up in the glossary. I'll use the pronunciation guide in parentheses to help me say the word. The definition is "tendon." I go back and reread the sentence with *sinew* to see if tendon makes sense. It does.

Words to Know

- lair
- ravine
- gnawed
- sinew
- shellfish
- kelp
- headland

Vocabulary Strategy for Unfamiliar Words

Dictionary/Glossary Sometimes when you read, you come across a word you do not know. You can use a glossary or dictionary to find out the meaning of the word. A glossary is a list of important words in a book and their meanings. A dictionary lists all words, in alphabetical order, and gives their meanings, pronunciations, and other helpful information.

1. Check the back of your book for a glossary. If there is no glossary, look up the word in a dictionary.
2. Find the entry for the word. Dictionary entries are in alphabetical order.
3. Read the pronunciation to yourself. Saying the word may help you recognize it.
4. Read all the meanings given for the word.
5. Choose the one that makes sense in your sentence.

As you read "Island Survival," use the glossary or a dictionary to find out the meanings of the vocabulary words.

70

DAY 2 Grouping Options

Reading

Whole Group Discuss the Question of the Day. Then use pp. 70–73.

Group Time Differentiated Instruction

Read *Island of the Blue Dolphins.* See pp. 68h–68i for the small group lesson plan.

Whole Group Use p. 89a.

Language Arts

Use pp. 89e–89k.

Strategic Intervention

Dictionary/Glossary Walk students through the steps of finding a word in the glossary or a dictionary. Then give partners the words *lair* and *ravine* to find in the glossary or dictionary.

Access Content Use ELL Poster 3 to preteach vocabulary. Choose from the following to meet language proficiency levels.

Beginning Use the Multilingual Lesson Vocabulary list that begins on p. 272 of the ELL Teaching Guide, as well as other home-language resources, to provide translations of the tested words.

Intermediate Have students use a T-chart labeled *word* and *definition* to make their own dictionary of the vocabulary words.

Advanced Teach the lesson on pp. 70–71. Have students complete the four-column chart they began on p. 70b for the remaining words.

Resources for home-language words may include parents, bilingual staff members, bilingual dictionaries, or online translation sources.

Island Survival

Have you ever imagined being shipwrecked on an island? What would you do to survive? First, you would take a look around to see how you could get food, water, and shelter. A lot would depend on what kind of land your island had.

A rocky, hilly island might have a cave you could use as your home—unless it was already a lair for a wild animal. As you explored, you would keep an eye out for things you could use for building or for hunting. Small trees growing in a ravine might be cut down to build a lean-to.

If you were able to hunt game, you might save parts of animals to use in your home. After you gnawed the flesh, you would have hides to make a blanket. Sinew could serve as a kind of rope. In shallow waters you would find shellfish to eat. The kelp floating there could be used as "wallpaper" or even as food.

If your island had a headland, it would provide a good high point from which to look out for rescue. You might build a fire there to draw the attention of passing ships.

Words to Write

Write a story about a wild animal that lives on an island. Use as many words in the Words to Know list as you can.

71

PRACTICE AND ASSESS

- Have students use their glossaries or dictionaries to find meanings of the remaining lesson vocabulary words.
- Remind students that a dictionary lists all the meanings of a word. They should read all the meanings before deciding which one fits best in the story or selection they are reading.
- If you began a four-column chart (p. 70b), have students complete it now or see if they can think of more synonyms and antonyms to add to the chart.
- Have students complete Practice Book p. 25.

WRITE Students' stories should include vocabulary words that relate to island animals, including *lair, gnawed, sinew, kelp,* and *shellfish.* Remind students to consult the glossary or a dictionary for help with word meanings.

Monitor Progress

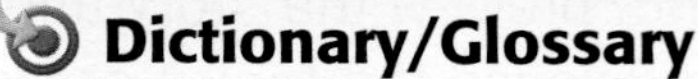

Dictionary/Glossary

If... students need more practice with the lesson vocabulary,	**then...** use Tested Vocabulary Cards.

Vocabulary • Unfamiliar Words

- When you see an unfamiliar word, use a dictionary or glossary to learn the word's meaning.
- A **dictionary** lists words in alphabetical order and gives their meanings, pronunciations, and other helpful information. A **glossary** is a list of important words and their meanings that are used in a book.

Directions Read the following passage about fishermen. Then answer the questions below. Look up unfamiliar words in a dictionary or glossary.

People who make their living from the ocean need more than good fishing skills. Of course they need to know about what kinds of shellfish live in the area, and how much kelp floats in the waters they fish. But they also need to know about water quality: how brackish is the water? Is it polluted? Knowing which are the best fishing coves and how near the shore the larger fish travel is essential. We view a coastline from a headland and appreciate its beauty, but a fisherman sees a completely different world. He or she sees a deep-sea ravine, the lair of a myriad of different fish. Many fishing decisions are left to the brain of the person fishing, not his or her luck, muscle, or sinew.

1. What is *kelp?* Why should people who fish for a living know about kelp?
   seaweed; Possible answer: Where there is kelp, there are likely to be fish.
2. How do *shellfish* differ from other fish?
   Shellfish have shells, whereas other fish do not.
3. If you are standing on a *headland,* where is the water?
   It is beneath you.
4. What is a *lair?* How does it apply to schools of fish?
   a hiding place; Possible answer: It is the place where the fish spend their time.
5. What does *myriad* mean? Would a person who fishes for a living be pleased to see a myriad of fish?
   many; Yes, because there would be many fish to catch.

School + Home **Home Activity** Your child identified and used vocabulary words from a passage about fishermen. Read a nonfiction article with your child. Have him or her point out unfamiliar words. Together, look up the words in a dictionary or glossary.

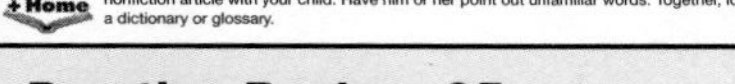

▲ **Practice Book** p. 25

BEFORE READING

Prereading Strategies

OBJECTIVES

- Identify setting and theme to improve comprehension.
- Use setting to visualize parts of the story.

GENRE STUDY

Historical Fiction

Island of the Blue Dolphins is historical fiction. Explain that historical fiction is a combination of imagination and fact, with fictional characters and plot placed in a factual historical setting.

PREVIEW AND PREDICT

Have students preview the story title and illustrations and discuss the topics or ideas they think it will cover. Have students use selection vocabulary words as they talk about what they expect to learn.

Strategy Response Log

Predict Have students try to picture the home that Karana will make for herself on the island. Have students describe their predictions in their strategy response logs. Students will check their predictions in the Strategy Response Log activity on p. 79.

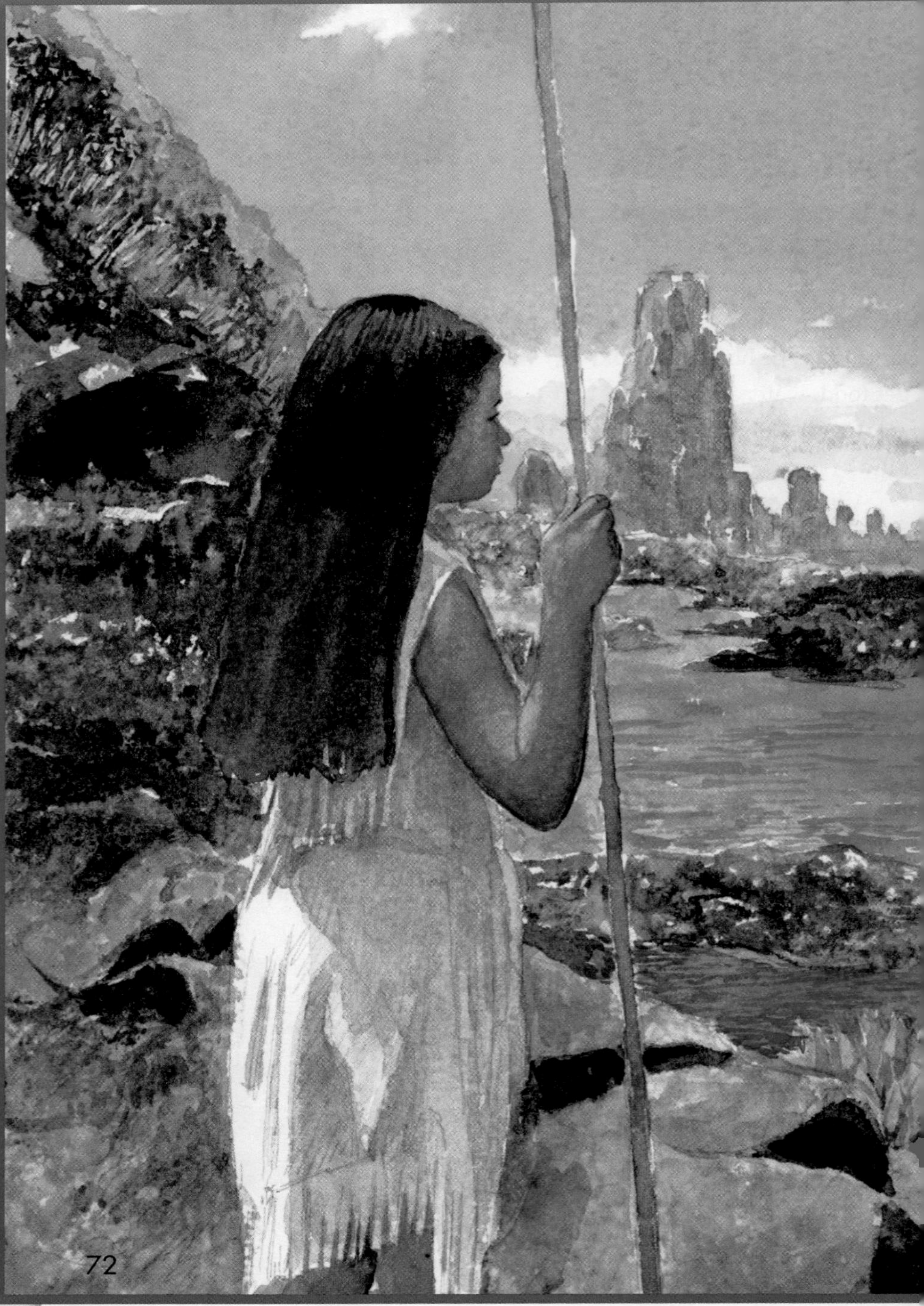

72

Access Content Lead students on a picture walk to identify things Karana will encounter on the island.

Consider having students read the story summary in English or in students' home languages. See the Multilingual Summaries in the ELL Teaching Guide, pp. 19–21.

ISLAND
of the
BLUE
DOLPHINS
by Scott O'Dell illustrated by E. B. Lewis
How will Karana meet the physical challenges that face her?
Genre
Historical fiction is realistic fiction that takes place in the past and is often full of adventure. As you read, keep asking yourself what might happen next.
73

SET PURPOSE

Discuss the illustration on pp. 72–73. Ask students where they think the character is and what she is doing. Ask them what they hope to find out about her as they read.

Remind students to think about the setting and theme of the story as they read.

STRATEGY RECALL

Students have now used these before-reading strategies:

- preview the selection to be aware of its genre, features, and possible content;
- activate prior knowledge about that content and what to expect of that genre;
- make predictions;
- set a purpose for reading.

Remind students to be aware of and flexibly use the during-reading strategies they have learned:

- link prior knowledge to new information;
- summarize text they have read so far;
- ask clarifying questions;
- answer questions they or others pose;
- check their predictions and either refine them or make new predictions;
- recognize the text structure the author is using, and use that knowledge to make predictions and increase comprehension;
- visualize what the author is describing;
- monitor their comprehension and use fix-up strategies.

After reading, students will use these strategies:

- summarize or retell the text;
- answer questions they or others pose;
- reflect to make new information become part of their prior knowledge.

AudioText

DURING READING

Guiding Comprehension

1 **Setting • Inferential**
Reread p. 75. Describe the setting of this historical fiction story.
This story is set on an island called the Island of the Blue Dolphins. The island has a cove, springs, rocks, and headland. The weather is both clear and windy.

Monitor Progress

Setting and Theme

If... students are unable to determine the setting,	**then...** use the skill and strategy instruction on p. 75.

2 **Compare and Contrast • Inferential**
How was the spring Karana visited near the dog's lair different from the spring near the headland?
The spring near the dog's lair had a steadier flow of water, was easier to reach, and was near a cliff that provided shelter.

3 **Theme • Critical**
Based on pp. 74–75, what do you think the big idea, or theme, for the story will be?
Possible response: I think the big idea or theme for this story will be overcoming obstacles and surviving on your own.

Students can use a student-friendly search engine and the keywords *California history* or *California islands* to learn more about the setting of this story. Be sure to follow classroom guidelines for Internet use.

From 1835 to 1853, a young Native American girl named Karana lived alone on a rugged island seventy-five miles off the coast of California. The author has fashioned this story out of the few facts known about her.

Karana and her people lived on the island until Aleut hunters killed some of the men. A friendly ship later took her people off the island, but she stayed there to be with her brother, who was left behind by the ship's crew. After her brother was killed by wild dogs, Karana faced the challenge of living alone on the island.

74

Extend Language Point to the word *spring* and tell students that it is a multiple-meaning word. Help them identify as many meanings as they can (a season, a metal coil, a jump or leap, and a place where underground water comes out of the earth). Ask students which meaning the author uses here.

The Island of the Blue Dolphins was my home; I had no other. It would be my home until the white men returned in their ship. But even if they came soon, before next summer, I could not live without a roof or a place to store my food. I would have to build a house. But where?

That night I slept on the rock, and the next day I began the search. The morning was clear, but to the north, banks of clouds hung low. Before long they would move in across the island, and behind them many other storms were waiting. I had no time to waste.

I needed a place that was sheltered from the wind, not too far from Coral Cove, and close to a good spring. There were 1 two such places on the island—one on the headland and the other less than a league to the west. The headland seemed to be the more favorable of the two, but since I had not been to the other for a long time, I decided to go there and make certain.

The first thing I found, which I had forgotten, was that this place was near the wild dogs' lair. As soon as I drew near to it the leader came to the opening of the cave and watched me with his yellow eyes. If I built a hut here I would have to kill him and his pack. I planned to do this anyway, but it would take much time.

The spring was better than the one near the headland, being less brackish and having a steadier flow of water. Besides it was much easier to reach, since it came from the side of a hill and  not from a ravine as the other one did. It was also close to the cliff and a ridge of rocks which would shelter my house. 

75

Map and Globe Skills

Time for SOCIAL STUDIES

A map or globe could provide a visual representation of Karana's island's location and distance in relation to the mainland and other landmarks. Karana lived on one of the Channel Islands, located less than 100 miles off the coast of Southern California in the Pacific Ocean.

  SKILLS ↔ STRATEGIES IN CONTEXT

Setting and Theme

TEACH

- Remind students that a setting is the time and place in which a story occurs.
- A theme is the big idea that the reader determines from the setting, events, and characters in a story.
- Model finding the setting on p. 75.

MODEL I know that the setting is the time and place in which a story takes place so I am going to look for clues about the time and place. The first paragraph on p. 75 tells me that the Island of the Blue Dolphins is Karana's home. The second paragraph says that there are rocks and that the weather is clear but storms are coming. From the third paragraph, I learn that there is a cove, a spring, and a headland on the island and that it can be windy.

PRACTICE AND ASSESS

Have students reread p. 75. Have them use details provided about the setting to determine which of the following is the theme for the selection. *(Choice b)*

a) Wild dogs killed Karana's brother.

b) Karana faced challenges living alone on the island.

c) A friendly ship took Karana's people off the island.

EXTEND SKILLS

Preface

Point out to students that the introductory part of the story on p. 74 is called a preface. This preface, a quick introductory remark, is used to set the scene and introduce the main character, Karana. Most novels begin with a preface. Have students find other books in the library that have a preface.

DURING READING

Guiding Comprehension

4 Character/Plot • Critical

***Text to Self* How would you describe the way Karana approached the job of finding a place to build her hut? Tell about a time you wish you had acted in a similar way.**

Possible response: She was very wise and cautious; she considered a lot of things first. It reminds me of the time I had to decide whether to study for a test or watch a television show. I wish I had thought through my decision more carefully!

Monitor Progress	
REVIEW **Character/Plot**	
If... students have difficulty describing Karana,	**then...** use the skill and strategy instruction on p. 77.

The rocks were not so high as those on the headland and therefore would give me less protection from the wind, yet they were high enough, and from them I could see the north coast and Coral Cove.

76

Access Content Tell students that *shelter* is used as a verb in the last sentence of p. 76 and that it means "to protect."

The thing that made me decide on the place to build my house was the sea elephants.

The cliffs here fell away easily to a wide shelf that was partly covered when the tide came in. It was a good place for sea elephants because they could crawl halfway up the cliff if the day were stormy. On fair days they could fish among the pools or lie on the rocks. 4

The bull is very large and often weighs as much as thirty men. The cows are much smaller, but they make more noise than the bulls, screaming and barking through the whole day and sometimes at night. The babies are noisy too.

On this morning the tide was low and most of the animals were far out, just hundreds of specks against the waves, yet the noise they made was deafening. I stayed there the rest of the day, looking around, and that night. At dawn when the clamor started again I left and went back to the headland.

There was another place to the south where I could have built my house, near the destroyed village of Ghalas-at, but I did not want to go there because it would remind me of the people who were gone. Also the wind blew strong in this place, blowing against the dunes which cover the middle part of the island so that most of the time sand is moving everywhere.

Rain fell that night and lasted for two days. I made a shelter of brush at the foot of the rock, which kept off some of the water, and ate the food I had stored in the basket. I could not build a fire because of the rain and I was very cold.

77

Time for SOCIAL STUDIES

Channel Islands

Because of the isolation and harsh island environment of the Channel Islands, there are about 65 species of plants there that are not found anywhere else in the world. Also unique to the Channel Islands is the island fox. It's similar to the gray fox but much smaller—about the size of a house cat. Birds on the islands include brown pelicans, albatrosses, terns, barn owls, and meadowlarks. There are also many species of fish, including various types of sharks, and other marine life, such as dolphins, sea lions, blue and gray whales, and elephant seals.

SKILLS ↔ STRATEGIES IN CONTEXT

Character and Plot REVIEW

TEACH

- Remind students that a character can be a person or animal. A character takes part in the action and events in a story.
- A plot is a pattern of events organized around some type of problem or conflict.

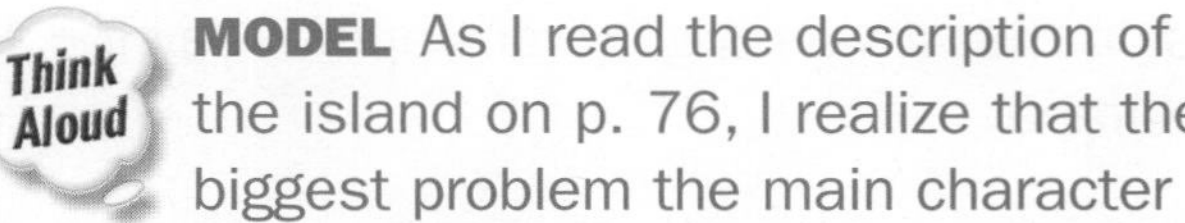

Think Aloud **MODEL** As I read the description of the island on p. 76, I realize that the biggest problem the main character faces at this point is deciding the best place to build her home. I realize that it is a risky decision for her to make.

PRACTICE AND ASSESS

- Have students read p. 75, paragraph 4. What does the description of the leader say about what kind of dog he is? *(It says he is watching Karana with yellow eyes, and she realizes she will have to kill him. It suggests that the dog is very dangerous.)*
- To assess, use Practice Book p. 26.

Character and Plot

Directions Read the article. Then answer the questions below.

George was lost. He could see the darkening blue sky when he looked up through the dense tree cover. He'd never make it back to base camp in the dark. Darkness was falling fast and the night time sounds of the mountains were growing louder. He knew he'd have to survive out here alone. He had forgotten his emergency kit, too, which only made him angrier at himself. He searched the rocks for a crevice or opening of some kind where he could sleep safely. He had two granola bars in his pack, and he'd been drinking his water sparingly. Every new rustle he heard put him on edge. Bears ruled these mountains, and he didn't want to meet one at night. He found a small opening at the base of a large rock formation. He eased himself into the space slowly, squinting and listening as hard as he could. When he was completely inside, he stood up. Inside the cave, everything seemed quiet and safe.

1. Why does George have to sleep overnight in the mountains?
   He gets lost during a hike and it becomes too dark to find his way back to camp.
2. Why is George angry with himself?
   He didn't pack his emergency kit.
3. Why does George look for a safe place to sleep for the night?
   He doesn't want a bear or other wild animal to see him.
4. The night sounds put George on edge. What might he be imagining?
   Possible answer: He might be imagining wild animals ready to attack him.
5. On a separate sheet of paper, describe the resolution to George's problem. What do you think will happen next?
   Possible answer: The resolution is that George found a safe place to sleep for the night. I predict George will find the base camp in the morning.

School + Home **Home Activity** Your child has read a fictional passage and answered questions about the plot and the main character. Have your child summarize this passage to you. Then ask your child to explain how he or she would feel if stuck in the same situation.

▲ **Practice Book** p. 26

Guiding Comprehension

5 Imagery/Sensory Words • Inferential
What do the images and sensory words on p. 78, paragraph 2, suggest about what kind of day it was for Karana?

Possible response: The images and sensory words "fresh," "sweet odors," and "I sang as I went down the trail" give the impression that it was a good or hopeful day for Karana.

6 Vocabulary • Dictionary/Glossary
Have students use a dictionary to determine the meaning of *omen* on p. 78, paragraph 2.

Meaning: a sign of what will happen

Monitor Progress

Dictionary/Glossary

If... students have difficulty using a dictionary to find the meaning of *omen*,	**then...** use vocabulary strategy instruction on p. 79.

7 Theme • Inferential
What does the strong fence around Karana's house show about her situation?

She built a strong fence around her shelter to protect herself and her supplies, showing that there are threats to her survival on the island.

On the third day the rain ceased and I went out to look for things which I would need in building the house. I likewise needed poles for a fence. I would soon kill the wild dogs, but there were many small red foxes on the island. They were so numerous that I could never hope to get rid of them either by traps or with arrows. They were clever thieves and nothing I stored would be safe until I had built a fence.

The morning was fresh from the rain. The smell of the tide pools was strong. Sweet odors came from the wild grasses in the ravines and from the sand plants on the dunes. I sang as I went
5 down the trail to the beach and along the beach to the sandspit.
6 I felt that the day was an omen of good fortune.

It was a good day to begin my new home.

Many years before, two whales had washed up on the sandspit. Most of the bones had been taken away to make ornaments, but the ribs were still there, half-buried in the sand.

These I used in making the fence. One by one I dug them up and carried them to the headland. They were long and curved, and when I had scooped out holes and set them in the earth they stood taller than I did.

I put the ribs together with their edges almost touching, and standing so that they curved outward, which made them impossible to climb. Between them I wove many strands of bull kelp, which shrinks as it dries and pulls very tight. I would have used seal sinew to bind the ribs together, for this is stronger than kelp, but wild animals like it and soon would have gnawed the
7 fence down. Much time went into its building. It would have taken me longer except that the rock made one end of the fence and part of a side.

Access Content Reread aloud the sentence "They were clever thieves and nothing I stored would be safe until I had built a fence." Tell students that *thieves* steal things secretly. Ask students who the thieves are that Karana is referring to here.

For a place to go in and out, I dug a hole under the fence just wide and deep enough to crawl through. The bottom and sides I lined with stones. On the outside I covered the hole with a mat woven of brush to shed the rain, and on the inside with a flat rock which I was strong enough to move.

79

VOCABULARY STRATEGY

Dictionary/ Glossary

TEACH

Model looking up the word *ornaments* from p. 78, paragraph 4 in the dictionary.

MODEL I'm familiar with one meaning of ornaments having to do with holiday tree decorations, but I'm not sure that makes sense here. I'm going to look it up in the dictionary. I'll flip to the *Os*, then to *O-R-N*. I see *ornament* means "any pretty decoration," so the whale bones must have been used to make pretty decorations.

PRACTICE AND ASSESS

Have students use a dictionary to find the meaning of *dunes* in paragraph 2. *(mounds or ridges of loose sand heaped up by the wind)*

Confirm Predictions Provide the following prompt: Was your prediction accurate? (See p. 72.) Revise your old prediction or make a new prediction about the rest of the story.

Develop Vocabulary

PRACTICE LESSON VOCABULARY

Students orally respond *yes* or *no* to each question and provide a reason for each answer.

1. Do wild dogs live in a *lair? (Yes, wild dogs make their home in a lair.)*
2. Do foxes *gnaw* at stones? *(No, foxes chew on bones, sinew, and other hard things they like to eat.)*
3. Could a wild dog fall into a *ravine? (Yes, a wild dog could stumble and fall into a deep trench between rocks.)*

BUILD CONCEPT VOCABULARY

Review previous concept words with students. Ask if students have come across any words today in their reading that they would like to add to the Wilderness Survival Concept Web, such as *sheltered* and *favorable*.

EXTEND SKILLS

Imagery/Sensory Words

Sensory words help readers to understand setting and to experience how something looks, smells, tastes, and feels. Imagery provides details, showing readers how something looks. Carefully chosen sensory words and imagery support the plot and characterization in a story. Have students read p. 78, paragraph 2, and note sensory words, phrases, and imagery.

If you want to teach this selection in two sessions, stop here.

Guiding Comprehension

If you are teaching the selection in two days, discuss the setting and theme so far and review the vocabulary.

8  **Visualize • Critical**

Read paragraph 6 on p. 81 and visualize Karana's shelter. Describe what you see.

Possible response: Karana used rock for the back of the house and left the front open. For walls and the roof, she used poles bound with sinew and covered with kelp leaves.

Monitor Progress

If... students have difficulty visualizing the setting,	then... use the skill and strategy instruction on p. 81.

9 **Summarizing • Inferential**

What are the things that Karana has done so far to survive in this setting?

Karana has found food, chosen a safe place for her home, built a fence of whale bones to keep the dogs and foxes out, and built a house of wood to stay warm in cold weather.

DAY 3 Grouping Options

Reading

Whole Group Discuss the Question of the Day.

Group Time Differentiated Instruction

Read *Island of the Blue Dolphins.* See pp. 68h–68i for the small group lesson plan.

Whole Group Discuss the Reader Response questions on page 84. Then use p. 89a.

Language Arts

Use pp. 89e–89k.

80

Fluency Help students "chunk," or group, words into meaningful phrases. For example, from p. 81:

The poles I made of equal length, / using fire to cut them / as well as a stone knife / which caused me much difficulty / because I had never made such a tool before.

I was able to take eight steps between the sides of the fence, which gave me all the room I would need to store the things I gathered and wished to protect.

I built the fence first because it was too cold to sleep on the rock, and I did not like to sleep in the shelter I had made until I was safe from the wild dogs.

The house took longer to build than the fence because it rained many days and because the wood I needed was scarce.

There was a legend among our people that the island had once been covered with tall trees. This was a long time ago, at the beginning of the world when Tumaiyowit and Mukat ruled. The two gods quarreled about many things. Tumaiyowit wished people to die. Mukat did not. Tumaiyowit angrily went down, down to another world under this world, taking his belongings with him, so people die because he did.

In that time there were tall trees, but now there were only a few in the ravines and these were small and crooked. It was very hard to find one that would make a good pole. I searched many days, going out early in the morning and coming back at night, before I found enough for a house.

I used the rock for the back of the house and the front I left open since the wind did not blow from this direction. The poles I made of equal length, using fire to cut them as well as a stone knife which caused me much difficulty because I had never made such a tool before. There were four poles on each side, set in the earth, and twice that many for the roof. These I bound together with sinew and covered with female kelp, which has broad leaves. 8

The winter was half over before I finished the house, but I slept there every night and felt secure because of the strong fence. 9 The foxes came when I was cooking my food and stood outside gazing through the cracks, and the wild dogs also came, gnawing at the whale ribs, growling because they could not get in.

81

Native Americans

Time for SOCIAL STUDIES

Before Europeans arrived, California had a large population of Native Americans. These peoples included the Paiutes, Shoshones, Utes, and other groups. In the early 1800s, the Spanish and later the Mexicans came to California, taking the land away from the indigenous people. Many Native Americans were put in missions to learn Western ways and religion, and to work. Many died during this period, mostly of disease. In 1850, California became part of the United States and more Native American lives and territories were lost.

DURING READING

SKILLS ↔ STRATEGIES IN CONTEXT

Setting/Theme Visualize

TEACH

When students visualize, they create a mental picture of something in their reading. Model visualizing Karana's house as it is described in the first two sentences in paragraph 6 on p. 81.

Think Aloud **MODEL** First, it says Karana used the rock for the back of her house, so I'm picturing a big rock. Next, she cut the poles using fire and a stone knife. Now, I'm picturing Karana holding a large pole over a small fire while cutting a pole with a knife. I imagine the burning wood gives off a smoky odor, and that her hands must be very hot so close to the fire.

PRACTICE AND ASSESS

Have students visualize Karana's completed house. Ask for volunteers to share what they pictured in their minds. *(Possible response: A hut made from whale bones and covered with kelp with a large rock at the back.)*

To find out more about the Native Americans living in the area of the *Island of the Blue Dolphins* in the mid-1800s, students can type the keywords *History of Californian Native Americans* into a student-friendly search engine. Be sure to follow classroom guidelines for using the Internet.

Guiding Comprehension

10 **Visualize • Inferential**
How were Karana's cooking utensils made?
She made them from two stones with hollow places in the center that had been worn smooth by the sea.

11 **Plot • Inferential**
What has Karana accomplished by the end of the selection?
Karana has created a safe and warm home for herself where she can cook, sleep, and find shelter from the weather and the animals on the island.

12 **Compare and Contrast • Critical**
Text to Text **Compare and contrast another selection you've read where the main character had to overcome many difficult obstacles. Describe similarities and differences.**
Possible response: I remember reading about a baseball player and how hard he had to work to realize his dream of being a professional baseball player. Unlike Karana, however, his survival didn't depend upon his success.

I shot two of them, but not the leader.

While I was building the fence and the house, I ate shellfish and perch which I cooked on a flat rock. Afterwards I made two utensils. Along the shore there were stones that the sea had worn
10 smooth. Most of them were round, but I found two with hollow places in the center which I deepened and broadened by rubbing them with sand. Using these to cook in, I saved the juices of the fish which are good and were wasted before.

For cooking seeds and roots I wove a tight basket of fine reeds, which was easy because I had learned how to do it from my sister Ulape. After the basket had dried in the sun, I gathered lumps of pitch on the shore, softened them over the fire, and rubbed them on the inside of the basket so that it would hold water. By heating small stones and dropping them into a mixture of water and seeds in the basket I could make gruel.

I made a place for fire in the floor of my house, hollowing it out and lining it with rocks. In the village of Ghalas-at we made new fires every night, but now I made one fire which I covered with ashes when I went to bed. The next night I would remove the ashes and blow on the embers. In this way I saved myself much work.

There were many gray mice on the island and now that I had food to keep from one meal to other, I needed a safe place to put it. On the face of the rock, which was the back wall of my house, were several cracks as high as my shoulder. These I cut out and smoothed to make shelves where I could store my food and the mice could not reach it.

11 By the time winter was over and grass began to show green on the hills, my house was comfortable. I was sheltered from the
12 wind and rain and prowling animals. I could cook anything I wished to eat. Everything I wanted was there at hand.

82

Strategy Response Log

Summarize When students finish reading the selection, provide this prompt: Describe *Island of the Blue Dolphins* to a friend. Write four or five sentences that highlight the most important events and tell what the story is about.

ELL

Access Content Tell students that the word *utensil* has a Spanish cognate *(utensilio)*. Explain that a *utensil* is "a tool or container used in a kitchen or on a farm." Ask students to name the two utensils that Karana made.

STRATEGY SELF-CHECK

Visualize

Ask students to visualize the two places that Karana considered as sites for her house.

Students can use their visualizations to write a sentence describing the theme of the selection.

Use Practice Book p. 27.

SELF-CHECK

Students can ask themselves these questions to assess their ability to use the skill and strategy.

- Did I visualize the island, characters, and setting as I read?
- Did I think about the period in history when the story took place?
- How did these things help me understand the theme?

Monitor Progress

Setting and Theme

If... students have difficulty describing the setting and theme in their illustrations and sentences,	**then...** use the Reteach lesson on p. 89b.

Develop Vocabulary

PRACTICE LESSON VOCABULARY

Students orally respond *yes* or *no* to each question and provide a reason for each answer.

1. Is *sinew* strong? *(Yes, Karana used it to bind her fence together.)*
2. Are *shellfish* a part of Karana's diet? *(Yes, she eats the seafood that lives in a shell that she finds in the water.)*
3. Is the *headland* miles from the water? *(No, the headland juts out into the water.)*

BUILD CONCEPT VOCABULARY

Review previous concept words with students. Ask if students have come across any words today in their reading that they would like to add to the Wilderness Survival Concept Web, such as *secure* and *comfortable*.

Theme and Setting

- The **theme** is the underlying meaning of a story. It is often not stated. You can figure out a theme from events and other evidence in the story.
- The **setting** is where and when the story takes place. Writers use details, such as sights and sounds, to describe it.

Directions Read the following passage. Then answer the questions below.

Jessica had never seen a real Native American village. Standing in the pueblo, she realized that her books hadn't prepared her for what it would be like. Under the pale spring sunshine, the red clay buildings at the center of the pueblo looked so different than the ones she had read about and seen in books back home. But when she entered one of the shops, it looked very familiar. It had the same kind of display cases, the same food, even the same posters she saw in shops at home.

The lady behind the counter gave Jessica a big smile and said hello. The lady was wearing a t-shirt with the name of the same college Jessica's father attended, the same college Jessica hoped to attend one day. Jessica didn't feel so far away from home anymore.

1. What is the setting of the above passage?
   in a Native American pueblo in springtime
2. Where had Jessica learned about pueblos before her arrival?
   Jessica read about pueblos in books.
3. Why does everything in the store look so familiar to Jessica?
   It has the same equipment and sells the same products as what she is used to back home.
4. What is the underlying theme of this passage?
   Possible answer: Even though we might have different cultural backgrounds, we have more in common than we think.
5. On a separate sheet of paper, write down the visual memories you have of a place you visited for the first time. It could be a new town, someone's home, a new school, etc.

Students' responses should include specific visual details of a place they visited for the first time.

Home Activity Your child answered questions about setting and theme in a fictional passage. Find a family photo that shows a place you have been to and have your child describe the setting in his or her own words. Try to make up a story with your child based on the picture.

▲ **Practice Book** p. 27

Reader Response

Open for Discussion **Personal Response**

MODEL When I think about Karana and how much work she puts into building her house, I think she has a good chance of surviving.

Comprehension Check **Critical Response**

1. Possible response: To make it more realistic and personal so you feel like you know her. ***Author's Purpose***
2. Theme: A person with determination can meet great challenges. Evidence: Karana builds a house, defends herself against wild animals, and gathers food. ***Theme***
3. Possible response: The house is made of wood poles, sinew and kelp. It has a boulder for the back wall. ***Visualize***
4. Responses will vary but may include *spring, cliff, ridge, shelf, dunes,* and *hills.* ***Vocabulary***

Look Back and Write For test practice, assign a 10–15 minute time limit. For assessment, see the Scoring Rubric at the right.

Retell

Have students retell *Island of the Blue Dolphins.*

Monitor Progress

Check Retelling Rubric 4 3 2 1

If...	then...
students have difficulty retelling the story,	use the Retelling Cards and the Scoring Rubric for Retelling on p. 85 to assist fluent retelling.

SUCCESS PREDICTOR

Check Retelling Let beginning ELL students listen to others before attempting their own retellings. For more ideas on assessing students' retellings, see the ELL and Transition Handbook.

Reader Response

Open for Discussion For a little while, you watched Karana, all alone on the island. Now report back: What do you think are her chances for survival? What is your evidence?

1. The author wrote *Island of the Blue Dolphins* in the first perso as if Karana is speaking to the reader. Why do you think he chose to tell the story in this way? **Think Like an Author**
2. Write a sentence that states the theme of the story. What evidence can you find to support your theme? **Theme and Settin**
3. Visualize the house Karana builds. Describe her house using details from the story. **Visualize**
4. Words from the Words to Know list, such as *lair, ravine,* and *headland,* give you a sense of place. Identify other words from the story that add to your understanding of Karana's island. **Vocabulary**

Look Back and Write What is th most important physical challenge th Karana faces? How does she meet th challenge? Use story details to suppo your answer.

Meet author **Scott O'Dell on page 768.**

84

Scoring Rubric **Look Back and Write**

Top-Score Response A top-score response will identify building a house as Karana's greatest challenge and mentions her difficulties in finding wood, making tools, and assembling the structure.

Example of a Top-Score Response Karana's most important physical challenge is building a shelter. This is difficult becaus there is hardly any wood on the island, and it rains a lot. After many days of searching, she finds enough poles. Then she mu meet a new challenge—making a stone knife to cut them.

For additional rubrics, see p. WA10.

DURING READING

Write Now

Friendly or Thank-You Letter

Prompt

In *Island of the Blue Dolphins,* the narrator describes a place as she might in a letter to a friend.
Think about a place you could describe.
Now write a friendly or thank-you letter about the place.

Writing Trait

A friendly letter has a certain **organization** or format—greeting, body, closing, signature. The body may have one or more **paragraphs.**

Student Model

Dear Aunt Gracie,

Thank you so much for inviting me along on the trip to Prince Edward Island. Mom has always told me how beautiful it is. It was so cool to finally see where you and Mom grew up.

I enjoyed our bike ride around the island and our picnic on the beach. My favorite day was when we went out on the boat. I couldn't believe the size of the fish Uncle Jim helped me catch!

Now that I have seen your favorite places, I can't wait to show you mine. I'm looking forward to your visit with us next summer.

Love,
Julie

Correct friendly letter format includes greeting, body, closing, and signature.

Purpose of letter is stated in first sentence.

Letter is organized so that each paragraph focuses on one main idea.

Use the model to help you write your own friendly or thank-you letter.

85

Write Now

Look at the Prompt Have students identify and discuss key words and phrases in the prompt. *(a place, describe, friendly or thank-you letter about the place)*

Strategies to Develop Organization/ Paragraphs

Have students

- use a graphic organizer, such as a flowchart, to arrange ideas logically.
- read their first drafts aloud and listen for choppy sentences or awkward transitions.
- add transitions to make connections between ideas easier to understand.

NO: I went to school. I went to the store.
YES: First, I went to school. Afterwards, I went to the store.

For additional suggestions and rubric, see pp. 89g–89h.

Hints for Better Writing

- Carefully read the prompt.
- Use a graphic organizer to plan your writing.
- Support your ideas with information and details.
- Use words that help readers understand.
- Proofread and edit your work.

Scoring Rubric Narrative Retelling

Rubric 4 3 2 1	4	3	2	1
Connections	Makes connections and generalizes beyond the text	Makes connections to other events, stories, or experiences	Makes a limited connection to another event, story, or experience	Makes no connection to another event, story, or experience
Author's Purpose	Elaborates on author's purpose	Tells author's purpose with some clarity	Makes some connection to author's purpose	Makes no connection to author's purpose
Characters	Describes the main character(s) and any character development	Identifies the main character(s) and gives some information about them	Inaccurately identifies some characters or gives little information about them	Inaccurately identifies the characters or gives no information about them
Setting	Describes the time and location	Identifies the time and location	Omits details of time or location	Is unable to identify time or location
Plot	Describes the problem, goal, events, and ending using rich detail	Tells the problem, goal, events, and ending with some errors that do not affect meaning	Tells parts of the problem, goal, events, and ending with gaps that affect meaning	Retelling has no sense of story

Retelling Plan

- ☑ **Week 1** Assess Strategic Intervention students.
- ☑ **Week 2** Assess Advanced students.
- ☑ **This week assess Strategic Intervention students.**
- ☐ **Week 4** Assess On-Level students.
- ☐ **Week 5** Assess any students you have not yet checked during this unit.

Use the Retelling Chart on p. TR16 to record retelling.

Selection Test To assess with *Island of the Blue Dolphins*, use Selection Tests, pp. 9–12.

Fresh Reads for Differentiated Test Practice For weekly leveled practice, use pp. 13–18.

DAY 4

Science in Reading

OBJECTIVES

- Examine features of an interview.
- Practice a test-taking strategy.
- Compare and contrast across texts.

PREVIEW/USE TEXT FEATURES

As students preview "Seven Survival Questions," have them note the interview's question-and-answer format. After they preview ask:

- **How can the question-and-answer format help you quickly locate specific information about what to do if you get lost?** *(The questions tell what information is provided in each section.)*

Link to Reading

Students can search the Internet to find out about state and national parks in their area. Have them use a student-friendly search engine and the keywords *park* and *(name of state)*.

Science in Reading

Interview

Genre

- **In an interview the interviewer asks questions. The other person, the subject, answers.**
- **Interviews usually appear in magazines or newspapers.**

Text Features

- **An interview first introduces the subject, or the person being interviewed.**
- **Questions and answers begin with a name in bold type followed by a colon.**
- **The words on the page are the actual words spoken by the subject and the interviewer.**

Link to Reading

Do research to find state and national parks in your area. What safety rules help keep visitors from getting lost?

SEVEN SURVIVAL QUESTIONS

by Buck Tilton
from Boys' Life *Magazine*

When you're lost, being a good leader can mean the difference between life and death. John Gookin, an authority on wilderness survival at the National Outdoor Leadership School (NOLS), shares his expert advice:

1 **Boys' Life:** Why do people get lost?

Gookin: Reasons vary. For one thing, people go out prepared for one activity, but they end up doing another. They may plan to go fishing, for instance, but then decide to leave the lake and try rock climbing. That often leads to trouble.

The other big mistake is overcorrecting for minor navigation errors. Instead of calmly retracing their steps, people head off in the wrong direction at a fast pace.

86

Content-Area Vocabulary — Science

debris	scattered fragments, such as fallen leaves or branches, tree bark
navigation	skill or process of finding a position and course

DAY 4 Grouping Options

Reading

Whole Group Discuss the Question of the Day.

Group Time Differentiated Instruction

Read "Seven Survival Questions." See pp. 68h–68i for the small group lesson plan.

Whole Group Use p. 89a.

Language Arts

Use pp. 89e–89k.

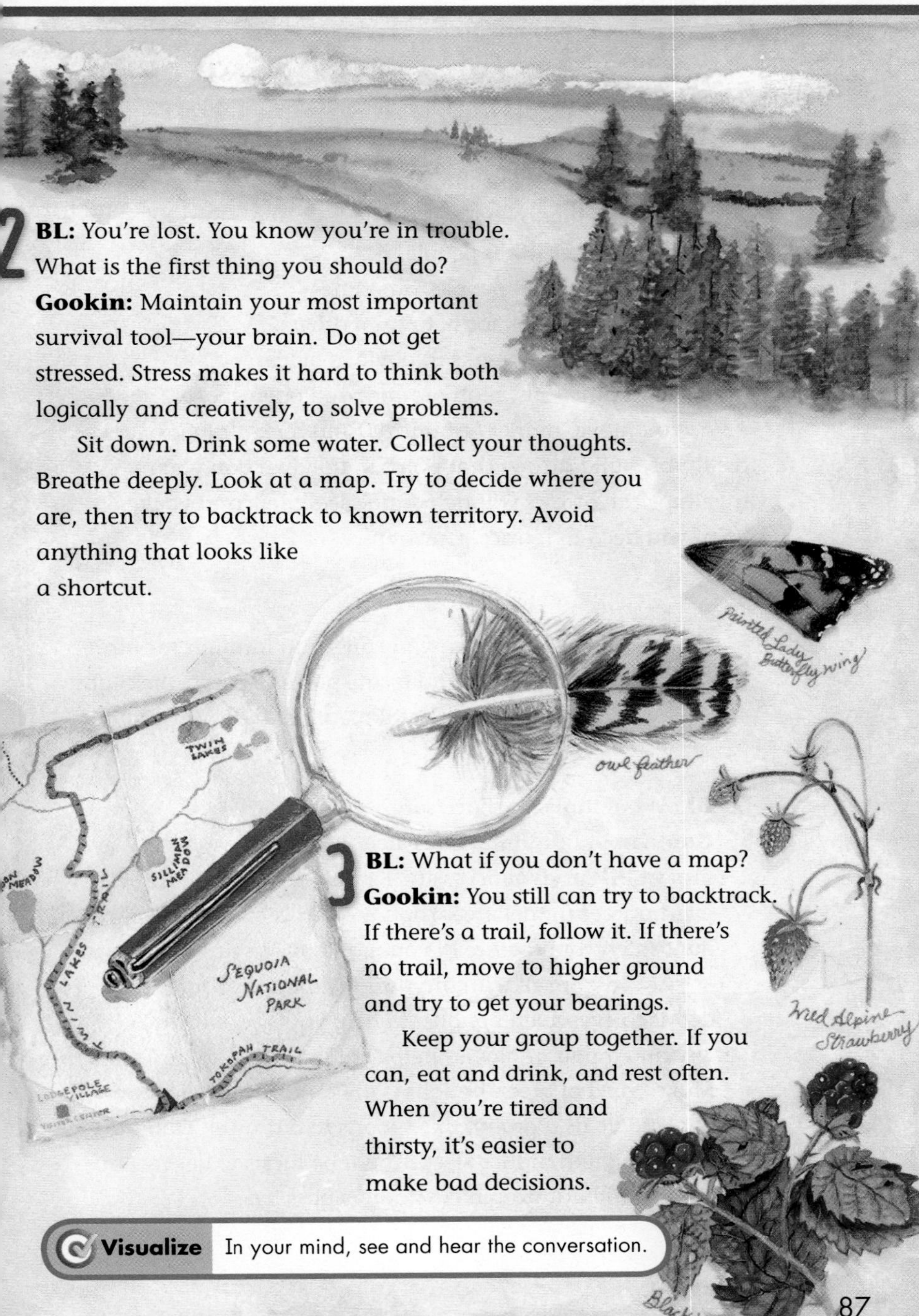

2 **BL:** You're lost. You know you're in trouble. What is the first thing you should do?

Gookin: Maintain your most important survival tool—your brain. Do not get stressed. Stress makes it hard to think both logically and creatively, to solve problems.

Sit down. Drink some water. Collect your thoughts. Breathe deeply. Look at a map. Try to decide where you are, then try to backtrack to known territory. Avoid anything that looks like a shortcut.

3 **BL:** What if you don't have a map?

Gookin: You still can try to backtrack. If there's a trail, follow it. If there's no trail, move to higher ground and try to get your bearings.

Keep your group together. If you can, eat and drink, and rest often. When you're tired and thirsty, it's easier to make bad decisions.

Visualize In your mind, see and hear the conversation.

87

INTERVIEW

Use the sidebar on p. 86 to guide discussion.

- Explain to students that an interview is a written record of a conversation between two people.
- Point out that each speaker's name is followed by a colon and then the words spoken by that person.
- Discuss with students why an interview is a good genre for presenting expert advice on what to do if you get lost.

AudioText

Visualize

Have students describe scenes that they see and hear as they visualize the conversation.

Map and Globe Skills

Time for SOCIAL STUDIES

Knowing how to use a map and compass can help you avoid getting lost in the wilderness. A topographical ("topo") map gives a complete picture of the terrain. It shows water sources, such as streams. It shows the elevation (distance above sea level) of the land. You can tell from a topo map how far and steeply you must travel to your destination. A compass shows you the direction in which you must travel. By using a map and compass together, you can tell where you are on a trail or in the backcountry.

Access Content Preview the text, reading the questions aloud and asking students to predict the answers to some of them.

- Point out the compound words *overcorrecting* (p. 86), *backtrack*, *shortcut* (p. 87), and *evergreen* (p. 88) and help students determine their meanings.
- After reading, ask students to check and correct their predictions.

Strategies for Nonfiction

USE INTRODUCTIONS Remind students that an interview begins by introducing the person being interviewed and often includes the topic of the interview. Sometimes the introduction gives information that can help us answer test questions. Provide the following strategy.

Use the Strategy

1. Read the test question carefully and make sure you understand it.
2. Ask yourself if the question is looking for information about the person being interviewed or the topic of the interview.
3. Scan the introduction, looking for answers to the question.

GUIDED PRACTICE Have students discuss how they would use the strategy to answer the following question.

What is the focus of John Gookin's interview with *Boys' Life Magazine*?

INDEPENDENT PRACTICE After students answer the following test question, discuss the process they used to find information.

Why is John Gookin a good person to interview for an article on surviving in the backcountry?

4 **BL:** Are there things you should do while you're trying to backtrack?
Gookin: If you see other people, ask for directions. Lost people sometimes are embarrassed to ask for help from others.

Stay visible. Take breaks in obvious places such as trail junctions, high ground, and open spaces.

As you move, mark your path. Using rocks or logs or tree limbs, build arrows that point in the direction you're traveling. The arrows will help guide searchers and you, too, if you need to retrace your steps.

5 **BL:** What if you can't find familiar terrain?
Gookin: Find a safe place to spend the night while there is still plenty of light. Stay calm.

6 **BL:** What makes a place safe?
Gookin: Maintaining body heat is often the most important survival necessity. Find shelter such as a rock overhang or a thick tree. High ground is best. If you can do it safely, build a fire big enough to help you stay warm.

Cover yourself with anything available, from forest debris to evergreen boughs, to help you stay warm. Even wearing a pair of glasses helps hold in a little bit of heat. Make a bed of green boughs if the ground is cold or snowy.

Huddle as a group, like spoons in a drawer. Don't expect a great night's sleep. You'll be lucky to get catnaps.

Stay near a trail in case others pass by.

Ponderosa Pine Needles

88

Test Practice Write the Independent Practice test question on the board. Read the strategy steps aloud as students follow along. Help students as needed to locate and scan the introduction. Point out that the introduction tells about Gookin, whereas the interview itself tells what Gookin said.

7 **BL:** What about the next day?

Gookin: Make yourself easy to find. Stay put, and sit in open spaces or on high points.

Searchers most easily spot geometric shapes (like a triangle or SOS) from the sky. Build one or more using your gear or anything else available, including people. Keep any reflective material out in the open. Signal mirrors are excellent survival tools. Used correctly, they can be seen for 20 miles. If you don't have a mirror, improvise with glass or even eyeglass lenses. A smoky fire can also be seen from far away in calm conditions.

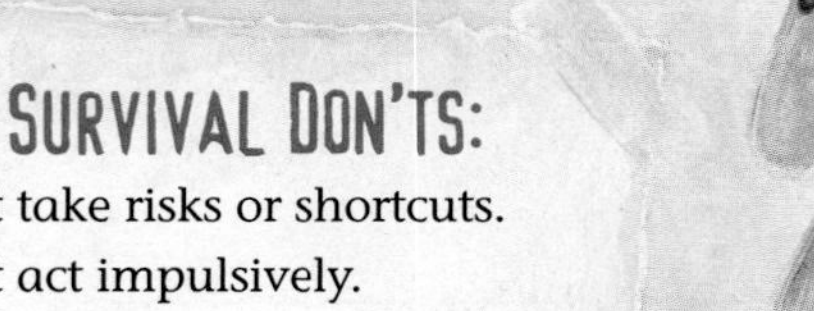

Top Survival Dos:

- Stay calm.
- Be methodical.
- Drink water.
- Keep warm.
- Build a fire—it's good for signaling and warmth.

Top Survival Don'ts:

- Don't take risks or shortcuts.
- Don't act impulsively.
- Don't hike after dark.
- Don't avoid people. Ask for help.
- Don't lose your spirit. Think positive thoughts.

Pine nuts

Reading Across Texts

If Karana listed survival tips for life on her island, what might they be?

Writing Across Texts Make a list of Karana's top five tips.

Visualize Can you see yourself lost but remaining calm?

89

DURING READING

CONNECT TEXT TO TEXT

Reading Across Texts

Have students reread *Island of the Blue Dolphins*, paying careful attention to the process Karana went through in deciding where to build her shelter.

Writing Across Texts To help choose Karana's top five tips, encourage students to think about which of the tips they wrote are most important to surviving.

Visualize

Possible response: Yes, especially since I have done a lot of camping, and I'm familiar with the survival tips.

DAY 5

Fluency Assessment Plan

- ☑ **Week 1** Assess Advanced students.
- ☑ **Week 2** Assess Strategic Intervention students.
- ☑ **This week assess On-Level students.**
- ☐ **Week 4** Assess Strategic Intervention students.
- ☐ **Week 5** Assess any students you have not yet checked during this unit.

Set individual goals for students to enable them to reach the year-end goal.

- Current Goal: 105–110 wcpm
- Year-End Goal: 140 wcpm

English language learners may be able to decode some English words but still not know the meanings. Help students recognize that they will understand sentences better and read more fluently as they learn more English words.

To develop fluent readers, use Fluency Coach.

DAY 5 Grouping Options

Reading

Whole Group
Revisit the Question of the Week.

Group Time
Differentiated Instruction
Reread this week's Leveled Readers. See pp. 68h–68i for the small group lesson plan.

Whole Group
Use p. 89b–89c.

Language Arts
Use pp. 89d–89l.

PITCH

Fluency

DAY 1

Model Reread "The Sign of the Beaver" on p. 68m. Explain that you will change the pitch of your voice to indicate dialogue and important moments in the story. Model for students as you read.

DAY 2

Choral Reading Read aloud the first two paragraphs on p. 75. Have students notice the drop in pitch at periods and the rise in pitch at the question mark. Have students practice as a class doing three choral readings of this section of p. 75.

DAY 3

Model Read aloud the last two paragraphs on p. 82. Have students notice how you lower your pitch slightly at the end of a paragraph, and then raise it again at the start of the succeeding paragraph. Practice as a class by doing three choral readings.

DAY 4

Partner Reading Partners practice reading aloud the last two paragraphs on p. 82, three times. Students should read with the proper pitch and offer each other feedback.

Monitor Progress — Check Fluency WCPM

As students reread, monitor their progress toward their individual fluency goals. Current Goal: 105–110 words correct per minute. End-of-Year Goal: 140 words correct per minute.

If... students cannot read fluently at a rate of 105–110 words correct per minute,
then... make sure students practice with text at their independent level. Provide additional fluency practice, pairing nonfluent readers with fluent readers.

If... students already read at 140 words correct per minute,
then... they do not need to reread three to four times.

SUCCESS PREDICTOR

DAY 5

Assessment

Individual Reading Rate Use the Fluency Assessment Plan and do a one-minute timed reading of either selection from this week to assess students in Week 3. Pay special attention to this week's skill, pitch. Provide corrective feedback for each student.

RETEACH

Setting and Theme

TEACH

Review the definitions of *setting* and *theme* on p. 68. Students can complete Practice Book p. 28 on their own, or you can complete it as a class. Point out that students should first fill in the graphic organizer by answering questions 1–4 and use that information to state the theme of the passage in question 5.

ASSESS

Have partners reread p. 78, paragraph 2, in their books and determine the setting and theme of the paragraph. (Setting: morning on the beach; theme: Karana is optomistic about the dog.)

For additional instruction on setting and themes, see DI • 54.

EXTEND SKILLS

Imagery

TEACH

Imagery is the use of words to help readers experience the way things look, sound, smell, taste, or feel.

- An image is any detail that stimulates any of your five senses or your imagination.
- Writers use imagery to make characters and setting seem real.
- The writer's choice of words and images helps to set the mood (the atmosphere or feeling of a written work) and tone (the writer's attitude toward the subject or toward the audience) of a piece of writing.

Work with students to explain how Scott O'Dell uses imagery on p. 77, paragraph 4. Make sure students note both the visual and auditory imagery provided in the description of the bulls and cows.

ASSESS

Have students discuss with partners how Scott O'Dell uses imagery on p. 82, paragraph 2. Have students write a descriptive paragraph about how two of the five senses are stimulated by the writer's words. (Students paragraphs should describe how their sense of taste and touch are affected.)

OBJECTIVES

- Determine the setting and theme of a fictional passage.
- Identify imagery and sensory words.

Skills Trace

Setting and Theme

Introduce/Teach	TE: 5.1 18–19, 68–69; 5.5 512–513
Practice	Practice Book: 3, 7, 8, 16, 23, 26, 27, 28, 96, 203, 207, 208
Reteach/Review	**TE: 5.1 41b, 49, 61, 77, 89b, DI•52, DI•54; 5.2 237; 5.5 535b, DI•52**
Test	Selection Test: 1-4, 9-12, 81-84; Benchmark Test: Unit 1

Access Content Reteach the skill by reviewing the Picture It! lesson on setting and theme in the ELL Teaching Guide, pp. 15–16.

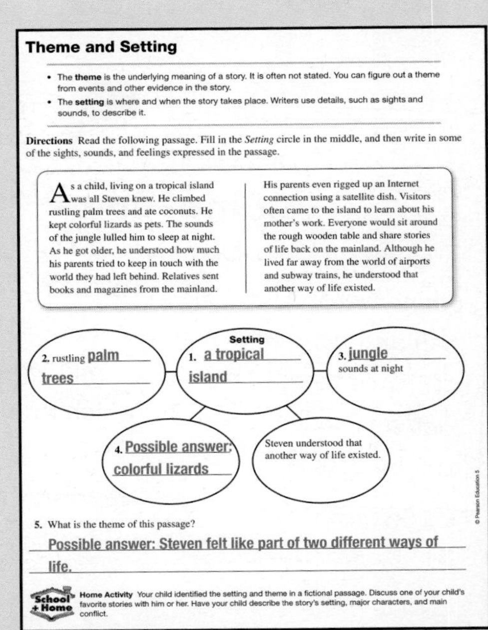

Theme and Setting

- The **theme** is the underlying meaning of a story. It is often not stated. You can figure out a theme from events and other evidence in the story.
- The **setting** is where and when the story takes place. Writers use details, such as sights and sounds, to describe it.

Directions Read the following passage. Fill in the *Setting* circle in the middle, and then write in some of the sights, sounds, and feelings expressed in the passage.

As a child, living on a tropical island was all Steven knew. He climbed rustling palm trees and ate coconuts. He kept colorful lizards as pets. The sounds of the jungle lulled him to sleep at night. As he got older, he understood how much his parents tried to keep in touch with the world they had left behind. Relatives sent books and magazines from the mainland. His parents even rigged up an Internet connection using a satellite dish. Visitors often came to the island to learn about his mother's work. Everyone would sit around the rough wooden table and share stories of life back on the mainland. Although he lived far away from the world of airports and subway trains, he understood that another way of life existed.

Setting

1. a tropical island
2. rustling palm trees
3. jungle sounds at night
4. Possible answer: colorful lizards

Steven understood that another way of life existed.

5. What is the theme of this passage?

Possible answer: Steven felt like part of two different ways of life.

Home Activity Your child identified the setting and theme in a fictional passage. Discuss one of your child's favorite stories with him or her. Have your child describe the story's setting, major characters, and main conflict.

▲ **Practice Book** p. 28

Words Correct Per Minute

SUCCESS PREDICTOR

Vocabulary and Word Study

VOCABULARY STRATEGY

Dictionary/ Glossary

UNFAMILIAR WORDS Remind students that they can use a dictionary or glossary to check the meaning of an unfamiliar word that they cannot define with context clues. Have students use a dictionary to look up the meaning and part of speech of these words from *Island of the Blue Dolphins* and then write a sentence using each word.

Word	Meaning	Part of speech	Sentence
cliffs	very steep, rocky slopes	noun	The sea lions climbed halfway up the cliffs during the storm.
tide			
gruel			
broadened			

Compound Words

In *Island of the Blue Dolphins*, there are several compound words that relate to the ocean, including *shellfish* and *headland*. Ask teams of students to brainstorm lists of other ocean-related compound words. Set a time limit and see which group comes up with the most words.

BUILD CONCEPT VOCABULARY

Survival

LOOKING BACK Remind students of the question of the week: *How do people survive in the wilderness?* Discuss how this week's Concept Web of vocabulary words relates to the theme of survival. Ask students if they have any words or categories to add. Discuss whether the words and categories are appropriately related to the concept.

MOVING FORWARD Preview the title of the next selection, *Satchel Paige.* Ask students which Concept Web words might apply to the new selection based on the title alone.

Put a star next to these words on the web.

Display the Concept Web and revisit the vocabulary words as you read the next selection to check predictions.

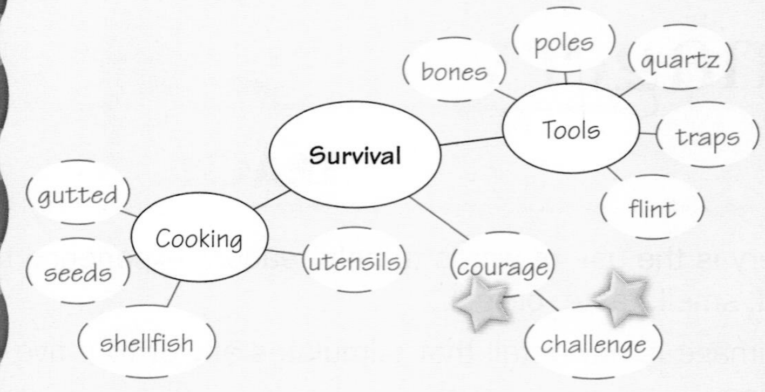

Monitor Progress

Check Vocabulary

If... students suggest words or categories that are not related to the concept,	**then...** review the words and categories on the Concept Web and discuss how they relate to the lesson concept.

Speaking and Viewing

SPEAKING

Group Review

SET-UP Have students work in small groups to reread *Island of the Blue Dolphins* as necessary to be able to review and summarize the story for classmates.

ORGANIZATION Have students decide in their groups which literary feature of the story (for example, character, plot, setting, theme) each student will focus on. Remind them that time is limited, so they should discuss and summarize only the most important elements of each feature.

TEAM PRESENTATION Provide time for students to rehearse their presentations. Share these ideas:

- Define literary terms for the audience, if necessary.
- Cite specific passages from the story to support statements.
- Allow each person in the group a turn speaking. Prepare a speaking order in advance.
- Use an outline to help present ideas.

Listening Tips

- Be courteous. Listen attentively.
- Take notes on things you don't understand, so that you can ask questions about them.
- Ask appropriate questions at the appropriate times.

VIEWING

Analyze Media

Discuss with students any television shows, movies, or radio interviews that focus on surviving in the out-of-doors, on land or water. Have students answer these questions orally, in groups, or individually, in writing.

1. **What is the mood of the program or film, and how is the mood conveyed?** *(Possible response: The mood is suspenseful. It's conveyed by the first scene, which shows a sailor on a small boat in a fierce storm.)*
2. **What is the greatest challenge faced by the main character(s)?** *(Responses will vary but should reflect the specifics of the film chosen.)*
3. **How does the main character(s) deal with his or her situation?** *(Responses will vary but should discuss how the main character(s) attempts to survive in the situation he or she is in.)*
4. **What is the main purpose of the program?** *(Possible responses: to entertain, inform, or both)*

ELL

Support Vocabulary Use the following to review and extend vocabulary and to explore lesson concepts further:

- ELL Poster 3, Days 3–5 instruction
- Vocabulary Activities and Word Cards in ELL Teaching Guide, pp. 17–18

Assessment For information on assessing students' speaking, listening, and viewing, see the ELL and Transition Handbook.

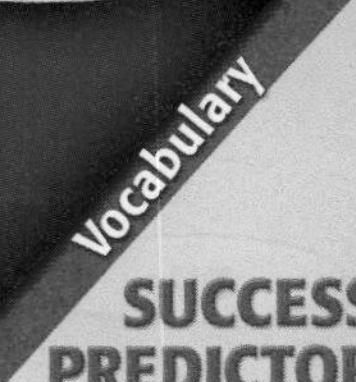

AFTER READING

Grammar Independent and Dependent Clauses

OBJECTIVES

- Define and identify independent and dependent clauses.
- Build sentences by combining an independent and a dependent clause.
- Use independent and dependent clauses in writing.
- Become familiar with independent and dependent clause assessment on high-stakes tests.

Monitor Progress

Grammar

If... students have difficulty distinguishing independent and dependent clauses,	**then...** provide additional instruction and practice in The Grammar and Writing Book pp. 62–65.

DAILY FIX-IT

This week use Daily Fix-It Transparency 3.

Grammar Support See the Grammar Transition lessons in the ELL and Transition Handbook.

▲ **The Grammar and Writing Book** For more instruction and practice, use pp. 62–65.

DAY 1 Teach and Model

DAILY FIX-IT

1. Marge like to read adventur stories. *(likes; adventure)*
2. She readed a book set in spain. *(read; Spain)*

READING-GRAMMAR CONNECTION

Write this sentence from *Island of the Blue Dolphins* on the board:

It would be my home until the white men returned in their ship.

Explain that this sentence begins with an **independent clause** *(It would be my home)* and ends with a **dependent clause** *(until the white men returned in their ship).*

Display Grammar Transparency 3. Read aloud the definitions and example sentence. Work through the items.

Independent and Dependent Clauses

A related group of words with a subject and a predicate is called a **clause.** A clause that makes sense by itself is an **independent clause.** A clause that does not make sense by itself is a **dependent clause.** A **complex sentence** contains an independent and a dependent clause.

Independent Clause ↓ **Dependent Clause** ↓

Native Americans lived on the island *until they were attacked.*

- In the example sentence, *Native Americans lived on the island* could stand alone as a sentence, so it is an independent clause. The second clause *(until they were attacked)* cannot stand alone. It must be combined with an independent clause to make sense, so it is a dependent clause.
- If the dependent clause comes first, set it off with a comma: *Until they were attacked, Native Americans lived on the island.* If the independent clause is first, no comma is needed: *Native Americans lived on the island until they were attacked.*

Directions Write *I* after each independent clause. Write *D* after each dependent clause.

1. if you live on an island D
2. the tides affect your life I
3. the water level rises I
4. when the tide comes in D
5. much of the beach disappears under water I
6. until the tide goes out D

Directions Write sentences combining each pair of clauses from the first exercise. Use correct capitalization and punctuation.

7. (Clauses 1 and 2) If you live on an island, the tides affect your life.
8. (Clauses 3 and 4) The water level rises when the tide comes in.
9. (Clauses 5 and 6) Much of the beach disappears under water until the tide goes out.

© Pearson Education

Unit 1 Island of the Blue Dolphins Grammar 3

▲ **Grammar Transparency** 3

DAY 2 Develop the Concept

DAILY FIX-IT

3. Mr. Jones is a expert on Native american history. *(an; American)*
4. Him gived a talk about the Cherokee to our class. *(He gave)*

GUIDED PRACTICE

Review the concept of independent and dependent clauses.

- A related group of words with a subject and a predicate is called a **clause.**
- A clause that makes sense by itself is an **independent clause.**
- A clause that does not make sense by itself is a **dependent clause.**

HOMEWORK Grammar and Writing Practice Book p. 9. Work through the first two items with the class.

Independent and Dependent Clauses

A related group of words with a subject and a predicate is called a **clause.** A clause that makes sense by itself is an **independent clause.** A clause that does not make sense by itself is a **dependent clause.** A **complex sentence** contains an independent and a dependent clause.

Independent Clause They came to the island in canoes.
Dependent Clause even though it was a long trip

If the dependent clause comes first, set it off with a comma: *Until they were attacked, Native Americans lived on the island.* If the independent clause is first, no comma is needed. *Native Americans lived on the island until they were attacked.*

Directions Write *I* if the underlined group of words is an independent clause. Write *D* if it is a dependent clause.

1. If you live on an island, you become independent. D
2. Natives made their own clothes because they could not buy them. I
3. Since there were no stores, they hunted for food. I
4. A seal provided meat while people used its hide for clothes. D
5. A hunting party paddled boats out to sea so that they could catch fish. I
6. Women gathered berries and roots before winter came. D
7. Because they needed containers for the food, they made baskets out of grasses. D

Directions Underline the dependent clause in each sentence.

8. Because they cooked with fire, the natives kept live coals.
9. After food was prepared, they covered the embers with ashes.
10. While they slept through the night, the coals stayed warm.
11. The coals smoldered until morning came.
12. When the cook blew on the coals, they glowed brightly.
13. She fed wood to the coals so that the fire would catch again.
14. If her husband had caught fish that morning, they would eat well for breakfast.

School-Home CONNECTION **Home Activity** Your child learned about independent and dependent clauses. Ask your child to write a sentence about Native Americans using an independent clause and a dependent clause and explain the difference between the two.

▲ **Grammar and Writing Practice Book** p. 9

DAY 3 Apply to Writing

DAILY FIX-IT

5. If you go to south Dakota. You should see the Badlands. *(South; Dakota, you)*
6. Thay look like a sene from another planet. *(They; scene)*

COMBINE CLAUSES

Explain the differences between simple and complex sentences.

Explain that complex sentences add interest to writing and help show relationships between ideas.

- Have students review something they have written to see if they can elaborate by joining or adding clauses with subordinating conjunctions such as *when, if, because* or *after.*

HOMEWORK Grammar and Writing Practice Book p. 10.

Independent and Dependent Clauses

Directions Add an independent clause to each dependent clause to create a sentence that makes sense. Write the sentence. **Possible answers:**

1. because the natives depended on the sea for food
   Because the natives depended on the sea for food, they built boats.
2. so that they could make a boat
   They found a large, sturdy tree so that they could make a boat.
3. after the tree was cut down
   After the tree was cut down, it was hollowed out with fire.
4. when the ashes were scraped out
   When the ashes were scraped out, a round-bottomed boat shape was left.
5. since the boat was made by digging out wood
   Since the boat was made by digging out wood, it was called a dugout.
6. so that they would be watertight
   Many boats were sealed with tar so that they would be watertight.
7. because the boats were so well made
   A hunting party could spend long days at sea because the boats were so well made.

School-Home Connection **Home Activity** Your child learned how to write sentences that combine an independent and a dependent clause. With your child, read an article about Native Americans. Have your child look for sentences that have both kinds of clauses.

▲ **Grammar and Writing Practice Book** p. 10

DAY 4 Test Preparation

DAILY FIX-IT

7. Natives on the cost hunted, and fished at sea. *(coast hunted and)*
8. They lived near the water. Because it was their source of food? *(water because; food.)*

STANDARDIZED TEST PREP

Test Tip

A dependent clause may come before or after an independent clause. When it comes first, it is set off by a comma.

Beginning: When the salmon swam upriver, natives caught many fish.

Ending: Natives caught many fish when the salmon swam upriver.

HOMEWORK Grammar and Writing Practice Book p. 11.

Independent and Dependent Clauses

Directions Mark the letter of the sentence that contains both an independent clause and a dependent clause.

1. A Natives used different kinds of natural materials as tools.
   B A sharp-edged rock could serve as a knife.
   C Hot rocks were placed into the fire.
   (D) When they got hot, they acted like an oven.
2. A Bones of some animals became tools too.
   (B) Because bone is so hard, it can pass through leather.
   C A long, thin piece of bone with a sharp end served as a needle.
   D A large bone could serve as a club or even a ladle.
3. A Bones were also used as decoration.
   (B) Artists might carve bone if the weather was bad.
   C A knife of stone could slice into the bone.
   D Some were cut into interesting shapes.
4. A Hides of animals provided clothing.
   B The hide was scraped long and hard.
   (C) Deerskin made soft, warm clothing after it was tanned.
   D Tougher parts of the deerskin were suitable for moccasins.
5. A Natives on the seacoast gathered beautiful shells.
   B Some colors and types of shells were especially valuable.
   C These shells were used as a form of money for trade.
   (D) Until white people arrived, gold and silver coins were unknown.
6. A The natives respected all forms of life.
   B They depended on animals for food and clothing.
   (C) They used every part of the animal so that nothing was wasted.
   D Animals always appeared in Native American tales and myths.
7. (A) The coyote was respected because it was intelligent.
   B It could be a competitor for small game and berries.
   C Coyotes and humans are omnivores.
   D They eat both animals and plants.
8. A The bison was the mainstay of life on the Great Plains.
   B These huge beasts covered the plains until the late 1800s.
   C White hunters killed bison for sport or for their tongues.
   (D) Although most of the bison were killed, the species survived.

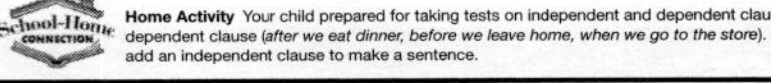
School-Home Connection **Home Activity** Your child prepared for taking tests on independent and dependent clauses. Say a dependent clause (*after we eat dinner, before we leave home, when we go to the store*). Have your child add an independent clause to make a sentence.

▲ **Grammar and Writing Practice Book** p. 11

DAY 5 Cumulative Review

DAILY FIX-IT

9. After white settlers took there land many Native Americans lived on reservations. *(their land,)*
10. With little land, it was dificult to hunt with bow and arow. *(difficult; arrow)*

ADDITIONAL PRACTICE

Assign pp. 62–65 in The Grammar and Writing Book.

EXTRA PRACTICE Grammar and Writing Practice Book p. 124.

ASSESSMENT

CUMULATIVE REVIEW Grammar and Writing Practice Book p. 12.

Independent and Dependent Clauses

Directions Write *I* after each independent clause. Write *D* after each dependent clause.

1. some Native Americans built homes of wood __I__
2. where they lived year-round __D__
3. others made tipis of skins and poles __I__
4. so that they could move their homes __D__
5. the cone-shaped tipi was useful __I__
6. because it was efficient and portable __D__
7. when the herd moved on __D__
8. the tipis were quickly taken down __I__
9. the natives followed the bison __I__
10. until the herd reached new grazing land __D__

Directions: Write sentences combining each pair of clauses in the first exercise. Use correct capitalization and punctuation.

11. (Clauses 1 and 2) Some Native Americans built homes of wood where they lived year-round.
12. (Clauses 3 and 4) Others made tipis of skins and poles so that they could move their homes.
13. (Clauses 5 and 6) The cone-shaped tipi was useful because it was efficient and portable.
14. (Clauses 7 and 8) When the herd moved on, the tipis were quickly taken down.
15. (Clauses 9 and 10) The natives followed the bison until the herd reached new grazing land.

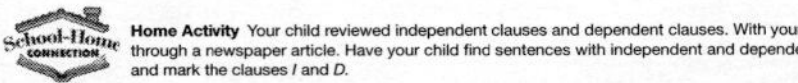
School-Home Connection **Home Activity** Your child reviewed independent clauses and dependent clauses. With your child, look through a newspaper article. Have your child find sentences with independent and dependent clauses and mark the clauses *I* and *D*.

▲ **Grammar and Writing Practice Book** p. 12

AFTER READING

Writing Workshop Friendly or Thank-You Letter

OBJECTIVES

- Identify qualities of a friendly or thank you letter.
- Write a letter using transitions to connect ideas smoothly.
- Focus on organization/paragraphs.
- Use a rubric.

Genre Friendly or Thank-You Letter
Writer's Craft Transitions
Writing Trait Organization/ Paragraphs

ELL

Organization/Paragraphs Explain that transition words make order clear in writing. Write *first, next, then, after, before, also,* and *but* on index cards, one to a card, and model their meaning and use. Help language learners use these transition words in their writing. Display cards for reference.

Writing Traits

FOCUS/IDEAS Important, interesting details clarify description and meaning.

ORGANIZATION/PARAGRAPHS The letter's paragraphs and details are carefully built; use of transitions makes them flow smoothly.

VOICE The writer's personality shows in caring and honest interaction with reader.

WORD CHOICE The writer uses specific words *(whitest, fiery hot)* and strong verbs *(dart).*

SENTENCES Use of dependent clauses adds interest to sentence structures and shows relationships between ideas.

CONVENTIONS There is excellent control and accuracy.

DAY 1 Model the Trait

READING-WRITING CONNECTION

- *Island of the Blue Dolphins* tells about a girl's island adventure.
- The story builds narrative paragraphs carefully, using many time and place transitions.
- Students will write a **friendly or thank-you letter** with transitions and paragraph organization. Explain that an informal friendly letter can share news and make requests, as well as say thanks.

MODEL ORGANIZATION/ PARAGRAPHS Discuss Writing Transparency 3A. Then discuss the model and the writing trait of organization/paragraphs.

Think Aloud The letter is organized using correct format. The writer begins with a greeting and ends with the closing "Love" and a signature. Each paragraph is about one idea. Details describe the beach. The transition, "As soon as we arrived," helps the paragraph fit in smoothly.

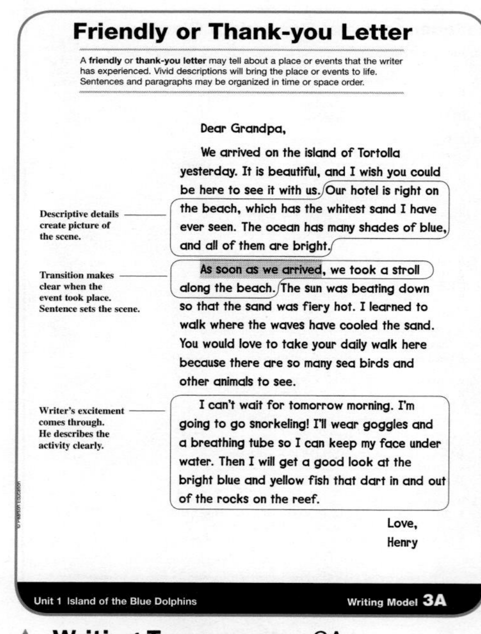

Friendly or Thank-you Letter

A **friendly** or **thank-you letter** may tell about a place or events that the writer has experienced. Vivid descriptions will bring the place or events to life. Sentences and paragraphs may be organized in time or space order.

Dear Grandpa,

We arrived on the island of Tortolla yesterday. It is beautiful, and I wish you could be here to see it with us. Our hotel is right on the beach, which has the whitest sand I have ever seen. The ocean has many shades of blue, and all of them are bright.

As soon as we arrived, we took a stroll along the beach. The sun was beating down so that the sand was fiery hot. I learned to walk where the waves have cooled the sand. You would love to take your daily walk here because there are so many sea birds and other animals to see.

I can't wait for tomorrow morning. I'm going to go snorkeling! I'll wear goggles and a breathing tube so I can keep my face under water. Then I will get a good look at the bright blue and yellow fish that dart in and out of the rocks on the reef.

Love,
Henry

Descriptive details create picture of the scene.

Transition makes clear when the event took place. Sentence sets the scene.

Writer's excitement comes through. He describes the activity clearly.

Unit 1 Island of the Blue Dolphins — Writing Model 3A

▲ **Writing Transparency** 3A

DAY 2 Improve Writing

WRITER'S CRAFT Transitions

Display Writing Transparency 3B. Read the directions and work together to understand the purpose of and use transitions.

CONNECT IDEAS WITH TRANSITIONS Tomorrow, we will write a **friendly or thank-you letter.** I could write to my sister telling her about the trail ride I took. Each paragraph in the body of the letter would tell about what happened that day. Transitions such as "first thing in the morning," "as we started out," and "by the time we stopped for lunch" would show the sequence of events clearly.

GUIDED WRITING Some students may need more help with transitions. Work with them to identify transitions and their purpose in the selection.

Transitions

- **Transitions** are words or phrases that connect sentences or paragraphs. They show how one thought leads to the next.
- Some transitions show time order, or sequence of events: *first, next, then.*
- Some transitions describe space order, or where one place is in relationship to another: *above, below, nearby.*
- Some transitions compare and contrast *(similarly, on the other hand)* or point out a cause and effect *(because, as a result).*

Directions Mark the letter of the phrase that tells the purpose of the underlined transitions.

1. The road sliced through the desert in a straight line. On the horizon, long ridges of sand lay like an ocean. Far in the distance, hazy blue mountains pointed skyward. High above their peaks, the sun shone down.
   A time order — (B) space order — C compare/contrast — D cause and effect
2. At first, the snake appeared lifeless. It lay still and coiled on a large, flat rock. Then, as the sun rose, the air grew warmer. A little later, the snake uncoiled itself and tested the air with its forked tongue.
   (A) time order — B space order — C compare/contrast — D cause and effect
3. By day the desert is hot as a firecracker. Every living thing seeks shelter from the punishing sun. In contrast, by night it becomes very cool, and its many animals emerge from burrows, tunnels, and rocky shelters.
   A time order — B space order — (C) compare and contrast — D cause and effect

Directions Add transitions from the box to make the sentences flow more smoothly. Use punctuation and capital letters correctly.

as soon as — when — then — at that moment — first

(4) First I want to thank you for my surprise party. (5) When I walked to your house, I didn't suspect a thing. (6) As soon as I opened the door, I thought I heard whispering. (7) Then I called, "Anybody home?" and walked into the den. (8) At that moment, twenty kids jumped out and yelled, "Surprise!"

Unit 1 Island of the Blue Dolphins — Writer's Craft 3B

▲ **Writing Transparency** 3B

Trait of the Week

Organization/ Paragraphs

DAY 3 Prewrite and Draft

READ THE WRITING PROMPT

on page 85 in the Student Edition.

In Island of the Blue Dolphins, *the narrator describes a place as she might in a letter to a friend.*

Think about a place you could describe.

Now write a friendly or thank-you letter about the place.

Writing Test Tips

- Include details that will interest your friend.
- Choose words that give a clear picture of events or things.
- Use transitions to show connections between ideas.

GETTING STARTED Students can do any of the following:

- Use a graphic organizer such as a sequence chart to list events in time order.
- Brainstorm a list of vivid adjectives and strong verbs to describe the place.
- Begin with an attention-getting sentence.

DAY 4 Draft and Revise

EDITING/REVISING CHECKLIST

☑ Have I used transitions to connect sentences and paragraphs smoothly?

☑ Are my sentences and paragraphs organized logically?

☑ Have I combined dependent and independent clauses in some sentences?

☑ Are words with long vowel digraphs spelled correctly?

See *The Grammar and Writing Book,* pp. 62–67.

Revising Tips

Organization/ paragraphs

- Arrange paragraphs logically, to show time order or space order.
- Use transitions that make sentences flow logically.
- Include supporting details that create a clear picture of each event or place described.

PUBLISHING Invite students to read their letters to a small group.

ASSESSMENT Use the scoring rubric to evaluate students' work.

DAY 5 Connect to Unit Writing

Personal Narrative

Week 1	Character Sketch 41g–41h
Week 2	Tall Tale 67g–67h
Week 3	Friendly or Thank-You Letter 89g–89h
Week 4	Feature Article 111g–111h
Week 5	Narrative Writing 133g–133h

PREVIEW THE UNIT PROMPT

Write a personal narrative about a challenge or difficult problem. Describe what the challenge was and tell how you met it. Use details that make the events clear and interesting.

APPLY

- The use of transitions can help connect the ideas and events in a personal narrative.

Writing Trait Rubric

	4	3	2	1
Organization/ Paragraphs	Ideas well developed from beginning to end; strong attention-getter and closure	Ideas that progress from beginning to end; good attention-getter and closure	Some sense of movement from beginning to end; weak attention-getter and closure	No sense of movement from beginning to end; no attention-getter or closure
	Letter organized with helpful transitions	Letter organized with some logical order and some transitions	Letter not clearly organized; uses few transitions	Letter not organized; no transitions

Spelling & Phonics Long Vowel Digraphs

OBJECTIVE

- Spell words with long vowel digraphs *ai, ee, ea, oa,* and *ow.*

Generalization

Connect to Phonics Long *a* is sometimes spelled *ai: paint.* Long *e* is sometimes spelled *ee* or *ea: speech, feast.* Long *o* is sometimes spelled *oa* or *ow: coast, arrow.* If a word has two vowels in a row, the first vowel is usually long, and the second vowel is silent.

Spelling Words

1. coast*	11. faint
2. feast	12. maintain
3. speech	13. crease
4. wheat	14. groan
5. Spain	15. breeze
6. paint	16. willow
7. arrow*	17. appeal
8. needle	18. bowling
9. charcoal	19. complain
10. praise	20. sneeze

Challenge Words

21. dungarees	24. speedometer
22. bungalow	25. referee
23. campaign	

* Words from the selection

Spelling/Phonics Support See the ELL and Transition Handbook for spelling support.

DAY 1 Pretest and Sort

PRETEST

Use the Dictation Sentences from Day 5 to administer the pretest. Read the word, read the sentence, and then read the word again. Guide students in self-correcting their pretests and correcting any misspellings.

Monitor Progress

Spelling

If... students misspell more than 5 pretest words,	**then...** use words 1–10 for Strategic Intervention.
If... students misspell 1–5 pretest words,	**then...** use words 1–20 for On-Level practice.
If... students correctly spell all pretest words,	**then...** use words 1–25 for Advanced Learners.

HOMEWORK Spelling Practice Book, p. 9.

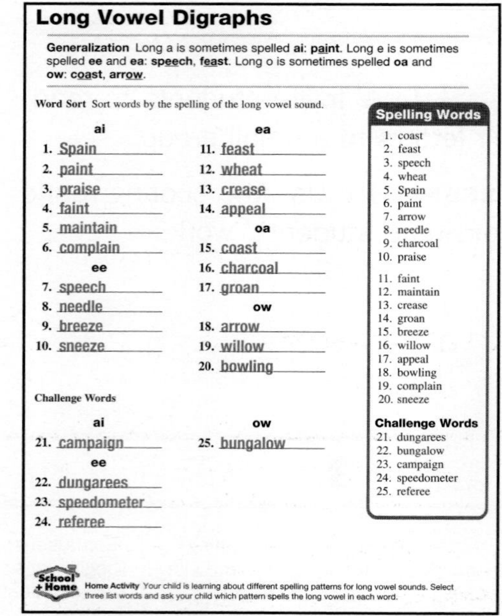

Long Vowel Digraphs

Generalization Long a is sometimes spelled **ai**: **paint**. Long e is sometimes spelled **ee** and **ea**: **speech**, **feast**. Long o is sometimes spelled **oa** and **ow**: **coast**, **arrow**.

Word Sort Sort words by the spelling of the long vowel sound.

ai
1. Spain
2. paint
3. praise
4. faint
5. maintain
6. complain

ee
7. speech
8. needle
9. breeze
10. sneeze

ea
11. feast
12. wheat
13. crease
14. appeal

oa
15. coast
16. charcoal
17. groan

ow
18. arrow
19. willow
20. bowling

Challenge Words

ai
21. campaign

ee
22. dungarees
23. speedometer
24. referee

ow
25. bungalow

Spelling Words
1. coast
2. feast
3. speech
4. wheat
5. Spain
6. paint
7. arrow
8. needle
9. charcoal
10. praise
11. faint
12. maintain
13. crease
14. groan
15. breeze
16. willow
17. appeal
18. bowling
19. complain
20. sneeze

Challenge Words
21. dungarees
22. bungalow
23. campaign
24. speedometer
25. referee

School + Home **Home Activity** Your child is learning about different spelling patterns for long vowel sounds. Select three list words and ask your child which pattern spells the long vowel in each word.

▲ **Spelling Practice Book** p. 9

DAY 2 Think and Practice

TEACH

Two vowels in a row usually stand for one sound—the long sound of the first letter. Write *praise* on the board. Underline vowel digraph *ai.* Say *praise* and point out that the letters *ai* spell the long *a* sound. Guide students in finding vowel digraphs that stand for the long vowel sounds in *sneeze, wheat, groan,* and *willow.*

praise

CIRCLE THE DIGRAPHS Have students write the list words and highlight each digraph. If colors are available, they may use one color for *ai,* and different colors for *ee, ea, oa,* and *ow.*

HOMEWORK Spelling Practice Book, p. 10.

Long Vowel Digraphs

Spelling Words				
coast	feast	speech	wheat	Spain
paint	arrow	needle	charcoal	praise
faint	maintain	crease	groan	breeze
willow	appeal	bowling	complain	sneeze

Words in Context Complete each sentence with a list word.

1. I am dizzy and may ____. 1. faint
2. A perfect ____ score is 300. 2. bowling
3. I heard the accident victim ____ because he was hurt. 3. groan
4. High ____ tells you that you did a great job. 4. praise
5. Make a ____ in the paper to fold it in half. 5. crease
6. Food grilled over a ____ fire tastes great. 6. charcoal
7. It is generally better to be positive rather than to ____. 7. complain
8. A sailboat needs a strong ____ to go fast. 8. breeze
9. Antique car owners spend a lot of time and money to ____ their vehicles so they will continue to run. 9. maintain
10. Two countries that border ____ are Portugal and France. 10. Spain

Classifying Write the list word that belongs in each group.

11. bow, feather, ____ 11. arrow
12. sew, thread, ____ 12. needle
13. glide, cruise, ____ 13. coast
14. cold, cough, ____ 14. sneeze
15. elm, oak, ____ 15. willow
16. talk, lecture, ____ 16. speech

Synonyms Write the list word that has the same or nearly the same meaning.

17. request 17. appeal
18. banquet 18. feast
19. grain 19. wheat
20. color 20. paint

School + Home **Home Activity** Your child wrote words with long vowel digraphs. Have your child tell you two ways to spell long e.

▲ **Spelling Practice Book** p. 10

AFTER READING

DAY 3 Connect to Writing

WRITE ABOUT FAMOUS PEOPLE

Ask students to list four famous people and write a sentence about each one, using at least one spelling word in each sentence.

Frequently Misspelled Words

Halloween *really*

These words may seem easy to spell, but they are often misspelled by fifth-graders. Alert students to these frequently misspelled words. Point out the long vowel digraphs in the words. Reinforce the double *l* in *really* by writing *real* and adding the suffix *-ly*.

HOMEWORK Spelling Practice Book, p. 11.

Long Vowel Digraphs

Proofread a Report Miguel wrote about his family's trip. Circle six spelling errors. Find one punctuation error. Write the corrections on the lines.

This summer, my family traveled to Spain. We felt very lucky to stay in a hotel right on the caost. The weather was always beautiful with a light breaze blowing in off the ocean. Outside my window, the branches of a wilow tree dipped into a small pond. The sky was the same color as the baby blue color in my pante box. On our last night we had a wonderful feest. I thought I would fante at the sight of so much food! Everything was really delicious? I felt my stomach groan when we got to dessert. Is that anything to complain about?

1. coast 2. breeze
3. willow 4. paint
5. feast 6. faint
7. Everything was really delicious.

Spelling Words: coast, feast, speech, wheat, Spain, paint, arrow, needle, charcoal, praise, faint, maintain, crease, groan, breeze, willow, appeal, bowling, complain, sneeze

Frequently Misspelled Words: Halloween, really

Proofread Words Circle the correct spelling of the word.

8.	weat	wheet	wheat
9.	charcole	charcoal	charcol
10.	maintain	maintane	mantain
11.	boling	bolling	bowling
12.	complain	complane	complan
13.	creese	creaze	crease
14.	arow	arrow	arro

School + Home **Home Activity** Your child corrected misspelled list words in a paragraph and selected the correctly spelled word in a group of words. Select three list words and ask your child to spell them.

▲ **Spelling Practice Book** p. 11

DAY 4 Review

REVIEW LONG VOWEL DIGRAPHS

Have students make a word web for each vowel digraph. Have them write *ai, ee, ea, oa,* or *ow* in the center circle of a web and then write the appropriate list words in smaller circles around the center circles.

Spelling Strategy
Rhyming Helpers

Use rhymes to help spell. Rhyming helpers are spelled the same at the end. Watch out! Rhyming words are not always good helpers. *Coast* and *toast* are rhyming helpers, but *groan* and *stone* are not.

HOMEWORK Spelling Practice Book, p. 12.

Long Vowel Digraphs

Spelling Words				
coast	feast	speech	wheat	Spain
paint	arrow	needle	charcoal	praise
faint	maintain	crease	groan	breeze
willow	appeal	bowling	complain	sneeze

Crossword Puzzle Write list words to complete the puzzle.

Across
2. fold
4. compliment
6. glide or slide
7. bow and ___
11. used to sew
12. kind of tree
13. a talk
14. use color
15. moan
16. light wind
17. request
18. to keep up

Down
1. banquet
2. used to BBQ
3. a country
5. family sport
8. pass out
9. cough and ___
10. whine
12. a grain

School + Home **Home Activity** Your child has learned to read, write, and spell words with long vowel digraph patterns. Look through books with your child to find three new words with long vowel digraphs.

▲ **Spelling Practice Book** p. 12

DAY 5 Posttest

DICTATION SENTENCES

1. California is on the west coast.
2. We filled our plates at the feast.
3. Do you enjoy making a speech?
4. These rolls are made from wheat.
5. Soccer is a popular sport in Spain.
6. We will paint the walls blue.
7. An arrow points to the exit.
8. A dropped needle is hard to find.
9. Dad filled the grill with charcoal.
10. I hope the critics praise the play.
11. We heard a faint sound outside.
12. Who will maintain the new garden?
13. Jim pressed the crease out of his shirt.
14. We groan when we hear a bad joke.
15. The breeze made the flag wave.
16. A weeping willow has long branches.
17. The library made an appeal for book donations.
18. Don't drop the heavy bowling ball!
19. People often complain about rainy days.
20. Some flowers make me sneeze.

CHALLENGE

21. My blue dungarees are worn out.
22. We stayed in a bungalow in the country.
23. What office would you like to campaign for?
24. The speedometer says we're going too fast.
25. The referee blew the whistle.

OBJECTIVES

- Formulate an inquiry question that is connected to this week's lesson focus.
- Effectively and efficiently find, evaluate, and communicate information related to an inquiry question using electronic sources.

New Literacies

Day 1	**Identify Questions**
Day 2	**Navigate/Search**
Day 3	**Analyze**
Day 4	**Synthesize**
Day 5	**Communicate**

NEW LITERACIES

Internet Inquiry Activity

EXPLORE WILDERNESS SURVIVAL

Use the following 5-day plan to help students conduct this week's Internet inquiry activity on wilderness survival. Remind students to follow classroom rules when using the Internet.

DAY 1

Identify Questions Discuss the lesson focus question: *How do people survive in the wilderness?* Brainstorm ideas for specific inquiry questions about wilderness survival. For example, students might investigate how campers and hikers can avoid being struck by lightning. Have students work individually, in pairs, or in small groups to write inquiry questions.

DAY 2

Navigate/Search Before students begin their search, review the steps for using a student-friendly search engine. Have students brainstorm keywords or phrases that might help them narrow their searches. Encourage them to try several keywords to get a range of information. Explain that it is often a process of trial and error to find the appropriate information.

DAY 3

Analyze Have students review the Web sites they identified on Day 2. Tell them to scan each site for information that helps answer their inquiry questions. They can check a Web site's publication date to see if the information is up-to-date.

DAY 4

Synthesize Have students synthesize information they gathered from the most useful Web sites they found on Day 3. Remind students that to avoid plagiarism they should use their own words to restate the information they have read.

DAY 5

Communicate Have students share their inquiry results. For example, students can use a word processing program to create lists of wilderness safety tips. They can use boldface, italics, different font types, or different font sizes to emphasize the most important information.

RESEARCH/STUDY SKILLS

SPQ3R

TEACH

Ask students what they can do to make sure they understand a selection before, during, and after reading it. Students may need prompting before they mention surveying, predicting, questioning, reading, reciting, and reviewing. Define each element of **SPQ3R.**

- When you **survey** a selection, you look for information in the title, author name, chapter headings, and illustrations to get ideas of what you are about to read.
- When you **predict**, you imagine (based on your survey) what the selection will be about.
- When you **question**, you ask what you want to find out as you read.
- When you **read** for understanding, you keep your questions and predictions in mind.
- When you **recite**, you tell or write about what you learned from reading.
- When you **review**, you look back at the predictions you made, the questions you asked, the answers you found, and the information you learned.

Have students reread "Seven Survival Questions," on pp. 86–89, or another nonfiction selection of their choice, using SPQ3R. Then discuss these questions:

1. **Before you read the selection, what questions do you want to have answered?** *(Possible response: How can you survive outside, if you are lost?)*
2. **Based on your review of what you learned, how accurate was your initial prediction? Explain.** *(Possible response: Fairly accurate, only I thought the selection would tell what to do if you got hurt.)*

ASSESS

As students apply SPQ3R, check that they follow all six steps. Make sure students' work incorporates their surveys, predictions, and questions. Encourage them to record their questions, answers, and what they learned.

For more practice or to assess students, use Practice Book pp. 29–30.

AFTER READING

OBJECTIVES

- Review steps in SPQ3R.
- Use SPQ3R to understand a nonfiction selection.

SPQ3R

SPQ3R is an acronym for a set of study skills that can help you when you read any text. It is especially helpful when reading nonfiction. Here's what it means: **Survey:** Look at the title, author name, chapter headings, and illustrations to get an idea of what you are about to read. **Predict:** Imagine what the story you're going to read is about. **Question:** Generate questions you want answered when reading the story. **Read:** Read the story, keeping your predictions and questions in mind. **Recite:** Recite or write down what you learned from reading the story. **Review:** Look back at the story, the predictions you made, the questions you posed, the answers you found in the text, and the information you learned from your reading.

Directions Use SPQ3R in reading the passage and answering the questions that follow.

Hawaii: A Remote State

Hawaii is a group of volcanic islands in the central Pacific Ocean some 2,300 miles west of San Francisco, California. Hawaii became the fiftieth state in the United States in 1959. Because of its location in the ocean, it is an important military location of the U.S. Because it is so beautiful, it is also one of the most popular vacation spots for Americans even though the flight to Hawaii is long.

Possible answers given.

1. Before you read this passage, what could you tell about the passage by surveying the map?
   The passage is going to be about Hawaii.
2. Before you read this passage, what did you predict the passage would be about?
   the distance between Hawaii and other places
3. What was a question you wanted the passage to answer before you read it?
   Where are Hawaii's best beaches?
4. When did Hawaii become a state? What is one of the things that Hawaii is known for?
   1959; It is an important military location.
5. Write down a brief review of what you learned from this passage? In your review, discuss whether your questions were answered and whether your prediction was true.
   As I predicted, the passage was about Hawaii, but it didn't tell me where the beaches are. I learned when it became a state, that it has military bases, that and is popular for vacations.

▲ **Practice Book** p. 29

Directions Use SPQ3R in reading the passage and answering the questions that follow.

Assateague Island's Wild Horses

Assateague Island is a 37-mile long barrier island, a thin strip of land that helps to protect Maryland's shoreline. It has been an outpost for the U.S. Coast Guard for nearly 50 years. But what's most unique about the island is the horses which roam freely on the beaches and marshland. While the origin of the horses is unclear, the popular myth claims the horses jumped from a sinking Spanish ship and swam to reach this island. It is more likely the horses were taken to the island by landowners trying not to pay taxes on livestock, perhaps as long ago as the seventeenth century.

Possible answers given.

1. Before you read this passage, what could you tell about the passage by surveying the illustration?
   The passage is probably about horses.
2. Before you read this passage, what did you predict the passage would be about?
   It will be about wild horses on an island.
3. Before you read this passage, what questions did you want the passage to answer?
   Do any people live on the island? What do the horses eat?
4. What is most unique about Assateague Island?
   There are horses that roam the island freely.
5. Write down a brief review of what you learned from this passage. In your review, discuss whether your questions were answered and whether your prediction was true.
   As I predicted, the passage was about wild horses on an island. My questions were not answered. I learned that no one really knows how the horses got to the island.

School + Home **Home Activity** Your child learned about the SPQ3R study skill and applied it to two nonfiction passages. Have your child explain the study skill to you. Then, with your child, apply it to a newspaper or magazine article.

▲ **Practice Book** p. 30

AFTER READING

Assessment Checkpoints *for the Week*

Selection Assessment

Use pp. 9–12 of Selection Tests to check:

 **Selection Understanding**

 **Comprehension Skill** *Theme and Setting*

 **Selection Vocabulary**

gnawed	*ravine*
headland	*shellfish*
kelp	*sinew*
lair	

Selection Tests
ASSESSMENT
Scott Foresman
Selection Tests
Teacher's Manual
• Assess comprehension of weekly selections
• Assess understanding of weekly comprehension skills
• Assess knowledge of selection vocabulary
Reading Street
Grade 5

Leveled Assessment

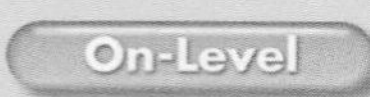

On-Level

Strategic Intervention

Advanced

Use pp. 13–18 of Fresh Reads for Differentiated Test Practice to check:

 **Comprehension Skill** *Theme and Setting*

 REVIEW **Comprehension Skill** *Character and Plot*

 **Fluency** *Words Correct Per Minute*

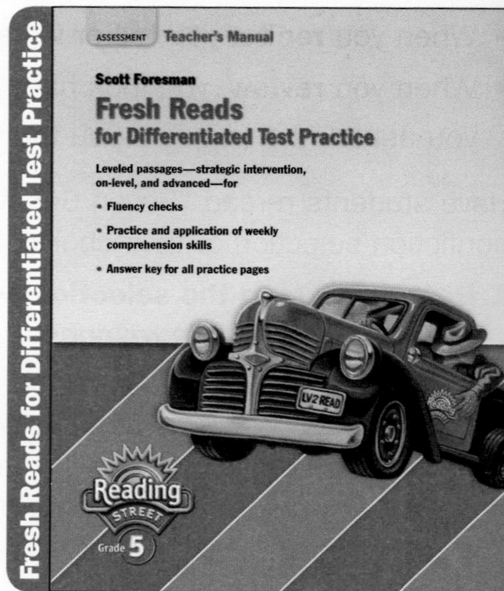

Fresh Reads for Differentiated Test Practice
ASSESSMENT Teacher's Manual
Scott Foresman
Fresh Reads
for Differentiated Test Practice
Leveled passages—strategic intervention, on-level, and advanced—for
• Fluency checks
• Practice and application of weekly comprehension skills
• Answer key for all practice pages
Reading Street
Grade 5

Managing Assessment

Use Assessment Handbook for:

 **Observation Checklists**

 **Record-Keeping Forms**

 **Portfolio Assessment**

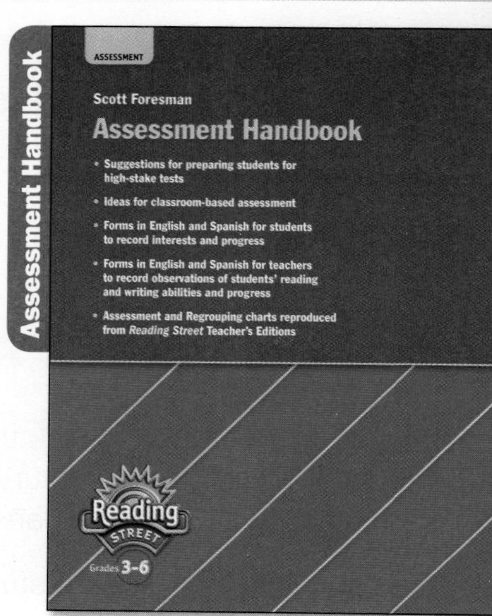

Assessment Handbook
ASSESSMENT
Scott Foresman
Assessment Handbook
• Suggestions for preparing students for high-stake tests
• Ideas for classroom-based assessment
• Forms in English and Spanish for students to record interests and progress
• Forms in English and Spanish for teachers to record observations of students' reading and writing abilities and progress
• Assessment and Regrouping charts reproduced from Reading Street Teacher's Editions
Reading Street
Grades 3–6

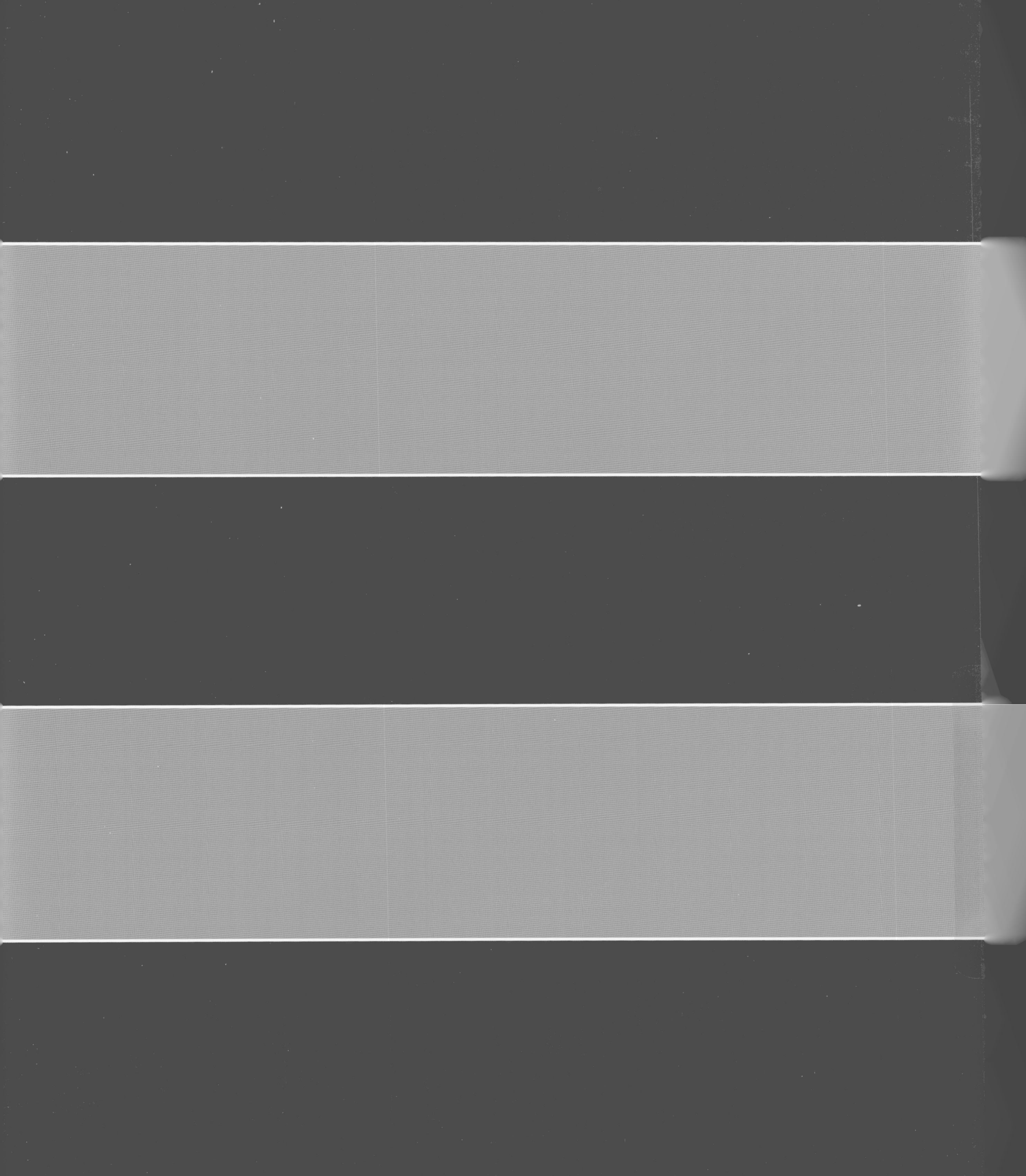

Unit 1

Meeting Challenges

CONCEPT QUESTION

What kinds of challenges do people face and how do they meet them?

Week 1

How do we meet the challenges of learning?

Week 2

How can nature challenge us?

Week 3

How do people survive in the wilderness?

Week 4

How do we face personal challenges?

Week 5

What challenges do immigrants encounter?

Week 4

EXPAND THE CONCEPT

How do we face personal challenges?

Time for SOCIAL STUDIES

Satchel Paige

by Lesa Cline-Ransome
paintings by James E. Ransome

Besides athletic ability, what makes an athlete great?

Social Studies in Reading

Expository Nonfiction

Genre

- Expository nonfiction deals with real people and events.
- Expository articles often appear in magazines.

Text Features

- Some articles deal with how things were different in the past.
- Expository articles about the past often include pictures that show what people and places looked like.

Link to Social Studies
Women couldn't vote in the 1870s, but they could play baseball. Do some research in books or on the Internet to find out when women finally did gain the right to vote and how they gained that right.

THE GIRLS of SUMMER

by Ellen Klages

Baseball is largely considered a man's game. But what if you take a closer look at its history?

The first team of professional baseball players, the Cincinnati Red Stockings, took the field in 1869. They were all male–the first boys of summer. The first girls of summer, women who were paid to play baseball, competed in their first game in 1875.

In the 1870s, an American woman could not vote. She could not own property in her own name after marriage. But she could play ball–as well as it could be played in an outfit that weighed as much as thirty pounds and included a floor-length skirt, underskirts, a long-sleeved, high-necked blouse, and high button shoes.

Amelia Bloomer designed and wore the loose-fitting, Turkish-style trousers that carried her name and made sports more practical for women athletes. In the 1890s, scores of "Bloomer Girls" baseball teams were formed all over the country.

The Bloomer Girls era lasted from the 1890s until 1934. Hundreds of teams–All Star Ranger Girls, Philadelphia Bobbies, New York Bloomer Girls–offered employment, travel, and adventure for young women who could hit, field, slide, or catch.

The Bloomer Girls teams dwindled as more and more minor league teams–farm clubs–were formed to provide experience for young men on their climb up to the majors. A few women were signed, briefly, to minor league contracts, but they were exceptions.

Although women had been playing pro ball on Bloomer Girls teams for more than forty years, in the 1930s public opinion was that they had inferior abilities when it came to sports. Women's professional baseball disappeared when the last of the Bloomer Girls teams disbanded in 1934.

Briefly, in the late 1940s and early 1950s, women played again. But in 1952 they were banned from professional baseball. The ban still holds today.

Reading Across Texts
This selection and *Satchel Paige* show how two groups of people had difficulties playing professional baseball for different reasons. What were those reasons?

Writing Across Texts Present your response in a two-column chart.

Sequence How do the dates help you with the sequence of events?

110

111

CONNECT THE CONCEPT

▶ **Build Background**
courage, hardships, taunts

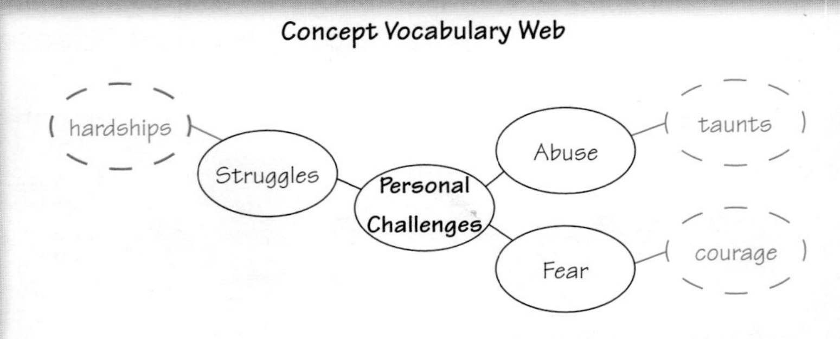

▶ **Social Studies Content**
History of Baseball, Segregation, Women in Sports

▶ **Writing**
Feature Article

▶ **Internet Inquiry**
Athletes Meeting Challenges

Preview Your Week

How do we face personal challenges?

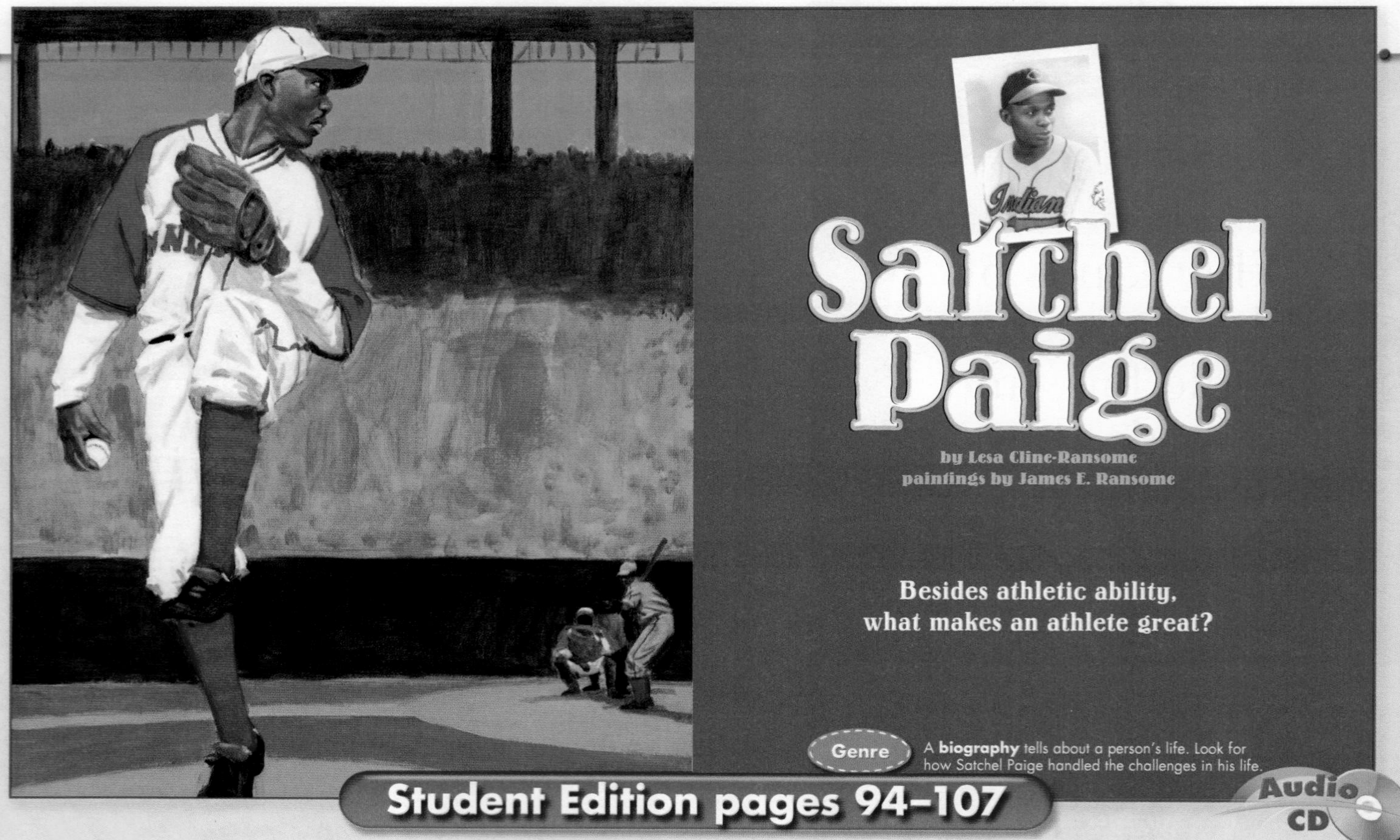
Satchel Paige
by Lesa Cline-Ransome
paintings by James E. Ransome
Besides athletic ability, what makes an athlete great?
Genre
A **biography** tells about a person's life. Look for how Satchel Paige handled the challenges in his life.
Student Edition pages 94–107

Audio CD

Genre Biography

Vocabulary Strategy Context Clues

Comprehension Skill Sequence

Comprehension Strategy Ask Questions

Paired Selection

SOCIAL STUDIES

Reading Across Texts

Compare the Difficulties that Two Groups Experienced

Genre

Expository Nonfiction

Text Features

Pictures

Social Studies in Reading

Expository Nonfiction

Genre
- Expository nonfiction deals with real people and events.
- Expository articles often appear in magazines.

Text Features
- Some articles deal with how things were different in the past.
- Expository articles about the past often include pictures that show what people and places looked like.

Link to Social Studies
Women couldn't vote in the 1870s, but they could play baseball. Do some research in books or on the Internet to find out when women finally did gain the right to vote and how they gained that right.

THE GIRLS of SUMMER

by Ellen Klages

Baseball is largely considered a man's game. But what if you take a closer look at its history?

The first team of professional baseball players, the Cincinnati Red Stockings, took the field in 1869. They were all male–the first boys of summer. The first girls of summer, women who were paid to play baseball, competed in their first game in 1875.

In the 1870s, an American woman could not vote. She could not own property in her own name after marriage. But she could play ball–as well as it could be played in an outfit that weighed as much as thirty pounds and included a floor-length skirt, underskirts, a long-sleeved, high-necked blouse, and high button shoes.

Amelia Bloomer designed and wore the loose-fitting, Turkish-style trousers that carried her name and made sports more practical for women athletes. In the 1890s, scores of "Bloomer Girls" baseball teams were formed all over the country.

The Bloomer Girls era lasted from the 1890s until 1934. Hundreds of teams–All Star Ranger Girls, Philadelphia Bobbies, New York Bloomer Girls–offered employment, travel, and adventure for young women who could hit, field, slide, or catch.

The Bloomer Girls teams dwindled as more and more minor league teams–farm clubs–were formed to provide experience for young men on their climb up to the majors. A few women were signed, briefly, to minor league contracts, but they were exceptions.

Although women had been playing pro ball on Bloomer Girls teams for more than forty years, in the 1930s public opinion was that they had inferior abilities when it came to sports. Women's professional baseball disappeared when the last of the Bloomer Girls teams disbanded in 1934.

Briefly, in the late 1940s and early 1950s, women played again. But in 1952 they were banned from professional baseball. The ban still holds today.

Reading Across Texts

This selection and *Satchel Paige* show how two groups of people had difficulties playing professional baseball for different reasons. What were those reasons?

Writing Across Texts Present your response in a two-column chart.

Sequence How do the dates help you with the sequence of events?

110

Student Edition pages 110–111

Audio
CD

- Student Edition
- Leveled Readers

Leveled Readers

Skill Sequence

Strategy Ask Questions

Lesson Vocabulary

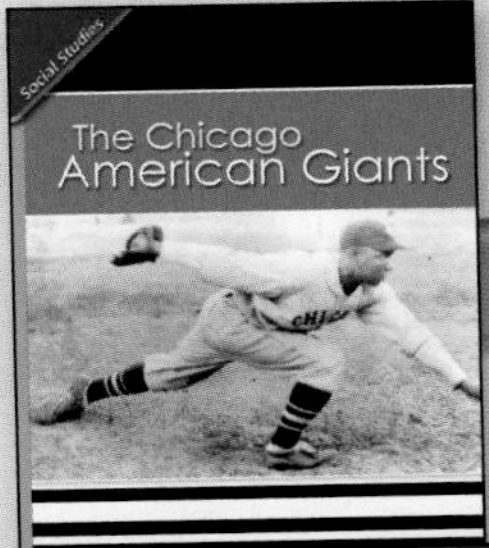

Below-Level

On-Level

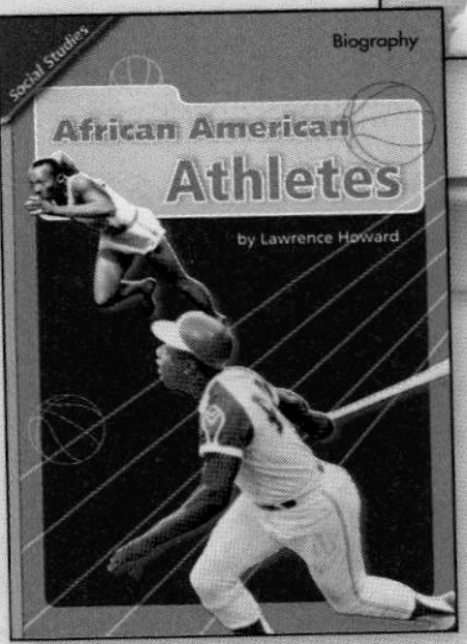

Advanced

ELL Reader

- Concept Vocabulary
- Text Support
- Language Enrichment

Time for SOCIAL STUDIES

Integrate Social Studies Standards

- Sports
- Contributions of Women
- Segregation

Satchel Paige,
pp. 94–107

"The Girls of Summer,"
pp. 110–111

Leveled Readers

Below-Level
- Support Concepts

On-Level
- Develop Concepts

Advanced
- Extend Concepts
- Social Studies Extension Activity

ELL Reader

Build **Concept Vocabulary**
Personal Challenges,
pp. 90l–90m

Teach **Social Studies Concepts**
History of Baseball, p. 97
Segregation, p. 101
Women in Sports, p. 111

Explore **Social Studies Center**
Find Out About Uniforms,
p. 90k

Weekly Plan

READING

45–90 minutes

TARGET SKILLS OF THE WEEK

Comprehension Skill
Sequence

Comprehension Strategy
Ask Questions

Vocabulary Strategy
Context Clues

DAY 1

PAGES 90l–92b, 111a, 111e–111k

Oral Language

QUESTION OF THE WEEK *How do we face personal challenges?*

Read Aloud: "Teammates," 90m
Build Concepts, 90l

Comprehension/Vocabulary

Comprehension Skill/Strategy Lesson, 90–91
- Sequence **T**
- Ask Questions

Build Background, 92a

Introduce Lesson Vocabulary, 92b
confidence, fastball, mocking, outfield, unique, weakness, windup **T**

Read Leveled Readers

Grouping Options 90f–90g

Fluency

Model Phrasing, 90l–90m, 111a

DAY 2

PAGES 92–103, 111a, 111e–111k

Oral Language

QUESTION OF THE DAY *How did Satchel's personality help him meet personal challenges?*

Comprehension/Vocabulary

Vocabulary Strategy Lesson, 92–93
- Context Clues **T**

Read *Satchel Paige,* 94–103

Grouping Options 90f–90g

- Sequence **T**
- Ask Questions
- Context Clues **T**
- REVIEW Compare and Contrast **T**

Develop Vocabulary

Fluency

Echo Reading, 111a

LANGUAGE ARTS

30–60 minutes

Trait of the Week

Word Choice

Day 1

Grammar, 111e
Introduce Compound and Complex Sentences **T**

Writing Workshop, 111g
Introduce Feature Article
Model the Trait of the Week: Word Choice

Spelling, 111i
Pretest for Adding *-ed, -ing*

Internet Inquiry, 111k
Identify Questions

Day 2

Grammar, 111e
Develop Compound and Complex Sentences **T**

Writing Workshop, 111g
Improve Writing with Tone

Spelling, 111i
Teach the Generalization

Internet Inquiry, 111k
Navigate/Search

DAILY WRITING ACTIVITIES

Day 1 Write to Read, 90

Day 2 Words to Write, 93
Strategy Response Log, 94, 103

DAILY SOCIAL STUDIES CONNECTIONS

Day 1 Personal Challenges Concept Web, 90l

Day 2 Time for Social Studies: U.S. History and Baseball, 97; Segregation and Jim Crow Laws, 101; Revisit the Personal Challenges Concept Web, 103

DAILY SUCCESS PREDICTORS

for Adequate Yearly Progress

Monitor Progress and Corrective Feedback

	Day 1	Day 2
Vocabulary	Check Vocabulary, *90l*	

RESOURCES FOR THE WEEK

- Practice Book, *pp. 31–40*
- Word Study and Spelling Practice Book, *pp. 13–16*
- Grammar and Writing Practice Book, *pp. 13–16*
- Selection Test, *pp. 13–16*
- Fresh Reads for Differentiated Test Practice, *pp. 19–24*
- The Grammar and Writing Book, *pp. 68–73*

Grouping Options for Differentiated Instruction

Turn the page for the small group lesson plan.

DAY 3 PAGES 104–109, 111a, 111e–111k

Oral Language

QUESTION OF THE DAY *How would Satchel's reputation be different if Josh had hit a homer?*

Comprehension/Vocabulary

Read *Satchel Paige,* 104–108

Grouping Options 90f–90g

Sequence **T**

Ask Questions

Develop Vocabulary

Reader Response

Selection Test

Fluency

Model Phrasing, 111a

Grammar, 111f
Apply Compound and Complex Sentences in Writing **T**

Writing Workshop, 109, 111h
Write Now
Prewrite and Draft

Spelling, 111j
Connect Spelling to Writing

Internet Inquiry, 111k
Analyze Sources

Day 3 Strategy Response Log, 106
Look Back and Write, 108

Day 3 Social Studies Center: Find Out About Uniforms, 90k; Revisit the Personal Challenges Concept Web, 107

DAY 4 PAGES 110–111a, 111e–111k

Oral Language

QUESTION OF THE DAY *Why do you think many people look to athletes for inspiration?*

Comprehension/Vocabulary

Read "The Girls of Summer," 110–111

Grouping Options 90f–90g

Expository Nonfiction

Reading Across Texts

Content-Area Vocabulary

Fluency

Partner Reading, 111a

Grammar, 111f
Practice Compound and Complex Sentences for Standardized Tests **T**

Writing Workshop, 111h
Draft, Revise, and Publish

Spelling, 111j
Provide a Strategy

Internet Inquiry, 111k
Synthesize Information

Day 4 Writing Across Texts, 111

Day 4 Time for Social Studies: Women in Sports, 111

DAY 5 PAGES 111a–111l

Oral Language

QUESTION OF THE WEEK *To wrap up the week, revisit the Day 1 question.*

Build Concept Vocabulary, 111c

Fluency

Read Leveled Readers

Grouping Options 90f–90g

Assess Reading Rate, 111a

Comprehension/Vocabulary

Reteach Sequence, 111b **T**

Author's Viewpoint/Bias, 111b

Review Context Clues, 111c **T**

Speaking and Listening, 111d
Sportscast
Listen to Audio CD

Grammar, 111f
Cumulative Review

Writing Workshop, 111h
Connect to Unit Writing

Spelling, 111j
Posttest for Adding *-ed, -ing*

Internet Inquiry, 111k
Communicate Results

Research/Study Skills, 111l
Newspaper/Newsletter

Day 5 Author's Viewpoint/Bias, 111b

Day 5 Revisit the Personal Challenges Concept Web, 111c

KEY ◉ = Target Skill **T** = Tested Skill

Comprehension	Fluency	Vocabulary
Check Retelling, *108*	Check Fluency WCPM, *111a*	Check Vocabulary, *111c*

SUCCE
PREDICT

Small Group Plan *for Differentiated Instructio*

Daily Plan AT A GLANCE

Reading

Whole Group
- Oral Language
- Comprehension/Vocabulary

Group Time

Differentiated Instruction

Meet with small groups to provide:
- Skill Support
- Reading Support
- Fluency Practice

Read

This week's lessons for daily group time can be found behind the Differentiated Instruction (DI) tab on pp. DI • 32–DI • 41.

Whole Group
- Fluency

Language Arts
- Grammar
- Writing
- Spelling
- Research/Inquiry
- Speaking/Listening/Viewing

***Use My Sidewalks on Reading Street* for Tier III intensive reading intervention.**

DAY 1

On-Level	Strategic Intervention	Advanced
Teacher-Led *Page DI • 33* • Develop Concept Vocabulary • **Read** On-Level Reader *Famous Women Athletes*	**Teacher-Led** *Page DI • 32* • Reinforce Concepts • **Read** Below-Level Reader *The Chicago American Giants*	**Teacher-Led** *Page DI • 33* • **Read** Advanced Reader *African American Athletes* • Independent Extension Activity

Independent Activities

While you meet with small groups, have the rest of the class...

- Visit the Reading/Library Center
- Listen to the Background Building Audio
- Finish Write to Read, p. 90
- Complete Practice Book pp. 33–34
- Visit Cross-Curricular Centers

DAY 2

On-Level	Strategic Intervention	Advanced
Teacher-Led *Pages 96–103* • **Read** *Satchel Paige*	**Teacher-Led** *Page DI • 34* • Practice Lesson Vocabulary • Read Multisyllabic Words • **Read** or Listen to *Satchel Paige*	**Teacher-Led** *Page DI • 35* • Extend Vocabulary • **Read** *Satchel Paige*

Independent Activities

While you meet with small groups, have the rest of the class...

- Visit the Reading/Library Center
- Listen to the AudioText for *Satchel Paige*
- Finish Words to Write, p. 93
- Complete Practice Book pp. 35–36
- Write in their Strategy Response Logs, pp. 94, 103
- Visit Cross-Curricular Centers
- Work on inquiry projects

DAY 3

On-Level	Strategic Intervention	Advanced
Teacher-Led *Pages 104–107* • **Read** *Satchel Paige*	**Teacher-Led** *Page DI • 36* • Practice Sequence and Ask Questions • **Read** or Listen to *Satchel Paige*	**Teacher-Led** *Page DI • 37* • Extend Sequence and Ask Questions • **Read** *Satchel Paige*

Independent Activities

While you meet with small groups, have the rest of the class...

- Visit the Reading/Library Center
- Listen to the AudioText for *Satchel Paige*
- Write in their Strategy Response Logs, p. 106
- Finish Look Back and Write, p. 108
- Complete Practice Book p. 37
- Visit Cross-Curricular Centers
- Work on inquiry projects

1 Begin with whole class skill and strategy instruction.

2 Meet with small groups to provide differentiated instruction.

3 Gather the whole class back together for fluency and language arts.

DAY 4

On-Level

Teacher-Led
Pages 110–111

Read "The Girls of Summer"

Strategic Intervention

Teacher-Led
Page DI • 38

- Practice Retelling
- **Read** or Listen to "The Girls of Summer"

Advanced

Teacher-Led
Page DI • 39

- **Read** "The Girls of Summer"
- Genre Study

Independent Activities

While you meet with small groups, have the rest of the class...

- Visit the Reading/Library Center
- Listen to the AudioText for "The Girls of Summer"
- Visit the Writing/Vocabulary Center
- Finish Writing Across Texts, p. 111
- Visit Cross-Curricular Centers
- Work on inquiry projects

DAY 5

On-Level

Teacher-Led
Page DI • 41

- **Reread** Leveled Reader *Famous Women Athletes*

Retell *Famous Women Athletes*

Strategic Intervention

Teacher-Led
Page DI • 40

- **Reread** Leveled Reader *The Chicago American Giants*
- Retell *The Chicago American Giants*

Advanced

Teacher-Led
Page DI • 41

- **Reread** Leveled Reader *African American Athletes*
- Share Extension Activity

Independent Activities

While you meet with small groups, have the rest of the class...

- Visit the Reading/Library Center
- Complete Practice Book pp. 38–40
- Visit Cross-Curricular Centers
- Work on inquiry projects

Grouping Place English language learners in the groups that correspond to their reading abilities in English.

Use the appropriate Leveled Reader or other text at students' instructional level.

TiP Send home the appropriate Multilingual Summary of the main selection on Day 1.

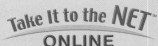

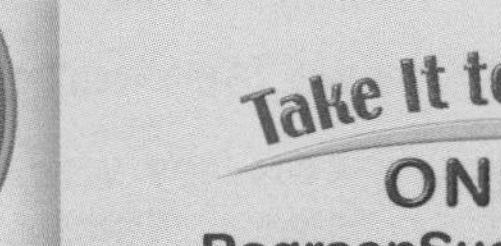

PearsonSuccessNet.com

Susan Watts-Taffe
For activities to build vocabulary, see the article "The Place of Word Consciousness in a Research-based Vocabulary Program" by M. Graves and Scott Foresman author S. Watts-Taffe.

TEACHER TALK

Phonics is instruction in the relationships between letters and sounds.

Looking Ahead

Be sure to schedule time for students to work on the unit inquiry project "Facing Challenges." This week students combine relevant information they've collected from different sources to answer their inquiry questions about an event in the Special Olympics.

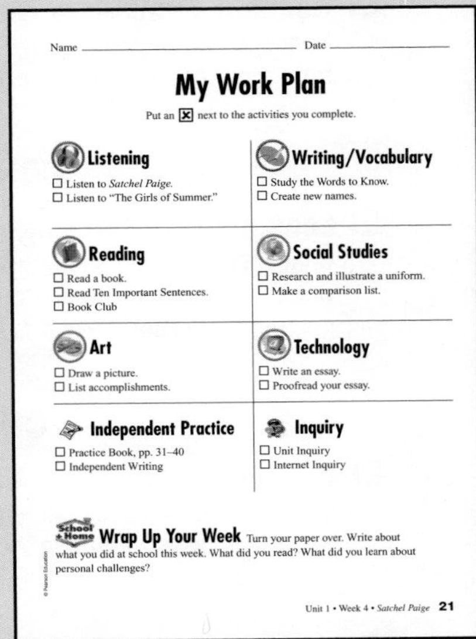

Name ______ Date ______

My Work Plan

Put an ☒ next to the activities you complete.

Listening
- ☐ Listen to *Satchel Paige*.
- ☐ Listen to "The Girls of Summer."

Writing/Vocabulary
- ☐ Study the Words to Know.
- ☐ Create new names.

Reading
- ☐ Read a book.
- ☐ Read Ten Important Sentences.
- ☐ Book Club

Social Studies
- ☐ Research and illustrate a uniform.
- ☐ Make a comparison list.

Art
- ☐ Draw a picture.
- ☐ List accomplishments.

Technology
- ☐ Write an essay.
- ☐ Proofread your essay.

Independent Practice
- ☐ Practice Book, pp. 31–40
- ☐ Independent Writing

Inquiry
- ☐ Unit Inquiry
- ☐ Internet Inquiry

School + Home **Wrap Up Your Week** Turn your paper over. Write about what you did at school this week. What did you read? What did you learn about personal challenges?

© Pearson Education

Unit 1 • Week 4 • *Satchel Paige* 21

▲ **Group-Time Survival Guide** p. 21, Weekly Contract

Customize Your Plan *by Stran*

ORAL LANGUAGE

SOCIAL STUDIES

Concept Development

How do we face personal challenges?

CONCEPT VOCABULARY

courage *hardships* *taunts*

BUILD

- ❑ **Question of the Week** Introduce and discuss the question of the week. This week students will read a variety of texts and work on projects related to the concept *personal challenges.* Post the question for students to refer to throughout the week. DAY 1 *90d*

- ❑ **Read Aloud** Read aloud "Teammates." Then begin a web to build concepts and concept vocabulary related to this week's lesson and the unit theme, Meeting Challenges. Introduce the concept words *courage, hardships,* and *taunts* and have students place them on the web. Display the web for use throughout the week. DAY 1 *90l-90m*

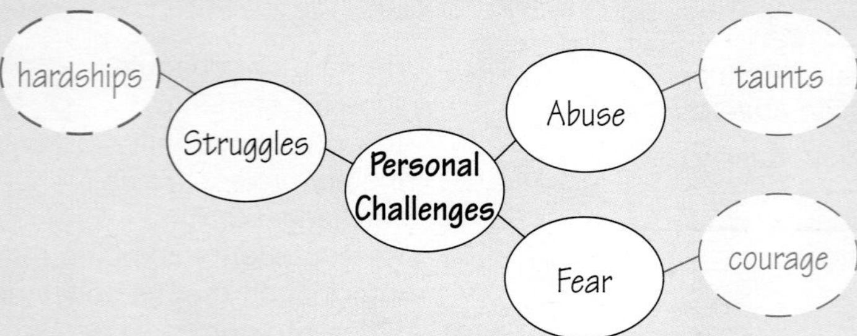

DEVELOP

- ❑ **Question of the Day** Use the prompts from the Weekly Plan to engage students in conversations related to this week's reading and the unit theme. EVERY DAY *90d-90e*

- ❑ **Concept Vocabulary Web** Revisit the Personal Challenges Concept Web and encourage students to add concept words from their reading and life experiences. DAY 2 *103,* DAY 3 *107*

CONNECT

- ❑ **Looking Back/Moving Forward** Revisit the Personal Challenges Concept Web and discuss how it relates to this week's lesson and the unit theme. Then make connections to next week's lesson. DAY 5 *111c*

CHECK

- ❑ **Concept Vocabulary Web** Use the Personal Challenges Concept Web to check students' understanding of the concept vocabulary words *courage, hardships,* and *taunts.* DAY 1 *90l,* DAY 5 *111c*

VOCABULARY

STRATEGY CONTEXT CLUES
When you are reading, you may come to a word you do not know. You may find a clue about the word's meaning in the words near the unknown word. An antonym, or a word with the opposite meaning of the unknown word, can be used to help figure out the unknown word's meaning.

LESSON VOCABULARY

confidence *fastball* *mocking* *outfield* *unique* *weakness* *windup*

TEACH

- ❑ **Words to Know** Give students the opportunity to tell what they already know about this week's lesson vocabulary words. Then discuss word meaning. DAY 1 *92b*

- ❑ **Vocabulary Strategy Lesson** Use the vocabulary strategy lesson in the Student Edition to introduce and model this week's strategy, *context clues.* DAY 2 *92-93*

Vocabulary Strategy Lesson

PRACTICE/APPLY

- ❑ **Leveled Text** Read the lesson vocabulary in the context of leveled text. DAY 1 *LR28-LR36*

Leveled Readers

- ❑ **Words in Context** Read the lesson vocabulary and apply *context clues* in the context of *Satchel Paige.* DAY 2 *94-103,* DAY 3 *104-108*

Main Selection—Nonfiction

- ❑ **Writing/Vocabulary Center** Invent new names for pitches using synonyms for *slow, fast,* and *curve.* ANY DAY *90k*

- ❑ **Homework** Practice Book pp. 34-35. DAY 1 *92b,* DAY 2 *93*

- ❑ **Word Play** Have students compile a list of specialized baseball vocabulary from *Satchel Paige.* ANY DAY *111c*

ASSESS

- ❑ **Selection Test** Use the Selection Test to determine students' understanding of the lesson vocabulary words. DAY 3

RETEACH/REVIEW

- ❑ **Reteach Lesson** If necessary, use this lesson to reteach and review *context clues.* DAY 5 *111c*

1 Use assessment data to determine your instructional focus.

2 Preview this week's instruction by strand.

3 Choose instructional activities that meet the needs of your classroom.

COMPREHENSION

SKILL SEQUENCE Sequence is the order in which events happen in a selection. Clue words such as *first, next,* and *last* indicate order.

STRATEGY ASK QUESTIONS Asking questions about important information, such as sequence of events, is a strategy good readers use. Asking questions *before* you read will help you connect what you will read to what you already know (prior knowledge). Asking questions *as* you read helps you understand what you are reading. Asking questions *after* you read helps you remember important information.

TEACH

- ❑ **Skill/Strategy Lesson** Use the skill/strategy lesson in the Student Edition to introduce and model *sequence* and *ask questions.* DAY 1 *90-91*

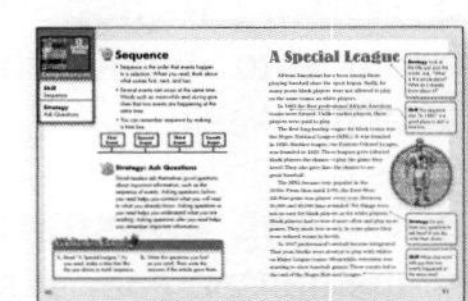
Skill/Strategy Lesson

- ❑ **Extend Skills** Teach author's viewpoint/bias. ANY DAY *111b*

PRACTICE/APPLY

- ❑ **Leveled Text** Apply *sequence* and *ask questions* to read leveled text. DAY 1 *LR28-LR36*

Leveled Readers

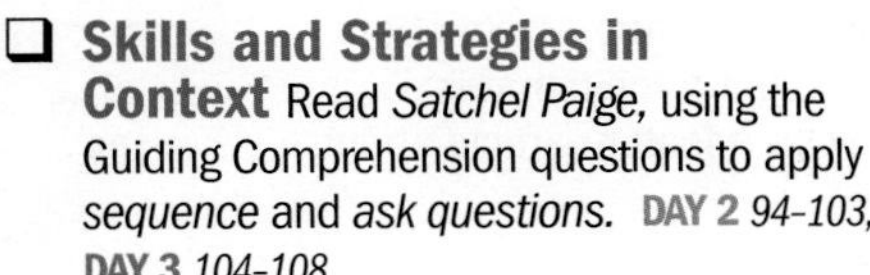

- ❑ **Skills and Strategies in Context** Read *Satchel Paige,* using the Guiding Comprehension questions to apply *sequence* and *ask questions.* DAY 2 *94-103,* DAY 3 *104-108*

Main Selection—NonFiction

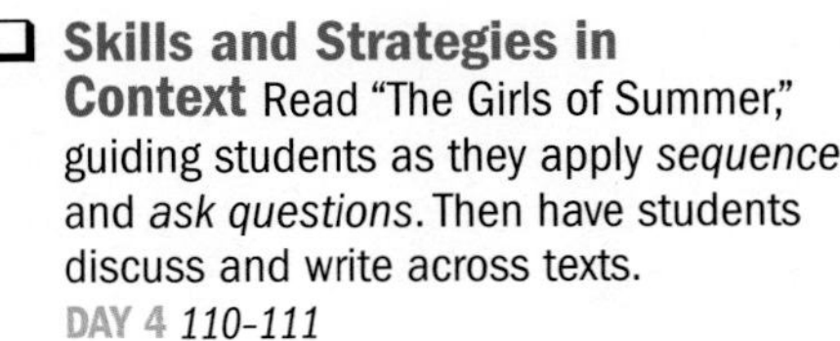

- ❑ **Skills and Strategies in Context** Read "The Girls of Summer," guiding students as they apply *sequence* and *ask questions*. Then have students discuss and write across texts. DAY 4 *110-111*

Paired Selection—Nonfiction

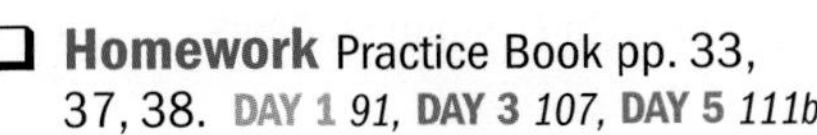

- ❑ **Homework** Practice Book pp. 33, 37, 38. DAY 1 *91,* DAY 3 *107,* DAY 5 *111b*
- ❑ **Fresh Reads for Differentiated Test Practice** Have students practice *sequence* with a new passage. DAY 3

ASSESS

- ❑ **Selection Test** Determine students' understanding of the selection and their use of *sequence.* DAY 3
- ❑ **Retell** Have students retell *Satchel Paige.* DAY 3 *108-109*

RETEACH/REVIEW

- ❑ **Reteach Lesson** If necessary, reteach and review *sequence.* DAY 5 *111b*

FLUENCY

SKILL PHRASING Phrasing is grouping related words, such as prepositional phrases, verbal phrases, and other clauses, to reinforce meaning. Phrasing allows the reader and listener to better understand the text.

TEACH

- ❑ **Read Aloud** Model fluent reading by rereading "Teammates." Focus on this week's fluency skill, phrasing. DAY 1 *90l-90m, 111a*

PRACTICE/APPLY

- ❑ **Echo Reading** Read aloud selected paragraphs from *Satchel Paige,* placing emphasis on grouping related words together. Then practice as a class by doing three echo readings of the selected paragraphs. DAY 2 *111a,* DAY 3 *111a*
- ❑ **Partner Reading** Have partners practice reading aloud, reading with careful phrasing, and offering each other feedback. As students reread, monitor their progress toward their individual fluency goals. DAY 4 *111a*
- ❑ **Listening Center** Have students follow along with the AudioText for this week's selections. ANY DAY *90j*
- ❑ **Reading/Library Center** Have students reread a selection of their choice. ANY DAY *90j*
- ❑ **Fluency Coach** Have students use Fluency Coach to listen to fluent readings or practice reading on their own. ANY DAY

ASSESS

- ❑ **Check Fluency WCPM** Do a one-minute timed reading, paying special attention to this week's skill—phrasing. Provide feedback for each student. DAY 5 *111a*

Customize Your Plan by Stran

GRAMMAR

SKILL COMPOUND AND COMPLEX SENTENCES A *simple sentence* expresses a complete thought and has a subject and a predicate. A *compound sentence* contains two simple sentences joined by a comma and a conjunction such as *and, but,* or *or. A complex sentence* contains an independent clause, which can stand alone, and a dependent clause, which cannot stand alone.

TEACH

- ☐ **Grammar Transparency 4** Use Grammar Transparency 4 to teach compound and complex sentences. DAY 1 *111e*

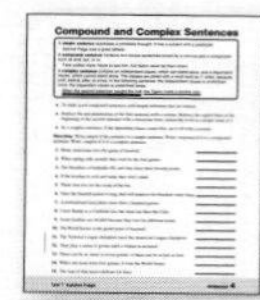

Grammar Transparency 4

PRACTICE/APPLY

- ☐ **Develop the Concept** Review the concept of compound and complex sentences and provide guided practice. DAY 2 *111e*
- ☐ **Apply to Writing** Have students review something they have written and apply compound and complex sentences. DAY 3 *111f*
- ☐ **Test Preparation** Examine common errors in compound and complex sentences to prepare for standardized tests. DAY 4 *111f*
- ☐ **Homework** Grammar and Writing Practice Book pp. 13–15. DAY 2 *111e*, DAY 3 *111f*, DAY 4 *111f*

ASSESS

- ☐ **Cumulative Review** Use Grammar and Writing Practice Book p. 16. DAY 5 *111f*

RETEACH/REVIEW

- ☐ **Daily Fix-It** Have students find and correct errors in grammar, spelling, and punctuation. **EVERY DAY** *111e–111f*
- ☐ **The Grammar and Writing Book** Use pp. 68–71 of The Grammar and Writing Book to extend instruction for compound and complex sentences. **ANY DAY**

The Grammar and Writing Book

WRITING

Trait of the Week

WORD CHOICE Good writers choose their words carefully. Strong verbs, specific nouns, and vivid adjectives help writers elaborate on their ideas. Well-chosen and precise words make writing clear and lively.

TEACH

- ☐ **Writing Transparency 4A** Use the model to introduce and discuss the Trait of the Week. DAY 1 *111g*
- ☐ **Writing Transparency 4B** Use the transparency to show students how tone can improve their writing. DAY 2 *111g*

Writing Transparency 4A

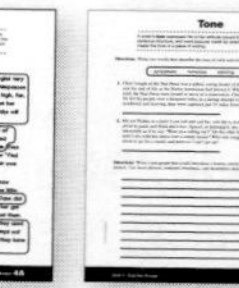

Writing Transparency 4B

PRACTICE/APPLY

- ☐ **Write Now** Examine the model on Student Edition p. 109. Then have students write their own feature article. **DAY 3** *109, 111h*, **DAY 4** *111h*

  Prompt *Satchel Paige* is a feature article about a baseball legend. Think about a topic that is interesting to you. Now write a feature article about that topic.

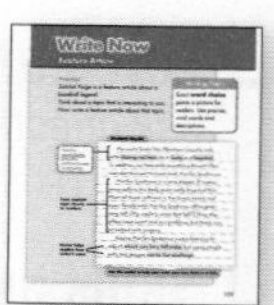

Write Now p. 109

- ☐ **Writing/Vocabulary Center** Invent new names for pitches using synonyms for *slow, fast,* and *curve.* **ANY DAY** *90k*

ASSESS

- ☐ **Writing Trait Rubric** Use the rubric to evaluate students' writing. DAY 4 *111h*

RETEACH/REVIEW

- ☐ **The Grammar and Writing Book** Use pp. 68–73 of The Grammar and Writing Book to extend instruction for compound and complex sentences, tone, and feature articles. **ANY DAY**

The Grammar and Writing Book

1 Use assessment data to determine your instructional focus.

2 Preview this week's instruction by strand.

3 Choose instructional activities that meet the needs of your classroom.

SPELLING

GENERALIZATION ADDING *-ED, -ING* In words that end in *e,* drop the *e: decided, deciding.* In words that end with CVC, double the final consonant: *admitted, admitting.* In words that end in *y,* change *y* to *i* when adding *-ed* and keep the *y* when adding *-ing: supplied, supplying.* Some base words change when endings are added.

TEACH

- ❑ **Pretest** Give the pretest for words with adding *-ed, -ing.* Guide students in self-correcting their pretests and correcting any misspellings. DAY 1 *111i*
- ❑ **Think and Practice** Connect spelling to the phonics generalization for adding *-ed, -ing.* DAY 2 *111i*

PRACTICE/APPLY

- ❑ **Connect to Writing** Have students use spelling words to write about a shopping experience. Then review frequently misspelled words: *getting, decided, stopped.* DAY 3 *111j*
- ❑ **Homework** Word Study and Spelling Practice Book pp. 13–16. **EVERY DAY**

RETEACH/REVIEW

- ❑ **Review** Review spelling words to prepare for the posttest. Then provide students with a spelling strategy—words with endings. DAY 4 *111j*

ASSESS

- ❑ **Posttest** Use dictation sentences to give the posttest for words with adding *-ed, -ing.* DAY 5 *111j*

Spelling Words

1. supplied
2. supplying
3. denied
4. denying
5. decided*
6. deciding
7. included
8. including
9. admitted
10. admitting
11. occurred
12. occurring
13. qualified
14. qualifying
15. identified
16. identifying
17. delayed
18. delaying
19. satisfied
20. satisfying

Challenge Words

21. occupied
22. occupying
23. criticized
24. criticizing
25. omitted
26. omitting

*Word from the selection

RESEARCH AND INQUIRY

- ❑ **Internet Inquiry** Have students conduct an Internet inquiry on athletes who, like Satchel Paige, succeed in spite of challenges. **EVERY DAY** *111k*
- ❑ **Newspaper/Newsletter** Review the terms, features, and purposes associated with newspapers and newsletters and discuss how students can use these resources to find information. DAY 5 *111l*
- ❑ **Unit Inquiry** Allow time for students to combine relevant information they have collected from different sources to answer their inquiry questions about an event in the Special Olympics. **ANY DAY** *17*

SPEAKING AND LISTENING

- ❑ **Sportscast** Have students prepare and deliver a sportscast of Paige and Gibson's meeting in the Negro World Series. **DAY 5** *111d*
- ❑ **Listen to Audio CD** Have students listen to the AudioText of *Satchel Paige* and answer questions. DAY 5 *111d*

Resources for

Differentiated Instruction

LEVELED READERS

- **Comprehension**
  - **Skill** Sequence
  - **Strategy** Ask Questions
- **Lesson Vocabulary**
  - Context Clues

- **Social Studies Standards**
  - Sports
  - Contributions of Women
  - Segregation

PearsonSuccessNet.com

Use the Online Database of over 600 books to

- Download and print additional copies of this week's leveled readers.
- Listen to the readers being read online.
- Search for more titles focused on this week's skills, topic, and content.

On-Level

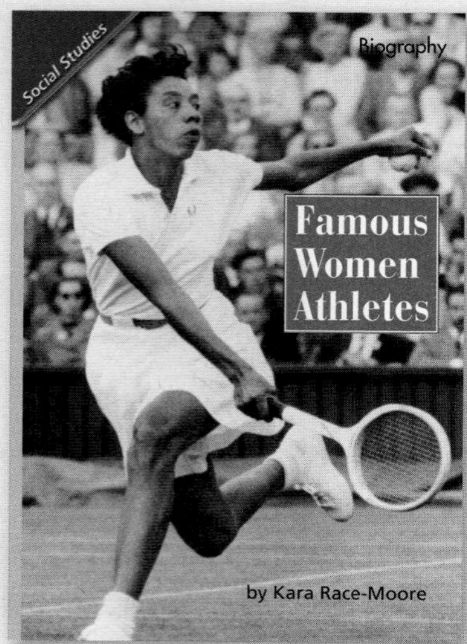

Social Studies
Biography
Famous Women Athletes
by Kara Race-Moore

On-Level Reader

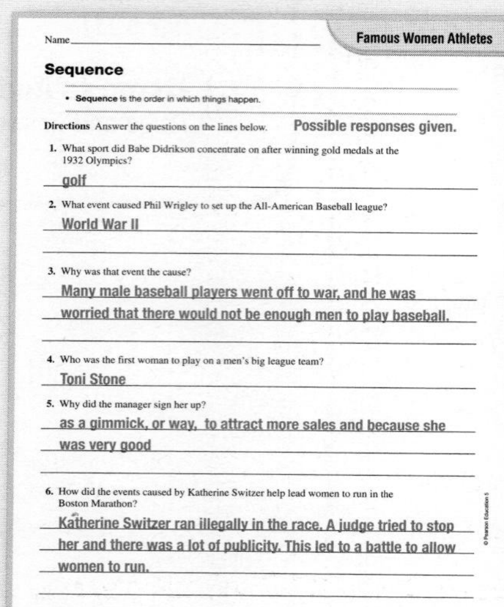

Name________ **Famous Women Athletes**

Sequence

- **Sequence** is the order in which things happen.

Directions Answer the questions on the lines below. Possible responses given.

1. What sport did Babe Didrikson concentrate on after winning gold medals at the 1932 Olympics?
   golf
2. What event caused Phil Wrigley to set up the All-American Baseball league?
   World War II
3. Why was that event the cause?
   Many male baseball players went off to war, and he was worried that there would not be enough men to play baseball.
4. Who was the first woman to play on a men's big league team?
   Toni Stone
5. Why did the manager sign her up?
   as a gimmick, or way, to attract more sales and because she was very good
6. How did the events caused by Katherine Switzer help lead women to run in the Boston Marathon?
   Katherine Switzer ran illegally in the race. A judge tried to stop her and there was a lot of publicity. This led to a battle to allow women to run.

© Pearson Education 5

On-Level Practice TE p. LR32

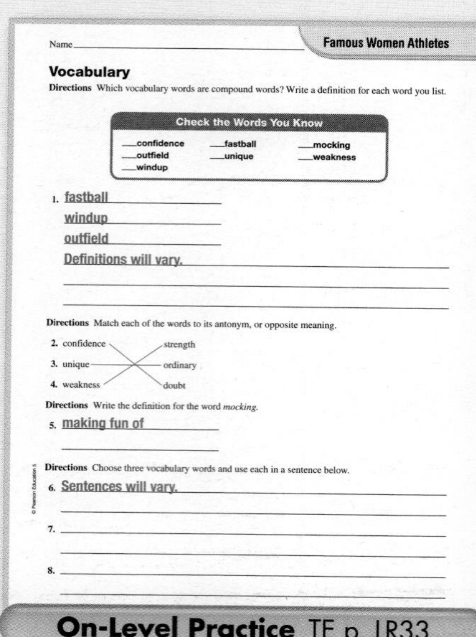

Name________ **Famous Women Athletes**

Vocabulary

Directions Which vocabulary words are compound words? Write a definition for each word you list.

Check the Words You Know
__confidence __fastball __mocking
__outfield __unique __weakness
__windup

1. fastball
   windup
   outfield
   Definitions will vary.

Directions Match each of the words to its antonym, or opposite meaning.

2. confidence — doubt
3. unique — ordinary
4. weakness — strength

Directions Write the definition for the word *mocking*.

5. making fun of

Directions Choose three vocabulary words and use each in a sentence below.

6. Sentences will vary.
7. ________
8. ________

© Pearson Education 5

On-Level Practice TE p. LR33

Strategic Intervention

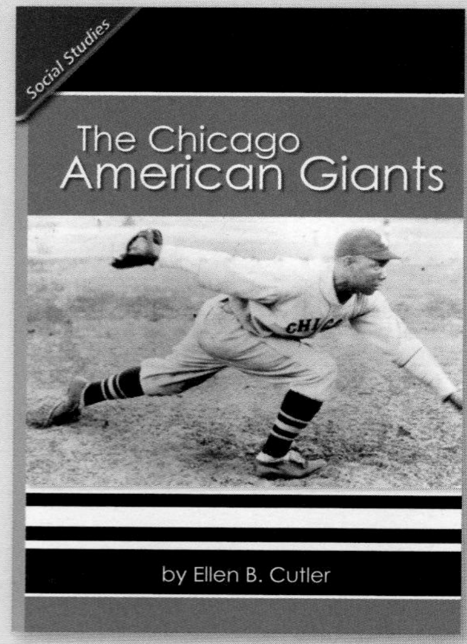

Social Studies
The Chicago American Giants
by Ellen B. Cutler

Below-Level Reader

Name________ **The Chicago American Giants**

Sequence

- **Sequence** is the order in which events happen.

Directions Answer the questions on the lines below.

1. Before telling you the sequence of events in the history of the Negro League, the author shows you a baseball game. Why do you think that is? Possible responses given.
   To get you involved with the story and to get you interested in learning more facts about the history of the game.
2. What did Rube Foster do that gave him enough experience to be manager of the Chicago American Giants?
   Before becoming a manager, he played baseball for more than twenty years.
3. What event most likely caused the end of the Negro American League?
   Baseball was integrated and black players could play on major league teams.
4. What event was the first step in desegregating baseball?
   Jackie Robinson joins the Brooklyn Dodgers.
5. Which event came first? Circle the letter of the correct answer.
   A. The international league bans teams with white players from signing African American players.
   (B.) Professional African American teams begin forming.

© Pearson Education 5

Below-Level Practice TE p. LR29

Name________ **The Chicago American Giants**

Vocabulary

Directions Complete each sentence with a word from the word box.

Check the Words You Know
__confidence __fastball
__mocking __outfield
__unique __weakness
__windup

1. Being the only one of its kind unique
2. A failing weakness
3. Pitch thrown at a high speed with very little curve fastball
4. Laughing at; making fun of mocking
5. Firm belief in yourself confidence
6. A swinging movement of the arms while twisting the body just before pitching the ball windup
7. The part of a basball field beyond the diamond or infield outfield

Directions Select three vocabulary words and use each in a sentence below.

8. Sentences will vary.
9. ________
10. ________

© Pearson Education 5

Below-Level Practice TE p. LR30

Advanced

Advanced Reader

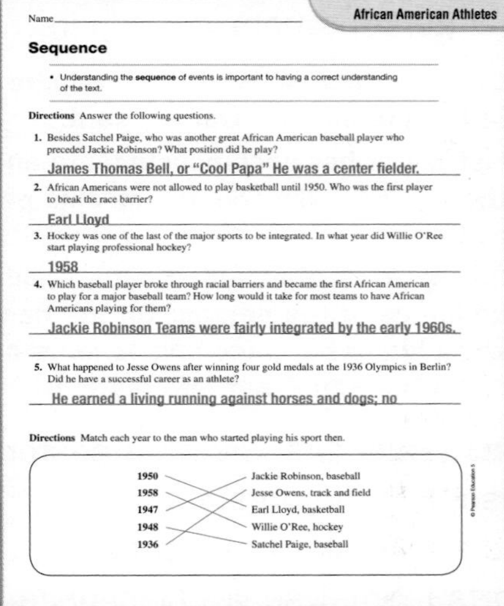

Name ______ African American Athletes

Sequence

- Understanding the **sequence** of events is important to having a correct understanding of the text.

Directions Answer the following questions.

1. Besides Satchel Paige, who was another great African American baseball player who preceded Jackie Robinson? What position did he play?
   James Thomas Bell, or "Cool Papa" He was a center fielder.
2. African Americans were not allowed to play basketball until 1950. Who was the first player to break the race barrier?
   Earl Lloyd
3. Hockey was one of the last of the major sports to be integrated. In what year did Willie O'Ree start playing professional hockey?
   1958
4. Which baseball player broke through racial barriers and became the first African American to play for a major baseball team? How long would it take for most teams to have African Americans playing for them?
   Jackie Robinson Teams were fairly integrated by the early 1960s.
5. What happened to Jesse Owens after winning four gold medals at the 1936 Olympics in Berlin? Did he have a successful career as an athlete?
   He earned a living running against horses and dogs; no

Directions Match each year to the man who started playing his sport then.

1950	Jackie Robinson, baseball
1958	Jesse Owens, track and field
1947	Earl Lloyd, basketball
1948	Willie O'Ree, hockey
1936	Satchel Paige, baseball

Advanced Practice TE p. LR35

Name ______ African American Athletes

Vocabulary

Directions Draw a line from each word to its definition.

Check the Words You Know

- __adversity
- __discrimination
- __integrated
- __prohibited
- __amateur
- __inferior
- __prejudiced
- __taunts

1. adversity — jeers; mocking or insulting remarks
2. amateur — below most others; low in quality
3. taunts — condition of misfortune or distress
4. discrimination — forbidden by law from doing something
5. inferior — when a public place or group has been opened to all races.
6. integrated — someone who plays something for pleasure, instead of for money or as a profession.
7. prejudiced — having an unreasonable dislike for someone or something
8. prohibited — act of showing an unfair difference in treatment

Directions Select four vocabulary words and use each in a sentence.

9. Sentences will vary.
10. ______
11. ______
12. ______

Advanced Practice TE p. LR36

ELL

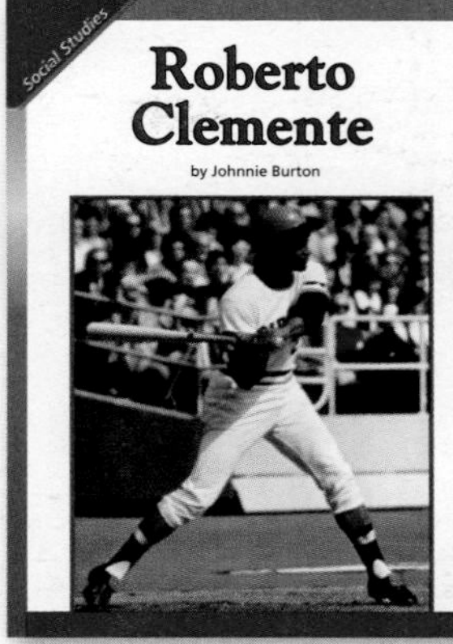

ELL Reader

ELL Poster 4

Teacher's Edition Notes

ELL notes throughout this lesson support instruction and reference additional resources at point of use.

Teaching Guide pp. 22–28, 218–219

- Multilingual summaries of the main selection
- Comprehension lesson
- Vocabulary strategies and word cards
- ELL Reader 5.1.4 lesson

ELL and Transition Handbook

Ten Important Sentences

- Key ideas from every selection in the Student Edition
- Activities to build sentence power

More Reading

Readers' Theater Anthology

- Fluency practice
- Five scripts to build fluency
- Poetry for oral interpretation

Leveled Trade Books

- Extended reading tied to the unit concept
- Lessons in the Trade Book Library Teaching Guide

Homework

- Family Times Newsletter
- ELL Multilingual Selection Summaries

Take-Home Books

- Leveled Readers

Cross-Curricular Centers

Listening

Listen to the Selections

MATERIALS
CD player, headphones, AudioText CD, student book

SINGLES

LISTEN TO LITERATURE Listen to *Satchel Paige* and "The Girls of Summer" as you follow or read along in your book. Listen for the sequence of events that occurs in *Satchel Paige*.

If there is anything you don't understand, you can listen again to any section.

Audio CD

Reading/Library

Read It Again!

MATERIALS
Collection of books for self-selected reading, reading logs, student book

SINGLES PAIRS GROUPS

Select a book you have already read. Record the title of the book in your reading log. You may want to read with a partner.

Choose from the following:

- **Leveled Readers**
- **ELL Readers**
- **Stories Written by Classmates**
- **Books from the Library**
- ***Satchel Paige***

TEN IMPORTANT SENTENCES Read the Ten Important Sentences for *Satchel Paige*. Then locate the sentences in the student book.

BOOK CLUB Form a group to discuss the ways in which the author brings Satchel Paige to life. Discuss other biographies you may have read.

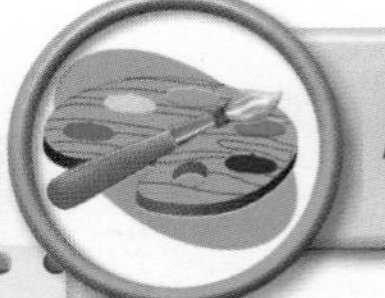

Art

Make a Trading Card

MATERIALS
Writing and art materials, index card

PAIRS GROUPS

Satchel Paige had many qualities that made him a talented and popular baseball player. Design a trading card featuring an athlete or other person whom you admire.

1. **Choose a person whom you admire to feature on your trading card.**
2. **List his or her accomplishments and the reasons why you admire this person.**
3. **On the front of an index card, create an image of the person. On the back, write his or her accomplishments and any other important information.**

EARLY FINISHERS Create a poster presenting the person on your card as the star of a fictitious sports team. Use vivid language and images to show off his or her feats.

Scott Foresman Reading Street Centers Survival Kit

Use the *Satchel Paige* materials from the Reading Street Centers Survival Kit to organize this week's centers.

Writing/ Vocabulary

Explore Word Meanings

MATERIALS
Writing and art materials

SINGLES

Invent new names for pitches.

1. **Look back at the selection. Satchel Paige had special names for each of his pitches, like "hesitation" for his slowball.**
2. **Create new names for a slowball, a fastball, and a curveball.**
3. **Use a thesaurus to find words to use that are synonyms for "slow," "fast," and "curve." Be sure to use vivid language.**

EARLY FINISHERS Draw a picture of Satchel Paige throwing one of his three special pitches.

Slow adjective	**Slow** means taking a long time to go or do or happen. *When traffic is this slow, downtown seems far away.* **Leisurely** means relaxed and without hurry. *Sandra and her father spent a leisurely afternoon at the beach.*

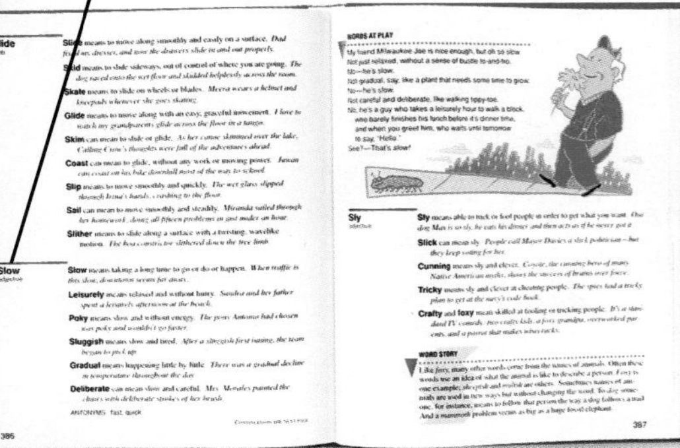

Social Studies

Find Out About UNIFORMS

MATERIALS
Writing and art materials, research materials, Internet access

SINGLES

Find out what men's and women's baseball uniforms looked like in the early 1900s.

1. **Use the Internet and a student-friendly search engine or other resources to research images of baseball uniforms from this time period.**
2. **Draw a picture of an old baseball uniform and label each part.**
3. **List the drawbacks and advantages to wearing one of these older uniforms versus today's uniforms.**

EARLY FINISHERS Write one or two paragraphs telling why you think players from the early 1900s dressed the way they did.

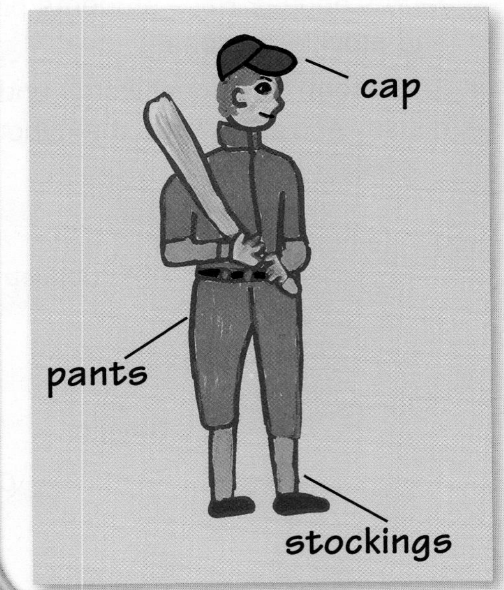

Technology

Create a Document

MATERIALS
Word processing program, copy of chart below

SINGLES

Find details from the selection that support the main idea that Satchel Paige was a great pitcher.

1. **Use the main idea chart below to help organize your ideas.**
2. **Use a word processing program. Create a new document.**
3. **Use your completed chart to help you write a half-page essay on the topic.**
4. **Proofread your essay before printing it out.**

EARLY FINISHERS Use the word processing program to format your essay differently.

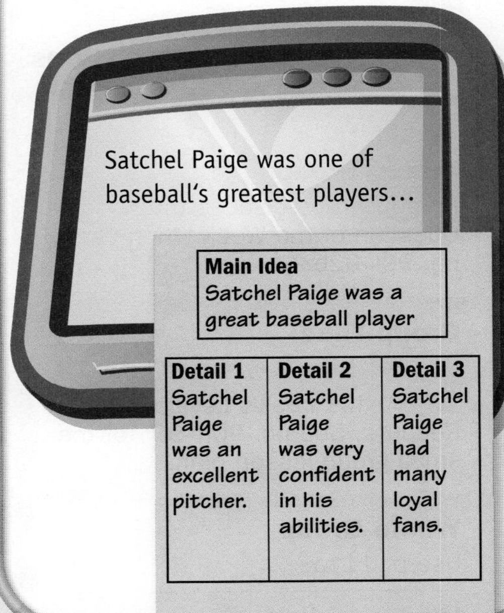

Satchel Paige was one of baseball's greatest players...
Main Idea
Satchel Paige was a great baseball player
Detail 1
Satchel Paige was an excellent pitcher.
Detail 2
Satchel Paige was very confident in his abilities.
Detail 3
Satchel Paige had many loyal fans.

ALL CENTERS

DAY 1

OBJECTIVES

- Build vocabulary by finding words related to the lesson concept.
- Listen to draw conclusions about a character or an event.

Concept Vocabulary

courage bravery
hardships hard condition of living
taunts mocking or insulting remarks

Monitor Progress
Check Word Use

If...	then...
students are unable to place words on the web,	review the lesson concept. Place the words on the web and provide additional words for practice, such as *isolation* and *hostility.*

SUCCESS PREDICTOR

DAY 1 Grouping Options

Reading
Whole Group
Introduce and discuss the Question of the Week. Then use pp. 90l–92b.

Group Time
Differentiated Instruction
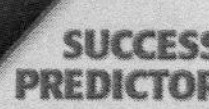 this week's Leveled Readers. See pp. 90h–90i for the small group lesson plan.

Whole Group
Use p. 111a.

Language Arts
Use pp. 111e–111k.

Build Concepts

FLUENCY

MODEL PHRASING As you read "Teammates," model phrasing by grouping prepositional phrases together, such as "on the mound," and "from the first breath of spring till the cool rush of fall."

LISTENING COMPREHENSION

After reading "Teammates," use the following questions to assess listening comprehension.

1. **Draw conclusions about the kind of person Pee Wee Reese was.** *(Possible responses: honorable, brave, loyal, kind)* ***Draw Conclusions***
2. **What was the effect of Pee Wee's standing beside Jackie in the crowd?** *(Possible responses: Pee Wee's action silenced many people in the crowd; they felt ashamed of their behavior.)* ***Cause and Effect***

BUILD CONCEPT VOCABULARY

Start a web to build concepts and vocabulary related to this week's lesson and the unit theme.

- Draw the Personal Challenges Concept Web.
- Read the sentence with the word *hardships* again. Ask students to pronounce *hardships* and discuss its meaning.
- Place *hardships* in an oval attached to *Struggles.* Explain that the word *hardships* is related to this concept. Read the sentences in which *courage* and *taunts* appear. Have students pronounce the words, place them on the web, and provide reasons.
- Brainstorm additional words and categories for the web. Keep the web on display and add words throughout the week.

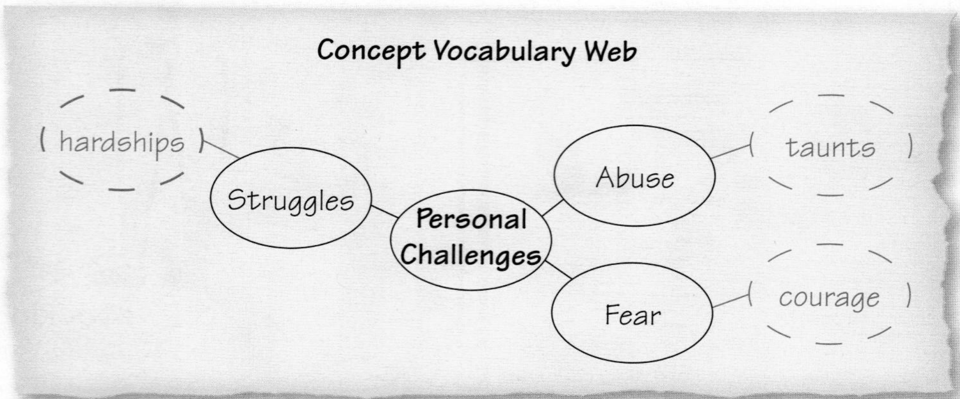

TEAMMATES

by Peter Golenbock

In the beginning of the sport, African Americans and other people were not allowed to play professional baseball together. In 1947, Jackie Robinson broke the color barrier when he signed on to play for the Brooklyn Dodgers. It was not easy. Jackie endured hardships such as verbal abuse, isolation, and death threats. Fortunately, Pee Wee Reese was also on the Brooklyn Dodgers team and Pee Wee was a man of honor and courage.

Very early in the season, the Dodgers traveled west to Ohio to play the Cincinnati Reds. Cincinnati is near Pee Wee's hometown of Louisville [Kentucky].

The Reds played in a small ballpark where the fans sat close to the field. The players could almost feel the breath of the fans on the backs of their necks. Many who came that day screamed terrible, hateful things at Jackie when the Dodgers were on the field.

More than anything else, Pee Wee Reese believed in doing what was right. When he heard the fans yelling at Jackie, Pee Wee decided to take a stand.

With his head high, Pee Wee walked directly from his shortstop position to where Jackie was playing first base. The taunts and shouting of the fans were ringing in Pee Wee's ears. It saddened him, because he knew it could have been his friends and neighbors. Pee Wee's legs felt heavy, but he knew what he had to do.

As he walked toward Jackie wearing the same gray Dodger uniform, he looked into his teammate's bold, pained eyes. The first baseman had done nothing to provoke the hostility except that he sought to be treated equal. Jackie was grim with anger. Pee Wee smiled broadly as he reached Jackie. Jackie smiled back.

Stopping beside Jackie, Pee Wee put his arm around Jackie's shoulders. An audible gasp rose up from the crowd when they saw what Pee Wee had done. Then there was silence.

Outlined on a sea of green grass stood these two great athletes, one black, one white, both wearing the same team uniform.

"I am standing by him," Pee Wee Reese said to the world. "This man is my teammate."

Activate Prior Knowledge

Before students listen to the Read Aloud, ask them what they know about racial segregation.

Set Purpose

Read aloud the title and have students predict what the selection will be about.

Read the introduction aloud. Have students use their prior knowledge and listen for facts and details to decide what kind of person Pee Wee Reese was.

Creative Response

Have students work with partners to reenact the turning point in the selection, when Pee Wee faces the crowd's hostility and stands by Jackie. ***Drama***

Access Content Before reading, share this summary: When the fans yell at Jackie Robinson, Pee Wee Reese, a teammate, decides to take a stand. He walks over to Robinson, puts his arm around his shoulders, and tells the world that he is standing by his teammate.

Homework Send home this week's Family Times newsletter.

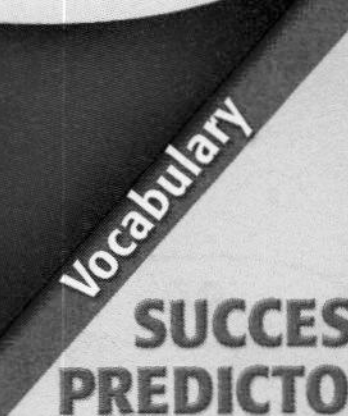

SKILLS ↔ STRATEGIES IN CONTEXT

Sequence Ask Questions

OBJECTIVES

- Use clue words to determine sequence.
- Ask questions to remember sequence.

Skills Trace	Sequence
Introduce/Teach	**TE: 5.1 90–91; 5.2 230–231; 5.6 726–727**
Practice	Practice Book: 33, 37, 38, 66, 76, 93, 97, 98, 256, 266, 293, 297, 298
Reteach/Review	TE: 5.1 111b, 121, DI•55; 5.2 173, 199, 253b, DI•56; 5.6 641, 655, 753b, DI•56
Test	Selection Test: 13–16, 37–40, 117–120; Benchmark Test: Units 2, 6

INTRODUCE

Write the title *Morning Routine* on the board. Add these events: *Catch bus. Brush teeth. Turn off alarm clock.* Have students order the events. *(Turn off alarm clock; brush teeth; catch bus.)*

Have students read the information on p. 90. Explain the following:

- Sequence is the order of events in a selection, which you can remember by asking yourself what comes first, next, and last.
- Asking questions as you read can help you keep track of important text information and understand what you are reading.

Use Skill Transparency 4 to teach sequence and ask questions.

Comprehension

Skill
Sequence

Strategy
Ask Questions

Sequence

- Sequence is the order that events happen in a selection. When you read, think about what comes first, next, and last.
- Several events can occur at the same time. Words such as *meanwhile* and *during* give clues that two events are happening at the same time.
- You can remember sequence by making a time line.

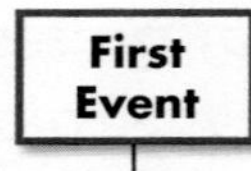

First Event	Second Event	Third Event	Fourth Event

Strategy: Ask Questions

Good readers ask themselves *good* questions about *important* information, such as the sequence of events. Asking questions *before* you read helps you connect what you will read to what you already know. Asking questions *as* you read helps you understand what you are reading. Asking questions *after* you read helps you remember important information.

Write to Read

1. Read "A Special League." As you read, make a time line like the one above to track sequence.
2. Write the questions you had as you read. Then write the answers if the article gave them.

90

Strategic Intervention

Sequence Explain that the order of events in a selection is just like the order of events in the school day. One event comes first, one event comes next, and so on. Draw on the board a time line like the one on p. 90. Have students guide you to complete the time line by naming the first four events in the school day. Tell students that they can use the same process to sequence events in a selection.

Access Content

Beginning/Intermediate For a Picture It! lesson on sequence, see ELL Teaching Guide, pp. 22–23.

Advanced As students read "A Special League," ask them to take notes on what comes first, next, and last. Have them use these notes to retell the selection.

A Special League

African Americans have been among those playing baseball since the sport began. Sadly, for many years black players were not allowed to play on the same teams as white players.

In 1882 the first professional African American teams were formed. Unlike earlier players, these players were paid to play.

The first long-lasting league for black teams was the Negro National League (NNL). It was founded in 1920. Another league, the Eastern Colored League, was founded in 1923. These leagues gave talented black players the chance to play the game they loved. They also gave fans the chance to see great baseball.

The NNL became very popular in the 1930s. From then until 1950, the East-West All-Star game was played every year. Between 30,000 and 40,000 fans attended! Yet things were not as easy for black players as for white players. Black players had to travel more often and play more games. They made less money. In some places they were refused rooms in hotels.

In 1946 professional baseball became integrated. That year, blacks were allowed to play with whites on Major League teams. Meanwhile, television was starting to show baseball games. These events led to the end of the Negro National League.

1 **Strategy** Look at the title and scan the article. Ask, "What is this article about? What do I already know about it?"

2 **Skill** The sequence clue "In 1882" is a good place to start a time line.

3 **Strategy** Do you have any questions to ask here? If you do, write them down.

4 **Skill** What clue word tells you that two events happened at the same time?

91

Available as **Skill Transparency** 4

Sequence

- **Sequence** is the order in which events happen in a selection. When you read, think about what comes first, next, and last.
- Several events can occur at the same time. Words such as *meanwhile* and *during* give clues that two events are happening at the same time.

Directions Read the following passage.

Jackie Robinson was the first African American baseball player to play in the modern Major Leagues. He played in the Negro Leagues until 1947 when he was signed to the Brooklyn Dodgers. Despite controversy about Robinson breaking the color barrier, he was an immediate success. During his first season, he led the National League in stolen bases, and after the season ended he was named Rookie of the Year. During his third season, he won the league's batting title and was later named baseball's Most Valuable Player.

Directions Fill in the time line below with the events from Jackie Robinson's career. List them in the order in which they happened.

Events in Jackie Robinson's Career

Played in the Negro Leagues.
1. Signed with the Brooklyn Dodgers.
2. Led National League in stolen bases.
3. Named Rookie of the Year.
4. Won the batting title.
5. Named Most Valuable Player.

School + Home **Home Activity** Your child read a short passage and identified its sequence of events using a time line. Read a newspaper article about a current event with your child. Have your child put the events in sequence using a time line.

Practice Book p. 33

TEACH

1 **STRATEGY** Model how asking questions before reading can help you think about the content and what you already know about it.

MODEL After reading the title and scanning the article, I can tell that the article is about African American baseball players. I do know that a long time ago, African American players were not allowed to play with white players.

2 **SKILL** Use clue words.

MODEL The date 1882 signals the first event, so I'll begin my time line there. I'll look for more dates or clue words to help me sequence events as I read on.

PRACTICE AND ASSESS

3 **SKILL STRATEGY** Possible response: How were things harder for black players?

4 **SKILL** *meanwhile*

WRITE Have students complete steps 1 and 2 of the Write to Read activity. You may wish to have students compare the questions that they asked.

Monitor Progress

Sequence

If... students are unable to complete **Write to Read** on p. 90,	**then...** use Practice Book p. 33 to provide additional practice.

Tech Files
ONLINE

Students can find out more about this subject by using a student-friendly search engine and the keyword *baseball*. Be sure to follow classroom guidelines for Internet use.

Build Background Use ELL Poster 4 to build background and vocabulary for the lesson concept of succeeding in spite of challenges.

▲ **ELL Poster** 4

Build Background

ACTIVATE PRIOR KNOWLEDGE

BEGIN A KWL CHART about baseball pitching.

- Give students a KWL chart and allow them two to three minutes to brainstorm things they know about baseball pitching. Record what they know in the first column of the chart.
- Give students two to three more minutes to ask questions they would like answered about baseball pitching. Record the questions in the second column of the chart.
- Tell students that, as they read, they should look for the answers to the questions and add any new information they learn to the chart throughout the week.

Topic Baseball Pitching

K	W	L
Pitchers throw the ball to batters.	How does a pitcher learn to pitch?	
Pitchers stand on a pitching mound.	What are the names of some famous pitchers?	
There are different kinds of pitches.	What kinds of pitches are there?	

▲ **Graphic Organizer** 4

BACKGROUND BUILDING AUDIO This week's audio is an interview with Buck O'Neil from the Negro Leagues. After students listen, discuss what interesting information they found out about the Negro Leagues.

Background Building Audio

Introduce Vocabulary

DISCUSS THE VOCABULARY

Share the lesson vocabulary with students. Have students locate each word in their glossaries and note each word's pronunciation and meaning. Ask students questions, such as the following, that include the new vocabulary. This will help clarify the new words' meanings.

- **How many objects, persons, or ideas can be *unique?***
- **If you have *confidence,* how do you feel when you meet new people?**
- **Where is the *outfield* in relation to the batter?**
- **How would you say "Just try" in a *mocking* voice?**
- **What word is the opposite of *weakness?***
- **Why is it hard to hit a *fastball?***

Have students write sentences that include the vocabulary words. You may expand this activity by using the More Words to Know.

If students have difficulty decoding multisyllabic words, have them use these steps for reading them. (See the Multisyllabic Word Routine on p. DI·1.)

1 **Look for Meaningful Word Parts** (base words, endings, prefixes, suffixes, roots) Think about the meaning of each part. Use the parts to read the word. Model: I see *-ness* at the end of *weakness. Weak* means "not strong" or "easy to bend," and adding the suffix *-ness* gives the word the quality of being weak. Therefore, *weakness* means "anything that lacks strength or is a weak point."

2 **Chunk Words with No Recognizable Parts** Say each chunk slowly. Then say the chunks fast to make a word. Model: *u, nique—unique.*

Lesson Vocabulary

WORDS TO KNOW

T confidence firm belief in yourself

T fastball a pitch thrown at high speed with very little curve

T mocking laughing at; making fun of

T outfield the three players in the outfield

T unique having no like or equal

T weakness a weak point; slight fault

T windup a swinging movement of the arms while twisting the body just before pitching the ball

MORE WORDS TO KNOW

duo pair

potholes deep holes in the surface of a street or road

semi-pro a part-time professional athlete

T = Tested Word

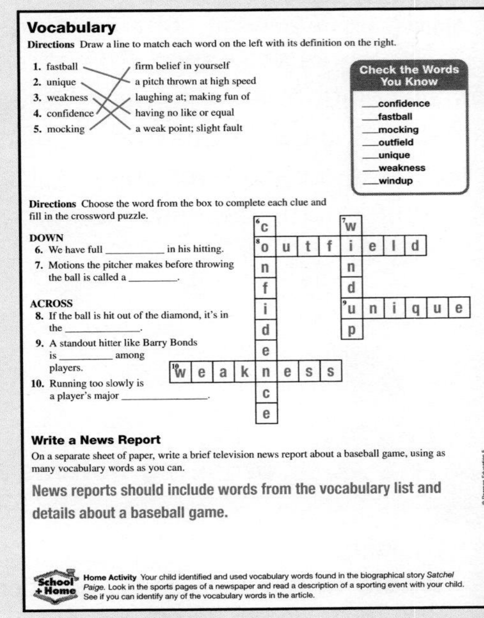

Vocabulary

Directions Draw a line to match each word on the left with its definition on the right.

1. fastball — firm belief in yourself
2. unique — a pitch thrown at high speed
3. weakness — laughing at; making fun of
4. confidence — having no like or equal
5. mocking — a weak point; slight fault

Check the Words You Know

__confidence
__fastball
__mocking
__outfield
__unique
__weakness
__windup

Directions Choose the word from the box to complete each clue and fill in the crossword puzzle.

DOWN

6. We have full ________ in his hitting. confidence
7. Motions the pitcher makes before throwing the ball is called a ________. windup

ACROSS

8. If the ball is hit out of the diamond, it's in the ________. outfield
9. A standout hitter like Barry Bonds is ________ among players. unique
10. Running too slowly is a player's major ________. weakness

Write a News Report

On a separate sheet of paper, write a brief television news report about a baseball game, using as many vocabulary words as you can.

News reports should include words from the vocabulary list and details about a baseball game.

School + Home **Home Activity** Your child identified and used vocabulary words found in the biographical story *Satchel Paige.* Look in the sports pages of a newspaper and read a description of a sporting event with your child. See if you can identify any of the vocabulary words in the article.

▲ **Practice Book** p. 34

DAY 2

Vocabulary Strategy

OBJECTIVE

Use context clues to determine word meaning.

INTRODUCE

Discuss the strategy for antonyms as context clues using the steps on p. 92.

TEACH

- Have students read "Play Ball," paying attention to how vocabulary is used.
- Model using an antonym to determine the meaning of *weakness*, which appears in the last paragraph of "Play Ball."

MODEL The author tells me that *weakness* is something a great player works to change. The phrase *until it finally* points to an antonym, *strength*, whose meaning I know. In this context, it means something a ball player does well. So, *weakness* means the opposite, "something a player does poorly."

Words to Know

- confidence
- windup
- fastball
- outfield
- mocking
- weakness
- unique

Remember

Try the strategy. Then, if you need more help, use your glossary or dictionary.

Vocabulary Strategy for Antonyms

Context Clues When you read, you may come to a word you do not know. You may find a clue about the word's meaning in the words near the unknown word. For example, you may find an antonym, or a word with the opposite meaning of the unknown word. You can use the antonym to figure out the unknown word's meaning.

1. Reread the sentence with the unknown word.
2. Look at the words nearby for words that signal opposites, such as *unlike, but,* and *on the other hand*. They may point to an antonym.
3. Decide what the antonym means.
4. Give the unknown word the opposite meaning. Does this meaning make sense in the sentence?

As you read "Play Ball!" check the context of words you don't know. See if an antonym gives you a clue to meaning.

92

DAY 2 Grouping Options

Reading

Whole Group Discuss the Question of the Day. Then use pp. 92–95.

Group Time Differentiated Instruction

Read *Satchel Paige*. See pp. 90h–90i for the small group lesson plan.

Whole Group Use p. 111a.

Language Arts

Use pp. 111e–111k.

Strategic Intervention

Context Clues Write the sentence in which *unique* appears. Read the sentence aloud. Guide students to identify an antonym in the next sentence that can help them determine the meaning of *unique*.

Access Content Use ELL Poster 4 to preteach vocabulary. Choose from the following to meet language proficiency levels.

Beginning Point out clues on p. 93 that show that *windup* and *fastball* are words related to baseball.

Intermediate After reading, have students use a web to show home-language terms that are related to baseball. Have them write *baseball* in the center oval and the baseball-related words in the ovals around it.

Advanced Teach the lesson on pp. 92–93. Have students find home-language terms for words that relate to baseball.

Resources for home-language words may include parents, bilingual staff members, bilingual dictionaries, or online translation sources.

Play Ball!

Many young people dream of becoming a great baseball player. Only a few will be able to do this. One reason is that you must first have a lot of talent. Another is that you must be willing to work very hard. With work comes skill. With skill comes the confidence a great player needs.

For a pitcher, every windup and throw of the ball helps him or her learn something. Whether learning to deliver a smoking fastball or a dancing curve, the pitcher must master difficult moves. A hitter learns with every at-bat which pitch should go by and which should be slammed into the outfield. Even the mocking "Heybatterbatterbatter" of the other team can help build a hitter's concentration.

Being dedicated, the great player of tomorrow is willing to work on a weakness until it finally becomes a strength. The really great player is unique. He or she has passed the common level of play expected and has invented a style that stands out. Every player who tries hard and loves the game, though, is a winner, no matter what.

Words to Write

Look at the pictures in *Satchel Paige*. Choose one to write about. Use as many words in the Words to Know list as you can.

93

PRACTICE AND ASSESS

- Have students figure out the meanings of the remaining words and explain the context clues they used to identify them.
- Point out that context does not work with every word. Students may have to use the glossary or a dictionary to determine word meaning.
- If students had trouble answering the vocabulary discussion questions (p. 92b), give students another opportunity to answer them. Students may also pose their own questions using lesson vocabulary words to a partner.
- Have students complete Practice Book p. 35.

WRITE Writing should include vocabulary words and other vocabulary relating to baseball.

Monitor Progress

Context Clues

If... students need more practice with the lesson vocabulary,	**then...** use Tested Vocabulary Cards.

Vocabulary • Context Clues

- An **antonym** is a word that means the opposite of another word.
- Look for clue words such as *unlike, no, but,* and *on the other hand* to identify antonyms.

Directions Read the following passage and look for antonyms as you read. Then answer the questions below.

Pat was the sort of person who could teach herself to sing, play guitar, and tap dance all at the same time. Most people would have doubts about their ability to do such a thing, but Pat had confidence in herself. Her performances always had an unforgettable style. She was also the star pitcher for her baseball team. Her windup was as flashy as her tap dancing, and nobody could hit her fastball.

Her obvious strength was pitching. On the other hand, her weakness was hitting. She frequently swung at the ball, but she seldom hit it past the bases into the outfield. Unlike people who would become discouraged by this weakness, Pat remained undaunted. She kept working to improve her swing. As you can guess, Pat was no ordinary young woman. She was unique!

1. Find the antonym in the passage for *confidence*. How does this antonym help define *confidence*?
   doubt; I know that it means the opposite of *doubt*.
2. Find the antonym in the passage for *weakness*. How does this antonym help to define *weakness*?
   strength; I know that it means the opposite of *strength*.
3. What is the definition of *seldom*? What clues in the passage support your definition?
   rarely; The clue word *but* tells you that it means the opposite of "frequently."
4. Find the antonym in the passage for *unique*. How does this antonym help to define *unique*?
   ordinary; I know that it means the opposite of *ordinary*.
5. How would you define *undaunted*, based on the passage? What clues support your definition?
   The word *unlike* tells me that *undaunted* is the opposite of *discouraged*.

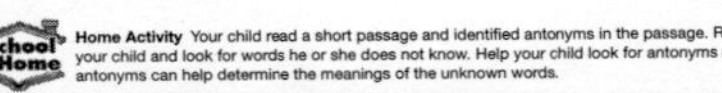

School + Home **Home Activity** Your child read a short passage and identified antonyms in the passage. Read a story with your child and look for words he or she does not know. Help your child look for antonyms and see if the antonyms can help determine the meanings of the unknown words.

▲ **Practice Book** p. 35

BEFORE READING

Prereading Strategies

OBJECTIVES

- Track the sequence of events to improve comprehension.
- Ask questions to understand the sequence of events.

GENRE STUDY

Biography

Satchel Paige is a biography. Explain that a biography is a selection about a real person's life that is written by another person.

PREVIEW AND PREDICT

Have students look at the selection title and illustrations. Have students identify the subject of the biography and predict how he earned a living and what made him great at what he did. Have students use lesson vocabulary words in their discussion.

Strategy Response Log

Ask Questions Have students write two questions about Satchel Paige and his life. Students will answer their questions in the Strategy Response Log activity on p. 103.

94

ELL

Build Background Use pictures in the story or pantomime to reinforce baseball vocabulary, such as *strike, batter, catcher, mitt* (p. 98), *outfield, bases* (p. 99), *home plate, outfielder* (p. 102), *inning,* and *bases loaded* (p. 104). Write the words on the board and help students define any unfamiliar terms.

Consider having students read the selection summary in English or in students' home languages. See the Multilingual Summaries in the ELL Teaching Guide, pp. 26–28.

Satchel Paige

by Lesa Cline-Ransome
paintings by James E. Ransome

Besides athletic ability, what makes an athlete great?

A **biography** tells about a person's life. Look for how Satchel Paige handled the challenges in his life.

95

SET PURPOSE

Read the first page of the selection aloud to students. Have them consider the two questions about Satchel Paige they wrote for their Strategy Response Logs and share what they hope to learn about him.

Tell students to notice which events happened first, next, and so on as they read. Explain that some events will be told out of sequence.

AudioText

DURING READING

Guiding Comprehension

1  **Sequence • Inferential**

Did Leroy Paige get the nickname "Satchel" after he became a ball player? Explain.

No. Satchel got his nickname before he became a ball player, when he carried suitcases, or satchels, for passengers at Union Station.

Monitor Progress

Sequence

If... students are unable to tell when Satchel earned his nickname,	**then...** use the skill and strategy instruction on p. 97.

2 **Vocabulary • Antonyms**

In 1923, baseball was a segregated sport. An antonym for *segregated* is *integrated.* What does *integrated* mean?

Integrated means "brought together." On an integrated team, all races play together.

Students who have access to the Internet can use the keywords *Negro League* to search for information about other teams and players who played with Satchel Paige.

1 *Leroy "Satchel" Paige earned his nickname as a young man. He carried suitcases—satchels—for passengers at Union Station in Mobile, Alabama. Satchel was a natural athlete. People said that by the age of ten he could outpitch grown men. So in 1923, at the age of 19, he decided to earn his living as a baseball player. In those days baseball was*
2 *a segregated sport. African Americans were forced to play in their own leagues, separate from whites.*

As a semipro pitcher, Satchel developed his own unique style. He'd pick up a tip here and there, put his Satchel spin on it, and polish it off with a brand-new name. Got so Satch began to think of his pitches as his children. The "hesitation" was his magic slow ball. The "trouble ball" caused all sorts of havoc. And then there was the "bee ball," which, according to Satch, would "always be where I want it to be."

96

Access Content Point to the word "hesitation." Explain that the word appears in quotation marks to show that this is what Satchel called this type of pitch. Tell students that *hesitate* means "to stop or wait a moment." Ask them to act out what a "hesitation" pitch might look like.

97

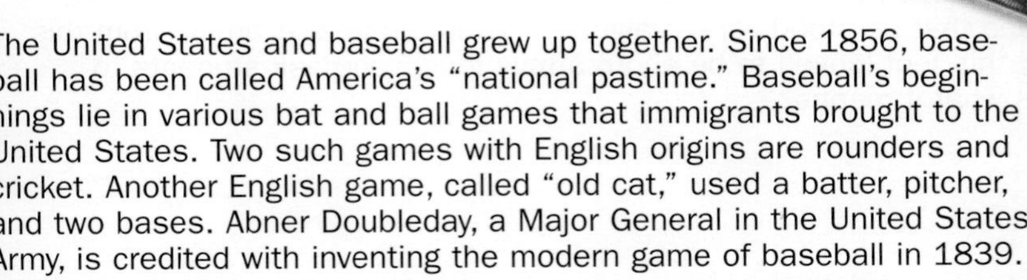

U.S. History and Baseball

The United States and baseball grew up together. Since 1856, baseball has been called America's "national pastime." Baseball's beginnings lie in various bat and ball games that immigrants brought to the United States. Two such games with English origins are rounders and cricket. Another English game, called "old cat," used a batter, pitcher, and two bases. Abner Doubleday, a Major General in the United States Army, is credited with inventing the modern game of baseball in 1839.

 **SKILLS ↔ STRATEGIES IN CONTEXT**

Sequence

TEACH

- Sequence means the order in which events take place.
- Clue words like *first*, *next*, and *last* help us learn about sequence.
- If there are no clue words in the text, the reader has to determine what happens first, next, and last.

MODEL First I'll read the headnote and ask questions like, *What happened first to Satchel? What happened next? What happened last?* If I put this information together, I can learn about the sequence of events in Satchel's life.

PRACTICE AND ASSESS

Have students reread the headnote on p. 96. Ask them to put these events in order. (*a, c, b*)

a) Satchel carries suitcases.

b) Satchel decides to earn his living as a baseball player.

c) Satchel gets his nickname.

DURING READING

Guiding Comprehension

3 Character • Inferential
Question the Author **The author talks about Satchel's grin. What is she trying to tell you about him?**

Possible response: The grin shows Satchel's joy for the game and his confidence.

4 Context Clues • Inferential
Use context clues to determine the meaning of the word *squint* on p. 98.

Clues: strain his eyes. Meaning: to look with the eyes partly closed.

Monitor Progress

Context Clues

If... students have difficulty using context clues to determine meaning,	**then...** use vocabulary strategy instruction on p. 99.

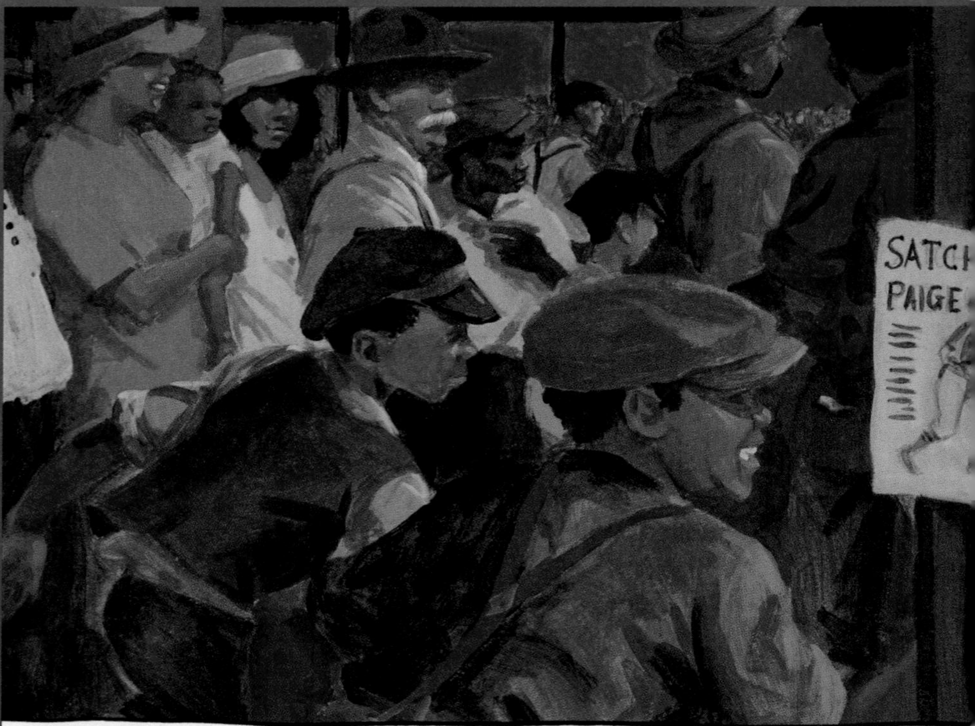

There was an odd way about his pitching. He would stand tall and straight as an oak tree on the mound. His foot looked to be about a mile long, and when he shot it into the air, it seemed to block out the sun. Satch's arm seemed to stretch on forever, winding, bending, twisting. And then there was
3 that grin he flashed just as he released the ball. It seemed to say, "Go ahead, just try and get a hit off of that."

"Strike one!"

And you never saw it coming. I mean, one minute it was there, plain as day in his hand, and then, all of a sudden . . .

"Strike two!"

It was in the catcher's mitt. The batter would strain his
4 eyes, squint a little.

Here it comes, got it now.

Extend Language Reread aloud the phrase "straight as an oak tree." Help students understand the use of figurative language to emphasize the idea that he stood very straight. Point out another example from this page, "his foot looked to be about a mile long," and ask students to guess what it means.

"Strike three!"

Just like that. All over.

"Next batter up!"

"Give it to 'em, Satch. Show your stuff," fans and teammates would shout. And he did. Every time. Folks would pack the stands to see how many Satchel could strike out in one game. He made the crowds laugh with his fast talking and slow walking ("A man's got to go slow to go long and far," he'd say), but mostly he made them cheer. Never in his nineteen years had he heard a sweeter sound. The more cheers he heard, the more his confidence grew. A kind of confidence that made him call to the outfield with the bases loaded and the last hitter up to bat, "Why don't you all have a seat. Won't be needing you on this one."

 **VOCABULARY STRATEGY**

Context Clues

TEACH

Read the fifth paragraph on p. 98. Model using context clues to determine the meaning of *squint.*

MODEL In the fifth paragraph on p. 98, it says, "the batter would strain his eyes, squint a little." I know that when you strain your eyes, you look really hard at something. When you do that, your eyes close a bit, so I think *squint* must mean to look with your eyes partly closed.

PRACTICE AND ASSESS

- Have students use context clues to determine the meaning of *confidence* in the last paragraph on p. 99 *(a strong, firm belief in oneself.)*

Guiding Comprehension

5 Cause and Effect • Inferential
Text to World **What was the effect of having large crowds at the games? What would be the effect if fewer fans came?**

The players made more money when the crowds came—that is, when attendance was high. If fewer fans came, the players' paychecks would be lower.

6 Compare and Contrast • Inferential
Compare a player's life in the Negro Leagues to a player's life in the Major Leagues.

Black players played two or three games a day, had long seasons, and couldn't eat in restaurants or sleep in hotels. White players enjoyed short seasons, train travel, rooms in hotels, and restaurant meals.

Monitor Progress

REVIEW **Compare and Contrast**

If... students have difficulty comparing and contrasting,	**then...** use the skill and strategy instruction on p. 101.

7 Vocabulary • Context Clues
Have students use context clues to determine the meaning of *on the road* on p. 101.

Clues: refused meals in restaurants; rooms in hotels; traveling. Meaning: they ate wherever they could.

ELL

Access Content Reread aloud the sentence: "Life in the Negro Leagues suited Satchel." Explain that *suited* means "it fit," or "satisfied," him. Ask students to tell why they think this life "suited" Satchel.

Wherever the crowds went, a good paycheck followed, so he 5
made sure to keep them coming. After just one year he was playing in the Negro major leagues for the Chattanooga Black Lookouts, and the folks were still cheering and shouting, "Give it to 'em, Satch. Show your stuff."

There were two major leagues back in 1924, when Satchel was called up. Because the white major-league ball clubs wouldn't allow blacks to play in their leagues, blacks had created their own in 1920 and named them the Negro Leagues. The white major-league players enjoyed trains, hotels, hot meals, and short seasons.

Negro League players were often refused meals in restaurants 6
and rooms in hotels. They ate on the road and slept where they
could—in train depots or on baseball fields. They played two, some- 7
times three games a day, nearly every day, in a season as long as the weather would hold. And when the season ended in America, Satch went right on playing and traveling in other parts of the world.

Life in the Negro Leagues suited Satchel. He was a traveling man. One city could never hold him for long. He moved from Alabama, where he played with the Birmingham Black Barons, to Tennessee, where he played with the Nashville Elite Giants, and to Pennsylvania, where he played with the Pittsburgh Crawfords.

From the first breath of spring till the cool rush of fall he would ride. Sometimes he joined his teammates on rickety old buses, bumping along on back roads studded with potholes so deep, players would have to hold on to their seats (and stomachs) just to keep from spilling into the aisles. But mostly he drove alone, in cars that would take him wherever he wanted to go. The fans would always be waiting in the next town. Their wait could be a long one—he was never much for keeping anyone's time but his own.

101

Segregation and Jim Crow Laws

During the first half of the 1900s, contact between blacks and whites was forbidden not only in baseball but in other areas as well. Segregation, or separation of the races, was almost complete. In many states segregation was enforced through Jim Crow laws. Jim Crow laws forbade intermarriage and required business owners and public institutions to keep blacks and whites separated. Apartment buildings, drinking fountains, restaurants, waiting rooms, parks, and many other facilities were segregated under Jim Crow laws.

SKILLS ↔ STRATEGIES IN CONTEXT

Compare and Contrast REVIEW

TEACH

- Remind students that comparisons tell how things are alike and contrasts tell how things are different.
- Explain that many comparisons and contrasts do not use clue words. The reader must then detect the comparison.

MODEL A sentence in the last paragraph on p. 99 describes how cheers made Satchel's confidence grow. I wonder how players feel when fans boo or are silent.

PRACTICE AND ASSESS

- Have students read the last paragraph on p. 99. Ask them to compare and contrast the effect cheers and boos have on a ballplayer. *(Possible response: Cheering makes players feel good about themselves, but booing makes them feel nervous or less confident.)*
- To assess, use Practice Book p. 36.

Compare and Contrast

Directions Read the passage. Then answer the questions below.

In 1999, the U.S. Women's Soccer team won the World Cup. Like the men's team in 1998, the women's team had high hopes of winning the international competition. Unlike the men's team from the year before, the U.S. women's team took first place in the contest. Mia Hamm, the leader of the team, was unlike any women's soccer player before. She became known as one of the greatest athletes, male or female, ever to play the game. Her success, however, was not a solo effort. On the American World Cup and Olympic teams, she was surrounded by many great players, and Hamm was always eager to praise her teammates. Like so many figures in women's sports, Hamm appreciates how hard it is to gain recognition. Hamm retired from soccer after leading the U.S. Olympic women's soccer team to a gold medal in 2004. For other women who still play soccer, she remains an inspiration.

1. How was the 1999 U.S. women's soccer team like the 1998 men's team?
   They both had high hopes of winning the World Cup.
2. How was the women's team different than the men's team?
   The women's team won the World Cup, and the men's team did not.
3. How was Mia Hamm different from previous women's soccer players?
   Possible answer: She was better than any of them.
4. How is Mia Hamm different from women who play soccer today?
   Possible answer: She didn't have role models to look up to.
5. On a separate sheet of paper, describe someone who interests you who did great things in his or her field. How was he or she similar to or different from other people who did the same activity?
   Students' answers should identify the individual and explain how he or she excelled, along with making comparisons and contrasts with others in his or her field.

School + Home **Home Activity** Your child has read a short passage and made comparisons and contrasts about the subject. Talk with your child about two different people in his or her life. Ask your child to compare and contrast these two people.

▲ **Practice Book** p. 36

DURING READING

Guiding Comprehension

8 **Vocabulary • Context Clues**

What context clues could you use to determine the meaning of *comforts* on p. 102?

Clues: settled life; warm smile; tender heart. Meaning: something that makes life easier and more comfortable.

9 **Cause and Effect • Inferential**

What caused Satchel to get married and start a family?

He longed for a more settled life and was tired of being on the road.

10 **Ask Questions • Critical**

What questions could you ask to determine the sequence of events so far in the selection?

Possible responses: What happened first? What happened next? What happened last?

Once he reached his mid-thirties, the joys of traveling
began to wear thin for Satchel. He found himself longing for
a more settled life and the comforts of a home. In 1941 he
8 finally found it in the warm smile and tender heart of Lahoma
9 Brown. Satch rested his travel-weary legs and happily began
his second career as husband and father. But even though he
had finally found what he thought he'd been searching for, it
was only a year before he took to the road again with his first
and only true love—baseball. His family would have to wait.

Satchel's teammates were in love with the game, too. And out of that love grew players better than anyone could ever dream. His teammates included "Cool Papa" Bell, a hitter who ran bases so fast, if you blinked you'd swear he'd never left home plate. Oscar Charleston was an outfielder who could tell just where a ball would land as soon as it hit the bat. And then there was Josh Gibson, who some said could hit a ball so hard and so far, it would land somewhere in the middle

102

Understanding Idioms Restate the idea "land somewhere in the middle of next week" (land somewhere very far away). Ask students who could "hit a ball so hard and so far, it would land somewhere in the middle of next week" and what he was sometimes called. Be sure students understand "the middle of next week" refers to distance not time.

of next week. Because of his powerful hitting and home run record, Josh was sometimes called "the black Babe Ruth," but many wondered if the Babe should have been called "the white Josh Gibson."

Back in 1923, when Gibson and Satch were teammates on the Pittsburgh Crawfords, they were considered a mighty powerful duo. Posters for the Crawfords read,

Josh Gibson and Satchel Paige
THE GREATEST BATTERY IN BASEBALL
Gibson guaranteed to hit two home runs and Paige guaranteed to strike out the first nine men.

"Someday we'll meet up and see who's best," they would often joke with each other. In 1942, soon after Satchel's return to the road, they got their chance. 10

Josh Gibson of the Homestead Grays

103

Develop Vocabulary

PRACTICE LESSON VOCABULARY

Students orally respond *yes* or *no* to each question and provide a reason for each answer.

1. Is a *windup* something a player does after a game? *(No, it is a part of a pitch.)*

2. If someone uses a *mocking* tone with you, is he or she teasing you? *(Yes, mocking is like teasing.)*

3. Is strength an antonym for *weakness?* *(Yes, they are opposites.)*

BUILD CONCEPT VOCABULARY

Review previous concept words with students. Ask if students have come across any words today in their reading or elsewhere that they would like to add to their Personal Challenges Concept Web, such as *rickety* and *bumping*.

STRATEGY SELF-CHECK

Ask Questions

TEACH

Ask students to identify the sequence of events in the selection so far. Remind them to ask questions such as "what happened first, next, and last" to help them. Students can record their questions and answers. *(Possible responses: First, Satchel decides to become a baseball player. Next, as a semi-pro pitcher he develops a unique way of pitching and the crowds love him. Finally, he gets called up to the major leagues and joins the Negro League, traveling from one city to another.)*

SELF-CHECK

Students can ask themselves these questions to assess their ability to use the skill and strategy.

- Did I ask what happened first, next, and last?
- Did the questions I asked help me correctly identify the sequence of events?

Monitor Progress

Sequence

If... students have difficulty asking questions to identify the sequence of events,	**then...** revisit the skill lesson on pp. 90–91. Reteach as necessary.

Strategy Response Log

Answer Questions Have students answer the two questions they posed at the beginning of the selection. (See p. 94.) Then have them ask another question they would like to have answered about Paige.

If you want to teach this selection in two sessions, stop here.

DAY 3

Guiding Comprehension

If you are teaching the selection in two days, discuss the sequence so far and review the vocabulary.

11 Details and Facts • Inferential

Explain how Satchel raised the stakes toward the end of the big game.

With one man on base, Satchel walked two players before Gibson's turn at bat. If Gibson got a hit, the Homestead Grays could score three runs and a home run.

12 Sequence • Literal

Which of these events from the World Series took place first: Josh Gibson came up to bat or Satchel walked two players?

Satchel walked two players before Josh Gibson came up to bat.

Monitor Progress

Sequence

If... students have difficulty answering the question to determine the sequence,	**then...** use the skill and strategy instruction on p. 105.

DAY 3 Grouping Options

Reading

Whole Group Discuss the Question of the Day.

Group Time Differentiated Instruction

Read *Satchel Paige.* See pp. 90h–90i for the small group lesson plan.

Whole Group Discuss the Reader Response questions on p. 108. Then use p. 111a.

Language Arts

Use pp. 111e–111k.

It was September 10, 1942, the second game of the Negro World Series. Satch's team, the Kansas City Monarchs, was in a heated best-of-seven matchup against the Homestead Grays, led by Josh Gibson. Toward the end of the game, Satch decided
11 to raise the stakes. With two outs in the inning and one man on base, he walked two players so the bases would be loaded
12 when Josh Gibson came up to bat. "Someday we'll meet up and

104

Access Content Tell students that "bases loaded" means that there are runners on all three bases, so they have a good chance of scoring a home run.

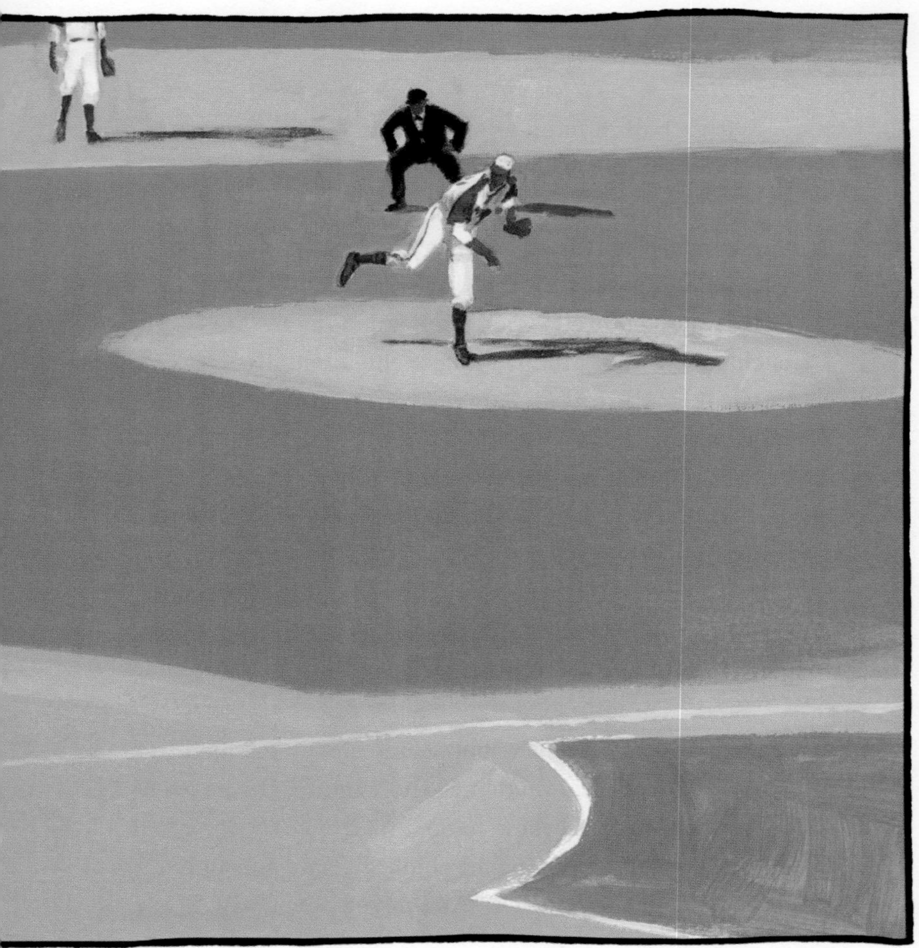

see who's best" rang in Satch's ears as he prepared to face the man who would now determine the fate of his team and Satch's reputation. Satchel called to Josh, "Remember back when we were playing with the Crawfords and you said you was the best hitter in the world and I was the best pitcher?"

"Yeah, I remember," Josh called back.

"Well, now we're going to see what's what," Satch said.

105

SKILLS ↔ STRATEGIES IN CONTEXT

Sequence
Ask Questions

TEACH

Have students read the first paragraph on pp. 104–105. Ask them in which order these two events took place: Josh's coming up to bat and Satchel's walking two players. Use this information to model how questions can help determine the sequence of events.

MODEL It says that Satchel walked two players so that when Josh came up to bat, the bases would be loaded. This makes me think that he must have walked the players before Josh came up to bat.

PRACTICE AND ASSESS

- Have students reread the first paragraph on pp. 104–105.
- Have students identify an event from the past involving Josh and Satchel that is mentioned on page 105. *(Satchel refers to the time he and Josh played for the same team, the Crawfords.)*
- Ask what question the comment "Well, now we're going to see what's what" raises. *(Possible response: Which player really was better?)*

EXTEND SKILLS

Author's Viewpoint/Bias

Point out that an author's viewpoint is the way the author looks at his or her subject. Explain that when you read a biography, you can determine the author's viewpoint by noticing the words he or she uses to describe the subject. Looking at the words the author uses, you can ask yourself: How does the author view the subject? Have students find examples of sentences in *Satchel Paige* that show the author's viewpoint.

Guiding Comprehension

13 **Vocabulary • Antonyms**
On p. 106, in describing Satchel's final pitch to Josh, the author says he "exhaled the breath he'd been holding since the windup." What is an antonym for *exhaled*?

Inhaled is an antonym for *exhaled*.

14 **Compare and Contrast • Critical**
Text to World **Have students identify a time when they or someone they know "raised the stakes" like Satchel did with Josh. Ask them to describe the situation and results.**

Possible responses: My mom challenged me to a running race, but this time, she wouldn't give me a head start like she did when I was little. It made me run even harder.

Strategy Response Log

Summarize When students finish reading the selection, provide this prompt: Write three sentences that summarize the main events of *Satchel Paige*. Do not include unnecessary details. Use the text structure, especially the sequence of events, to help you.

With a ball in hand and a grin on his face, Satch told Josh, "I'm gonna throw a fastball letter high."

"Strike one!"

Josh shook his head, tightened his grip on the bat, and resumed his position as he tried to stare into Satchel's eyes.

But Satch stared straight ahead at Josh's knees. His coach back at the Mount Meigs School had always told him,

"Look at the knees, Satch. Every weakness a batter has, you can spot in the knees."

"Now I'm gonna throw this one a little faster and belt high," Satch said during the windup.

"Strike two!"

In typical Satch style, he called in a mocking voice, "Now I got you oh-and-two and I'm supposed to knock you down, but instead I'm gonna throw a pea at your knee."

"Strike three!"

13 Josh never moved the bat. Satch slowly exhaled the breath he'd been holding since the windup. It was over. He'd done what he'd come to do.

"Nobody hits Satchel's fastball," he said through a smile as bright as the sun. "And nobody ever will."

14

106

Extend Language Reread the following phrase aloud: "stare into Satchel's eyes." Show students what it means to stare into someone's eyes.

STRATEGY SELF-CHECK

Ask Questions

Draw a time line listing the years 1920 to 1945 in five-year increments. List these events from the selection: Satchel and Josh play for the Pittsburgh Crawfords *(1923);* Satchel gets married *(1941);* Satchel and Josh meet in the Negro World Series *(1942).*

Have students list the sequence of events from the selection. Students can use the list to ask questions they might have about the selection. *(Responses will vary but should demonstrate knowledge of the sequence.)*

Use Practice Book p. 37

SELF-CHECK

Students can ask themselves these questions to assess their understanding of the selection.

- Did I keep track of the sequence of events as I read *Satchel Paige*?
- Was I able to generate questions to help me?

Monitor Progress

Sequence

If... students have difficulty sequencing events or asking questions,	**then...** use the Reteach lesson on p. 111b.

Sequence

- **Sequence** is the order in which events happen in a selection. When you read, think about what comes first, next, and last.
- Several events can occur at the same time. Words such as *meanwhile* and *during* give clues that two events are happening at the same time.

Directions Read the following passage. Then answer the questions below.

Alan had to find a way to dunk a basketball through the hoop in the driveway. He just had to! Both of his brothers could, and so could his older sister. Even though he was still only seven, he wanted to know how it felt to slam the ball through the hoop. First, he tried to run as far away as he could and jump to the hoop. Then he set up a box under the net and tried to jump from there to reach the rim. That didn't work, either. Meanwhile, his brothers and sister were watching him as he struggled. Just as Alan was about to give up, they rushed out to him. Before he knew it, he was being lifted up into the air. Then he caught the pass his sister threw. Within a second, the hoop was within reach. He reached out, and *swoosh!* At last, the ball dove through the hoop.

1. What does Alan really want to do as the story begins?
   He wants to dunk a basketball.
2. What does he try first? What word helps you find what he did first?
   He tries running up to the hoop; first.
3. What does he try next? What word tells you this?
   He jumps off a box; then.
4. What is happening at the same time Alan is trying to dunk the ball? What words tell you this?
   His brothers and sister are watching him; meanwhile.
5. What is the last thing that happens? How can you tell?
   The ball goes through the hoop; at last.

School + Home **Home Activity** Your child read a short passage and answered questions about its sequence of events. Work with your child to develop a sequential solution to a problem he or she is facing.

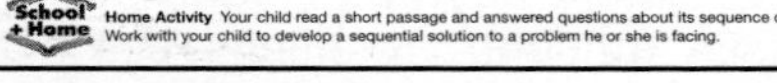

▲ **Practice Book** p. 37

Develop Vocabulary

PRACTICE LESSON VOCABULARY

As a class, have students complete the following sentences orally.

1. With Satchel on the mound, players on his team had little to do in the *(outfield).*
2. Satchel's foot appeared to be a mile long and his arm seemed to stretch on forever during the *(windup).*
3. The more cheers Satchel heard, the greater his *(confidence).*
4. Satchel's *(fastball)* moved so fast that no one could hit it.

BUILD CONCEPT VOCABULARY

Review previous concept words with the students. Ask if students have come across any words today in their reading or elsewhere that they would like to add to their Personal Challenges Concept Web such as *fate* and *reputation.*

DURING READING

Reader Response

Open for Discussion Personal Response

MODEL The part that really made Satchel come alive for me was the part that describes his pitching. So I would start reading aloud on p. 98.

Comprehension Check Critical Response

1. Possible response: She chose details that showed why Satchel Paige was one of the greatest pitchers of all time. ***Author's Purpose***
2. Possible response: First Satchel issued a "reminder challenge"; then, with each pitch, he taunted Gibson; while he was pitching, Satchel avoided Gibson's eyes and stared straight at his knees. ***Sequence***
3. Possible response: Fans liked Satchel Paige. They saw him as a talented and entertaining pitcher. ***Ask Questions***
4. List words: *outfield, windup, fastball.* Other terms: *home plate, World Series*
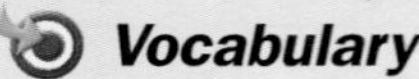 ***Vocabulary***

Look Back and Write For test practice, assign a 10–15 minute time limit. For assessment, see the Scoring Rubric at the right.

Retell

Have students retell *Satchel Paige.*

Monitor Progress

Check Retelling Rubric 4 | 3 | 2 | 1

If... students have difficulty retelling the story,	**then...** use the Retelling Cards and the Scoring Rubric for Retelling on p. 109 to assist fluent retelling.

Check Retelling Have beginning ELL students listen to other retellings before attempting their own. For more ideas on assessing students' retellings, see the ELL and Transition Handbook.

Reader Response

Open for Discussion A good biography helps you, the reader, see and hear the person the book is about. It brings that person to life. Reread aloud the part of *Satchel Paige* that did the most to bring him alive for you.

1. A good biographer must select which details to include about the subject's life. How do you think Lesa Cline-Ransome decided what to include about the life of Satchel Paige? **Think Like an Author**
2. Reread pages 104–106. In your own words, describe how Satchel Paige defeated Josh Gibson, in sequence from start to finish. **Sequence**
3. Ask yourself this question: How did fans feel about Satchel Paige? Look back at page 99 and answer it. **Ask Questions**
4. To understand the story of Satchel Paige, it helps to know the game of baseball. Which words on the Words to Know list are baseball terms? Choose three other words from the text that could be used to talk about baseball. **Vocabulary**

Look Back and Write From the information in the selection, describe what kind of person Satchel Paige was. Use details from the text to support your answer.

Meet author **Lesa Cline-Ransome on page 762 and** illustrator **James E. Ransome on page 775.**

108

Scoring Rubric Look Back and Write

Top-Score Response A top-score response will recognize Satchel Paige's colorful personality, his love of fame, and his ambition and devotion to baseball and will use text details for support.

Example of a Top-Score Response Satchel Paige had a colorful personality that drew big crowds. He even named his pitches and gave dramatic, humorous pitching performances. Paige loved being famous. Cheering fans gave him confidence. Most of all, Paige was ambitious and loved the game. He was determined to strike out the great Josh Gibson. He played and traveled constantly.

For additional rubrics, see p. WA10.

Write Now

Feature Article

Prompt

Satchel Paige is a feature article about a baseball legend.
Think about a topic that is interesting to you.
Now write a feature article about that topic.

Writing Trait

Exact **word choice** paints a picture for readers. Use precise, vivid words and descriptions.

Student Model

My uncle looks like Abraham Lincoln, only with blazing red hair. He is lanky and bearded. In addition, he lives with something Honest Abe was also thought to have had: Marfan Syndrome.

Marfan Syndrome is a rare disease. It makes some cells in the body grow really long and thin. Most of these cells are in the bones, heart, and eyes. People with Marfan Syndrome often grow very tall. (My uncle is seven feet tall!) They also often have heart and eye problems, but these can be helped with surgery.

Having Marfan Syndrome means learning to adjust, which can be a tall order, but many people with this disease rise to the challenge.

Careful word choice provides striking image in opening.

Facts explain topic clearly to readers.

Humor helps readers hear writer's voice.

Use the model to help you write your own feature article.

Write Now

Look at the Prompt Explain that each sentence in the prompt has a purpose.

- Sentence 1 presents a topic.
- Sentence 2 suggests students think about the topic.
- Sentence 3 tells what to write—a feature article.

Strategies to Develop Word Choice

Have students

- think of comparisons that will give readers a clearer picture.

NO: Micah was embarrassed.
YES: Micah turned red as a tomato.

- replace vague nouns with exact nouns.

NO: We met at a place downtown.
YES: We met at a café in the square.

For additional suggestions and rubric, see pp. 111g–111h.

Writer's Checklist

- ☑ **Focus** Is the topic clear?
- ☑ **Organization** Do ideas flow smoothly?
- ☑ **Support** Is the topic supported with strong, vivid details?
- ☑ **Conventions** Are commas and apostrophes used correctly?

Scoring Rubric Expository Retelling

Rubric 4 3 2 1	4	3	2	1
Connections	Makes connections and generalizes beyond the text	Makes connections to other events, texts, or experiences	Makes a limited connection to another event, text, or experience	Makes no connection to another event, text, or experience
Author's Purpose	Elaborates on author's purpose	Tells author's purpose with some clarity	Makes some connection to author's purpose	Makes no connection to author's purpose
Topic	Describes the main topic	Identifies the main topic with some details early in retelling	Identifies the main topic	Retelling has no sense of topic
Important Ideas	Gives accurate information about events, steps, and ideas using details and key vocabulary	Gives accurate information about events, steps, and ideas with some detail and key vocabulary	Gives limited or inaccurate information about events, steps, and ideas	Gives no information about events, steps, and ideas
Conclusions	Draws conclusions and makes inferences to generalize beyond the text	Draws conclusions about the text	Is able to draw few conclusions about the text	Is unable to draw conclusions or make inferences about the text

Retelling Plan

- ☑ **Week 1** Assess Strategic Intervention students.
- ☑ **Week 2** Assess Advanced students.
- ☑ **Week 3** Assess Strategic Intervention students.
- ☑ **This week assess On-Level students.**
- ☐ **Week 5** Assess any students you have not yet checked during this unit.

Use the Retelling Chart on p. TR17 to record retelling.

Selection Test To assess with *Satchel Paige*, use Selection Tests, pp. 13–16.

Fresh Reads for Differentiated Test Practice For weekly leveled practice, use pp. 19–24.

DAY 4

Social Studies in Reading

OBJECTIVES

- Examine features of expository nonfiction.
- Practice a test-taking strategy.
- Compare and contrast across texts.

PREVIEW/USE TEXT FEATURES

As students preview "The Girls of Summer," have them look at the illustrations. Then ask:

- **What do the illustrations tell you about the girls of summer?** *(Possible response: They played baseball.)*

Link to Social Studies

Discuss with students sources they might use for their research on women's voting rights.

EXPOSITORY NONFICTION

Use the sidebar on p. 110 to guide discussion.

- Explain that expository nonfiction provides information about the real world.
- Point out that expository nonfiction contains factual information and very often includes illustrations to help readers better understand the text.

DAY 4 Grouping Options

Reading

Whole Group Discuss the Question of the Day.

Group Time Differentiated Instruction

Read "The Girls of Summer." See pp. 90h–90i for the small group lesson plan.

Whole Group Use p. 111a.

Language Arts

Use pp. 111e–111k.

Social Studies in Reading

Expository Nonfiction

Genre

- **Expository nonfiction deals with real people and events.**
- **Expository articles often appear in magazines.**

Text Features

- **Some articles deal with how things were different in the past.**
- **Expository articles about the past often include pictures that show what people and places looked like.**

Link to Social Studies

Women couldn't vote in the 1870s, but they could play baseball. Do some research in books or on the Internet to find out when women finally did gain the right to vote and how they gained that right.

THE GIRLS of SUMMER

by Ellen Klages

Baseball is largely considered a man's game. But what if you take a closer look at its history?

The first team of professional baseball players, the Cincinnati Red Stockings, took the field in 1869. They were all male—the first boys of summer. The first girls of summer, women who were paid to play baseball, competed in their first game in 1875.

In the 1870s, an American woman could not vote. She could not own property in her own name after marriage. But she could play ball—as well as it could be played in an outfit that weighed as much as thirty pounds and included a floor-length skirt, underskirts, a long-sleeved, high-necked blouse, and high button shoes.

110

Content-Area Vocabulary Social Studies

era	a period of time or history
public opinion	opinion of the people in a country, community, etc.
vote	a formal expression of a choice about a proposal, motion, candidate for office, etc.

AudioText

Amelia Bloomer designed and wore the loose-fitting, Turkish-style trousers that carried her name and made sports more practical for women athletes. In the 1890s, scores of "Bloomer Girls" baseball teams were formed all over the country.

The Bloomer Girls era lasted from the 1890s until 1934. Hundreds of teams—All Star Ranger Girls, Philadelphia Bobbies, New York Bloomer Girls—offered employment, travel, and adventure for young women who could hit, field, slide, or catch.

The Bloomer Girls teams dwindled as more and more minor league teams—farm clubs—were formed to provide experience for young men on their climb up to the majors. A few women were signed, briefly, to minor league contracts, but they were exceptions.

Although women had been playing pro ball on Bloomer Girls teams for more than forty years, in the 1930s public opinion was that they had inferior abilities when it came to sports. Women's professional baseball disappeared when the last of the Bloomer Girls teams disbanded in 1934.

Briefly, in the late 1940s and early 1950s, women played again. But in 1952 they were banned from professional baseball. The ban still holds today.

Reading Across Texts

This selection and *Satchel Paige* show how two groups of people had difficulties playing professional baseball for different reasons. What were those reasons?

Writing Across Texts Present your response in a two-column chart.

Sequence How do the dates help you with the sequence of events?

111

Time for SOCIAL STUDIES

Women in Sports

Women athletes have played many sports besides baseball that were originally designed for men. The first women's intercollegiate basketball championship was held in 1896, five years after the game was invented. In the 1920s and 1930s, women competed fiercely—and to much popular acclaim—in rodeo events, such as calf roping, barrel racing, and sharp-shooting. In 1998, women's ice hockey became an Olympic medal sport.

DURING READING

Strategies for Nonfiction

USE ILLUSTRATIONS Explain that expository articles often include illustrations to support information in the text. Students can use illustrations to help answer test questions. Present the following strategy.

Use the Strategy

1. Read the test question.
2. Look at the illustrations and see if they provide information that will help you answer the question.

GUIDED PRACTICE Have students discuss how they would use the strategy to answer the following question.

What time period does this article tell about?

INDEPENDENT PRACTICE After students answer the following test question, discuss the process they used to find information.

What did women wear to play baseball?

Sequence

The dates tell in what order the events took place.

CONNECT TEXT TO TEXT

Reading Across Texts

Discuss why African Americans and women had difficulties playing professional baseball.

Writing Across Texts Help students begin their charts by having the class generate one reason for each column.

DAY 5

Fluency Assessment Plan

- ☑ **Week 1** Assess Advanced students.
- ☑ **Week 2** Assess Strategic Intervention students.
- ☑ **Week 3** Assess On-Level students.
- ☑ **This week assess Strategic Intervention students.**
- ☐ **Week 5** Assess any students you have not yet checked during this unit.

Set individual goals for students to enable them to reach the year-end goal.

- Current Goal: 105–110 wcpm
- Year-End Goal: 140 wcpm

Provide opportunities for English language learners to read aloud to younger children. This allows them to practice their oral reading and improve their fluency.

To develop fluent readers, use Fluency Coach.

DAY 5 Grouping Options

Reading

Whole Group
Revisit the Question of the Week.

Group Time
Differentiated Instruction
Reread this week's Leveled Readers. See pp. 90h–90i for the small group lesson plan.

Whole Group
Use p. 111b–111c.

Language Arts
Use pp. 111d–111l.

PHRASING

Fluency

DAY 1

Model Reread "Teammates" on p. 90m. Explain that you will group words together, such as prepositional phrases, verbal phrases, and other clauses, as you read the selection. Model for students as you read.

DAY 2

Echo Reading Read aloud the last paragraph on p. 101. Have students notice that you take a breath between phrases or chunks of meaningful words, but you do not pause in the middle of the group of words. Have students practice as a class doing three echo readings of the last paragraph on p. 101.

DAY 3

Model Read aloud the first paragraph on p. 102. Have students notice how you group words together to create the natural phrasing heard in spoken language. Practice as a class by doing three echo readings.

DAY 4

Partner Reading Partners practice reading aloud the first paragraph on p. 102, three times. Students should read with appropriate phrasing and offer each other feedback.

Monitor Progress — Check Fluency WCPM

As students reread, monitor their progress toward their individual fluency goals. Current Goal: 105–110 words correct per minute. End-of-Year Goal: 140 words correct per minute.

If... students cannot read fluently at a rate of 105–110 words correct per minute,
then... make sure students practice with text at their independent level. Provide additional fluency practice, pairing nonfluent readers with fluent readers.

If... students already read at 140 words correct per minute,
then... they do not need to reread three to four times.

SUCCESS PREDICTOR

DAY 5

Assessment
Individual Reading Rate Use the Fluency Assessment Plan and do a one-minute timed reading of either selection from this week to assess students in Week 4. Pay special attention to this week's skill, phrasing. Provide corrective feedback for each student.

RETEACH

Sequence

TEACH

Review the definition of *sequence* on p. 90. Students can complete Practice Book p. 38 on their own, or you can complete it as a class. Point out that the information to complete the time line is in the passage. Students should put the steps in sequential order and record them in their own words.

ASSESS

Have partners put these five events from "The Girls of Summer," pp. 110–111 in sequential order: women are banned from professional baseball *(5);* the first "Bloomer Girls" baseball teams are formed *(1);* the Bloomer Girls play for some 40 years *(3);* the first girls of summer compete in their first game *(2);* and Bloomer Girls teams dwindle *(4).*

For additional instruction on sequence, see DI • 55.

EXTEND SKILLS

Author's Viewpoint/Bias

TEACH

An author's viewpoint is the way an author looks at the subject he or she is writing about.

- You can learn an author's viewpoint by looking at the words he or she uses and the opinions expressed.
- Sometimes you can figure out an author's viewpoint even when it is not stated directly.

Work with students to explain the author's viewpoint of Satchel's wife, Lahoma Brown, by rereading p. 102, paragraph 1. Have students identify words that express the author's viewpoint. *(warm smile, tender heart)*

ASSESS

Have students reread p. 101, paragraphs 2–3, to figure out the author's viewpoint about how the white and black players were treated on the road. Have students write a response to this question:

- **What does the author's comparison of the treatment the white and black baseball players received show about her beliefs? Use words from the text to support your answer.**

OBJECTIVES

- Order events of a story sequentially.
- Identify author's viewpoint.

Skills Trace

Sequence

Introduce/Teach	TE: 5.1 90–91; 5.2 230–231; 5.6 726–727
Practice	Practice Book: 6, 33, 37, 38, 66, 76, 93, 97, 98, 106, 256, 266, 293, 297, 298
Reteach/Review	**TE: 5.1 111b, 121, DI•55; 5.2 173, 199, 253b, DI•56; 5.6 641, 655, 753b, DI•56**
Test	Selection Test: 13–16, 37–40, 117–120; Benchmark Test: Units 2, 6

Access Content Reteach the skill by reviewing the Picture It! lesson on sequence in the ELL Teaching Guide, pp. 22–23.

Sequence

- **Sequence** is the order in which events happen in a selection. When you read, think about what comes first, next, and last.
- Several events can occur at the same time. Words such as *meanwhile* and *during* give clues that two events are happening at the same time.

Directions Read the following passage.

There are many ways you can break in a new baseball mitt, but this is one of the tried-and-true, old-fashioned ways. First, get the mitt wet with warm water. Don't get it too soaked! Without putting the mitt on, spend some time opening and closing it with both hands to loosen up the leather. Next, you want to rub a little bit of oil (not motor oil) into the palm of the mitt where it creases. Put a baseball right in the heart of the mitt and then wrap it tightly with a rubber band. Let it sit that way overnight. The next morning, take the rubber band off the mitt and resume opening and closing it with both hands. You'll need to repeat the overnight process a few times before your mitt really loosens up. But when it does, it'll feel like that mitt was grown on your hand.

Directions Fill in the diagram below with the steps to breaking in a mitt. List them in the order in which they are supposed to be done.

Possible answers given.

How to Break in a Baseball Mitt

Get the mitt wet with warm water	1. Rub a little bit of oil in the mitt.	2. Put a ball in the mitt and wrap it tightly with a rubber band.	3. Let it sit overnight.	4. Unwrap the mitt and open and close it a few times.	5. Repeat the process a few times.

School + Home **Home Activity** Your child read a short passage and identified the order of steps in a process. With your child, write down the sequence of steps he or she must follow to do something he or she regularly does around the house.

▲ **Practice Book** p. 38

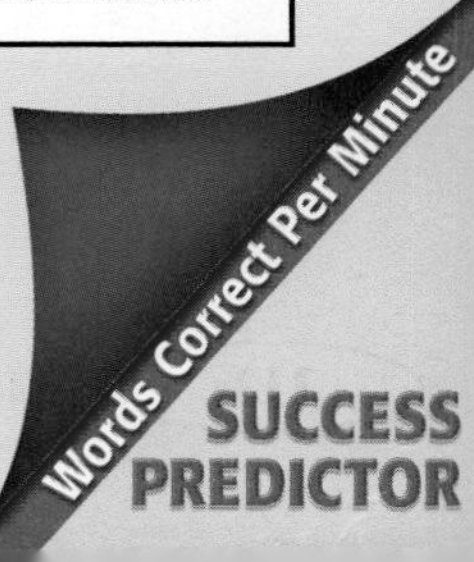

AFTER READING

Vocabulary and Word Study

VOCABULARY STRATEGY

Context Clues

UNFAMILIAR WORDS Remind students that they can use context clues to determine the meanings of unfamiliar words. Have students list any unknown words they encountered as they read *Satchel Paige.* They can create a chart identifying the words, any context clues, and definitions of the words based on their context. Students can confirm word meanings using a dictionary.

Word	Context Clues	Meaning
unique	put his Satchel spin on it	one of a kind
interprets		
domed		

Specialized Vocabulary

Specialized vocabulary words, such as *outfield,* all relate to the same category—in this case, baseball. Have partners make a list of specialized baseball vocabulary from *Satchel Paige.* Students can add other baseball terms they know or locate baseball words in a specialized dictionary.

Baseball Terms

1. pitcher
2. batter up
3. outfielder
4. World Series
5. ______
6. ______

BUILD CONCEPT VOCABULARY

Personal Challenges

LOOKING BACK Remind students of the question of the week: *How do we face personal challenges?* Discuss how this week's Concept Web of vocabulary words relates to the theme of personal challenges. Ask students if they have any words or categories to add. Discuss whether the words and categories are appropriately related to the concept.

MOVING FORWARD Preview the title of the next selection, *Shutting Out the Sky.* Ask students which Concept Web words might apply to the new selection based on the title alone.

Put a star next to these words on the web. Display the Concept Web and revisit the vocabulary words as you read the next selection to check predictions.

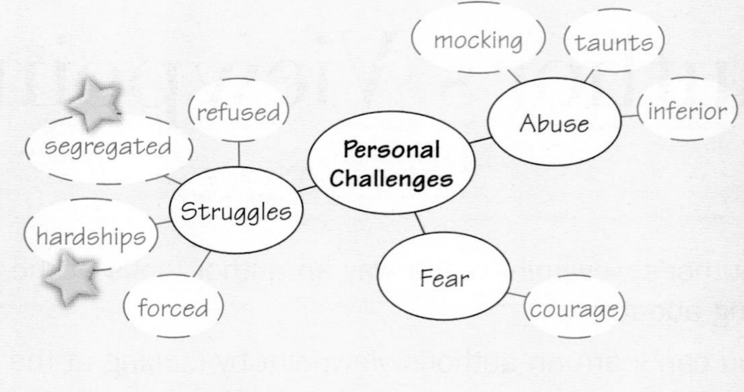

Monitor Progress

Check Word Use

If... students suggest words or categories that are not related to the concept, **then...** review the words and categories on the Concept Web and discuss how they relate to the lesson concept.

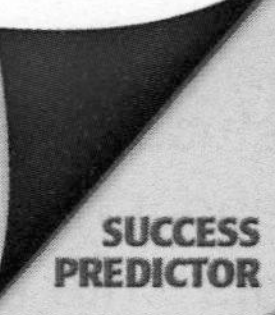

Speaking and Listening

SPEAKING

Sportscast

SET-UP Have students prepare and deliver a sportscast of Paige and Gibson's meeting in the Negro World Series. Students can base their sportscasts on information provided in the selection (pp. 104–106).

TEAM PRESENTATION Allow students to work in pairs, both acting as professional broadcasters describing and analyzing events in the game.

PLANNING Have students review pp. 104–106 of the selection. Provide them with time to record important events and details about the game on note cards. Students may want to prepare minute-by-minute outlines so that they can remember all of the details of play.

Delivery Tips

- Avoid long pauses.
- Vary your pace, pitch, and volume.
- Speak clearly, so the audience will know what happens in each moment of play.
- Use descriptive and expressive language. Allow yourself to express enthusiasm in ways that sportscasters do.

LISTENING

Listen to Audio CD

Have students listen to the AudioText of *Satchel Paige.* They can discuss these questions as a class or answer them in writing.

1. **Describe the tone used by the speaker. What mood does the speaker create?**
2. **Does the reader's delivery help you better understand the information? If so, how?**
3. **What is one advantage of hearing an informative text like this one read aloud?**

Support Vocabulary Use the following to review and extend vocabulary and to explore lesson concepts further:

- ELL Poster 4, Days 3–5 instruction
- Vocabulary Activities and Word Cards in ELL Teaching Guide, pp. 24–25

Assessment For information on assessing students' speaking and listening, see the ELL and Transition Handbook.

Grammar Compound and Complex Sentences

OBJECTIVES

- Define and identify compound and complex sentences.
- Punctuate compound and complex sentences correctly.
- Use compound and complex sentences correctly in writing.
- Become familiar with sentence assessment on high-stakes tests.

Monitor Progress

Grammar

If... students have difficulty identifying compound and complex sentences,	**then...** provide additional instruction and practice in The Grammar and Writing Book pp. 68–71.

DAILY FIX-IT

This week use Daily Fix-It Transparency 4.

Support Grammar See the Grammar Transition lessons in the ELL and Transition Handbook.

▲ **The Grammar and Writing Book**
For more instruction and practice, use pp. 68–71.

DAY 1 Teach and Model

DAILY FIX-IT

1. Wich sport do you like best. *(Which; best?)*
2. I love baseball but Im not a good baseball player. *(baseball,; I'm)*

READING-GRAMMAR CONNECTION

Write this sentence about *Satchel Paige* on the board:

African Americans have played baseball since the sport began.

Explain that this is a **complex sentence.** It has an independent clause and a dependent clause connected by the joining word *since.*

Explain that the subject and verb within each clause of a complex sentence must agree.

Display Grammar Transparency 4. Read aloud the definitions and sample sentences. Work through the items.

Compound and Complex Sentences

A **simple sentence** expresses a complete thought. It has a subject and a predicate.
Satchel Paige was a great athlete.
A **compound sentence** contains two simple sentences joined by a comma and a conjunction such as *and, but,* or *or.*
Fans waited many hours to see him, but Satch never let them down.
A **complex sentence** contains an independent clause, which can stand alone, and a dependent clause, which cannot stand alone. The clauses are joined with a word such as *if, when, because, until, before, after,* or *since.* In the following sentence, the independent clause is underlined once; the dependent clause is underlined twice.
When the second baseman caught the ball, the Tigers made a double play.

- To make good compound sentences, join simple sentences that are related.
- Replace the end punctuation of the first sentence with a comma. Replace the capital letter at the beginning of the second sentence with a lowercase letter, unless the word is a proper noun or *I.*
- In a complex sentence, if the dependent clause comes first, set it off with a comma.

Directions Write *simple* if the sentence is a simple sentence. Write *compound* if it is a compound sentence. Write *complex* if it is a complex sentence.

1. Many Americans love the game of baseball. simple
2. When spring rolls around, they wait for the first games. complex
3. The bleachers of ballparks fill, and fans cheer their favorite teams. compound
4. If the weather is cold and rainy, they don't mind. complex
5. These fans live for the crack of the bat. simple
6. Since the baseball season is long, they will return to the bleachers many times. complex
7. A professional team plays more than a hundred games. simple
8. Uncle Randy is a Cardinals fan, but Aunt Jan likes the Cubs. compound
9. Some families are divided because they root for different teams. complex
10. The World Series is the grand prize of baseball. simple
11. The National League champion faces the American League champion. simple
12. They play a series of games until a winner is declared. complex
13. There can be as many as seven games, or there can be as few as four. compound
14. When one team wins four games, it wins the World Series. complex
15. The fans of that team celebrate for days. simple

Unit 1 Satchel Paige — Grammar 4

▲ **Grammar Transparency** 4

DAY 2 Develop the Concept

DAILY FIX-IT

3. For years black player were denyed the right to play in the white major leagues. *(players; denied)*
4. The league beginned admiting them in 1947. *(began admitting)*

GUIDED PRACTICE

Review the concept of compound and complex sentences.

- A **compound sentence** contains two simple sentences joined by a comma and a conjunction. A semicolon (;) can be used between the two parts of a compound sentence when a conjunction is not used.
- A **complex sentence** contains an independent clause, which can stand alone, and a dependent clause, which cannot stand alone.

HOMEWORK Grammar and Writing Practice Book p. 13. Work through the first two items with the class.

Compound and Complex Sentences

A **simple sentence** expresses a complete thought. It has a subject and a predicate.
The Negro League formed in 1920.
A **compound sentence** contains two simple sentences joined by a comma and a conjunction such as *and, but,* or *or.*
The athletes played several games a day, and they traveled on a bus.
A **complex sentence** contains an independent clause, which can stand alone, and a dependent clause, which cannot stand alone. The clauses are joined by a word such as *if, when, because, until, before, after,* or *since.* In the following sentence, the independent clause is underlined once; the dependent clause is underlined twice.
Many years would pass before the major leagues were integrated.

Directions Join each pair of simple sentences with *and, but,* or *or.* Write the compound sentence on the lines. Change punctuation and capital letters as necessary.

1. My sister can hit the ball hard. She pitches well too.
My sister can hit the ball hard, and (*or* but) she pitches well too.
2. The game should have started at one o'clock. A thunderstorm began at 12:45.
The game should have started at one o'clock, but a thunderstorm began at 12:45.
3. The teams will make up the game next Sunday. They will wait until the end of the season.
The teams will make up the game next Sunday, or they will wait until the end of the season.

Directions Write *compound* after each compound sentence. Write *complex* after each complex sentence. Underline the word that joins the two clauses in each sentence.

4. All players are important to a team, but the pitcher may be most important. compound
5. If a pitcher strikes out batters, the opposing team cannot score. complex
6. Outfielders must catch the ball when the batter hits a pop fly. complex
7. The game was tied, and no one left the bleachers. compound
8. The pitcher struck out two batters, but the third batter hit a home run. compound

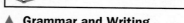

School-Home Connection **Home Activity** Your child learned about compound and complex sentences. Have your child write a paragraph about a baseball game, using at least one compound sentence and one complex sentence.

▲ **Grammar and Writing Practice Book** p. 13

DAY 3 Apply to Writing

DAILY FIX-IT

5. Jackie Robinson becomed the first African American player in the white major leagues. *(became; American)*

6. His many talents showed that him was more than qualifid. *(he; qualified)*

COMBINE IDEAS

Explain that combining simple sentences or clauses to form compound and complex sentences makes writing more interesting and easier to understand.

- Have students review something they have written. See if they can improve it by changing simple sentences into compound or complex sentences, and eliminating any run-on sentences or sentence fragments.

HOMEWORK Grammar and Writing Practice Book p. 14.

Compound and Complex Sentences

Directions Add a clause from the box to complete each sentence. Write *compound* or *complex* to tell what kind of sentence each one is.

He was the first African American player in the white major leagues
and a hero's skin color does not matter to them
the jeers soon turned to cheers
Since Jackie Robinson was the only African American on the field
and in 1962 he was elected to the Baseball Hall of Fame

1. Baseball fans love the stars of the game, and a hero's skin color does not matter to them. compound
2. Since Jackie Robinson was the only African American on the field, he endured anger and jeers at first. complex
3. Because he showed great skill and grace, the jeers soon turned to cheers. complex
4. The public admired Robinson, and in 1962 he was elected to the Baseball Hall of Fame. compound
5. He was the first African American player in the white major leagues, but he soon was not the only one. compound

Directions Write several sentences about your favorite sports hero or performer. Use at least one compound sentence and one complex sentence. Use commas and conjunctions correctly.

Possible answer: Lou Gehrig is considered one of the greatest baseball players of all time. He was twice elected the American League's Most Valuable Player. Because he never missed a game, Gehrig played in 2,130 consecutive New York Yankee games in 14 years. Gehrig had a natural talent for the game, but he was forced to retire because of ill health.

School-Home CONNECTION **Home Activity** Your child learned how to use compound and complex sentences in writing. Ask your child to read you a story and to point out examples of compound and complex sentences.

▲ **Grammar and Writing Practice Book** p. 14

DAY 4 Test Preparation

DAILY FIX-IT

7. Nobody culd hit you're curve ball. *(could; your)*

8. Touch the runer with the ball and tag she out. *(runner; her)*

STANDARDIZED TEST PREP

Test Tip

A compound sentence always joins clauses with a comma and a conjunction. In a complex sentence, use a comma only if the first clause is a dependent clause.

Compound Sentence: I wore my Cubs hat, and I carried a pennant.

Complex Sentence (dependent clause first): When the team took the field, fans rose to their feet.

Complex Sentence (dependent clause second): Fans rose to their feet when the team took the field.

HOMEWORK Grammar and Writing Practice Book p. 15.

Compound and Complex Sentences

Directions Mark the letter of the phrase that correctly identifies each underlined word, group of words, or sentence.

1. Every day Ted and I play catch, or we join our friends in a game.
   A dependent clause
   (B) independent clause
   C compound sentence
   D complex sentence
2. We love the game, but we aren't the best players.
   (A) conjunction
   B independent clause
   C dependent clause
   D complex sentence
3. If you practice every day, you will do better.
   (A) dependent clause
   B independent clause
   C compound sentence
   D complex sentence
4. A game is more fun when the crowd cheers you on.
   A dependent clause
   B independent clause
   C compound sentence
   (D) complex sentence
5. Although our team played well, we still lost.
   A dependent clause
   (B) independent clause
   C compound sentence
   D complex sentence
6. Rub this oil into your glove, and you will catch balls more easily.
   A dependent clause
   B independent clause
   (C) compound sentence
   D complex sentence
7. Before you play a big game, you should relax.
   A conjunction
   (B) dependent clause
   C independent clause
   D complex sentence
8. Aleesha plays third base, or she is catcher.
   (A) conjunction
   B independent clause
   C compound sentence
   D complex sentence
9. We keep score, but we really play just for fun.
   A dependent clause
   B independent clause
   (C) compound sentence
   D complex sentence
10. Because we have fun, we don't mind an occasional loss.
    A dependent clause
    (B) independent clause
    C compound sentence
    D complex sentence

School-Home CONNECTION **Home Activity** Your child prepared for taking tests on compound and complex sentences. Have your child read a sports article in the newspaper and identify compound sentences and complex sentences.

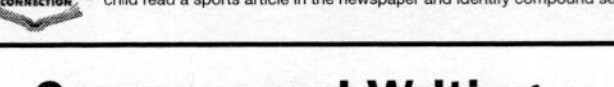

▲ **Grammar and Writing Practice Book** p. 15

DAY 5 Cumulative Review

DAILY FIX-IT

9. The Umpire said that pitch was an strike. *(umpire; a strike)*

10. After we play a game Dan and me ride our bikes home. *(game,; Dan and I)*

ADDITIONAL PRACTICE

Assign pp. 68–71 in The Grammar and Writing Book.

EXTRA PRACTICE Grammar and Writing Practice Book p. 125.

ASSESSMENT

CUMULATIVE REVIEW Grammar and Writing Practice Book p. 16.

Compound and Complex Sentences

Directions Join each pair of simple sentences to form a compound sentence. Use the conjunction that makes sense (*and, but,* or *or*). Put a comma before the conjunction. Write the compound sentence on the lines.

1. Julia loves sports.
   She cannot decide which one to try first.
   Julia loves sports, but (*or* and) she cannot decide which one to try first.
2. She could play softball.
   She could join a soccer team.
   She could play softball, or (*or* and) she could join a soccer team.
3. Her older brother plays on a traveling soccer team.
   Her mom is an umpire for the softball league.
   Her older brother plays on a traveling soccer team, and her mom is an umpire for the softball league.
4. Marcus runs like the wind.
   He is quite strong.
   Marcus runs like the wind, and he is quite strong.

Directions Write *compound* after each compound sentence and underline the conjunction. Write *complex* after each complex sentence and underline the dependent clause.

5. His name was George Herman Ruth, but everyone called him Babe. compound
6. He was a left-handed pitcher when he began his career in 1914. complex
7. He pitched 163 games, and he won 92 of them. compound
8. If you can believe it, he was greatest of all at hitting home runs. complex

School-Home CONNECTION **Home Activity** Your child reviewed compound and complex sentences. Ask your child to explain how a game is played, using some compound and complex sentences.

▲ **Grammar and Writing Practice Book** p. 16

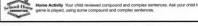

AFTER READING

Writing Workshop Feature Article

OBJECTIVES

- Identify qualities of a feature article about a famous person.
- Write a feature article with a recognizable tone.
- Focus on word choice.
- Use a rubric.

Genre Feature Article
Writer's Craft Tone
Writing Trait Word Choice

ELL

Word Choice To help students use exact words rather than vague ones, develop a web with a word such as *nice* in the center and around it strong words that can replace it *(friendly, helpful, kind, polite, generous).*

Writing Traits

FOCUS/IDEAS Relevant facts and vivid details create a clear image of Goodall.

ORGANIZATION/PARAGRAPHS The introduction grabs attention, and events are in a logical sequence or chronological order.

VOICE The writer expresses admiration for Goodall.

WORD CHOICE The writer uses exact description *(crawling on her belly)* and adjectives *(exhausted, bruised, heroic)* to give a sense of the person.

SENTENCES Use of varied sentence structures clarifies meaning and adds interest.

CONVENTIONS There is excellent control and accuracy.

DAY 1 Model the Trait

READING-WRITING CONNECTION

- *Satchel Paige* tells about a baseball legend.
- The article uses colorful language to capture Paige's flamboyant style.
- Students will write a **feature article** using exact, vivid words to create a tone.

MODEL WORD CHOICE Discuss Writing Transparency 4A. Then discuss the model and the writing trait of word choice.

Think Aloud: The writer has used exact description to create a sense of what is happening at the moment. For example, "crawling on her belly with vines catching her hair" helps me to feel what it is like to follow chimpanzees through the jungle. Adjectives like *exhausted, bruised,* and *happy* help me to sense how Jane feels and understand her determination.

Feature Article

A **feature article** tells about an interesting person or experience. It answers the questions *Who? What? When? Where? Why?* It grabs your attention at the beginning. Descriptive details and facts provide information about the person or experience. A feature article may tell a story or use quotations.

Jane Goodall

Details paint a vivid picture and make an attention-grabbing opener.

Jane Goodall's favorite kind of day begins very early in the African forest. She follows a chimpanzee mother and her family. This means climbing high, far, and fast. It also means hours of crawling on her belly with vines catching her hair. At dusk, she will be exhausted, bruised, and very happy.

Facts answer *who, what, when, where,* and *why.*

Jane Goodall began her amazing study of African chimpanzees in 1960. She was 26 and finally about to realize her childhood dream. Even as a little girl, Jane knew she must somehow "find a way to watch free, wild animals living their own undisturbed lives."

Word choices add to picture of Goodall's personality.

Sentence structure emphasizes Goodall's achievement.

At first, the chimps ran whenever they saw Jane. She used binoculars, but she could see little of their behavior. Patient and determined, Jane did not give up. As time passed, the chimps let her get closer. She learned amazing new things about them. For example, she was the first to see that they used tools. She was the first to observe that chimps eat meat. She was the first to understand that they have lasting family relationships.

Unit 1 Satchel Paige Writing Model **4A**

▲ **Writing Transparency** 4A

DAY 2 Improve Writing

WRITER'S CRAFT
Tone

Display Writing Transparency 4B. Read the directions and work together to identify tone and create a suitable tone.

Think Aloud: **CREATE APPROPRIATE TONE** Tomorrow, we will write a **feature article.** I could write about my Uncle Dan's triathlon. How could I develop an admiring tone? I might say, "Every morning at 5 A.M., you could see him running in sleet, rain, or blasting heat." These details show dedication. I could say, "his tall, lean body became as strong as iron." This comparison shows his success. These words suggest someone admirable.

GUIDED WRITING Some students may need more help with tone. Work with them to identify the tone of the narrator in the reading selection.

Tone

A writer's **tone** expresses his or her attitude toward the subject. Word choice, sentence structure, and word pictures made by details and comparisons create the tone in a piece of writing.

Directions Write two words that describe the tone of each selection.

sympathetic humorous admiring affectionate

1. Chief Joseph of the Nez Perce was a gifted, caring leader of his people. Unfortunately, his era saw the end of life as the Native Americans had known it. When gold was discovered on their land, the Nez Perce were forced to move to a reservation. Chief Joseph rejected the agreement. He led his people over a thousand miles in a daring attempt to escape to Canada. Greatly outnumbered and starving, they were captured just 30 miles from the border and freedom.
   admiring, sympathetic
2. My cat Pickles is a pain! I can call and call her, and she is nowhere to be found. Just when I'm about to panic and think she's lost, injured, or kidnapped, she ambles in, yawning and blinking innocently as if to say, "Were you calling me?" On the other hand, who else makes me laugh until I cry with her antics over a catnip mouse? Who else snuggles in my lap (just when I was about to go fix a snack) and purrs so I can't get up?
   humorous, affectionate

Directions Write a paragraph that could introduce a feature article about an interesting or unusual person. Use word choices, sentence structures, and descriptive details that create a suitable tone.

Possible answer: She bounces rather than walks into a room. A crazy purple top hat with blue feathers is perched on her huge mop of orange curls. "Hi, boys and girls!" she shouts in a high, silly voice. Tootsie the Clown's huge black eyebrows, bright red nose, and great big painted mouth always make me want to laugh!

Unit 1 Satchel Paige Writer's Craft **4B**

▲ **Writing Transparency** 4B

DAY 3 Prewrite and Draft

READ THE WRITING PROMPT on page 109 in the Student Edition.

Satchel Paige *is a feature article about a baseball legend.*

Think about a topic that is interesting to you.

Now write a feature article about that topic.

Writing Test Tips

- Answer the *5W* questions about your topic to show why it is well-known.
- Use vivid, interesting details and important facts about your topic.
- For a person, include words and actions that show personality.

GETTING STARTED Students can do any of the following:

- Write the topic in the center of a word web and interesting facts and key details around this.
- List and order significant events.
- Brainstorm details such as special or unusual features or striking actions about the topic for an attention-grabbing opener.

DAY 4 Draft and Revise

EDITING/REVISING CHECKLIST

- ☑ Does the tone of the writing fit the subject?
- ☑ Do my word choices show how I feel about the subject?
- ☑ Have I used some compound and complex sentences?
- ☑ Are words that end with *-ed* and *-ing* spelled correctly?

See *The Grammar and Writing Book*, pp. 68–73.

Revising Tips

Word Choice

- Support description with words that describe appearance and action exactly and vividly.
- Be sure facts telling who, what, when, where, and why are included.
- Use quotations or a sequence of events to sharpen the picture.

PUBLISHING Display pictures of the people students wrote about. Have students read their feature articles. Ask listeners to choose the pictures that match.

ASSESSMENT Use the scoring rubric to evaluate students' work.

DAY 5 Connect to Unit Writing

Personal Narrative	
Week 1	Character Sketch 41g–41h
Week 2	Tall Tale 67g–67h
Week 3	Friendly or Thank-You Letter 89g–89h
Week 4	Feature Article 111g–111h
Week 5	Narrative Writing 131g–131h

PREVIEW THE UNIT PROMPT

Write a personal narrative about a challenge or difficult problem. Describe what the challenge was and tell how you met it. Use details that make the events clear and interesting.

APPLY

- Word choice, sentence structure, and word pictures create an identifiable tone in a personal narrative.

Writing Trait Rubric

	4	3	2	1
Word Choice	Vivid style created by use of exact nouns, strong verbs, exciting adjectives, and clear figurative language	Some style created by strong and precise words	Little style created by strong, precise words; some lack of clarity	Word choice vague or incorrect
	Uses strong, specific words that make feature article clear, detailed, and vivid	Uses some specific words that make feature article clear with adequate details and facts	Needs more precise word choice to create style and clarity in feature article	Feature article made dull or unclear by poor word choice

Spelling & Phonics Adding *-ed, -ing*

OBJECTIVE

- Spell words that end with *-ed* and *-ing*.

Generalization

Connect to Phonics In words that end in *e*, drop the *e*: *decided, deciding*. In words that end with CVC, double the final consonant: *admitted, admitting*. In words that end in *y*, change *y* to *i* when adding *-ed* and keep the *y* when adding *-ing*: *supplied, supplying*. Some base words change when endings are added.

Spelling Words

1. supplied	11. occurred
2. supplying	12. occurring
3. denied	13. qualified
4. denying	14. qualifying
5. decided*	15. identified
6. deciding	16. identifying
7. included	17. delayed
8. including	18. delaying
9. admitted	19. satisfied
10. admitting	20. satisfying

Challenge Words

21. occupied	24. criticizing
22. occupying	25. omitted
23. criticized	26. omitting

* Word from the selection

Spelling/Phonics Support See the ELL and Transition Handbook for spelling support.

DAY 1 Pretest and Sort

PRETEST

Use the Dictation Sentences from Day 5 to administer the pretest. Read the word, read the sentence, and then read the word again. Guide students in self-correcting their pretests and correcting any misspellings.

Monitor Progress

Spelling

If... students misspell more than 5 pretest words,	**then...** use words 1–10 for Strategic Intervention.
If... students misspell 1–5 pretest words,	**then...** use words 1–20 for On-Level practice.
If... students correctly spell all pretest words,	**then...** use words 1–26 for Advanced Learners.

HOMEWORK Spelling Practice Book, p. 13.

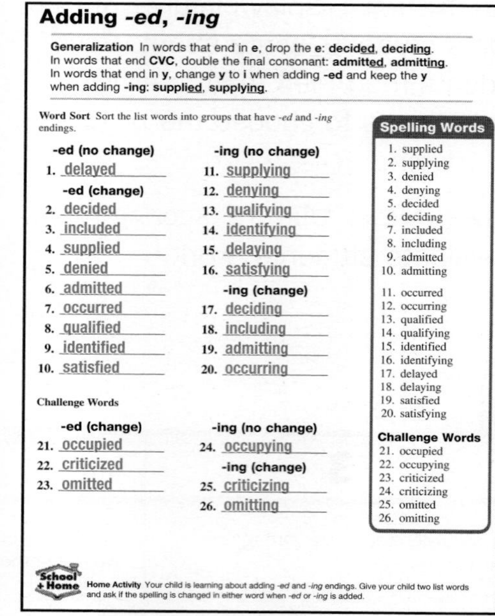

Adding *-ed, -ing*

Generalization In words that end in **e**, drop the **e**: **decided**, **deciding**. In words that end **CVC**, double the final consonant: **admitted**, **admitting**. In words that end in **y**, change **y** to **i** when adding **-ed** and keep the **y** when adding **-ing**: **supplied**, **supplying**.

Word Sort Sort the list words into groups that have *-ed* and *-ing* endings.

-ed (no change)
1. delayed

-ed (change)
2. decided
3. included
4. supplied
5. denied
6. admitted
7. occurred
8. qualified
9. identified
10. satisfied

-ing (no change)
11. supplying
12. denying
13. qualifying
14. identifying
15. delaying
16. satisfying

-ing (change)
17. deciding
18. including
19. admitting
20. occurring

Challenge Words

-ed (change)
21. occupied
22. criticized
23. omitted

-ing (no change)
24. occupying

-ing (change)
25. criticizing
26. omitting

Spelling Words
1. supplied
2. supplying
3. denied
4. denying
5. decided
6. deciding
7. included
8. including
9. admitted
10. admitting
11. occurred
12. occurring
13. qualified
14. qualifying
15. identified
16. identifying
17. delayed
18. delaying
19. satisfied
20. satisfying

Challenge Words
21. occupied
22. occupying
23. criticized
24. criticizing
25. omitted
26. omitting

School + Home **Home Activity** Your child is learning about adding *-ed* and *-ing* endings. Give your child two list words and ask if the spelling is changed in either word when *-ed* or *-ing* is added.

▲ **Spelling Practice Book** p. 13

DAY 2 Think and Practice

TEACH

Look at a base word's final letters to decide whether to make changes when adding endings. Write *include* on the board. Cross out *e*. Explain that *e* must be dropped before adding *-ed* or *-ing*. Erase the *e* and add *-ing*. Model how to add endings to *occur* and *satisfy*. Point out that the *y* in *delay* does not change because a vowel precedes the *y*.

include

FIND BASE WORDS Have students apply the generalization in reverse to write the base word for each pair of list words.

HOMEWORK Spelling Practice Book, p. 14.

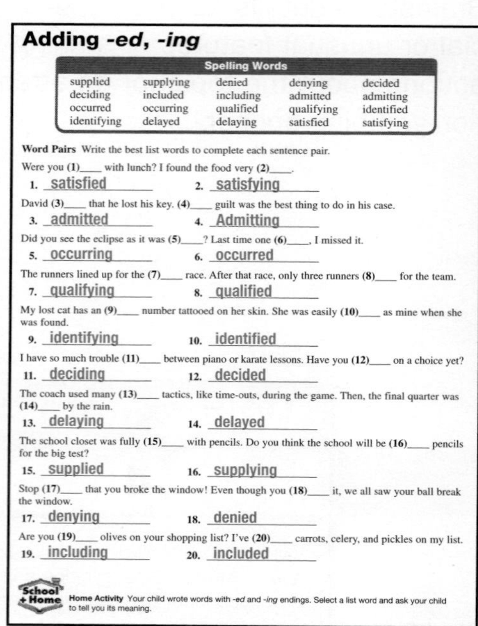

Adding *-ed, -ing*

Spelling Words				
supplied	supplying	denied	denying	decided
deciding	included	including	admitted	admitting
occurred	occurring	qualified	qualifying	identified
identifying	delayed	delaying	satisfied	satisfying

Word Pairs Write the best list words to complete each sentence pair.

Were you **(1)**____ with lunch? I found the food very **(2)**____.
1. satisfied 2. satisfying

David **(3)**____ that he lost his key. **(4)**____ guilt was the best thing to do in his case.
3. admitted 4. Admitting

Did you see the eclipse as it was **(5)**____? Last time one **(6)**____, I missed it.
5. occurring 6. occurred

The runners lined up for the **(7)**____ race. After that race, only three runners **(8)**____ for the team.
7. qualifying 8. qualified

My lost cat has an **(9)**____ number tattooed on her skin. She was easily **(10)**____ as mine when she was found.
9. identifying 10. identified

I have so much trouble **(11)**____ between piano or karate lessons. Have you **(12)**____ on a choice yet?
11. deciding 12. decided

The coach used many **(13)**____ tactics, like time-outs, during the game. Then, the final quarter was **(14)**____ by the rain.
13. delaying 14. delayed

The school closet was fully **(15)**____ with pencils. Do you think the school will be **(16)**____ pencils for the big test?
15. supplied 16. supplying

Stop **(17)**____ that you broke the window! Even though you **(18)**____ it, we all saw your ball break the window.
17. denying 18. denied

Are you **(19)**____ olives on your shopping list? I've **(20)**____ carrots, celery, and pickles on my list.
19. including 20. included

School + Home **Home Activity** Your child wrote words with *-ed* and *-ing* endings. Select a list word and ask your child to tell you its meaning.

▲ **Spelling Practice Book** p. 14

DAY 3 Connect to Writing

WRITE ABOUT A SHOPPING EXPERIENCE

Ask students to use at least four spelling words to write about a good or bad experience they had at a particular store or business.

Frequently Misspelled Words

getting *decided*
stopped

These words may seem easy to spell, but they are often misspelled by fifth-graders. Alert students to these frequently misspelled words. Have students apply this lesson's spelling generalization to the words.

HOMEWORK Spelling Practice Book, p. 15.

Adding *-ed, -ing*

Proofread a Newspaper Article This is an article from a local weekly newspaper. Circle six spelling errors. Write the sentence with a punctuation error correctly. Write the corrections on the lines below.

Three Caught After Holdup
by Rosy Redeye

The crime ocurred after midnight. The store's videotape identifyed three suspects. The store owner supplyed the license plate number to the police department. Geting the results took no time. The police quickly located the car and suspects. They had trouble admiting their wrongdoing. However, in front of the judge, they deceided to admit everything. The police were satisfied that they solved the case.

Spelling Words
supplied, supplying, denied, denying, decided, deciding, included, including, admitted, admitting, occurred, occurring, qualified, qualifying, identified, identifying, delayed, delaying, satisfied, satisfying

Frequently Misspelled Words
getting, decided, stopped

1. occurred 2. indentified
3. supplied 4. Getting
5. admitting 6. decided
7. The police quickly located the car and suspects.

Proofread Words Circle the correct spelling of the word.

8.	occured	occurred	ocured
9.	included	includid	includ
10.	qualifed	qualifide	qualified
11.	deceided	decided	decieded
12.	satesfying	satisfying	satisfiying
13.	admitted	admited	admetted
14.	suppliing	sapplying	supplying

School + Home **Home Activity** Your child identified misspelled list words. Select three list words and ask your child to spell them.

▲ **Spelling Practice Book** p. 15

DAY 4 Review

REVIEW ADDING *-ED* AND *-ING*

Have pairs of students write the list words on individual note cards and turn the cards face down. Tell students to take turns turning two cards face up. If both list words have the same base word, the student who turned up the cards should explain how the endings were added.

Spelling Strategy
Words with Endings

Step 1: Draw a line between the base words and their endings.

Step 2: Study the word one part at a time.

HOMEWORK Spelling Practice Book, p. 16.

Adding *-ed, -ing*

Spelling Words

supplied	supplying	denied	denying	decided
deciding	included	including	admitted	admitting
occurred	occurring	qualified	qualifying	identified
identifying	delayed	delaying	satisfied	satisfying

Adding -ed Write list words that tell about an action that happened in the past.

Two -ed words in which the final consonant is doubled:

1. admitted 2. occurred

One -ed word in which the final e is dropped.

3. decided

Five -ed words in which y is changed to i

4. supplied 5. qualified 6. identified
7. denied 8. satisfied

Word Endings Write list words by adding the ending in parentheses.

9. supply (ing) 9. supplying
10. deny (ing) 10. denying
11. decide (ing) 11. deciding
12. include (ing) 12. including
13. admit (ing) 13. admitting
14. occur (ing) 14. occurring
15. qualify (ing) 15. qualifying
16. identify (ing) 16. identifying
17. delay (ed) 17. delayed
18. satisfy (ing) 18. satisfying
19. delay (ing) 19. delaying
20. include (ed) 20. included

School + Home **Home Activity** Your child has learned to read, write, and spell words with *-ed* and *-ing* endings. Have your child pick the five hardest words on the list. Go over the spellings with your child.

▲ **Spelling Practice Book** p. 16

DAY 5 Posttest

DICTATION SENTENCES

1. Mom supplied food for the picnic.
2. Who will be supplying the drinks?
3. Ann denied that she was tired.
4. There's no use denying that we like snow days.
5. Have you decided what to wear?
6. We are deciding which movie to watch.
7. The tip is included with our meal.
8. Everyone, including me, left early.
9. No one will be admitted after the show starts.
10. Are you admitting that you did it?
11. A great idea just occurred to me.
12. Accidents keep occurring on that road.
13. My team qualified for the playoffs.
14. Qualifying for the playoffs is hard.
15. The winner was identified at last.
16. After identifying my lost dog, I brought her home.
17. Our flight was delayed.
18. Delaying the game caused a penalty.
19. Are you satisfied now?
20. The holiday meal was satisfying.

CHALLENGE

21. The army occupied the city.
22. The baby was occupying himself with toys.
23. The coach criticized the game.
24. Write an essay criticizing the play.
25. My name was omitted from the list.
26. I lost points for omitting an answer.

AFTER READING

OBJECTIVES

- Formulate an inquiry question that is connected to this week's lesson focus.
- Effectively and efficiently find, evaluate, and communicate information related to an inquiry question using electronic sources.

New Literacies	
Day 1	**Identify Questions**
Day 2	**Navigate/Search**
Day 3	**Analyze**
Day 4	**Synthesize**
Day 5	**Communicate**

NEW LITERACIES

Internet Inquiry Activity

EXPLORE ATHLETES MEETING CHALLENGES

Use the following 5-day plan to help students conduct this week's Internet inquiry activity on athletes who, like Satchel Paige, succeed in spite of challenges. Remind students to follow classroom rules when using the Internet.

DAY 1

Identify Questions Discuss the lesson focus question: *How do we face personal challenges?* Brainstorm ideas for specific inquiry questions about how people succeed as athletes in spite of challenges. For example, students might want to find out about the Special Olympics. Have students work individually, in pairs, or in small groups to write inquiry questions they want to answer.

DAY 2

Navigate/Search Talk about the meaning of URL endings such as *.com, .org, .edu,* etc. Discuss how not all Web sites are reliable since their material can be biased towards the publishers' viewpoints.

DAY 3

Analyze Have students explore the Web sites they identified on Day 2. Tell them to scan each site for information that helps answer their inquiry questions. Suggest that they use links to gather more information. Show students how to click on a hypertext link in one of the documents that they found, to go to another document with related information.

DAY 4

Synthesize Have students synthesize information from Day 3 to develop answers to their inquiry questions and think about the best ways to communicate their findings to the rest of the class.

DAY 5

Communicate Have students share their inquiry results in the form of posters with illustrations and text that they can present orally to the class.

RESEARCH/STUDY SKILLS

Newspaper/Newsletter

TEACH

Ask students where they can expect to find timely news about a local or regional sports team. Students will likely mention newspapers. Show a newspaper to students and discuss these features.

- A **newspaper** contains current news and information.
- An **article** is a newspaper story. Most newspapers have three basic kinds of articles—news articles, feature stories, and editorials giving opinions in a persuasive way.
- A **headline** is like a chapter title. It tells you what an article is about.
- A **photograph** shows information visually.
- A **caption** explains what a photograph shows.
- Most newspapers are divided into **sections** that are devoted to certain subjects, such as sports, business, or entertainment.
- A **newsletter** is a brief publication of a group containing news of interest about and to that group's members.

Have students work in small groups, and give each group an article from a section of a newspaper. Tell students to read the article and discuss these questions in their groups:

1. **In what section would you find this article?** *(Possible response: sports)*
2. **If the article has a photograph, what purpose does the photo serve?** *(Possible response: It helps show readers what happened.)*
3. **Does the headline reflect the contents of the article?** *(Responses will vary but students should describe how the headline relates to the information in the article.)*

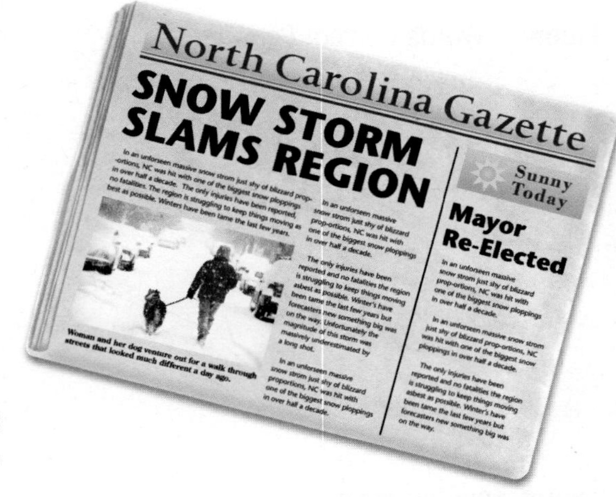

ASSESS

Check that students can identify headlines, photos, and captions and explain their purposes.

Check whether students can distinguish articles that summarize events and articles that use persuasive techniques to convince the reader of something.

For more practice or to assess students, use Practice Book pp. 39–40.

OBJECTIVES

- Discuss terms associated with newspapers and newsletters.
- Read a newspaper article and identify specific features and their purposes.

Newspaper/Newsletter

- A **newspaper** is a daily (or weekly) periodical that contains timely news and information on current events and issues. Daily newspapers generally cover local, regional, national, and international news. Most newspapers organize information from most important to least important. There are three basic kinds of articles found in a newspaper: news stories, editorials (opinions pieces), and feature stories.
- A **newsletter** is a brief publication by a group or organization that contains news of interest to that group's members.

Directions Read the newspaper page and answer the questions below.

HOMETOWN NEWS

JULY 17, 2004 — **Cloudy, 72°**

BARR HITS THE CYCLE–AGAIN

Hometown hero Billy Barr has been having the kind of week baseball players can only dream of. Last night, for the third game in a row, Barr hit for the cycle, which means he hit a single, a double, a triple, and a home run.

"I guess my grandfather was looking out for me tonight," said Barr after the game, referring to his grandfather Alan Barr, one of the first Negro League players to break into Major League baseball in the 1950s. Billy Barr frequently makes reference to his grandfather, who inspired his grandson to play baseball.

The last time a Major League player hit for the cycle in three consecutive games was in 1971, when Sal Bando did it for the Oakland Athletics.

1. Where do you find the date on a newspaper's front page?
   It is at the top under the name of the newspaper.
2. How does the headline give you a clue to what the article will be about?
   It tells you who the article is about and what that person did.
3. Most newspapers give the daily weather forecast somewhere on the front page. What is the forecast for this day's newspaper?
   Cloudy, 72 degrees
4. Why does the writer mention the last time this event occurred at the very end of the article?
   Mentioning the last occurrence shows how rarely it happens.
5. Which of the three basic types of articles is this one?
   This article is a news story.

▲ **Practice Book** p. 39

Directions Read the selection from the newsletter and answer the questions below.

EVANSTON SOCCER NEEDS VOLUNTEERS

Hello Evanston soccer families!

The new season starts soon, and we're busy getting our teams and coaches organized and ready to play. As you can imagine, it's a lot of work. So once again we are asking for volunteers to help us out for the new season. We are an all-volunteer organization. In 2006 we won the Regional Youth Soccer Organization of the year award because of the great support our volunteers gave us. We want to make it two in a row for this year!

Volunteering only requires a few hours of your time each week. Currently, we need about 40 parents to volunteer to be coaches, referees, and board members.

We know how busy everyone's lives are, but our organization can only succeed if everyone pitches in. We hope you'll consider volunteering this year!

6. To whom is this newsletter story directed?
   It's directed to parents of Evanston youth soccer players.
7. Who do you think would receive a copy of this newsletter?
   Families and individuals involved in the Evanston soccer program would receive it.
8. Name two things this newsletter specifically asks soccer parents to volunteer to do.
   Possible answer: coach or referee
9. Based on this newsletter article, who runs this youth soccer organization?
   The organization is run by volunteers.
10. If you wanted to find out about a big event happening in your city, where would you go to find out the information—a newspaper or a newsletter? Why?
    A newspaper would be better, because they cover important events for a big audience. Newsletters are written for specific groups.

School + Home **Home Activity** Your child answered questions about newspapers and newsletters. With your child, sketch out the front page of a newspaper based on your family's activities for the day.

▲ **Practice Book** p. 40

AFTER READING

Assessment Checkpoints *for the Week*

Selection Assessment

Use pp. 13–16 of Selection Tests to check:

 **Selection Understanding**

 **Comprehension Skill** *Sequence*

 **Selection Vocabulary**

confidence *unique*
fastball *weakness*
mocking *windup*
outfield

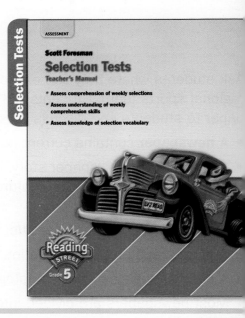

Selection Tests

ASSESSMENT

Scott Foresman
Selection Tests
Teacher's Manual

- Assess comprehension of weekly selections
- Assess understanding of weekly comprehension skills
- Assess knowledge of selection vocabulary

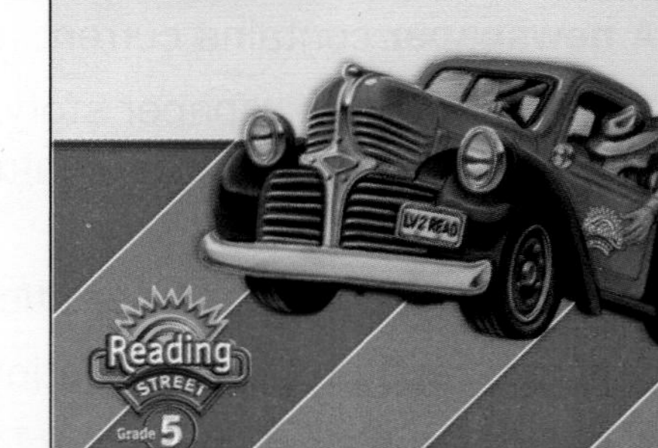

Leveled Assessment

On-Level

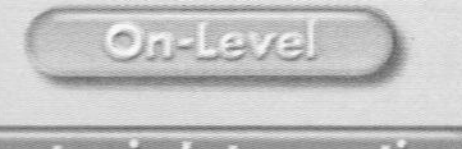

Advanced

Use pp. 19–24 of Fresh Reads for Differentiated Test Practice to check:

 **Comprehension Skill** *Sequence*

 REVIEW **Comprehension Skill** *Compare and Contrast*

 **Fluency** *Words Correct Per Minute*

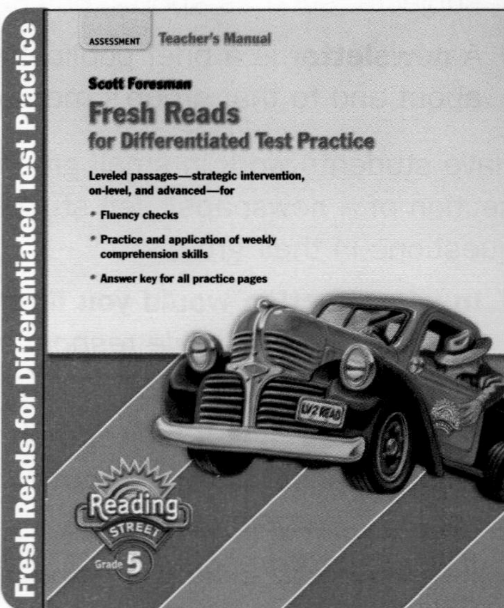

Managing Assessment

Use Assessment Handbook for:

 **Record-Keeping Forms**

 **Portfolio Assessment**

Assessment Handbook

ASSESSMENT

Scott Foresman
Assessment Handbook

- Suggestions for preparing students for high-stake tests
- Ideas for classroom-based assessment
- Forms in English and Spanish for students to record interests and progress
- Forms in English and Spanish for teachers to record observations of students' reading and writing abilities and progress
- Assessment and Regrouping charts reproduced from *Reading Street* Teacher's Editions

Reading Street Grades 3–6

Unit 1
Meeting Challenges

CONCEPT QUESTION

What kinds of challenges do people face and how do they meet them?

Week 1

How do we meet the challenges of learning?

Week 2

How can nature challenge us?

Week 3

How do people survive in the wilderness?

Week 4

How do we face personal challenges?

Week 5

What challenges do immigrants encounter?

Week 5

EXPAND THE CONCEPT

What challenges do immigrants encounter?

Time for SOCIAL STUDIES

CONNECT THE CONCEPT

▶ **Build Background**
Ellis Island, immigration, Registry Room

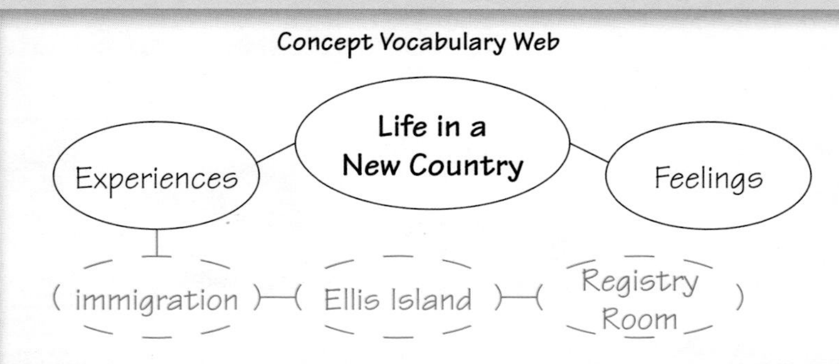

▶ **Social Studies Content**
Tenement Museum, Ellis Island

▶ **Writing**
Narrative Writing

▶ **Internet Inquiry**
The Immigrant Experience

Preview Your Week

What challenges do immigrants encounter?

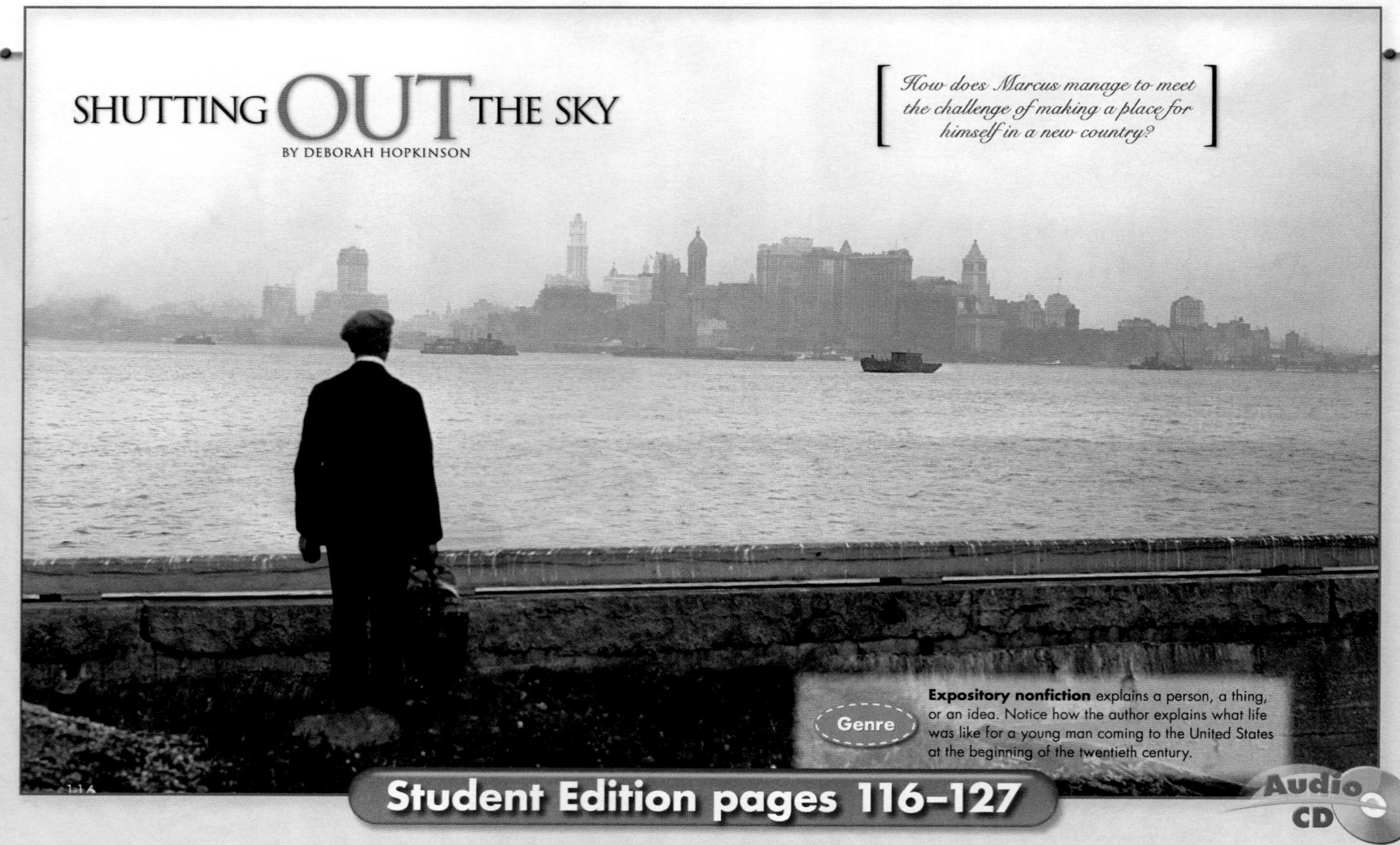

SHUTTING OUT THE SKY
BY DEBORAH HOPKINSON
How does Marcus manage to meet the challenge of making a place for himself in a new country?
Genre
Expository nonfiction explains a person, a thing, or an idea. Notice how the author explains what life was like for a young man coming to the United States at the beginning of the twentieth century.

Student Edition pages 116–127

Audio CD

Genre Expository Nonfiction

Vocabulary Strategy Context Clues

Comprehension Skill Cause and Effect

Comprehension Strategy Summarize

SOCIAL STUDIES

Paired Selection

Reading Across Texts

Compare Situations

Genre

E-mail

Text Features

Address Box

Message

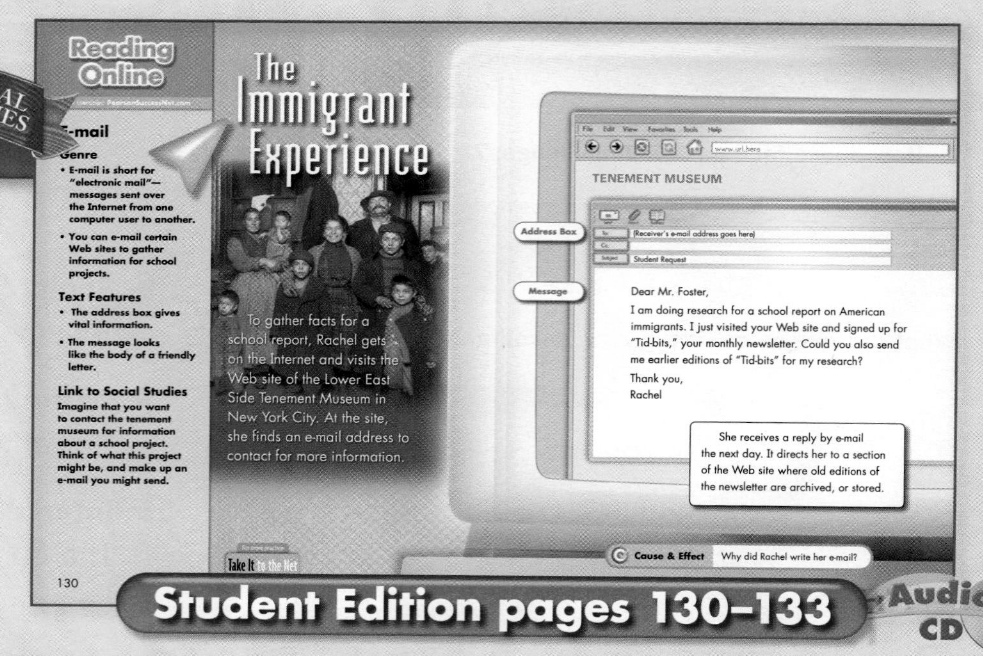

Reading Online
E-mail
Genre
• E-mail is short for "electronic mail"—messages sent over the Internet from one computer user to another.
• You can e-mail certain Web sites to gather information for school projects.
Text Features
• The address box gives vital information.
• The message looks like the body of a friendly letter.
Link to Social Studies
Imagine that you want to contact the tenement museum for information about a school project. Think of what this project might be, and make up an e-mail you might send.
The Immigrant Experience
To gather facts for a school report, Rachel gets on the Internet and visits the Web site of the Lower East Side Tenement Museum in New York City. At the site, she finds an e-mail address to contact for more information.
TENEMENT MUSEUM
Address Box
Message
Student Request
Dear Mr. Foster,
I am doing research for a school report on American immigrants. I just visited your Web site and signed up for "Tid-bits," your monthly newsletter. Could you also send me earlier editions of "Tid-bits" for my research?
Thank you,
Rachel
She receives a reply by e-mail the next day. It directs her to a section of the Web site where old editions of the newsletter are archived, or stored.
Cause & Effect Why did Rachel write her e-mail?
130

Student Edition pages 130–133

Audio CD

- Student Edition
- Leveled Readers

Leveled Readers

Skill Cause and Effect

Strategy Summarize

Lesson Vocabulary

Below-Level

On-Level

Advanced

ELL Reader

- Concept Vocabulary
- Text Support
- Language Enrichment

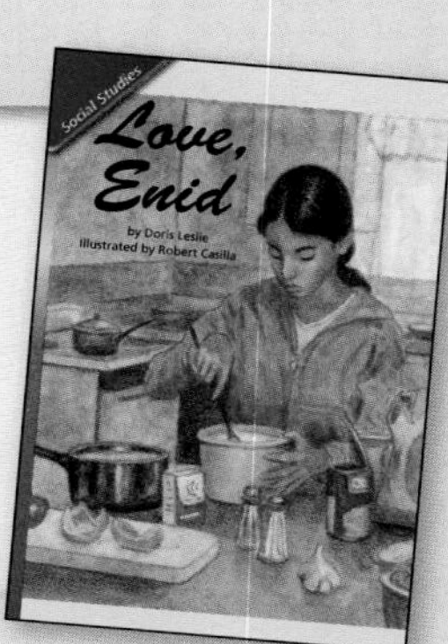

Time for SOCIAL STUDIES

Integrate Social Studies Standards

- Ethnic Groups
- Cultures
- Immigration
- Customs
- U.S. History

Shutting Out the Sky, pp. 116–127

"The Immigrant Experience," pp. 130–133

Leveled Readers

Below-Level
- Support Concepts

On-Level
- Develop Concepts

Advanced
- Extend Concepts
- Social Studies Extension Activity

ELL Reader

Build **Concept Vocabulary**
Life in a New Country, pp. 112l–112m

Teach **Social Studies Concepts**
Tenement Museum, p. 119
Ellis Island, p. 125

Explore **Social Studies Center**
Learn About Immigration, p. 112k

Weekly Plan

PearsonSuccessNet.com

READING

45–90 minutes

TARGET SKILLS OF THE WEEK

Comprehension Skill
Cause and Effect

Comprehension Strategy
Summarize

Vocabulary Strategy
Context Clues

DAY 1

PAGES 112l–114b, 133a, 133e–133k

Oral Language

QUESTION OF THE WEEK *What challenges do immigrants encounter?*

Read Aloud: "Journey to Ellis Island," 112m
Build Concepts, 112l

Comprehension/Vocabulary

Comprehension Skill/Strategy Lesson, 112–113
Cause and Effect T
Summarize
Build Background, 114a
Introduce Lesson Vocabulary, 114b
advice, advised, circumstances, elbow, hustled, immigrants, luxury, newcomer, peddler T

Read Leveled Readers

Grouping Options 112f–112g

Fluency

Model Pauses, 112l–112m, 133a

DAY 2

PAGES 114–123, 133a, 133e–133k

Oral Language

QUESTION OF THE DAY *In what ways is America different from Romania?*

Comprehension/Vocabulary

Vocabulary Strategy Lesson, 114–115
Context Clues T

Read *Shutting Out the Sky,* 116–123

Grouping Options
112f–112g

Cause and Effect T
Context Clues T
REVIEW Sequence T
Develop Vocabulary

Fluency

Echo Reading, 133a

LANGUAGE ARTS

30–60 minutes

Trait of the Week

Word Choice

Day 1

Grammar, 133e
Introduce Common and Proper Nouns T

Writing Workshop, 133g
Introduce Narrative Writing
Model the Trait of the Week: Word Choice

Spelling, 133i
Pretest for Contractions

Internet Inquiry, 133k
Identify Questions

Day 2

Grammar, 133e
Develop Common and Proper Nouns T

Writing Workshop, 111g
Improve Writing with Show, Don't Tell

Spelling, 133i
Teach the Generalization

Internet Inquiry, 133k
Navigate/Search

DAILY WRITING ACTIVITIES

Day 1 Write to Read, 112

Day 2 Words to Write, 115
Strategy Response Log, 116, 123

DAILY SOCIAL STUDIES CONNECTIONS

Day 1 Life in a New Country Concept Web, 112l

Day 2 Time for Social Studies: Tenement Museum, 119; Revisit the Life in a New Country Concept Web, 123

DAILY SUCCESS PREDICTORS

for Adequate Yearly Progress

Monitor Progress and Corrective Feedback

	Day 1	Day 2
Vocabulary	Check Vocabulary, *112l*	

RESOURCES FOR THE WEEK

- Practice Book, *pp. 41–50*
- Word Study and Spelling Practice Book, *pp. 17–20*
- Grammar and Writing Practice Book, *pp. 17–20*
- Selection Test, *pp. 17–20*
- Fresh Reads for Differentiated Test Practice, *pp. 25–30*
- The Grammar and Writing Book, *pp. 74–79*

Grouping Options for Differentiated Instruction

Turn the page for the small group lesson plan.

DAY 3 PAGES 124–129, 133a, 133e–133k

Oral Language

QUESTION OF THE DAY *How are Marcus's expectations of America different from what he finds?*

Comprehension/Vocabulary

Read *Shutting Out the Sky,* 124–128

Grouping Options 112f–112g

Cause and Effect **T**

Summarize

Develop Vocabulary

Reader Response

Selection Test

Fluency

Model Pauses, 133a

Grammar, 133f
Apply Common and Proper Nouns in Writing **T**

Writing Workshop, 129, 133h
Write Now
Prewrite and Draft

Spelling, 133j
Connect Spelling to Writing

Internet Inquiry, 133k
Analyze Sources

Day 3 Strategy Response Log, 126
Look Back and Write, 128

Day 3 Time for Social Studies: Ellis Island, 125
Revisit the Life in a New Country Concept Web, 127

DAY 4 PAGES 130–133a, 133e–133k

Oral Language

QUESTION OF THE DAY *What thoughts and feelings might an immigrant experience upon leaving his or her homeland?*

Comprehension/Vocabulary

Read "The Immigrant Experience," 130–133

Grouping Options 112f–112g

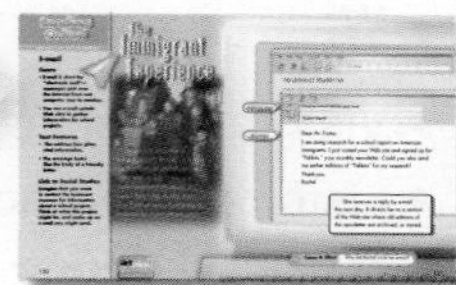

E-mail

Reading Across Texts

Fluency

Partner Reading, 133a

Grammar, 133f
Practice Common and Proper Nouns for Standardized Tests **T**

Writing Workshop, 133h
Draft, Revise, and Publish

Spelling, 133j
Provide a Strategy

Internet Inquiry, 133k
Synthesize Information

Day 4 Writing Across Texts, 133

Day 4 Social Studies Center: Learn About Immigration, 112k

DAY 5 PAGES 133a–133l

Oral Language

QUESTION OF THE WEEK *To wrap up the week, revisit the Day 1 question.*

Build Concept Vocabulary, 133c

Fluency

Read Leveled Readers

Grouping Options 112f–112g

Assess Reading Rate, 133a

Comprehension/Vocabulary

Reteach Cause and Effect, 133b **T**

Paraphrase, 133b

Review Context Clues, 133c **T**

Speaking and Viewing, 133d
Interview
Analyze a Photo

Grammar, 133f
Cumulative Review

Writing Workshop, 133h
Connect to Unit Writing

Spelling, 133j
Posttest for Contractions

Internet Inquiry, 133k
Communicate Results

Research/Study Skills, 133l
Electronic Encyclopedia

Day 5 Paraphrase, 133b

Day 5 Revisit the Life in a New Country Concept Web, 133c

KEY ◎ = Target Skill **T** = Tested Skill

SUCCESS PREDICTOR

Comprehension	Fluency	Vocabulary
Check Retelling, *128*	Check Fluency WCPM, *133a*	Check Vocabulary, *133c*

Small Group Plan *for Differentiated Instructio*

Daily Plan AT A GLANCE

Reading

Whole Group
- Oral Language
- Comprehension/Vocabulary

Group Time

Differentiated Instruction

Meet with small groups to provide:
- Skill Support
- Reading Support
- Fluency Practice

Read

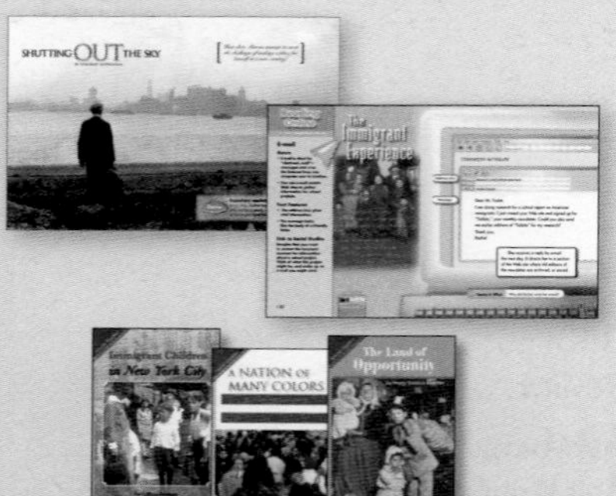

This week's lessons for daily group time can be found behind the Differentiated Instruction (DI) tab on pp. DI • 42–DI • 51.

Whole Group
- Fluency

Language Arts
- Grammar
- Writing
- Spelling
- Research/Inquiry
- Speaking/Listening/Viewing

Use *My Sidewalks on Reading Street* for Tier III intensive reading intervention.

DAY 1

On-Level	Strategic Intervention	Advanced
Teacher-Led *Page DI • 43*	Teacher-Led *Page DI • 42*	Teacher-Led *Page DI • 43*
• Develop Concept Vocabulary • **Read** On-Level Reader *A Nation of Many Colors*	• Reinforce Concepts • **Read** Below-Level Reader *Immigrant Children in New York City*	• **Read** Advanced Reader *The Land of Opportunity* • Independent Extension Activ

i Independent Activities

While you meet with small groups, have the rest of the class...

- Visit the Reading/Library Center
- Listen to the Background Building Audio
- Finish Write to Read, p. 112
- Complete Practice Book pp. 43–44
- Visit Cross-Curricular Centers

DAY 2

On-Level	Strategic Intervention	Advanced
Teacher-Led *Pages 118–123*	Teacher-Led *Page DI • 44*	Teacher-Led *Page DI • 45*
• **Read** *Shutting Out the Sky*	• Practice Lesson Vocabulary • Read Multisyllabic Words • **Read** or Listen to *Shutting Out the Sky*	• Extend Vocabulary • **Read** *Shutting Out the Sky*

i Independent Activities

While you meet with small groups, have the rest of the class...

- Visit the Reading/Library Center
- Listen to the AudioText for *Shutting Out the Sky*
- Finish Words to Write, p. 115
- Complete Practice Book pp. 45-46
- Write in their Strategy Response Logs, pp. 116, 123
- Visit Cross-Curricular Centers
- Work on inquiry projects

DAY 3

On-Level	Strategic Intervention	Advanced
Teacher-Led *Pages 124–127*	Teacher-Led *Page DI • 46*	Teacher-Led *Page DI • 47*
• **Read** *Shutting Out the Sky*	• Practice Cause and Effect and Summarize • **Read** or Listen to *Shutting Out the Sky*	• Extend Cause and Effect and Summarize • **Read** *Shutting Out the Sky*

i Independent Activities

While you meet with small groups, have the rest of the class...

- Visit the Reading/Library Center
- Listen to the AudioText for *Shutting Out the Sky*
- Write in their Strategy Response Logs, p. 126
- Finish Look Back and Write, p. 128
- Complete Practice Book p. 47
- Visit Cross-Curricular Centers
- Work on inquiry projects

1. Begin with whole class skill and strategy instruction.
2. Meet with small groups to provide differentiated instruction.
3. Gather the whole class back together for fluency and language arts.

DAY 4

On-Level	Strategic Intervention	Advanced
Teacher-Led *Pages 130–133*	**Teacher-Led** *Page DI • 48*	**Teacher-Led** *Page DI • 49*
• **Read** "The Immigrant Experience"	• Practice Retelling • **Read** or Listen to "The Immigrant Experience"	• **Read** "The Immigrant Experience" • Genre Study

i Independent Activities

While you meet with small groups, have the rest of the class...

- Visit the Reading/Library Center
- Listen to the AudioText for "The Immigrant Experience"
- Visit the Writing/Vocabulary Center
- Finish Writing Across Texts, p. 133
- Visit Cross-Curricular Centers
- Work on inquiry projects

DAY 5

On-Level	Strategic Intervention	Advanced
Teacher-Led *Page DI • 51*	**Teacher-Led** *Page DI • 50*	**Teacher-Led** *Page DI • 51*
• **Reread** Leveled Reader *A Nation of Many Colors* • Retell *A Nation of Many Colors*	• **Reread** Leveled Reader *Immigrant Children in New York City* • Retell *Immigrant Children in New York City*	• **Reread** Leveled Reader *The Land of Opportunity* • Share Extension Activity

i Independent Activities

While you meet with small groups, have the rest of the class...

- Visit the Reading/Library Center
- Complete Practice Book pp. 48–50
- Visit Cross-Curricular Centers
- Work on inquiry projects

Grouping Place English language learners in the groups that correspond to their reading abilities in English.

Use the appropriate Leveled Reader or other text at students' instructional level.

Tip Send home the appropriate Multilingual Summary of the main selection on Day 1.

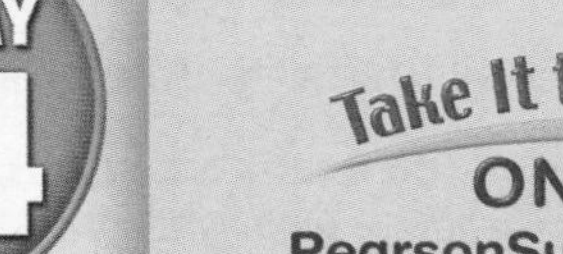

Take It to the NET ONLINE
PearsonSuccessNet.com

Jeanne Paratore
For ideas for successful home-school programs, see the article "Home and School Together" by Scott Foresman author Jeanne Paratore.

TEACHER TALK

Explicit instruction is teaching in which the teacher explains a skill (what it is and when and why to use it), models how to perform it, guides practice, and offers independent practice.

Looking Ahead

Be sure to schedule time for students to work on the unit inquiry project "Facing Challenges." This week students prepare posters or newspaper articles about their Special Olympics events.

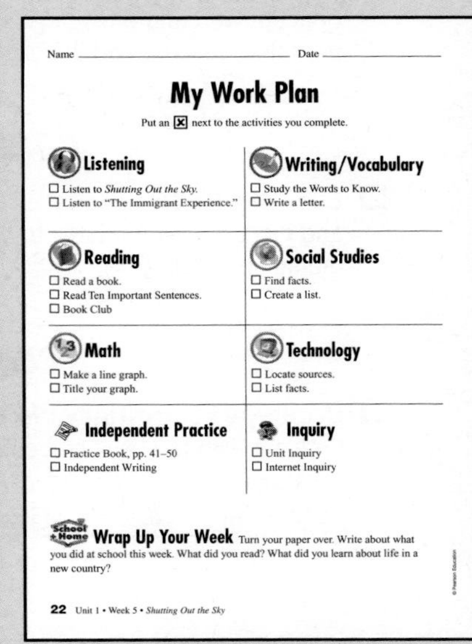

Name ______ Date ______

My Work Plan

Put an ☒ next to the activities you complete.

Listening
☐ Listen to *Shutting Out the Sky.*
☐ Listen to "The Immigrant Experience."

Writing/Vocabulary
☐ Study the Words to Know.
☐ Write a letter.

Reading
☐ Read a book.
☐ Read Ten Important Sentences.
☐ Book Club

Social Studies
☐ Find facts.
☐ Create a list.

Math
☐ Make a line graph.
☐ Title your graph.

Technology
☐ Locate sources.
☐ List facts.

Independent Practice
☐ Practice Book, pp. 41–50
☐ Independent Writing

Inquiry
☐ Unit Inquiry
☐ Internet Inquiry

Wrap Up Your Week Turn your paper over. Write about what you did at school this week. What did you read? What did you learn about life in a new country?

22 Unit 1 • Week 5 • *Shutting Out the Sky*

▲ **Group-Time Survival Guide** p. 22, Weekly Contract

Customize Your Plan by Stran

ORAL LANGUAGE

Concept Development

What challenges do immigrants encounter?

CONCEPT VOCABULARY

Ellis Island *immigration* *Registry Room*

BUILD

- ❑ **Question of the Week** Introduce and discuss the question of the week. This week students will read a variety of texts and work on projects related to the concept *life in a new country.* Post the question for students to refer to throughout the week. DAY 1 *112d*
- ❑ **Read Aloud** Read aloud "Journey to Ellis Island." Then begin a web to build concepts and concept vocabulary related to this week's lesson and the unit theme, Meeting Challenges. Introduce the concept words *Ellis Island, immigration,* and *Registry Room* and have students place them on the web. Display the web for use throughout the week. DAY 1 *112l–112m*

DEVELOP

- ❑ **Question of the Day** Use the prompts from the Weekly Plan to engage students in conversations related to this week's reading and the unit theme. EVERY DAY *112d–112e*
- ❑ **Concept Vocabulary Web** Revisit the Life in a New Country Concept Web and encourage students to add concept words from their reading and life experiences. DAY 2 *123,* DAY 3 *127*

CONNECT

- ❑ **Looking Back** Revisit the Life in a New Country Concept Web and discuss how it relates to this week's lesson and the unit theme. DAY 5 *133c*

CHECK

- ❑ **Concept Vocabulary Web** Use the Life in a New Country Concept Web to check students' understanding of the concept vocabulary words *Ellis Island, immigration,* and *Registry Room.* DAY 1 *112l,* DAY 5 *133c*

VOCABULARY

STRATEGY CONTEXT CLUES
When you read, you may find that the meaning of a word you know does not make sense in a sentence. Some words have more than one meaning, and are multiple-meaning words. Finding clues in nearby words can help determine which meaning is being used.

LESSON VOCABULARY

advice *advised* *circumstances* *elbow* *hustled* *immigrants* *luxury* *newcomer* *peddler*

TEACH

- ❑ **Words to Know** Give students the opportunity to tell what they already know about this week's lesson vocabulary words. Then discuss word meaning. DAY 1 *114b*
- ❑ **Vocabulary Strategy Lesson** Use the vocabulary strategy lesson in the Student Edition to introduce and model this week's strategy, *context clues.* DAY 2 *114–115*

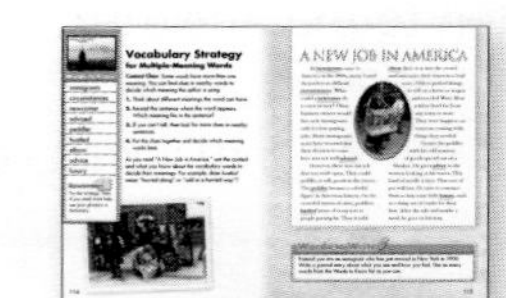

Vocabulary Strategy Lesson

PRACTICE/APPLY

- ❑ **Leveled Text** Read the lesson vocabulary in the context of leveled text. DAY 1 *LR37–LR45*

Leveled Readers

- ❑ **Words in Context** Read the lesson vocabulary and apply *context clues* in the context of *Shutting Out the Sky*. DAY 2 *116–123,* DAY 3 *124–128*

Main Selection—Nonfiction

- ❑ **Writing/Vocabulary Center** Imagine you are Marcus Ravage, a new arrival to New York in 1900. Write a letter to your family in Romania. ANY DAY *112k*
- ❑ **Homework** Practice Book pp. 44–45. DAY 1 *114b,* DAY 2 *115*
- ❑ **Word Play** Have students work with a partner and compile a list of all the proper nouns from *Shutting Out the Sky* and "The Immigrant Experience." ANY DAY *133c*

ASSESS

- ❑ **Selection Test** Use the Selection Test to determine students' understanding of the lesson vocabulary words. DAY 3

RETEACH/REVIEW

- ❑ **Reteach Lesson** If necessary, use this lesson to reteach and review *context clues.* DAY 5 *133c*

1 Use assessment data to determine your instructional focus.

2 Preview this week's instruction by strand.

3 Choose instructional activities that meet the needs of your classroom.

COMPREHENSION

SKILL CAUSE AND EFFECT The cause is what made something happen. The effect is what happened as the result of a cause.

STRATEGY SUMMARIZE Summarizing is a short retelling of a portion of the text that includes the main ideas and leaves out unimportant details.

TEACH

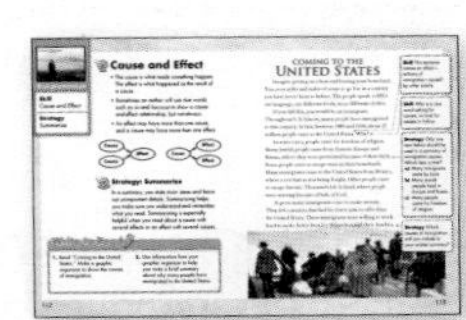
Skill/Strategy Lesson

- ❑ **Skill/Strategy Lesson** Use the skill/strategy lesson in the Student Edition to introduce and model *cause and effect* and *summarize*. DAY 1 *112-113*
- ❑ **Extend Skills** Teach paraphrase. **ANY DAY** *133b*

PRACTICE/APPLY

Leveled Readers

- ❑ **Leveled Text** Apply *cause and effect* and *summarize* to read leveled text. DAY 1 *LR37-LR45*

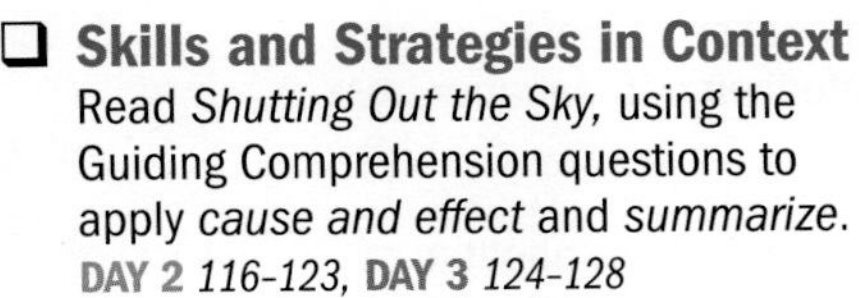

- ❑ **Skills and Strategies in Context** Read *Shutting Out the Sky,* using the Guiding Comprehension questions to apply *cause and effect* and *summarize*. DAY 2 *116-123,* DAY 3 *124-128*

Main Selection—Nonfiction

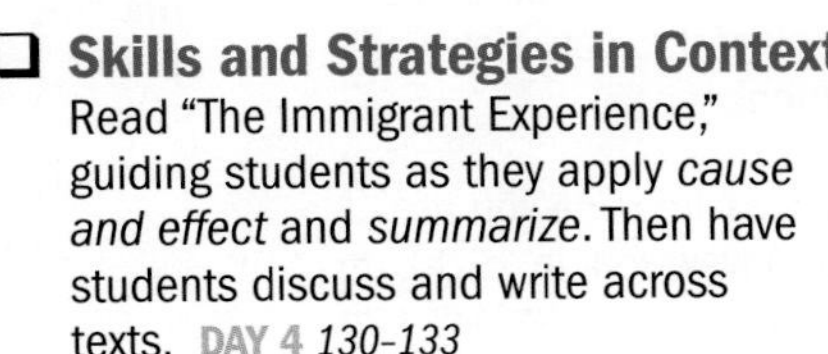

- ❑ **Skills and Strategies in Context** Read "The Immigrant Experience," guiding students as they apply *cause and effect* and *summarize*. Then have students discuss and write across texts. DAY 4 *130-133*

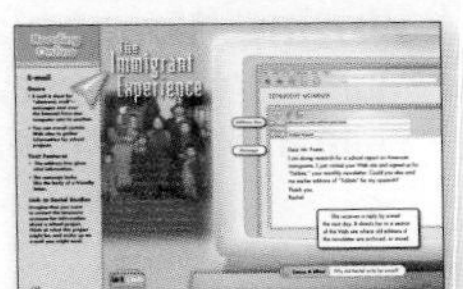
Paired Selection—Nonfiction

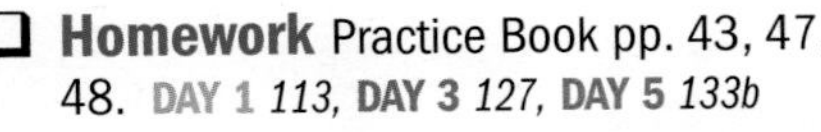

- ❑ **Homework** Practice Book pp. 43, 47, 48. DAY 1 *113,* DAY 3 *127,* DAY 5 *133b*
- ❑ **Fresh Reads for Differentiated Test Practice** Have students practice *cause and effect* with a new passage. DAY 3

ASSESS

- ❑ **Selection Test** Determine students' understanding of the selection and their use of *cause and effect*. DAY 3
- ❑ **Retell** Have students retell *Shutting Out the Sky*. DAY 3 *128-129*

RETEACH/REVIEW

- ❑ **Reteach Lesson** If necessary, reteach and review *cause and effect*. DAY 5 *133b*

FLUENCY

SKILL PAUSES Pauses in reading are natural stopping points in a text. A fluent reader will pause at logical breaks, such as after phrases, at the end of a complete thought, or between paragraphs, to make it easier for listeners to understand and to emphasize the feelings or mood in the text.

TEACH

- ❑ **Read Aloud** Model fluent reading by rereading "Journey to Ellis Island." Focus on this week's fluency skill, pauses. DAY 1 *112l-112m, 133a*

PRACTICE/APPLY

- ❑ **Echo Reading** Read aloud selected paragraphs from *Shutting Out the Sky,* emphasizing the pauses. Then practice as a class, doing three echo readings of the selected paragraphs. DAY 2 *133a,* DAY 3 *133a*
- ❑ **Partner Reading** Have partners practice reading aloud, inserting pauses at logical breaks, at the end of complete thoughts, and between paragraphs. Have partners offer each other feedback. As students reread, monitor their progress toward their fluency goals. DAY 4 *133a*
- ❑ **Listening Center** Have students follow along with the AudioText for this week's selections. **ANY DAY** *112j*
- ❑ **Reading/Library Center** Have students reread a selection of their choice. **ANY DAY** *112j*
- ❑ **Fluency Coach** Have students use Fluency Coach to listen to fluent readings or practice reading on their own. **ANY DAY**

ASSESS

- ❑ **Check Fluency WCPM** Do a one-minute timed reading, paying special attention to this week's skill—pauses. Provide feedback for each student. DAY 5 *133a*

Customize Your Plan by Stran

GRAMMAR

SKILL COMMON AND PROPER NOUNS A *proper noun* names a particular person, place, or thing. The first word and each important word of a proper noun is capitalized. All other nouns are *common nouns* and are not capitalized.

TEACH

- ❑ **Grammar Transparency 5** Use Grammar Transparency 5 to teach common and proper nouns. DAY 1 *133e*

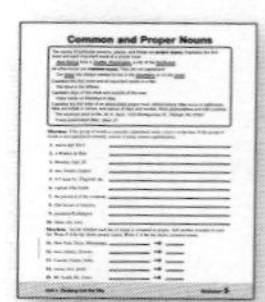

Grammar Transparency 5

PRACTICE/APPLY

- ❑ **Develop the Concept** Review the concept of common and proper nouns and provide guided practice. DAY 2 *133e*
- ❑ **Apply to Writing** Have students review something they have written and apply common and proper nouns. DAY 3 *133f*
- ❑ **Test Preparation** Examine common errors in common and proper nouns to prepare for standardized tests. DAY 4 *133f*
- ❑ **Homework** Grammar and Writing Practice Book pp. 17–19. DAY 2 *133e*, DAY 3 *133f*, DAY 4 *133f*

ASSESS

- ❑ **Cumulative Review** Use Grammar and Writing Practice Book p. 20. DAY 5 *133f*

RETEACH/REVIEW

- ❑ **Daily Fix-It** Have students find and correct errors in grammar, spelling, and punctuation. EVERY DAY *133e–133f*
- ❑ **The Grammar and Writing Book** Use pp. 74–77 of The Grammar and Writing Book to extend instruction for common and proper nouns. ANY DAY

The Grammar and Writing Book

WRITING

Trait of the Week

WORD CHOICE Good writers choose their words carefully. Strong verbs, specific nouns, and vivid adjectives help writers elaborate on their ideas. Well-chosen words make writing clear, colorful, and interesting.

TEACH

- ❑ **Writing Transparency 5A** Use the model to introduce and discuss the Trait of the Week. DAY 1 *133g*
- ❑ **Writing Transparency 5B** Use the transparency to show students how showing not just telling, can improve their writing. DAY 2 *133g*

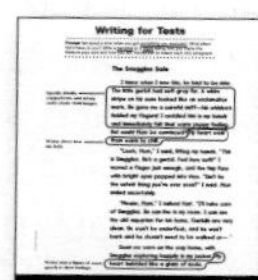

Writing Transparency 5A

Writing Transparency 5B

PRACTICE/APPLY

- ❑ **Write Now** Examine the model on Student Edition p. 129. Then have students write their own narrative. DAY 3 *129, 133h*, DAY 4 *133h*

  Prompt *Shutting Out the Sky* tells about a boy's experiences in a new country. Think about an experience that was meaningful to you. Now write a narrative about that experience.

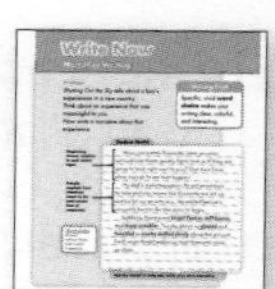

Write Now p. 129

- ❑ **Writing/Vocabulary Center** Imagine you are Marcus Ravage, a new arrival to New York in 1900. Write a letter to your family in Romania. ANY DAY *112k*

ASSESS

- ❑ **Writing Trait Rubric** Use the rubric to evaluate students' writing. DAY 4 *133h*

RETEACH/REVIEW

- ❑ **The Grammar and Writing Book** Use pp. 74–79 of The Grammar and Writing Book to extend instruction for common and proper nouns, showing and not telling, and narrative writing. ANY DAY

The Grammar and Writing Book

1 Use assessment data to determine your instructional focus.

2 Preview this week's instruction by strand.

3 Choose instructional activities that meet the needs of your classroom.

SPELLING

GENERALIZATION CONTRACTIONS In contractions, an apostrophe (') takes the place of letters that are left out: *they are* becomes *they're*. A contraction is a combination of two words. To read a contraction, figure out which letters the apostrophe replaced.

TEACH

- ❑ **Pretest** Give the pretest for words with contractions. Guide students in self-correcting their pretests and correcting any misspellings. DAY 1 *133i*
- ❑ **Think and Practice** Connect spelling to the phonics generalization for contractions. DAY 2 *133i*

PRACTICE/APPLY

- ❑ **Connect to Writing** Have students use spelling words to write an anecdote. Then review frequently misspelled words: *that's, you're, doesn't.* DAY 3 *133j*
- ❑ **Homework** Word Study and Spelling Practice Book pp. 17–20. **EVERY DAY**

RETEACH/REVIEW

- ❑ **Review** Review spelling words to prepare for the posttest. Then provide students with a spelling strategy—meaning helpers. DAY 4 *133j*

ASSESS

- ❑ **Posttest** Use dictation sentences to give the posttest for words with contractions. DAY 5 *133j*

Spelling Words

1. they're	8. what'll	15. wouldn't*
2. you've	9. doesn't	16. who've
3. weren't	10. hadn't*	17. shouldn't
4. needn't	11. could've	18. who'd
5. there'd	12. would've	19. this'll
6. they've	13. should've	20. couldn't
7. mustn't	14. might've	

Challenge Words

21. there've	23. what've	25. there'll
22. mightn't	24. needn't	

*Word from the selection

RESEARCH AND INQUIRY

- ❑ **Internet Inquiry** Have students conduct an Internet inquiry on the immigrant experience. **EVERY DAY** *133k*
- ❑ **Electronic Encyclopedia** Review the terms associated with an electronic encyclopedia and discuss how students can use an electronic encyclopedia to locate information. DAY 5 *133l*
- ❑ **Unit Inquiry** Allow time for students to prepare posters or newspaper articles about their Special Olympics events. **ANY DAY** *17*

SPEAKING AND VIEWING

- ❑ **Interview** Have students work in pairs to write questions and perform a mock interview with Marcus. DAY 5 *133d*
- ❑ **Analyze a Photo** Have students examine the photograph on p.121 of *Shutting Out the Sky* and answer questions. DAY 5 *133d*

Resources for

Differentiated Instruction

LEVELED READERS

- **Comprehension**
  - **Skill** Cause and Effect
  - **Strategy** Summarize
- **Lesson Vocabulary**
  - Context Clues

- **Social Studies Standards**
  - Ethnic Groups
  - Cultures
  - Immigration
  - Customs
  - U.S. History

PearsonSuccessNet.com

Use the Online Database of over 600 books to

- Download and print additional copies of this week's leveled readers.
- Listen to the readers being read online.
- Search for more titles focused on this week's skills, topic, and content.

On-Level

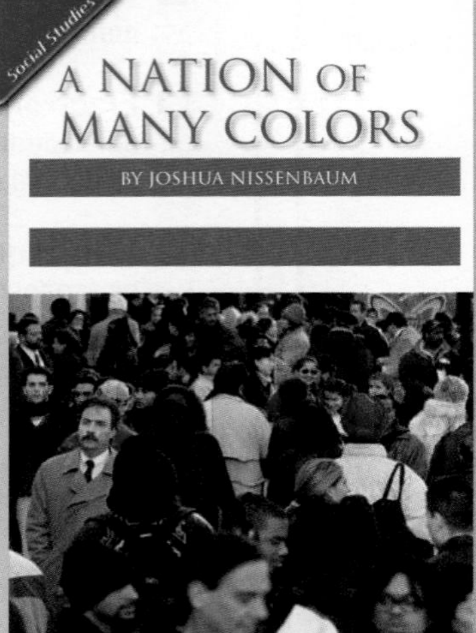

On-Level Reader

Name________________ **A Nation of Many Colors**

Cause and Effect

- A **cause** tells why something happened.
- An **effect** tells what happened.

Directions Using the graphic organizer, list three causes and three effects of immigration in the United States. One cause and one effect are done for you.

Causes	Effects
Cubans felt threatened by Castro's communist government.	200,000 Cubans immigrated to U.S. from 1959–1962.
Many ethnic groups immigrated in the late 1800s.	U.S. became a melting pot of customs and cultures.
Immigrants found it difficult to adapt to American life.	Immigrant communities were formed.

On-Level Practice TE p. LR41

Name________________ **A Nation of Many Colors**

Vocabulary

Directions Underline the context clue that explains what each of the boldface words mean.

Check the Words You Know

___advice	___advised	___circumstances
___elbow	___hustled	___immigrants
___luxury	___newcomer	___peddler

1. Sam's words of wisdom are always the best **advice**.
2. The teacher counseled Adrian and said the principal **advised** him to do so.
3. All the situations created by the picnic were **circumstances** beyond control.
4. The joint between the upper and lower arm makes the **elbow** very important.
5. Everyone that was pushed inside felt **hustled** by the guards.
6. The **immigrants** were new settlers on the plains and needed help.
7. The **luxury** apartment was comfortable and richly decorated.
8. Every **newcomer** was welcomed just as they moved into town.
9. The **peddler** sold more pots than any of the other market sellers.

Directions Write a paragraph about what life is often like for an immigrant, using as many vocabulary words as possible.

Responses will vary.

On-Level Practice TE p. LR42

Strategic Intervention

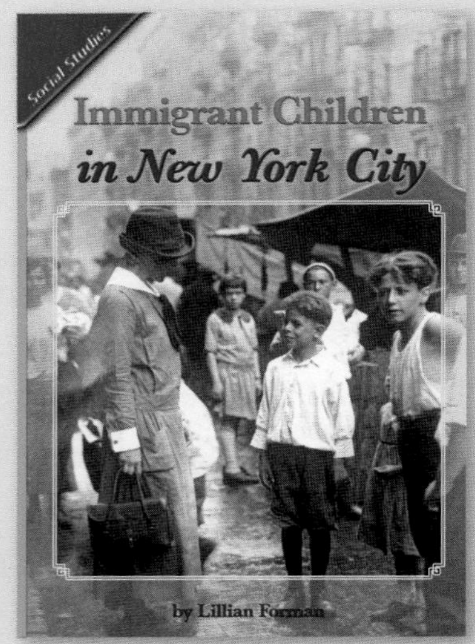

Below-Level Reader

Name________________ **Immigrant Children**

Cause and Effect

- A **cause** tells why something happened.
- An **effect** tells what happened.

Directions Use the information in the chart to answer the questions below.

Causes	Effects
Causes of Immigration	**Effects of Immigration**
better life more money better education	little money little education had to work hard nowhere to safely play

1. What caused many immigrant children to work so hard?
   Their families were poor and needed help.
2. What effect did education have on immigrant children?
   It gave them opportunities for better jobs and a better life.
3. What effects did new playgrounds have on immigrant children?
   They had a safe, fun place to play.
4. What caused parents to take their children from their homes and move them to America?
   a better life, freedom, an education
5. What caused overcrowded schools?
   There were a large number of children who immigrated to America.

Below-Level Practice TE p. LR38

Name________________ **Immigrant Children**

Vocabulary

Directions Complete each sentence with a word from the word box.

Check the Words You Know

___advice	___advised	___circumstances
___elbow	___hustled	___immigrants
___luxury	___newcomer	___peddler

1. The __peddler__ sold us wood.
2. We were __hustled__ by the bad salesman.
3. Her good __advice__ helped him get a job.
4. The __circumstances__ of his arrival were mysterious.
5. The __luxury__ of a house was a dream of ours.
6. The __newcomer__ asked us directions.
7. We __advised__ the boy not to talk to strangers.
8. A basketball player should never __elbow__ another player.
9. The __immigrants__ were anxious to get to the new country.

Directions Write the vocabulary word that is a synonym for each pair of words.

10. shove, nudge __elbow__
11. tricked, cheated __hustled__
12. opinions, guidance __advice__
13. happenings, situations __circumstances__
14. wealth, comfort __luxury__
15. beginner, novice __newcomer__
16. colonists, settlers __immigrants__
17. dealer, merchant __peddler__
18. directed, counseled __advised__

Directions Select two vocabulary words and use each in a sentence below.

19. Sentences will vary.
20. ________________

Below-Level Practice TE p. LR39

Advanced

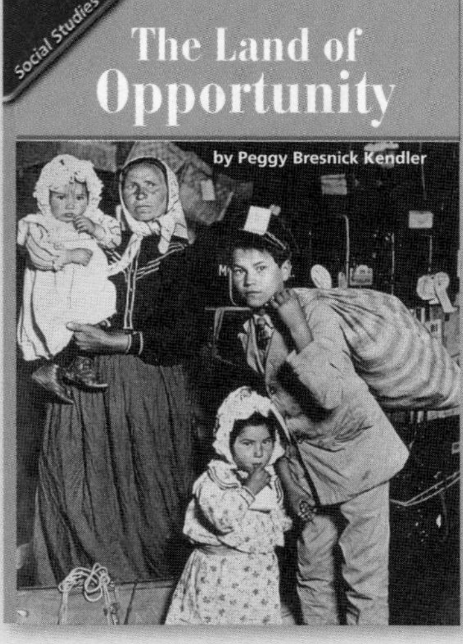

Advanced Reader

Name ________________ The Land of Opportunity

Cause and Effect

- A **cause** tells why something happened.
- An **effect** tells what happened.

Directions Answer the following questions.

1. What caused many people to leave their homes and come to the United States?
They were poor and wanted a better life in America.
They wanted a better life for their families.
2. What effect did immigration have on New York?
overcrowding
3. What caused immigrants to work so hard?
They wanted to provide a better life for their families.
4. What caused immigrant neighborhoods to spring up in many major cities?
Immigrants helped other immigrants from their homeland, sharing their resources.
5. What effect did crowded, run-down tenements have on immigrants?
They were disappointed, sad.

Directions Write whether the following are causes or effects of immigration.

6. Immigrants were poor in their home countries. cause
7. So many people immigrated to New York that it became overcrowded. effect
8. Children were given a better education in America. effect
9. America provided freedom from a harsh government. cause
10. Immigrants heard that America was the land of opportunity. cause

Advanced Practice TE p. LR44

Name ________________ The Land of Opportunity

Vocabulary

Directions Write the vocabulary word that matches each defintion.

Check the Words You Know

___barracks ___citizens ___detainees ___emigrate
___interpreter ___naturalized ___steerage ___tenements

1. steerage — part of the ship occupied by passengers traveling at the cheapest rate
2. citizens — people who are members of a nation
3. emigrate — to leave your own country to settle in another
4. tenements — buildings that are divided into sets of rooms occupied by separate families
5. interpreter — someone who orally translates from one language to another
6. detainees — people who are kept from moving forward; delayed
7. naturalized — having been made a citizen of a country by an official act
8. barracks — group of buildings for people to live in, usually in a fort or camp

Directions Write two sentences using at least two vocabulary words in each.

9. Sentences will vary.
10. ________________

Advanced Practice TE p. LR45

ELL

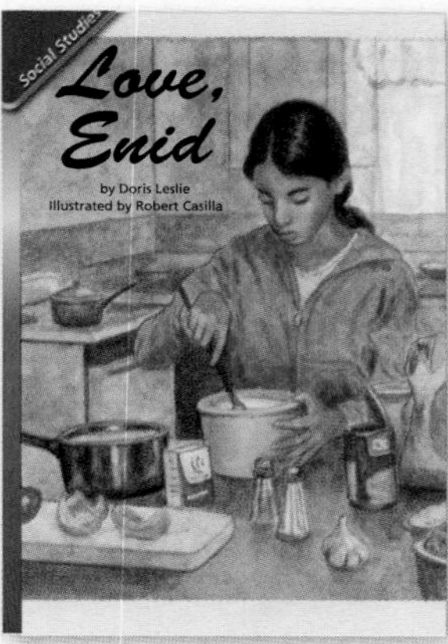

ELL Reader

ELL Poster 5

Teacher's Edition Notes

ELL notes throughout this lesson support instruction and reference additional resources at point of use.

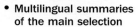

Teaching Guide pp. 29–35, 220–221

- Multilingual summaries of the main selection
- Comprehension lesson
- Vocabulary strategies and word cards
- ELL Reader 5.1.5 lesson

ELL and Transition Handbook

Ten Important Sentences

- Key ideas from every selection in the Student Edition
- Activities to build sentence power

More Reading

Readers' Theater Anthology

- Fluency practice
- Five scripts to build fluency
- Poetry for oral interpretation

Leveled Trade Books

- Extended reading tied to the unit concept
- Lessons in the Trade Book Library Teaching Guide

Homework

- Family Times Newsletter
- ELL Multilingual Selection Summaries

Take-Home Books

- Leveled Readers

Cross-Curricular Centers

Listening

Listen to the SELECTIONS

MATERIALS
CD player, headphones, Audio Text CD, student book

SINGLES

LISTEN TO LITERATURE Listen to *Shutting Out the Sky* and "The Immigrant Experience" as you follow or read along in your book. Listen for the causes and effects that occur in the selections.

If there is anything you don't understand, you can listen again to any section.

Reading/ Library

Read it AGAIN!

MATERIALS
Collection of books for self-selected reading, reading logs, student book

SINGLES
PAIRS
GROUPS

Select a book you have already read. Record the title of the book in your reading log. You may want to read with a partner.

Choose from the following:

- **Leveled Readers**
- **ELL Readers**
- **Stories Written by Classmates**
- **Books from the Library**
- ***Shutting Out the Sky***

TEN IMPORTANT SENTENCES Read the Ten Important Sentences for *Shutting Out the Sky*. Then locate the sentences in the student book.

BOOK CLUB Look at the photographs in *Shutting Out the Sky*. Discuss how the photographs help you to imagine the time period and the similarities and differences between life today and life for immigrants in the 1800s.

Math

Make a Line Graph

MATERIALS
Paper, pencil, copy of table below, graph paper

SINGLES

Use the data in the table below to create a line graph showing how the number of Irish immigrants who came through Ellis Island changed over time.

1. **Label the horizontal axis: "Number of Immigrants." Label the vertical axis: "Years." Include the scale on each axis.**
2. **Plot the data for each year shown. Connect the points for each set of data.**
3. **Title your graph.**

EARLY FINISHERS Make a bar graph or a pictograph to display the same information in a different way.

Number of Irish Immigrants Who Came Through Ellis Island

1790–1820	1820–1880	1880–1930
25,000	2,800,000	1,700,000

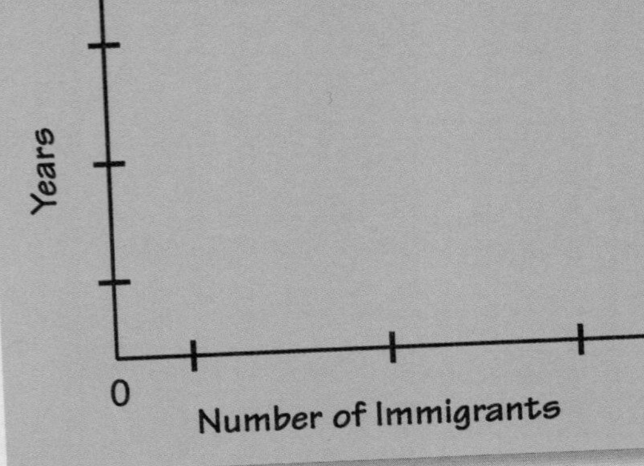

Scott Foresman Reading Street Centers Survival Kit

Use the *Shutting Out the Sky* materials from the Reading Street Centers Survival Kit to organize this week's centers.

Writing/ Vocabulary

Write a Letter

MATERIALS
Writing and art materials

SINGLES

Imagine you are Marcus Ravage and you have just arrived in New York in 1900.

1. **Write a letter to your family in Romania telling them about what you have done and seen in your first few days in America.**
2. **Use details from the selection in your letter. As Marcus, think about your impressions of New York.**

EARLY FINISHERS Draw a postcard showing one of the sights you saw in New York.

Dear Family,

Social Studies

Learn About Immigration

MATERIALS
Books on immigration in America, Internet access, writing materials, index cards

SINGLES

PAIRS

Find out more about Ellis Island in New York or Angel Island in San Francisco.

1. **Find three or four interesting facts about one of these places and list them, along with some details, on index cards.**
2. **Use your findings to create a "Did You Know?" list of facts about Ellis Island or Angel Island.**

EARLY FINISHERS Write a paragraph using the facts you gathered.

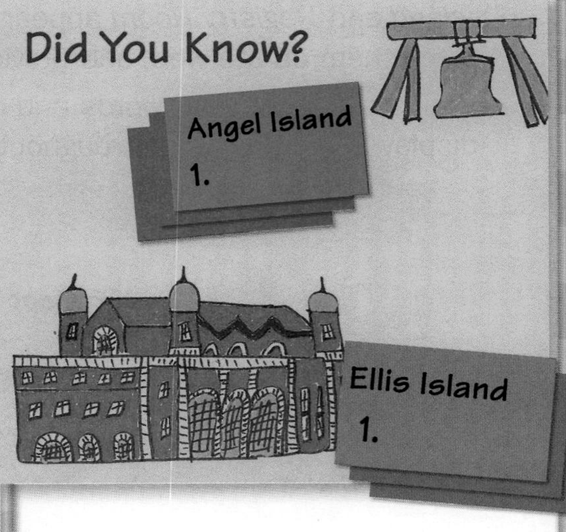

Technology

Compare Sources

MATERIALS
Internet access, writing materials

SINGLES

PAIRS

Use a student-friendly search engine to search for information on Ellis Island.

1. **Locate three different Internet sources for Ellis Island. List the source and one fact from each source.**
2. **Tell about the most helpful source you found.**

EARLY FINISHERS Narrow your Internet search to find out the number of daily visitors to Ellis Island today.

DAY 1

Build Concepts

OBJECTIVES

- Build vocabulary by finding words related to the lesson concept.
- Listen for causes and effects.

Concept Vocabulary

Ellis Island small island in the harbor of New York, just south of Manhattan. From 1891 to 1943 it housed reception facilities for new immigrants.

immigration act of coming into a country or region to live

Registry Room place on Ellis Island in which registration of new immigrants took place

Monitor Progress

Check Vocabulary

If...	then...
students are unable to place words on the web,	review the lesson concept. Place the words on the web and provide additional words for practice, such as *struggled* and *anxiously.*

DAY 1 Grouping Options

Reading

Whole Group
Introduce and discuss the Question of the Week. Then use pp.112l–114b.

Group Time
Differentiated Instruction
Read this week's Leveled Readers. See pp. 112h–112i for the small group lesson plan.

Whole Group
Use p. 133a.

Language Arts
Use pp. 133e–133k.

FLUENCY

MODEL PAUSES As you read "Journey to Ellis Island," model pausing at points to help convey the tension and anxiety felt by the characters in this story. For example, when you read the sentence "Finally, they heard their name: 'WEINSTEIN! Weinstein family, this way, please!'" Pause at the colon.

LISTENING COMPREHENSION

After reading "Journey to Ellis Island," use the following questions to assess listening comprehension.

1. **What causes the man with the bucket of milk to get angry at Yehuda?** *(Yehuda tricks the man into getting an extra drink of milk.)* ***Cause and Effect***
2. **How does the Weinstein family feel on this day?** *(nervous; excited)* ***Draw Conclusions***

BUILD CONCEPT VOCABULARY

Start a web to build concepts and vocabulary related to this week's lesson and the unit theme.

- Draw the Life in a New Country Concept Web.
- Read the sentence with the word *immigration* again. Ask students to pronounce *immigration* and discuss its meaning.
- Place *immigration* in an oval attached to the *Experiences* oval. Explain that *immigration* is related to this concept. Read the sentences in which *Ellis Island* and *Registry Room* appear. Have students pronounce the words, place them on the web, and provide reasons.
- Brainstorm additional words and categories for the web. Keep the web on display and add words throughout the week.

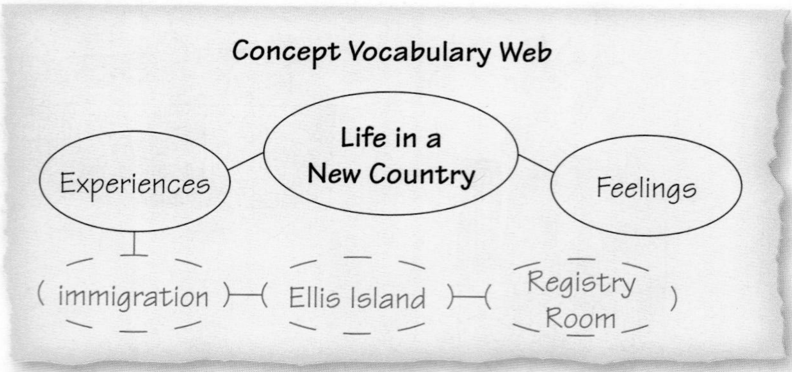

by Carol Bierman

In September of 1922, Yehuda Weinstein and his family moved from Russia to America o join his older brother, Abe. This passage describes what it was like to wait at Ellis Island efore being called by immigration officials.

The next morning, the Weinsteins were taken to the Main Building on Ellis sland. Yehuda and Esther thought it looked like a castle, with its massive red brick valls edged in white stone and its four tall towers.

"America must really be a rich country if they have such a beautiful building just or people arriving!" Yehuda exclaimed. Rachel nodded, but she was too nervous o answer. They struggled up the staircase to the huge Registry Room with the bags hat held everything they owned. Yehuda had never been in a room so large. There vere rows and rows of wooden benches crowded with men, women, and children nd their bundles of belongings. The hall was hot and stuffy, and it echoed with oise — babies crying, people talking anxiously to each other in many different anguages, and officials calling out names. The Weinsteins sat on a bench to wait. sther curled up against Rachel and soon fell asleep.

Yehuda saw a man approaching with a big bucket filled with milk and a basket f long yellow fruit. He was stopping at every child, giving each one a cup of milk nd one of the strange pieces of fruit. Yehuda watched as one boy bit right into the ellow skin, made a face, and spit it out. Then he saw someone pull the skin down n strips and eat the soft white fruit inside. Yehuda smiled to himself — every day in America he was learning something new!

When the man reached Yehuda, he gave him a banana and one to save for Esther. Yehuda ate his banana hungrily and gulped down the warm milk. But he was still thirsty.

He noticed that the man with the bucket had moved on a few rows and was still giving out milk. Yehuda quietly slipped away from his mother's side and took a seat n a row that the man had not yet reached. When the man came to Yehuda, he hardly glanced up, and the boy got another delicious drink of milk.

Yehuda moved on a few rows to try his luck again. But this time the man looked closely at him. "Hey, wait a minute! Didn't I give you some before?"

Yehuda understood the man's tone of voice and shook his head nervously. "Nayn," he said.

"It was you, all right!" The man wagged his finger at Yehuda. "You can't fool me, son. No more milk for you." Yehuda returned to his mother's side, with the milk-and-banana man's stern eyes watching him all the way.

"Where have you been?" Rachel asked.

"Just wandering around," Yehuda replied sheepishly.

"Stay here," his mother said firmly, pointing to the seat beside her. "We don't know when Abe will come. We don't want to miss him now."

Finally, they heard their name: "WEINSTEIN! Weinstein family, this way, please!"

Activate Prior Knowledge

Before students listen to the Read Aloud, have them share what they know about immigration.

Set Purpose

Read aloud the title and have students predict what the selection will be about.

Read the introduction aloud. Have students listen for the cause of the banana man's anger at Yehuda.

Creative Response

Invite small groups of students to role-play the scene in which Yehuda tries to get more milk from the Ellis Island worker. ***Drama***

Access Content Before reading, share this summary: The Weinstein family waits in the Registry Room for their name to be called. A man gives all the children a cup of milk and a banana. Yehuda wants more, so he moves around the room, hoping the man will not notice.

Homework Send home this week's Family Times newsletter.

SUCCESS PREDICTOR

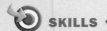

 SKILLS ↔ STRATEGIES IN CONTEXT

Cause and Effect Summarize

OBJECTIVES

- Identify causes and effects.
- Use causes and effects to summarize.

Skills Trace

Cause and Effect

Introduce/Teach	**TE: 5.1 42–43, 112–113; 5.5 582–583**
Practice	Practice Book: 6, 13, 17, 18, 43, 47, 48, 106, 233, 237, 238
Reteach/Review	TE: 5.1 27, 67b, 133b; 5.3 267, DI•53, DI•56; 5.5 603b, DI•55
Test	Selection Test: 5–8, 17–20, 93–96; Benchmark Test: Unit 1

INTRODUCE

Place a book on the edge of a desk and then bump into the desk, causing the book to fall to the floor. Ask students what happened *(The book fell off the desk)* and why it happened. *(You bumped into the desk).* Point out that why something happens is the *cause* and what happens is the *effect.*

Have students read the information on p. 112. Explain the following:

- *Cause* answers the question, "Why did it happen?" *Effect* answers the question, "What happened?" A cause can have several effects, and an effect can have several causes.
- Cause-effect relationships can be used to help summarize a selection.

Use Skill Transparency 5 to teach cause and effect and summarize.

Comprehension

Skill
Cause and Effect

Strategy
Summarize

Cause and Effect

- The cause is what made something happen. The effect is what happened as the result of a cause.
- Sometimes an author will use clue words such as *so* and *because* to show a cause-and-effect relationship, but not always.
- An effect may have more than one cause, and a cause may have more than one effect.

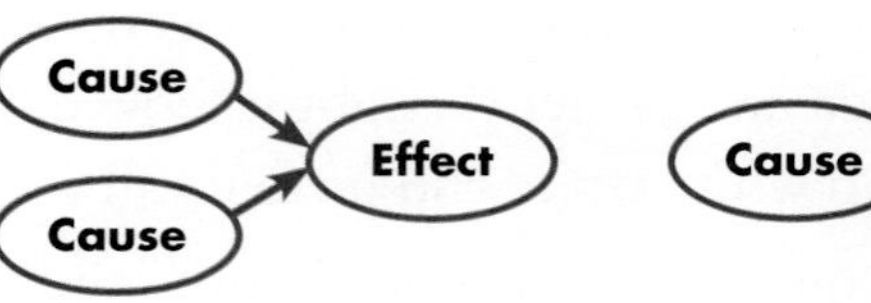

Strategy: Summarize

In a summary, you state main ideas and leave out unimportant details. Summarizing helps you make sure you understand and remember what you read. Summarizing is especially helpful when you read about a cause with several effects or an effect with several causes.

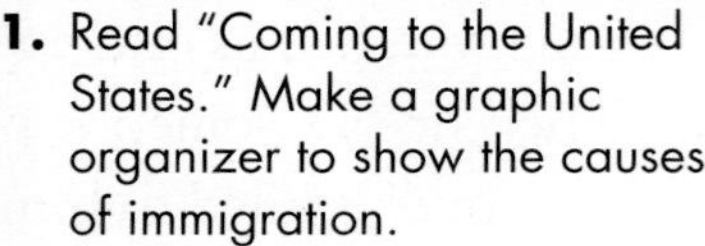

1. Read "Coming to the United States." Make a graphic organizer to show the causes of immigration.
2. Use information from your graphic organizer to help you write a brief summary about why many people have immigrated to the United States.

112

Strategic Intervention

Cause and Effect Write several cause-effect sentences on the board. *(for example, The sun came out and caused the snowman to melt. Sean forgot his key, so he had to wait outside.)* Work with students to identify the cause and effect in each sentence.

Access Content

Beginning/Intermediate For a Picture It! lesson on cause and effect, see the ELL Teaching Guide, pp. 29–30.

Advanced Before students read "Coming to the United States," ask them to name reasons why people come to this country. Explain that people coming to the United States is the effect. Tell students that the reasons they give are the causes.

COMING TO THE UNITED STATES

Imagine getting on a boat and leaving your homeland. ou cross miles and miles of ocean to go live in a country ou have never been to before. The people speak a differ- nt language, eat different foods, wear different clothes.

If you did this, you would be an immigrant. 'hroughout U.S. history, many people have immigrated) this country. In fact, between 1880 and 1930, about 27 ıillion people came to the United States. Why?

In some cases, people came for freedom of religion. Iany Jewish people came from Eastern Europe and ussia, where they were persecuted because of their faith. ome people came to escape wars in their homelands. Iany immigrants came to the United States from Mexico, here a revolution was being fought. Other people came) escape famine. Thousands left Ireland, where people ere starving because of lack of food.

A great many immigrants came to make money. 'hey left countries that had far fewer jobs to offer than ıe United States. These immigrants were willing to work ard to make better lives for themselves and their families.

1 **Skill** This sentence names an effect—millions of immigrants—caused by other events.

2 **Skill** *Why* is a clue word asking for causes, so look for causes to follow.

3 **Strategy** Only one item below should be used in a summary of immigration causes. Which item is that?
a) Many immigrants came by boat.
b) Many Jewish people lived in Europe and Russia.
c) Many people came for freedom of religion.

4 **Strategy** Which causes of immigration will you include in your written summary?

113

Available as **Skill Transparency** 5

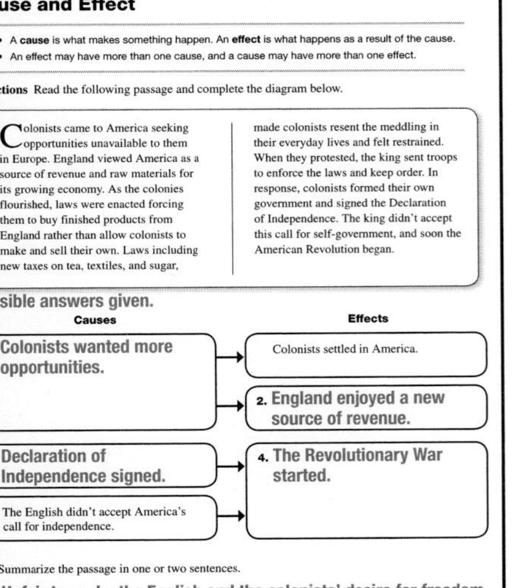

use and Effect

- A **cause** is what makes something happen. An **effect** is what happens as a result of the cause.
- An effect may have more than one cause, and a cause may have more than one effect.

ctions Read the following passage and complete the diagram below.

Colonists came to America seeking opportunities unavailable to them in Europe. England viewed America as a source of revenue and raw materials for its growing economy. As the colonies flourished, laws were enacted forcing them to buy finished products from England rather than allow colonists to make and sell their own. Laws including new taxes on tea, textiles, and sugar, made colonists resent the meddling in their everyday lives and felt restrained. When they protested, the king sent troops to enforce the laws and keep order. In response, colonists formed their own government and signed the Declaration of Independence. The king didn't accept this call for self-government, and soon the American Revolution began.

ssible answers given.

Causes	Effects
Colonists wanted more opportunities.	Colonists settled in America.
	2. England enjoyed a new source of revenue.
Declaration of Independence signed.	4. The Revolutionary War started.
The English didn't accept America's call for independence.	

Summarize the passage in one or two sentences.

Unfair taxes by the English and the colonists' desire for freedom caused the American Revolutionary War.

hool Home **Home Activity** Your child read a short passage and identified causes and effects. Look up an event in the U.S. Revolutionary War and discuss causes and effects described in the selection.

Practice Book p. 43

TEACH

1 **SKILL** Model how to identify an effect.

MODEL I know that an effect answers the question, "What happened?" The answer to this question (about 27 million people came to the United States) can be found at the end of paragraph 2. If I read on, I will find out what caused this effect.

3 **STRATEGY** Use paragraph 3 to model how to summarize.

MODEL A summary should contain only the main ideas. Paragraph 3 is about why people came to the United States. My summary should include the reasons why they came. It should not include how they came or who came. So the summary should include *c*.

PRACTICE AND ASSESS

2 **SKILL** Causes answer the question "Why?" Read on to find out why people came to the United States.

4 **STRATEGY** Some people came for freedom of religion. Others came to escape wars or famine in their homelands. And still others came to make money.

WRITE Have students complete steps 1 and 2 of the Write to Read activity. You might consider using this as a whole-class activity.

Monitor Progress

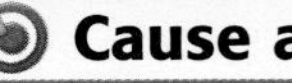

Cause and Effect

If... students are unable to complete **Write to Read** on p. 112,	**then...** use Practice Book p. 43 to provide additional practice.

Build Background

ACTIVATE PRIOR KNOWLEDGE

BRAINSTORM about immigration.

- Give students two to three minutes to write words and phrases they associate with immigration.
- Discuss students' responses. Explain that as they read, students should think about the challenges immigrants encounter when arriving in a new country.

BACKGROUND BUILDING AUDIO This week's audio explores challenges and hardships that immigrants to New York City faced at the turn of the century. After students listen, discuss how they might have tried to overcome these challenges or hardships.

Background Building Audio

ONLINE

To find information about Ellis Island and immigration, students can use a student-friendly search engine and use the keywords *Ellis Island*. Be sure to follow classroom guidelines for Internet use.

ELL

Build Background Use ELL Poster 5 to build background and vocabulary for the lesson concept of immigration.

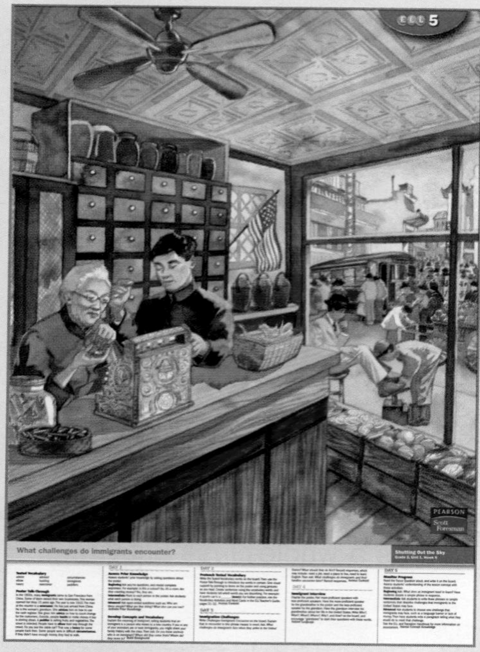

▲ **ELL Poster** 5

Introduce Vocabulary

DISCUSS THE VOCABULARY

Have volunteers read aloud the lesson vocabulary. Then have students locate each word in their glossaries, noting each word's pronunciation and meaning. Ask questions that include the new vocabulary, such as the following.

What might a *peddler* sell?

If you *elbow* your way to the head of the crowd, what are you doing?

What is a *luxury* in your home?

Ask students which vocabulary words they've heard or used before, and in what context. ***Activate Prior Knowledge***

Remind students that a word's connotation is a meaning suggested by the word, and is an important part of building vocabulary. Discuss connotations for the word *immigrant* vs. connotations for *newcomer*. ***Connotation***

After discussing word connotations, students can write sentences that include the vocabulary words.

At the end of the week, have students review their sentences and improve upon them using what they have learned.

Use the Multisyllabic Word Routine on p. DI•1 to help students read multisyllabic words.

Lesson Vocabulary

WORDS TO KNOW

T advice an opinion about what should be done

T advised gave advice to; offered an opinion

T circumstances conditions that accompany an act or event

T elbow to push with the elbow; make your way by pushing

T hustled hurried along

T immigrants people who come into a country or region to live

T luxury something pleasant but not necessary

T newcomer a person who has just come or who came not long ago

T peddler a person who travels about selling things carried in a pack or in a truck, wagon, or cart

MORE WORDS TO KNOW

crannies small, narrow openings; cracks; crevices

greenhorn a person without training or experience

pushcarts light carts pushed by hand

T = Tested Word

Vocabulary

Directions Choose the word from the box that best completes each sentence. Write the word on the line.

1. Immigrants come from one country to another to live. A 2. newcomer faces many challenges when moving to a new home. They don't have the 3. luxury of familiar surroundings. Sometimes, they find themselves in strange and confusing 4. circumstances. To find jobs and homes, they often rely on the 5. advice of their new friends and acquaintances.

Check the Words You Know

___advice
___advised
___circumstances
___elbow
___hustled
___immigrants
___luxury
___newcomer
___peddler

Directions Circle the word that has the same or nearly the same meaning as the first word in each group.

6. peddler	walker	(salesperson)	bicyclist
7. elbow	disappear	(push)	bend
8. hustled	eased	slipped	(hurried)
9. circumstances	happenings	(situation)	ideas
10. advised	thought	decided	(suggested)

Journal Entry

On a separate sheet of paper, write a journal entry as if you have just moved to another country. Use as many vocabulary words as you can.

Journal entry should include words from the vocabulary list and details about what it would be like to move to another country.

School + Home **Home Activity** Your child identified and used vocabulary words from *Shutting Out the Sky*. Together with your child, read an article about life in another country. Talk with your child about what it might be like to live in that country.

▲ **Practice Book** p. 44

DAY 2

Vocabulary Strategy

OBJECTIVE

Use context clues to determine correct meaning of multiple-meaning words.

INTRODUCE

Discuss the strategy for context clues using the steps on p. 114.

TEACH

- Have students read "A New Job in America," paying attention to how words, including examples, are used to identify word meanings.
- Model using context clues to determine the meaning of *elbow*.

MODEL I know that *elbow* means "the joint between the upper and lower parts of my arm," and "to push with the elbow." The sentence says they would "elbow their way into the crowd." I put the clues together with the meanings I know and decide that in this sentence, *elbow* means "to push."

DAY 2 Grouping Options

Reading

Whole Group Discuss the Question of the Day. Then use pp. 114–117.

Group Time Differentiated Instruction

Read *Shutting Out the Sky.* See pp. 112h–112i for the small group lesson plan.

Whole Group Use p. 133a.

Language Arts

Use pp. 133e–133k.

Words to Know

immigrants
circumstances
newcomer
advised
peddler
hustled
elbow
advice
luxury

Remember

Try the strategy. Then, if you need more help, use your glossary or dictionary.

Vocabulary Strategy for Multiple-Meaning Words

Context Clues Some words have more than one meaning. You can find clues in nearby words to decide which meaning the author is using.

1. Think about different meanings the word can hav
2. Reread the sentence where the word appears. Which meaning fits in the sentence?
3. If you can't tell, then look for more clues in nearb sentences.
4. Put the clues together and decide which meaning works best.

As you read "A New Job in America," use the conte and what you know about the vocabulary words to decide their meanings. For example, does *hustled* mean "hurried along" or "sold in a hurried way"?

114

Strategic Intervention

Context Clues Have students use context clues to determine the meaning of *sort* on p. 115. Explain that one meaning is "to categorize or arrange," but that is not the meaning in this selection.

Access Content Use ELL Poster 5 to preteach vocabulary. Choose from the following to meet language proficiency levels.

Beginning Read the sentence on p. 115 with the word *hustled*. Point out clues that show *hustled* does not mean "push roughly and hurriedly" but "to sell in a rough, hurried, or illegal manner."

Intermediate Have students create a web with people in the center and words that are related to people in the ovals around it.

Advanced Teach the lesson on pp. 114–115. Have students find home-language terms for some of the vocabulary words.

Resources for home-language words may include parents, bilingual staff members, bilingual dictionaries, or online translation sources.

A NEW JOB IN AMERICA

As immigrants came to America in the 1800s, many found themselves in difficult circumstances. What could a newcomer do to earn money? Often business owners would hire new immigrants only for low-paying jobs. Many immigrants must have worried that their decision to come here was not well advised.

However, there was one job that was wide open. They could peddle, or sell, goods in the streets. The peddler became a colorful figure in American history. On the crowded streets of cities, peddlers hustled items of every sort to people passing by. They would elbow their way into the crowd and announce their wares in a loud voice. Others packed things to sell on a horse or wagon and traveled West. Most settlers lived far from any town or store. They were happy to see someone coming with things they needed.

Picture the peddler with his odd mixture of goods spread out on a blanket. He gives advice to the women looking at his wares. This kind of needle is best. That sort of pot will last. He tries to convince them to buy some little luxury, such as a shiny set of combs for their hair. After the sale and maybe a meal, he goes on his way.

Words to Write

Pretend you are an immigrant who has just arrived in New York in 1900. Write a journal entry about what you see and how you feel. Use as many words from the Words to Know list as you can.

115

BEFORE READING

PRACTICE AND ASSESS

- Have students determine the meanings of the remaining words. Ask them to explain the context clues they used.
- Remind students that if the meanings they know for a word don't work in the context and the clues around the word don't help, they can consult a dictionary or glossary to find the correct meaning of the word.
- Have students look at the sentences they wrote (p. 114b) and assess whether or not they used the words correctly. Have them write new sentences using vocabulary words.
- Have students complete Practice Book p. 45.

WRITE Students' journal entries might include words such as *advised, peddler,* and *circumstances* from the lesson vocabulary to describe an experience as an immigrant.

Monitor Progress

Context Clues

If... students need more practice with the lesson vocabulary,	**then...** use Tested Vocabulary Cards.

Vocabulary • Context Clues

- Some words have more than one meaning. They are called **multiple-meaning words.**
- When you see a word you don't know, you may find a clue about the word's meaning in the words near the unknown word.

Directions Read the following passage. Then answer the questions below.

Cara had to elbow her way through the crowd to get close enough to see the stage. She wanted to get a spot with a good view before her brother's mariachi band played. Like most of the other latecomers, she was stuck at the back of the crowd. The judges had the luxury of folding chairs on a platform with a good view.

Even though she had hustled as quickly as she could, Cara could barely see. The only advice she could suggest for herself was to make the best of the jam she was in.

1. *Elbow* can mean "a part of the arm" or "to push." How do you think these two meanings are related to one another?
   You could use your elbow to push your way through a crowd.
2. A *band* can be "a group of musicians" or "a thin, flat strip of material." Which of these meanings is used in the second sentence? How do you know?
   "A group of musicians"; Cara wants to hear the band play.
3. *Luxury* can mean "use of the best and most costly food, clothes, houses, and amusements" or "something pleasant but not necessary." How is it used in this passage? How can you tell?
   "Something pleasant but not necessary"; A folding chair can't be described as the best and most costly.
4. *Hustled* can mean "pushed or shoved roughly" or "moved quickly or with energy." How is it used in this passage? How can you tell?
   "Moved quickly or with energy"; Cara moved quickly.
5. A *jam* can be "a thick preserve made of sugar and fruit' or "a difficult situation." Which of these meanings is used in the passage? How do you know?
   "A difficult situation"; Cara has to make the best of it.

School + Home **Home Activity** Your child identified words with multiple meanings in a fictional passage. With your child, make a list of words he or she uses that have different meanings.

▲ **Practice Book** p. 45

BEFORE READING

Prereading Strategies

OBJECTIVES

- Identify causes and effects to improve comprehension.
- Summarize to identify causes and effects.

GENRE STUDY

Expository Nonfiction

Shutting Out the Sky is expository nonfiction. Explain that expository nonfiction is informational text that tells a real-life story and attempts to explain the nature of a person, a thing, or an idea.

PREVIEW AND PREDICT

Have students preview the selection by discussing the photographs and reading the captions. Ask them to think about the title. When they hear "shutting out the sky," what are they reminded of and what do they predict the title describes? Have students use selection vocabulary words as they discuss their ideas.

Strategy Response Log

Predict Have students write their predictions in their strategy response logs. Students will check their predictions in the Strategy Response Log activity on p. 123.

Access Content Guide students in reading the captions and examining the pictures for details about the selection. Invite students to name other words they know that apply to the immigrant experience.

Consider having students read the selection summary in English or in students' home languages. See the Multilingual Summaries in the ELL Teaching Guide, pp. 33–35.

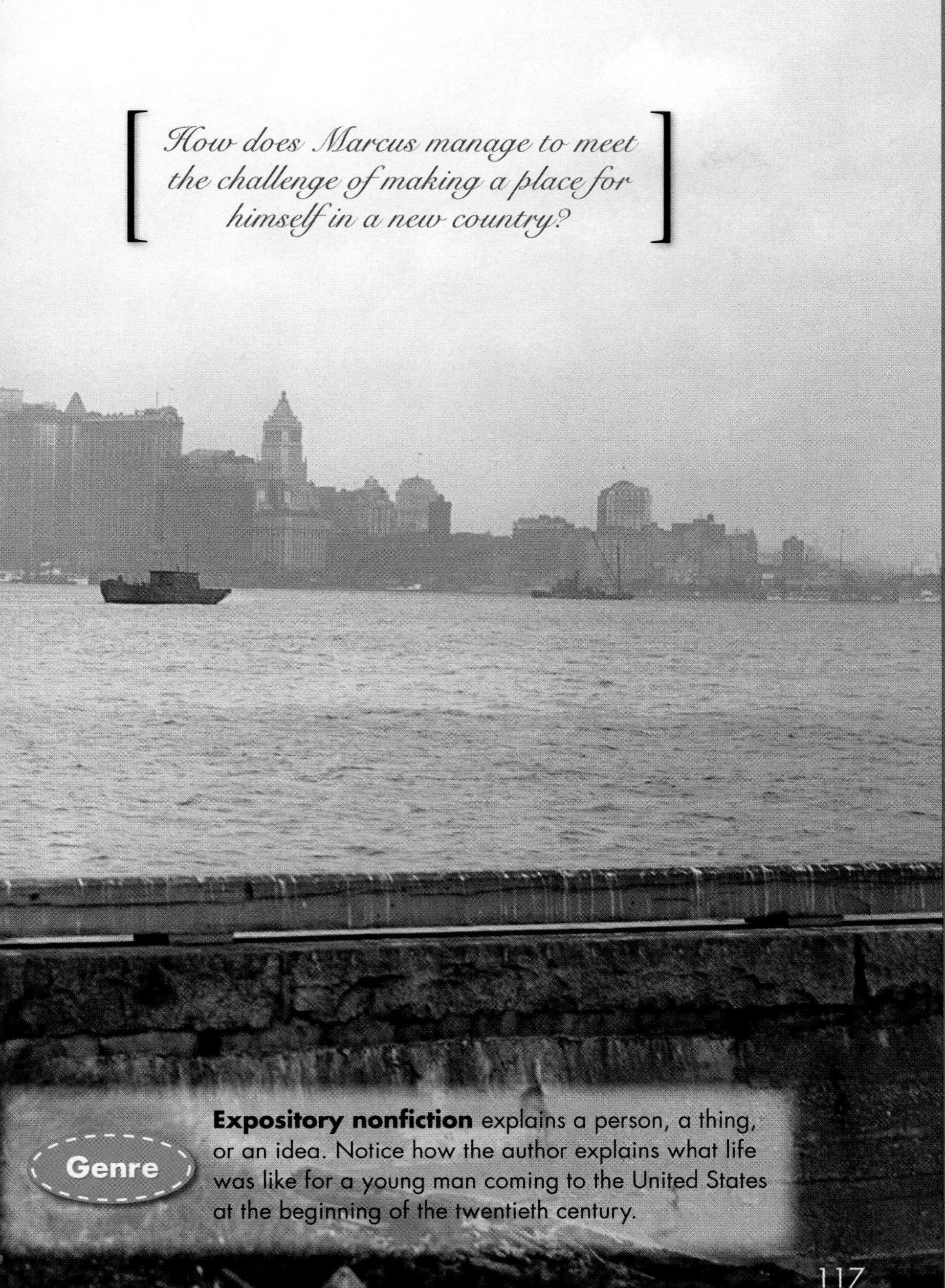

How does Marcus manage to meet the challenge of making a place for himself in a new country?
Genre
Expository nonfiction explains a person, a thing, or an idea. Notice how the author explains what life was like for a young man coming to the United States at the beginning of the twentieth century.
117

BEFORE READING

SET PURPOSE

Read the first page of the selection aloud to students. Have them consider their preview discussion and tell what they hope to find out as they read.

Remind students to look for causes and effects as they read.

STRATEGY RECALL

Students have now used these before-reading strategies:

- preview the selection to be aware of its genre, features, and possible content;
- activate prior knowledge about that content and what to expect of that genre;
- make predictions;
- set a purpose for reading.

Remind students to be aware of and flexibly use the during-reading strategies they have learned:

- link prior knowledge to new information;
- summarize text they have read so far;
- ask clarifying questions;
- answer questions they or others pose;
- check their predictions and either refine them or make new predictions;
- recognize the text structure the author is using, and use that knowledge to make predictions and increase comprehension;
- visualize what the author is describing;
- monitor their comprehension and use fix-up strategies.

After reading, students will use these strategies:

- summarize or retell the text;
- answer questions they or others pose;
- reflect to make new information become part of their prior knowledge.

AudioText

DURING READING

Guiding Comprehension

1 Cause and Effect • Critical
Text to World **Reread the headnote on p. 118. Aside from becoming crowded, how do you think the arrival of 23 million immigrants affected New York City?**

Answers will vary, but students should discuss resulting changes in foods, languages, customs, and religions of New York City.

Monitor Progress	
Cause and Effect	
If... students are unable to recognize cause and effect,	**then...** use the skill and strategy instruction on p. 119.

2 Details and Facts • Inferential
Which details about the Segals' apartment made Marcus feel they were rich?

Possible responses: Five-room apartment on the third floor, the sofa, kitchen table, and many chairs.

Students can learn more about the millions who immigrated to the United States in the late 1800s by typing the keywords *Ellis Island* into a student-friendly search engine. Be sure to follow classroom guidelines for Internet use.

1 *At the end of the nineteenth century, 23 million immigrants came to New York City from Europe. Marcus Ravage was one of them. Like many new immigrants, Marcus thought that he would soon be rich. He was about to learn that life in New York would be a lot harder than he thought.*

118

ELL

Build Background Tell students that a *tenement* is an apartment building made specifically for multiple working-class families. Explain that tenements were built in New York City from the mid-1800s until 1929. Until 1867, laws did not require developers to provide running water, gas, or adequate light and ventilation, so most early tenements did not have them.

RICH, OR POOR?

One early morning in December 1900, a sixteen-year-old boy left Ellis Island and made his way alone into New York City. Struggling with his heavy bundles, Marcus Ravage elbowed his way through the crowded streets of the Lower East Side.

Marcus shivered in the bitter cold. If only he'd followed his mother's advice and brought his heavy coat to America. He'd been so sure he wouldn't need it. After all, he'd argued, why should he bother carrying old clothes when he'd soon be rich enough to buy new ones!

But Marcus had brought something almost as precious as a warm coat, and with cold fingers he dug into his bundles to find it. It was just a crumpled bit of paper, but it was a link between his old life in Romania and his new one. On the paper was scribbled the New York address of distant relatives from back home.

Before long, Marcus found himself in the apartment of the Segal family, who had arrived from Romania just three months before. Mrs. Segal, along with her son and five daughters, lived in a five-room apartment on the third floor of a Rivington Street tenement. Looking around at the sofa, kitchen table, and ever so many chairs, Marcus felt sure that the Segals were already rich. And he wouldn't be far behind.

Mrs. Segal told Marcus he could stay for free for a few days. After that, he would be expected to find a job and pay fifty cents a week for his bed. With seven members of the Segal family plus him, the apartment would be crowded, Marcus thought, but it was better than being out on the street.

119

Tenement Museum

Time for SOCIAL STUDIES

The Lower East Side Tenement Museum, which opened in New York City in 1988, is in an original tenement building that was boarded up in 1935. The building was restored, but everything found inside was left intact. The mission of the museum is to both preserve the history of the urban immigrants and working-class people who came to this country, and to promote tolerance and understanding of other cultures and our shared American heritage.

SKILLS ↔ STRATEGIES IN CONTEXT

Cause and Effect

TEACH

- Remind students that a *cause* is why something happened and an *effect* is what happened as a result.
- Clue words such as *because, so,* and *since* can signal a cause-effect relationship.
- Model recognizing a cause-effect relationship on p. 119, paragraph 2.

MODEL In the second paragraph, I see that "Marcus shivered in the bitter cold." In the next sentence, I see that he didn't bring his heavy coat to America. This is an example of cause and effect. Marcus left his heavy coat at home (cause), so he shivers in the cold (effect).

PRACTICE AND ASSESS

Have students read these three statements. Ask them to identify the causes *(Choices a, b)* and the effect *(Choice c)*.

a) Marcus has no money.

b) Marcus is hungry.

c) Marcus is sad and frightened.

DURING READING

Guiding Comprehension

3 **Sequence • Literal**

Name in order three things that have happened to Marcus in the selection thus far.

Possible responses: First, Marcus arrives in New York City. Next, he goes to live with Mrs. Segal. Last, he finds out she has many boarders in her apartment.

Monitor Progress	
REVIEW **Sequence**	
If... students have difficulty sequencing the events so far,	**then...** use the skill and strategy instruction on p. 121.

4 **Compare and Contrast • Inferential**

Compare and contrast Marcus to the boarders at this point in the story.

Like the boarders, Marcus is new to the city and needs a place to stay. Unlike the boarders, he stays in Mrs. Segal's apartment for free.

5 **Simile • Inferential**

Question the Author **The phrase "huddling like seals on a rock" is an example of a simile. Why do you think the author used this feature?**

Possible response: It makes it easier for the reader to "see" what the scene looks like.

Immigrants at Ellis Island (right)

3 That evening, people Marcus had never seen before began to stream into the apartment, tired from a long day of work. *Who were all these strangers?* Marcus thought. As the hours ticked by and the strangers didn't leave, Marcus realized they were boarders—they lived there too! They paid Mrs. Segal for a bed, **4** and perhaps for meals and laundry. *Where would everyone sleep?* he wondered.

Marcus soon found out. It wasn't long before everyone began to rush about, lining up chairs in rows to make beds. Marcus and three other young men shared the sofa, sleeping with their heads on the cushions and feet propped awkwardly on chairs. Nine bodies pressed together on the floor, huddling like seals on a rock. In the **5** kitchen, Mrs. Segal and one child cuddled on top of the washtubs while the rest of the children slept on the floor. And the room Marcus thought was the children's bedroom? A family of five had taken it over.

Immigrant family in a crowded apartment

120

ELL

Extend Language Point to the word *boarders* and have students repeat it. Explain that *boarders* are people who pay for food and lodging in someone else's home. Tell students that *borders* means "lines or places where one area ends and another begins." Explain that the words sound the same but have different spellings and meanings.

SKILLS ↔ STRATEGIES IN CONTEXT

Sequence REVIEW

TEACH

- Remind students that sequence refers to the order of events.
- Time order is a way of organizing text. Dates, times of day, and other clue words can help determine time order.
- To model the strategy, sequence the events from p. 120, paragraph 1.

Think Aloud **MODEL** As I read, I'll look for clues that suggest the time order of the events. The clue words "that evening," "the long day," and "the hours ticked by" suggest that the people stayed long after they streamed into the apartment.

PRACTICE AND ASSESS

- Have students reread p. 120, paragraph 1 and 2. Ask in what order these events took place. *(c, b, a)*
  a) People slept wherever they could.
  b) Chairs were lined up in rows to make beds.
  c) People streamed into the apartment.
- To assess, use Practice Book p. 46.

Sequence

Directions Read the passage. Then answer the questions below.

Mike Nee came to America in 1927. He was 21 years old and had spent his entire life on the west coast of Ireland. Once in America, he found work with the local gas company. He was young, strong, and a tireless worker. Within a couple of years, he was able to buy himself a house. Soon after that, he met Ellen, who was also from Ireland. They married in 1932 and hoped to have a large family just like the ones they grew up in. They had many struggles in their first years of marriage. But they were determined to share the good life in their new country with children of their own. After many years, Mike and Ellen welcomed their daughter Mary into the world in 1943. There truly couldn't have been two happier parents.

1. When did Mike Nee come to America?
   Mike came to America in 1927.
2. How many years passed after coming to America before Mike and Ellen got married?
   They got married five years later.
3. Which did Mike do first—get married or buy a house?
   He bought a house first.
4. How many years passed between Mike and Ellen's marriage and the birth of their daughter?
   Eleven years passed before their daughter was born.
5. How old was Mike when he became a father?
   Mike was 37 years old when he became a father.

School + Home **Home Activity** Your child has read a short passage and answered questions about the sequence of events. Together, read one of your child's favorite stories and discuss the sequence in which events in the story occur.

▲ **Practice Book** p. 46

DURING READING

Guiding Comprehension

6 Author's Craft • Inferential

Question the Author **Why do you think the author wrote, "Soon the rooms were filled with deep breathing, dreadful snoring, and smells of all kinds"?**

Possible response: Phrases like *deep breathing, dreadful snoring,* and *smells of all kinds* help us "hear" and "see" the action the author describes.

7 Vocabulary • Context Clues

What is the meaning of *fine* in paragraph 2 on p. 123? What other meaning could this word have?

On p. 123, *fine* means "of very high quality" because it's talking about the nice apartment. Another meaning for *fine* is "thin or slender," like a fine-tooth comb.

Monitor Progress

Context Clues

If... students have difficulty finding multiple meanings for the word,	**then...** use vocabulary strategy instruction on p. 123.

6 Soon the rooms were filled with deep breathing, dreadful snoring, and smells of all kinds. Yet despite his new, strange circumstances, Marcus fell asleep right away. Next morning he woke to the puffing of steam engines and clatter of wheels outside the windows. Once again the rooms hummed with activity. People raced to put the furniture back into place; the men scrambled to get dressed before the girls awoke. Mrs. Segal crammed extra feather beds into nooks and crannies and made coffee.

After everyone else had hurried off to work or school, Marcus and Mrs. Segal were left alone in the now neat and tidy apartment. Since Marcus was still considered a guest, Mrs. Segal wouldn't hear of him helping with the housework or marketing. He was thoroughly surprised to see Mrs. Segal clean the kitchen floor with precious soap rather than sand, as his mother would have back home.

When Mrs. Segal came back from the market, Marcus felt more confused then ever. She'd brought the largest eggplant (which some immigrants called a "blue tomato") he'd ever seen, as well as an

Fruit and vegetable stand in New York City

122

Access Content Recite the phrase "crammed extra feather beds into nooks and crannies." Explain that *crammed* means "forced into a crowded space" and *nooks* and *crannies* are "tiny corners or openings." Ask if students have ever crammed things into tiny places in their homes.

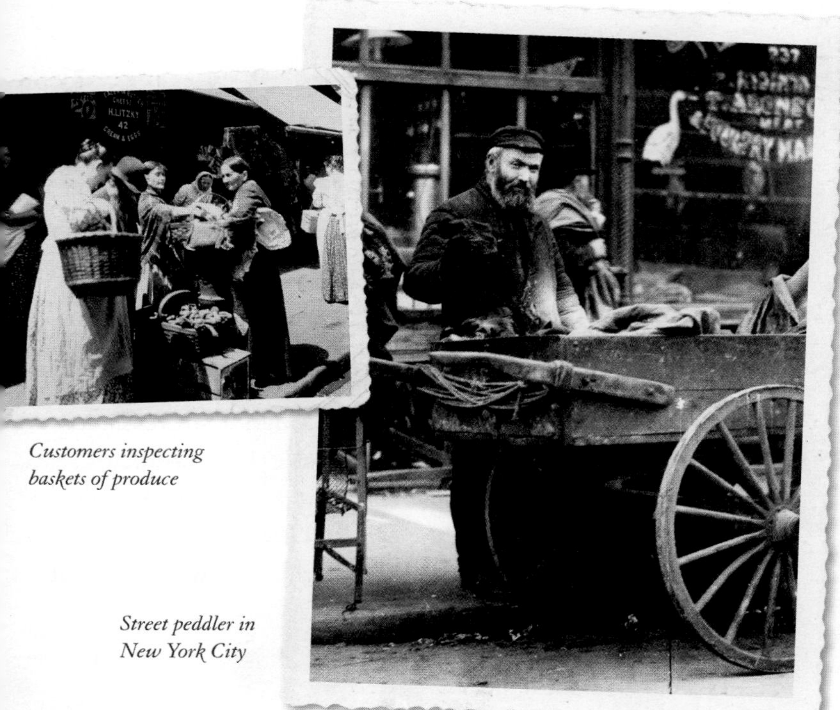
Customers inspecting baskets of produce

Street peddler in New York City

exotic yellow fruit in the shape of a cucumber—a banana. And then there was a cauliflower, a vegetable his father had eaten only once in a big city and had talked about ever since. To say nothing of meat—which she cooked for lunch!

Back home in his village only rich people could indulge in the luxury of meat in the middle of the day, eat such extraordinary vegetables, use soap instead of sand to clean floors, or live on the second floor of such a nice apartment.

But, Marcus puzzled, if the Segals were rich, if they had *already* made their million dollars in three months, why did they share their fine apartment with so many borders? 7

To a newcomer, or "greenhorn" like Marcus, it was all very confusing.

123

Develop Vocabulary

PRACTICE LESSON VOCABULARY

Students orally respond *yes* or *no* to each question and provide a reason for each answer.

1. **Does *hustled* mean pushed around?** *(No; hustled means selling aggressively in order to make money.)*
2. **Are the Segals *immigrants?*** *(Yes; they arrived from Romania three months before Marcus.)*
3. **Were the people in Marcus's village used to *luxury?*** *(No; only rich people could afford big apartments.)*

BUILD CONCEPT VOCABULARY

Review previous concept words with students. Ask if students have come across any words today in their reading that they would like to add to the Life in a New Country Concept Web, such as *boarders* and *crowded.*

VOCABULARY STRATEGY

Context Clues

TEACH

Read paragraph 2 on p. 123. Model using context clues to determine the correct meaning of *fine*.

Think Aloud

MODEL The first sentence in the paragraph contains the words *rich* and *million dollars*. The word *fine* in the next sentence has multiple meanings such as, "of very high quality," "very small or thin," or "a sum of money paid as a punishment for breaking the law." Because the paragraph has to do with Marcus puzzling out whether or not the Segals are rich, I assume that in this case, *fine* means "of very high quality."

PRACTICE AND ASSESS

Have students use context clues to determine the meaning of *luxury* in paragraph 1. *(Clues: rich people* and *extraordinary. Meaning: really special, expensive things)*

Strategy Response Log

Confirm Predictions Provide the following prompt: Was your earlier prediction accurate? (See p. 116.) Revise your old prediction or write a new one about the rest of the story.

EXTEND SKILLS

Parentheses

Often an author will add factual information to a story by using parentheses. The information inside these punctuation marks is interesting, but not of primary importance to the sentence. It is included to increase the reader's background knowledge. Have students explain why the author uses parentheses in paragraph 3 on p. 122 when talking about Mrs. Segal's eggplant.

If you want to teach this selection in two sessions, stop here.

DAY 3

Guiding Comprehension

If you are teaching the selection in two days, discuss the cause-effect relationships so far and review the vocabulary.

8 **Cause and Effect • Inferential**
Why did Marcus take a job as a peddler?
Mrs. Segal tells him he must earn his keep. She tells him to be a peddler like others.

Monitor Progress
Cause and Effect

If... students have difficulty recognizing cause and effect,	**then...** use the skill and strategy instruction on p. 125.

9 **Draw Conclusions • Inferential**
How does Marcus feel about becoming a peddler?
He feels ashamed; he thinks it might be beneath him.

10 **Draw Conclusions • Inferential**
Marcus paid for two boxes of chocolates. How will he make money selling them?
He will sell the chocolates for more money than what he paid for them.

DAY 3 Grouping Options

Reading
Whole Group Discuss the Question of the Day.

Group Time Differentiated Instruction
Read *Shutting Out the Sky.* See pp. 112h–112i for the small group lesson plan.

Whole Group Discuss the Reader Response questions on p. 128. Then use p. 133a.

Language Arts
Use pp. 133e–133k.

MARCUS THE PEDDLER

Sixteen-year-old Marcus Ravage was in trouble. No matter how he tried, he couldn't find a job. But Mrs. Segal, his relative (and now landlady), didn't seem to think he was trying quite hard enough. It 8 was time he began to earn his keep, she told him firmly. After all, he was sleeping in her apartment and eating her food.

Mrs. Segal gave Marcus a dollar and pushed him out onto the street to get started as a peddler. This was America, she reminded him, where "everyone hustled, and nearly everybody peddled."

9 Marcus was ashamed and nervous at the same time. A lowly peddler! This certainly wasn't the way he'd imagined his start in America. He'd been so sure he could get rich right away. But what other choice did he have?

So Marcus took Mrs. Segal's dollar and one of her nice brass trays to Orchard Street. There he bought two boxes of chocolates. Open- 10 ing the boxes, he arranged the candy pieces on the tray. Now he was in business.

Marcus stood on a busy corner trying to catch the attention of the crowds rushing off to work. Marcus shivered. More than ever, he wished he'd brought his heavy winter coat.

A busy market

Boys selling newspapers (right)

124

ELL

Access Content Tell students that "to earn his keep" means to earn money to support himself. Ask students what Marcus finally does to earn his keep and how Mrs. Segal helps him.

SKILLS ↔ STRATEGIES IN CONTEXT

Cause/Effect Summarize

TEACH

Read aloud p. 124. Have students take turns summarizing what has happened up to this point. Model how to use the summary to explore cause and effect in the story.

Think Aloud **MODEL** I understand that Marcus is new to the country. He needs money, so he has to find a job. The cause is he needs money, and the effect is he has to find a job.

PRACTICE AND ASSESS

Have students work in pairs to summarize paragraph 3 on p. 124 and talk about what caused Marcus to feel ashamed and nervous.

EXTEND SKILLS

Stereotype

A stereotype is an oversimplified idea about a person or a group of people. A stereotype is judged on certain familiar traits that cause him or her to be seen as a member of a certain group but not judged on any other traits that might cause him or her to be seen as an individual. On page 124, for example, Mrs. Segal claims that all Americans "hustled, and nearly everybody peddled." But Marcus thinks peddlers are a lowly shameful group. Have students look for other examples of stereotyping in *Shutting Out the Sky*.

Time for SOCIAL STUDIES

Ellis Island

In 1952, Ellis Island was closed and declared excess Federal Property. Thirteen years later, in 1965, President Lyndon B. Johnson directed that Ellis Island be added to the Statue of Liberty National Monument. As a result, it became open to the public on a limited basis. Starting in 1984, Ellis Island underwent a $160 million restoration—the largest historic restoration in U.S. history. Today, almost 2 million people visit Ellis Island each year.

DURING READING

Guiding Comprehension

11 Graphic Sources • Critical
How do the photographs help set the mood of the story?
The photographs are dark and grim. They match Marcus's feelings about New York City throughout most of the story.

12 Compare and Contrast • Critical
How is the Marcus at the end of the story different from the Marcus we met at the beginning of the story?
At the end, he is happy and encouraged, unlike the beginning, when he was scared and discouraged. At the end of the story, he buys himself dinner and feels that he is "on his way."

13 Compare and Contrast • Critical
Text to Self **Think about a time you went through a new or difficult change in your life. What happened? How did you feel?**
Work with students to compare their experiences and feelings to those of Marcus.

Strategy Response Log

Summarize When students finish reading the selection, provide this prompt: Tell a friend what *Shutting Out the Sky* is about in four or five sentences.

11

A policeman and a dog

A policeman chased him to another corner, where a boy ran by and tried to spill all his chocolates as a joke. And still, every person brushed by him without buying a thing. As the minutes went by, Marcus became even more cold and miserable. How could he face Mrs. Segal? Would she kick him out?

After about two hours, Marcus noticed the streets beginning to fill with pushcarts and other peddlers. Marcus later remembered "peddlers with pushcarts and peddlers with boxes, peddlers with movable stands and peddlers with baskets, peddlers with bundles, with pails, with satchels and suitcases and trunks. . . . They came pouring in from all directions—men with white beards, old women draped in fantastic shawls, boys with piping voices, young mothers with babes in their arms."

A man selling tablecloths nearby called out, "How is business?"

Context Clues Use gestures and facial expressions to convey the meaning of *astonished,* as you say, "I'm astonished." Read aloud the sentence in paragraph 2, p. 127 with the word *astonishment.* Guide students in using the context of the paragraph and your pantomime to tell what it means *(great surprise or amazement).*

Marcus shook his head sadly. He hadn't made a single sale. As it happened, the man was also from Romania, and he took Marcus under his wing, "Move along, elbow your way through the crowds in front of the stores, seek out the women with kids; shove your tray into their faces," the older man advised. "Don't be timid. . . . And yell, never stop yelling: 'Candy, ladies! Finest in America. Only a nickel, a half-a-dime, five cents.'"

Then it was Marcus's turn to try. To his astonishment and delight, it began to work. His candy started to sell! By the end of the day, Marcus was glowing with pride.

That night Marcus went to a Romanian restaurant on Allen Street. For ten cents, he ordered the first meal he'd ever paid for in America: pot roast with mashed potatoes and gravy and a dish of chopped eggplant with olive oil. While he ate, Marcus counted his earnings: seventy cents, not counting the chocolates he had eaten himself.

Marcus was on his way.

Boys playing marbles

12

Marcus Ravage quickly made friends with other Romanian immigrants and started feeling at home in the United States. Later, he got a better job at a tailor shop and went to school at night. Nine years after coming to America, Marcus graduated from the University of Missouri and became a journalist and writer. He died in 1965 at the age of 81.

127

STRATEGY SELF-CHECK

Summarize

Have students list the causes and effects in the story. Students can use these events to write a summary. Encourage them to paraphrase, or use their own words, for their summary. Use Practice Book p. 47.

SELF-CHECK

Students can ask themselves these questions to assess their ability to use the skill and strategy.

- Did I identify causes and effects as I read *Shutting Out the Sky?*
- Was I able to summarize story events in my own words?
- Did I think about the effects these events had on Marcus and others?

Monitor Progress

Summarize Text

If... students have difficulty summarizing events,	**then...** use the Reteach lesson on p. 133b.

Cause and Effect

- A **cause** is what makes something happen. An **effect** is what happens as a result of the cause.
- An effect may have more than one cause, and a cause may have more than one effect.

Directions Read the following passage. Then answer the questions below.

In the early part of the twentieth century, there were a large number of immigrants who came to the United States. Many people came from eastern European countries like Poland, Italy, and Russia. Because large U.S. cities offered an easier transition into American culture many ethnic neighborhoods developed in major cities. These cities offered jobs and public transportation was widespread. Immigrants were able to be near other relatives who'd moved to the U.S., and a community of familiar languages and customs was welcoming to newcomers. These areas where immigrants settled helped define the neighborhoods that became a part of big cities like Chicago, New York, and Boston.

Possible answers given.

1. What were the nationalities of many immigrants in the early twentieth Century?
   Polish, Italian, and Russian
2. What features of big cities appealed to immigrants?
   These cities offered jobs and public transportation was widespread.
3. What do you think happened to the population in big cities during this time? What do you think was the cause of this effect?
   The population of the big cities increased; Many immigrants moved into the city in a short amount of time.
4. How were the immigrants' cultural backgrounds preserved in the new country?
   Immigrants shared languages and other customs.
5. Write a summary of the passage in one or two sentences.
   New immigrants to the U.S. in the early twentieth century preserved their cultural backgrounds by creating ethnic neighborhoods in large cities.

School + Home **Home Activity** Your child read a short passage and answered questions about cause and effect. Read an article about your city or a neighborhood where you live. See if you can identify some of the reasons why your city or neighborhood is the way that it is.

▲ **Practice Book** p. 47

Develop Vocabulary

PRACTICE LESSON VOCABULARY

Students orally respond *true* or *false* to each question. If *false,* then students should provide a reason for their answers.

1. When you want to know someone's opinion about something, you ask for his or her advice. *(True)*
2. A *newcomer* is someone who is always late. *(False: A newcomer is someone who has just arrived.)*
3. *Hustled* means pushed away. *(False: Hustled means worked quickly or with energy.)*

BUILD CONCEPT VOCABULARY

Review previous concept words with students. Ask if students have come across any words today in their reading that they would like to add to the Life in a New Country Concept Web, such as *keep* and *nervous.*

Reader Response

Open for Discussion Personal Response

MODEL If I were Marcus I would not want my family and friends back home to worry. I'd write that I am okay, but that life in America is challenging.

Comprehension Check Critical Response

1. Possible response: The author might have researched Ellis Island, used the Internet, or interviewed some of Marcus's relatives. ***Author's Purpose***
2. Possible response: He was surprised by the cold, the crowded apartment, and how hard it was to find a job. ***Cause and Effect***
3. Possible response: He takes a dollar from Mrs. Segal and buys chocolate to sell. ***Summarize***
4. Possible response: Marcus's mother *advised* him to bring a heavy coat. Marcus might have *advised* other *immigrants* to copy the way he *hustled* to find a job. ***Vocabulary***

Look Back and Write For test practice, assign a 10–15 minute time limit. For assessment, see the Scoring Rubric at the right.

Retell

Have students retell *Shutting Out the Sky*.

Monitor Progress

Check Retelling Rubric 4 3 2 1

If... students have difficulty retelling the selection,	**then...** use the Retelling Cards and the Scoring Rubric for Retelling on p. 129 to assist fluent retelling.

SUCCESS PREDICTOR

Check Retelling Model retelling for students by talking about the photograph on pp. 116–117. Then have students use the photographs and the headings to retell the selection. For more ideas on assessing students' retellings, see the ELL and Transition Handbook.

Reader Response

Open for Discussion If Marcus wrote home to Romania, what would he say? Would he tell all or only the bright side? If you were Marcus, what would you write? Why?

1. The author isn't making up Marcus; he really lived. How do you think the author got her information about him? List three possible ways. **Think Like an Author**
2. Several surprises greet Marcus on his arrival in New York City. What are three things that surprise him and why? Look back at pages 119–123 to find answers. **Cause and Effect**
3. What steps does Marcus take to start earning a living? Look back at pages 124–127 to summarize his progress. **Summarize**
4. What advice did Marcus's mother give him when he came to America? What other advice do you think he might have for newcomers? Use words from the Words to Know list to tell about it. **Vocabulary**

Look Back and Write Marcus the peddler got some advice. What was it, who gave it, and how did it work? After rereading pages 126–127, write the answer in your own words.

Meet author **Deborah Hopkinson on page 767.**

128

Scoring Rubric Look Back and Write

Top-Score Response A top-score response will use details from pp. 126–127 to identify a tablecloth salesman as the person who gave Marcus advice, to explain the advice, and to tell how it helped Marcus succeed.

Example of a Top-Score Response A tablecloth peddler sees that Marcus is not selling anything. He advises him to be more aggressive. He tells Marcus to elbow his way through the crowd, yell, and push his wares in the faces of women with kids. Marcus finds that this method works, and he is able to sell all his candy.

For additional rubrics, see p. WA10.

Write Now

Narrative Writing

Prompt

Shutting Out the Sky tells about a boy's experiences in a new country. Think about an experience that was meaningful to you. Now write a narrative about that experience.

Writing Trait

Specific, vivid **word choice** makes your writing clear, colorful, and interesting.

Student Model

Beginning draws readers in and states topic.

When you watch fireworks, have you ever noticed how those sparkly lights look as if they are going to land right next to you? One time I was close enough to see that happen!

Details explain how situation came to be and create hint of suspense.

My dad is a photographer. He got permission to take pictures where the fireworks are set up, and he let me go with him. We waited behind a concrete barrier for the show to begin.

Word choice shows rather than tells what happens.

Suddenly, there were bright flashes, soft booms, and sharp crackles. The sky above us glowed and twinkled as smoke drifted slowly along the ground. I will never forget watching that fireworks show up close.

Use the model to help you write your own narrative.

Write Now

Look at the Prompt Have students identify and discuss key words and phrases in the prompt. *(experience, meaningful to you, narrative)*

Strategies to Develop Word Choice

Have students

- make lists of describing words for their topic, one for each of the five senses.
- brainstorm descriptions and comparisons about their topic with a partner.
- replace weak verbs with strong ones.

NO: James walked into the room.
YES: James swaggered into the room.

For additional suggestions and rubric, see pp. 133g–133h.

Hints for Better Writing

- Carefully read the prompt.
- Use a graphic organizer to plan your writing.
- Support your ideas with information and details.
- Use words that help readers understand.
- Proofread and edit your work.

Scoring Rubric Expository Retelling

Rubric 4|3|2|1	4	3	2	1
Connections	Makes connections and generalizes beyond the text	Makes connections to other events, texts, or experiences	Makes a limited connection to another event, text, or experience	Makes no connection to another event, text, or experience
Author's Purpose	Elaborates on author's purpose	Tells author's purpose with some clarity	Makes some connection to author's purpose	Makes no connection to author's purpose
Topic	Describes the main topic	Identifies the main topic with some details early in retelling	Identifies the main topic	Retelling has no sense of topic
Important Ideas	Gives accurate information about events, steps, and ideas using details and key vocabulary	Gives accurate information about events, steps, and ideas with some detail and key vocabulary	Gives limited or inaccurate information about events, steps, and ideas	Gives no information about events, steps, and ideas
Conclusions	Draws conclusions and makes inferences to generalize beyond the text	Draws conclusions about the text	Is able to draw few conclusions about the text	Is unable to draw conclusions or make inferences about the text

Retelling Plan

- ☑ **Week 1** Assess Strategic Intervention students.
- ☑ **Week 2** Assess Advanced students.
- ☑ **Week 3** Assess Strategic Intervention students.
- ☑ **Week 4** Assess On-Level students.
- ☑ **This week assess any students you have not yet checked during this unit.**

Use the Retelling Chart on p. TR17 to record retelling.

Selection Test To assess with *Shutting Out the Sky*, use Selection Tests, pp. 17–20.

Fresh Reads for Differentiated Test Practice For weekly leveled practice, use pp. 25–30.

DAY 4

Reading Online

OBJECTIVES

- Examine the features of e-mail.
- Compare and contrast across texts.

PREVIEW/USE TEXT FEATURES

Have students preview "The Immigrant Experience." Ask:

- **What information goes in the box labeled *To:* on p. 131?** *(The address of the person to whom the e-mail is being sent.)*
- **What are the purposes of the buttons above the address box?** *(They allow you to send the e-mail, attach a file, and access the address book.)*

If students have trouble identifying e-mail features, use the Technology Tools Box below.

Link to Social Studies

Have students work in pairs or groups to brainstorm project ideas. Remind them to use formal, polite language when writing e-mails to organizations.

DAY 4 Grouping Options

Reading

Whole Group Discuss the Question of the Day.

Group Time Differentiated Instruction

Read "The Immigrant Experience." See pp. 112h–112i for the small group lesson plan.

Whole Group Use p. 133a.

Language Arts

Use pp. 133e–133k.

Reading Online

New Literacies: PearsonSuccessNet.com

E-mail

Genre

- **E-mail is short for "electronic mail"—messages sent over the Internet from one computer user to another.**
- **You can e-mail certain Web sites to gather information for school projects.**

Text Features

- **The address box gives vital information.**
- **The message looks like the body of a friendly letter.**

Link to Social Studies

Imagine that you want to contact the tenement museum for information about a school project. Think of what this project might be, and make up an e-mail you might send.

The Immigrant Experience

To gather facts for a school report, Rachel gets on the Internet and visits the Web site of the Lower East Side Tenement Museum in New York City. At the site, she finds an e-mail address to contact for more information.

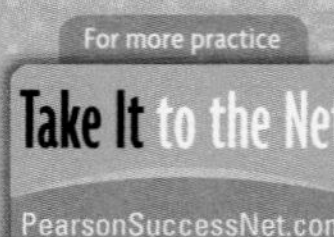

For more practice
Take It to the Net
PearsonSuccessNet.com

130

TECHNOLOGY TOOLS

E-MAIL

To: The e-mail address of the person you are writing to goes here. Use the **Cc:** box to send copies of your letter to other e-mail addresses if you wish.

Subject: In a few words, tell what you are writing about.

Click *Attach* to attach a file (such as a word processing document or a picture) to your e-mail.

Click *Send* to send your message. This step is the last thing you do when sending e-mail.

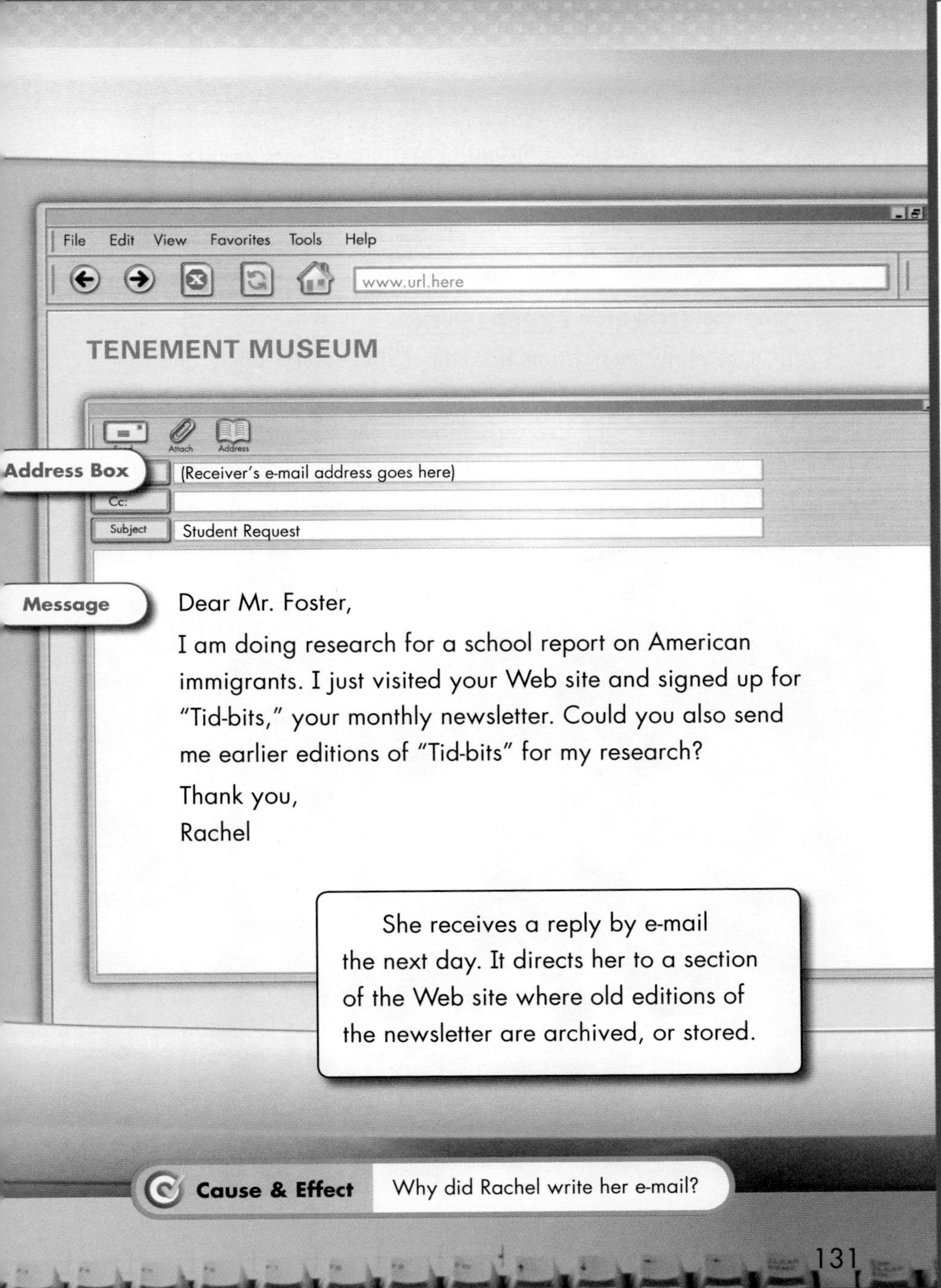

File Edit View Favorites Tools Help
www.url.here
TENEMENT MUSEUM
Address Box
(Receiver's e-mail address goes here)
Cc:
Subject
Student Request
Message
Dear Mr. Foster,
I am doing research for a school report on American immigrants. I just visited your Web site and signed up for "Tid-bits," your monthly newsletter. Could you also send me earlier editions of "Tid-bits" for my research?
Thank you,
Rachel
She receives a reply by e-mail the next day. It directs her to a section of the Web site where old editions of the newsletter are archived, or stored.
Cause & Effect
Why did Rachel write her e-mail?
131

WEB-IQUETTE

E-mail

Tell students that while e-mail is a quick and efficient way to exchange information, there are rules of etiquette they should follow:

- Remember your audience. There is a big difference between writing a quick e-mail to a friend and writing to an adult to ask for information for school.
- If you receive an e-mail message from a friend or trusted adult, reply promptly.
- Do not open, read, or respond to e-mail from addresses you don't recognize.

NEW LITERACIES: E-MAIL

Use the sidebar on p. 130 to guide discussion.

- E-mail—"electronic mail"—makes the trip from one computer to another in a very short time and is used for both personal and business correspondence.
- Tell students e-mail can be written in a variety of formats, depending on the audience. Here, Rachel writes a business letter asking for information. Ask how this e-mail is different from an e-mail someone might send to a friend.
- Discuss with students how they could use e-mail to get information. Have students name places they could send e-mails to gather information for projects.

AudioText

Cause and Effect

Possible response: She figured the museum newsletter would have information she could use in her report, so she asked Mr. Foster to send her earlier editions of the publication.

Access Content Preview the text with students, reading titles aloud. Point out that the screen on p. 131 depicts e-mail, while the illustrations on pp. 132 and 133 show a Web site. Explain these terms if necessary.

Strategies for Navigation

USE FOLDERS Explain to students that using folders in their e-mail accounts is a lot like using paper folders at home or at school to organize assignments and information. When using folders in e-mail, students should label them according to the topic, date, sender of the e-mail, or the type of e-mail that they are receiving. Tech-savvy students can set up their e-mail accounts so e-mail will be entered directly into the appropriate folders when it is received.

Use the Strategy

1. The next time you are using your e-mail account, look for information on how to create, name, and use folders.
2. When you send or receive an e-mail, save or drag it into the correctly named folder.
3. Then, when you are looking for an e-mail message, it will be easy to find.

PRACTICE Think about the ways you use e-mail at home and at school.

Make a list of folders that you could create in your e-mail inbox.

The next time you access your e-mail account, try adding a folder. Don't forget to name it.

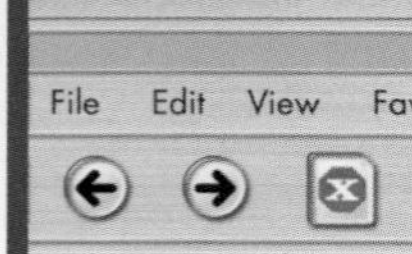

File Edit View Fa

Rachel looks through the archived newsletters and sees this article. She finds it useful for her report. She also finds it surprising.

THE IMMIGRANT EXPERIENCE

Like many immigrants from the 19th century, Emily Zhou's father left his home and family to seek prosperity in America. Once he settled in New York, though, Mr. Zhou could only find low-paying, menial jobs: he worked twelve hour days for $20 in the basement of a Chinese restaurant.

132

Guided Practice If time allows, have students log onto the Internet. Show them how to make a folder in an e-mail account. Help students make connections between the steps they are doing and related vocabulary terms.

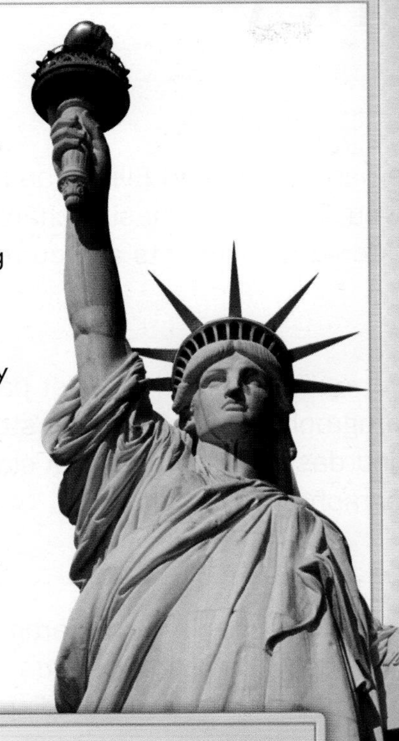

Though he longed to return home, Mr. Zhou was deeply in debt and could not leave America. So, Mrs. Zhou joined her husband in New York City, leaving young Emily in the care of her grandparents. Emily did not see her parents for nearly a decade, finally reuniting with her family in New York when she was eighteen.

However, the Zhous are not immigrants from the 19th or early 20th centuries: Emily and her family are part of the recent surge of immigrants to New York City. Indeed, 37% of New Yorkers were born in another country.

Reading Across Texts

Compare this newsletter article with what you read in *Shutting Out the Sky*. How are the situations of Mr. Zhou today and Marcus Savage one-hundred plus years ago similar?

Writing Across Texts Write your response in a paragraph.

Summarize What steps did Rachel follow to get her information?

133

DURING READING

CONNECT TEXT TO TEXT

Reading Across Texts

Discuss the similarities and differences between Marcus Ravage and Mr. Zhou. Focus on dates, places, ages, jobs and wages, family situations, and other facts.

Have students make a two-column chart to record the information.

Writing Across Texts Before writing, students may want to reorder the facts in their two-column charts so the attributes such as dates and ages appear across from one another.

Summarize

Rachel found a logical place on the Internet where she could gather information about immigrants to America. Then, she signed up for an e-mail newsletter and sent an e-mail to Mr. Foster asking for earlier editions. Finally, she looked at the newsletters and found information for her project.

DAY 5

Fluency Assessment Plan

- ☑ **Week 1** Assess Advanced students.
- ☑ **Week 2** Assess Strategic Intervention students.
- ☑ **Week 3** Assess On-Level students.
- ☑ **Week 4** Assess Strategic Intervention students.
- ☑ **This week assess any students you have not yet checked during this unit.**

Set individual goals for students to enable them to reach the year-end goal.

- Current Goal: 105–110 wcpm
- Year-End Goal: 140 wcpm

Provide opportunities for students to read one-on-one with an aide or parent volunteer, if possible. The adult models by reading first, and the child reads and rereads the same text, with adult guidance. Allow extra repetitions for English language learners, to improve their fluency.

To develop fluent readers, use Fluency Coach.

DAY 5 Grouping Options

Reading
Whole Group
Revisit the Question of the Week.

Group Time
Differentiated Instruction
Reread this week's Leveled Readers. See pp. 112h–112i for the small group lesson plan.

Whole Group
Use p. 133b–133c.

Language Arts
Use pp. 133d–133l.

PAUSES

Fluency

DAY 1

Model Reread "Journey to Ellis Island" on p. 112m. Explain that you will pause as you read to emphasize characters' feelings and the mood of the story. Model for students as you read.

DAY 2

Echo Reading Read aloud the last paragraph on pp. 122–123 and the first full paragraph on p. 123. Have students notice how you pause at commas and dashes. Practice as a class by doing three echo readings of these paragraphs.

DAY 3

Model Read aloud the first two paragraphs on p. 127. Have students listen for pauses at commas, periods, and colons. Have students practice as a class by doing three echo readings.

DAY 4

Partner Reading Partners practice reading the first two paragraphs on p. 127, three times. Students should read with appropriate pauses and offer each other feedback.

Monitor Progress — Check Fluency WCPM

As students reread, monitor their progress toward their individual fluency goals. Current Goal: 105–110 words correct per minute. End-of-Year Goal: 140 words correct per minute.

If... students cannot read fluently at a rate of 105–110 words correct per minute,
then... make sure students practice with text at their independent level. Provide additional fluency practice, pairing nonfluent readers with fluent readers.

If... students already read at 140 words correct per minute,
then... they do not need to reread three to four times.

SUCCESS PREDICTOR

DAY 5

Assessment
Individual Reading Rate Use the Fluency Assessment Plan and do a one-minute timed reading of either selection from this week to assess students in Week 5. Pay special attention to this week's skill, pauses. Provide corrective feedback for each student.

RETEACH

Cause and Effect

TEACH

Review the definitions of *cause* and *effect* on p. 112. Students can complete Practice Book p. 48 on their own, or you can complete it as a class. Explain they must complete the sentences in the cause and effect bubbles using information from the passage provided. When they have finished, they should use their answers to write a summary of the passage.

ASSESS

Have partners reread p. 133, paragraph 1 in their books to identify the cause for Mr. Zhou's inability to leave America and return home. *(Mr. Zhou was deeply in debt).*

For additional instruction on cause and effect, see DI•56.

EXTEND SKILLS

Paraphrase

TEACH

To paraphrase something is to put it in your own words. A paraphrase should keep the author's ideas and overall meaning, but it should be easier to read than the original.

- When you paraphrase, think about what the author is trying to say.
- Do not add any opinions of your own.
- Use your own words.

Have small groups of students work together to paraphrase p. 119 from *Shutting Out the Sky.*

ASSESS

Have students write out their paraphrase for p. 124.

Remind students that they should use their own choice of words to describe what the author was trying to say.

OBJECTIVES

- Recognize cause and effect.
- Paraphrase a passage.

Skills Trace	
Cause and Effect	
Introduce/Teach	TE: 5.1 42–43, 112–113; 5.5 582–583
Practice	Practice Book: 6, 13, 17, 18, 43, 47, 48, 233, 237, 238
Reteach/Review	**TE: 5.1 27, 67b, 133b; 5.3 267, DI•53, DI•56; 5.5 603b, DI•55**
Test	Selection Test: 5-8, 17-20, 93-96; Benchmark Test: Unit 1

Access Content Reteach the skill by reviewing the Picture It! lesson on cause and effect in the ELL Teaching Guide, pp. 29–30.

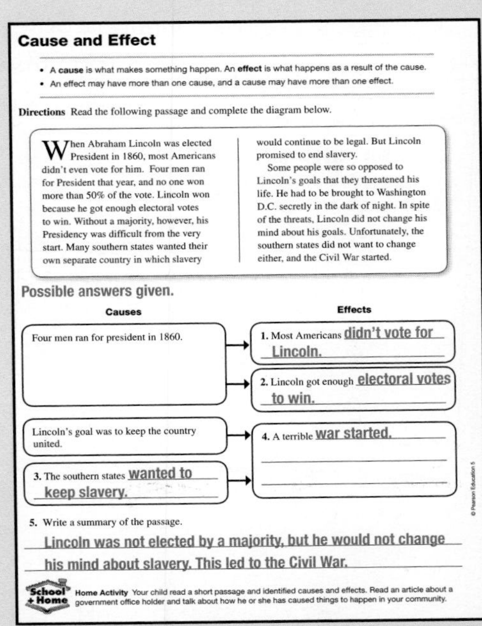

Cause and Effect

- A **cause** is what makes something happen. An **effect** is what happens as a result of the cause.
- An effect may have more than one cause, and a cause may have more than one effect.

Directions Read the following passage and complete the diagram below.

When Abraham Lincoln was elected President in 1860, most Americans didn't even vote for him. Four men ran for President that year, and no one won more than 50% of the vote. Lincoln won because he got enough electoral votes to win. Without a majority, however, his Presidency was difficult from the very start. Many southern states wanted their own separate country in which slavery would continue to be legal. But Lincoln promised to end slavery.

Some people were so opposed to Lincoln's goals that they threatened his life. He had to be brought to Washington D.C. secretly in the dark of night. In spite of the threats, Lincoln did not change his mind about his goals. Unfortunately, the southern states did not want to change either, and the Civil War started.

Possible answers given.

Causes	Effects
Four men ran for president in 1860.	1. Most Americans didn't vote for Lincoln.
	2. Lincoln got enough electoral votes to win.
Lincoln's goal was to keep the country united.	4. A terrible war started.
3. The southern states wanted to keep slavery.	

5. Write a summary of the passage.
Lincoln was not elected by a majority, but he would not change his mind about slavery. This led to the Civil War.

School + Home **Home Activity** Your child read a short passage and identified causes and effects. Read an article about a government office holder and talk about how he or she has caused things to happen in your community.

▲ **Practice Book** p. 48

Words Correct Per Minute

SUCCESS PREDICTOR

Vocabulary and Word Study

VOCABULARY STRATEGY

Context Clues

MULTIPLE-MEANING WORDS Point out to students that many words in English have more than one meaning. One way to tell which meaning the author intended is to look for context clues in surrounding words. Have students use context clues to determine the correct meaning of the multiple-meaning words from *Shutting Out the Sky* below. Then have them write a second definition for each word. Encourage students to use a dictionary if necessary.

Word	Meaning in Story	Second Definition
left	went away	opposite of right
trunks		
still		

Proper Nouns

The two selections, *Shutting Out the Sky* and "The Immigrant Experience" contain many proper nouns. Have students work with partners to list people, places, and things mentioned.

People	Places	Things
1. Marcus	1. Ellis Island	1. Web site
2.	2. Romania	2.
3.	3.	3.

BUILD CONCEPT VOCABULARY

Life in a New Country

LOOKING BACK Remind students of the unit theme: Meeting Challenges. Discuss the unit focus question: *What kinds of challenges do people face and how do they meet them?* Ask students how the Concept Vocabulary from each week of this unit relates to the unit theme and unit focus question. Ask students if they have any words or categories to add. If time permits, create a Unit Concept Web.

Monitor Progress

Check Vocabulary

If... students suggest words or categories that are not related to the concept,	**then...** review the words and categories on the Concept Web and discuss how they relate to the lesson concept.

Speaking and Viewing

SPEAKING

Interview

SET-UP Have students use information from the selection to perform a mock interview with Marcus.

PLANNING Allow students to work in pairs, one acting as the interviewer and one as Marcus. Encourage them to review the selection to gather ideas for questions and answers. Students should come up with several questions they would like to ask Marcus about his experiences as a newcomer in America. The student playing Marcus should think about how he or she will answer the questions based on information from the selection.

PRESENTATION Student pairs may want to begin by briefly introducing Marcus to the audience with general background information. Then they should conduct the interview with questions and answers. They can conclude by wrapping up the most important points of the interview.

VIEWING

Analyze a Photo

Have students examine the photograph on p. 121 of *Shutting Out the Sky*. They can answer these questions in writing.

1. **What is your first impression looking at this photo?** *(Possible response: It is very crowded, and people are tired)*
2. **Identify details you notice when you look more closely at the photo.** *(Possible responses: dark; many women and children, few men in the back; immigrants don't have many possessions)*
3. **What message do you think the photographer wishes to convey in the photo?** *(Possible response: Immigrating is tiring, difficult, and scary.)*

Support Vocabulary Use the following to review and extend vocabulary and to explore lesson concepts further:

- ELL Poster 5, Days 3–5 instruction
- Vocabulary Activities and Word Cards in ELL Teaching Guide, pp. 31–32

Assessment For information on assessing students' speaking, listening, and viewing, see the ELL and Transition Handbook.

AFTER READING

Grammar Common and Proper Nouns

OBJECTIVES

- Define and identify common and proper nouns.
- Use common and proper nouns correctly in writing.
- Become familiar with common and proper noun identification assessment on high-stakes tests.

Monitor Progress

Grammar

If... students have difficulty identifying common and proper nouns,	**then...** provide additional instruction and practice in The Grammar and Writing Book pp. 74–77.

DAILY FIX-IT

This week use Daily Fix-It Transparency 5.

Support Grammar See the Grammar Transition lessons in the ELL and Transition Handbook.

▲ **The Grammar and Writing Book** For more instruction and practice, use pp. 74–77.

DAY 1 Teach and Model

DAILY FIX-IT

1. Our adress is 610 East River drive. *(address; Drive)*
2. The driver doe'snt know how to get their. *(doesn't; there)*

READING-GRAMMAR CONNECTION

Write this sentence from *Shutting Out the Sky* on the board:

One early morning in December 1900, a sixteen-year-old boy left Ellis Island and made his way alone into New York City.

Explain that the sentence contains three **proper nouns:** *December, Ellis Island, New York City.* They are capitalized because they name a particular month, island, and city.

Display Grammar Transparency 5. Read aloud the definitions and sample sentences. Work through the items.

Common and Proper Nouns

The names of particular persons, places, and things are **proper nouns.** Capitalize the first word and each important word of a proper noun.

Alexi Bishop lives in Seattle, Washington, a city of the Northwest.

All other nouns are **common nouns.** They are not capitalized.

Our family has always wanted to live in the mountains or on the coast.

Capitalize the first word and all important words in a title.

The Wind in the Willows

Capitalize days of the week and months of the year.

Class meets on Mondays in May.

Capitalize the first letter of an abbreviated proper noun. Abbreviations often occur in addresses, titles and initials in names, and names of days and months. Most abbreviations end with a period.

The envelope went to Ms. M. R. Ryan, 1410 Montgomery St., Raleigh, NC 27607.
It was postmarked Wed., Sept. 27.

Directions If the group of words is correctly capitalized, write *correct* on the line. If the group of words is not capitalized correctly, rewrite it using correct capitalization.

1. mississippi River — Mississippi River
2. *A Wrinkle In Time* — *A Wrinkle in Time*
3. Monday, Sept. 26 — correct
4. mrs. Juanita campos — Mrs. Juanita Campos
5. 907 main St., Flagstaff, Az. — 907 Main St., Flagstaff, AZ
6. captain John Smith — Captain John Smith
7. the president of the company — correct
8. Girl Scouts of America — correct
9. president Washington — President Washington
10. Sioux city, iowa — Sioux City, Iowa

Directions Decide whether each list of nouns is common or proper. Add another example to each list. Write *P* if the list shows proper nouns. Write *C* if the list shows common nouns. Possible answers:

11. New York, Texas, Mississippi, Indiana → P
12. trees, bushes, flowers, grass → C
13. Canada, France, India, Brazil → P
14. ocean, river, pond, lake → C
15. Mr. Smith, Ms. Jones, Dr. Johnson → P

Unit 1 Shutting Out the Sky Grammar 5

▲ **Grammar Transparency** 5

DAY 2 Develop the Concept

DAILY FIX-IT

3. Ask grandpa Otie about our familys history. *(Grandpa; family's)*
4. His parents came hear from germany. *(here; Germany)*

GUIDED PRACTICE

Review the concept of proper and common nouns.

- Names of particular persons, places, and things are **proper nouns.** Capitalize the first word and each important word of a proper noun.
- All other nouns are **common nouns.** They are not capitalized.

Say that words formed from proper nouns are called proper adjectives, such as England (proper noun) and English tea (proper adjective).

HOMEWORK Grammar and Writing Practice Book p. 17.

Common and Proper Nouns

The names of particular persons, places, and things are **proper nouns.** Capitalize the first word and each important word of a proper noun.

I love Harry Potter in the books by J. K. Rowling.

All other nouns are **common nouns**. They are not capitalized.

That author has written five best-selling novels.

Capitalize the first word and all important words in a title.

Reflections on a Gift of Watermelon Pickle

Capitalize days of the week and months of the year.

Saturday, October 14

Capitalize the first letter of an abbreviated proper noun. Abbreviations often occur in addresses, titles and initials in names, and names of days and months. Most abbreviations end with a period. In addresses, state names are abbreviated using two capital letters and no period.

The envelope went to Mr. L. Cho, 11 E. 3rd St., Rochester, MN 55901.
It was postmarked Mon., Nov. 6.

Directions Write the proper noun from the box that matches each common noun. Add capital letters where they are needed.

sears tower | *my side of the mountain*
argentina | president jefferson
rebecca | "america the beautiful"

	Common Noun	Proper Noun
1.	girl	Rebecca
2.	president	President Jefferson
3.	country	Argentina
4.	book	*My Side of the Mountain*
5.	building	Sears Tower
6.	song	"America the Beautiful"

School-Home Connection **Home Activity** Your child learned about common and proper nouns. Take a walk with your child. Have him or her pick out proper nouns on signs and buildings in your community and practice writing them using proper capitalization.

▲ **Grammar and Writing Practice Book** p. 17

DAY 3 Apply to Writing

DAILY FIX-IT

5. do your family have old photographs of relatives. *(Does; relatives?)*
6. look at this picture of grandma Lila. *(Look; Grandma)*

USE COMMON AND PROPER NOUNS

Explain that using proper nouns can make writing clearer and more specific.

- Have students review something they have written to see if they can improve it by adding proper nouns.

HOMEWORK Grammar and Writing Practice Book p. 18.

Common and Proper Nouns

Directions Rewrite each sentence. Capitalize all proper nouns.

1. Many immigrants to the united states came to new york.
   Many immigrants to the United States came to New York.
2. The statue of liberty and the empire state building inspired them.
   The Statue of Liberty and the Empire State Building inspired them.
3. Men like john d. rockefeller and jacob astor had become rich in america.
   Men like John D. Rockefeller and Jacob Astor had become rich in America.
4. Even a poor person could one day live at 1600 pennsylvania ave., washington, d.c.
   Even a poor person could one day live at 1600 Pennsylvania Ave., Washington, D.C.

Directions Add the date, greeting, signature, and information needed in the body of the letter. Use correct capitalization. Possible answers:

November 12, 2006

Dear Pat,

Please come to a birthday party for Uncle Norm (person) on Friday (day of week), November 20, (date), at 7 P.M. (time of day). The party will be held at The Courthouse Grill (name of place) 600 W. State Street (address) Indianapolis, IN 46226

We really hope you can come and help us celebrate.

Best wishes,
Rob (signature)

School-Home Connection **Home Activity** Your child learned how to use common and proper nouns in writing. Ask your child to write a note inviting a friend to a special event. He or she should capitalize all proper nouns.

▲ **Grammar and Writing Practice Book** p. 18

DAY 4 Test Preparation

DAILY FIX-IT

7. Whod guess that tiny baby in lace would become the mother of ten chilren? *(Who'd; children)*
8. A hundred years ago, familes was much larger. *(families were)*

STANDARDIZED TEST PREP

Test Tip

You may need to decide which titles should be capitalized as proper nouns. A title used as part of a name is capitalized, even if it is abbreviated:

Title as part of name: General Robert E. Lee

Title abbreviations as part of name: Sen. John Smith, Jr.

Not part of name: The general and the senator talked for hours.

HOMEWORK Grammar and Writing Practice Book p. 19.

Common and Proper Nouns

Directions Mark the letter of the correct answer.

1. A mr. william baird, jr.
   B Mr. William Baird, jr.
   (C) Mr. William Baird, Jr.
   D mr. William Baird, jr.
2. A sunday, march 14
   (B) Sunday, March 14
   C Sunday, march 14
   D sunday, March 14
3. (A) Sugarland, TX 77478
   B Sugarland, tx 77478
   C sugarland, TX 77478
   D Sugarland, Tx. 77478
4. A dr. wilson adair
   B dr. Wilson adair
   C Dr. wilson Adair
   (D) Dr. Wilson Adair
5. A Rome, italy
   B rome, italy
   (C) Rome, Italy
   D rome, Italy
6. (A) a park on the Missouri River
   B a Park on the Missouri river
   C a park on the missouri River
   D a Park on the missouri river
7. A the movie *Beauty and The Beast*
   B the movie *beauty and the beast*
   C the Movie *Beauty And the Beast*
   (D) the movie *Beauty and the Beast*
8. A 190 n. Clark st.
   (B) 190 N. Clark St.
   C 190 n. Clark St.
   D 190 N. Clark st.
9. A *a Light in the Attic*
   B *A Light in The Attic*
   C *A Light In The Attic*
   (D) *A Light in the Attic*
10. A Miss Anna kowalski
    B miss Anna kowalski
    (C) Miss Anna Kowalski
    D miss Anna Kowalski

Directions Match each capitalization rule with the mistake in each sentence. Write the letter on the line.

A Capitalize the first and all important words in a book title.
B Capitalize days of the week and months of the year.
C Capitalize the first letter of an abbreviated proper noun.
D Capitalize titles before people's names.

D 11. Did you know major Segal was born in Romania?
A 12. He wrote a book called *coming to america*.
B 13. The group meets the first monday in each month.
C 14. April's meeting is at the library on w. Oak st.

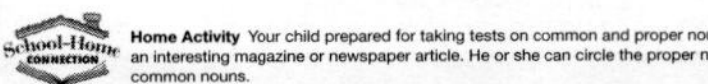

School-Home Connection **Home Activity** Your child prepared for taking tests on common and proper nouns. Have your child read an interesting magazine or newspaper article. He or she can circle the proper nouns and underline the common nouns.

▲ **Grammar and Writing Practice Book** p. 19

DAY 5 Cumulative Review

DAILY FIX-IT

9. Many imigrants came from europe. *(immigrants; Europe)*
10. They weren't afraid to work or try knew things? *(new things.)*

ADDITIONAL PRACTICE

Assign pp. 74–77 in The Grammar and Writing Book.

EXTRA PRACTICE Grammar and Writing Practice Book p. 126.

ASSESSMENT

CUMULATIVE REVIEW Grammar and Writing Practice Book p. 20.

Common and Proper Nouns

Directions Match the letter of each common noun on the right with a proper noun on the left. Then write another proper noun that fits in that category. Possible answers:

B	1. Japan	England	A. city
D	2. *Oliver Twist*	*Charlotte's Web*	B. country
E	3. Ms. Kopeki	Mr. Dean	C. team
C	4. Atlanta Braves	New York Yankees	D. book
A	5. London	Paris	E. teacher

Directions Write *C* if the group of words is capitalized correctly. If the group of words is not capitalized correctly, rewrite it using correct capitalization.

6. Helen and her cousins C
7. mr. Jorge Ruiz, sr. Mr. Jorge Ruiz, Sr.
8. the greatest City in the Midwest the greatest city in the Midwest
9. fourth of july Fourth of July
10. Mississippi River C
11. holidays in november holidays in November
12. south bend, In 46614 South Bend, IN 46614

Directions Rewrite each sentence. Use capital letters where they are needed.

13. On friday we went to a restaurant on east 18th st. called hot tamales.
    On Friday we went to a restaurant on East 18th St. called Hot Tamales.
14. It is owned by ms. marie dablontez, who is from mexico.
    It is owned by Ms. Marie Dablontez, who is from Mexico.

School-Home Connection **Home Activity** Your child reviewed common and proper nouns. Ask your child to write a note inviting a friend to do something. Have him or her check to be sure proper nouns are capitalized correctly.

▲ **Grammar and Writing Practice Book** p. 20

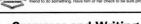

Writing for Tests **Narrative Writing**

OBJECTIVES

- Write a narrative for a test.
- Identify key words in a prompt.
- Focus on word choice.
- Use a rubric.

Genre Narrative Writing
Writer's Craft Show, Don't Tell
Writing Trait Word Choice

Word Choice If students write home-language words, use the following resources to find replacement words:

- conversations with you,
- other home-language speakers,
- bilingual dictionaries,
- online translation sources.

Writing Traits

FOCUS/IDEAS Strong supporting details show what happens instead of telling what happens.

ORGANIZATION/PARAGRAPHS The paragraphs are sequenced logically to show when events occurred.

VOICE The writer's personality shows in the writing. The writer is engaged with the subject.

WORD CHOICE The writer uses vivid words to create strong pictures and figures of speech.

SENTENCES The writing includes different kinds of sentences, such as questions and exclamations.

CONVENTIONS There is excellent control and accuracy, including capitalization of proper nouns.

DAY 1 Model the Trait

READING-WRITING CONNECTION

- When you write a response for tests, remember that sensory details and colorful word choice can strengthen your answer.
- Think about how the writer uses words in *Shutting Out the Sky* to show how crowded the immigrants were.

MODEL WORD CHOICE Discuss Writing Transparency 5A. Point out underlined words in the prompt. Then discuss the model and the writing trait of word choice.

Think Aloud The writer of this narrative has chosen words that appeal to the senses and create word pictures, such as "his whiskers tickled my fingers" and "popped into view." All the details and the simile in the last sentence help me understand how the writer felt.

Writing for Tests

Prompt Tell about a time when you got something you treasured. What effect did it have on you? Write a narrative to a friend telling how you made this treasure your own and how you felt. Remember to indent each new paragraph.

The Snuggles Sale

I knew when I saw him, he had to be mine. The little gerbil had soft gray fur. A white stripe on his nose looked like an exclamation mark. He gave me a careful sniff—his whiskers tickled my fingers! I cuddled him in my hands and immediately felt that warm puppy feeling. But could Mom be convinced? My heart went from warm to chill.

"Look, Mom," I said, lifting my hands. "This is Snuggles. He's a gerbil. Feel how soft!" I moved a finger just enough, and the tiny face with bright eyes popped into view. "Isn't he the cutest thing you've ever seen?" I said. Mom smiled uncertainly.

"Please, Mom," I talked fast. "I'll take care of Snuggles. He can live in my room. I can use the old aquarium for his home. Gerbils are very clean. He won't be underfoot, and he won't bark and he doesn't need to be walked or— "

Soon we were on the way home, with Snuggles exploring happily in my jacket. My heart bubbled like a glass of soda.

Specific details, comparisons, and strong verbs create vivid images.

Writer *shows* how she feels.

Writer uses a figure of speech to show feelings.

Unit 1 Shutting Out the Sky — Writing Model **5A**

▲ **Writing Transparency** 5A

DAY 2 Improve Writing

WRITER'S CRAFT
Show, Don't Tell

Display Writing Transparency 5B. Work with students to identify writing that shows rather than tells.

Think Aloud **SHOW, DON'T TELL, FEELINGS** Tomorrow we will write a **narrative** about getting a precious thing. How could I show rather than tell about my excitement when I found my grandmother's lost ring? I might say, "My breath caught in my throat. Slowly I stretched my shaking hand toward the ring." These sentences show that I felt surprised and excited.

GUIDED WRITING Some students may need more help writing with sensory details.

- Help them find sentences in the selection that *show,* not *tell.*
- Work with them to improve this sentence: *I was worried.*

Show, Don't Tell

When you write about yourself, **show—don't tell**—how you feel.
No I felt relieved.
Yes I let out a huge breath and leaned back. I felt the knots in my stomach relax.

Directions Underline the sentence ending that shows rather than tells. For the last sentence, write your own ending to show how you would feel in this situation.

1. The early fog hung around me like a thick wall of smoke. / was hard to see through.
2. Rays of sun burned the fog off in about an hour. / cut into the fog like a laser until the air was clear and clean.
3. My spirits soon were soaring like the hawks over the fields I passed. / had been low, but they were lifted by the bright sunshine.
4. Fields of corn were ripe and ready for harvest. / had turned from green to pale gold, and dry stalks rustled.
5. A day of travel seemed like an opportunity instead of a chore. / stretched before me, rich with blue sky and new sights.
6. For the moment, I felt Possible answer: For the moment, I felt as free as a cloud on a sunny sky.

Directions Imagine that you are walking home after school. It is autumn, but you do not have your coat, and the wind is cold. Write about your walk, showing rather than telling what you see, hear, feel, smell, and taste, as well as how you feel. Possible answer:

The wind blows through my thin shirt. It whistles around my ears and knocks over the empty trash cans. Leaves of gold, orange, and red wave on the trees or fly and bounce across brown yards. They smell musty and sharp—like fall. Brrrr. I'm shaking, too. If only I had my coat!

Unit 1 Shutting Out the Sky — Writer's Craft **5B**

▲ **Writing Transparency** 5B

Trait of the Week

Word Choice

DAY 3 Prewrite and Draft

READ THE WRITING PROMPT on page 129 in the Student Edition.

Shutting Out the Sky *tells about a boy's experiences in a new country. Think about an experience that was meaningful to you. Now write a narrative about that experience.*

Writing Test Tips

1. **Read the prompt carefully.**
   - Find key words.
   - Consider the purpose and audience. How will they affect your writing?
2. **Develop a plan.** Think of what you want to say before writing. Fill out a simple graphic organizer. For example, for a story, think of a beginning, middle, and end. For a comparison/contrast essay, fill out a T-chart or a Venn diagram.
3. **Support your ideas.** Use facts, examples, and details to strengthen your response. Avoid making general statements that are unsupported.
4. **Choose clear, precise words.** Use words that create pictures and help readers understand what you mean.
5. **Check your writing.** If this is a timed test, you may not have time to recopy your work. However, you can neatly add, delete, or change words and make corrections in spelling, punctuation, or grammar. Make sure your handwriting is legible. Reread your work before handing it in.

DAY 4 Draft and Revise

EDITING/REVISING CHECKLIST

☑ **Focus** Do all sentences focus on the topic of getting the treasured thing?

☑ **Organization** Is narrative developed in logical order with transition words?

☑ **Support** Do descriptive words and sentence structures make the writing clear and lively?

☑ **Conventions** Have I capitalized all proper nouns correctly? Are apostrophes used correctly in contractions?

See *The Grammar and Writing Book*, pp. 74–79.

Revising Tips

Word Choice

- Support narrative with words that show exactly how people and things look, sound, smell, taste, and feel.
- Change vague or ordinary action words to more specific, vivid ones.
- Add vivid nouns and descriptive words to any details that tell instead of show.

ASSESSMENT Use the scoring rubric to evaluate students' work.

DAY 5 Connect to Unit Writing

Personal Narrative

Week 1	Character Sketch 41g–41h
Week 2	Tall Tale 67g–67h
Week 3	Friendly or Thank you Letter 89g–89h
Week 4	Feature Article 111g–111h
Week 5	Narrative Writing 133g–133h

PREVIEW THE UNIT PROMPT

Write a personal narrative about a challenge or difficult problem. Describe what the challenge was and tell how you met it. Use details that make the events clear and interesting.

APPLY

- Use vivid details to show readers the events and people in narrative writing.

Writing Trait Rubric

	4	3	2	1
Word Choice	Vivid style created by use of exact nouns, strong verbs, exciting adjectives, and clear figurative language	Some style created by strong and precise words	Little style created by strong, precise words; some lack of clarity	Word choice vague or incorrect
	Uses strong, specific words that make narrative vivid, and description of experience clear	Uses some specific words that make narrative clear	Needs more precise word choice to create style and clarity in narrative	Narrative made dull or unclear by poor word choice

AFTER READING

Spelling & Phonics Contractions

OBJECTIVE

- Spell contractions.

Generalization

Connect to Phonics In contractions, an apostrophe (') takes the place of letters that are left out: *they are* becomes *they're.* A contraction is a combination of two words. To read a contraction, figure out which letters the apostrophe replaced.

Spelling Words

1. they're	11. could've
2. you've	12. would've
3. weren't	13. should've
4. needn't	14. might've
5. there'd	15. wouldn't*
6. they've	16. who've
7. mustn't	17. shouldn't
8. what'll	18. who'd
9. doesn't	19. this'll
10. hadn't*	20. couldn't

Challenge Words

21. there've	24. those'll
22. mightn't	25. there'll
23. what've	

* Words from the selection

Spelling/Phonics Support See the ELL and Transition Handbook for spelling support.

DAY 1 Pretest and Sort

PRETEST

Use the Dictation Sentences from Day 5 to administer the pretest. Read the word, read the sentence, and then read the word again. Guide students in self-correcting their pretests and correcting any misspellings.

Monitor Progress

Spelling

If... students misspell more than 5 pretest words,	**then...** use words 1–10 for Strategic Intervention.
If... students misspell 1–5 pretest words,	**then...** use words 1–20 for On-Level practice.
If... students correctly spell all pretest words,	**then...** use words 1–25 for Advanced Learners.

HOMEWORK Spelling Practice Book, p. 17.

Contractions

Generalization In contractions an apostrophe (') takes the place of letters that are left out: **they are** becomes **they're**.

Word Sort Sort the list words into nouns/pronouns and verbs.

nouns/pronouns	verbs
1. they're	9. weren't
2. you've	10. needn't
3. there'd	11. mustn't
4. they've	12. doesn't
5. what'll	13. hadn't
6. who've	14. could've
7. who'd	15. would've
8. this'll	16. should've
	17. might've
	18. wouldn't
	19. shouldn't
	20. couldn't

Challenge Words

nouns/pronouns	verbs
21. there've	25. mightn't
22. what've	
23. those'll	
24. there'll	

Spelling Words
1. they're
2. you've
3. weren't
4. needn't
5. there'd
6. they've
7. mustn't
8. what'll
9. doesn't
10. hadn't
11. could've
12. would've
13. should've
14. might've
15. wouldn't
16. who've
17. shouldn't
18. who'd
19. this'll
20. couldn't

Challenge Words
21. there've
22. mightn't
23. what've
24. those'll
25. there'll

School + Home **Home Activity** Your child is learning about contractions. Ask your child to tell you what role the apostrophe plays in contractions.

▲ **Spelling Practice Book** p. 17

DAY 2 Think and Practice

TEACH

To spell a contraction, use an apostrophe to show that letters have been replaced. Write *you have* on the board. Cross out *ha* and write an apostrophe above the crossed out letters. Then write *you've* as one word. Guide students in forming the contractions for *must not, could have,* and *there would.* Point out that *'d* can stand for *would* or *had* and give an example sentence for each use.

you have

CONTRACTION CHART Have students write the list words and then write the two words each contraction stands for.

HOMEWORK Spelling Practice Book, p. 18.

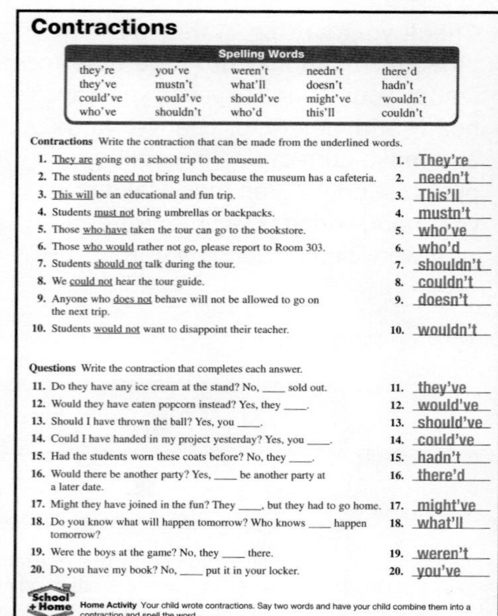

Contractions

Spelling Words

they're	you've	weren't	needn't	there'd
they've	mustn't	what'll	doesn't	hadn't
could've	would've	should've	might've	wouldn't
who've	shouldn't	who'd	this'll	couldn't

Contractions Write the contraction that can be made from the underlined words.

1. They are going on a school trip to the museum. — 1. They're
2. The students need not bring lunch because the museum has a cafeteria. — 2. needn't
3. This will be an educational and fun trip. — 3. This'll
4. Students must not bring umbrellas or backpacks. — 4. mustn't
5. Those who have taken the tour can go to the bookstore. — 5. who've
6. Those who would rather not go, please report to Room 303. — 6. who'd
7. Students should not talk during the tour. — 7. shouldn't
8. We could not hear the tour guide. — 8. couldn't
9. Anyone who does not behave will not be allowed to go on the next trip. — 9. doesn't
10. Students would not want to disappoint their teacher. — 10. wouldn't

Questions Write the contraction that completes each answer.

11. Do they have any ice cream at the stand? No, ____ sold out. — 11. they've
12. Would they have eaten popcorn instead? Yes, they ____. — 12. would've
13. Should I have thrown the ball? Yes, you ____. — 13. should've
14. Could I have handed in my project yesterday? Yes, you ____. — 14. could've
15. Had the students worn these coats before? No, they ____. — 15. hadn't
16. Would there be another party? Yes, ____ be another party at a later date. — 16. there'd
17. Might they have joined in the fun? They ____, but they had to go home. — 17. might've
18. Do you know what will happen tomorrow? Who knows ____ happen tomorrow? — 18. what'll
19. Were the boys at the game? No, they ____ there. — 19. weren't
20. Do you have my book? No, ____ put it in your locker. — 20. you've

School + Home **Home Activity** Your child wrote contractions. Say two words and have your child combine them into a contraction and spell the word.

▲ **Spelling Practice Book** p. 18

AFTER READING

DAY 3 Connect to Writing

WRITE AN ANECDOTE

Ask students to write a personal anecdote. Tell them to use at least five spelling words to make the story sound informal, as if they were speaking to a friend.

Frequently Misspelled Words

that's *you're*
doesn't

These words may seem easy to spell, but they are often misspelled by fifth-graders. Alert students to these frequently misspelled words. Point out that all the words are contractions that need apostrophes. Discuss when to use *your* and *you're.* Remind students that *doesn't* has an *e* because it is the contraction for *does not.*

HOMEWORK Spelling Practice Book, p. 19.

Contractions

Proofread a Conversation Jack wrote this conversation between a waiter and a diner. Find six spelling errors and one punctuation error. Write the corrections on the lines.

"Whatll you have for lunch?" asked the waiter.
"I'm not sure," said the diner.
"Maybe this'll tempt you—lima bean casserole!" said the waiter. "Who'ud eat that for lunch?" asked the diner.
"That's a very popular dish around here," said the waiter. "Theyr'e already lining up outside the door for the beans."
"You arn't kidding about a long line," said the diner.
You mustn't miss this tasty treat," said the waiter.
"Okay, I wouldn't want to miss your special dish!" said the diner. "Hey, this doesnt taste too bad at all!"
"See what you would've been missing if you had'nt tried our special dish?" said the waiter.

1. What'll
2. Who'd
3. They're
4. aren't
5. doesn't
6. hadn't
7. "You mustn't miss this tasty treat," said the waiter.

Spelling Words
they're, you've, weren't, needn't, there'd, they've, mustn't, what'll, doesn't, hadn't, could've, would've, should've, might've, wouldn't, who've, shouldn't, who'd, this'll, couldn't

Frequently Misspelled Words
that's, you're, doesn't

Proofread Words Circle the correct spelling of the word.

8.	wood've	woud've	would've
9.	dosn't	doesn't	dosen't
10.	weren't	wearn't	wheren't
11.	coudn't	culdn't	couldn't
12.	might've	mihgt've	mitgth've
13.	whatll	whatl'l	what'll
14.	who'd	who'ld	whod'd

School + Home **Home Activity** Your child identified misspelled list words. Select contractions and ask your child to tell you how they were formed.

▲ **Spelling Practice Book** p. 19

DAY 4 Review

REVIEW CONTRACTIONS

Have students write ten sentences. In each sentence, they should use the two words that one of the list word contractions stands for. Have students trade papers with a partner, and have the partner underline the two words and write the contraction.

Spelling Strategy
Meaning Helpers

Even short words can be hard to spell until you discover where they come from.

Example: doesn't

You don't hear the *e* in *doesn't,* but because you know *doesn't* stands for *does not,* you remember to write it. *Does not* is a meaning clue for *doesn't.*

HOMEWORK Spelling Practice Book, p. 20.

Contractions

Spelling Words

they're	you've	weren't	needn't	there'd
they've	mustn't	what'll	doesn't	hadn't
could've	would've	should've	might've	wouldn't
who've	shouldn't	who'd	this'll	couldn't

Contractions Complete the chart.

	Word	Word	Contraction
1.	should	have	should've
2.	who	would	who'd
3.	this	will	this'll
4.	should	not	shouldn't
5.	had	not	hadn't
6.	what	will	what'll
7.	they	have	they've
8.	does	not	doesn't
9.	could	have	could've
10.	they	are	they're

Writing Contractions Put the apostrophe in the correct place in each word. Write each word.

11. w o u l d n ' t — 11. wouldn't
12. w h o ' v e — 12. who've
13. w e r e n ' t — 13. weren't
14. w o u l d ' v e — 14. would've
15. m u s t n ' t — 15. mustn't
16. c o u l d n ' t — 16. couldn't
17. y o u ' v e — 17. you've
18. t h e r e ' d — 18. there'd
19. n e e d n ' t — 19. needn't
20. m i g h t ' v e — 20. might've

School + Home **Home Activity** Your child has learned to spell contractions. Have your child pick the five hardest words on the list. Go over the spellings with your child.

▲ **Spelling Practice Book** p. 20

DAY 5 Posttest

DICTATION SENTENCES

1. They're both coming to the party.
2. Tell us what you've learned.
3. We weren't allowed to go outside.
4. You needn't be so rude.
5. Mom hoped there'd be enough food.
6. They've finally chosen a name for the puppy.
7. You mustn't tell my secret.
8. What'll we do if it rains?
9. The store doesn't have my size.
10. Maggie hadn't been there before.
11. I wish we could've visited you.
12. We would've done it another way.
13. We should've done our chores first.
14. The team might've won if the star had not been ill.
15. The pony wouldn't jump over the fence.
16. People who've seen the movie liked it.
17. You shouldn't have done that.
18. Who'd like a second helping?
19. This'll only take a minute.
20. We couldn't see through the fog.

CHALLENGE

21. There've been too many accidents here.
22. It mightn't have been all his fault.
23. What've I done with my keys?
24. Those'll have to be enough for now.
25. There'll be another bus in ten minutes.

OBJECTIVES

- Formulate an inquiry question that is connected to this week's lesson focus.
- Effectively and efficiently find, evaluate, and communicate information related to an inquiry question using electronic sources.

New Literacies

Day 1	Identify Questions
Day 2	Navigate/Search
Day 3	Analyze
Day 4	Synthesize
Day 5	Communicate

NEW LITERACIES

Internet Inquiry Activity

EXPLORE THE IMMIGRANT EXPERIENCE

Use the following 5-day plan to help students conduct this week's Internet inquiry activity on the immigrant experience. Remind students to follow classroom rules when using the Internet.

DAY 1

Identify Questions Discuss the lesson focus question: *What challenges do immigrants encounter?* As a group, brainstorm ideas for questions about the immigrant experience. For example, students might like to learn more about Ellis Island, or they might want to learn about the living conditions of immigrants like Marcus. Have students work individually, in pairs, or in small groups to write inquiry questions they want to answer.

DAY 2

Navigate/Search Introduce or review key Internet terms, including *URL* ("uniform resource locator"—the World Wide Web address of a site on the Internet); *browser* (a software tool used to surf the Web); and *link* (a connection from one site to another). Then have students locate two or more Web sites they can use to find information related to their inquiry question.

DAY 3

Analyze Discuss with students how to use the search feature to find keywords in a Web site document. Then have students skim and scan the Web sites they identified on Day 2 and analyze each site for usefulness. Encourage them to note information they can use to answer their inquiry questions.

DAY 4

Synthesize Have students synthesize information from Day 3. On the board, draw a graphic organizer, such as a web, chart, or table, that they can use to help them synthesize effectively.

DAY 5

Communicate Have students share their inquiry results. Provide appropriate presentation software and ask them to use it to create three-minute presentations of their research.

RESEARCH/STUDY SKILLS

Electronic Encyclopedia

TEACH

Ask students where they might find information about a subject like Angel Island or Ellis Island. Help them understand that they could consult an electronic encyclopedia for information. If possible, show an example of an electronic encyclopedia to students and define these features.

An **encyclopedia** gives general information about many topics. It can be a general or technical encyclopedia. (A **technical encyclopedia** gives information on topics related to a specialized field such as medicine or engineering.)

- **Electronic encyclopedias** are on CD-ROMS or online.
- Encyclopedias are organized alphabetically by **entries**. Entries are the topics contained in the encyclopedia.
- **Keyword searches** are used to locate entries in an electronic encyclopedia.
- Many entries in an electronic encyclopedia include **cross-references**, or **links**, to more information about the topic you are researching.
- Electronic entries often include graphics, maps, and audio files related to the topics.

Have students work in groups, and provide each group with access to either a print or an electronic encyclopedia (online or CD-ROM). Have groups identify features of encyclopedia entries as they review the encyclopedias. Discuss these questions:

1. **What keywords or entry words would you use to find information about Angel Island?** *(Possible response: Angel Island California)*
2. **If you wanted more information about Angel Island, what part of the entry would help you?** *(The cross-references or links)*

ASSESS

As students work with encyclopedias, check that they know how to select keywords or entry words for their searches and can identify parts of entries. For electronic versions, check that students can easily navigate the various pages on the site.

For more practice or to assess students, use Practice Book pp. 49–50.

OBJECTIVES

- Review terms associated with electronic encyclopedias.
- Use an electronic encyclopedia to locate information.

Electronic Encyclopedia

An **encyclopedia** gives general information about many different subjects. An electronic encyclopedia can be found on a CD-ROM or on the Internet. They often have interactive graphics and maps, as well as audio files. They are organized alphabetically by **entries,** which are the topics. You can locate topics by using **keyword searches.** Keyword searches give you a list of topics to choose from. Cross-referencing is represented by hotlinks, which are underlined words.

Directions Read the entry from an online encyclopedia and answer the questions below.

Online Student Encyclopedia home

Keyword Search

Print Article E-Mail Article to Friend Bookmark Article

Ellis Island
Ellis Island is located in New York Harbor. It was named after its owner in the 1770s, Samuel Ellis. Sixteen million immigrants to the United States passed through Ellis Island between 1892 and 1954. In 1965 the island became part of the Statue of Liberty National Monument. The immigration processing center is no longer used; however, it was made into a museum in 1990. The museum houses 400 years' worth of documents and artifacts about American immigration.

See also **Immigration**.

Back to top

Possible answers given.

1. How would you search for information about Samuel Ellis in this online encyclopedia?
   You would enter "Samuel Ellis" in the Keyword Search box at the top of the screen.
2. Can you e-mail this article to a friend? Why do you think e-mailing an article would be useful?
   Yes; It would be useful for doing research with a project team.
3. Why do you think you would bookmark this page?
   It would be helpful for doing future research on the subject.
4. When was Ellis Island made into a museum?
   Ellis Island became a museum in 1990.
5. What is a simple way you could learn more about immigration?
   You could click on the underlined words *See also Immigration.*

▲ **Practice Book** p. 49

Directions Read the entry from an online encyclopedia and answer the questions below.

Online Student Encyclopedia home

Keyword Search

Print Article E-Mail Article to Friend Bookmark Article

Ethnic Diversity
Most contemporary societies are, to some extent, ethnically diverse. History has played a part in making societies more diverse. Conquerors brought people from different societies to live under their rule. Sometimes people were brought to a new society as slaves. When they are not forced to move, people are often motivated to move to new societies to pursue economic improvement or to flee political and religious persecution. See also ethnicity, immigration.

Assimilation occurs when a newly arrived group takes on some (or all) of the customs and values of the dominant group. Assimilation can occur voluntarily or it can be forced by the dominant group.

Back to top

Possible answers given.

6. This selection is part of a larger topic entitled *Ethnic Groups*. What keywords would you use if you wanted to learn about how the Irish moved to America?
   Irish immigrant or *Irish immigration* would be possible keywords.
7. If you wanted to learn about people who moved to flee religious persecution, what words would you use in the keyword search?
   Immigration and *religious persecution* are possible keywords.
8. How would you print this article?
   Click on *Print Article* at the top of the screen.
9. According to the entry, what are three reasons people leave their native lands?
   Economic, political, and religious freedom are three reasons people may move.
10. What is the difference between a dictionary and an encyclopedia?
    Dictionaries provide definitions to words; Encyclopedias provide in-depth information about a topic.

School + Home **Home Activity** Your child answered questions about electronic encyclopedias. With your child, search an encyclopedia for information about your family's ancestors and their native land or lands.

▲ **Practice Book** p. 50

AFTER READING

Assessment Checkpoints *for the Week*

Selection Assessment

Use pp. 17–20 of Selection Tests to check:

 **Selection Understanding**

 **Comprehension Skill** *Cause and Effect*

 **Selection Vocabulary**

advice	*immigrants*
advised	*luxury*
circumstances	*newcomer*
elbow	*peddler*
hustled	

Selection Tests
ASSESSMENT
Scott Foresman
Selection Tests
Teacher's Manual
• Assess comprehension of weekly selections
• Assess understanding of weekly comprehension skills
• Assess knowledge of selection vocabulary
Reading Street
Grade 5

Leveled Assessment

On-Level

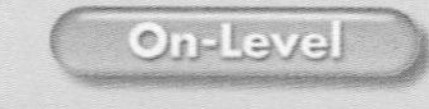
Strategic Intervention

Advanced

Use pp. 25–30 of Fresh Reads for Differentiated Test Practice to check:

 **Comprehension Skill** *Cause and Effect*

 REVIEW **Comprehension Skill** *Sequence*

 **Fluency** *Words Correct Per Minute*

Fresh Reads for Differentiated Test Practice
ASSESSMENT Teacher's Manual
Scott Foresman
Fresh Reads
for Differentiated Test Practice
Leveled passages—strategic intervention, on-level, and advanced—for
• Fluency checks
• Practice and application of weekly comprehension skills
• Answer key for all practice pages
Reading Street
Grade 5

Managing Assessment

Use Assessment Handbook for:

 **Observation Checklists**

 **Record-Keeping Forms**

 **Portfolio Assessment**

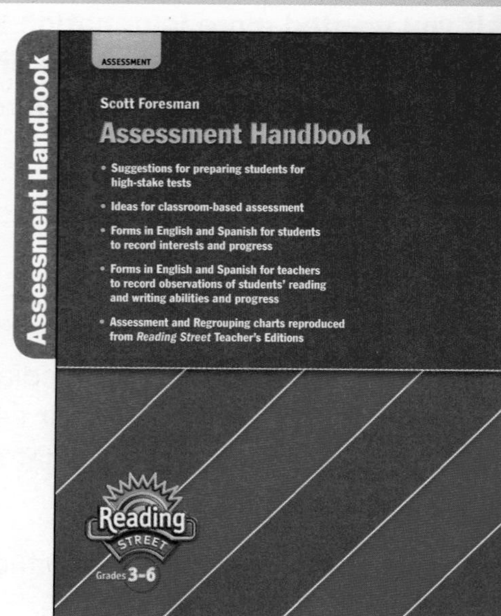
Assessment Handbook
ASSESSMENT
Scott Foresman
Assessment Handbook
• Suggestions for preparing students for high-stake tests
• Ideas for classroom-based assessment
• Forms in English and Spanish for students to record interests and progress
• Forms in English and Spanish for teachers to record observations of students' reading and writing abilities and progress
• Assessment and Regrouping charts reproduced from Reading Street Teacher's Editions
Reading Street
Grades 3–6

Unit 1
Concept Wrap-Up

CONCEPT QUESTION
What kinds of challenges do people face and how do they meet them?

Students are ready to express their understanding of the unit concept question through discussion and wrap-up activities and to take the Unit 1 Benchmark Test.

Unit Poetry

Use the poetry on pp. 134-137 to help students appreciate poetry and further explore their understanding of the unit theme, Meeting Challenges. It is suggested that you

- **read the poems aloud**
- **discuss and interpret the poems with students**
- **have students read the poems for fluency practice**
- **have students write interpretive responses**

Unit Wrap-Up

Use the Unit Wrap-Up on pp. 138-139 to discuss the unit theme, Meeting Challenges, and to have students show their understanding of the theme through cross-curricular activities.

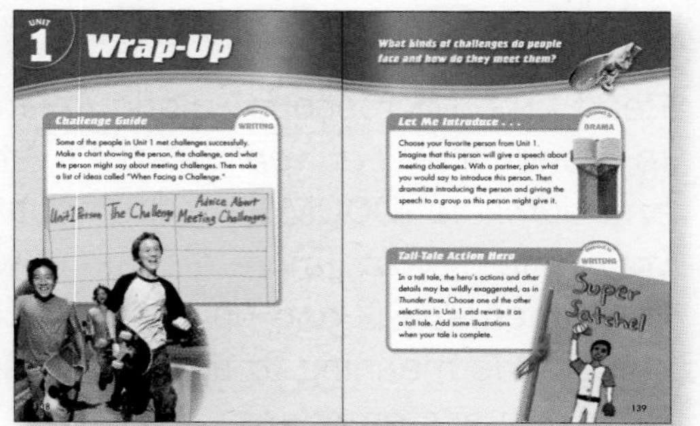

Unit Project

On p. 17, you assigned students a unit-long inquiry project, a poster of information advertising Special Olympics events. Students have investigated, analyzed, and synthesized information during the course of the unit as they prepared their posters. Schedule time for students to present their posters. The project rubric can be found to the right.

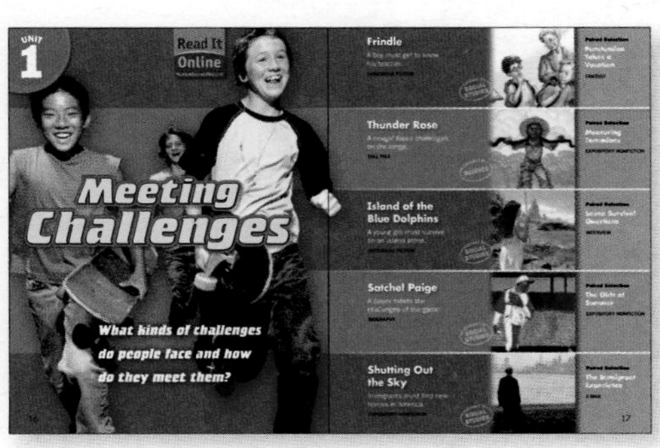

Unit Inquiry Project Rubric

4	3	2	1
• Research is accurate and very detailed. Sources are reliable and relevant to inquiry question. • Poster presents clear and complete information. It is visually appealing.	• Research is generally accurate and detailed. Most sources are reliable and relevant. • Poster is generally clear and visually appealing, but may omit some information.	• Research includes inaccuracies, irrelevant information, or little detail. Some sources are unreliable. • Poster has some visual appeal, but key information may be unclear or missing.	• Research is not accurate, detailed, or relevant. Most sources are unreliable. • Poster is incomplete or confusing. It is not visually appealing.

Unit 1

Reading Poetry

OBJECTIVES

- Listen and respond to poems.
- Identify how meaning is conveyed through word choice.
- Read poetry fluently.
- Connect ideas and themes across texts.

Model Fluent Reading

Read "The Microscope" aloud, taking care to pronounce *Leeuwenhoek* (LAY ven hook) and *dumkopf* (DOOM kawpf) smoothly. Make your tone of voice more disdainful when the Dutchmen speak and point out that tone of voice adds meaning to a poem by showing the speaker's emotions.

Discuss the Poem

1 Rhyme • Critical

What are some examples of end rhyme in this poem? Why do you think the poet uses so many end rhymes?

Possible responses: End rhymes include *Dutch* and *such, fussed* and *dust, store* and *for, lice* and *mice, gear* and *smear,* and so on. The rhyming creates a playful, lighthearted tone.

2 Plot • Literal

What does Anton spend his time doing instead of waiting on customers in his store?

Possible responses: Anton makes a microscope lens and spends his time looking at tiny things, such as *mosquito's wings, the hairs of sheep, the legs of lice, the skin of people,* and bugs that swim in a drop of water.

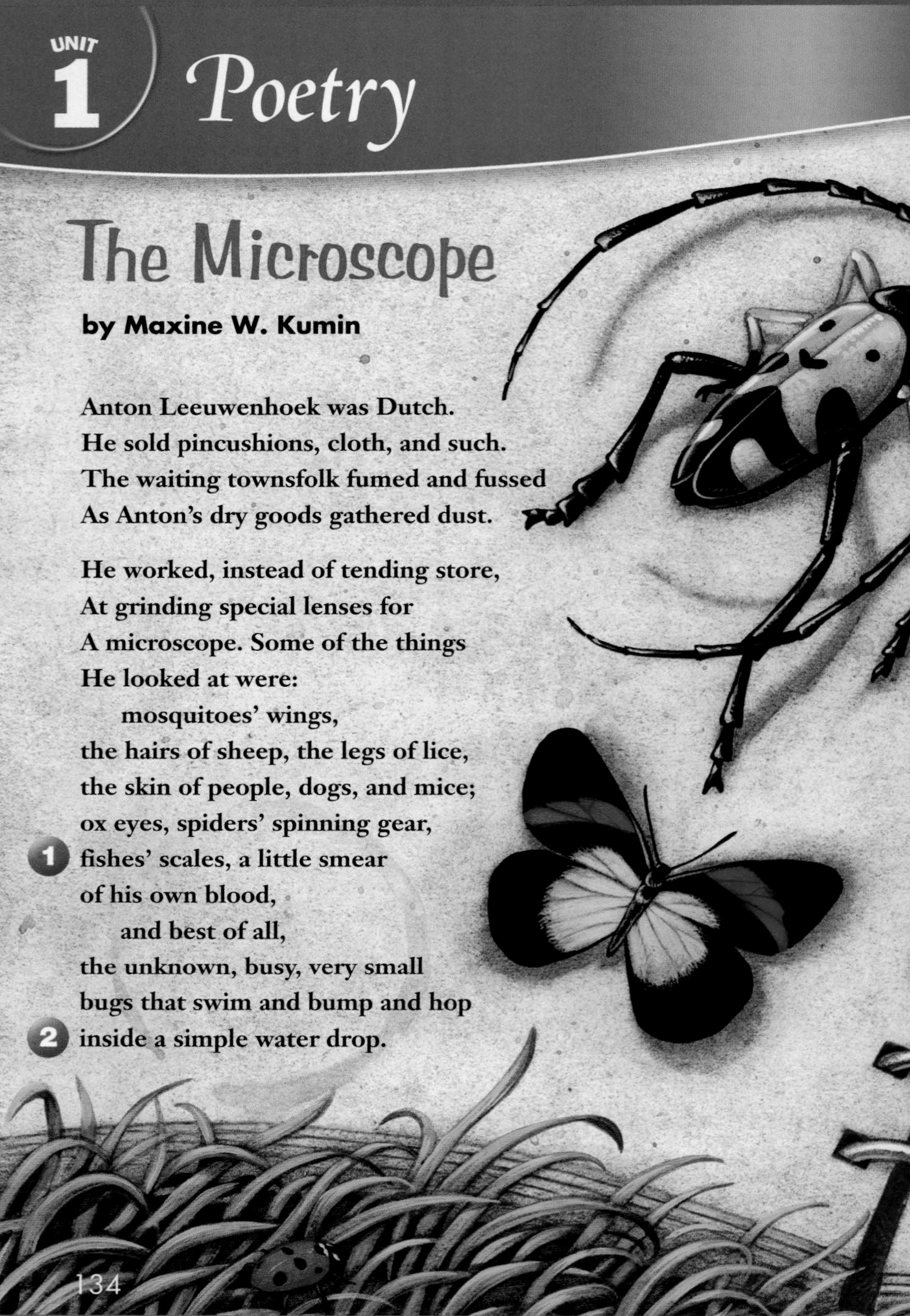

UNIT 1 Poetry

The Microscope

by Maxine W. Kumin

Anton Leeuwenhoek was Dutch.
He sold pincushions, cloth, and such.
The waiting townsfolk fumed and fussed
As Anton's dry goods gathered dust.

He worked, instead of tending store,
At grinding special lenses for
A microscope. Some of the things
He looked at were:
    mosquitoes' wings,
the hairs of sheep, the legs of lice,
the skin of people, dogs, and mice;
ox eyes, spiders' spinning gear,
1 fishes' scales, a little smear
of his own blood,
    and best of all,
the unknown, busy, very small
bugs that swim and bump and hop
2 inside a simple water drop.

134

Practice Fluent Reading

Have partners take turns reading "The Microscope" aloud, using different tones of voice. Ask students to discuss how the different tones of voice change the meaning of the poem. Then have students listen to the AudioText of the poem and compare and contrast their readings with the CD recording.

AudioText

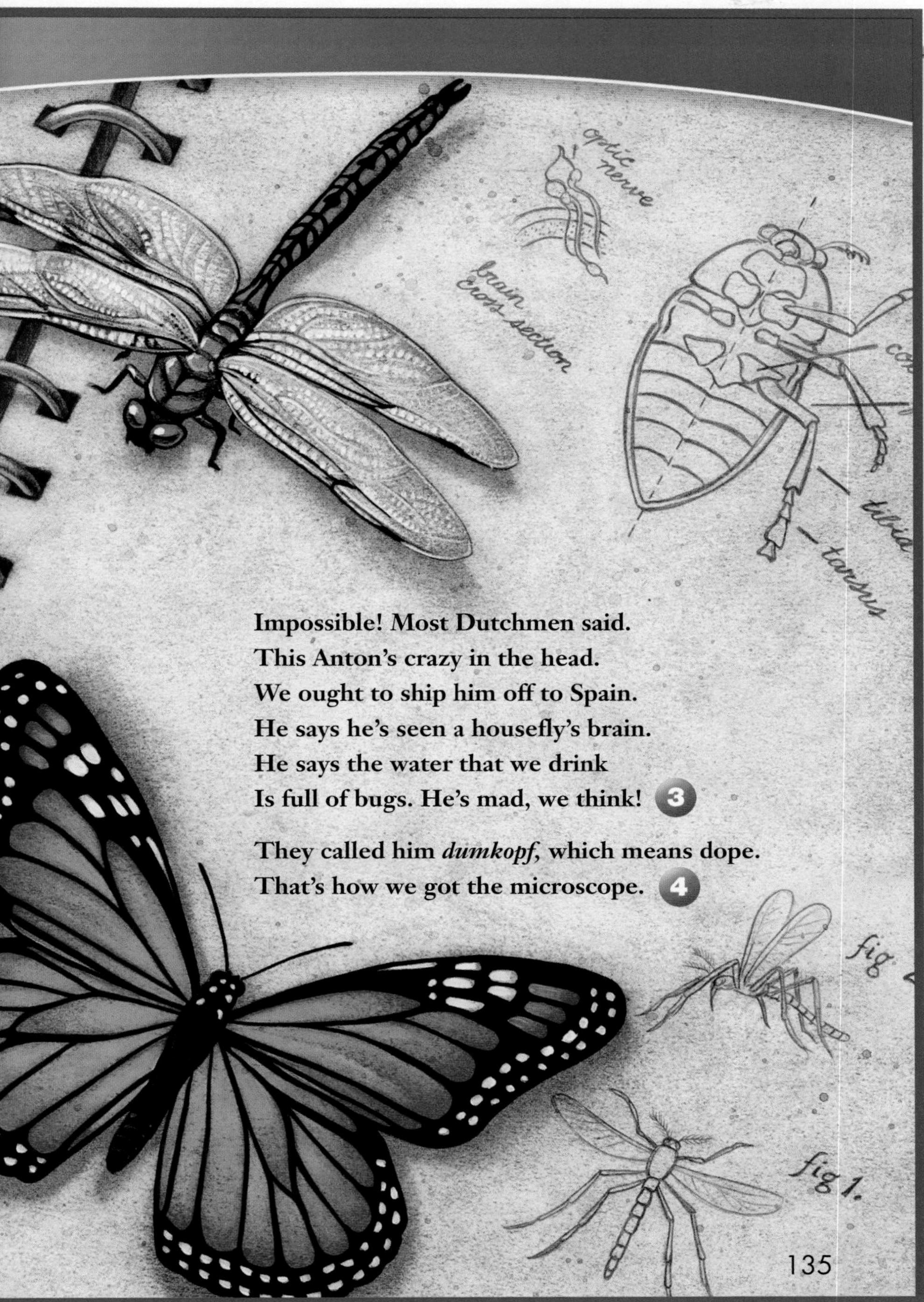

optic nerve
brain cross-section
tibia
tarsus
fig 1.
Impossible! Most Dutchmen said.
This Anton's crazy in the head.
We ought to ship him off to Spain.
He says he's seen a housefly's brain.
He says the water that we drink
Is full of bugs. He's mad, we think! 3
They called him *dumkopf,* which means dope.
That's how we got the microscope. 4
135

3 Draw Conclusions • Inferential

What do you think the townsfolk think of Anton?

Possible responses: The townspeople may be angry with him for seemingly wasting his time and not selling what is in his store. They say he's crazy.

4 Author's Viewpoint • Critical

What is the poet's attitude toward Anton? How can you tell?

Possible responses: The poet seems to respect Anton and the contribution he makes to science. She makes the townspeople appear foolish for thinking Anton is crazy.

Writing Poetry

Have students write poems about a modern device and how it would have looked to their great-grandparents. For example, students may write about what someone from long ago would think of cell phones, notebook computers, microwave ovens, or dishwashers.

Extend Skills

Irony

Explain that irony is the contrast between what appears to be and what actually is. Although the poem at first appears to be criticizing Anton, the end of the poem shows the result of all his "wasted time"—the microscope, an invaluable and very widely used invention.

Unit 1

Reading Poetry

Model Fluent Reading

Read "Full Day" aloud. Point out that you can't get the full meaning of the poem if you pause at the end of every line. Instead, you should let the punctuation guide your reading.

Discuss the Poem

1 **Draw Conclusions • Inferential**

Why do you think the speaker describes the clouds as "mountains of froth and foam"?

Possible response: When you are looking down on clouds from a plane, they look like they are froth and foam. They look as if they have little substance to them at all.

2 **Imagery • Inferential**

What visual images does the poem create?

Possible responses: From a plane, the travelers see *mountains of froth and foam.* From the covered wagons, people saw *the long grass and sweet shine of evening settling on the fields.*

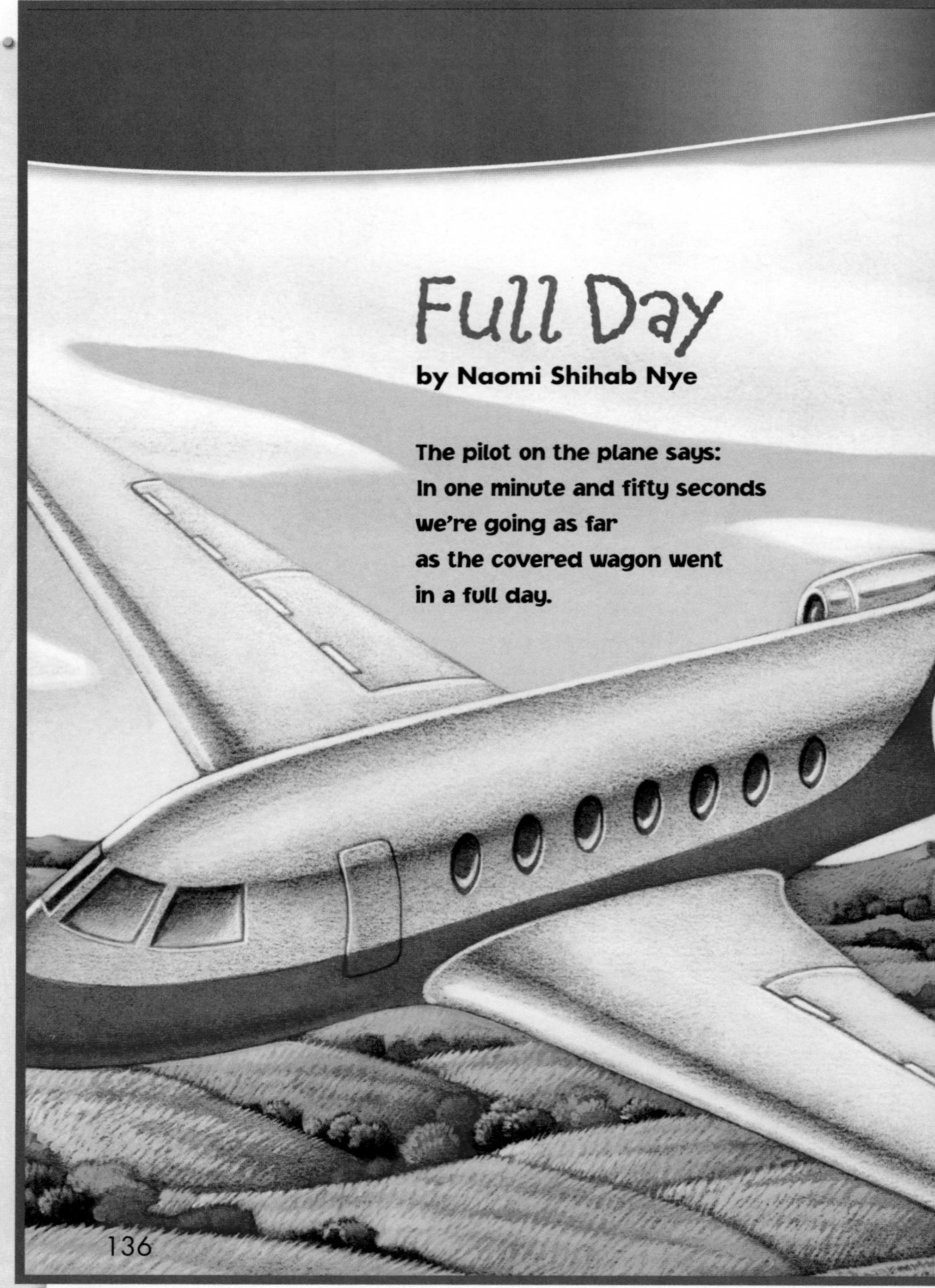

Full Day
by Naomi Shihab Nye
The pilot on the plane says:
In one minute and fifty seconds
we're going as far
as the covered wagon went
in a full day.
136

EXTEND SKILLS

Author's Viewpoint

Explain that readers can sometimes figure out an author's viewpoint, or his or her attitude toward the subject being described. In "Full Day," while the poet admires air travel for its speed, she seems to have greater respect for travel by covered wagon. The poet describes the hardships these travelers had to endure and points out how they got to enjoy the beautiful countryside and carry their treasures with them. They *experienced* their trip in a way that passengers in a plane never can.

Practice Fluent Reading

Have partners take turns reading "Full Day" aloud. Tell students to read the poem twice—once pausing at the end of every line and once pausing for punctuation; that is, where punctuation indicates complete phrases or sentences. Point out how using punctuation to determine phrasing helps make the poem more meaningful.

AudioText

We look down
on clouds,
1 mountains of froth and foam.
We eat a neat
and subdivided lunch.

How was it for the people in
the covered wagon?
They bumped and jostled.
Their wheels broke.
Their biscuits were tough.
They got hot and cold and old.
Their shirts tore on the branches
they passed.

But they saw the pebbles
and the long grass
and the sweet shine of evening
settling on the fields. 2
They knew the ruts and the rocks.
They threw their furniture out
to make the wagons lighter. 3
They carried their treasures
in a crooked box. 4

Writing Poetry

Have students write poems, in rhyme or free verse, comparing different ways of traveling. It could be walking instead of taking the bus, bicycling instead of running, or driving in a car instead of taking a train. Encourage students to include details about what they see and do as they travel. Have students recite their poems for the class.

3 Details and Facts • Inferential

What details does the speaker give about travel by covered wagon?

Possible responses: The speaker describes the travelers' physical discomforts, such as being *bumped, jostled, hot,* and *cold.* She describes how they had to wear torn shirts and throw away furniture to make the load lighter.

4 Compare and Contrast • Inferential

According to the speaker, how is traveling in a plane different from traveling in a covered wagon?

Possible responses: People travel faster in planes than they did in covered wagons. They also see clouds, rather than beautiful landscape. People traveling in planes eat prepackaged food, while those in covered wagons ate tough biscuits and experienced all of the good and bad details of their trip firsthand.

Connect Ideas and Themes

Remind students this unit deals with the challenges people face and how they meet them. Ask students to discuss the challenges faced by the individuals in each poem. Then have students recall times when they have faced personal challenges and share how they overcame them.

Extend Skills

Free Verse

Free verse is a form of poetry that doesn't have familiar rhythm or even words that rhyme. The poet creates a form especially for that poem. "Full Day" is an example of free verse.

Unit 1
Wrap-Up

OBJECTIVES

- Critically analyze unit theme.
- Connect content across selections.
- Combine content and skills in meaningful activities that build literacy.
- Respond to unit selections through a variety of modalities.

MEETING CHALLENGES

Discuss the Big Idea

What kinds of challenges do people face and how do they meet them?

Write the unit theme and Big Idea question on the board. Ask students to think about the selections they have read in the unit. Discuss how each selection and lesson concept can help them answer the Big Idea question from this unit.

Model this for students by choosing a selection and explaining how the selection and lesson concept address the Big Idea.

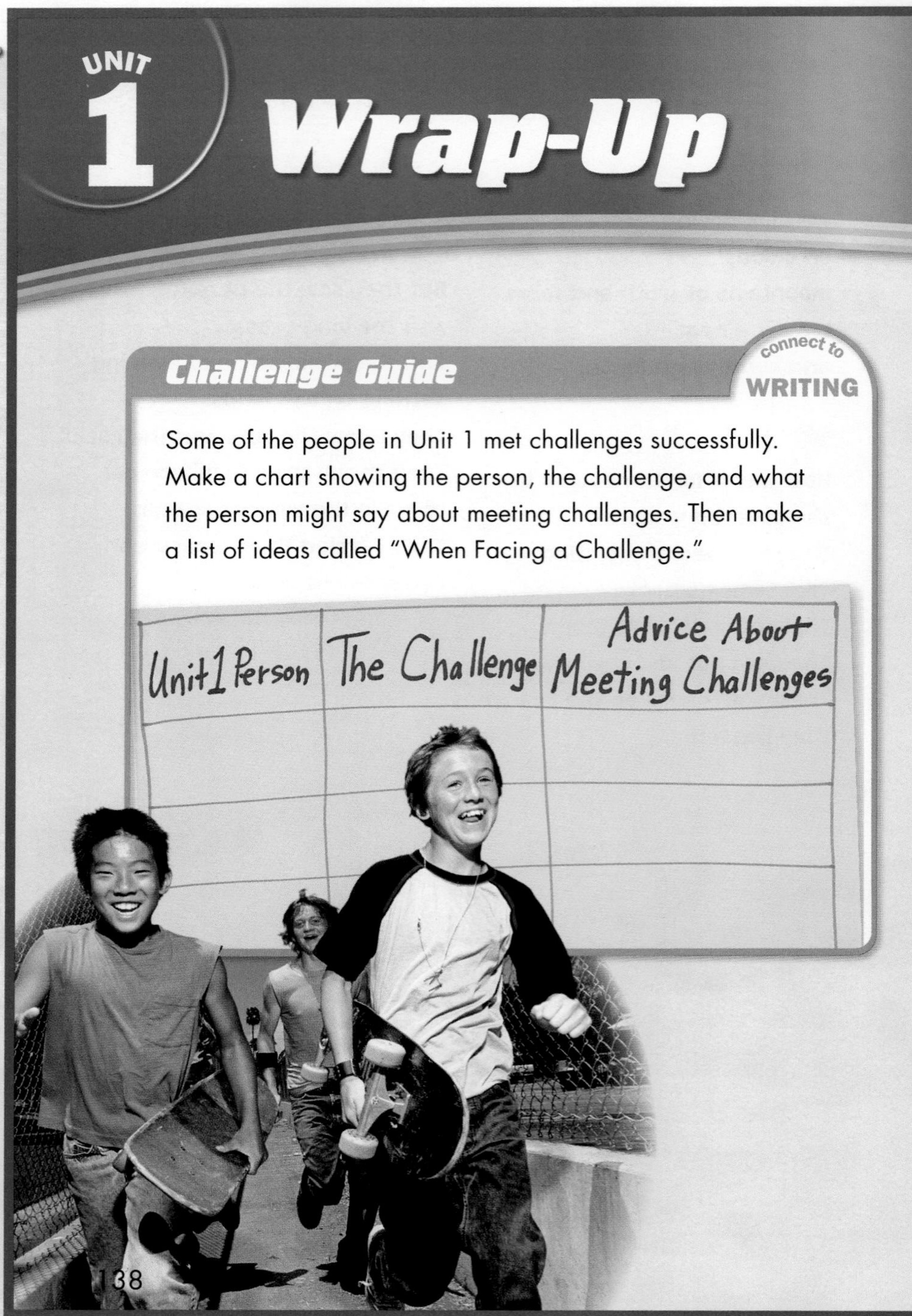
UNIT 1 Wrap-Up

Challenge Guide

connect to WRITING

Some of the people in Unit 1 met challenges successfully. Make a chart showing the person, the challenge, and what the person might say about meeting challenges. Then make a list of ideas called "When Facing a Challenge."

Unit 1 Person	The Challenge	Advice About Meeting Challenges

138

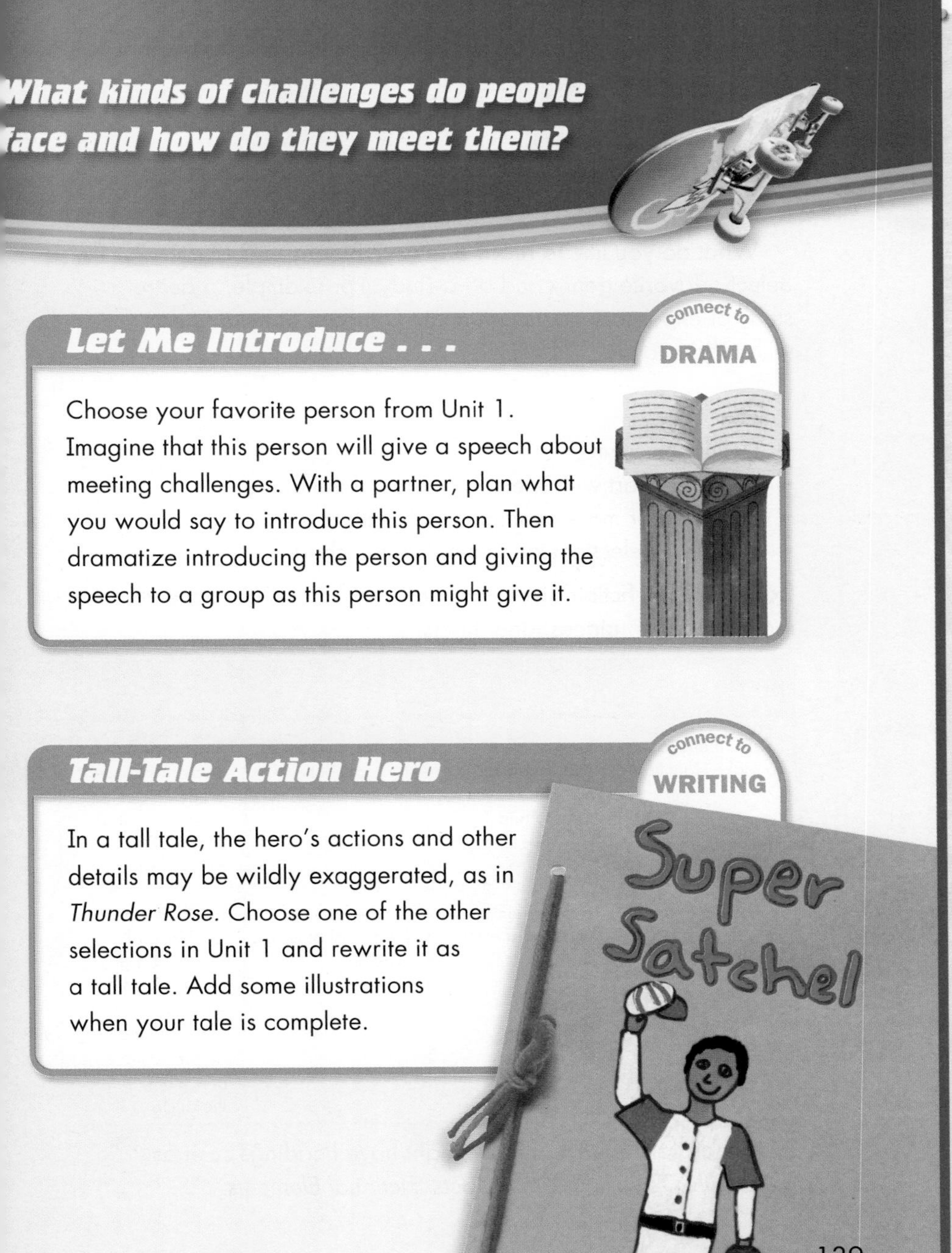
What kinds of challenges do people
face and how do they meet them?
Let Me Introduce . . .
connect to
DRAMA
Choose your favorite person from Unit 1. Imagine that this person will give a speech about meeting challenges. With a partner, plan what you would say to introduce this person. Then dramatize introducing the person and giving the speech to a group as this person might give it.
Tall-Tale Action Hero
connect to
WRITING
In a tall tale, the hero's actions and other details may be wildly exaggerated, as in Thunder Rose. Choose one of the other selections in Unit 1 and rewrite it as a tall tale. Add some illustrations when your tale is complete.
Super
Satchel
139

ACTIVITIES

Challenge Guide

Make a Chart Discuss with students how different characters or people met challenges in the unit. Elicit ideas about what advice these characters or people might give about overcoming challenges.

Let Me Introduce . . .

Write a Speech Each student should first select a favorite person or character from the unit. Help students plan their speeches by making a list of important details about the character or person and thinking about what he or she would want to say to others about meeting challenges. Have students chose one important detail to include in the introduction.

Tall-Tale Action Hero

Rewrite a Story After students choose a selection to rewrite as a tall tale, point out that they can give the main characters superpowers, change the setting, or rewrite the action. Have students work in pairs or small groups to discuss ideas before they begin writing.

Genre and Author Study

GENRE STUDY

Explain that understanding the conventions and elements of a genre can help students

- know what to expect and better understand a story
- recognize a genre when the genre is not identified
- gain insight into the author's purpose or author's thoughts
- read more critically
- create and organize their own writing

Think Aloud **MODEL** If I'm reading a story that I know is a fable, I know to look for a moral. If I don't know the genre but am reading a short tale with talking animals and a moral, I know it's a fable. Based on what the moral is, I will know something about the author's beliefs. Comparing fables and recognizing the best ones could help me create my own fable.

Expository Nonfiction

Point out the definition of expository nonfiction on p. 760. Add that selections in this genre supply information. Have students look at the chart for *Special Effects* and *Ghost Towns.* Ask students how knowing the elements of this genre might help them decide if a selection is a good example of this genre.

Other Genres/Other Features

Discuss other genres, as well as other possible headings for charts (for example, for expository nonfiction, one might add *style* or *organization*, while other genres might add *rhyme, setting, theme*, or *point of view*). Have students name a few favorite books and create simple genre charts.

Genre Study

What do you like to read? Fantasy? Biography? Mystery? Select a favorite genre and do a study. For example, a genre study of expository nonfiction might compare *Special Effects* with *Ghost Towns*.

Try It

- Define the genre.
- Set up a chart with special features of the genre.
- Read two or more examples of the genre.
- Compare selections and complete the chart.

Expository nonfiction gives facts and, sometimes, opinions about real-life people, places, and things.

Selection	Topic	Text Features	Example Facts
Special Effects by Jake Hamilton	How some special effects are created for movies and TV	Photos, numbered text, call-outs	The movie-makers study this concept model to decide on the size and shape of the finished product.
Ghost Towns by Raymond Bial	How settlements became ghost towns	Modern and historic photos, captions	In 1848, James W. Marshall discovered gold at Sutter's Mill when he shut down the water on the millrace and glanced into the ditch.

A chart for historical fiction might have headings such as these: *Title, Topic, Historical Facts, Fictional Elements.*

760

Other Genres and Their Features

Genre	Characteristics
Expository nonfiction	topic, organization, text features, style
Biography	main subject, facts, organization, illustrations
Mystery	detective, suspects, plot, clues, style
Science fiction	theme, science-related plot, characters, futuristic setting
Myth	country or culture of origin, characters, plot
Legend	hero, hero's traits, setting, conflict
Fantasy	characters, setting, plot, fantastical elements
Narrative poetry	subject, plot, rhyme, rhythm
Lyric poetry	subject, figurative language, sound devices, rhythm

Author Study

Do you have a favorite selection? Make a note of the author's name and look for books by that author. You will probably enjoy other works by him or her.

Try It

- Find three or four works by one author.
- Read the book jackets or use the Internet to learn about the author's life to see what may have influenced his or her writing.
- Read the author's works.
- Compare topics, genres, and so on.
- Tell which work is your favorite and why.

Read this author study of Julius Lester.

Julius Lester

Julius Lester has written more than thirty books and won many honors. When he was growing up in the 1940s and 1950s, he never dreamed he would become a writer. He wanted to be a musician. After recording two albums and hosting radio and television shows, he turned to writing. His love of music may have inspired him to write about Mahalia Jackson. The Blues Singers is about real people, but some of his books are fiction. My favorite book is a true story—Black Cowboy, Wild Horses.

761

Additional Questions to Consider

- Where and when did/does the author live? How did this affect his or her work?
- Why was the author drawn to his or her favorite genre or topic?
- Are events in the author's life reflected in his or her work?
- Can you identify with any ideas or events from the author's life?
- How does knowing more about the author help you better understand his or her work?

AUTHOR STUDY

Explain to students that an author study is a great opportunity to learn more about favorite authors and their writing. Reading other works by the same author can help students

- identify an author's craft
- make connections to similar genres of writing
- experience good writing models

Author's Craft

Authors make choices about the elements, the language, and the style of their works. By studying an author's work, students will begin to see the writing traits of their favorite authors. Are their characters funny? Are their books easy to read? Do they have great illustrations? Identifying choices an author makes helps students understand their own interests.

Genre

An author study can also help students understand genres. Are all the books by their favorite author science fiction? Does the author write only biographies of famous sports legends? Connecting with a genre can encourage students to read similar works of the same genre by other authors.

Writing

What inspires your favorite author to write? How does he or she come up with ideas? These are the kinds of discoveries students will make by doing an author study. When students experience good writing models, they learn to understand the writing process. Imitating the style of their favorite authors is a great springboard for writing.

DISCUSS AUTHORS

The following information will add to students' understanding of the writing done by the authors whose biographical information appears on pages 762–763.

- Writers of biographies are called **biographers.** Writers of autobiographies are called **autobiographers.**
- Biographers and autobiographers can write about a person's entire life, part of the person's life, or a single incident in the person's life.
- Biographers must do a lot of research to recreate the life and times of the people about whom they write. Because autobiographers write about themselves, they use their memories, but they might still do research about locations they visited. Or they might talk to relatives and friends who went through events and situations with them.
- Biographies and autobiographies are works of nonfiction. However, some writers include fictional elements, such as dialogue and details that make the subject "come alive." These fictional elements are based on research and evidence. Dialogue should include words or ideas that the person would likely have said in a given situation, and details should be true to the time and place of the story.
- An autobiography is usually told from the first-person point of view, because the writer is writing about himself or herself. A biography is usually written in the third person. However, a biographer might use another character to tell the story from the first-person point of view, as Ken Mochizuki did in *Passage to Freedom.*

Meet Authors of Biography and Autobiography

Lesa Cline-Ransome

The author of *Satchel Paige*, p. 94

Lesa Cline-Ransome was working in the fashion world when she became interested in education. She started teaching and then turned to writing for children. Ms. Cline-Ransome works with her illustrator husband, James Ransome. She says that she trusts completely his artistic judgments and that he sometimes comes to her for ideas about how to illustrate a story. **Other books: *Major Taylor, Champion Cyclist* and *The Wagon***

Jean Fritz

The author of *Leonardo's Horse*, p. 292

Jean Fritz writes books about history because she enjoys doing research. She says, "For every book I write, I have to read a great deal and usually travel to the place I'm writing about." While writing *Leonardo's Horse*, Ms. Fritz went to Italy. She was there when the 24-foot bronze horse was presented as a gift from the American people to the Italian people. **Other books: *Bully for You, Teddy Roosevelt* and *Can't You Make Them Behave, King George?***

Barbara Kerley

The author of *The Dinosaurs of Waterhouse Hawkins*, p. 320

Barbara Kerley says she got the idea for writing *The Dinosaurs of Waterhouse Hawkins* when her daughter asked how big a T. rex was. "I had no idea, so we got a book on dinosaurs from the library. In it was this incredible drawing of a dinner party, with formal waiter, candlesticks on the table, and all these elegant gentlemen stuffed into a dinosaur. I was hooked—I just had to find out the story behind that picture." **Another book: *Songs of Papa's Island***

762

Ken Mochizuki

The author of *Passage to Freedom*, p. 166

Passage to Freedom is Mr. Mochizuki's first children's nonfiction book. He approached the story as a journalist, gathering whatever information he could. He decided to tell the story from the point of view of Chiune Sugihara's son. But Hiroki Sugihara was only five years old at the time. Mr. Mochizuki says, "Having someone recall specific incidents that occurred over fifty years ago is no easy task." Fortunately Hiroki was able to remember many details. Chiune Sugihara is one of Mr. Mochizuki's personal heroes. "He was a man willing to suffer the consequences and risk his life and career to save the lives of others." **Other books: *Baseball Saved Us* and *Heroes***

Gary Soto

The author of "The Gymnast," p. 488

Gary Soto says, "It appears these days I don't have much of a life because my nose is often stuck in a book. But I discovered that reading builds a life inside the mind. I enjoy biographies and novels and reading in Spanish. Also, I like theater, tennis, basketball, traveling (especially London), and working in the garden . . . sometimes." Born in Fresno, California, Mr. Soto was the second of three children. Although his writing comes from his experiences growing up in a Mexican American community, he says that his stories are not all based on actual events. Mr. Soto has taught at the University of California but today is a full-time writer. Does Mr. Soto revise his writing? He says, "Yes, all writers revise, and almost all writers have friends who look at their work. My first reader is my wife, poor thing. I bother her almost daily." **Other books: *Off and Running* and *The Pool Party***

763

More About Jean Fritz

Ms. Fritz has been writing about history and famous people in history for more than forty years. She says that when she is asked how she chooses her subjects, she tells people that her subjects choose her. "A character in history will suddenly step out of the past and demand a book," she says.

Jean Fritz's first biography was *The Cabin Faced West,* which included a visit by George Washington to a pioneer family.

Ms. Fritz has won many awards for her writing, including the Laura Ingalls Wilder Award from the American Library Association.

More About Barbara Kerley

Barbara Kerley clearly remembers being in fifth grade. She remembers reading constantly, playing soccer (which she liked), and playing piano (which she didn't like).

As an adult, Ms. Kerley worked with the Peace Corps in Nepal. She taught math, science, and English. She felt the Peace Corps work was important because it gave her the opportunity to do something for those less fortunate than she had been.

Ms. Kerley says she writes every day. She feels it is important for a writer to have a routine. Otherwise, she says, "...half the morning is frittered away with nothing but clean socks to show for it."

Students can use a student-friendly search engine to learn more about the authors and their subjects. Keywords might include authors' names; the names of the subjects of the biographies; or an event, place, or time period mentioned in the author information or in the stories.

DISCUSS AUTHORS

The following information will add to students' understanding of the writing done by the authors whose biographical information appears on pages 764–765.

Myths and Tales

- Myths, folk tales, and tall tales were passed down for generations before being written down. They reflect something about the cultures to which they belong.
- Writers who write down myths and tales are usually reflecting their own values, their own cultures, or their appreciation for the histories behind the stories.
- Myths, folk tales, and tall tales highlight human behavior and what a culture values. Choices that the culture views as unwise have bad results, while behavior that a culture values will lead to a happy ending.
- Tall tales tend to show both the values and the hardships of those living in difficult places. Qualities that are necessary for survival (strength, bravery) are humorously exaggerated in tall tales.

Narrative Nonfiction

- Writers of narrative nonfiction tell good stories with interesting characters, plots, and settings, but their stories are about real people, places, and events, not imaginary ones.
- Writers of narrative nonfiction must be good researchers. They must be able to dig into history, news reports, reference works, or journals to gather the details needed to make people and events come to life for the reader.

Meet Authors of Myths and Tales

Charlotte Craft

The author of *King Midas and the Golden Touch*, p. 678

Charlotte Craft is the daughter of the illustrator of *King Midas*, Kinuko Craft. She lives in Scotland with her family. Her inspiration for the story of *King Midas and the Golden Touch* was Nathaniel Hawthorne's retelling of the Greek myth.

Linda Fang

The author of "The Ch'i-lin Purse," p. 190

As a ten-year-old girl living in Shanghai, China, Linda Fang was too shy to speak up in class. So one day her teacher handed her a picture book, told her to read it that night, and said, "Come back tomorrow and see if you can tell it to me." The teacher's goal was to help her student overcome her shyness. The teacher's plan must have worked, because today Ms. Fang is a professional storyteller and winner of the 1998 Storyteller of the Year Award. Ms. Fang first heard "The Ch'i-lin Purse" from her mother. **Other books about China: *Fa Mulan* and *Da Wei's Treasure***

Jerdine Nolen

The author of *Thunder Rose*, p. 46

Jerdine Nolen says that as a child she was never bored. Ms. Nolen says she can't remember a time when she wasn't writing and collecting words. "My mother encouraged me to do that. She was always eager to hear my new list of 'favorite words.'" Once you have a story, Ms. Nolen says, it's important to keep revising and reworking it. "It is like sculpting or wiring the pieces together in a way, so the words on the page have enough life—they could stand up and walk around all on their own."

764

Meet Authors of Narrative Nonfiction and Case Studies

Dr. Robert Ballard

The author of *The Unsinkable Wreck of the R.M.S.* Titanic, p. 540

Dr. Robert Ballard was born in Wichita, Kansas, but grew up in San Diego, California, near the water. He says that growing up he always wanted to be Captain Nemo from Jules Verne's science-fiction novel *20,000 Leagues Under the Sea*. Dr. Ballard has led or taken part in more than one hundred deep-sea expeditions. Another of his accomplishments is founding the JASON Foundation for Education. He did this in response to the thousands of letters from schoolchildren wanting to know how he discovered the R.M.S. *Titanic*. **Other books about shipwrecks: *The Wreck of the Zanzibar* and *The Story of the H.L. Hunley and Queenie's Coin***

Susan E. Quinlan

The author of "The Mystery of Saint Matthew Island," p. 658

Susan E. Quinlan loves wildlife. She says, "It's hard to draw a line between what I do for a living and what I do for hobbies." As a biologist and naturalist guide, she has explored environments in many parts of the world. "The Mystery of Saint Matthew Island" is one of fourteen accounts in *The Case of the Mummified Pigs and Other Mysteries in Nature*. To write the book she followed up on "wisps of knowledge" she had collected from her experiences in the field and from interviewing scientists. Ms. Quinlan says, "Through my years of educational work as a wildlife biologist, I gradually realized that people who are trained as biologists look at nature differently from other people. ... One of my goals as a writer is to help others learn to look at nature in the ways that a biologist might. I also want to interpret the research work of scientists in ways that children and nonscientists can understand and enjoy." **Other books: *The Case of the Monkeys That Fell from the Trees* and *The Case of the Mummified Pigs***

More About Linda Fang

Linda Fang credits the start of her professional career to good luck. She was working for a television station in Washington, D.C., in 1987. "They had a storytelling show. I saw that they didn't have any Chinese stories, so I sent them one. The station liked the story, but they didn't have the right person to tell it. They tried me on camera and thought I did well."

Soon, Ms. Fang was performing at theaters, museums, festivals, and competitions. People often asked where they could find a book that included her stories. "Since the stories were never published in English, I decided to write one."

More About Dr. Robert Ballard

Dr. Ballard has tracked down many other important shipwrecks besides the *Titanic.* He located the German battleship *Bismarck,* the U.S. aircraft carrier *Yorktown* (sunk in the World War II Battle of Midway), and most recently John F. Kennedy's boat, *PT-109.* He is an explorer-in-residence for the National Geographic Society and president of the Institute for Exploration. Dr. Ballard's JASON Project uses telecommunications technology to enable schoolchildren around the country to "come along" on undersea explorations around the globe.

Students can use a student-friendly search engine to learn more about the authors and their subjects. Keywords might include authors' names, the cultures that gave rise to the fictional stories, or the real events and people of the narrative nonfiction. Students might also search out other myths, tall tales, and folk tales, using these terms as keywords.

DISCUSS AUTHORS

The following information will add to students' understanding of the writing done by the authors whose biographical information appears on pages 766–767.

- Writers of expository nonfiction may write to explain, to give directions, to persuade, or to share information.
- Because there is no plot in expository nonfiction, writers must find another way to organize their information. A writer might use chronological order or cause-and-effect or compare-and-contrast structure. A writer might also use sequential order, as in the numbered steps for directions.
- Some expository nonfiction is intended to be persuasive. The author may select the facts, ideas, and opinions he or she includes to get you to reach a specific conclusion. Students can recognize persuasive writing if the writing asks them to think, believe, or do something. It is always wise in these cases to get more facts on the topic to discover whether you truly agree with the point being made.
- Often, the writer simply wishes to supply information on an interesting topic. For some authors, writing expository nonfiction is their job. This applies to newspaper reporters, magazine writers, and encyclopedia writers. They research a topic that interests them and write about it. However, some authors are scientists, researchers, or historians who are simply writing about the topics they know best. Biologist Dr. Joanne Settel is an example.

Meet Authors of Expository Nonfictio

Raymond Bial

The author of *Ghost Towns of the American West*, p. 608

A photographer who works in both color and black and white, Raymond Bial has published more than thirty books. *Ghost Towns of the American West* is a blend of photographs and text called a photo essay. **Other books: *Tenement* and *The Farms***

Alden Carter

The author of *Stretching Ourselves*, p. 416

Alden Carter and his wife, Carol, worked as a team to write *Stretching Ourselves*. Mr. Carter says, "We knew a little girl (Emily in the book) with cerebral palsy. Our son and her brother played on the same basketball team." **Other books: *I'm Tougher Than Diabetes!* and *I'm Tougher Than Asthma!***

Jane Goodall

The author of "10 Ways to Help Save Wildlife," p. 212

"It is quite possible that today's teenagers will raise their children in a world with no wild chimpanzees, gorillas, orangutans, and bonobos," Dr. Jane Goodall said. "It's a tragic prospect, but there is still time to act." **Other books: *With Love* and *Chimps***

Jake Hamilton

The author of *Special Effects in Film and Television*, p. 368

Jake Hamilton has always loved movies. Today Mr. Hamilton gets to watch movies as part of his job. He is a film critic for newspapers and magazines. This is his first book for young people. **Other books about special effects: *Computer Animation From Start to Finish* and *Virtual Reality***

Deborah Hopkinson

The author of *Shutting Out the Sky*, p. 116

Deborah Hopkinson is interested in both nonfiction and historical fiction. Many of Ms. Hopkinson's award-winning books are about a woman or girl who has led an unusual life. **Other books: *A Band of Angels* and *Girl Wonder***

Julius Lester

The author of "Mahalia Jackson," p. 350

Julius Lester says, "I write because the lives of all of us are stories." Mr. Lester has published more than thirty books and won many honors. It is important to him to help African American children become aware of their heritage. **Other books: *Black Cowboy, Wild Horses* and *The Knee-High Man and Other Tales***

Patrick O'Brien

The author and illustrator of *The Hindenburg*, p. 704

Patrick O'Brien says, "I began working on *The Hindenburg* after my editor asked me if I would be interested. I did a lot of research. For the explosions, I watched historical films of the actual event and other movies with big explosions." **Other books: *Duel of the Ironclads* and *The Great Ships***

Joanne Settel

The author of *Exploding Ants*, p. 440

Dr. Joanne Settel says, "I love making science exciting and accessible for others. There are so many amazing things going on in the natural world. It's tremendous fun letting people know about them." **Other books: *Why Does My Nose Run?* and *Why Do Cats' Eyes Glow in the Dark?***

767

More About Deborah Hopkinson

Deborah Hopkinson knew she wanted to be a writer, but she didn't know what to write. Then, when her daughter Rebekah was about three, she found herself reading a lot of children's books. Ms. Hopkinson says, "I thought, 'Maybe I'll try writing for children. At least the books are short.' I have since found out that because a story is short doesn't mean that it is easy to write."

More About Julius Lester

When he was growing up in the 1940s and 1950s, Julius Lester never dreamed he would one day become a writer. He wanted to be a musician. After recording two albums and hosting television shows, he turned to writing. He hopes that, if enough stories are written about people's lives, readers will begin to recognize how much we all have in common.

More About Joanne Settel

Dr. Joanne Settel, a biologist with a specialty in zoology, relates, "I have been collecting journal articles with interesting animal facts for more than 30 years. Every few years I pull out the ones that are the most interesting and put them together in a book. This time, I was particularly looking for items...that would make kids go 'wow' or 'gross' or 'yuk.' I wanted a book that would stand out from the crowd."

Students can search electronic reference works to find out more about these authors and the topics covered in their expository writing. Keywords might include authors' names, an interesting detail, or the general topic of their work.

DISCUSS AUTHORS

The following information will add to students' understanding of the writing done by the authors whose biographical information appears on pages 768–769.

Realistic and Historical Fiction

- In addition to good imaginations and storytelling skills, writers of realistic and historical fiction need the research skills of a nonfiction writer.
- Writers of historical fiction must study the time period of their story and the real people and events that surround the fictional elements of their stories. It takes much research to write good historical fiction.
- Writers of realistic fiction need to know about the settings of their stories and what people's lives there are like. They may use places they know or research new places.

Humorous Fiction

- Writers of humorous fiction must be good observers of human behavior. They need to see the humor in a wide range of situations—from the difficult to the silly. They also need to know what makes people laugh, whether it's a surprise ending or a kitten playing in a big paper bag.
- In many ways, writers of humorous fiction need the same skills as writers of realistic fiction. We generally view things as being funnier if we can identify in some way with the characters, situations, or events of the story.

Meet Authors of Realistic and Historical Fiction

Lulu Delacre

The author of "At the Beach: Abuelito's Story," p. 638

Lulu Delacre grew up in Puerto Rico. For "At the Beach," Ms. Delacre says, "I wanted to write about an adventure at the beach. When I was a child I went to the beach with my father and sister most weekends." Like the boy in the story, Ms. Delacre has actually stepped on a sea urchin! "It is indeed very painful," she says. **Other books: *Salsa Stories* and *Arroz con Leche***

Francisco Jiménez

The author of "Inside Out," p. 146

Francisco Jiménez was born in Mexico. When he was four years old, he came to the United States with his family. His parents were looking for a better life. They followed the crops from place to place in California. They often lived in tents or one-room shacks. School was the only stable thing in his life. He knew that what he learned in school would stay with him no matter how often he moved. "Inside Out" comes from his childhood experiences. **Other books: *The Christmas Gift* and *The Circuit***

Scott O'Dell

The author of *Island of the Blue Dolphins*, p. 72

Island of the Blue Dolphins was Scott O'Dell's first book for young people. It won the Newbery Medal. Mr. O'Dell believed that writing stories for young readers was more rewarding than writing for adults. One of the frequent questions young readers asked him was, "What's the most important thing a writer should do?" His answer was to stick with it. "Writing is hard, harder than digging a ditch, and it requires patience," he said. **Other books: *The Black Pearl* and *Carlota***

Meet Authors of Humorous Fiction

Andrew Clements

The author of *Frindle*, p. 22

Author Andrew Clements had a thought: *What would happen if a kid started using a new word, and other kids really liked it, but his English teacher didn't?* The result was *Frindle*. Mr. Clements says, "*Frindle* includes a lot of material drawn from my own experiences as a kid and a teacher and a parent. One of the things I love about Nick is that he's right on the edge—he's what a good friend of mine calls 'Very Nearly Naughty.' But Nick is so smart and funny, and he has such a good heart and such good ideas that you have to forgive him." **Other books: *The School Story* and *The Landry News***

Richard Peck

The author of "The Three-Century Woman," p. 516

Richard Peck often writes about grandparents. One of his most memorable characters is Grandma Dowdel, who stars in his Newbery Award-winning novel, *A Year Down Yonder*. Many of Mr. Peck's characters are independent people. He says that he tries to give readers leading characters they can look up to and reasons to believe that problems can be solved. He also hopes his readers will learn that they can be different from the group. Mr. Peck grew up in a small town in Illinois. He was a high school teacher for many years. He quit teaching to write, but he draws on his experiences with students in his books. "Ironically, it was my students that taught me to be a writer, though I had been hired to teach them," he said in a speech once. "They taught me that a novel must entertain first before it can be anything else." **Other books about family life: *Fair Weather* and *Misty of Chincoteague***

769

More About Francisco Jiménez

Francisco Jiménez once said, "I write in both English and Spanish. The language I use is determined by what period in my life I write about. Since Spanish was the dominant language during my childhood, I generally write about those experiences in Spanish."

As a child, Mr. Jiménez helped his family pick crops: strawberries in the summer, grapes in the fall, cotton in the winter. He always missed the beginning of the school year because he was picking grapes. At first, he didn't speak much English. Starting late and not speaking English made school more challenging, but Mr. Jiménez knew education was important. His belief in the importance of education has stayed with him. Today, Mr. Jiménez teaches at the University of Santa Clara in California. His wife is also a teacher.

More About Scott O'Dell

Scott O'Dell got the idea for *Island of the Blue Dolphins* from an article he read about a young girl, Karana, who lived alone for eighteen years on an island off the California coast. The book became a best seller, and Mr. O'Dell went on to write another twenty-five books for young readers. His book *The Black Pearl* was another Newbery award winner and is an American Library Association Notable Book.

Mr. O'Dell died in 1989. His widow completed two books that he had left unfinished.

Students can search the Internet, using authors' names as keywords. Remind students to follow classroom guidelines for Internet use.

DISCUSS AUTHORS

The following information will add to students' understanding of the writing done by the authors whose biographical information appears on pages 770–771.

Fiction and Science Fiction

- Writers of fiction need to combine an understanding of human behavior, emotions, and experiences with active imaginations.
- Writers of science fiction need to add to the above an interest in science—because good science fiction needs to include some scientific facts, theories, or ideas.
- In both types of fiction, writers need to make sure the reactions and emotions of the characters are believable, or readers will not connect with the story.

Plays

- Writers of plays—or **playwrights**—need to understand the theater. Everything an audience learns must be said by the actors. Action and dialogue establish the characters, emotions, and background.
- Playwrights must also write words that can be spoken. If the sentences they write do not flow—that is, if they are difficult to say— they will not work well on stage.

Poetry

- Writers of poetry—or **poets**—must be disciplined. Words must be carefully chosen to carry the most meaning but also to fit into the rhythm patterns or rhyme schemes.
- Poets must find ways of fitting ideas into a short amount of space. Figurative language helps, but it must be used effectively to get the writer's ideas across.

Meet Authors of Fiction and Science Fiction

Paul Fleischman

The author of *Weslandia*, p. 396

When he was asked if his childhood was like Wesley's in *Weslandia*, Paul Fleischman replied, "Yes and no. I felt different from my peers because I was so short—the shortest boy in my grade all the way through 10th grade. And like Wesley, my friends and I made up an alternate world—our own games, our own underground school newspaper." On the other hand, he says, "Unlike Wesley, I wasn't an outcast. I was president of my grammar school and had a great pack of friends." Mr. Fleischman grew up in Santa Monica, California, where he listened to his father, well-known writer Sid Fleischman, read chapters of his books to the family. Paul Fleischman says, "We grew up knowing that words felt good in the ears and on the tongue, that they were as much fun to play with as toys." **Other books: *Lost! A Story in String* and *Joyful Noise***

Jules Verne

The author of *Journey to the Center of the Earth*, p. 586

Jules Verne was born in France in 1828. He studied to become a lawyer, but from the beginning he knew he would be a better writer than lawyer. His books are read throughout the world. *Journey to the Center of the Earth* is just one of his stories about extraordinary voyages. Mr. Verne's books are a mix of fact and fantasy. They combine science with action and adventure. He created what he called a "novel of science," or "scientific novel." Today we call the genre science fiction. In modern times, many of his books, including *Journey to the Center of the Earth,* have been made into movies. **Other science fiction books: *A Wrinkle in Time* and *20,000 Leagues Under the Sea***

Meet Authors of Plays and Poetry

Lydia R. Diamond

The author of *The Stormi Giovanni Club*, p. 462

Playwright Lydia R. Diamond said, "I think kids are a little more brave than adults sometimes." She was thinking about her own school days when she moved around a lot. The move from Mississippi to Massachusetts was especially hard. "It was cold in Massachusetts and warm in Mississippi, and that was strange. I made new friends quickly, though. I wasn't afraid." When she moves to new places now, with a husband and baby, it's different. "It's harder to leave friends when you're an adult. But my character Stormi Giovanni has taught me to have more faith, that I will make new friends, that it will be OK." Lydia Diamond's plays have been performed in U.S. cities from New York to California. One of them, *Here I Am . . . See Can You Handle It*, is based on the writings of Nikki Giovanni. Ms. Diamond lives in Massachusetts with her husband and her son. **Other books about family life: *A Family Apart* and *Flip-Flop Girl***

Henry Wadsworth Longfellow

The author of *The Midnight Ride of Paul Revere*, p. 234

Henry Wadsworth Longfellow became the most popular poet of his day. Mr. Longfellow was one of the first American poets to write about people, traditions, and events with American themes. Mr. Longfellow climbed the steps of the Old North Church and visited an inn in New England. These experiences may have inspired him to write *The Midnight Ride of Paul Revere*. Mr. Longfellow died in 1882. **Another book: *Paul Revere's Ride***

More About Jules Verne

Jules Verne is generally considered the inventor of science fiction. He was a man of great imagination, but he was also a man of great humor and brilliance. He described engineering marvels, both real and imagined, with incredible technical accuracy. In books such as *From the Earth to the Moon, Mysterious Island, Twenty Thousand Leagues Under the Sea,* and *Around the World in Eighty Days,* Mr. Verne predicted such developments as elevated trains, automobiles, fax machines, computer-like banking machines, submarines, the Aqua-Lung, television, and space travel.

More About Henry Wadsworth Longfellow

Longfellow began publishing poetry while at college. He spent several years in Europe learning French, Spanish, and Italian. When he was offered a position with Harvard University, he settled down and began writing seriously. His narrative poems were a huge success and helped develop audiences for poetry in America. Admired both in the United States and overseas, he was the first American poet to be honored with a memorial in Poets' Corner in London's Westminster Abbey.

Students can use a student-friendly search engine to learn more about the authors on these pages. They might also wish to find additional works by the authors or other works in these genres.

DISCUSS ILLUSTRATORS

The following information will add to students' understanding of the work done by the illustrators whose biographical information appears on pages 772–775.

- An illustrator must use the author's words and his or her own knowledge and imagination to create images to go with those words.
- Often an illustrator can rely on his or her own experiences to come up with images. However, in some cases, an illustrator must do research to determine the right clothes, plants, houses, foods, transportation, or objects that are used by the characters in a story, especially for a story with a historical or real-world setting. For science fiction, a knowledge of the scientific aspects of the story is necessary.
- Sometimes illustrators and authors work closely together, talking regularly, each one modifying his or her work as the other produces images or words. Other times, a story is completed and given to an illustrator, and the illustrator must fit the pictures to the words.
- In some cases, illustrations simply help readers visualize a story. Sometimes they offer clues about the story. Other times, they are a necessary part of the information being shared, as the reader may have no knowledge of the location, people, objects, or events being described.
- Encourage students to look carefully at illustrations as they read and to think about what those illustrations contribute to the stories.

Meet Illustrators

Christopher Bing

The illustrator of *The Midnight Ride of Paul Revere*, p. 234

Christopher Bing has said, "When people pick up one of my books, I want them to become absorbed into the work and feel like they are experiencing the time and period of the event that they're looking at or reading about." He uses maps and re-created documents to make characters and settings come alive. In the illustrations for *The Midnight Ride of Paul Revere*, Mr. Bing used a pen, ink, and a brush on white scratchboard to create the look of an old book.

Another book: *Casey at the Bat*

Carol Carter

The illustrator of *Stretching Ourselves*, p. 416

Carol Carter and her husband, Alden, worked as a team to write *Stretching Ourselves*. They knew a little girl (Emily in the book) with cerebral palsy, and they recruited several more people with CP for the project. Then they had to make layouts because the pictures and text had to work together. After they had a layout, Mr. Carter wrote copy. Then Ms. Carter could start taking photographs. Ms. Carter said, "Photo shoots are hard work and are also very exciting because we never know exactly what's going to happen."

R. Gregory Christie

The illustrator of *The Stormi Giovanni Club*, p. 462

Illustrator R. Gregory Christie has won awards for his work on books of fiction and poetry for young people. One reviewer has said that his unique illustrations, which combine realism and exaggeration, "create harmony with the words."

772

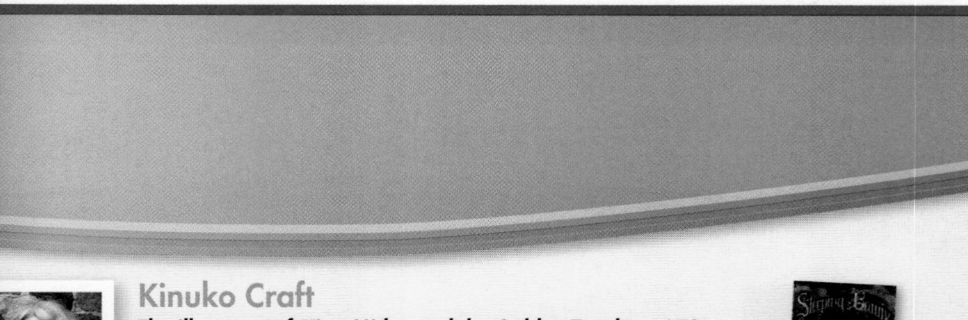

Kinuko Craft

The illustrator of *King Midas and the Golden Touch*, p. 678

Kinuko Craft says, "I feel that, throughout time, each generation has a person with a 'golden touch' who learns the same lesson Midas did." In her paintings for some of the scenes in the book, she used geometric patterns. These come from the designs on small objects found at a burial site believed to be that of the real King Midas. Archaeologists found the objects during a dig at the site in Turkey. Kinuko Craft is one of the most widely respected illustrators of fantasy in the United States today. In an interview, she said, "From grade school through my high school days, my effort was to imitate nature—anything natural." **Other books: *Sleeping Beauty* and *The Adventures of Tom Thumb***

Franklin Hammond

The illustrator of *Wings for the King*, p. 266

Growing up in Canada, Franklin Hammond had asthma. Back then, doctors didn't let kids with asthma play sports, so Mr. Hammond explored art instead. He wasn't a great student, but he worked hard so that he could one day attend his dream school, the Ontario College of Art and Design. As a professional artist, Mr. Hammond says he especially loves working on children's books. He is well known for his unique three-dimensional art, which includes real-life objects and materials. He had a great opportunity to experiment in three dimensions when he created the flying machine in *Wings for the King*. He carefully assembled this fantastic structure using wood, wire, and metal. He says, "There are lots of small details in my work, so I hope kids look closely and find them." **Other books of plays: *Folktales on Stage* and *Cinderella Outgrows the Glass Slipper and Other Zany Fractured Fairy Tale Plays***

773

More About R. Gregory Christie

R. Gregory Christie began his art career creating covers for jazz record albums. In 1996, editors at a major publisher invited him to illustrate *The Palm of My Heart: Poetry by African American Children.* The book won the Coretta Scott King Honor Award for illustration, as well as other awards. Mr. Christie was soon illustrating other books for young readers, focusing primarily on historical and cultural characters, such as Sojourner Truth, Langston Hughes, and Richard Wright.

More About Kinuko Craft

Kinuko Craft was born in Japan. She studied fine arts at the Kanazawa Municipal College of Fine and Industrial Arts before coming to the United States in the early 1960s to study design and illustration at the School of the Art Institute of Chicago. Ms. Craft has won numerous awards, not only for her children's books, but for her other artwork as well. She has painted book covers and opera posters and has done covers and illustrations for *Time, Newsweek,* and *National Geographic,* among other magazines.

Students can use a student-friendly search engine to learn more about the illustrators on these pages or elsewhere in the book. Students may wish to find the personal Web pages for some of the illustrators.

More About Dom Lee

As a child Dom Lee was not a particularly avid reader. "I went to the movies instead. The many movies that I saw during my childhood help me with my illustrations today."

Dom Lee moved to the United States from Seoul, South Korea, with his wife, Keunhee, to pursue a career as an illustrator. After he earned a masters degree in Fine Art, Mr. Lee got his first illustrating project from an editor who had seen Mr. Lee's art at an exhibition.

Mr. Lee's wife, Keunhee, is also an artist and the two have collaborated on books in Korea and now in the U.S. *Journey Home* by Lawrence McKay is the first U.S. book to showcase their collaborative work.

More About Frank Morrison

Frank Morrison has illustrated books by a number of different writers—including one by Queen Latifah. He won the Coretta Scott King/John Steptoe Award for the illustrations for *Jazzy Miz Mozetta.* One critic wrote, "Morrison captures the exuberant spirit of Miz Mozetta with . . .dynamic illustrations that dance to the beat of a fresh, rhythmic story."

Students can use a student-friendly search engine to find images of historic time periods, real places, or real people illustrated in the books and compare them with the illustrators' interpretations of those times and places.

Meet Illustrators

Dom Lee

The illustrator of *Passage to Freedom*, p. 166

Passage to Freedom is the third book Dom Lee has illustrated for writer Ken Mochizuki. Before Mr. Lee began working on the illustrations, he researched the time period to make sure the details he used were accurate. "When I first began my research for *Passage to Freedom,* I only knew a few facts about the Holocaust. But after visiting the Holocaust Museum at Washington, D.C., I was shocked by what I saw. I will never forget the impact that museum left on me."

Frank Morrison

The illustrator of *Sweet Music in Harlem*, p. 730

Frank Morrison is a noted painter whose works are collected for their artistic value. He brings a canvas alive with beauty. He is known for his special style with its long, thin, dramatic figures. Although he had an interest in art early in life, he didn't know that it was to be his calling. While visiting the Louvre Museum in Paris, he suddenly realized he wanted to paint. Comedian Bill Cosby, who takes pride in discovering the artistic talents of African Americans, is a collector of Mr. Morrison's paintings. Mr. Morrison's works have been seen on television shows, and he was commissioned to create a work, titled *Duet,* for the annual music festival sponsored by *Essence* magazine. Mr. Morrison gets inspiration from his mother and his grandparents. He was born in Massachusetts but now lives with his wife, Connie, and their three children in New Jersey. **Other books: *Duke Ellington* and *M Is for Music***

Kadir Nelson

The illustrator of *Thunder Rose*, p. 46

Kadir Nelson says that as a child, "I always knew I'd be an artist. My mother was so supportive, and she never talked me out of it. I was also fortunate that I had an uncle who was an art teacher. He introduced me to the seriousness of taking care of my gift." Mr. Nelson's paintings can be found in the private collections of famous actors, sports figures, and musicians. **Other books: *Big Jabe* and *Ellington Was Not a Street***

James E. Ransome

The illustrator of *Satchel Paige*, p. 94

James E. Ransome and his wife, Lesa Cline-Ransome, who wrote *Satchel Paige*, live in upstate New York with their four children. Mr. Ransome says that he did not have the opportunity to meet artists or visit art galleries while growing up. "I do not remember how my interest in art began," he writes, "but I do remember that some of my first drawings were of hot-rod cars and images copied from the pages of comic books and the Bible."

Brian Selznick

The illustrator of *The Dinosaurs of Waterhouse Hawkins*, p. 320

Once Barbara Kerley had written the manuscript, Brian Selznick got a call from his editor. She described *The Dinosaurs of Waterhouse Hawkins*. Mr. Selznick said the story left his head spinning, and all he could say was "I'll do it!" Mr. Selznick has also written and illustrated his own books. **Another book: *A Week in the Woods***

775

More About James E. Ransome

James E. Ransome has been named one of seventy-five authors and illustrators everyone should know by the Children's Book Council. Mr. Ransome says, "What makes illustrating books so exciting is that not only am I learning about the characters, the environment they live in, and the history of the period, but I can also allow the story to dictate the palette and design that I use to illustrate it, thus giving each book an original, different look and feel."

More About Brian Selznick

Brian Selznick enjoyed the research for *The Dinosaurs of Waterhouse Hawkins.* "The real fun began when I went to England to see Waterhouse's dinosaurs for myself! A park ranger led me across the park onto Dinosaur Island. There they were! The dinosaurs loomed larger and more magnificent than I could ever have imagined. It was like stepping back in time."

For his work on the book, Mr. Selznick won the 2001 Caldecott Honor. "I was very proud, and it made me extra happy because it meant that lots more kids would get to learn about Waterhouse Hawkins."

Students can use a student-friendly search engine to find out about awards given for book illustration. Have students locate an award-winning illustrator whose images they like, and then pick a book they might like to read illustrated by that artist.

Glossary

Glossary

How to Use This Glossary

This glossary can help you understand and pronounce some of the words in this book. The entries in this glossary are in alphabetical order. There are guide words at the top of each page to show you the first and last words on the page. A pronunciation key is at the bottom of every other page. Remember, if you can't find the word you are looking for, ask for help or check a dictionary.

The entry word is in dark type. It shows how the word is spelled and how the word is divided into syllables.

The pronunciation is in parentheses. It also shows which syllables are stressed.

Part-of-speech labels show the function or functions of an entry word and any listed form of that word.

ad·vise (ad vīz′), **1.** *V.* to give advice to; offer an opinion to; counsel: *I shall act as you advised.* **2.** *V.* to give notice; inform: *We were advised that a storm was approaching, so we didn't go sailing.* ❑ *V.* **ad·vised, ad·vis·ing.**

Sometimes, irregular and other special forms will be shown to help you use the word correctly.

The definition and example sentence show you what the word means and how it is used.

Aa

ab·do·men (ab′də mən), *N.* the part of the body containing the stomach, the intestines, and other important organs; belly.

ab·o·rig·i·ne (ab′ə rij′ə nē), *N.* one of the earliest known inhabitants of Australia. ❑ *N. PL.* **ab·o·rig·i·nes.**

ab·sence (ab′səns), *N.* condition of being without; lack: *Darkness is the absence of light.*

ac·com·plish·ment (ə kom′plish mənt), *N.* something that has been done with knowledge, skill, or ability; achievement: *The teachers were proud of the pupils' accomplishments.*

a·chieve (ə chēv′), *V.* to carry out to a successful end; accomplish; do: *Have you achieved your purpose?* ❑ *V.* **a·chieved, a·chiev·ing.**

ac·quaint (ə kwānt′), *V.* to make aware; let know; inform: *Let me acquaint you with your new duties.* ❑ *V.* **ac·quain·ted, ac·quain·ting.**

ad·mir·ing·ly (ad mīr′ing lē), *ADV.* With wonder, pleasure, and approval: *We gazed admiringly at the beautiful painting.*

a·dorn (ə dôrn′), *V.* to add beauty to; put ornaments on; decorate: *She adorned her hair with flowers.* ❑ *V.* **a·dorned, a·dorn·ing.**

ad·vice (ad vīs′), *N.* opinion about what should be done; suggestion: *My advice is that you study more.*

ad·vise (ad vīz′), **1.** *V.* to give advice to; offer an opinion to; counsel: *I shall act as you advised.* **2.** *V.* to give notice; inform: *We were advised that a storm was approaching, so we didn't go sailing.* ❑ *V.* **ad·vised, ad·vis·ing.**

a·gree·ment (ə grē′mənt), *N.* harmony in feeling or opinion: *The coaches are in complete agreement that she will be a superb gymnast.*

air·time (âr′tim), *N.* specific amount of time in a television, radio, or any broadcast media program.

al·gae (al′jē), *N. PL.* group of related living things, mostly living in water.

Alz·heim·er's (älts′hī mərz), *N.* disease of the brain that causes confusion and gradual loss of memory.

a·nat·o·my (ə nat′ə mē), *N.* structure of a living thing: *the anatomy of an earthworm.*

ap·pre·ci·ate (ə prē′shē āt), *V.* to think highly of; recognize the worth or quality of; value; enjoy: *Almost everybody appreciates good food.* ❑ *V.* **ap·pre·ci·at·ed, ap·pre·ci·at·ing.**

ar·chi·tect (är′kə tekt), *N.* person who designs and makes plans for buildings. (*Architect* comes from two Greek words, *archi* meaning "chief" and *tekton* meaning "builder.")

ar·mor (är′mər), *N.* any kind of protective covering. The steel plates of a warship and the bony shell of an armadillo are armor.

armor

ar·ti·fi·cial (är′tə fish′əl), *ADJ.* made by human skill or labor; not natural: *Plastics are artificial substances that do not occur in nature.*

as·cent (ə sent′), *N.* act of going up; upward movement; rising: *The sudden ascent of the elevator made us dizzy.*

as·sign·ment (ə sīn′mənt), *N.* something assigned, especially a piece of work to be done: *Today's assignment in arithmetic consists of ten problems.*

as·ton·ish (ə ston′ish), *V.* to surprise greatly; amaze: *We were astonished by the child's remarkable memory.* ❑ *V.* **as·ton·ished, as·ton·ish·ing.**

au·da·cious (ò dā′shəs), *ADJ.* rudely bold; impudent: *The audacious waiter demanded a larger tip.*

Bb

back·flip (bak′ flip), *N.* backward somersault performed in the air. ❑ *N. PL.* **back·flips.**

back·ground (bak′ ground), *N.* the part of a picture or scene toward the back: *The cottage stands in the foreground with the mountains in the background.*

bar·ber (bär′bər), *N.* person whose business is cutting hair and shaving or trimming beards.

bass[1] (bās), **1.** *N.* the lowest male voice in music. **2.** *N.* the largest, lowest sounding stringed instrument in an orchestra or band.

bass[2] (bas), **1.** *N.* North American freshwater or saltwater fish with spiny fins, used for food.

be·hav·ior (bi hā′vyər), *N.* manner of behaving; way of acting: *Her sullen behavior showed that she was angry.*

bel·fry (bel′frē), *N.* space in a tower in which a bell or bells may be hung.

a	in hat	ō	in open	sh	in she
ā	in age	ò	in all	th	in thin
â	in care	ô	in order	ᴛʜ	in then
ä	in far	oi	in oil	zh	in measure
e	in let	ou	in out	ə	= a in about
ē	in equal	u	in cup	ə	= e in taken
ėr	in term	ů	in put	ə	= i in pencil
i	in it	ü	in rule	ə	= o in lemon
ī	in ice	ch	in child	ə	= u in circus
o	in hot	ng	in long		

ben·e·fac·tor (ben′ə fak′tər), *N.* person who has given money or kindly help. (*Benefactor* comes from two Latin words, *bene* meaning "well" or "good" and *facere* meaning "do.")

be·queath (bi kwēth′), *V.* to give or leave by means of a will when a person dies: *He bequeathed his fortune to his children.* ❑ *V.* **be·queathed, be·queath·ing.**

bleach (blēch), *V.* to whiten by exposing to sunlight or by using chemicals: *animal skulls bleached by the desert sun.* ❑ *V.* **bleached, bleach·ing.**

blen·der (blen′dər), *N.* an electric kitchen appliance for grinding, mixing, or beating various foods.

blu·ish (blü′ish), *ADJ.* somewhat blue; somewhat like the color of the clear sky in daylight.

bluish

blun·der (blun′dər), *N.* a stupid mistake: *Misspelling the title of a book is a silly blunder to make in a book report.* ❑ *N. PL.* **blun·ders.**

bound·ar·y (boun′dər ē), *N.* a limiting line or thing; limit; border: *the boundary between Canada and the United States.* ❑ *N. PL.* **bound·aries.**

brack·ish (brak′ish), **1.** *ADJ.* slightly salty. Coastal marshes often have brackish waters. **2.** *ADJ.* bad-tasting.

brand (brand), **1.** *N.* a certain kind, grade, or make: *Do you like this brand of flour?* **2.** *V.* to mark by burning the skin with a hot iron: *The cowboys branded the cows.* ❑ *V.* **brand·ed, brand·ing.**

break·fast (brek′fəst), *V.* to eat the first meal of the day. ❑ *V.* **break·fast·ed, break·fast·ing.**

bronze (bronz), *N.* a dark yellow-brown alloy of copper and tin.

Cc

ca·ble (kā′bəl), *N.* a message sent through wires by electric current or electronic signals.

cal·cu·la·tion (kal′kyə lā′shən), *N.* careful thinking; deliberate planning: *The success of the expedition was the result of much calculation.* ❑ *N. PL.* **cal·cu·la·tions.**

cam·e·o (kam′ē ō), *N.* a semiprecious stone carved so that there is a raised design on a background, usually of a different color.

can·non (kan′ən), *N.* a big gun, especially one that is mounted on a base or wheels.

can·tan·ker·ous (kan tang′kər əs), *ADJ.* ready to make trouble; ill-natured; quarrelsome.

car·cass (kär′kəs), *N.* body of a dead animal. ❑ *N. PL.* **car·cass·es.**

cart·wheel (kärt′wēl′), *N.* a sideways handspring with the legs and arms kept straight. ❑ *N. PL.* **cart·wheels.**

cat·er·pil·lar (kat′ər pil′ər), *N.* the wormlike larvae of insects such as butterflies and moths.

cav·i·ty (kav′ə tē), *N.* hollow place; hole. Cavities in teeth are caused by decay. ❑ *N. PL.* **cav·i·ties.**

ce·re·bral pal·sy (ser′ə brəl pòl′zē), *N.* paralysis caused by damage to the brain before or at birth. Persons suffering from cerebral palsy have trouble coordinating their muscles.

choir (kwīr), *N.* group of singers who sing together, often in a church service.

cir·cum·stance (sėr′kəm stans), **1.** *N.* condition that accompanies an act or event: *Unfavorable circumstances such as fog and rain often delayed us in our trip to the mountains.* **2.** *N.* the existing condition or state of affairs: *He was forced by circumstances to resign.* ❑ *N. PL.* **cir·cum·stanc·es.**

civ·i·li·za·tion (siv′ə lə zā′shən), *N.* the ways of living of a people or nation: *The civilizations of ancient Egypt and ancient Greece had many contacts over the centuries.*

clar·i·net (klar′ə net′), *N.* a woodwind instrument, having a mouthpiece with a single reed and played by means of holes and keys.

cleanse (klenz), **1.** *V.* to make clean: *cleanse a wound before bandaging it.* **2.** *V.* to make pure: *cleanse the soul.* ❑ *V.* **cleansed, cleans·ing.**

close-up (klōs′up′), *N.* picture taken with a camera at close range.

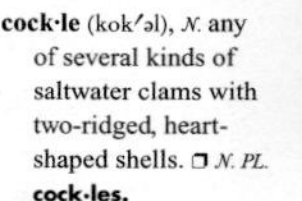

close-up of chimpanzee

cock·le (kok′əl), *N.* any of several kinds of saltwater clams with two-ridged, heart-shaped shells. ❑ *N. PL.* **cock·les.**

co·coon (kə kün′), *N.* case of silky thread spun by the larvae of various insects, to live in while they are developing into adults. Most moth larvae form cocoons.

com·bi·na·tion (kom′bə nā′shən), *N.* series of numbers or letters dialed in opening a certain kind of lock: *Do you know the combination of the safe?*

com·plex (kom′pleks), *ADJ.* hard to understand: *The instructions for building the radio were complex.*

con·ceal (kən sēl′), *V.* to put out of sight; hide: *The murky water concealed the crabs.* ❑ *V.* **con·cealed, con·ceal·ing.**

con·fi·dence (kon′fə dəns), *N.* firm belief in yourself; self-confidence: *Years of experience at her work have given her great confidence.*

con·ser·va·tion (kon′sər vā′shən), *N.* preservation from harm or decay; protection from loss or from being used up: *Conservation of energy saves fuel.*

con·struct (kən strukt′), *V.* to put together; fit together; build: *construct a bridge.* ❑ *V.* **con·struct·ed, con·struct·ing.**

con·tri·bute (kən trib′yüt), *V.* to help bring about: *A poor diet contributed to the child's bad health.* ❑ *V.* **con·tri·but·ed, con·tri·but·ing.**

cove (kōv), *N.* a small, sheltered bay; inlet on the shore.

cramp (kramp), *V.* to shut into a small space; limit: *Living in only three rooms, the family was cramped.* ❑ *V.* **cramped, cramp·ing.**

a	in hat	ō	in open	sh	in she
ā	in age	ò	in all	th	in thin
â	in care	ô	in order	ᴛʜ	in then
ä	in far	oi	in oil	zh	in measure
e	in let	ou	in out	ə	= a in about
ē	in equal	u	in cup	ə	= e in taken
ėr	in term	ů	in put	ə	= i in pencil
i	in it	ü	in rule	ə	= o in lemon
ī	in ice	ch	in child	ə	= u in circus
o	in hot	ng	in long		

cranny • distribution

cran·ny (kran′ē), *N.* a small, narrow opening; crack; crevice: *She looked in all the nooks and crannies of the house for the misplaced book.* ❐ *N. PL.* **cran·nies.**

crit·i·cal (krit′ə kəl), *ADJ.* being important to the outcome of a situation: *Help arrived at the critical moment.*

crit·i·cize (krit′ə sīz), *V.* to find fault with; disapprove of; blame: *Do not criticize him until you know all the circumstances.* ❐ *V.* **crit·i·cized, crit·i·ciz·ing.**

cruise (krüz), *V.* to travel in a car, airplane, boat, etc. at the speed at which the vehicle operates best. ❐ *V.* **cruised, cruis·ing.**

Dd

dain·ti·ly (dān′ti lē), *ADV.* with delicate beauty; freshly and prettily: *She daintily wiped her mouth with her napkin.*

deaf·en·ing (def′ən ing), *ADJ.* very loud; amazingly noisy.

de·bris (də brē′), *N.* scattered fragments; ruins; rubbish: *The street was covered with broken glass, stone, and other debris from the storm.*

debris in a landfill

de·cay (di kā′), *N.* process of rotting: *The decay in the tree trunk proceeded so rapidly that the tree fell over in a month.*

dem·on·strate (dem′ən strāt), *V.* to show how a thing is done; explain by using examples. ❐ *V.* **dem·on·strates, dem·on·strat·ed, dem·on·strat·ing.**

de·pressed (di prest′), *ADJ.* gloomy; low-spirited; sad. (*Depressed* comes from the Latin word *depressum* meaning "pressed down.")

de·vas·ta·tion (dev′ə stā′shən), *N.* the act of laying waste, destroying.

die-off (dī′ ôf), *N.* to die one after another until all are dead: *The entire herd experienced a die-off during the drought.*

dig·ni·tar·y (dig′nə ter′ē), *N.* person who has a position of honor: *We saw several foreign dignitaries when we visited the United Nations.* ❐ *N. PL.* **dig·ni·tar·ies.**

di·gress (dī gres′), *V.* to turn aside from the main subject in talking or writing: *I lost interest in the book because the author digressed too much.* ❐ *V.* **di·gressed, di·gres·sing.**

dip·lo·mat (dip′lə mat), *N.* person whose work is to manage the relations between his or her nation and other nations.

dir·i·gi·ble (dir′ə jə bəl), *N.* an airship made with a rigid framework. It is filled with gas that is lighter than air.

dis·lodge (dis loj′), *V.* to drive or force out of a place, position, etc.: *She used a crowbar to dislodge a heavy stone.* ❐ *V.* **dis·lodged, dis·lodg·ing.**

dis·re·spect (dis′ri spekt′), *V.* to show a lack of respect; to be rude. ❐ *V.* **dis·re·spect·ed, dis·re·spect·ing.**

dis·tri·bu·tion (dis′trə byü′shən), *N.* the act of giving some of to each, of dividing and giving out in shares.

780

drench • explosion

drench (drench), *V.* to wet thoroughly; soak: *A sudden, heavy rain drenched us.* ❐ *V.* **drenched, drench·ing.**

drift·wood (drift′wu̇d′), *N.* wood carried along by water or washed ashore from the water.

du·o (dü′ō), *N.* pair.

Ee

e·co·nom·ic (ek′ə nom′ik), *ADJ.* of or about the management of the income, supplies, and expenses of a household, government, etc.

eer·ie (ir′ē), *ADJ.* causing fear because of strangeness or weirdness: *a dark and eerie old house.*

el·bow (el′bō), **1.** *N.* joint between the upper and lower arm. **2.** *V.* to push with the elbow; make your way by pushing: *Don't elbow me off the sidewalk.* ❐ *V.* **el·bow·ed, el·bow·ing.**

e·merge (i mėrj′), *V.* to come into view; come out; come up: *The sun emerged from behind a cloud.* ❐ *V.* **e·merged, e·mer·ging.**

em·phat·i·cal·ly (em phat′i cal lē), *ADV.* said or done forcefully; strongly.

en·a·ble (en ā′bəl), *V.* to give ability, power, or means to; make able: *The airplane enables people to travel great distances rapidly.* ❐ *V.* **en·abled, en·a·bling.**

en·case (en kās′), *V.* to cover completely; enclose: *A cocoon encased the caterpillar.* ❐ *V.* **en·cases, en·cased, en·cas·ing.**

en·thu·si·as·tic (en thü′zē as′tik), *ADJ.* full of enthusiasm; eagerly interested: *My little brother is very enthusiastic about going to kindergarten.*

en·vi·ron·ment (en vī′rən ment), *N.* condition of the air, water, soil, etc.: *working for a pollution-free environment.*

en·vy (en′vē), *N.* feeling of discontent, dislike, or desire because another person has what you want: *The children were filled with envy when they saw her new bicycle.*

ep·i·sode (ep′ə sōd), *N.* one part of a story that is published or broadcast in several parts, one at a time.

er·a (ir′ə), *N.* a period of time or history: *We live in the era of space exploration.*

e·rect (i rekt′), *V.* to put up; build: *That house was erected 40 years ago.* ❐ *V.* **e·rec·ted, e·rec·ting.**

es·sen·tial (ə sen′shəl), *ADJ.* absolutely necessary; very important: *Good food and enough rest are essential to good health.*

ex·pand (ek spand′), *V.* to make or grow larger; increase in size; enlarge: *The balloon expanded as it was filled with air.* ❐ *V.* **ex·pan·ded, ex·pan·ding.**

ex·plo·sion (ek splō′zhən), *N.* act of bursting with a loud noise; a blowing up: *The explosions of the bombs shook the whole city.*

a	in hat	ō	in open	sh	in she
ā	in age	ȯ	in all	th	in thin
â	in care	ô	in order	ᴛʜ	in then
ä	in far	oi	in oil	zh	in measure
e	in let	ou	in out	ə	= a in about
ē	in equal	u	in cup	ə	= e in taken
ėr	in term	u̇	in put	ə	= i in pencil
i	in it	ü	in rule	ə	= o in lemon
ī	in ice	ch	in child	ə	= u in circus
o	in hot	ng	in long		

781

exquisite • greenhorn

ex·qui·site (ek′skwi zit, ek skwiz′it), *ADJ.* very lovely; delicate: *These violets are exquisite.*

an **exquisite** pattern

ex·tinct (ek stingkt′), *ADJ.* no longer existing.

ex·tra·ter·res·tri·al (ek′strə tə res′trē əl), *N.* a creature from outer space.

Ff

fash·ion (fash′ən), *V.* to make, shape, or form: *He fashioned a whistle out of wood.* ❐ *V.* **fash·ioned, fash·ion·ing.**

fast·ball (fast′bȯl′), *N.* a pitch thrown at high speed with very little curve.

fate (fāt), *N.* what becomes of someone or something: *The Revolutionary War decided the fate of the United States.*

fear·less (fir′lis), *ADJ.* without fear; afraid of nothing; brave; daring.

fidg·et·y (fij′ə tē), *ADJ.* restless; uneasy: *That fidgety child keeps twisting and moving.*

flee (flē), *V.* to run away; get away by running: *The robbers were fleeing, but the police caught them.* ❐ *V.* **fled, flee·ing.**

fo·cus (fō′kəs), **1.** *N.* the correct adjustment of a lens, the eye, etc., to make a clear image: *If the camera is not brought into focus, the photograph will be blurred.* **2.** *N.* the central point of attraction, attention, activity, etc.: *The new baby was the focus of attention.*

foot·man (fu̇t′mən), *N.* a uniformed male servant who answers the bell, waits on the table, goes with a car or carriage to open the door, etc. ❐ *N. PL.* **foot·men.**

for·get·ful (fər get′fəl), *ADJ.* apt to forget; having a poor memory: *When I get too tired, I become forgetful.*

foun·da·tion (foun dā′shən), *N.* part on which the other parts rest for support; base: *the foundation of a house.* ❐ *N. PL.* **foundations.**

Gg

gait (gāt), *N.* the kind of steps used in moving; manner of walking or running: *A gallop is one of the gaits of a horse.*

ges·ture (jes′chər), *V.* to make a movement to help express an idea or feeling. ❐ *V.* **ges·tured, ges·tur·ing.**

glim·mer (glim′ər), *N.* a faint, unsteady light.

gnaw (nȯ), *V.* to bite at and wear away: *A mouse has gnawed the cover of this box.* ❐ *V.* **gnawed, gnaw·ing.**

gos·pel (gos′pəl), *N.* religious music with much emotion and enthusiasm, including features of spirituals and jazz.

grat·i·tude (grat′ə tüd), *N.* kindly feeling because of a favor received; desire to do a favor in return; thankfulness. (*Gratitude* comes from the Latin word *gratia* meaning "favor.")

grav·i·ty (grav′ə tē), *N.* the natural force that causes objects to move or tend to move toward the center of the earth. Gravity causes objects to have weight.

green·horn (grēn′hôrn′), *N.* person without training or experience.

782

grenadier • ichthyosaurus

gren·a·dier (gren′ə dir′), *N.* a member of a specially chosen unit of foot soldiers. ❐ *N. PL.* **gren·a·diers.**

guar·an·tee (gar′ən tē′), *V.* to make certain that something will happen as a result: *Not studying for a test is a guaranteed way to make a poor grade.* ❐ *V.* **guar·an·teed, guar·an·tee·ing.**

gym·nas·tics (jim nas′tiks), *N.* a sport in which very difficult exercises are performed.

girl doing **gymnastics**

Hh

ham·mock (ham′ək), *N.* a hanging bed or couch made of canvas, cord, etc. It has cords or ropes at each end for hanging it between two trees or posts. ❐ *N. PL.* **ham·mocks.**

hand·i·capped (han′dē kapt′), *ADJ.* having a physical or mental disability.

Ha·nuk·kah (hä′nə kə), *N.* a yearly Jewish festival that lasts eight days, mostly in December. It celebrates the rededication of the temple in Jerusalem after a victory over the Syrians in 165 B.C. Candles are lighted on each of the eight days of Hanukkah.

head·land (hed′lənd), *N.* narrow ridge of high land jutting out into water; promontory.

hes·i·ta·tion (hez′ə tā′shən), *N.* act of failing to act promptly; doubt; indecision.

hid·e·ous (hid′ē əs), *ADJ.* very ugly; frightful; horrible: *a hideous monster.*

hu·mane (hyü mān′), *ADJ.* not cruel or brutal; kind; merciful: *We believe in the humane treatment of animals.*

hus·tle (hus′əl), **1.** *V.* to push or shove roughly or hurriedly; jostle rudely: *Guards hustled the demonstrators away from the mayor's office.* **2.** *V.* to hurry along: *He had to hustle to get the lawn mowed before dinner.* **3.** *V.* INFORMAL. get or sell in a hurried or illegal way. ❐ *V.* **hus·tled, hus·tling.**

hy·dro·gen (hī′drə jən), *N.* a colorless, odorless gas that burns easily. Hydrogen is a chemical element that weighs less than any other element. It combines with oxygen to form water and is present in most organic compounds.

Ii

ich·thy·o·sau·rus (ik′thē ə sôr′əs), *N.* large, fishlike reptile, now extinct, that lived in the sea. It had a long beak, paddlelike flippers, and a tail with a large fin.

a	in hat	ō	in open	sh	in she
ā	in age	ȯ	in all	th	in thin
â	in care	ô	in order	ᴛʜ	in then
ä	in far	oi	in oil	zh	in measure
e	in let	ou	in out	ə	= a in about
ē	in equal	u	in cup	ə	= e in taken
ėr	in term	u̇	in put	ə	= i in pencil
i	in it	ü	in rule	ə	= o in lemon
ī	in ice	ch	in child	ə	= u in circus
o	in hot	ng	in long		

783

Glossary

immigrant • linger

im·mi·grant (im′ə grənt), *N.* someone who comes into a country or region to live there: *Canada has many immigrants from Europe.* ❑ *N. PL.* **im·mi·grants.**

in·con·ceiv·a·ble (in′kən sē′və bəl), *ADJ.* hard to imagine or believe; incredible: *It is inconceivable that two nations so friendly for centuries should now be at odds.*

in·con·ven·ience (in′kən vē′nyəns), *N.* something inconvenient; cause of trouble, difficulty, or bother.

in·de·pend·ence (in′di pen′dəns), *N.* freedom from the control, influence, support, or help of others: *The American colonies won independence from England.*

in·no·va·tion (in′ə vā′shən), *N.* change made in the established way of doing things: *The principal made many innovations.* ❑ *N. PL.* **in·no·va·tions.**

in·spire (in spīr′), *V.* to fill with a thought or feeling; influence: *A chance to try again inspired her with hope.* ❑ *V.* **in·spired, in·spir·ing.**

in·tact (in takt′), *ADJ.* with nothing missing or broken; whole; untouched; uninjured: *The missing money was found and returned to the bank intact.*

in·ter·i·or (in tir′ē ər), *N.* inner surface or part; inside: *The interior of the house was beautifully decorated.*

theater **interior**

in·ter·sec·tion (in′tər sek′shən), *N.* point, line, or place where one thing crosses another: *a dangerous intersection.*

in·ves·ti·ga·tion (in ves′tə gā′shən), *N.* a careful search; detailed or careful examination: *An investigation of the accident by the police put the blame on the drivers of both cars.*

i·ras·ci·ble (i ras′ə bəl), *ADJ.* easily made angry.

is·sue (ish′ü), *V.* to send out; put forth: *The government issues money and stamps.* ❑ *V.* **is·sued, is·su·ing.**

Jj

jam (jam), **1.** *V.* to press or squeeze tightly between two surfaces: *The ship was jammed between two rocks.* **2.** *V.* to make music with other musicians without having practiced (*SLANG*). ❑ *V.* **jammed, jamm·ing. 3.** *N.* preserve made by boiling fruit with sugar until thick: *strawberry jam.*

Kk

kelp (kelp), *N.* any of various large, tough, brown seaweeds.

Ll

lair (lâr), *N.* den or resting place of a wild animal.

la·ment (lə ment′), **1.** *V.* to feel or show grief for; mourn aloud for: *We lament the dead.* **2.** *V.* to say sadly, with grief: *She lamented his absence.* ❑ *V.* **la·ment·ed, la·ment·ing.**

land·scape (land′ skāp), **1.** *N.* view of scenery on land. **2.** *N.* picture showing a land scene.

life·less (līf′lis), *ADJ.* without life: *a lifeless statue.*

lime·light (līm′līt′), *N.* center of public attention and interest: *Some people are never happy unless they are in the limelight.*

lin·ger (ling′gər), *V.* to stay on; go slowly, as if unwilling to leave: *He lingers after the others leave.* ❑ *V.* **ling·ered, ling·er·ing.**

784

logger • nutritious

log·ger (lò′gər), *N.* a person whose work is cutting down and removing trees. ❑ *N. PL.* **log·gers.**

lul·la·by (lul′ə bī), *N.* song for singing to a child in a cradle; soft song to lull a baby to sleep.

lux·ur·y (luk′shər ē), **1.** *N.* use of the best and most costly food, clothes, houses, furniture, and amusements: *The movie star was accustomed to luxury.* **2.** *N.* something pleasant but not necessary: *Candy is a luxury.*

Mm

mag·ni·fy (mag′nə fī), *V.* to cause something to look larger than it actually is; increase the apparent size of an object: *A microscope magnifies bacteria so that they can be seen and studied.* ❑ *V.* **mag·ni·fied, mag·ni·fy·ing.**

match·mak·er (mach′mā′kər), *N.* person who arranges, or tries to arrange, marriages for others.

mer·can·tile (mėr′kən tīl), *ADJ.* of merchants or trade; commercial: *a mercantile company.*

midst (midst), *N.* in the middle of.

mi·grant (mī′ grənt), *ADJ.* migrating; roving: *a migrant worker.*

min·i·a·ture (min′ē ə chůr, min′ə chər), *ADJ.* a reduced image or likeness: *miniature furniture for a dollhouse.*

mock (mok), *V.* to laugh at; make fun of: *The student was punished for mocking the kindergartner.* ❑ *V.* **mocked, mock·ing.**

mold[1] (mōld), *N.* a hollow shape in which anything is formed, cast, or solidified, such as the mold into which melted metal is poured to harden into shape, or the mold in which gelatin is left to stiffen.

mold[2] (mōld), *N.* loose or broken earth.

mon·i·tor (mon′ə tər), **1.** *N.* a television set connected to a computer. ❑ *N. PL.* **mon·i·tors. 2.** *V.* to listen to and check radio or television transmissions, telephone messages, etc., by using a receiver. ❑ *V.* **mon·i·tored, mon·i·tor·ing.**

mon·u·men·tal (mon′yə men′tl), *ADJ.* very great: *monumental ignorance.*

mu·cus (myü′kəs), *N.* a slimy substance produced in the nose and throat to moisten and protect them.

Nn

nau·se·at·ing (nò′shē āt ing), *ADJ.* sickening; causing nausea.

Na·zi (nä′tsē *or* nat′sē), *N.* member of the National Socialist Party, a fascist political party in Germany, led by Adolf Hitler. ❑ *N. PL.* **Nazis.**

new·com·er (nü′kum′ər), *N.* person who has just come or who came not long ago.

news·reel (nüz rēl′), *N.* a short news story for a movie audience. ❑ *N. PL.* **news·reels.**

night·time (nīt′tīm′), *N.* time between evening and morning.

nu·tri·tious (nü trish′əs), *ADJ.* valuable as food; nourishing.

a	in hat	ō	in open	sh	in she
ā	in age	ò	in all	th	in thin
â	in care	ô	in order	ᴛʜ	in then
ä	in far	oi	in oil	zh	in measure
e	in let	ou	in out	ə	= a in about
ē	in equal	u	in cup	ə	= e in taken
ėr	in term	ů	in put	ə	= i in pencil
i	in it	ü	in rule	ə	= o in lemon
ī	in ice	ch	in child	ə	= u in circus
o	in hot	ng	in long		

785

occasion • ponder

Oo

oc·ca·sion (ə kā′zhən), *N.* a special event: *The jewels were worn only on great occasions.*

on·stage (on′stāj′), *ADV.* on the part of a stage that the audience can see: *walk onstage.*

ooze (üz), *N.* a soft mud or slime, especially at the bottom of a pond or river or on the ocean bottom.

out·field (out′fēld′), **1.** *N.* the part of a baseball field beyond the diamond or infield. **2.** *N.* the three players in the outfield.

o·ver·run (ō′vər run′), *V.* to spread over: *Vines overran the wall.* ❑ *V.* **o·ver·ran, o·ver·run·ning.**

Pp

par·a·pet (par′ə pet), *N.* a low wall at the edge of a balcony, roof, or bridge.

parapet

par·a·site (par′ə sīt), *N.* any living thing that lives on or in another, from which it gets its food, often harming the other in the process. Lice and tapeworms are parasites. ❑ *N. PL.* **par·a·sites.**

pa·vil·ion (pə vil′yən), *N.* a light building, usually somewhat open, used for shelter, pleasure, etc.: *The swimmers took shelter from the sudden storm in the beach pavilion.*

ped·dler (ped′lər), *N.* person who travels about selling things carried in a pack or in a truck, wagon, or cart.

per·mit (pər mit′), **1.** *V.* to let; allow: *My parents will not permit me to stay up late.* ❑ *V.* **per·mit·ted, per·mit·ting. 2.** *N.* license or written order giving permission to do something: *Do you have a permit to fish in this lake?*

phi·los·o·pher (fə los′ə fər), *N.* a person who attempts to discover and understand the basic nature of knowledge and reality. (*Philosopher* comes from a Greek word *philosophia* meaning "love of wisdom.")

pitch (pich), **1.** *V.* to throw or fling; hurl; toss: *They were pitching horseshoes.* ❑ *V.* **pitched, pitch·ing. 2.** *N.* thick, black, sticky substance made from tar or turpentine, used to fill the seams of wooden ships, to cover roofs, to make pavements, etc.

ple·si·o·saur·us (plē′sē ə sôr′əs), *N.* any of several large sea reptiles that lived about 200 million years ago. They had long necks and flippers instead of legs.

plesiosaurus

plunge (plunj), *V.* to fall or move suddenly downward or forward: *The sea turtle plunged into the water.* ❑ *V.* **plunged, plung·ing.**

pon·der (pon′dər), *V.* to consider carefully; think over: *ponder a problem.* ❑ *V.* **pon·dered, pon·der·ing.** (*Ponder* comes from a Latin word *pondus* meaning "weight.")

786

posthumously • religious

post·hu·mous·ly (pos′chə məs lē), *ADV.* happening after death: *The author was honored posthumously.*

pot·hole (pot′hōl′), *N.* a deep hole in the surface of a street or road. ❑ *N. PL.* **pot·holes.**

pre·cious (presh′əs), *ADJ.* having great value; worth much; valuable. Gold, platinum, and silver are often called the precious metals. Diamonds, rubies, and sapphires are precious stones.

pred·a·tor (pred′ə tər), *N.* animal or person that lives by killing and eating other animals.

pre·his·tor·ic (prē′hi stôr′ ik), *ADJ.* Of or belonging to periods before recorded history: *Some prehistoric people lived in caves.*

pro·ce·dure (prə sē′jər), *N.* way of proceeding; method of doing things: *What is your procedure in making bread?* ❑ *N. PL.* **pro·ce·dures.**

pro·ces·sion (prə sesh′ən), *N.* something that moves forward; persons marching or riding: *The opening procession started at noon.*

pro·file (prō′fīl), **1.** *N.* a side view, especially of the human face. **2.** *N.* low profile; moderate attitude or position, deliberately chosen in order to avoid notice (*IDIOMATIC*).

pro·por·tion (prə pôr′shən), *N.* a proper relation among parts: *The dog's short legs were not in proportion to its long body.*

pros·per·i·ty (pro sper′ə tē), *N.* prosperous condition; good fortune; success: *a time of peace and prosperity.*

pro·to·type (prō′ tə tīp), *N.* the first or primary type of anything: *A modern ship has its prototype in the hollowed log used by primitive peoples.*

push·cart (pu̇sh′kärt′), *N.* a light cart pushed by hand. ❑ *N. PL.* **push·carts.**

Rr

ra·vine (rə vēn′), *N.* a long, deep, narrow valley eroded by running water.

realm (relm), *N.* kingdom.

re·as·sem·ble (rē′ə sem′ bəl), *V.* come or bring together again. ❑ *V.* **re·as·sem·bled, re·as·sem·bling.**

rec·om·mend (rek′ə mend′), *V.* to speak in favor of; suggest favorably: *The teacher recommended him for the job.* ❑ *V.* **rec·om·men·ded, rec·om·men·ding.**

ref·u·gee (ref′yə jē′ *or* ref′yə jē′), *N.* person who flees for refuge or safety, especially to a foreign country, in time of persecution, war, or disaster: *Refugees from the war were cared for in neighboring countries.* ❑ *N. PL.* **refugees.**

re·lease (ri lēs′), *V.* to permit to be published, shown, sold, etc. ❑ *V.* **re·leased, re·leas·ing.**

re·li·gious (ri lij′əs), *ADJ.* much interested in the belief, study, and worship of God or gods; devoted to religion: *He is very religious and prays often.*

a	in hat	ō	in open	sh	in she
ā	in age	ò	in all	th	in thin
â	in care	ô	in order	ᴛʜ	in then
ä	in far	oi	in oil	zh	in measure
e	in let	ou	in out	ə	= a in about
ē	in equal	u	in cup	ə	= e in taken
ėr	in term	ů	in put	ə	= i in pencil
i	in it	ü	in rule	ə	= o in lemon
ī	in ice	ch	in child	ə	= u in circus
o	in hot	ng	in long		

787

Ren·ais·sance (ren′ə säns′ *or* ren′ə säns), *N.* the great revival of art and learning in Europe during the 1300s, 1400s, and 1500s; the period of time when this revival occurred.

rep·re·sent·a·tive (rep′ri zen′tə tiv), *N.* person appointed or elected to act or speak for others: *She is the club's representative at the convention.* ❑ *N. PL.* **rep·re·sent·a·tives.**

re·proach·ful·ly (ri prōch′fəl lē), *ADV.* with disapproval.

rep·u·ta·tion (rep′yə tā′shən), *N.* what people think and say the character of someone or something is; character in the opinion of others; name; repute: *This store has an excellent reputation for fair dealing.*

re·source·ful (ri sôrs′fəl), *ADJ.* good at thinking of ways to do things; quick-witted: *The resourceful children mowed lawns to earn enough money to buy new bicycles.*

ri·val (rī′vəl), *N.* person who wants and tries to get the same thing as another or who tries to equal or do better than another; competitor: *The two girls were rivals for the same class office.*

ro·bo·tic (rō bot′ik), *ADJ.* of or for a machine with moving parts and sensing devices controlled by a computer: *robotic design.*

role (rōl), **1.** *N.* an actor's part in a play, movie, etc.: *She played the leading role in the school play.* **2.** *N.* role model, a person whose patterns of behavior influence someone else's actions and beliefs: *Parents are important role models for children.*

rus·tle (rus′əl), *V.* to make or cause to make a light, soft sound of things gently rubbing together: *The leaves were rustling in the breeze.* ❑ *V.* **rus·tled, rus·tling.**

Ss

sa·cred (sā′krid), **1.** *ADJ.* worthy of reverence: *the sacred memory of a dead hero.* **2.** *ADJ.* not to be violated or disregarded: *a sacred promise.* (*Sacred* comes from a Latin word *sacrare* meaning "holy.")

scarce (skârs), *ADJ.* hard to get; rare: *Water is becoming scarce.*

scin·til·late (sin′tl āt), *V.* to sparkle; flash: *Her brilliant wit scintillates.* ❑ *V.* **scin·til·lat·ed, scin·til·lat·ing.**

scoun·drel (skoun′drəl), *N.* an evil, dishonorable person; villain; rascal: *The scoundrels who set fire to the barn have been caught.*

scrawl (skról), *V.* to write or draw poorly or carelessly. ❑ *V.* **scrawled, scrawl·ing.**

scraw·ny (skró′nē), *ADJ.* having little flesh; lean; thin; skinny: *Turkeys have scrawny necks.*

sea ur·chins (sē′ ėr′chəns), *N.* any of numerous small, round sea animals with spiny shells.

sec·ond·hand (sek′ənd hand′), **1.** *ADJ.* not new; used already by someone else: *secondhand clothes.* **2.** *ADV.* from other than the original source; not firsthand: *The information came to us secondhand.*

sed·i·ment (sed′ə mənt), *N.* material that settles to the bottom of a liquid: *A film of sediment covered the underwater wreck.*

seed·ling (sēd′ling), *N.* a young plant grown from a seed. ❑ *N. PL.* **seed·lings.**

sem·i·pro (sem′i prō′), *N.* a part-time professional athlete.

ser·pent (sėr′pənt), *N.* snake, especially a big snake.

se·vere (sə vir′), *ADJ.* serious; grave: *a severe illness.*

shell·fish (shel′fish′), *N.* a water animal with a shell. Oysters, clams, crabs, and lobsters are shellfish.

shut·down (shut′doun′), **1.** *N.* act of closing of a factory, or the like, for a time: *The factory had a partial shutdown last week to fix some faulty equipment.* **2.** *N.* a stopping; a checking of (*INFORMAL*): *His reply was a real shutdown to her negative comment.*

side·track (sīd′trak′), *V.* to draw someone's attention away from something: *Don't sidetrack me with pointless questions.* ❑ *V.* **side·tracked, side·track·ing.**

sin·ew (sin′yü), *N.* tendon.

sketch (skech), *V.* to draw roughly and quickly. ❑ *V.* **sketched, sketch·ing.**

skid (skid), *V.* to slip or slide sideways while moving: *The car skidded on the slippery road.* ❑ *V.* **skid·ded, skid·ding.**

slav·er·y (slā′vər ē), *N.* the condition of being owned by another person and being made to work without wages.

sol·i·tar·y (sol′ə ter′ē), *ADJ.* without companions; away from people; lonely.

som·ber (som′bər), **1.** *ADJ.* having deep shadows; dark; gloomy: *A cloudy winter day is somber.* **2.** *ADJ.* sad; gloomy; dismal: *His losses made him somber.*

a **somber** picture (def. 2)

som·er·sault (sum′ər sólt), *V.* to run or jump, turning the heels over the head. ❑ *V.* **som·er·saul·ted, som·er·saul·ting.**

so·nar (sō′när), *N.* device for finding the depth of water or for detecting and locating underwater objects. Sonar sends sound waves into water, and they are reflected back when they strike the bottom or any object.

So·vi·et (sō′vē et), *N.* a person belonging to or fighting for the former Soviet Union. ❑ *N. PL.* **So·vi·ets.**

spe·cial·ize (spesh′ə līz), *V.* to develop in a special way: *Animals and plants are specialized to fit their surroundings.* ❑ *V.* **spe·cial·ized, spe·cial·iz·ing.**

spe·cif·ic (spi sif′ik), *ADJ.* definite; precise; particular: *There was no specific reason for the party.*

spec·ta·cles (spek′tə kəlz), *N. PL.* eyeglasses. (*Spectacles* comes from a Latin word *spectare* meaning "to watch.")

spec·tac·u·lar (spek tak′ yə lər), *ADJ.* making a great display or show; very striking or imposing to the eye: *a spectacular storm.*

spin·dly (spind′lē), *ADJ.* very long and slender; too tall and thin: *a spindly plant.*

spir·i·tu·al (spir′ə chü əl), *N.* a religious song which originated among African Americans of the southern United States. ❑ *N. PL.* **spir·i·tu·als.**

a in hat	ō in open	sh in she
ā in age	ó in all	th in thin
â in care	ô in order	ᴛʜ in then
ä in far	oi in oil	zh in measure
e in let	ou in out	ə = a in about
ē in equal	u in cup	ə = e in taken
ėr in term	ů in put	ə = i in pencil
i in it	ü in rule	ə = o in lemon
ī in ice	ch in child	ə = u in circus
o in hot	ng in long	

spoon·ful (spün′fůl), *N.* as much as a spoon can hold.

star·va·tion (stär vā′shən), *N.* suffering from extreme hunger; being starved: *Starvation caused his death.*

stealth·y (stel′thē), *ADJ.* done in a secret manner; secret; sly: *The cat crept in a stealthy way toward the bird.*

steed (stēd), *N.* horse, especially a riding horse.

ster·ile (ster′əl), *ADJ.* free from germs: *Bandages should always be kept sterile.*

stern·ly (stėrn′ lē), *ADV.* strictly; firmly: *The teacher frowned sternly.*

strat·e·gy (strat′ə jē), *N.* the skillful planning and management of anything.

strict (strict), *ADJ.* very careful in following a rule or in making others follow it: *The teacher was strict but fair.*

stroke (strōk), *N.* a sudden attack of illness, especially one caused by a blood clot or bleeding in the brain; apoplexy.

sub·ject (sub′jikt), **1.** *N.* something that is thought about, discussed, investigated, etc.; topic: *The subject for our composition was "An Exciting Moment."* **2.** *N.* person under the power, control, or influence of another: *subjects of the king.*

su·per·i·or (sə pir′ē ər), *N.* person who is higher in rank, position, or ability: *A captain is a lieutenant's superior.* ❑ *N. PL.* **su·per·i·ors.**

sus·pend·ers (sə spen′dərz), *N. PL.* straps worn over the shoulders to hold up the trousers.

sus·pi·cion (sə spish′ən), *N.* belief; feeling; thought: *I have a suspicion that the weather will be very hot today.* ❑ *N. PL.* **sus·pi·cions.**

Tt

tape·worm (tāp′wėrm′), *N.* any of the numerous long, flat worms that live during their adult stage as parasites in the intestines of human beings and other animals. ❑ *N. PL.* **tape·worms.**

teen·ag·er (tēn′ā′jər), *N.* person in his or her teens.

ther·a·pist (ther′ə pist), *N.* person who specializes in the treatment of diseases, injuries, or disorders.

thieve (thēv), *V.* to steal. ❑ *V.* **thieved, thiev·ing.**

throb (throb), *V.* to beat rapidly or strongly: *My injured foot throbbed.* ❑ *V.* **throb·bed, throb·bing.**

ti·dy (tī′dē), *V.* to put in order; make neat: *I tidied the room.* ❑ *V.* **ti·died, ti·dy·ing.**

to·ga (tō′gə), *N.* a loose, outer garment worn in public. ❑ *N. PL.* **to·gas.**

tra·di·tion (trə dish′ən), *N.* custom or belief handed down from generation to generation: *According to tradition, Betsy Ross made the first American flag.* ❑ *N. PL.* **tra·di·tions.**

trans·at·lan·tic (tran′sət lan′tik), *ADJ.* crossing the Atlantic: *a transatlantic liner.*

tum·ble·down (tum′bəl doun′), *ADJ.* ready to fall down; not in good condition; dilapidated: *a tumbledown shack in the mountains.*

tun·dra (tun′drə), *N.* a vast, level, treeless plain in the arctic regions. The ground beneath its surface is frozen even in summer.

tweez·ers (twē′zərz), *N.* small pincers for pulling out hairs, picking up small objects, etc.

Uu

u·nique (yü nēk′), *ADJ.* having no like or equal; being the only one of its kind: *a unique specimen of rock, a unique experience.*

un·screw (un skrü′), *V.* to loosen or take off by turning: *Can you help me unscrew this tight lid?* ❑ *V.* **un·screwed, un·screw·ing.**

Vv

va·cant (vā′kənt), *ADJ.* not occupied: *a vacant chair, a vacant house.*

var·mint (vär′mənt), *N.* an objectionable animal or person (*DIALECT*).

vein (vān), *N.* **1.** membranous tubes forming part of the system of vessels that carry blood to the heart. **2.** a small natural channel within the earth through which water trickles or flows. ❑ *N. PL.* **veins.**

vi·bra·phone (vī′brə fōn), *N.* musical instrument similar to the xylophone, with metal bars and artificially increased vibration; vibraharp.

view·port (vyü′pôrt), *N.* small window in a small vessel, such as a space capsule or mini-submarine.

vi·sa (vē′zə), *N.* an official signature or endorsement upon a passport, showing that it has been examined and approved. A visa is granted by the consul or other representative of the country to which a person wishes to travel.

Ww

wai·tress (wā′tris), *N.* woman who serves or brings food to people in a restaurant.

weak·ness (wēk′nis), *N.* a weak point; slight fault: *Putting things off is her weakness.*

weight·less·ness (wāt′lis nis), *N.* the condition of being free from the pull of gravity: *weightless travelers in space.*

wheel·chair (wēl′châr′), *N.* chair on wheels, used especially by people who are sick or unable to walk. It can be moved by the person who is sitting in the chair.

wince (wins), *V.* to draw back suddenly; flinch slightly: *I winced when the dentist's drill touched my tooth.* ❑ *V.* **winced, winc·ing.**

wind·up (wīnd′up′), *N.* (in baseball), a swinging movement of the arms while twisting the body just before pitching the ball.

with·er (wiᴛʜ′ər), *V.* to lose or cause to lose freshness; make or become dry and lifeless; dry up; fade; shrivel: *Age had withered the old woman's face.* ❑ *V.* **with·ered, with·er·ing.**

work·shop (wėrk′shop′), *N.* space or building where work is done.

wor·ship (wėr′ship), *V.* to pay great honor and reverence to: *to worship God.* ❑ *V.* **wor·shipped, wor·ship·ping.**

worth·less (wėrth′lis), *ADJ.* without value; good-for-nothing; useless: *Throw those worthless, broken toys away.*

a in hat	ō in open	sh in she
ā in age	ó in all	th in thin
â in care	ô in order	ᴛʜ in then
ä in far	oi in oil	zh in measure
e in let	ou in out	ə = a in about
ē in equal	u in cup	ə = e in taken
ėr in term	ů in put	ə = i in pencil
i in it	ü in rule	ə = o in lemon
ī in ice	ch in child	ə = u in circus
o in hot	ng in long	

English/Spanish Selection Vocabulary List

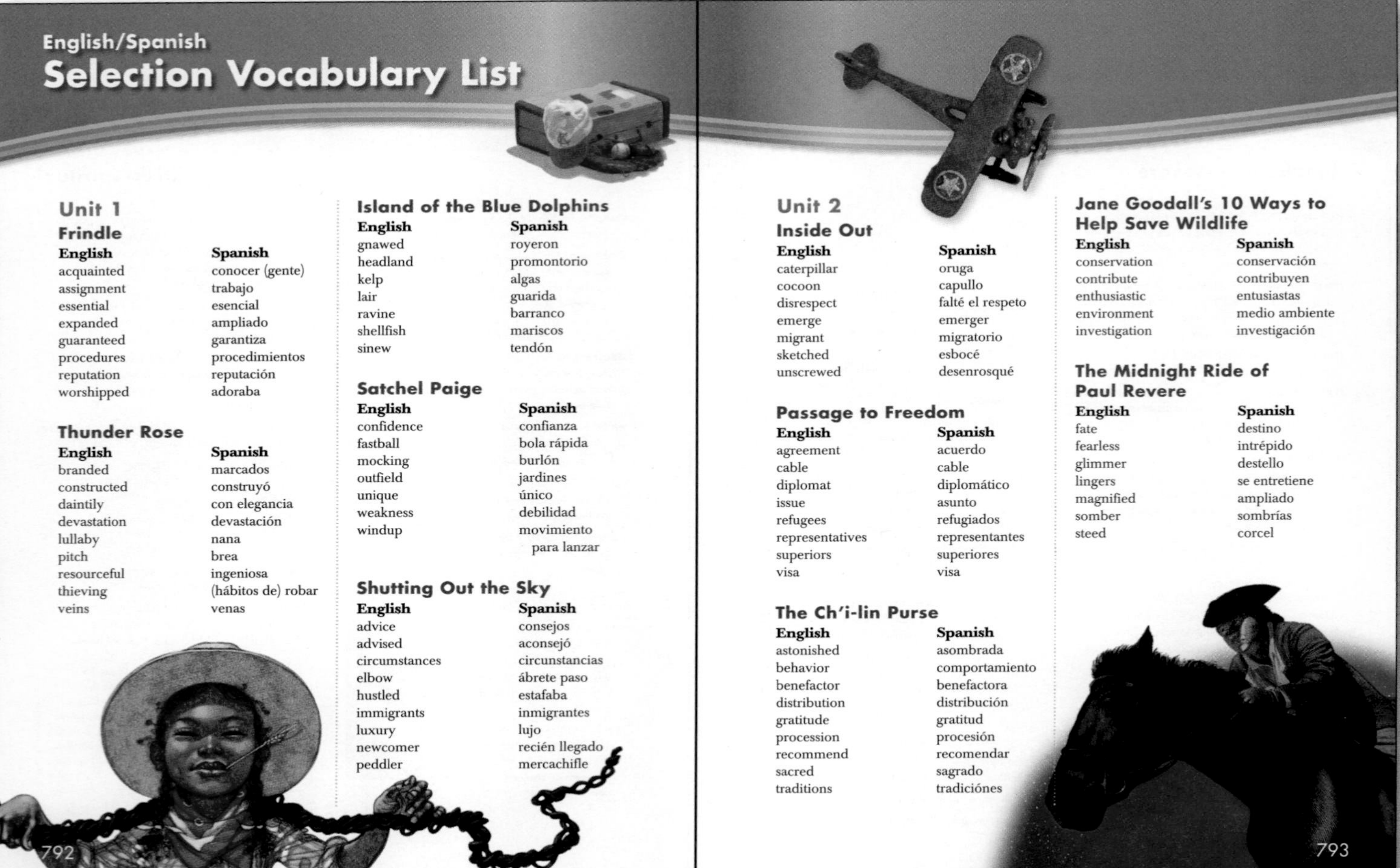

English/Spanish

Selection Vocabulary List

Unit 1

Frindle

English	Spanish
acquainted	conocer (gente)
assignment	trabajo
essential	esencial
expanded	ampliado
guaranteed	garantiza
procedures	procedimientos
reputation	reputación
worshipped	adoraba

Thunder Rose

English	Spanish
branded	marcados
constructed	construyó
daintily	con elegancia
devastation	devastación
lullaby	nana
pitch	brea
resourceful	ingeniosa
thieving	(hábitos de) robar
veins	venas

Island of the Blue Dolphins

English	Spanish
gnawed	royeron
headland	promontorio
kelp	algas
lair	guarida
ravine	barranco
shellfish	mariscos
sinew	tendón

Satchel Paige

English	Spanish
confidence	confianza
fastball	bola rápida
mocking	burlón
outfield	jardines
unique	único
weakness	debilidad
windup	movimiento para lanzar

Shutting Out the Sky

English	Spanish
advice	consejos
advised	aconsejó
circumstances	circunstancias
elbow	ábrete paso
hustled	estafaba
immigrants	inmigrantes
luxury	lujo
newcomer	recién llegado
peddler	mercachifle

792

Unit 2

Inside Out

English	Spanish
caterpillar	oruga
cocoon	capullo
disrespect	falté el respeto
emerge	emerger
migrant	migratorio
sketched	esbocé
unscrewed	desenrosqué

Passage to Freedom

English	Spanish
agreement	acuerdo
cable	cable
diplomat	diplomático
issue	asunto
refugees	refugiados
representatives	representantes
superiors	superiores
visa	visa

The Ch'i-lin Purse

English	Spanish
astonished	asombrada
behavior	comportamiento
benefactor	benefactora
distribution	distribución
gratitude	gratitud
procession	procesión
recommend	recomendar
sacred	sagrado
traditions	tradiciónes

Jane Goodall's 10 Ways to Help Save Wildlife

English	Spanish
conservation	conservación
contribute	contribuyen
enthusiastic	entusiastas
environment	medio ambiente
investigation	investigación

The Midnight Ride of Paul Revere

English	Spanish
fate	destino
fearless	intrépido
glimmer	destello
lingers	se entretiene
magnified	ampliado
somber	sombrías
steed	corcel

793

English/Spanish Selection Vocabulary List

Unit 3

Wings for the King

English	Spanish
admiringly	con admiración
permit	permítame
scoundrel	canalla
subject	súbdita
worthless	inútiles

Leonardo's Horse

English	Spanish
achieved	logrado
architect	arquitecto
bronze	bronce
cannon	cañón
depressed	deprimido
fashioned	elaboró
midst	(en) medio (de)
philosopher	filósofo
rival	rival

The Dinosaurs of Waterhouse Hawkins

English	Spanish
erected	erigió
foundations	cimientos
mold	molde
occasion	ocasión
proportion	proporción
tidied	ordenó
workshop	taller

Mahalia Jackson

English	Spanish
appreciate	apreciar
barber	barbero
choir	coro
released	se publicó
religious	religiosa
slavery	esclavitud
teenager	adolescente

Special Effects in Film and Television

English	Spanish
background	fondo
landscape	paisaje
miniature	miniatura
prehistoric	prehistórico
reassembled	reensamblados

794

Unit 4

Weslandia

English	Spanish
blunders	tropezones
civilization	civilización
complex	complejo
envy	envidia
fleeing	huir
inspired	inspiró
rustling	susurrando
strategy	estrategia

Stretching Ourselves: Kids with Cerebral Palsy

English	Spanish
abdomen	abdomen
artificial	artificial
gait	manera de caminar
handicapped	discapacitado
therapist	terapeuta
wheelchair	silla de ruedas

Exploding Ants: Amazing Facts About How Animals Adapt

English	Spanish
critical	críticos
enables	permite
mucus	mucus
scarce	escaso
specialize	se especializan
sterile	estériles

The Stormi Giovanni Club

English	Spanish
cavities	caries
combination	combinación
demonstrates	demuestra
episode	episodio
profile	(mantenerse en) segundo plano
strict	estricto

The Gymnast

English	Spanish
bluish	azulados
cartwheels	volteretas laterales
gymnastics	gimnástica
hesitation	duda
limelight	centro de atención
skidded	patinó
somersault	dar saltos mortales
throbbing	latía
wincing	haciendo una mueca de dolor

Unit 5

The Three-Century Woman

English	Spanish
eerie	escalofriante
intersection	intersección
pondered	reflexionó
severe	serio
spectacles	gafas
withered	marchita

The Unsinkable Wreck of the R.M.S. *Titanic*

English	Spanish
cramped	estrecho
debris	restos
interior	interior
ooze	limo
robotic	robótico
sediment	sedimento
sonar	sonar

Talk with an Astronaut

English	Spanish
accomplishments	logros
focus	atención
gravity	gravedad
monitors	monitores
role	ejemplo
specific	específico

Journey to the Center of the Earth

English	Spanish
armor	armadura
encases	reviste
extinct	extintas
hideous	horroroso
plunged	sumergido
serpent	serpiente

Ghost Towns of the American West

English	Spanish
economic	económico
independence	independencia
overrun	rebosante
scrawled	garabateó
vacant	vacantes

796

Unit 6

At the Beach

English	Spanish
algae	algas
concealed	ocultado
driftwood	madera flotante
hammocks	hamacas
lamented	lamentó
sea urchins	erizos de mar
sternly	severamente
tweezers	pinzas

The Mystery of Saint Matthew Island

English	Spanish
bleached	decolorados
carcasses	animales muertos
decay	descomposición
parasites	parásitos
scrawny	escuálido
starvation	inanición
suspicions	sospechas
tundra	tundra

King Midas and the Golden Touch

English	Spanish
adorn	adornar
cleanse	(te) bañas
lifeless	inanimada
precious	precioso
realm	reino
spoonful	cucharada

The *Hindenburg*

English	Spanish
criticizing	criticando
cruised	navegó
drenching	empapándolo
era	era
explosion	explosión
hydrogen	hidrógeno

Sweet Music in Harlem

English	Spanish
bass	bajo
clarinet	clarinete
fidgety	inquieto
forgetful	olvidadizo
jammed	improvisé
nighttime	noche
secondhand	segunda mano

797

Acknowledgments

Acknowledgments

Text

22: From *Frindle* by Andrew Clements. Text ©1996 by Andrew Clements. Reprinted by permission of Simon & Schuster Books for Young Readers, an imprint of Simon & Schuster Children's Publishing Division; **36:** *Punctuation Takes a Vacation* by Robin Pulver. Text ©2003 by Robin Pulver. All rights reserved. Reprinted by permission of Holiday House, Inc.; **46:** *Thunder Rose*, text ©2003 by Jerdine Nolen. Illustrations ©2003 by Kadir Nelson. Reprinted by permission of Harcourt, Inc.; **66:** "Measuring Tornadoes" from *Storm Chasers* by Trudi Strain Trueit. ©2002 Franklin Watts, a Division of Scholastic, Inc. Used by permission of Scholastic Library Publishing; **72:** From *Island of the Blue Dolphins*. ©1960, renewed 1988 by Scott O'Dell. Reprinted by permission of Houghton Mifflin Company. All rights reserved; **86:** "7 Survival Questions," by Buck Tilton. Used with permission of Buck Tilton and *Boys' Life*, April 2001. Published by the Boy Scouts of America; **94:** From *Satchel Paige* by Lesa Cline-Ransome, paintings by James E. Ransome. Text ©2000 Lesa Cline-Ransome. Illustrations ©2000 James E. Ransome. Reprinted with the permission of Simon & Schuster Books for Young Readers, an imprint of Simon & Schuster Children's Publishing Division; **110:** From "The Girls of Summer" by Ellen Klages. Adapted with permission, © Exploratorium, www.exploratorium.edu. Used by permission; **116:** From *Shutting Out the Sky* by Deborah Hopkinson. Published by Orchard Books, a division of Scholastic Inc. ©2003 by Deborah Hopkinson. Reprinted by permission of Scholastic Inc.; **130:** "The Immigrant Experience" from *Tenement Tid-Bits*, e-mail newsletter of The Lower East Side Tenement Museum, November 2003. Reprinted by permission of The Lower East Side Tenement Museum at www.tenement.org/immigrantexperience; **134:** "The Microscope" by Maxine W. Kumin. ©1968 by Maxine W. Kumin. Used by permission of The Anderson Literary Agency Inc; **136:** "Full Day" from *Come With Me: Poems For A Journey* by Naomi Shihab Nye. Text ©2000 by Naomi Shihab Nye, Greenwillow Books. Used by permission of HarperCollins Publishers; **146:** From "Inside Out," from *The Circuit* by Francisco Jiménez. ©1997 by Francisco Jiménez. Reprinted by permission of the University of New Mexico Press; **160:** "Random Acts of Kindness" from the Random Acts of Kindness Web site. Reprinted by permission of The Random Acts of Kindness Foundation at www.actsofkindness.org; **166:** *Passage to Freedom: The Sugihara Story*. Text ©1997 by Ken Mochizuki. Illustrations ©1997 by Dom Lee. Afterword ©1997 by Hiroki Sugihara. Permission arranged with Lee & Low Books Inc., New York, NY 10016; **180:** From "I Wanted My Mother," from *Hiding to Survive: Stories of Jewish Children Rescued from the Holocaust*. ©1994 by Maxine B. Rosenberg. Reprinted by permission of Clarion Books/Houghton Mifflin Company. All rights reserved; **190:** "The Ch'i-lin Purse" from *The Ch'i-lin Purse* by Linda Fang. ©1963 by Linda Fang. Reprinted by permission of Farrar, Straus & Giroux, LLC; **206:** "Lion and the Mouse" from *The Fables of Aesop* retold by Ruth Spriggs. ©1975 by Eurobook Limited, Oxfordshire, England. Used by permission; **212:** "Jane Goodall's 10 Ways to Help Save Wildlife," from *National Geographic KIDS*, April 2003. ©2003 National Geographic Society. Reprinted by permission; **226:** "Why Some Animals Are Considered 'Bad' or 'Scary'" from SanDiegoZoo.org. Used by permission of the Zoological Society of San Diego; **234:** Illustrations from *The Midnight Ride of Paul Revere* by Henry Wadsworth Longfellow, graved and painted by Christopher Bing. ©2001 Christopher Bing. Reproduced with permission of the publisher, Handprint Books, Inc.; **250:** "Deborah Sampson" by Michael Zullo from www2.1hric.org. Used by permission of Michael Zullo; **254:** "For Peace Sake" by Cedric McClester ©1990 by Cedric McClester. Used by permission of the author; **256:** "Two People I Want to Be Like" from *If Only I Could Tell You* by Eve Merriam. ©1983 Eve Merriam. Used by permission of Marian Reiner; **257:** "Strangers" from *Good Luck Gold and Other Poems* by Janet S. Wong. ©1994 by Janet S. Wong. Reprinted with the permission of Margaret K. McElderry Books, an imprint of Simon & Schuster Children's Publishing Division. All rights reserved; **266:** From *Wings for the King* by Anne Sroda from *Plays*, November 2000, Vol. 60, No.2. Reproduced with permission of Sterling Partners, Inc./PLAYS, P. O. Box 600160, Newton, MA 02460; **282:** "Becky Schroeder: Enlightened Thinker" from *Brainstorm! The Stories of Twenty American Kid Inventors* by Tom Tucker, illustrated by Richard Loehle. ©1996 by Tom Tucker. Reprinted by permission of Farrar, Straus & Giroux, LLC; **292:** *Leonardo's Horse* by Jean Fritz and illustrated by Hudson Talbott. Text ©Jean Fritz, 2001. Illustrations ©Hudson Talbott, 2001. Published by arrangement with G. P. Putnam's Sons, a division of Penguin Young Readers Group, a member of Penguin Group (USA) Inc. All rights reserved; **312:** "Humans with Wings," from *HumanPower* by Roger Yepsen. ©1992 Roger Yepsen. Reprinted with the permission of Simon & Schuster Books for Young Readers, an imprint of Simon & Schuster Children's Publishing Division; **320:** From *The Dinosaurs of Waterhouse Hawkins* by Barbara Kerley Kelly. Text ©2001 by Barbara Kerley Kelly. Illustrations ©2001 by Brian Selznick. Reprinted by permission of Scholastic, Inc; **340:** "A Model Scientist" adapted from *OWL Magazine*, Oct. 2002. Used by permission of Bayard Canada Inc.; **350:** "Mahalia Jackson" from *The Blues Singers* by Julius Lester. ©2001 Julius Lester. Illustrated by Lisa Cohen. Reprinted by permission of Hyperion Books for Children; **360:** From *Perfect Harmony* by Charles Smith. ©2002 Charles Smith. Reprinted by permission of Hyperion Books For Children; **368:** From *Special Effects in Film and Television* by Jake Hamilton. ©1998 Dorling Kindersley. Reprinted by permission; **380:** Adaptation of "A Trick of the Eye" by Brian Sibley from http://ww.bfi.org.uk. Used by permission of Sheil Land Associates Ltd.; **384:** "Chemistry 101" from *Carver: A Life In Poems* by Marilyn Nelson. ©2001 by Marilyn Nelson. Used by permission of Front Street, a division of Boyds Mill Press, Inc; **385:** "The Bronze Horse" by Beverly McLoughland, *Cricket*, November 1990. Used by permission of the author; **386:** "The Termites" from *Insectlopedia*, ©1998 by Douglas Florian, reprinted by permission of Harcourt, Inc. This material may not be reproduced in any form or by any means without the prior written permission of the publisher; **387:** "Stairs" from *Excuse It Please* by Oliver Herford, J. B. Lippincott Company, 1929; **396:** *Weslandia* by Paul Fleischman. Text ©1999 by Paul Fleischman. Illustrations ©1999 by Kevin Hawkes. Reproduced by the publisher Candlewick Press, Inc., Cambridge, MA; **410:** "Under the Back Porch" by Virginia Hamilton. ©1992, 2004 by Virginia Hamilton. Reprinted by permission of Arnold Adoff, 750 Union St., Yellow Springs, OH 45387; **411:** "Keziah," from *Bronzeville Boys and Girls* by Gwendolyn Brooks. ©1956 by Gwendolyn Brooks Blakely. Used by permission of HarperCollins Publishers; **416:** From *Stretching Ourselves* by Alden R. Carter, Photographs by Carol S. Carter. ©2000 Alden R. Carter. Reprinted by permission of John Hawkins & Associates, Inc.; **434:** "Helpful Tools" from *Do You Remember the Color Blue?* by Sally Hobart Alexander, ©2000 by Sally Hobart Alexander. Used by permission of Viking Children's Books, A Division of Penguin Young Readers Group, A Member of Penguin Group (USA) Inc., 345 Hudson Street, New York, NY 10014, the Author and BookStop Literary Agency. All rights reserved; **440:** From *Exploding Ants* by Joanne Settel, Ph.D. Text ©1999 by Joanne Settel. Reprinted with the permission of Atheneum Books for Young Readers, an imprint of Simon & Schuster Children's Publishing Division; **480:** "Think Dress Codes Are a Drag?" by Emilie Ostrander from the *Chicago Tribune*, April 15, 2003. Copyrighted 4/15/2003, Chicago Tribune Company. All rights reserved. Used with permission; **488:** "The Gymnast" by Gary Soto from *A Summer Life* ©1990 by University Press of New England. Reprinted with permission; **501:** From "Gymnastics" from *The Columbia Electronic Encyclopedia, 6th ed.* ©2003, Columbia University Press. Used by permission; **502:** *Random House Webster's Unabridged Dictionary*. New York: Random House, 1991. **504:** "the drum" from *Spin A Soft Black Song* by Nikki Giovanni. ©1971, 1985 by Nikki Giovanni. Reprinted by permission of Hill and Wang, a division of Farrar, Straus & Giroux, LLC; **505:** "Which Lunch Table?" from *Swimming Upstream: Middle Grade Poems* by Kristine O'Connell George. Text ©2002 by Kristine O'Connell

798

George. Reprinted by permission of Clarion Books, an imprint of Houghton Mifflin Company. All rights reserved; **506:** "Desert Tortoise" from *Desert Voices* by Byrd Baylor. Text ©1981 by Byrd Baylor. Reprinted with the permission of Atheneum Books for Young Readers, an imprint of Simon & Schuster Children's Publishing Division; **507:** "Camel" by Lillian M. Fisher. All other rights reserved, ©Lillian M. Fisher 2004. Used by permission of the author, Lillian M. Fisher; **516:** "The Three-Century Woman" ©1996 by Richard Peck. First published in *Second Sight: Stories for a New Millennium*, Philomel Books. All rights reserved. Used by permission of Sheldon Fogelman Agency, Inc; **540:** "The Unsinkable Wreck of the R.M.S. Titanic" from *Ghost Liners: Exploring the World's Greatest Lost Ships* by Robert D. Ballard and Rick Archbold, illustrations by Ken Marschall. Text ©1998 by Odyssey Corporation and Ken Marschall, from *Ghost Liners*, a Little Brown Madison Press Book. Used by permission; **554:** Excerpt from *Shipwreck Season* by Donna Hill. ©1998 by Donna Hill. Reprinted by permission of Clarion Books, an imprint of Houghton Mifflin Company. All rights reserved; **564:** "Talk with an Astronaut" from "Meet Famous Latinos: Ellen Ochoa" from scholastic.com. ©2004 by Scholastic Inc. Reprinted by permission of Scholastic Inc; **578:** "Crust, Mantle, Core," from Scott Foresman *Science for Texas* by Dr. Timothy Cooney, Michael Anthony DiSpezio, et al. ©2000, Addison-Wesley Educational Publishers, Inc. All Rights Reserved; **608:** Text and Photographs from *Ghost Towns of the American West* by Raymond Bial. ©2001 by Raymond Bial. Reprinted by permission of Houghton Mifflin Company. All rights reserved; **622:** "Dame Shirley Goes to the Gold Rush" from *Journeys in Time: A New Atlas of American History* by Elspeth Leacock and Susan Buckley. Text ©2001 by Elspeth Leacock and Susan Washburn Buckley. Reprinted with permission of Houghton Mifflin Company. All rights reserved; **626:** "Your World" from *The Selected Works of Georgia Douglas Johnson*, by Georgia Douglas Johnson, G. K. Hall ©1997, G. K. Hall. Reprinted by permission of The Gale Group; **627:** "Share the Adventure" ©1993 by Patricia and Fredrick McKissack. First appeared as a National Children's Book Week Poem by The Children's Book Council, Curtis Brown, Ltd., 1993; **628:** "A Path to the Moon," *Giants, Moosequakes and Other Disasters* by bp Nichol, Black Moss Press, 1985. Used by permission of the Estate of bp Nichol; **638:** "At the Beach," from *Salsa Stories* by Lulu Delacre. ©2000 Lulu Delacre. Reprinted by permission of Scholastic, Inc; **652:** "The Eagle and the Bat" from *The Sound of Flutes and Other Indian Legends* by Richard Erdoes and illustrated by Paul Goble, ©1976 by Richard Erdoes. Illustrations ©1976 by Paul Goble. Used by permission of Random House Children's Books, a division of Random House, Inc.; **658:** "The Mystery of Saint Matthew Island" from *The Case of the Mummified Pigs and Other Mysteries in Nature*, written by Susan E. Quinlan, illustrated by Jennifer Owings Dewey. Text ©1995 by Susan E. Quinlan; Illustrations ©1995 by Jennifer Owings Dewey. Published by Caroline House, Boyds Mills Press, Inc. Reprinted by permission; **670:** "Get the Lead Out" from *The Sky's the Limit: Stories of Discovery by Women and Girls* by Catherine Thimmesh, illustrated by Melissa Sweet. Text ©2002 by Catherine Thimmesh. Illustrations ©2002 by Melissa Sweet. Reprinted by permission of Houghton Mifflin Company. All rights reserved; **678:** *King Midas and the Golden Touch* as told by Charlotte Craft, illustrated by K. Y. Craft. Text ©1999 by Charlotte Craft. Illustrations ©1999 Kinuko Y. Craft. Used by permission of HarperCollins Publishers; **698:** "Jimmy Jet and His TV Set" from *Where the Sidewalk Ends* by Shel Silverstein. ©2004 by Evil Eye Music. Used by permission of HarperCollins Publishers; **705:** Adaptation of *The Hindenburg* by Patrick O'Brien, ©2000 by Patrick O'Brien. Reprinted by permission of Henry Holt and Company, LLC; **730:** *Sweet Music in Harlem*. Text ©2004 by Debbie A. Taylor. Illustrations ©2004 by Frank Morrison. Permission arranged with Lee & Low Books, Inc., New York, NY 10016; **754:** "A Sinister Spider Named Ruth" from *Pocketful of Nonsense* by James Marshall, Golden Books, Western Publishing Company, Inc., 1992; **755:** "Sunflakes" from *Country Pie* by Frank Asch, HarperCollins Publishers, 1979; **756:** "Almost Human" from *Earth Lines: Poems for the Green Age* by Pat Moon. ©1993 by Pat Moon. Used by permission of Greenwillow Books and HarperCollins Publishers; **757:** "The Bat", from *The Collected Poems of Theodore Roethke* by Theodore Roethke. ©1938 by Theodore Roethke. Used by permission of Doubleday, a division of Random House, Inc.

Illustrations

Cover: Greg Newbold; **12, 510, 630** Steven Adler; **22-34** James Bernardin; **37-41, 161** Laura Huliska-Beith; **44-45** Jason Wolff; **46-48** Darryl Ligasan; **69-84** E. B. Lewis; **86-88, 317** Maryjo Koch; **110** Charles Pyle; **134-136** Greg Newbold; **146-158** Raul Colon; **160, 206-207** Vladimir Radunsky; **181-185** John Sandford; **190-204** Ed Young; **226-229, 263-265** John Manders; **260, 388** Melissa Sweet; **266-280, 454, 546, 794** Franklin Hammond; **282-286** Leslie Cober-Gentry; **312-315** Dahl Taylor; **317, 340-344** Phil Wilson; **410** Jui Ishida; **437-451, 795** Robert Mancini; **462-478** Gregory Christie; **480-482** Robert Wagt; **504-506, 630** Bob Dacey; **513-530** Matt Faulkner; **532-534** Janan Cain; **554-558** Francis Livingston; **586-598** Marc Sasso; **601** Matt Zang; **622, 625** Rodica Prato; **626-628** Shelly Hehenberger; **637-650** Michael Steirnagle; **652** Amanda Hall; **657-665, 797** Tom McNeely; **666** John Burgoyne; **678-696, 704-720** Patrick O'Brien; **754-756** Laura Ovresat.

Photographs

Every effort has been made to secure permission and provide appropriate credit for photographic material. The publisher deeply regrets any omission and pledges to correct errors called to its attention in subsequent editions.

Unless otherwise acknowledged, all photographs are the property of Scott Foresman, a division of Pearson Education.

Photo locators denoted as follows: **Top (T), Center (C), Bottom (B), Left (L), Right (R), Background (Bkgd).**

4 ©Sean Murphy/Getty Images; **6** ©Gary Braasch/Corbis; **10** ©Gary Braasch/Corbis; **16** ©Sean Murphy/Getty Images; **17** ©Bettmann/Corbis; **19** Getty Images; **20** ©Jutta Klee/Corbis; **21** ©Corbis; **66** International Stock Photography/Taxi/Getty Images; **67** (TL, CL) ©Jim Reed/Corbis; **91** ©Vintage Military; **92** ©Stephen Dunn/Getty Images; **93** Getty Images; **95** Legends Archive; **113** Corbis; **114** Corbis; **115** Corbis; **116** ©Bettmann/Corbis; **118** (TL, CL) Bettmann/Corbis; (TR) Prints & Photographs Division/Library of Congress, (CR) Corbis; **120** ©Bettmann/Corbis; **121** Corbis; **122** Brown Brothers; **123** (TL) Getty Images, (TR) New York Public Library/Art Resource, NY; **124** Museum of the City of New York; **125** Getty Images; **126** Photo Collection Alexander Alland, Sr./Corbis; **127** Corbis; **128** ©Tony Linck/Time Life Pictures/Getty Images; **130** Corbis; **132** Corbis; **133** ©Joseph Sohm/ChromoSohm Inc./Corbis; **138** ©Sean Murphy/Getty Images; **139** (TR) Sports Icons/©Comstock, Inc., (CR) ©Brad Yeo Collection/the i spot; **140** ©Peter Beck/Corbis; **141** ©Michael Nichols/NGS Image Collection; **143** ©Larry Dale Gordon/Getty Images; **144** ©Tony Cordoza/Getty Images; **145** (T) ©Geoff Du Feu/Getty Images, (BR) ©Stephen Dalton/NHPA Limited; **163** Corbis; **164** ©Ken Davies/Masterfile Corporation; **165** Getty Images; **168** (Bkgd) ©Anne Frank House/Getty Images, (C) Courtesy of Joseph Shadur/United States Holocaust Museum; **170** (C) Courtesy of Joseph Shadur/United States Holocaust Museum, (Bkgd) ©Anne Frank House/Getty Images; **171** Bonhams, London, UK/Bridgeman Art Library; **172** (C) Courtesy of Joseph Shadur/United States Holocaust Museum, (Bkgd) Anne Frank House/Getty Images; **174** (C) Courtesy of Joseph Shadur/United States Holocaust Museum, (Bkgd) ©Anne Frank House/Getty Images; **175** ©Jeffrey Coolidge/Getty Images; **176** (C) Courtesy of Joseph Shadur/United States Holocaust Museum, (Bkgd) ©Anne Frank House/Getty Images; **187** Illustration Works, Inc.; **188** ©2000 Kinuko Y. Craft ; **189** ©2000 Kinuko Y. Craft; **209** (BL) ©Anup Shah/Nature Picture Library,

799

(TR) ©Renee Lynn/Corbis; **210** ©Lori Adamski Peek/Getty Images/Stone; **211** (BR) Melanie Acevedo/FoodPix, (BC, CC) ©Photodisc Green/Getty Images; **212** (TC, TL) ©Roger Eritja/Alamy, (C) ©Michael Nichols/NGS Image Collection; **214** (TC) ©JH Pete Carmichael/Getty Images, (R) ©David Fleetham/Mira; **216** (BR) ©Gay Bumgarner/Stone/Getty Images, (R) ©Anup Shah/Nature Picture Library; **218** ©Ariel Skelley/Corbis; **219** (CL, CC) ©Photodisc Green/Getty Images, (BC) ©Melanie Acevedo/FoodPix; **220** (BR) ©Ken J. Howard/Sea Images, (R) ©Michael & Patricia Fogden/Corbis; **222** ©Paco Feria/Peter Arnold, Inc.; **223** ©Bob Hallinen/Anchorage Daily News; **224** ©David Fleetham/Mira; **231** (BR) ©Freelance Photography Guild/Corbis, (BR) ©Comstock Inc.; **232** ©Kevin Fleming/Corbis; **233** ©Kevin Fleming/Corbis; **240** ©Hans Neleman/Getty Images; **241** (TR, BR, BL) ©Hans Neleman/Getty Images; **250** ©Bettmann/Corbis; **252** (TR) The Granger Collection, NY, (B) Corbis; **253** ©Bettmann/Corbis; **254** ©Images/Corbis; **256** ©Images/Corbis; **258** ©Gary Braasch/Corbis; **259** (TR) ©David A. Northcott/Corbis, (CR) Getty Images, (BL) ©Gavin Wickham/Eye Ubiquitous/Corbis; **261** ©Jim Henson's Creature Shop/©DK Images; **289** ©State Museum of Georgia/AKG London Ltd.; **290** ©Marc Moritsch/NGS Image Collection; **310** ©Leonardo da Vinci's Horse, Inc.; **341** ©Kevin Kelly; **345** ©Kevin Kelly; **347** ©Andy Warhol Foundation/Corbis; **348** ©Lewis W. Hine/Getty Images; **361** The Boys Choir of Harlem, Inc.; **363** ©Charles R. Smith, Jr.; **365** ©Tom Wagner/Corbis; **366** ©Richard Cummins/Corbis; **367** ©Mitchell Gerber/Corbis; **368** ©Jim Henson's Creature Shop/©DK Images; **369** ©Millenium FX Ltd/©DK Images; **370** ©Mike Valentine (BSC)/©DK Images; **371** Millenium FX Ltd/©DK Images; **372** ©Millenium FX Ltd/©DK Images; **373** (TL) ©Millenium FX Ltd/©DK Images, (R) ©Turbo Squid, Inc.; **374-376** ©Millenium FX Ltd/©DK Images; **377** ©Paramount/Everett Collection, Inc.; **378** ©Millenium FX Ltd/©DK Images; **381** Getty Images; **382** (CL, TR) ©American Artist, (BL) ©Matthias Kulka/Corbis; **384** (TR) Getty Images, (Bkgd) ©Steve Drake/Veer, Inc.; **385** ©Stuart McClymont/Getty Images; **386** ©Walter Bibikow/Index Stock Imagery; **387** ©Pete Turner/Getty Images; **389** ©Richard T. Nowitz/Corbis; **390** (C) ©Royalty-Free/Corbis, (Bkgd) ©Stephen Frink/Corbis; **393** ©PBNJ Productions/Corbis; **413** ©Tom Stewart/Corbis; **414** ©Tom Stewart/Corbis; **415** ©Royalty-Free/Corbis; **437** ©Hans Neleman/Getty Images; **438** (TL) ©1984 Defense Mechanisms in Social Insects, Hermann. Reproduced with permission of Greenwood Publishing Group, Inc., Westport, CT., (BL, BC) ©BSIP Agency/Index Stock Imagery; **439** ©BSIP Agency/Index Stock Imagery; **442** (BL) ©Steven Hunt/Getty Images, (TR) ©Oliver Strewe/Getty Images; **443** (TL) ©Fred Bavendam/Minden Pictures, (TR) ©Bob Elsdale/Getty Images; **444** (CL) ©Tim Flach/Getty Images, (BL) ©Ant Photo Library/NHPA Limited; **445** ©Studio Carlo Dani/Animals Animals/Earth Scenes; **446** (TL) ©Tim Flach/Getty Images, (TC) ©Premaphotos/Animals Animals/Earth Scenes; **447** (TL) ©Scott Camazine, (TR) ©Mitsuaki Iwago/Minden Pictures; **448** (TL) ©Tim Flach/Getty Images, (BL) ©Art Wolfe/Getty Images, (BR) ©David Tipling/Photographer's Choice/Getty Images; **450** (CL) ©Tim Flach/Getty Images, (T) ©Joe McDonald/Corbis, (BL) ©Michael & Patricia Fogden/Minden Pictures; **451** ©Michael & Patricia Fogden/Corbis; **459-461** ©Illustration Works, Inc.; **485** ©Rubberball Productions; **487** ©Reuters/Jeff J. Mitchell/Corbis; **490** Brand X Pictures; **493** Veer, Inc.; **498** Rubberball Productions; **500** ©Don Mason/Corbis; **502** (BL) Corbis, (BC) ©Jon Feingersh/Corbis, (BR) ©Caron P./Corbis; **503** ©Dave Black/Corbis; **508** Digital Vision; **509** ©Stuart Westmorland/Corbis; **514** ©Paul Barton/Corbis; **515** ©Royalty-Free/Corbis; **537** (B, BC) Getty Images; **538** ©Ralph White/Corbis; **539-542** ©1998 from Ghost Liners/Little Brown Madison Press Books; **543** (CR) The Granger Collection, NY, (BL) ©1998 from Ghost Liners/Little Brown Madison Press Books; **543-546** ©1998 from Ghost Liners/Little Brown Madison Press Books; **546** Woods Hole Oceanographic Institution; **547** Woods Hole Oceanographic Institution; **548-550** ©1998 from Ghost Liners/Little Brown Madison Press Books; **551** (TL, TR) Woods Hole Oceanographic Institution, (Inset) Michael Freeman/Corbis; **552** ©1998 from Ghost Liners/Little Brown Madison Press Books; **562** Corbis; **563** Corbis; **564** ©World Perspectives/Getty Images; **566** Getty Images; **567** ©Mark M. Lawrence/Corbis; **569** Corbis; **570** NASA; **573** NASA; **574** Digital image ©1996 Corbis/Original image courtesy of NASA/Corbis; **576** ©Digital image ©1996 Corbis/Original image courtesy of NASA/Corbis; **578** (C) Getty Images, (CR) Corbis, (T) NASA; **579** ©Premium Stock/Corbis; **580** ©Time Life Pictures/NASA/Getty Images; **581** ©NASA/Roger Ressmeyer/Corbis; **583** ©DK Images; **585** ©Illustration Works, Inc.; **602** (TL) ©DK Images, (CL) Colin Keates/©DK Images, (TC, CC, TR, CR) Harry Taylor/©DK Images; **605** ©Bettmann/Corbis; **606** ©K.D. Swan/Corbis; **607** (T) ©Joseph Sohm/Visions of America/Corbis, (CC) ©Lester Lefkowitz/Corbis; **608** ©James Nazz/Corbis; **609** ©Chris Collins/Corbis; **610** (L) ©DK Images, (C) ©Raymond Bial; **611** ©John Cancalosi/Peter Arnold, Inc.; **612** ©Bettmann/Corbis; **613** ©Western History Department/Denver Public Library, Western History Collection; **614** (T) Museum of History & Industry/Corbis, (BL) ©Raymond Bial; **616** (BL) ©Raymond Bial, (BR) David Stoecklein/Corbis; **617** ©Raymond Bial; **619** (T) ©Lynn Radeka/SuperStock, (BR) ©Western History Department/Denver Public Library/Denver Public Library, Western History Collection; **620** ©Bettmann/Corbis; **630** NASA; **632** ©Jerry Lofaro/Courtesy of Konica Minolta Business Solutions/American Artists Represents; **633** ©Natalie Fobes/Corbis; **635** (TC) Getty Image, (BL) Brand X Pictures/Getty Images; **636** ©Pat O'Hara/Corbis; **637** ©Martin Harvey/Peter Arnold, Inc.; **655** ©Paul Chinn/San Francisco Chronicle/Corbis; **656** ©Simon Battersby/©DK Images; **658** ©Natalie Fobes/Corbis; **663** ©David Klein; **664** (TC) ©Darrell Gulin/Corbis, (TL) ©David Muench/Corbis, (CR) ©Steve Austin/Papilio/Corbis; **667** (TR) ©David Roseneau, (CL) ©David Klein/George Allez; **668** ©David Klein; 670 (CR) ©Kathleen Murray, (TR) ©Royalty-Free/Corbis; **671** ©Royalty-Free/Corbis; **672** (BL) ©Kathleen Murray, (L, TR) ©Royalty-Free/Corbis; **673** Christine M. Douglas/©DK Images; **675** (BL) ©Images/Corbis, (TR) ©Royalty-Free/Corbis; **677** Brand X Pictures; **701** ©Tim Hawkins/Eye Ubiquitous/Corbis; **702** (BL) ©Lake County Museum/Corbis, (BC) ©Bettmann/Corbis; **703** ©Bettmann/Corbis; **722** ©Owen Franken/Corbis; **724** (CR) Corbis, (B) The Granger Collection, NY; **725** (TR, C) Corbis; **727** ©Underwood & Underwood/Corbis; **728** Corbis; **729** ©Bettmann/Corbis; **752** ©Art Kane Archives; **758** (CL) ©Werner Dieterich/Getty Images, (CR) Corbis, (BL) ©Jerry Lofaro/Courtesy of Konica Minolta Business Solutions/American Artists Represents; **762** ©William Philpott/Reuters America, Inc.; **764** (C) ©Linda Fang, (T) ©Charlotte Craft; **765** (T) ©UPP/Topham/The Image Works, Inc., (B) ©Susan Quinlan; **766** ©Sarah Bial; **767** ©Milan Sabatini; **769** AP Images; **770** Lebrecht Collection; **771** ©Michael Nicholson/Corbis; **772** ©Handprint Books; **774** Courtesy, Lee & Low Books; **777** (C) Art Resource, NY, (Bkgd, Insert) SuperStock; **778** Daemmrich Photography; **779** ©Tom McHugh/Photo Researchers, Inc.; **782** Planet Art; **786** SuperStock; **789** ©1996 Grant Wood/VAGA/SuperStock; **794** ©Millenium FX Ltd/©DK Images; **796** (TL) ©Corbis/Corbis, (BR) ©David Stoecklein/Corbis.

Glossary

The contents of this glossary have been adapted from *Thorndike Barnhart Advanced Dictionary*. Copyright ©1997, Pearson Education, Inc.

777 (C) Art Resource, NY, (Bkgd) SuperStock, (Insert) SuperStock; 778 Daemmrich Photography; 779 ©Tom McHugh/Photo Researchers, Inc.; 782 Planet Art; 786 SuperStock; 789 ©1996 Grant Wood/VAGA/SuperStock

800

Writing

Writing Trait of the Week

Writing Workshop

Rubrics

Rubric 4 3 2 1

Assessment

Assessment

Student Tips for Making Top Scores in Writing Tests

1. **Use transitions such as those below to relate ideas, sentences, or paragraphs.**

in addition	nevertheless	finally	however
then	instead	therefore	as a result
for example	in particular	first	such as

2. **Write a good beginning. Make readers want to continue.**
   - I shouldn't have opened that green box.
   - Imagine being locked in a crate at the bottom of the sea.
   - When I was four, I saw a purple dog.
   - Have you ever heard of a talking tree?

3. **Focus on the topic.**
   If a word or detail is off-topic, get rid of it. If a sentence is unrelated or loosely related to the topic, drop it or connect it more closely.

4. **Organize your ideas.**
   Have a plan in mind before you start writing. Your plan can be a list, bulleted items, or a graphic organizer. Five minutes spent planning your work will make the actual writing go much faster and smoother.

5. **Support your ideas.**
   - Develop your ideas with fully elaborated examples and details.
   - Make ideas clear to readers by choosing vivid words that create pictures.
   - Avoid dull *(get, go, say)*, vague *(thing, stuff, lots of)*, or overused *(really, very)* words.
   - Use a voice that is appropriate to your audience.

6. **Make writing conventions as error-free as possible.**
   Proofread your work line by line, sentence by sentence. Read for correct punctuation, then again for correct capitalization, and finally for correct spelling.

7. **Write a conclusion that wraps things up but is more than a repeating of ideas or "The end."**
   - After all, he was my brother, weird or not.
   - The Internet has changed our lives for better and for worse.
   - It's not the largest planet but the one I'd choose to live on.
   - Now tell me you don't believe in a sixth sense.

Focus/Ideas

Organization/ Paragraphs

Voice

Word Choice

Sentences

Conventions

Writing Traits

- **Focus/Ideas** refers to the main purpose for writing and the details that make the subject clear and interesting. It includes development of ideas through support and elaboration.

- **Organization/Paragraphs** refers to the overall structure of a piece of writing that guides readers. Within that structure, transitions show how ideas, sentences, and paragraphs are connected.

- **Voice** shows the writer's unique personality and establishes a connection between writer and reader. Voice, which contributes to style, should be suited to the audience and the purpose for writing.

- **Word Choice** is the use of precise, vivid words to communicate effectively and naturally. It helps create style through the use of specific nouns, lively verbs and adjectives, and accurate, well-placed modifiers.

- **Sentences** covers strong, well-built sentences that vary in length and type. Skillfully written sentences have pleasing rhythms and flow fluently.

- **Conventions** refers to mechanical correctness and includes grammar, usage, spelling, punctuation, capitalization, and paragraphing.

OBJECTIVES

- Develop an understanding of a personal narrative.
- Use vivid description to show, not tell, feelings and actions.
- Establish criteria for evaluating a personal narrative.

Key Features

Personal Narrative

In a personal narrative, a writer gives a firsthand account about something that happened in his or her life.

- Is about an interesting experience in the storyteller's life
- Tells the story using *I* or *me*
- Flows from beginning to middle to end
- Provides details to make the event vivid

Connect to Weekly Writing

Week 1	Character Sketch 41g–41h
Week 2	Tall Tale 67g–67h
Week 3	Friendly or Thank-You Letter 89g–89h
Week 4	Feature Article 111g–111h
Week 5	Narrative Writing 133g–133h

Strategic Intervention

See Differentiated Instruction p. WA8.

Advanced

See Differentiated Instruction p. WA9.

See Differentiated Instruction p. WA9.

Additional Resource for Writing
Writing Rubrics and Anchor Papers, pp. 39–45

Personal Narrative

Writing Prompt: Meeting Challenges
Write a personal narrative about a challenge or difficult problem. Describe what the challenge was and tell how you met it. Use details that make the events clear and interesting.
Purpose: Describe the steps you took to meet a challenge
Audience: Students in your class

READ LIKE A WRITER

Look back at *Island of the Blue Dolphins.* Remind students that the narrator tells the events about building a house in the order in which they happened. Point out that in a **personal narrative** events are often described in chronological order to create a beginning, middle, and end.

EXAMINE THE MODEL AND RUBRIC

GUIDED WRITING Read the model aloud. Have students point out sentences in which the writer uses vivid words to show how she feels and acts. Discuss how the model reflects traits of good writing.

Facing My Math Challenge

Two years ago I struggled with learning my multiplication facts. My stomach did flip-flops on tests. Mom called me "math-challenged." I just couldn't learn the multiplication facts! In March, I decided to face my math challenge.

First, I met with Ms. Egan after school to learn strategies for mastering multiplication. She told me to practice the multiplication facts every day (even on the weekends!). Then I created multiplication flashcards. I flipped through them whenever I had a free moment. I quizzed myself at the bus stop, in bed, and in the waiting room at the dentist's office. Next, my friend Jean and I composed a song about the multiplication facts by putting them to music. I don't think we'll ever get a record deal, but the song was music to my math-challenged ears!

Finally, the day of the quiz came. My mom quizzed me at breakfast, Jean and I sang the multiplication song all the way to school, and I whizzed through my flashcards one last time before class. When I got the quiz, I went to work. In my mind swirled pictures of flashcards and the melody of the multiplication song. Fifteen minutes later, I handed in my quiz.

The next day Ms. Egan handed me my quiz. Wow! I missed only one problem. Next to my name, Ms. Egan had written "You did it!"

Unit 1 Personal Narrative • PREWRITE — Writing Process 1

▲ **Writing Transparency** WP1

Traits of a Good Personal Narrative

Focus/Ideas	Narrative is well focused and developed with lively details.
Organization/ Paragraphs	Narrative includes a beginning that introduces the topic, a middle that progresses chronologically, and an end that resolves the problem.
Voice	Writer expresses his/her feelings and uses humor to give the narrator a distinctive voice. (*I don't think we'll ever get a record deal, but the song was music to my math-challenged ears!*)
Word Choice	Writer uses vivid words (*flip-flops, swirled*) to help readers visualize the experience. Time-order words show the sequence of events.
Sentences	Sentences are varied and of different lengths and patterns.
Conventions	Writer has good control of grammar, capitalization, spelling, and usage.

Unit 1 Personal Narrative • PREWRITE — Writing Process 2

▲ **Writing Transparency** WP2

FINDING A TOPIC

- With students, brainstorm problems or challenges that people their age might experience. Write a list on the board.
- Suggest that students sort through their memories by talking to their families and reviewing journals or photograph albums.
- Have students collaborate with others by having a discussion with a small group about problems they have solved or challenges they have met.

NARROW A TOPIC Have students look more closely at the ideas they have chosen to refine their topic.

Earned a brown belt in karate This is too complicated.
Learned to tell a joke This is too simple.
Swam across a lake This would be an exciting story.

PREWRITING STRATEGY

GUIDED WRITING Display Writing Transparency WP3.

Think Aloud **MODEL** This student will tell about an exciting experience swimming across a lake. The main ideas and events of the story are mapped out. Now the student can write a draft by adding details to each part of the story.

PREWRITING ACTIVITIES

- Have students use Grammar and Writing Practice Book p. 160 to help them organize information.
- Students can make a word web.

Notes for a Personal Narrative

Directions Fill in the graphic organizer with information about the event or experience that you plan to write about.

Possible title Swimming to the Other Side

Summary

What happened? I swam across Lake Wonder
When? last summer
Where? at Camp Wilderness
Who was there? camp staff and friends

Details

Beginning I wanted to swim across Lake Wonder at camp.

Middle I designed a training schedule.
Camp counselors helped me train in and out of the water.

End After four weeks of preparation, I swam across Lake Wonder.

Unit 1 Personal Narrative • PREWRITE   Writing Process 3

▲ **Writing Transparency** WP3

Monitor Progress

Differentiated Instruction

If...	**then...**
students have trouble deciding if a topic is suitable,	suggest that they think about whether they would enjoy telling a friend about the experience, and the friend would enjoy hearing about it.

Notes for a Personal Narrative

Directions Fill in the graphic organizer with information about the event or experience that you plan to write about.

Summary

What happened? Answers should include details
When? about each part of student's
Where? personal narrative.
Who was there?

Details

Beginning

Middle

End

▲ **Grammar and Writing Practice Book** p. 160

Think Like a Writer

Use Transitions to Show Time As you write your personal narrative, be sure you describe events in the order in which they happened. Transition words such as *first, then,* and *next* help prepare your reader for each step in the action.

Support Writing If students do not know some words on Writing Transparency WP4, offer meanings for them.

- Read and define words such as *confident, fidget,* and *strut,* and use them in sentences.
- Model the body language or movements characteristic of each describing word.

Words That Tell About *You*

Directions How did you feel about the challenge facing you at the beginning, middle, and end of your experience? Choose one or two words from the word bank to describe each part of your experience. Then add details that *show* readers each feeling.

anxious	thrilled	proud	inspired
disappointed	excited	contented	determined
dismayed	fearful	delighted	upset

Beginning Answers should be based on adjectives from the word bank and expand with details that show the feelings the adjectives suggest.

Middle ______

End ______

▲ **Grammar and Writing Practice Book** p. 161

WRITING THE FIRST DRAFT

GUIDED WRITING Use Writing Transparency WP4 to practice using words that tell about you.

- Have students identify the word or words in each sentence that describe the way the writer felt. Have them think about a way to describe the feeling so that the writer shows it instead of telling it.
- Point out that a vivid description helps a reader see, hear, touch, taste, or feel something in his or her imagination.

Think Aloud **MODEL** I know how I feel when I am frightened. If I describe sweaty hands and the way I fidget in my chair, readers will be able to clearly *see* how I feel. This is much more vivid than *telling* them I am frightened.

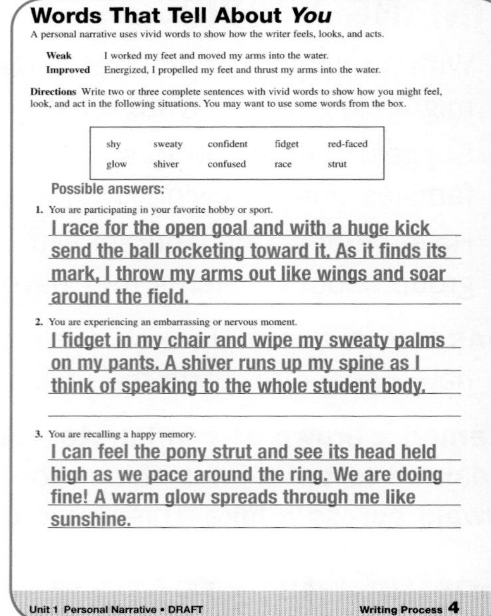
Words That Tell About *You*

A personal narrative uses vivid words to show how the writer feels, looks, and acts.

Weak I worked my feet and moved my arms into the water.
Improved Energized, I propelled my feet and thrust my arms into the water.

Directions Write two or three complete sentences with vivid words to show how you might feel, look, and act in the following situations. You may want to use some words from the box.

shy	sweaty	confident	fidget	red-faced
glow	shiver	confused	race	strut

Possible answers:

1. You are participating in your favorite hobby or sport.
I race for the open goal and with a huge kick send the ball rocketing toward it. As it finds its mark, I throw my arms out like wings and soar around the field.

2. You are experiencing an embarrassing or nervous moment.
I fidget in my chair and wipe my sweaty palms on my pants. A shiver runs up my spine as I think of speaking to the whole student body.

3. You are recalling a happy memory.
I can feel the pony strut and see its head held high as we pace around the ring. We are doing fine! A warm glow spreads through me like sunshine.

Unit 1 Personal Narrative • DRAFT Writing Process 4

▲ **Writing Transparency** WP4

WRITER'S CRAFT Show, Don't Tell

Here are some ways writers can show what happens instead of simply telling what happens:

- Instead of statements of emotion such as "I was so happy," use details that allow readers to picture the effects of the emotion.
- Appeal to the five senses by using descriptive details.
- Use vivid, specific verbs such as *soar* or *strut.*

DRAFTING STRATEGIES

- Have students review their notes before they write.
- Students should use time-order words and phrases such as *last summer, first, next,* and *after four weeks* as transitions from one part of the story to the next.
- Remind them to keep their audience and purpose in mind.
- Students should follow the directions above in order to show and not tell in their stories.
- Have students use Grammar and Writing Practice Book p. 161 to choose words that show their feelings.

WRITER'S CRAFT Elaboration

COMBINE SENTENCES Explain that one way to elaborate is to join two simple sentences to make compound or complex sentences. Two short, choppy sentences sound smoother when they are combined with words such as *and, but, or, if, when, before,* or *because.*

Choppy I like to swim. I hate getting my eyes wet. I put my face in the water. I come up spluttering.

Improved I like to swim, but I hate getting my eyes wet. When I put my face in the water, I come up spluttering.

Use Grammar and Writing Practice Book p. 162 to practice elaboration by combining sentences.

Trait Checklist

REVISING

Focus/Ideas

✔ Is the personal narrative focused?

✔ Are there enough details?

Organization/Paragraphs

✔ Do time-order words help make the sequence of events clear?

Voice

✔ Is the narrative interesting and lively?

Word Choice

✔ Do vivid words help show instead of merely tell?

Sentences

✔ Have short, choppy sentences been combined to sound smoother?

REVISING STRATEGIES

GUIDED WRITING Use Writing Transparency WP5 to model revising. Point out the Revising Marks, which students should use when they revise their work.

Think Aloud **MODEL** This is part of the narrative about swimming across Lake Wonder. In the first sentence, *that I had almost gotten there* has been replaced with *the shoreline* to add a specific detail that readers can picture. Adding *energized* to the next sentence gives a vivid sense of how the writer felt. In sentence 3, a general descriptive word *(happy)* is replaced with a precise one *(exhilarated)* that shows exactly how the writer felt. After sentence 4, the interjection *Wow!* is added to show the writer's excitement. The final sentence is deleted because it adds nothing to the narrative and makes the ending flat and uninteresting.

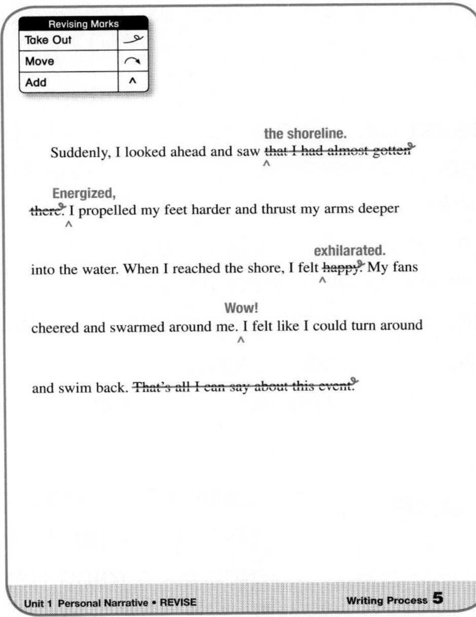
Revising Marks	
Take Out	
Move	
Add	^

Suddenly, I looked ahead and saw ~~that I had almost gotten~~ ^the shoreline. ~~there.~~ ^Energized, I propelled my feet harder and thrust my arms deeper into the water. When I reached the shore, I felt ~~happy.~~ ^exhilarated. My fans cheered and swarmed around me. ^Wow! I felt like I could turn around and swim back. ~~That's all I can say about this event.~~

Unit 1 Personal Narrative • REVISE Writing Process 5

▲ **Writing Transparency** WP5

PEER REVISION Write the Revising Checklist on the board, or make copies to distribute. Students can use this checklist to revise their personal narratives. Have partners read each other's first drafts. Remind them to be courteous and specific with suggestions.

Elaboration

Combine Sentences

When you write, you can elaborate by combining short simple sentences to make compound or complex sentences. This will create a smoother flow of ideas in your writing. The two sentences you combine must make sense together. You can create compound sentences by combining short sentences using the word *and, but,* or *or.* You can create complex sentences by combining short sentences with *if, because, before, after, since,* or *when.*

Directions Use the word in ( ) to combine the two sentences. Remember to capitalize the first word of the new sentence and to replace the first period with a comma.

1. (but) My big sister could climb the pine tree in the pasture. I had not tried.
My big sister could climb the pine tree in the pasture, but I had not tried.
2. (because) The first limbs were so high. I thought it was too hard.
Because the first limbs were so high, I thought it was too hard.
3. (when) She boosted me up. I could just reach the lowest limb.
When she boosted me up, I could just reach the lowest limb.
4. (and) The rough bark scratched my skin. Sticky pine resin oozed onto my hands.
The rough bark scratched my skin, and sticky pine resin oozed onto my hands.
5. (but) I was scared. I climbed to the very top of that pine.
I was scared, but I climbed to the very top of that pine.

▲ **Grammar and Writing Practice Book** p. 162

Monitor Progress

Differentiated Instruction

If... students are using only simple sentences,	**then...** review the grammar lesson on p. 111e.

Editing Checklist

- ✔Did I spell words with short vowels correctly?
- ✔Did I capitalize proper nouns correctly?
- ✔Did I use vivid descriptive words instead of weak, vague ones?
- ✔Did I indent each paragraph?

Support Writing Invite students to read their drafts aloud to you. Observe whether they seem to note any spelling or grammatical errors by stumbling or self-correcting. Return to those errors and how to correct them. Use the appropriate Grammar Transition Lessons in the ELL and Transition Handbook to explicitly teach the English conventions.

EDITING STRATEGY

SENTENCE BY SENTENCE Suggest that students use an editing strategy. They can check their work by reading sentence by sentence through the narrative. As they read each sentence, have them check to be sure it contains both a subject and a predicate, begins with a capital letter, and ends with an appropriate end mark.

GUIDED WRITING Use Writing Transparency WP6 to model the process of reading sentence by sentence. Indicate the Proofreading Marks, which students should use when they edit their work. Write the Editing Checklist on the board, or make copies to distribute. Students can use this checklist to edit their work.

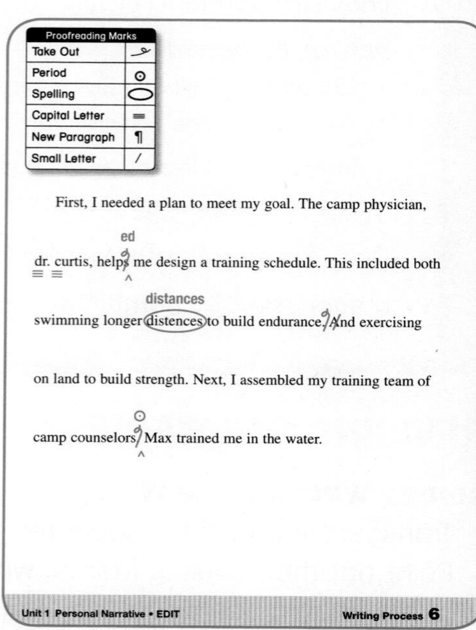

Proofreading Marks	
Take Out	
Period	⊙
Spelling	○
Capital Letter	≡
New Paragraph	¶
Small Letter	/

First, I needed a plan to meet my goal. The camp physician, dr. curtis, helps (ed) me design a training schedule. This included both swimming longer distences (distances) to build endurance. And exercising on land to build strength. Next, I assembled my training team of camp counselors, (⊙) Max trained me in the water.

Unit 1 Personal Narrative • EDIT — Writing Process 6

▲ **Writing Transparency** WP6

MODEL First I'll check spelling. A word with the short *i* sound was misspelled. The writer has corrected the spelling of *distances.* Next, I will check capitalization. The title and name *Dr. Curtis* have been capitalized, as proper nouns should be. Now I will read the sentences aloud. I can hear that *helps* is not the correct verb. The writer changed it to *helped.* Also, the fourth sentence is not a complete thought. It needs to be joined to the sentence before it, so the period has been deleted and the capital A changed to a small letter. Finally, the last sentence combines two complete ideas without a conjunction such as *and* or *when.* It needs to be broken into two sentences, so the comma after *counselors* is changed to a period.

USING TECHNOLOGY Students who have written or revised their personal narratives on computers should keep these points in mind as they edit:

- A computer grammar checker can catch some errors, but it should not be relied on exclusively. A good grammar book is the best source.
- Use the Format menu to set the margins, line lengths, paragraph indents, and other features for your paper.
- Using a print preview or page layout feature can show you how your work will appear before it is printed.

SELF-EVALUATION

Prepare students to fill out a Self-Evaluation Guide. Display Writing Transparency WP7 to model the self-evaluation process.

Think Aloud **MODEL** I would give the personal narrative a *4.*

Focus/Ideas This narrative is focused on the goal of swimming across a lake.

Organization/Paragraphs The events are described in order.

Voice The narrator's personality and feelings are clearly expressed.

Word Choice The writer uses words that show instead of tell and time-order words.

Sentences The types and lengths of sentences are varied.

Conventions Grammar, capitalization, and spelling are excellent.

Swimming to the Other Side

Last summer at Camp Wilderness I decided to swim across Lake Wonder. I knew it wouldn't be easy. Lake Wonder is humongous and always ice-cold. When you jump in the frigid water, your body feels like a popsicle!

First, I needed a plan to meet my goal. The camp physician, Dr. Curtis, helped me design a training schedule. This included both swimming longer distances to build endurance and exercising on land to build strength. Next, I assembled my training team of camp counselors. Max trained me in the water. He gave me tips on my stroke and showed me an awesome way to kick my feet like propellers. Judy was my "on-land" coach. Every day I swam, ran, lifted weights, and stretched my muscles for greater flexibility. When I got in bed at "lights out," my aching muscles begged me to stop. Would it be worth it? They don't call it Lake *Wonder* for nothing!

After four weeks of training, I finally felt ready to dive in! The water was cold, but I concentrated on the moves that Max taught me and thought about reaching the other side. I could hear the enthusiastic cheers of my friends. "Come on!" they shouted. "You're almost there!"

Suddenly, I looked ahead and saw the shoreline. Energized, I propelled my feet harder and thrust my arms deeper into the water. When I reached the shore, I felt exhilarated. My fans cheered and swarmed around me. Wow! I felt like I could turn around and swim back.

Unit 1 Personal Narrative • PUBLISH Writing Process 7

▲ **Writing Transparency** WP7

EVALUATION Assign Grammar and Writing Practice Book p. 163. Tell students that when they evaluate their own narratives, assigning a score of 3, 2, or even 1 does not necessarily indicate a bad paper. The ability to identify areas for improvement in future writing is a valuable skill.

Ideas for Publishing

Illustrated Books Students can illustrate their stories with drawings or magazine pictures. They can design a cover and make their own book.

Writer's Circle Students can take turns reading their narratives aloud in a small group. Classmates may ask questions about the narratives.

Self-Evaluation Guide

Personal Narrative

Directions Think about the final draft of your personal narrative. Then rate yourself on a scale of from 4 to 1 (4 is the highest) on each writing trait. After you fill out the chart, answer the questions.

Writing Traits	4	3	2	1
Focus/Ideas				
Organization/Paragraphs				
Voice				
Word Choice				
Sentences				
Conventions				

1. What is the best part of your personal narrative? Why?
Answers should show that students have given thought to the personal narratives they have written.

2. Write one thing you would change about this personal narrative if you had the chance to write it again. Why?

▲ **Grammar and Writing Practice Book** p. 163

Scoring Rubric Personal Narrative

Rubric 4 3 2 1	4	3	2	1
Focus/Ideas	Personal narrative well focused and developed with many supporting details	Personal narrative generally focused and developed with supporting details	Personal narrative often off topic; few supporting details	Personal narrative without focus or sufficient information
Organization/ Paragraphs	Clear sequence of events with time-order words	Reasonably clear sequence with one or two lapses	Confused sequence of events	No attempt to sequence events
Voice	Sincere, engaging, voice; feelings clear	Pleasant voice but not compelling or unique	No clear, original voice	Flat writing; no identifiable voice
Word Choice	Vivid descriptive words that show instead of tell;	Some vivid words that show instead of tell	Few vivid words that show instead of tell	No attempt to show instead of tell
Sentences	Clear sentences; variety of types, including use of compound and complex	Mostly clear sentences with some variety	Some sentences unclear; little variety or only simple sentences	Incomplete or run-on sentences; short, choppy sentences
Conventions	Few, if any, errors	Several minor errors	Errors that detract from writing and may interfere with understanding	Errors that detract from writing and prevent understanding

For 6-, 5-, and 3-point Scoring Rubrics, see pp. WA11–WA14.

Personal Narrative
Differentiated Instruction

WRITING PROMPT: Meeting Challenges

Write a personal narrative about a challenge or difficult problem. Describe what the challenge was and tell how you met it. Use details that make the events clear and interesting.

Purpose: Describe the steps you took to meet a challenge

Audience: Students in your class

MODIFY INSTRUCTION

Pick One

ALTERNATIVE PROMPTS

ALTERNATIVE PROMPTS: Narrative Writing

Strategic Intervention Think about a problem you solved by yourself. Write a paragraph telling what you did and how you decided on a solution. Tell how you felt when you succeeded.

On-Level Think about a challenging goal you would like to achieve. Write a journal entry. Ask yourself questions about the goal you want to reach, why you want to achieve it, and how you could accomplish it. Then answer the questions, and write two or three paragraphs based on the questions.

Advanced Write a personal narrative in the form of a tall tale that humorously relates the way you met a huge challenge. Use exaggeration and colorful details to paint vivid pictures of your superhuman efforts. Include dialogue between two or more people to make your story lively.

Strategic Intervention

MODIFY THE PROMPT

Ask emerging writers questions such as *Did you ever solve a problem you were having? Did you ever meet a challenge such as learning a new sport or overcoming a fear of heights?* Encourage discussion. Write possible topics and key details on the board.

PREWRITING SUPPORT

- Describe an experience of your own in which you worked to meet a challenge or solve a problem.
- Discuss personal narratives with which students are familiar. Help them characterize each narrator and summarize the main experience he or she describes.
- Students can dictate to you the event they want to describe in their personal narrative. Take notes that students can use for the narrative. Circle key words or concepts and prompt students for details about them.

OPTIONS

- Give students the option of writing a group narrative under your supervision.

CHECK PROGRESS Segment the assignment into manageable pieces. Check work at intervals, such as graphic organizers and first drafts, to make sure writing is on track.

Advanced

MODIFY THE PROMPT

Expect advanced writers to produce work with strong elaboration and some analytic thought about the meaning of the personal experience. A distinct and original voice should be evident, and description should show, rather than tell, emotions. Students should use compound and complex sentences as well as simple sentences fluently.

APPLY SKILLS

- As students revise their work, have them consider some ways to improve it.

  Add time-order words to make the order of events clearer.

  Look for opportunities to add sensory details that build a precise mood and tone.

  Include descriptive details that help show instead of tell about the experience.

OPTIONS

- Students can follow these steps to create their own class rubrics.
  1. Read examples of class personal narratives and rank them 1–4, with 4 the highest.
  2. Discuss how they arrived at each rank.
  3. Isolate the six traits and make a rubric based on them.

CHECK PROGRESS Discuss the students' Self-Evaluation Guides. Work with students to monitor their growth and identify their strengths and weaknesses as writers.

MODIFY THE PROMPT

Have students describe the main ideas they want to include in their narratives. Help students restate the key ideas as complete sentences. Record these on the board, leaving blanks. Have students copy the sentences, filling in the blanks.

BUILD BACKGROUND

- Write the word *personal* on the board. Explain that it describes anything relating to an individual. Write the word *narrative* and explain that it is another word for story. Discuss the fact that a personal narrative is simply a story about the writer. Discuss the list of Key Features of a personal narrative that appears in the left column of p. WA2.

OPTIONS

- As students write their personal narratives, guide them toward books, magazines, or Web sites that provide comprehension support through features such as:

  illustrated personal narratives and other pictures

  text in the home-language
- For more suggestions on scaffolding the Writing Workshop, see the ELL and Transition Handbook.

CHECK PROGRESS You may need to explain certain traits and help students fill out their Self-Evaluation Guides. Downplay conventions and focus more on ideas. Recognize examples of vocabulary growth and efforts to use language in more complex ways.

Scoring Rubric Look Back and Write

2 points The response indicates that the student has a complete understanding of the reading concept embodied in the task. The response is accurate, complete, and fulfills all the requirements of the task. Necessary support and/or examples are included, and the information given is clearly text-based.

1 point The response indicates that the student has a partial understanding of the reading concept embodied in the task. The response includes information that is essentially correct and text-based, but the information is too general or too simplistic. Some of the support and/or examples may be incomplete or omitted.

0 points The response indicates that the student does not demonstrate an understanding of the reading concept embodied in the task. The student has either failed to respond or has provided a response that is inaccurate or has insufficient information.

Scoring Rubric Look Back and Write

4 points The response indicates that the student has a thorough understanding of the reading concept embodied in the task. The response is accurate, complete, and fulfills all the requirements of the task. Necessary support and/or examples are included, and the information is clearly text-based.

3 points The response indicates that the student has an understanding of the reading concept embodied in the task. The response is accurate and fulfills all the requirements of the task, but the required support and/or details are not complete or clearly text-based.

2 points The response indicates that the student has a partial understanding of the reading concept embodied in the task. The response that includes information is essentially correct and text-based, but the information is too general or too simplistic. Some of the support and/or examples and requirements of the task may be incomplete or omitted.

1 point The response indicates that the student has a very limited understanding of the reading concept embodied in the task. The response is incomplete, may exhibit many flaws, and may not address all requirements of the task.

0 points The response indicates that the student does not demonstrate an understanding of the reading concept embodied in the task. The student has either failed to respond or has provided a response that is inaccurate or has insufficient information.

Scoring Rubric Narrative Writing

Rubric 3 2 1	6	5	4	3	2	1
us/Ideas	Excellent, focused narrative; well elaborated with quality details	Good, focused narrative; elaborated with telling details	Narrative focused; adequate elaboration	Generally focused narrative; some supporting details	Sometimes unfocused narrative; needs more supporting details	Rambling narrative; lacks development and detail
anization/ ragraphs	Strong beginning, middle, and end; appropriate order words	Coherent beginning, middle, and end; some order words	Beginning, middle, and end easily identifiable	Recognizable beginning, middle, and end; some order words	Little direction from beginning to end; few order words	Lacks beginning, middle, end; incorrect or no order words
Voice	Writer closely involved; engaging personality	Reveals personality	Pleasant but not compelling voice	Sincere voice but not fully engaged	Little writer involvement, personality	Careless writing with no feeling
rd Choice	Vivid, precise words that bring story to life	Clear words to bring story to life	Some specific word pictures	Language adequate but lacks color	Generally limited or redundant language	Vague, dull, or misused words
ntences	Excellent variety of sentences; natural rhythm	Varied lengths, styles; generally smooth	Correct sentences with some variations in style	Correctly constructed sentences; some variety	May have simple, awkward, or wordy sentences; little variety	Choppy; many incomplete or run-on sentences
ventions	Excellent control; few or no errors	No serious errors to affect understanding	General mastery of conventions but some errors	Reasonable control; few distracting errors	Weak control; enough errors to affect understanding	Many errors that prevent understanding

Scoring Rubric Narrative Writing

Rubric 3 2 1	5	4	3	2	1
cus/Ideas	Excellent, focused narrative; well elaborated with quality details	Good, focused narrative; elaborated with telling details	Generally focused narrative; some supporting details	Sometimes unfocused narrative; needs more supporting details	Rambling narrative; lacks development and detail
anization/ ragraphs	Strong beginning, middle, and end; appropriate order words	Coherent beginning, middle, and end; some order words	Recognizable beginning, middle, and end; some order words	Little direction from beginning to end; few order words	Lacks beginning, middle, end; incorrect or no order words
Voice	Writer closely involved; engaging personality	Reveals personality	Sincere voice but not fully engaged	Little writer involvement, personality	Careless writing with no feeling
rd Choice	Vivid, precise words that bring story to life	Clear words to bring story to life	Language adequate but lacks color	Generally limited or redundant language	Vague, dull, or misused words
entences	Excellent variety of sentences; natural rhythm	Varied lengths, styles; generally smooth	Correctly constructed sentences; some variety	May have simple, awkward, or wordy sentences; little variety	Choppy; many incomplete or run-on sentences
nventions	Excellent control; few or no errors	No serious errors to affect understanding	Reasonable control; few distracting errors	Weak control; enough errors to affect understanding	Many errors that prevent understanding

Scoring Rubric Narrative Writing

Rubric 3 2 1	3	2	1
cus/Ideas	Excellent, focused narrative; well elaborated with quality details	Generally focused narrative; some supporting details	Rambling narrative; lacks development and detail
anization/ ragraphs	Strong beginning, middle, and end; appropriate order words	Recognizable beginning, middle, and end; some order words	Lacks beginning, middle, end; incorrect or no order words
Voice	Writer closely involved; engaging personality	Sincere voice but not fully engaged	Careless writing with no feeling
rd Choice	Vivid, precise words that bring story to life	Language adequate but lacks color	Vague, dull, or misused words
entences	Excellent variety of sentences; natural rhythm	Correctly constructed sentences; some variety	Choppy; many incomplete or run-on sentences
nventions	Excellent control; few or no errors	Reasonable control; few distracting errors	Many errors that prevent understanding

Scoring Rubric Descriptive Writing

Rubric 4 3 2 1	6	5	4	3	2	1
Focus/Ideas	Excellent, focused description; well elaborated with quality details	Good, focused description; elaborated with telling details	Description focused; good elaboration	Generally focused description; some supporting details	Sometimes unfocused description; needs more supporting details	Rambling description development and de
Organization/ Paragraphs	Compelling ideas enhanced by order, structure, and transitions	Appealing order, structure, and transitions	Structure identifiable and suitable; transitions used	Adequate order, structure, and some transitions to guide reader	Little direction from beginning to end; few transitions	Lacks direction and identifiable structure no transitions
Voice	Writer closely involved; engaging personality	Reveals personality	Pleasant but not compelling voice	Sincere voice but not fully engaged	Little writer involvement, personality	Careless writing with no feeling
Word Choice	Vivid, precise words that create memorable pictures	Clear, interesting words to bring description to life	Some specific word pictures	Language adequate; appeals to senses	Generally limited or redundant language	Vague, dull, or misus words
Sentences	Excellent variety of sentences; natural rhythm	Varied lengths, styles; generally smooth	Correct sentences with variations in style	Correctly constructed sentences; some variety	May have simple, awkward, or wordy sentences; little variety	Choppy; many incom run-on sentences
Conventions	Excellent control; few or no errors	No serious errors to affect understanding	General mastery of conventions but some errors	Reasonable control; few distracting errors	Weak control; enough errors to affect understanding	Many errors that pre understanding

Scoring Rubric Descriptive Writing

Rubric 4 3 2 1	5	4	3	2	1
Focus/Ideas	Excellent, focused description; well elaborated with quality details	Good, focused description; elaborated with telling details	Generally focused description; some supporting details	Sometimes unfocused description; needs more supporting details	Rambling description; lacks development and detail
Organization/ Paragraphs	Compelling ideas enhanced by order, structure, and transitions	Appealing order, structure, and transitions	Adequate order, structure, and some transitions to guide reader	Little direction from beginning to end; few transitions	Lacks direction and identifiable structure; no transitions
Voice	Writer closely involved; engaging personality	Reveals personality	Sincere voice but not fully engaged	Little writer involvement, personality	Careless writing with no feeling
Word Choice	Vivid, precise words that create memorable pictures	Clear, interesting words to bring description to life	Language adequate; appeals to senses	Generally limited or redundant language	Vague, dull, or misused words
Sentences	Excellent variety of sentences; natural rhythm	Varied lengths, styles; generally smooth	Correctly constructed sentences; some variety	May have simple, awkward, or wordy sentences; little variety	Choppy; many incomplete or run-on sentences
Conventions	Excellent control; few or no errors	No serious errors to affect understanding	Reasonable control; few distracting errors	Weak control; enough errors to affect understanding	Many errors that prevent understanding

Scoring Rubric Descriptive Writing

Rubric 4 3 2 1	3	2	1
Focus/Ideas	Excellent, focused description; well elaborated with quality details	Generally focused description; some supporting details	Rambling description; lacks development and detail
Organization/ Paragraphs	Compelling ideas enhanced by order, structure, and transitions	Adequate order, structure, and some transitions to guide reader	Lacks direction and identifiable structure; no transitions
Voice	Writer closely involved; engaging personality	Sincere voice but not fully engaged	Careless writing with no feeling
Word Choice	Vivid, precise words that create memorable pictures	Language adequate; appeals to senses	Vague, dull, or misused words
Sentences	Excellent variety of sentences; natural rhythm	Correctly constructed sentences; some variety	Choppy; many incomplete or run-on sentences
Conventions	Excellent control; few or no errors	Reasonable control; few distracting errors	Many errors that prevent understanding

Scoring Rubric Persuasive Writing

Rubric 4 3 2 1	6	5	4	3	2	1
Focus/Ideas	Persuasive argument carefully built with quality details	Persuasive argument well supported with details	Persuasive argument focused; good elaboration	Persuasive argument with one or two convincing details	Persuasive piece sometimes unfocused; needs more support	Rambling persuasive argument; lacks development and detail
Organization/ Paragraphs	Information chosen and arranged for maximum effect	Evident progression of persuasive ideas	Progression and structure evident	Information arranged in a logical way with some lapses	Little structure or direction	No identifiable structure
Voice	Writer closely involved; persuasive but not overbearing	Maintains persuasive tone	Persuasive but not compelling voice	Sometimes uses persuasive voice	Little writer involvement, personality	Shows little conviction
Word Choice	Persuasive words carefully chosen for impact	Argument supported by persuasive language	Uses some persuasive words	Occasional persuasive language	Generally limited or redundant language	Vague, dull, or misused words; no persuasive words
Sentences	Excellent variety of sentences; natural rhythm	Varied lengths, styles; generally smooth	Correct sentences with variations in style	Carefully constructed sentences; some variety	Simple, awkward, or wordy sentences; little variety	Choppy; many incomplete or run-on sentences
Conventions	Excellent control; few or no errors	No serious errors to affect understanding	General mastery of conventions but some errors	Reasonable control; few distracting errors	Weak control; enough errors to affect understanding	Many errors that prevent understanding

Scoring Rubric Persuasive Writing

Rubric 4 3 2 1	5	4	3	2	1
Focus/Ideas	Persuasive argument carefully built with quality details	Persuasive argument well supported with details	Persuasive argument with one or two convincing details	Persuasive piece sometimes unfocused; needs more support	Rambling persuasive argument; lacks development and detail
Organization/ Paragraphs	Information chosen and arranged for maximum effect	Evident progression of persuasive ideas	Information arranged in a logical way with some lapses	Little structure or direction	No identifiable structure
Voice	Writer closely involved; persuasive but not overbearing	Maintains persuasive tone	Sometimes uses persuasive voice	Little writer involvement, personality	Shows little conviction
Word Choice	Persuasive words carefully chosen for impact	Argument supported by persuasive language	Occasional persuasive language	Generally limited or redundant language	Vague, dull, or misused words; no persuasive words
Sentences	Excellent variety of sentences; natural rhythm	Varied lengths, styles; generally smooth	Carefully constructed sentences; some variety	Simple, awkward, or wordy sentences; little variety	Choppy; many incomplete or run-on sentences
Conventions	Excellent control; few or no errors	No serious errors to affect understanding	Reasonable control; few distracting errors	Weak control; enough errors to affect understanding	Many errors that prevent understanding

Scoring Rubric Persuasive Writing

Rubric 4 3 2 1	3	2	1
Focus/Ideas	Persuasive argument carefully built with quality details	Persuasive argument with one or two convincing details	Rambling persuasive argument; lacks development and detail
Organization/ Paragraphs	Information chosen and arranged for maximum effect	Information arranged in a logical way with some lapses	No identifiable structure
Voice	Writer closely involved; persuasive but not overbearing	Sometimes uses persuasive voice	Shows little conviction
Word Choice	Persuasive words carefully chosen for impact	Occasional persuasive language	Vague, dull, or misused words; no persuasive words
Sentences	Excellent variety of sentences; natural rhythm	Carefully constructed sentences; some variety	Choppy; many incomplete or run-on sentences
Conventions	Excellent control; few or no errors	Reasonable control; few distracting errors	Many errors that prevent understanding

Scoring Rubric Expository Writing

Rubric 4 3 2 1	6	5	4	3	2	1
Focus/Ideas	Insightful, focused exposition; well elaborated with quality details	Informed, focused exposition; elaborated with telling details	Exposition focused, good elaboration	Generally focused exposition; some supporting details	Sometimes unfocused exposition needs more supporting details	Rambling exposition; la development and deta
Organization/ Paragraphs	Logical, consistent flow of ideas; good transitions	Logical sequencing of ideas; uses transitions	Ideas sequenced with some transitions	Sequenced ideas with some transitions	Little direction from beginning to end; few order words	Lacks structure and transitions
Voice	Writer closely involved; informative voice well suited to topic	Reveals personality; voice suited to topic	Pleasant but not compelling voice	Sincere voice suited to topic	Little writer involvement, personality	Careless writing with no feeling
Word Choice	Vivid, precise words to express ideas	Clear words to express ideas	Words correct and adequate	Language adequate but may lack precision	Generally limited or redundant language	Vague, dull, or misusec words
Sentences	Strong topic sentence; fluent, varied structures	Good topic sentence; smooth sentence structure	Correct sentences that are sometimes fluent	Topic sentence correctly constructed; some sentence variety	Topic sentence unclear or missing; wordy, awkward sentences	No topic sentence; ma incomplete or run-on sentences
Conventions	Excellent control; few or no errors	No serious errors to affect understanding	General mastery of conventions but some errors	Reasonable control; few distracting errors	Weak control; enough errors to affect understanding	Many errors that preve understanding

Scoring Rubric Expository Writing

Rubric 4 3 2 1	5	4	3	2	1
Focus/Ideas	Insightful, focused exposition; well elaborated with quality details	Informed, focused exposition; elaborated with telling details	Generally focused exposition; some supporting details	Sometimes unfocused exposition needs more supporting details	Rambling exposition; lacks development and detail
Organization/ Paragraphs	Logical, consistent flow of ideas; good transitions	Logical sequencing of ideas; uses transitions	Sequenced ideas with some transitions	Little direction from beginning to end; few order words	Lacks structure and transitions
Voice	Writer closely involved; informative voice well suited to topic	Reveals personality; voice suited to topic	Language adequate but may lack precision	Little writer involvement, personality	Careless writing with no feeling
Word Choice	Vivid, precise words to express ideas	Clear words to express ideas	Topic sentence correctly constructed; some sentence variety	Generally limited or redundant language	Vague, dull, or misused words
Sentences	Strong topic sentence; fluent, varied structures	Good topic sentence; smooth sentence structure	Sincere voice suited to topic	Topic sentence unclear or missing; wordy, awkward sentences	No topic sentence; many incomplete or run-on sentences
Conventions	Excellent control; few or no errors	No serious errors to affect understanding	Reasonable control; few distracting errors	Weak control; enough errors to affect understanding	Many errors that prevent understanding

Scoring Rubric Expository Writing

Rubric 4 3 2 1	3	2	1
Focus/Ideas	Insightful, focused exposition; well elaborated with quality details	Generally focused exposition; some supporting details	Rambling exposition; lacks development and detail
Organization/ Paragraphs	Logical, consistent flow of ideas; good transitions	Sequenced ideas with some transitions	Lacks structure and transitions
Voice	Writer closely involved; informative voice well suited to topic	Sincere voice suited to topic	Careless writing with no feeling
Word Choice	Vivid, precise words to express ideas	Language adequate but may lack precision	Vague, dull, or misused words
Sentences	Strong topic sentence; fluent, varied structures	Topic sentence correctly constructed; some sentence variety	No topic sentence; many incomplete or run-on sentences
Conventions	Excellent control; few or no errors	Reasonable control; few distracting errors	Many errors that prevent understanding

Unit 1

Monitoring Fluency

Ongoing assessment of student reading fluency is one of the most valuable measures we have of students' reading skills. One of the most effective ways to assess fluency is taking timed samples of students' oral reading and measuring the number of words correct per minute (WCPM).

How to Measure Words Correct Per Minute—WCPM

Choose a Text

Start by choosing a text for the student to read. The text should be:

- narrative
- unfamiliar
- on grade level

Make a copy of the text for yourself and have one for the student.

Timed Reading of the Text

Tell the student: As you read this aloud, I want you to do your best reading and to read as quickly as you can. That doesn't mean it's a race. Just do your best, fast reading. When I say *begin,* start reading.

As the student reads, follow along in your copy. Mark words that are read incorrectly.

Incorrect
- omissions
- substitutions
- mispronunciations
- reversals

Correct
- self-corrections within 3 seconds
- repeated words

After One Minute

At the end of one minute, draw a line after the last word that was read. Have the student finish reading but don't count any words beyond one minute. Arrive at the words correct per minute—WCPM—by counting the total number of words that the student read correctly in one minute.

Fluency Goals

Grade 5 End-of-Year Goal = 140 WCPM

Target goals by unit

Unit 1 105 to 110 WCPM	**Unit 4** 120 to 128 WCPM
Unit 2 110 to 116 WCPM	**Unit 5** 125 to 134 WCPM
Unit 3 115 to 122 WCPM	**Unit 6** 130 to 140 WCPM

More Frequent Monitoring

You may want to monitor some students more frequently because they are falling far below grade-level benchmarks or they have a result that doesn't seem to align with their previous performance. Follow the same steps above, but choose 2 or 3 additional texts.

Fluency Progress Chart Copy the chart on the next page. Use it to record each student's progress across the year.

Fluency Progress Chart, Grade 5

Name ______________________________

WCPM	1	2	3	4	5	6	7	8	9	10	11	12	13	14	15	16	17	18	19	20	21	22	23	24	25	26	27	28	29	30
175																														
170																														
165																														
160																														
155																														
150																														
145																														
140																														
135																														
130																														
125																														
120																														
115																														
110																														
105																														
100																														
95																														
90																														
85																														
80																														

Timed Reading

Name **Date**

Assessment Chart

Unit 1

Week	Day 3 Retelling Assessment			Day 5 Fluency Assessment			Reteach	Teacher's Comments	Grouping
	The assessed group is highlighted for each week.	Benchmark Score	Actual Score	*The assessed group is highlighted for each week.*	Benchmark WCPM	Actual Score	✓		
WEEK 1	***Frindle*** Character and Plot								
	Strategic	**1–2**		Strategic	Less than 105				
	On-Level	**3**		On-Level	105–110				
	Advanced	**4**		Advanced*	105–110				
WEEK 2	***Thunder Rose*** Cause and Effect								
	Strategic	**1–2**		Strategic	Less than 105				
	On-Level	**3**		On-Level	105–110				
	Advanced	**4**		Advanced*	105–110				
WEEK 3	***Island of Blue Dolphins*** Setting and Theme								
	Strategic	**1–2**		Strategic	Less than 105				
	On-Level	**3**		On-Level	105–110				
	Advanced	**4**		Advanced*	105–110				
WEEK 4	***Satchel Paige*** Sequence								
	Strategic	**1–2**		Strategic	Less than 105				
	On-Level	**3**		On-Level	105–110				
	Advanced	**4**		Advanced*	105–110				
WEEK 5	***Shutting Out the Sky*** Cause and Effect								
	Strategic	**1–2**		Strategic	Less than 105				
	On-Level	**3**		On-Level	105–110				
	Advanced	**4**		Advanced*	105–110				
	Unit 1 Benchmark Test Score								

- **RECORD SCORES** Use this chart to record scores for the Day 3 Retelling, Day 5 Fluency, and Unit Benchmark Test Assessments.

*Students in the advanced group should read above-grade-level materials.

- **REGROUPING** Compare the student's actual score to the benchmark score for each group level and review the *Questions to Consider.* Students may move to a higher or lower group level, or they may remain in the same group.
- **RETEACH** If a student is unable to complete any part of the assessment process, use the weekly Reteach lessons for additional support. Record the lesson information in the space provided on the chart. After reteaching, you may want to reassess using the Unit Benchmark Test.

See also *Assessment Handbook*, p. 175

Unit 1

Assess and Regroup

FYI In Grade 5 there are opportunities for regrouping every five weeks—at the end of Units 2, 3, 4, and 5. These options offer sensitivity to each student's progress, although some teachers may prefer to regroup less frequently.

Assess Unit 1

To assess student progress at the end of Unit 1, consider student's end-of-unit scores for

- Unit 1 Retelling
- Fluency (WCPM)
- Unit 1 Benchmark Test

Group Time

On-Level

For On-Level Unit 1 assessment, students should

- score 3 or better on their cumulative unit rubric scores for Retelling
- meet the current benchmark for fluency (105–110 WCPM), reading On-Level text such as Student Edition selections
- score 80% or better on the Unit 1 Benchmark Tests
- be capable of working in the On-Level group based on teacher judgment

Strategic Intervention

Students would benefit from Strategic Intervention if they

- score 2 or lower on their cumulative unit rubric scores for Retelling
- do not meet the current benchmark for fluency (105–110 WCPM)
- score below 60% on the Unit 1 Benchmark Tests
- are struggling to keep up with the On-Level group based on teacher judgment

Advanced

For Advanced group Unit 1 assessment, students should

- score 4 on their cumulative unit rubric scores for Retelling and demonstrate expansive vocabulary and ease of language in their retellings
- score 95% on the Unit 1 Benchmark Test
- read above-grade-level material fluently (105–110 WCPM)
- be capable of handling the problem solving and investigative work of the Advanced group based on teacher judgment

QUESTIONS TO CONSIDER

- What types of test questions did the student miss? Are they specific to a particular skill or strategy?
- Does the student have adequate background knowledge to understand the test passages or selections for retelling?
- Has the student's performance met expectations for daily lessons and assessments with little or no reteaching?
- Is the student performing more like students in another group?
- Does the student read for enjoyment, different purposes, and varied interests?

Benchmark Fluency Scores

Current Goal: **105–110 WCPM**

End-of-Year Goal: **140 WCPM**

Leveled Readers

Table of Contents

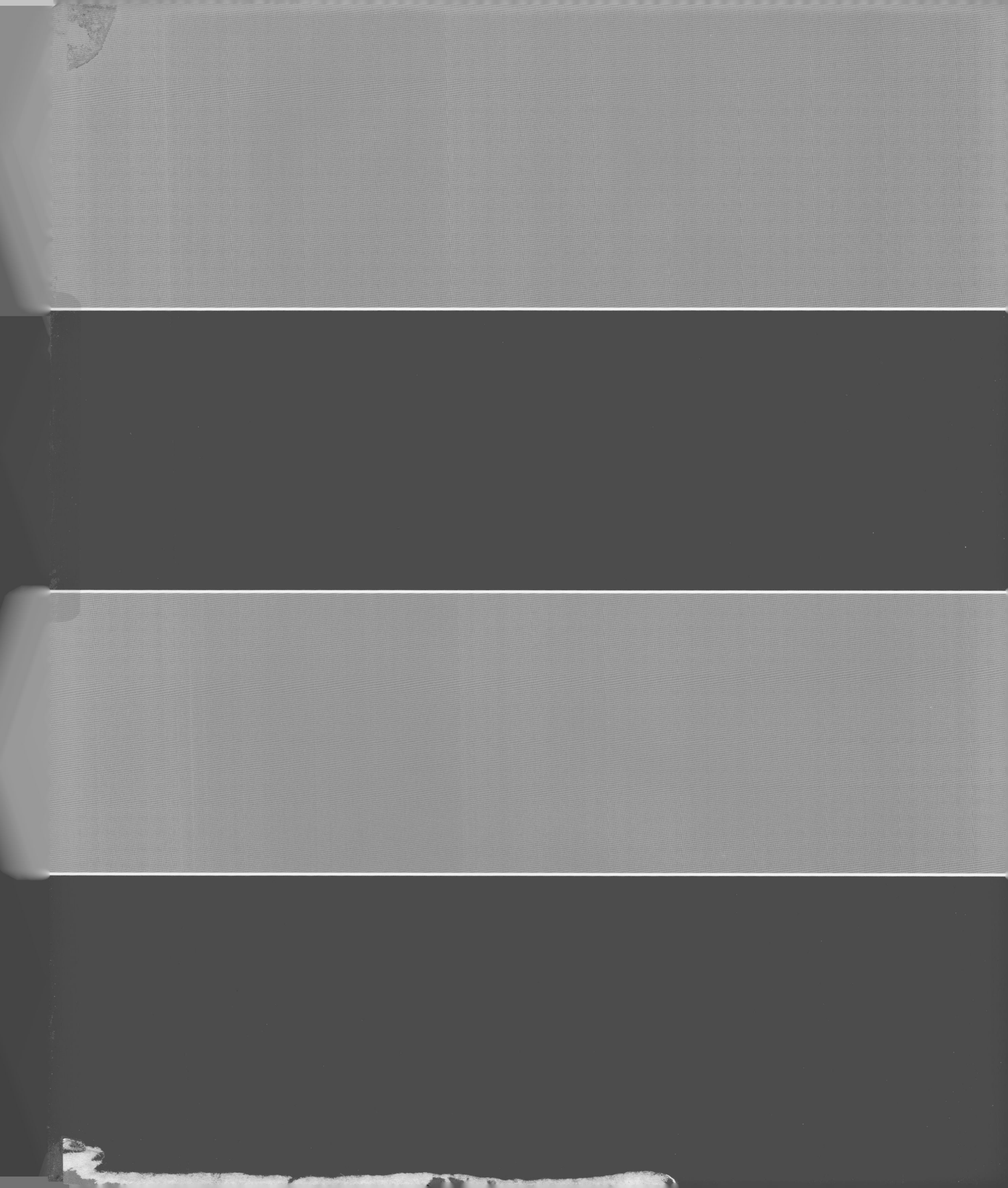

Unit 1 Week 1

The Spelling Bee

CHARACTER AND PLOT

PRIOR KNOWLEDGE

LESSON VOCABULARY acquainted, assignment, essential, expanded, guaranteed, procedures, reputation, worshipped

SUMMARY After being diagnosed with dyslexia, fifth-grader Kate worked on improving her reading over the summer. Her effort paid off when she succeeded in the school spelling bee.

INTRODUCE THE BOOK

BUILD BACKGROUND Ask students if they've ever been frustrated or had a hard time with something. How did they handle it? How did they try to make it better?

PREVIEW/USE ILLUSTRATIONS Invite students to look at the pictures in the book. Ask: Who is the main character? Have students look on pages 12 and 13. Ask: What is the main character doing? Why does she seem sad? How do you think this story will end?

TEACH/REVIEW VOCABULARY Review the vocabulary words with students. Have them write the words and then underline the base word in each word except *essential.*

TARGET SKILL AND STRATEGY

CHARACTER AND PLOT Have students create story maps to track the *plot,* or events, in the story. Make sure students understand that there is a shift in time, or flashback, that begins on page 9.

PRIOR KNOWLEDGE Tell students that when they read a story, they need to think about how it connects to their lives so they can draw on *prior knowledge* to understand more about the characters and plot. Have students brainstorm challenges that they, friends, or characters in other books have faced. Invite students to share their findings.

READ THE BOOK

Use the following questions to support comprehension.

PAGES 3–7 What did you learn about Kate's character through her interactions with Mr. Harper? *(She's a chatterbox; she has trouble following rules; she wants to try hard; she's worked hard this year.)*

PAGES 12–13 How did you feel when you read about Kate having to stay home from camp? *(Responses will vary.)*

ELL Invite students to retell the story.

TALK ABOUT THE BOOK

READER RESPONSE

1. He is strict but caring; contributed by emphasizing that Kate can overcome her reading difficulties if she didn't become distracted.
2. Know: Dyslexia is a disorder that causes people to have difficulty reading; Want to Know: Possible response: Whether scientists are working to find a cure for it.
3. *Assign* is a verb; *assignment* is a noun. *Assign* means "to give as a share; allot," while *assignment* means "something assigned, usually work to be done." Sentences will vary
4. Responses will vary.

RESPONSE OPTIONS

WRITING AND SPEAKING Hold a spelling bee. Afterwards, have students write how they felt about the experience.

CONTENT CONNECTIONS

Time for SOCIAL STUDIES

SOCIAL STUDIES Watch a portion of the documentary movie, *Spellbound,* to learn more about the national spelling bee and how contestants prepare.

Name ___________________________________

Character and Plot

- The **plot** is an organized sequence of events.
- A **character** is a person who takes part in the events of a story.

1. Name some main **characters** in *The Spelling Bee*.

____

____

2. How does *The Spelling Bee* **begin**?

____

____

3. What is the **problem** in the story?

____

____

4. What do we learn in **flashback**?

____

____

5. What is the **climax**?

____

____

6. What is the **resolution**?

____

____

Name ____________________

Vocabulary

Directions In each of the following sentences, underline the synonym for the vocabulary word in ( ). Note: Some synonyms may include more than one word.

Check the Words You Know

___acquainted	___assignment
___essential	___expanded
___guaranteed	___procedures
___reputation	___worshipped

1. Our teacher said it was necessary to bring our coats on the hike. (essential)

2. Paulo was friendly with all his neighbors. (acquainted)

3. Alice adored her new puppy. (worshipped)

4. "The project our teacher gave out yesterday was easy!" exclaimed Jasper. (assignment)

5. He had a good opinion of people about him. (reputation)

6. The two recipes showed different processes for making the same cookies. (procedures)

7. I made sure I had a chance for a good grade by studying hard. (guaranteed)

8. Reading that book stretched my horizons. (expanded)

Directions Select two vocabulary words and use each in a sentence below.

9. ____________________

____

10. ____________________

____

Unit 1 Week 1

Learning from Ms. Liang

Learning from Ms. Liang
by Juna Loch
illustrated by K. E. Lewis

CHARACTER AND PLOT

PRIOR KNOWLEDGE

LESSON VOCABULARY acquainted, assignment, essential, expanded, guaranteed, procedures, reputation, worshipped

SUMMARY When a new teacher arrives, a fifth-grade class learns what it feels like to walk around in somebody else's skin.

INTRODUCE THE BOOK

BUILD BACKGROUND Invite students to talk about how they feel on a bad day. Ask: Have you ever felt like a nobody? How did it feel? Have them talk about a time when they understood how someone else was feeling.

PREVIEW/USE ILLUSTRATIONS Have students preview the book by looking at the illustrations. Ask what they think the students in the story will learn from Ms. Liang.

TEACH/REVIEW VOCABULARY Invite students to use each of the vocabulary words in a sentence. Challenge them to write sentences related to the selection.

TARGET SKILL AND STRATEGY

CHARACTER AND PLOT Remind students that a *character* is a person who takes part in the events of a story. Explain how readers can determine character traits based on how other characters act toward the character and what they say about him/her. Say: The *plot* is an organized sequence of events, often sequential. Authors use *flashbacks* to explain what happened in the past and *foreshadowing* to hint at events to come. As they read, challenge students to notice how characters treat one another as clues to their traits. Tell students to look for flashbacks and foreshadowing.

ELL Help students brainstorm a list of words to describe characters. *(helpful, mean, friendly, untrustworthy, lonely)* Invite students to write a description of a character from the story using words from the list.

PRIOR KNOWLEDGE Remind students that *prior knowledge* is what a reader knows about a given topic from reading and from personal experience. Invite students to look for places in the text that make them think of their own lives. Explain that prior knowledge may help them understand the characters and the plot.

READ THE BOOK

PAGE 7 According to Ms. Liang, what have scientists discovered? *(The expressions that people make affect their feelings.)*

PAGE 11 What flashback does the narrator have in class when she's trying to think of something to write? *(She remembers times when she felt like a nobody.)*

PAGE 13 Why did Ms. Liang tell students not to sign their names on their first writing assignment? *(to protect students' feelings)*

TALK ABOUT THE BOOK

READER RESPONSE

1. Students might respond that the narrator changed by learning to understand how Lisa felt.
2. Possible responses: Emily Dickinson wrote the poem "Nobody" and never left home after age 18. Students might want to know what her parents and other people thought about her.
3. *acquaint, expand, guarantee,* and *worship;* sentences will vary.
4. Responses will vary.

RESPONSE OPTIONS

WRITING Invite students to write a paragraph about what people would understand about you if people could walk around in your skin. Tell them not to sign their names. Have them write a second paragraph about trying to get inside the skin of someone they don't like. Ask them to sign this one but not to use anyone's real name.

CONTENT CONNECTIONS

Time for SOCIAL STUDIES

SOCIAL STUDIES Students can learn more about Emily Dickinson by going to the library or using the Internet. Challenge them to read more of her poems and to find a favorite.

Name ______________________________

Character and Plot

- A **character** is a person who takes part in the events of a story.
- The **plot** is an organized sequence of events. Authors often use flashbacks to tell about something that has already happened and foreshadowing to hint at events to come.

Directions Fill in the graphic organizer. Under Plot, include flashback and foreshadowing.

Title ______________________________

Characters

Setting

Problem

Plot

____
____
____
____
____
____
____

Solution

Name ______________________________

Vocabulary

Directions Read each sentence. Write the word from the box that has the same meaning as the underlined word or phrase. Some words may be used more than once.

Check the Words You Know

___acquainted	___assignment
___essential	___expanded
___guaranteed	___procedures
___reputation	___worshipped

1. It wasn't long before Lisa adored Ms. Liang. ____________
2. Ms. Liang told the class that it was extremely important for them to get inside someone else's skin. ____________
3. She also established certain rules and regulations for participating in class. ____________
4. Slowly, the class's understanding of other people's feelings grew. ____________
5. By the end, even A.J. was ready to "get to know each other better." ____________
6. The narrator had trouble doing her writing homework. ____________
7. Ms. Liang assured her students that she had once been a nobody herself. ____________
8. Are you familiar with the poetry of Emily Dickinson? ____________
9. By the end of the story, Lisa's standing in the class had grown. ____________
10. The narrator promised she would not make mean remarks about Lisa again. ____________

Directions Write a summary of *Learning from Ms. Liang,* using as many vocabulary words as possible.

____

____

____

____

____

____

Unit 1 Week 1

This Is the Way We Go to School

This Is the Way We Go to School
by Colin Kong
illustrated by Burgandy Beam

CHARACTER AND PLOT

PRIOR KNOWLEDGE

LESSON VOCABULARY etiquette, expenses, podium, quills, segregation, tutors

SUMMARY Students from Miss Jacobson's class present three reports on education in the United States in 1725, in 1830, and in 1925. The class learns about the history of public education in this country.

INTRODUCE THE BOOK

BUILD BACKGROUND Ask: What is public education? When did it start? Ask students to tell what they know about the history of education in the United States.

PREVIEW/USE TEXT FEATURES Have students preview the book. During what period of time do they think the story will take place?

TEACH/REVIEW VOCABULARY Have students read the last paragraph on page 6. Ask: What words help you understand the meaning of *etiquette?*

TARGET SKILL AND STRATEGY

CHARACTER AND PLOT Have students look for clues, such as words and actions, that reveal what *characters* are like. Remind them that the *plot* is an organized sequence of events. Explain that authors use flashbacks to talk about events from the past and foreshadowing to hint at events to come.

PRIOR KNOWLEDGE Remind students that *prior knowledge* is what a reader knows about a given topic, from reading and from personal experience. Invite students to skim the book to get an overall idea of what it is about. Challenge them to scan the book for particular information to determine what they would like to focus on. Explain that prior knowledge may help you understand the characters and the plot.

ELL Invite students to tell what they know about education in their native country. Challenge them to explain what is similar and what is different between there and here.

READ THE BOOK

Use the following questions to support comprehension.

PAGE 3 What do you notice about Ben's character? *(He asks questions but forgets to raise his hand.)*

PAGE 15 How did public education change between the 1720s and the 1830s? *(By 1830s, boys and girls both attended public school.)*

PAGES 17–18 Why was education in the South different from education in New England? *(New England towns were close together so there were more schools; in the South, towns spread out, and it was harder for people to create schools.)*

TALK ABOUT THE BOOK

READER RESPONSE

1. Responses will vary.

2. Responses will vary.

3. *segregate;* to separate or set apart from others

4. Answers will vary.

RESPONSE OPTIONS

WRITING Challenge students to write a journal entry from the point of view of a student in 1725, in 1830, or in 1925. They should include details about their school and what they learn. Encourage them to base their writing on what they learned in this selection, as well as on prior knowledge.

CONTENT CONNECTIONS

Time for SOCIAL STUDIES

SOCIAL STUDIES Students can go to the library or use the Internet to learn more about courageous students and their families who challenged segregation laws in the 1960s. Invite them to research the Supreme Court ruling, *Brown vs. the Board of Education*, and other legislation that ended segregation in public schools.

Name

Character and Plot

- A **character** is a person who takes part in the events of a story.
- The **plot** is an organized sequence of events. Authors often use flashbacks to tell about something that has already happened and foreshadowing to hint at events to come.

Directions Fill in the graphic organizer below. Under Plot, include flashbacks and foreshadowing.

Title

Characters

Setting

Problem

Plot

Solution

Name ____

Vocabulary

Directions Draw a line from each word to its definition.

Check the Words You Know

___**etiquette**
___**podium**
___**segregation**
___**expenses**
___**quills**
___**tutors**

1. etiquette	separation of people based on race
2. expenses	feather pens
3. podium	household budget
4. quills	wooden lectern
5. segregation	special teachers
6. tutors	good manners

Directions Write a paragraph about the history of education in America. Use as many vocabulary words as you can.

____

____

____

____

____

____

____

____

____

____

____

____

Unit 1 Week 2

CAUSE AND EFFECT

MONITOR AND FIX UP

LESSON VOCABULARY branded, constructed, daintily, devastation, lullaby, pitch, resourceful, thieving, veins

Storm Danger!

SUMMARY Most storms cause few risks, but some—thunderstorms, flash floods, tornadoes, hurricanes, and blizzards—can be dangerous. This book describes the effects of storms and gives tips on how to stay safe.

INTRODUCE THE BOOK

BUILD BACKGROUND Ask students to describe their experiences—either personal or what they have seen in movies or TV—with thunderstorms, flash floods, tornadoes, hurricanes, and blizzards. Ask: What are some dangers of each storm?

ELL Point out that storms have different names depending on the geographical area in which they occur. Invite students to name the types of storms that occur in their native land, such as *typhoons* or *monsoons.*

PREVIEW/USE TEXT FEATURES Have students preview the book by looking at the photographs and the "Protect Yourself" charts throughout the text. Ask: What do you think you will learn from this book?

TEACH/REVIEW VOCABULARY Write the vocabulary words on the board and invite students to define them. Then have students work in small groups to act out the words in charades.

TARGET SKILL AND STRATEGY

CAUSE AND EFFECT Discuss how a *cause* (such as a storm) may have multiple effects, and an *effect* (such as flooding) may have more than one cause. Encourage students as they read to ask themselves: What happened? What caused it to happen? Point out that this book is organized to describe the effects of each type of storm.

MONITOR AND FIX UP Note that there are likely to be new words and challenging concepts in the text, so students will want to adopt strategies to *monitor* comprehension as they read. Review *fix-up* strategies, such as slowing reading rate and summarizing facts, and encourage students to use these strategies as they read.

READ THE BOOK

Use the following questions to support comprehension.

PAGES 6–7 What are some common effects of thunderstorms? *(strong winds that knock over trees or power lines; hail; lightning; flooding)*

PAGE 12 Where do tornadoes happen most often? *(in the plains of the U.S., between the Rocky Mountains and the Appalachian Mountains)*

PAGE 17 Name three ways to protect yourself during a blizzard. *(Possible responses: don't travel by car; have a battery-operated radio; wear layers)*

TALK ABOUT THE BOOK

READER RESPONSE

1. Answers will vary. Causes: hail, lightning, floods, strong winds; Effects: trees toppling, damage to buildings, fires, roads washed away
2. Flash floods happen because the rain comes so quickly that it cannot be absorbed.
3. *Pitch* (verb) means "to throw." *Veins* are also methods of expression or style. Sentences will vary.
4. Possible response: They are safety checklists.

RESPONSE OPTIONS

SPEAKING Have students use the selection's information on thunderstorms (or another type of storm common to your area) to present short radio or TV weather bulletins about how to prepare for such a storm.

CONTENT CONNECTIONS

TIME FOR Science

SCIENCE Have students work in small groups to research the causes and effects of a typhoon or monsoon. Have them work together to create a "Protect Yourself" bulleted list for the storm chosen.

Name ______________________________

Cause and Effect

- A **cause** is the reason something happens. The **effect** is what happens.
- A cause may have more than one effect, and an effect may have more than one cause.

Directions Read the following passage. Then fill in the chart that follows.

Tornadoes occur when a warm, humid air mass meets with a cool, dry air mass. This collision sometimes results in a powerful, swirling column of air. The tornado's swirling winds can exceed 300 mph. Tornadoes cause much damage by this sheer force of wind, but they also have a strong updraft that can lift and carry objects.

A tornado can lift cars into the air and tear trees out of the ground. It can pull roofs from houses, even if the houses are well constructed. Tornadoes can be strong enough to send glass and wood flying through the air.

Tornado: Causes	Tornado: Effects
1. ______________________________	1. ______________________________
2. ______________________________	2. ______________________________
	3. ______________________________
	4. ______________________________
	5. ______________________________

Name ____

Vocabulary

Directions Complete each sentence with a vocabulary word from the box. One word with two different meanings, is used twice.

Check the Words You Know

___branded	___constructed	___daintily
___devastation	___lullaby	___pitch
___resourceful	___thieving	___veins

1. The ______________________ mother found a new safe spot for her son to wait out the storm.
2. As the baby cried, her mother sang her a ______________________ to help her sleep.
3. Blood flows through your ______________________.
4. The tornado caused a massive amount of ______________________.
5. The men used ______________________ to repair the loose tiles on the roof.
6. The ______________________ teenagers began to hatch their plot to grab jewelry from the store.
7. The tree was ______________________ black after it was struck by lightning.
8. The ______________________ in the leaf helped distribute water.
9. Jenny's home is ______________________ of stucco, with a tile roof.
10. The ballerinas moved ______________________ across the stage.

Directions Write a paragraph about storms, using as many vocabulary words as you can.

____

____

____

____

____

____

____

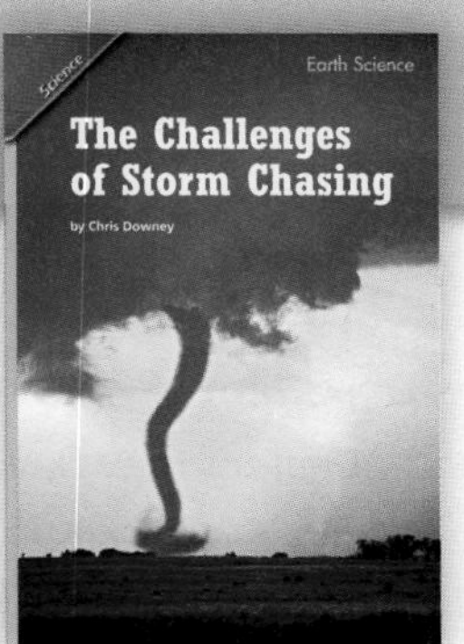

Unit 1 Week 2

The Challenges of Storm Chasing

CAUSE AND EFFECT

MONITOR AND FIX UP

LESSON VOCABULARY branded, constructed, daintily, devastation, lullaby, pitch, resourceful, thieving, veins

SUMMARY In Tornado Alley, which crosses the plains of the United States, storm chasers hunt down and track tornadoes to learn more about them and to experience the thrill of seeing them up close. But it can be dangerous, especially when practiced by novices.

INTRODUCE THE BOOK

BUILD BACKGROUND Ask: Have you ever seen a tornado live or on TV? What was it like? What other types of storms have you seen up close?

ELL Students may come from countries that do not have tornadoes. Show photographs of tornadoes to help students visualize them. Encourage students to describe a tornado and the kinds of damage it can do.

PREVIEW/USE TEXT FEATURES Have students preview the book by looking at the photographs, the map on pages 4–5, and the diagrams on pages 10–11 and 13. Ask: What do you think you will learn from this book?

TEACH/REVIEW VOCABULARY After you review the meanings of the vocabulary words with students, have volunteers use each word in a sentence.

TARGET SKILL AND STRATEGY

CAUSE AND EFFECT Remind students that sometimes clue words like *after* will help establish *cause* and *effect*. Encourage students as they read to pose questions to themselves, such as "What happened?" and "What caused it to happen?" This will work well when students look at the photographs on pages 14–15.

MONITOR AND FIX UP Note that there are likely to be new words and challenging concepts in the text, so students will want to adopt strategies to *monitor* comprehension as they read. Encourage them to use *fix-up* strategies: summarizing facts to clarify ideas (perhaps on paper); slowing their reading rate; and using diagrams, maps, and photos. Explain that they can use graphic sources such as the diagram on page 13 to help them understand how a tornado (effect) is caused.

READ THE BOOK

Use the following questions to support comprehension.

PAGE 9 What effect do "renegade" storm chasers have? *(They make roads more dangerous by speeding; they risk their own lives and the lives of others.)*

PAGES 12–13 What makes a tornado funnel? *(Cold air moves over warm air. Then lighter air rises up through cold air, creating the funnel cloud, which rotates.)*

PAGE 15 What were the effects of the May 1999 Oklahoma tornado? *(It destroyed houses and neighborhoods around Oklahoma City.)*

TALK ABOUT THE BOOK

READER RESPONSE

1. Tornado Alley has many storms in the spring because of weather patterns that occur during that time of year. This makes spring the best season to spot tornadoes, but it is a dangerous time as well.
2. Responses will vary. Learned: NSSL was set up to track storms and inform citizens; scientists study storms and improve forecasting by using Doppler on Wheels and other equipment. Want to Know: tornado frequency, safety precautions.
3. *brand, construct;* sentences will vary.
4. Responses will vary. Students should know which states are part of Tornado Alley and where it is located in the U.S.

RESPONSE OPTIONS

WRITING Have students prepare a list of things they would do or not do in order to remain safe during a tornado.

CONTENT CONNECTIONS

SCIENCE Have students research Hurricane Hunters, people who fly into the eye of a hurricane to study it.

Name ____________________

Cause and Effect

- A **cause** is the reason something happens. The **effect** is what happens.
- A cause may have more than one effect, and an effect may have more than one cause.
- Sometimes a cause is not directly stated, and you need to think about why something happened.

Directions Read the following passage. Then answer the questions that follow.

Tornadoes form when a layer of cold air moves over a layer of warm air. The lighter air rises up through the cold air. This makes the funnel cloud rotate as the air changes places. A tornado can do amazing damage to buildings, property, and land. Tornado winds, rising to a furious pitch, will rip through a town, and destroy everything in their path. Houses and mobile homes may be flattened, ripped apart, or carried away completely. A tornado can even peel the bark off trees!

But as dangerous as they are, tornadoes are a great source of delight for storm chasers. They love to seek out, or chase, tornadoes. Their task is a dangerous one. High winds can flip the chaser's vehicle or blow out car windows. Heavy rain and hail can make it hard to see. Flooding and fog can make traveling harder and might strand a chaser in the path of a storm. Lightning, a release of electricity in the atmosphere, is another danger for storm chasers. It can strike without warning!

1. Describe the cause of tornadoes.

____

____

2. What are two effects of tornadoes?

____

____

3. What is the cause for lightning, as stated in the passage?

____

____

4. What are two effects of tornadoes on storm chasers?

____

____

5. Would you like to be a storm chaser? Why or why not? Give examples from the reader to support your choice.

____

____

Name________________________________

Vocabulary

Directions Write the vocabulary word that best matches each definition below. One word, with two different meanings, is used twice.

Check the Words You Know

___branded	___constructed	___daintily
___devastation	___lullaby	___pitch
___resourceful	___thieving	___veins

1. the act of laying waste, destroying ____________
2. likely to steal ____________
3. with delicate beauty ____________
4. thick, black, sticky substance made from tar ____________
5. natural channels through which water flows ____________
6. soft song sung to put a baby to sleep ____________
7. good at thinking of ways to do things ____________
8. marked by burning ____________
9. tubes that carry blood through your body ____________
10. put together ____________

Directions Choose two vocabulary words and use each in a sentence below.

11. ____

____

12. ____

____

Unit 1 Week 2

Forecasting the Weather

CAUSE AND EFFECT

MONITOR AND FIX UP

LESSON VOCABULARY anemometer, atmosphere, barometer, Doppler radar, hygrometer, meteorologists, radiosondes troposphere, weather forecasts

SUMMARY This book notes the vital role that weather plays in our lives and the challenges that exist in predicting weather accurately. The book also describes the role of meteorologists and the tools they use to forecast weather on land, at sea, and in the air.

INTRODUCE THE BOOK

BUILD BACKGROUND Have students discuss ways in which they use weather forecasts in their daily lives. Ask: Has a sudden weather change ever caught you off-guard?

PREVIEW/USE TEXT FEATURES Have students preview the book by looking at the photographs. Then have students look at the diagram on pages 6–7 and the time-lapse photo on page 17. Ask: What do you think you will learn from this book?

TEACH/REVIEW VOCABULARY Write the vocabulary words on the board. Ask students to give the definitions of any words they know. Then have students identify parts of the words that give them clues. For example, the suffix *–ist* in *meteorologist* indicates that this word refers to someone who specializes in something. If there are any words with which students are unfamiliar, have them look up the definitions in the Glossary.

TARGET SKILL AND STRATEGY

CAUSE AND EFFECT Note that sometimes a *cause* may have multiple effects and an *effect* may have more than one cause. Encourage students as they read about forecasting weather to ask themselves: What causes this to happen?

MONITOR AND FIX UP Encourage students to develop a reading plan. Note that there are likely to be new words and challenging concepts in the text, so students will want to adopt strategies to *monitor* comprehension as they read. Encourage students to use *fix-up* strategies: summarizing facts to clarify ideas and pinpointing causes and effects; slowing their reading rate; rereading chunks of text; using diagrams and photos.

READ THE BOOK

Use the following questions to support comprehension.

PAGE 4 Which days in the 10-day forecast show a low temperature of 54 degrees or higher? *(Friday, Saturday, Sunday, and Monday)*

PAGE 13 What causes the cups to spin faster in an anemometer? *(increases in wind speeds)*

PAGE 21 How are the two weather maps different? *(Top map shows a temperature forecast; bottom shows a weather forecast.)*

TALK ABOUT THE BOOK

READER RESPONSE

1. The sun heats the atmosphere, which sets air in motion.
2. Students should be able to follow the path of the storm. They might want to know how long the storm lasted, or who was affected and how.
3. *Doppler effect;* possible response: The Doppler effect made the car's siren sound different in different places.
4. Answers will vary.

RESPONSE OPTIONS

SPEAKING Have students use the information on the weather page of a local newspaper to prepare and present short weather forecasts for the next two days.

ELL Tell students that there are nonscientific ways that people predict impending weather conditions. For example, some people say that if their knee aches, rain is on the way. Encourage students to tell similar common sayings they may have heard.

CONTENT CONNECTIONS

SCIENCE Have students research the differences between the causes and effects of tornadoes and hurricanes.

Name ____________________

Cause and Effect

- A **cause** is the reason something happens. The **effect** is what happens.
- A cause may have more than one effect, and an effect may have more than one cause.
- Sometimes a cause is not directly stated, and you need to think about why something happened.

Directions Read the following passage. Then answer the questions that follow.

Hurricanes are huge tropical storms. The warm humid air of the tropics rises. As the air rises, it cools, and the moisture condenses to cloud and rain drops. Heat energy is released in this condensation process. In addition, winds collide and push warm, moist air upward. This rising air reinforces the air that is already rising from the surface, so the circulation and wind speeds of the storm increase. A tropical storm with a wind speed of 74 miles per hour is classified as a hurricane. When a hurricane makes landfall it loses the tropical moisture and weakens rapidly. But it can cause massive damage before it does.

High winds are a primary cause of the loss of life and home destruction that can result from hurricanes. Winds create airborne projectiles out of trees and sharp objects that hurl through the air and then bang into homes, businesses and even people. In addition, flooding caused by the coastal storm surge of the ocean and the massive rains that come with hurricanes create damage. Hurricanes have destroyed fishing piers and other businesses, too.

1. What are two major causes of hurricanes?

____

____

2. Name two major causes of hurricane damage.

____

____

3. What is one major effect of hurricanes?

____

____

4. What is another major effect of hurricanes?

____

____

5. What might you do to prepare for a hurricane?

____

____

Name ______________________________

Setting and Theme

- **Setting** is the time and place in which a story occurs.
- **Theme** is the subject or idea that a story is about.

Directions Based on your understanding of *Stuk's Village*, answer the questions below.

1. What is the setting of the story?

2. How would the story be different if it were set in a different time?

3. What is the story's theme?

4. Does the theme depend on the setting of the story? Why or why not?

Name ______________________________

Vocabulary

Directions Complete each sentence with a word from the word box.

Check the Words You Know

___gnawed	___headland
___kelp	___lair
___ravine	___shellfish
___sinew	

1. The fish hide in the ______________________.
2. The dog ______________________ on the bone.
3. My family eats ______________________ on Fridays.
4. The ______________________ flooded when it rained a lot.
5. We made rope from the animal's ______________________.
6. She stood on the ______________________ to see the boats coming.
7. The fox sleeps in the ______________________ by the tree.

Directions Write the vocabulary word that belongs with each group of words below.

8. gully, valley, ______________________
9. tendon, vein, ______________________
10. chewed, nibbled, ______________________

Directions Write a summary of *Stuk's Village* using as many vocabulary words as you can.

Unit 1 Week 3

SETTING AND THEME

VISUALIZE

LESSON VOCABULARY gnawed, headland, kelp, lair, ravine, shellfish, sinew

Toby's Vacation

SUMMARY Toby and his family visit the Channel Islands off the California coast. Toby learns about the unique plants and animals on each island and the importance of respecting nature.

INTRODUCE THE BOOK

BUILD BACKGROUND Discuss what students know about endangered species. Ask them to name animals that are endangered, like the spotted owl. Prompt them to discuss why these animals are endangered.

PREVIEW/USE TEXT FEATURES As students preview the book, ask them to look at the photographs and read the captions. Based on these features, ask students what they think the book will be about.

ELL Have students write each vocabulary word on one side of an index card and its definition on the back. Then they take turns reading the definitions and guessing which words go with them.

TEACH/REVIEW VOCABULARY Have students look up each word in a dictionary and write the definitions. Then have volunteers write sentences using vocabulary words.

TARGET SKILL AND STRATEGY

SETTING AND THEME Remind students that *setting* is the time and place in which a story occurs, and *theme* is the underlying meaning of a story, a "big idea" that stands on its own outside a story. As students read, ask them to write down the setting of the story and to ask themselves: Does the theme depend on the setting of the story? What does the writer want me to learn or know from reading this story?

VISUALIZE Remind students that to *visualize* is to create a picture in the mind. As students read, prompt them to pay close attention to imagery and sensory details. Using a graphic organizer, have students write words and phrases that help them form mental pictures.

READ THE BOOK

Use the following questions to support comprehension.

PAGE 5 How many islands make up the Channel Islands? *(eight)*

PAGE 11 What is the setting? *(Santa Cruz Island)*

PAGE 11 What words or phrases on this page help you visualize the setting? *(largest island, mountain ranges, ravines, tide pools, deer, mice, many reptiles, sea lions)*

TALK ABOUT THE BOOK

READER RESPONSE

1. San Diego; palm trees, big buildings, wide roads, beaches, ocean
2. Possible responses: birds, trees, foxes, seals
3. A point of land extending out into water
4. Possible responses: cleaning up trash, not polluting

RESPONSE OPTIONS

WRITING Suggest students imagine what it would be like to visit one of the Channel Islands. Have them write a short description of the experience using vivid details.

CONTENT CONNECTIONS

Time for SOCIAL STUDIES

SOCIAL STUDIES Students can learn more about endangered animals by researching them on the Internet or in the library. Suggest that they choose an endangered animal that interests them most and then read about ways people are trying to preserve it. Encourage students to get involved in some way, such as writing a letter to the government for help.

Name____

Setting and Theme

- **Setting** is the time and place in which the story occurs.
- **Theme** is the subject or idea of a story.

Directions Based on your understanding of *Toby's Vacation*, answer the questions below.

1. What is the setting of the story?

2. What is the story's theme?

3. Does the theme depend on the setting of the story? Why or why not?

4. What is another setting where the theme of the story would still be the same? Why?

Name ______________________________

Vocabulary

Directions Write the vocabulary word that matches each definition.

Check the Words You Know

___gnawed	___headland
___kelp	___lair
___ravine	___shellfish
___sinew	

1. a type of seaweed ______________________
2. chewed ______________________
3. a sea animal that has a shell ______________________
4. gully ______________________
5. a vein ______________________
6. a point of land extending out into water ______________________
7. den or home ______________________

Directions Write three sentences, using as many vocabulary words as you can.

8. ____

9. ____

10. ____

Harvesting Medicine...

Unit 1 Week 3

SETTING AND THEME

VISUALIZE

LESSON VOCABULARY cultivated, idly, ominous, purify, quell, urgency

SUMMARY A Native American boy and his grandfather who are from the Chumash tribe, journey to gather healing plants. They worry that the new Spanish people settling in the area will bring sickness to the Native American tribes.

INTRODUCE THE BOOK

BUILD BACKGROUND Discuss what students know about different plants and their uses. Ask them if they know of plants that may harm them, such as poison ivy, or plants that have healing effects, such as aloe.

PREVIEW/USE PHOTOGRAPHS As students preview the book, ask them to look at the photographs and guess what they think the book will be about. Draw their attention to the photograph on page 7. Ask them what clues this photograph gives about the book's theme.

TEACH/REVIEW VOCABULARY Have students look up each word in a dictionary and write the definitions. Ask them to write the base word of each word with a suffix. How does the suffix change each word's meaning?

ELL Discuss each vocabulary word and its definition. Ask students if there are similarities between English and their home languages.

TARGET SKILL AND STRATEGY

SETTING AND THEME Remind students that *setting* is the time and place in which a story occurs. As students read, ask them to consider whether the setting is important to what happens in the story. Remind students that *theme* is the "big idea" that stands on its own outside a story. As students read, have them answer the following question: What does the author want me to learn from reading this story?

VISUALIZE Remind students that to *visualize* is to create a picture in one's mind. As students read, have them use a graphic organizer to write words and phrases that help them visualize what is happening.

READ THE BOOK

Use the following questions to support comprehension.

PAGE 4 What is the setting? *(hills full of wildflowers, weeds, and various plants)*

PAGE 15 What words or phrases on this page help you visualize the setting? (beautiful, twisted oaks make patterns against the yellow grass and blue sky; the autumn sun releases the rich smell of the grass)

PAGE 24 What is the theme? *(Possible response: Natural ways of healing have been with us for a long time, but they may be threatened by modern civilization.)*

READER RESPONSE

1. 1500s, a hill on the California coast; answers will vary.
2. Possible response: way of life and fears would be different; life would be different; relationships may be the same.
3. *'ap* means "home"; *idly* means "doing nothing."
4. Possible response: Many will become sick.

RESPONSE OPTIONS

WRITING Have students imagine what it would be like to live when there were no drugstores or hospitals. Ask them to write a list of ways they could stay healthy without the use of today's drugs. Prompt them to think of things like eating fruits and vegetables and exercising.

CONTENT CONNECTIONS

TIME FOR Science

SCIENCE Students can learn more about the healing benefits of plants by researching them on the Internet or in the library. Encourage them to use a graphic organizer to list the plants and their healing benefits.

Name ____

Setting and Theme

- **Setting** is the time and place in which a story occurs.
- **Theme** is the subject or idea that a story is about.

Directions Based on your understanding of *Harvesting Medicine on the Hill*, answer the questions below.

1. What is the setting of the story?

____

____

2. What is the story's theme?

____

____

____

3. Does the theme depend on the setting of the story? Why or why not?

____

____

____

____

Name ________________________________

Vocabulary

Directions Write each vocabulary word next to its definition.

Check the Words You Know

___cultivated	___idly
___ominous	___purify
___quell	___urgency

1. to clear from imperfection ________________
2. the state of needing immediate attention ________________
3. loosened the soil around plants ________________
4. to quiet, pacify ________________
5. foreboding ________________
6. inactively ________________

Directions Write four sentences using as many vocabulary words as you can.

7. ________________________________

____

8. ________________________________

____

9. ________________________________

____

10. ________________________________

____

The Chicago American Giants

Unit 1 Week 4

SEQUENCE

ASK QUESTIONS

LESSON VOCABULARY confidence, fastball, mocking, outfield, unique, weakness, windup

SUMMARY This book highlights the Chicago American Giants, part of the Negro League of the last century.

INTRODUCE THE BOOK

BUILD BACKGROUND Encourage students to discuss their knowledge of baseball history. Explore students' awareness of segregation in baseball. Let them know that black and white baseball players were not allowed to play on the same teams or in the same leagues.

PREVIEW/USE TEXT FEATURES Invite students to look through the book before reading. Ask them to note such features as photos, captions, and the time line on pages 18–19. Ask how these features aid understanding.

TEACH/REVIEW VOCABULARY Challenge students to write sentences that use the vocabulary words related to sports. Example: *The coach had great confidence that his team would win.*

ELL Ask volunteers to use gestures and illustrations to help students understand the meaning of the baseball-related words: *outfield, windup, fastball.*

TARGET SKILL AND STRATEGY

SEQUENCE Remind students that *sequence* is the order in which things happen. Since this book is historical, students should look for dates to help them organize and understand when the events take place and how one event might lead to another.

ASK QUESTIONS Students can *ask questions* to help them focus on the sequence of events in baseball history. Before reading, ask students to think of a question that relates to the sequence of events in the history of baseball and African American baseball players.

READ THE BOOK

Use the following questions to support comprehension.

PAGE 6 What were barnstormers? *(African American baseball teams that traveled around to play games.)*

PAGE 7 The sentence, *The first season for the Chicago American Giants started in 1911*, answers what question? *(When did they first play?)*

PAGE 16 Who was the first African American to play for a major league team? *(Jackie Robinson)*

TALK ABOUT THE BOOK

READER RESPONSE

1. Professional African American...;
   Rube Foster and others...;
   The Eastern Colored League is...;
   The Baseball Hall of Fame is...;
   Jackie Robinson plays his first game...
2. Responses will vary.
3. *fastball, outfield, windup*; sentences will vary.
4. Possible response: It showed how African Americans have been involved with baseball since it began.

RESPONSE OPTIONS

VIEWING Have students go back and look at the photos in the book. Discuss why the author could have used illustrations but chose to use photos. *(Photos lend authenticity and interest.)*

CONTENT CONNECTIONS

Time for SOCIAL STUDIES

SOCIAL STUDIES Encourage interested students to learn more about Jackie Robinson or other people mentioned in the book. They can do research in the library or on the Internet. Suggest they share with the class the information they found most interesting.

Sequence

- **Sequence** is the order in which events happen.

Directions Answer the questions on the lines below.

1. Before telling you the sequence of events in the history of the Negro League, the author shows you a baseball game. Why do you think that is?

2. What did Rube Foster do that gave him enough experience to be manager of the Chicago American Giants?

3. What event most likely caused the end of the Negro American League?

4. What event was the first step in desegregating baseball?

5. Which event came first? Circle the letter of the correct answer.
   A. The international league bans teams with white players from signing African American players.
   B. Professional African American teams begin forming.

Name ____

Vocabulary

Directions Complete each sentence with a word from the word box.

Check the Words You Know

___confidence	___fastball
___mocking	___outfield
___unique	___weakness
___windup	

1. Being the only one of its kind ______________________
2. A failing ______________________
3. Pitch thrown at a high speed with very little curve ______________________
4. Laughing at; making fun of ______________________
5. Firm belief in yourself ______________________
6. A swinging movement of the arms while twisting the body just before pitching the ball

   ____
7. The part of a basball field beyond the diamond or infield ______________________

Directions Select three vocabulary words and use each in a sentence below.

8. ____

   ____
9. ____

   ____
10. ____

    ____

Famous Women Athletes

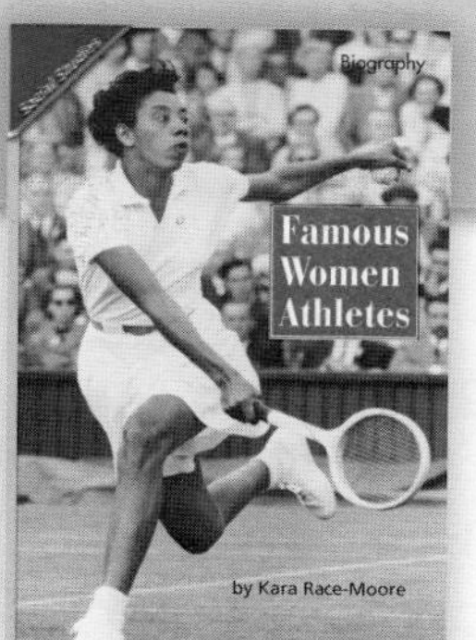

Biography
Famous
Women
Athletes
by Kara Race-Moore

Unit 1 Week 4

SEQUENCE

ASK QUESTIONS

LESSON VOCABULARY confidence, fastball, mocking, outfield, unique, weakness, windup

SUMMARY This book highlights the women who have broken gender and race barriers in the field of sports.

INTRODUCE THE BOOK

BUILD BACKGROUND Invite students to name famous women athletes. Ask: Do you think women in the past have had the same opportunity to compete in sports as men? What are you basing your knowledge on? Do you think that girls and women today have the same sports' opportunities as before?

PREVIEW/USE TEXT FEATURES Have students look at the features in the book before reading. Ask: Do you think the book is fiction or nonfiction? Why? What can you learn from the headings? *(the names of the women and their sports)* Remind students that reading the captions will give them important information about the athletes.

TEACH/REVIEW VOCABULARY Divide the group into teams. Play a quick game where students take turns giving definitions of the words while others guess the words.

ELL Students might not be familiar with sports terminology. Review *outfield, windup,* and *fastball* (page 3), as well as *croquet, badminton* and *bunt* (page 8).

TARGET SKILL AND STRATEGY

SEQUENCE Remind students that *sequence* is the order in which things happen. Point out that the information in this book tracks women's accomplishments in sports throughout the twentieth century. Suggest students take notes to help them keep track of these women's achievements.

ASK QUESTIONS *Asking questions* before, during, and after reading makes it easier to focus on information and to monitor, or check, understanding. Before students read, have them come up with a question about women's sports that they hope this book will answer, such as *Was there ever an all women's baseball team?* or *When did women become part of the Olympics?*

READ THE BOOK

Use the following questions to support comprehension.

PAGE 5 How many times did Trudy attempt to swim the English Channel? *(two)*

PAGES 8–9 What questions does the information on these pages answer about women and baseball? *(Responses will vary.)*

PAGE 18 Which two women worked together for the rights of female tennis players? *(Rosemary Casals and Billy Jean King)*

TALK ABOUT THE BOOK

READER RESPONSE

1. Gertrude Ederle swims...; Althea Gibson qualifies...; Toni Stone gets a hit...; Roberta Gibb runs...; Billie Jean helps...
2. Possible response: Was the official told to take her away? Answers will vary.
3. Possible responses: universe, unit, uniform; sentences will vary.
4. Responses will vary.

RESPONSE OPTIONS

WRITING/VIEWING Challenge students to design promotional posters for one of the sporting events mentioned in this book.

CONTENT CONNECTIONS

Time for SOCIAL STUDIES

SOCIAL STUDIES Have students study one of the female sports figures from this book. They can also find information from class books, the library, or the Internet. Encourage students to discuss why they studied a particular person.

Name ____________________

Sequence

- **Sequence** is the order in which things happen.

Directions Answer the questions on the lines below.

1. What sport did Babe Didrikson concentrate on after winning gold medals at the 1932 Olympics?

2. What event caused Phil Wrigley to set up the All-American Baseball league?

3. Why was that event the cause?

4. Who was the first woman to play on a men's big league team?

5. Why did the manager sign her up?

6. How did the events caused by Katherine Switzer help lead women to run in the Boston Marathon?

Name ____________________

Vocabulary

Directions Which vocabulary words are compound words? Write a definition for each word you list.

Check the Words You Know

- ___confidence
- ___outfield
- ___windup
- ___fastball
- ___unique
- ___mocking
- ___weakness

1. ____________________

____

____

____

____

____

Directions Match each of the words to its antonym, or opposite meaning.

2. confidence	strength
3. unique	ordinary
4. weakness	doubt

Directions Write the definition for the word *mocking*.

5. ____________________

____

Directions Choose three vocabulary words and use each in a sentence below.

6. ____________________

____

7. ____________________

____

8. ____________________

____

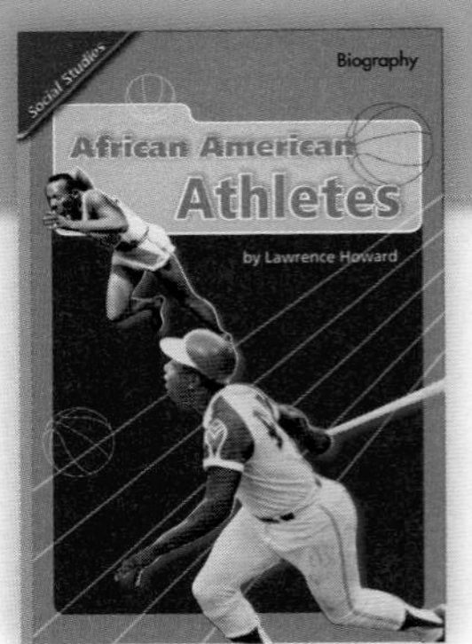

Unit 1 Week 4

African American Athletes

SEQUENCE

ASK QUESTIONS

LESSON VOCABULARY adversity, amateur, discrimination, inferior, integrated, prejudiced, prohibited, taunts

SUMMARY This book traces the history of African Americans in sports in the United States. Before 1945, African Americans were not allowed to play in most professional sports. This book looks at individual athletes who were able to break through the race barrier and set an example for others who follow.

INTRODUCE THE BOOK

BUILD BACKGROUND Have students name some famous African American athletes. Ask them if they knew there were times when African Americans were not allowed to play professional sports. Discuss what it would be like to be prevented from doing something you wanted to do, just because of the color of your skin.

PREVIEW/USE TEXT FEATURES Have students look at the section headings and the photographs and discuss how these text elements help organize the book. Ask students what information the section headings provide.

TEACH/REVIEW VOCABULARY To reinforce the contextual meaning of the word *discrimination* on page 3, discuss with students how the phrase "or unfair treatment" helps them guess the meaning of the word *discrimination.*

ELL Ask students to skim the story and write down any unfamiliar words. Suggest they look up the words in a dictionary and write the meanings in their notebooks.

TARGET SKILL AND STRATEGY

SEQUENCE Remind students that the *sequence* in a story or article is the order in which the events occur. To better understand what this means, ask students to write a short paragraph about how they clean their room, keeping the actions in sequence.

ASK QUESTIONS Remind students that *asking questions* before, during, and after they read will help them actively engage with the material. Example question: *How did the author organize the information?*

READ THE BOOK

Use the following questions to support comprehension.

PAGE 4 Satchel Paige had names for some of his pitches. Name a few. *(bee ball, trouble ball, Long Tom)*

PAGE 6 Who was the first African American to play professional basketball? *(Earl Lloyd)*

PAGE 7 Pro football was integrated from 1920 until 1933. What happened from 1934 to 1946? *(African Americans were barred from football.)*

TALK ABOUT THE BOOK

READER RESPONSE

1. Football, 1946; baseball, 1947; basketball, 1950; hockey, 1958
2. Responses will vary.
3. Possible response: Professional hockey was not integrated until the late 1950s.
4. Possible response: The photograph shows that baseball had been integrated.

RESPONSE OPTIONS

WRITING Have students write a brief paragraph in which they express their feelings about discrimination and prejudice.

CONTENT CONNECTIONS

Time for SOCIAL STUDIES

SOCIAL STUDIES Have students take one of the sports figures in this book and do further research on him or her. Students can use the Internet or the library to find information. How did the athlete deal with discrimination that he or she faced along the way?

Name ____________________

Sequence

- Understanding the **sequence** of events is important to having a correct understanding of the text.

Directions Answer the following questions.

1. Besides Satchel Paige, who was another great African American baseball player who preceded Jackie Robinson? What position did he play?

2. African Americans were not allowed to play basketball until 1950. Who was the first player to break the race barrier?

3. Hockey was one of the last of the major sports to be integrated. In what year did Willie O'Ree start playing professional hockey?

4. Which baseball player broke through racial barriers and became the first African American to play for a major baseball team? How long would it take for most teams to have African Americans playing for them?

5. What happened to Jesse Owens after winning four gold medals at the 1936 Olympics in Berlin? Did he have a successful career as an athlete?

Directions Match each year to the man who started playing his sport then.

1950	Jackie Robinson, baseball
1958	Jesse Owens, track and field
1947	Earl Lloyd, basketball
1948	Willie O'Ree, hockey
1936	Satchel Paige, baseball

Name____

Vocabulary

Directions Draw a line from each word to its definition.

Check the Words You Know

___adversity	___amateur
___discrimination	___inferior
___integrated	___prejudiced
___prohibited	___taunts

1. adversity	jeers; mocking or insulting remarks
2. amateur	below most others; low in quality
3. taunts	condition of misfortune or distress
4. discrimination	forbidden by law from doing something
5. inferior	when a public place or group has been opened to all races.
6. integrated	someone who plays something for pleasure, instead of for money or as a profession.
7. prejudiced	having an unreasonable dislike for someone or something
8. prohibited	act of showing an unfair difference in treatment

Directions Select four vocabulary words and use each in a sentence.

9. ____

____

10. ____

____

11. ____

____

12. ____

____

Unit 1 Week 5

CAUSE AND EFFECT

SUMMARIZE

LESSON VOCABULARY advice, advised, circumstances, elbow, hustled, immigrants, luxury, newcomer, peddler

Immigrant Children...

UMMARY In the early 1900s, many families traveled to he United States looking for a better life. These families aced difficult times. Immigrant children had a hard time etting educated or having fun.

NTRODUCE THE BOOK

UILD BACKGROUND Discuss with students what hallenges immigrant children might have faced. Ask hem to think about how they have felt being in a new ituation, such as the first day of school or moving to a ew house. Remind them that immigrant children had ttle money and education.

REVIEW/USE PHOTOGRAPHS AND CAPTIONS Ask students o look at the photographs in the book and read the aptions. Discuss what students believe they will learn bout in the book based on these observations.

EACH/REVIEW VOCABULARY Review vocabulary words nd their definitions with students. Have volunteers write a silly sentence on the board using one of the vocabulary vords correctly. Repeat this with all the vocabulary words.

ARGET SKILL AND STRATEGY

CAUSE AND EFFECT Remind students that *cause* xplains why something happened, and *effect* explains what happened. As students read the book, have them ist reasons why immigrants came to the United States. Suggest that they use a graphic organizer to list the auses of immigration.

ELL Help students fill in a graphic organizer showing he causes and effects of immigration.

SUMMARIZE Remind students that to *summarize* neans to briefly state what happened in a story. Have students list the main ideas in the story as they read.

READ THE BOOK

Use the following questions to support comprehension.

PAGE 6 What caused immigrants to move to the United States? *(desire for more money and a better life)*

PAGE 10 How did immigrant parents teach their children about their heritage? *(They taught them folk songs and stories and celebrated holidays by cooking traditional dishes.)*

PAGE 18 What did Alice and Irene Lewisohn do to improve the Lower East Side? *(They opened a playhouse.)*

TALK ABOUT THE BOOK

READER RESPONSE

1. Possible response: What They Did: gave advice to people from the Lower East Side, opened a theater, and built a playground. What Happened: immigrants learned about family health care and had to persuade their landlords to improve their buildings. They saw famous plays. Children had a safe place to play.
2. Possible response: improved apartment living by establishing fire safety regulations, ventilation, and improved indoor plumbing; it helped stop spread of diseases.
3. *immigrants* and *newcomers;* sentences will vary.
4. Responses will vary but should include specific references to details in photographs.

RESPONSE OPTIONS

WRITING Have students write a short journal entry as if they were immigrant children. Ask them to write about their new neighborhood and the games that they play there.

CONTENT CONNECTIONS

Time for SOCIAL STUDIES

SOCIAL STUDIES Encourage students to learn more about the life of immigrant children in the late nineteenth or early twentieth centuries from a book or the Internet.

Name ____________________

Cause and Effect

- A **cause** tells why something happened.
- An **effect** tells what happened.

Directions Use the information in the chart to answer the questions below.

Causes	Effects
Causes of Immigration	**Effects of Immigration**
better life **more money** **better education**	**little money** **little education** **had to work hard** **nowhere to safely play**

1. What caused many immigrant children to work so hard?

2. What effect did education have on immigrant children?

3. What effects did new playgrounds have on immigrant children?

4. What caused parents to take their children from their homes and move them to America?

5. What caused overcrowded schools?

Name ______________________________

Vocabulary

Directions Complete each sentence with a word from the word box.

Check the Words You Know		
___advice	___advised	___circumstances
___elbow	___hustled	___immigrants
___luxury	___newcomer	___peddler

1. The ______________ sold us wood.
2. We were ______________ by the bad salesman.
3. Her good ______________ helped him get a job.
4. The ______________ of his arrival were mysterious.
5. The ______________ of a house was a dream of ours.
6. The ______________ asked us directions.
7. We ______________ the boy not to talk to strangers.
8. A basketball player should never ______________ another player.
9. The ______________ were anxious to get to the new country.

Directions Write the vocabulary word that is a synonym for each pair of words.

10. shove, nudge ______________
11. tricked, cheated ______________
12. opinions, guidance ______________
13. happenings, situations ______________
14. wealth, comfort ______________
15. beginner, novice ______________
16. colonists, settlers ______________
17. dealer, merchant ______________
18. directed, counseled ______________

Directions Select two vocabulary words and use each in a sentence below.

19. ____

____

20. ____

____

Social Studies
A NATION OF MANY COLORS
BY JOSHUA NISSENBAUM

A Nation of Many Colors

CAUSE AND EFFECT

SUMMARIZE

LESSON VOCABULARY advice, advised, circumstances, elbow, hustled, immigrants, luxury, newcomer, peddler

SUMMARY This book explores how the United States became a diverse country with many immigrant groups. The selection also tells the story of the various immigrant groups that have helped to shape this country into what it is today.

INTRODUCE THE BOOK

BUILD BACKGROUND Discuss students' thoughts about what it means to start a new life in a new country. Do they know any families or friends who came from another country? Discuss how immigrants have contributed to the United States. Ask: What are some places, people, or things that show this country's diversity?

PREVIEW/USE PHOTOGRAPHS Invite students to take a picture walk through the photographs. Ask them how the photographs provide more information about the subject.

ELL Have students skim the story and write down any unfamiliar words. Suggest they look up the words in the dictionary and write the meanings in their notebooks.

TEACH/REVIEW VOCABULARY Review the vocabulary words. Then play "Vocabulary Master" with students. Give them three definitions for each word, including one that is fantastical or silly. Have them select the correct definition and then use the word in a sentence.

TARGET SKILL AND STRATEGY

CAUSE AND EFFECT Remind students that an *effect* is something that happens, and a *cause* is why something happens. Give students a pair of sentences related to the subject of this book that show cause and effect. Have students identify which of these sentences shows cause and which shows effect.

SUMMARIZE Remind students that *summarizing* is a good way to check understanding of a text. As students read, have them write down what they think are the main events.

READ THE BOOK

Use the following questions to support comprehension.

PAGE 4 What does the phrase "melting pot" mean? *(collection of ethnic groups represented in the U.S.)*

PAGE 5 What are some examples of what causes immigrants to come to the United States? *(the desire for an education, civil rights, and better employment)*

PAGE 22 Can you summarize what happened to Jewish Americans during the 1900s? *(Many moved to the suburbs and blended into mainstream American culture.)*

TALK ABOUT THE BOOK

READER RESPONSE

1. Cause: African Americans were tired of racism. Possible Effects: united African Americans; produced leaders like Martin Luther King, Jr.; caused whites to reconsider how they view ethnic groups
2. To get an education, to obtain civil and religious rights, to find employment, to escape war
3. *Advice* is a noun, and *advise* is a verb.
4. Responses will vary.

RESPONSE OPTIONS

WRITING Ask students to imagine they are a recent immigrant to the United States. Have them create a character with details such as what country they are from and what kind of life they will be leading. Have students write to relatives in their former countries about their new home.

CONTENT CONNECTIONS

SOCIAL STUDIES Ask students to research the life of an immigrant group not covered in this book.

Name ______________________________

Cause and Effect

- A **cause** tells why something happened.
- An **effect** tells what happened.

Directions Using the graphic organizer, list three causes and three effects of immigration in the United States. One cause and one effect are done for you.

Causes	Effects
Cubans felt threatened by Castro's communist government.	
	Immigrant communities were formed.

Name ____________________________________

Vocabulary

Directions Underline the context clue that explains what each of the boldface words mean.

Check the Words You Know

___advice	___advised	___circumstances
___elbow	___hustled	___immigrants
___luxury	___newcomer	___peddler

1. Sam's words of wisdom are always the best **advice**.
2. The teacher counseled Adrian and said the principal **advised** him to do so.
3. All the situations created by the picnic were **circumstances** beyond control.
4. The joint between the upper and lower arm makes the **elbow** very important.
5. Everyone that was pushed inside felt **hustled** by the guards.
6. The **immigrants** were new settlers on the plains and needed help.
7. The **luxury** apartment was comfortable and richly decorated.
8. Every **newcomer** was welcomed just as they moved into town.
9. The **peddler** sold more pots than any of the other market sellers.

Directions Write a paragraph about what life is often like for an immigrant, using as many vocabulary words as possible.

____

____

____

____

____

____

____

____

____

The Land of Opportunity
by Peggy Bresnick Kendler

The Land of Opportunity

CAUSE AND EFFECT

SUMMARIZE

LESSON VOCABULARY barracks, citizens, detainees, emigrate, interpreter, naturalized, steerage, tenements

SUMMARY Many people left their homes and came to America in the early 1900s. They had dreams of making good money and having a better life. The road to a better life, however, was often filled with hard times and disappointment.

INTRODUCE THE BOOK

BUILD BACKGROUND Ask students what challenges they think immigrants may experience. Then have them discuss a time when they tried something new or difficult.

PREVIEW/USE TEXT FEATURES Ask students to look at the photos in the book and read the captions. Draw their attention to the chart on page 7 and point out the massive number of people who immigrated to the U.S. As a class, summarize what students think the book will teach them.

TEACH/REVIEW VOCABULARY Divide students into small groups. Have each group choose a vocabulary word and write a sentence using that word. Each group writes its sentence on the board, leaving a blank where the vocabulary word should go. Have other groups guess which vocabulary word completes the sentences.

ELL Have students list vocabulary words and then write them in their home language.

TARGET SKILL AND STRATEGY

CAUSE AND EFFECT Remind students that *cause* explains why something happened and *effect* explains what happened. As students read, have them use a graphic organizer to list reasons why immigrants came to the United States.

SUMMARIZE Remind students that a summary tells what happens in a story. As they read, have students write a short sentence that describes the main idea of each paragraph. Later, they can use the sentences to form a summary.

READ THE BOOK

Use the following questions to support comprehension.

PAGE 4 Why did immigrants move to America? *(They wanted a better life, more money, and freedom from their government.)*

PAGE 12 What was life like for immigrants? *(They had little money and lived in run-down, crowded tenements.)*

TALK ABOUT THE BOOK

READER RESPONSE

1. Responses will vary.
2. Immigrants had to wait one year. They had to pass a test about United States history and how the government worked.
3. Responses will vary.
4. Responses will vary.

RESPONSE OPTIONS

WRITING Have students imagine they are an immigrant child writing about their new life to a friend back home. Have them list things they miss about their home country and things they like about their new country.

CONTENT CONNECTIONS

Time for SOCIAL STUDIES

SOCIAL STUDIES Encourage students to learn more about immigration by finding a book or Internet article about the subject.

Name ______________________________

Cause and Effect

- A **cause** tells why something happened.
- An **effect** tells what happened.

Directions Answer the following questions.

1. What caused many people to leave their homes and come to the United States?

____

____

2. What effect did immigration have on New York?

____

____

3. What caused immigrants to work so hard?

____

____

4. What caused immigrant neighborhoods to spring up in many major cities?

____

____

5. What effect did crowded, run-down tenements have on immigrants?

____

____

Directions Write whether the following are causes or effects of immigration.

6. Immigrants were poor in their home countries. ______________

7. So many people immigrated to New York that it became overcrowded. ______________

8. Children were given a better education in America. ______________

9. America provided freedom from a harsh government. ______________

10. Immigrants heard that America was the land of opportunity. ______________

Name ______________________________

Vocabulary

Directions Write the vocabulary word that matches each defintion.

Check the Words You Know

___barracks	___citizens	___detainees	___emigrate
___interpreter	___naturalized	___steerage	___tenements

1. ______________________ part of the ship occupied by passengers traveling at the cheapest rate
2. ______________________ people who are members of a nation
3. ______________________ to leave your own country to settle in another
4. ______________________ buildings that are divided into sets of rooms occupied by separate families
5. ______________________ someone who orally translates from one language to another
6. ______________________ people who are kept from moving forward; delayed
7. ______________________ having been made a citizen of a country by an official act
8. ______________________ group of buildings for people to live in, usually in a fort or camp

Directions Write two sentences using at least two vocabulary words in each.

9. ____

____

10. ____

____

Answer Key for Below-Level Reader Practice

The Spelling Bee LR1

Character and Plot, LR2

Possible responses given. **1.** Kate, Mr. Harper, Kate's mom **2.** We meet Kate who is a chatterbox. **3.** Kate is nervous and excited about the spelling bee. **4.** Kate has dyslexia and has to work hard to improve her reading. **5.** Kate isn't sure she can spell the first spelling word. **6.** Kate successfully spells the word and feels she can conquer any challenge.

Vocabulary, LR3

1. necessary. essential for necessary **2.** friendly. acquainted for friendly **3.** adored. worshipped for adored **4.** project. assignment for project **5.** good opinion. reputation for good opinion **6.** processes. procedures for processes **7.** made sure. guaranteed for made sure **8.** Stretched. expanded for stretched **9–10.** Sentences will vary.

Storm Danger! LR10

Cause and Effect, LR11

Possible responses given. Causes: **1.** warm humid air meets cool, dry air **2.** strong updraft can lift and carry objects
Effects: **1.** lift cars into the air **2.** tear trees out of the ground **3.** pull roofs from houses **4.** send glass flying **5.** send wood flying

Vocabulary, LR12

1. resourceful **2.** lullaby **3.** veins **4.** devastation **5.** pitch **6.** thieving **7.** branded **8.** veins **9.** constructed **10.** daintily Paragraphs will vary.

Stuk's Village LR19

Setting and Theme, LR20

Possible responses given. **1.** the village of Shisholop **2.** There would be easier, more modern ways to make crafts and get food. **3.** Trading is important to the whole village. **4.** Yes. The setting is at a time and place where Native Americans didn't have modern conveniences, so they had to trade to survive.

Vocabulary, LR21

1. kelp **2.** gnawed **3.** shellfish **4.** ravine **5.** sinew **6.** headland **7.** lair **8.** ravine **9.** sinew **10.** gnawed

The Chicago American Giants LR28

Sequence, LR29

Possible responses given. **1.** To get you involved with the story and to get you interested in learning more facts about the history of the game. **2.** Before becoming manager, he played baseball for more than twenty years. **3.** Baseball was integrated and black players could play on major league teams. **4.** Jackie Robinson joins the Brooklyn Dodgers. **5.** B

Vocabulary, LR30

1. unique **2.** weakness **3.** fastball **4.** mocking **5.** confidence **6.** windup **7.** outfield **8–10.** Sentences will vary.

Immigrant Children in New York City LR37

Cause and Effect, LR38

1. Their families were poor and needed help. **2.** It gave them opportunities for better jobs and a better life. **3.** They had a safe, fun place to play. **4.** a better life, freedom, an education **5.** There were a large number of children who immigrated to America.

Vocabulary, LR39

1. peddler **2.** hustled **3.** advice **4.** circumstances **5.** luxury **6.** newcomer **7.** advised **8.** elbow **9.** immigrants **10.** elbow **11.** hustled **12.** advice **13.** circumstances **14.** luxury **15.** newcomer **16.** immigrants **17.** peddler **18.** advised **19–20.** Sentences will vary.

.earning from Ms. Liang LR4

Character and Plot, LR5

ITLE: Learning from Ms. Liang CHARACTERS: Lisa Linney, Ms. Liang, arrator, A.J., Mary Alice SETTING: Ms. Liang's classroom. PROBLEM: ‹ids are treating Lisa and each other like nobodies. PLOT: New teacher omes to classroom and puts poem on the board ("I'm nobody! Who re you?") She gets the kids to think about what it feels like to live ı someone else's skin. Flashbacks: narrator remembers when a lassmate said mean things to her; when she and Mary Alice said ıean things about Lisa; Ms. Liang tells about how she was treated ke a nobody and how she became a teacher Foreshadowing: Lisa ; invisible at the beginning of the story, foreshadowing the lesson of I'm nobody." SOLUTION: Lisa is no longer invisible; everyone learns to ave more consideration of other people's feelings.

'ocabulary, LR6

. worshipped **2.** essential **3.** procedures **4.** expanded **5.** acquainted **.** assignment **7.** guaranteed **8.** acquainted **9.** reputation **10.** guaranteed entences will vary.

'he Challenges of Storm Chasing LR13

Cause and Effect, LR14

'ossible responses given. **1.** When a layer of cold air moves over a ayer of warm air, the lighter air rises up through the cold air and makes he funnel cloud rotate. **2.** Houses and mobile homes may be flattened, pped apart, or carried away. A tornado can even peel the bark off trees. **.** Lightning is a release of electricity in the atmosphere. **4.** High winds an flip the chaser's vehicle or blow out car windows. Heavy rain and ail can make it hard to see. **5.** Yes, because storms are amazing to ook at and you can learn a lot about them. I would like to work in a ruck with tracking equipment.

'ocabulary, LR15

. devastation **2.** thieving **3.** daintily **4.** pitch **5.** veins **6.** lullaby **'.** resourceful **8.** branded **9.** veins **10.** constructed **11–12.** Sentences vill vary.

Toby's Vacation LR22

Setting and Theme, LR23

Possible responses given. **1.** the Channel Islands **2.** If everybody respects nature, plants and animals can be saved from extinction. **3.** Responses will vary. Yes. The setting is a place where animals live undisturbed. **4.** a forest. Responses will vary.

Vocabulary, LR24

1. kelp **2.** gnawed **3.** shellfish **4.** ravine **5.** sinew **6.** headland **7.** lair **8–10.** Sentences will vary.

Famous Women Athletes LR31

Sequence, LR32

Possible responses given. **1.** golf **2.** World War II **3.** Many male baseball players went off to war, and he was worried that there would not be enough men to play baseball. **4.** Toni Stone **5.** as a gimmick, or way, to attract more sales and because she was very good **6.** Katherine Switzer ran illegally in the race. A judge tried to stop her and there was a lot of publicity. This led to a battle to allow women to run.

Vocabulary, LR33

1. fastball, windup, outfield; Definitions will vary. **2.** confidence/doubt **3.** unique/ordinary **4.** weakness/strength **5.** making fun of **6–8.** Sentences will vary.

A Nation of Many Colors LR40

Cause and Effect, LR41

Causes—Many ethnic groups immigrated in late 1800s./Immigrants found it difficult to adapt to American life. Effects—200,000 Cubans immigrated to U.S. from 1959–1962./U.S. became melting pot of customs and cultures.

Vocabulary, LR42

1. words of wisdom **2.** counseled **3.** situations **4.** joint **5.** pushed **6.** new settlers **7.** comfortable and richly decorated **8.** they moved into town **9.** market sellers Responses will vary.

This Is the Way We Go to School LR7

Character and Plot, LR8

CHARACTERS: Miss Jacobson, Ben, Lizzie, Haley, Greg, Jamie, Ben, Sofia, Katie, Tim, and Jeffrey SETTING: Miss Jacobson's classroom, a colonial New England schoolhouse, a 19th century one-room schoolhouse in Massachusetts, a classroom in Mississippi in 1925 PROBLEM: The class must take over and give three presentations on the history of education in America. PLOT: Miss Jacobson tells class they will take over and make three presentations on the history of education in America. Lizzie and Haley tell about Katie, a girl who lives on a farm in Connecticut in 1725 and goes to dame school while her brothers go to primary school. Greg and Jamie tell about Tim, a boy who goes to public school in Massachusetts in 1830. Ben and Sofia tell about Jeffrey, an African American boy who goes to school in Mississippi in 1925. The presentations are flashbacks. Foreshadowing: On page 17, Ben announces the Mississippi presentation very dramatically, foreshadowing the fact that Jeffrey is none other than Sofia's great-grandfather. SOLUTION: Presentations were wonderful and informative.

Vocabulary, LR9

1. good manners **2.** household budget **3.** wooden lectern **4.** feather pens **5.** separation of people based on race **6.** special teachers Possible response: In the 1700s, girls went to school to learn good manners and etiquette. They also learned to manage household expenses. Boys who came from wealthy families could afford luxuries such as quills, or feather pens. Their parents often hired tutors to teach them Greek, Latin, science, and algebra. In the 1920s, in the south, there were black and white students who did not study together because of segregation.

Forecasting the Weather LR16

Cause and Effect, LR17

Possible responses given. **1.** Warm humid air rises and then cools. Winds collide and push warm, moist air upward. **2.** high winds; flooding caused by coastal storm surge **3.** loss of life **4.** damages to residences and businesses **5.** temporarily move inland; board up doors and windows of home and businesses

Vocabulary, LR18

1. radiosondes **2.** Doppler radar **3.** barometer **4.** anemometer **5.** hygrometer **6.** weather forecasts **7.** troposphere **8.** meteorologists **9.** troposphere **10.** atmosphere **11–12.** Sentences will vary.

Harvesting Medicine on the Hill LR25

Setting and Theme, LR26

Possible responses given. **1.** nature's pharmacy of flowers, roots and leaves **2.** Red Hawk is learning from his grandfather about the differen healing plants. **3.** Yes. The setting is a place where Native Americans lived and where there were many plants.

Vocabulary, LR27

1. purify **2.** urgency **3.** cultivated **4.** quell **5.** ominous **6.** idly **7–10.** Sentences will vary.

African American Athletes LR34

Sequence, LR35

1. James Thomas Bell, or "Cool Papa" He was a center fielder. **2.** Earl Lloyd **3.** 1958 **4.** Jackie Robinson Teams were fairly integrated by the early 1960s. **5.** He earned a living running against horses and dogs; no

1950—Earl Lloyd, basketball. 1958—Willie O'Ree, hockey. 1947—Jackie Robinson, baseball. 1948—Satchel Paige, baseball. 1936—Jesse Owens, track and field

Vocabulary, LR36

1. adversity—condition of misfortune or distress **2.** amateur—someone who plays something for pleasure, instead of for money **3.** taunts—jeers; mocking or insulting remarks. **4.** discrimination—act of showing an unfair difference in treatment **5.** inferior—below most others; low in quality **6.** integrated—when a public place or group has been opened to all races **7.** prejudiced—having an unreasonable dislik for someone or something **8.** prohibited—forbidden by law from doing something **9–12.** Sentences will vary.

The Land of Opportunity LR43

Cause and Effect, LR44

1. They were poor and wanted a better life in America. **2.** overcrowding **3.** They wanted to provide a better life for their families. **4.** Immigrants helped other immigrants from their homeland, sharing their resources. **5.** They were disappointed, sad. **6.** cause **7.** effect **8.** effect **9.** cause **10.** cause

Vocabulary, LR45

1. steerage **2.** citizens **3.** emigrate **4.** tenements **5.** interpreter **6.** detainees **7.** naturalized **8.** barracks **9–10.** Sentences will vary.

Differentiated Instruction

Table of Contents

Routine Cards

Routine Card

Fluent Word Reading Routine

Teach students to read words fluently using this Routine.

1 Connect Write an example word. Isolate the sound-spelling or word structure element you will focus on and ask students to demonstrate their understanding.

2 Model When you come to a new word, look at all the letters in the word and think about its vowel sound. Say the sounds in the word to yourself and then read the word. Model reading the example words in this way. When you come to a new word, what are you going to do?

3 Group Practice Write other similar words. Let's read these words. Look at the letters, think about the vowel sounds, and say the sounds to yourself. When I point to the word, let's read it together. Allow 2-3 seconds previewing time for each word.

Routine Card

Oral Rereading Routine

Use this Routine when students read orally.

1 Read Have students read the entire book orally.

2 Reread For optimal fluency, students should reread the text three or four times.

3 Provide Feedback Listen as students read and provide corrective feedback regarding their oral reading and their use of decoding strategies.

Routine Card

Paired Reading Routine

Use this Routine when students read in pairs.

1 Reader 1 Begins Students read the entire book, switching readers at the end of each page.

2 Reader 2 Begins Have partners reread; now the other partner begins.

3 Reread For optimal fluency, students should reread three or four times.

4 Provide Feedback Listen as students read. Provide corrective feedback regarding their oral reading and their use of decoding strategies.

Routine Card

Choral Reading Routine

Use this Routine when students read chorally.

1 Select a Passage Choose an appropriate passage from the selection.

2 Divide into Groups Assign each group a part to read.

3 Model Have students track the print as you read.

4 Read Together Have students read along with you.

5 Independent Reading Have the groups read aloud without you. Monitor progress and provide feedback. For optimal fluency, students should reread three to four times.

Routine Cards

Routine Card

Multisyllabic Word Routine

Teach students this Routine to read long words with meaningful parts.

1 Teach Tell students to look for meaningful parts and to think about the meaning of each part. They should use the parts to read the word and determine meaning.

2 Model Think aloud to analyze a long word for the base word, ending, prefix, and/or suffix and to identify the word and determine its meaning.

3 Guide Practice Provide examples of long words with endings *(-ing, -ed, -s)*, prefixes *(un-, re-, dis-, mis-, non-)*, and/or suffixes *(-ly, -ness, -less, -ful,* and so on). Help students analyze base words and parts.

4 Provide Feedback Encourage students to circle parts of the words to help identify parts and determine meaning.

Routine Card

Multisyllabic Word Routine

Teach students this Routine to chunk words with no recognizable parts.

1 Teach Tell students to look for chunks in words with no meaningful parts. They should say each chunk slowly and then say the chunks fast to make a whole word.

2 Model Think aloud to demonstrate breaking a word into chunks, saying each chunk slowly, and then saying the chunks fast to make a word.

3 Guide Practice Provide examples of long words with no meaningful parts. Help students chunk the words.

4 Provide Feedback If necessary, reteach by modeling how to break words into chunks.

Routine Card

Picture Walk Routine

To build concepts and vocabulary, conduct a structured picture walk before reading.

1 Prepare Preview the selection and list key concepts and vocabulary you wish to develop.

2 Discuss As students look at the pages, discuss illustrations, have students point to pictured items, and/or ask questions that target key concepts and vocabulary.

3 Elaborate Elaborate on students' responses to reinforce correct use of the vocabulary and to provide additional exposure to key concepts.

4 Practice For more practice with key concepts, have each student turn to a partner and do the picture walk using the key concept vocabulary.

Routine Card

Concept Vocabulary

Use this Routine to teach concept vocabulary.

1 Introduce the Word Relate the word to the week's concept. Supply a student-friendly definition.

2 Demonstrate Provide several familiar examples to demonstrate meaning.

3 Apply Have students demonstrate understanding with a simple activity.

4 Display the Word Relate the word to the concept by displaying it on a concept web. Have students identify word parts and practice reading the word.

5 Use the Word Often Encourage students to use the word often in their writing and speaking. Ask questions that require students to use the word.

Group Time

DAY 1

Strategic Intervention

ROUTINE

1 Build Background

REINFORCE CONCEPTS Display the Challenges in Education Concept Web. This week's concept is *challenges in education*. Different things can make school challenging. Discuss the meaning of each word on the web, using the definitions on p. 18l and the Concept Vocabulary routine on p. DI•1.

CONNECT TO READING This week you will read about characters who face different challenges in school. Some are challenges in learning, some are challenges with understanding a new teacher, and some are challenges that real people faced, like segregation. What kinds of challenges have you faced in school? *(Answers will vary. Students may suggest such ideas as studying, doing homework, having conflicts with other students, and so on.)*

2 Read Leveled Reader *The Spelling Bee*

BEFORE READING Using the Picture Walk routine on p. DI•1, guide students through the text focusing on key concepts and vocabulary. Ask questions such as:

p. 3 The girl in the front row is the main character, Kate. What challenge do you think she has in class? *(The teacher looks upset because Kate is talking.)* You know from experience that teachers get frustrated and impatient when students don't pay attention!

pp. 4-7 How does Kate seem to change after talking to her teacher?

DURING READING Read pp. 3–5 aloud, while students track the print. Do a choral reading of pp. 6–9. If students are capable, have them read and discuss the remainder of the book with a partner. Ask: How do Kate's teachers and the school counselor help her? Why is the spelling bee especially challenging for her?

AFTER READING Encourage pairs of students to discuss Kate's challenges and how she meets them. We read *The Spelling Bee* to learn about the challenges that one character faces in school and the character traits she has that help her meet these challenges. Understanding the traits that help people meet challenges in school will help us as we read *Frindle*.

PearsonSuccessNet.com

Monitor Progress

Selection Reading and Comprehension

If...	then...
If... students have difficulty reading the selection with a partner,	**then...** have them follow along as they listen to the Online Leveled Reader Audio.
If... students have trouble understanding dyslexia and why having dyslexia would be a challenge,	**then...** reread pp. 10–12 and discuss the definition of dyslexia in the text.

For alternate Leveled Reader lesson plans that teach **Plot and Character, Prior Knowledge,** and **Lesson Vocabulary,** see pp. LR1–LR9.

On-Level

ROUTINE

DAY 1

1 Build Background

DEVELOP VOCABULARY Write the word *mistakes* and ask students to define it in their own words. *(Mistakes are things that you do wrong.)* What is another word that means the same thing or about the same thing as *mistake? (error, blunder, fault, goof-up)* Repeat this activity with the word *acquainted* and other words from the Leveled Reader *Learning from Ms. Liang*. Use the Concept Vocabulary routine on p. DI•1 as needed.

2 Read Leveled Reader *Learning from Ms. Liang*

BEFORE READING Have students create webs with *Ms. Liang* in the center. This book tells about a class with a new teacher, Ms. Liang. As you read, think of words that describe Ms. Liang. Add them to the web as you read.

DURING READING Have students follow along as you read pp. 3–9. Then let them complete the book on their own. Remind students to add character traits to their webs as they read.

AFTER READING Have students compare the character traits on their webs. Point out that being able to figure out what a character is like will help them as they read tomorrow's story *Frindle.*

Advanced

ROUTINE

DAY 1

1 Read Leveled Reader *This Is the Way We Go to School*

BEFORE READING Recall the Read Aloud "Understood Betsy." How was Betsy's school different from your school? Today you will read about what it was like to go to school in the past.

CRITICAL THINKING Have students read the Leveled Reader independently. Encourage them to think critically. For example, ask:

- How was school different in the past than it is today?
- At which time in history—1725, 1830, or 1925—do you think it was most difficult to go to school? What makes you think so?
- How was school different for students in the northern states than for those in the southern states of the United States? What made education so different in different parts of the country?

AFTER READING Have students review the selection to find five or more unfamiliar words and determine their meanings. Then ask them to use the words in statements that compare and contrast modern schools with schools in the past. Have students meet with you to discuss the selection and the statements they wrote.

2 Independent Extension Activity

EDUCATION LAWS Have students read "Laws for Public Schooling" on p. 24. Throughout the week, have students investigate laws about education in their community or in their state to see how useful or restrictive they are.

Group Time

Strategic Intervention

ROUTINE

1 Word Study/Phonics

LESSON VOCABULARY Use p. 20b to review the meanings of *acquainted, assignment, essential, expanded, guaranteed, procedures, reputation,* and *worshipped*. Have individuals practice reading the words from word cards.

DECODING MULTISYLLABIC WORDS Write *acceptable*, saying the word as you write it. Then model how to decode a base word with a suffix. This is a two-syllable word formed from the base word *accept* and the *suffix -able*. First I cover the suffix and read the base word: *accept.* Then I blend the base word and the suffix to read the whole word: *accept able, acceptable*. The suffix *-able* means "inclined to," so acceptable means "inclined to accept."

Use the Multisyllabic Word routine on p. DI • 1 to help students read these other words from *Frindle: attendance, vocabulary, syllable, frantically, hesitated,* and *shutdown*. Be sure students understand the meanings of words such as *vocabulary* and *frantically*.

Use *Strategies for Word Analysis,* Lesson 1, with students who have difficulty mastering word analysis and need practice with decodable text.

Audio CD AudioText

2 Read *Frindle*, pp. 22–29

BEFORE READING *The Spelling Bee* was about a student who overcame a challenge and had success in school. In this story, a teacher helps her students succeed—by challenging them.

Using the Picture Walk routine on p. DI • 1, guide students through the text, asking questions such as those listed below. Then read the question on p. 23. Together, set a purpose for reading.

p. 22–23 Nick is the student on the left. How do you think he feels about Mrs. Granger? How can you tell?

pp. 24–27 What kind of person do you think Mrs. Granger is? How do the illustrations make her look this way? As we read, let's pay attention to details about Mrs. Granger to find out what she is like.

DURING READING Follow the Guiding Comprehension routine on pp. 23–29. Have students read along with you while tracking the print or do a choral reading of the selection. Stop every two pages to ask what students have learned so far. Prompt as necessary

- What "special power" do all students think Mrs. Granger has?
- What about fifth grade worries Nick the most?

AFTER READING What has happened in the selection so far? What do you think will happen next? Reread passages as needed.

Monitor Progress

Word and Story Reading

If... students have difficulty reading multisyllabic words in the selection,	**then...** have them look for and read meaningful parts in the words or have them chunk words with no recognizable parts.
If... students need practice reading words fluently,	**then...** use the Fluent Word Reading Routine on the DI tab.
If... students have difficulty reading along with the group,	**then...** have them follow along as they listen to the AudioText.

Advanced

ROUTINE

1 Extend Vocabulary

WORD STRUCTURE Choose and read a sentence or passage with a word that can be examined according to its structure, such as this sentence from p. 3 of *This Is the Way We Go to School:* "Next week, there will be three presentations, each given by two students." What meaningful word parts do you see in the word *presentations*? *(The base word is* present. *The word has the suffix* -ation *and the ending* -s.) How do the word parts help you figure out the word's meaning? *(The suffix* -ation *changes the verb* present *into a noun that means "something you present." The ending* -s *means "more than one.")* Remind students to use the strategy as they read *Frindle*.

2 Read *Frindle*, pp. 22–29

BEFORE READING In *This Is the Way We Go to School,* you read about the challenges students faced when they went to school long ago. Today's selection tells about a challenge a student faces—how to deal with a strict teacher. As you read, think about challenges that other students have faced in school—and challenges you have faced yourself.

Have students preview the selection and write predictions in their Strategy Response Logs (p. 22) about what they expect to read. Have them keep track of their predictions as they read.

CREATIVE THINKING Have students read pp. 22–29 independently. Encourage them to think creatively. For example, ask:

- How would you feel if you had a teacher like Mrs. Granger? What would you do to get to know her and to survive in her class?

AFTER READING Have partners discuss the selection and share their Strategy Response Log entries. Have students record which parts of their predictions were right and record new predictions for the rest of the selection (p. 29). Then have students list three pieces of advice that they would give to Nick about surviving Mrs. Granger's class. They can write their advice in the form of a letter from a newspaper advice columnist. Students can share and compare their advice.

DAY 2

Frindle
by Andrew Clements
illustrated by James Bernardin

How do Nick and Mrs. Granger meet the challenge of getting to know each other?

Audio CD AudioText

Group Time

DAY 3

Audio CD AudioText

Strategic Intervention

ROUTINE

1 Reinforce Comprehension

SKILL CHARACTER AND PLOT Have students tell what a character is. *(a person or animal in a story)* Ask students what a plot is. *(The plot usually centers on the events that make up the story or a conflict.)* If necessary, review the meaning and provide a model. A character is a person or animal in a story. In *Frindle,* Nick is a character. The plot is the series of events that make up a story. The events center on a conflict. So far in *Frindle,* the conflict seems to be a conflict inside of Nick. He is worried about being in Mrs. Granger's class.

Tell students that Mrs. Granger is also a main character in the story. She is a person who is strong and who is set in her ways. Ask students to look for clues to support these statements about Mrs. Granger. *(Mrs. Granger wears the same serious suits every day. Mrs. Granger punishes children who chew gum. She asks the parents to buy dictionaries for their homes. If students forget to copy the word of the week, they have two words the next week.)*

2 Read *Frindle,* pp. 30–33

BEFORE READING Have students retell what happened in the selection so far. Ask: How are Nick's experiences before he starts a new school year similar to what has happened to you before you start school? Reread pp. 28–29. Model how to use your prior knowledge. As I read this part of the story, I thought about getting ready for school each year. I find out the names of my students, and I send a letter to their homes. This helps the students and their parents get to know me before school starts. When I read about Mrs. Granger doing this, it helped me realize that she cares about her students just like I do. Remind students to use their prior knowledge about schools and teachers as they read the rest of *Frindle.* **STRATEGY Prior Knowledge**

DURING READING Follow the Guiding Comprehension routine on pp. 30–33. Have students read along with you while tracking print or do a choral reading. Stop every page or two to ask students what has happened so far. Prompt as necessary

- What does Mrs. Granger do on the first day of class?
- How is Mrs. Granger different from the other fifth-grade teachers?
- How does Nick try to trick Mrs. Granger? What is the result?

AFTER READING Describe the challenges that Nick has in this story. Reread with students for comprehension as needed. Tell them that tomorrow they will read "Punctuation Takes a Vacation," a fantasy with another strong teacher, Mr. Wright.

Monitor Progress

Word and Story Reading

If... students have difficulty reading multisyllabic words in the selection,	**then...** have them look for and read meaningful parts in the words or have them chunk words with no recognizable parts.
If... students have difficulty reading along with the group,	**then...** have them follow along as they listen to the AudioText.

Advanced

ROUTINE

1 Extend Comprehension

SKILL PLOT AND CHARACTER Ask students to state the conflict in the story. Then ask them to think about Mrs. Granger. What inner conflict might she have leading up to the first day of school? What might have caused her feelings about the dictionary? her strictness in class?

STRATEGY PRIOR KNOWLEDGE Invite students to imagine that they are getting ready to enter sixth grade. What worries them about sixth grade? What fears or uncertainties do they have? Encourage them to share their ideas in a quickwrite. Then have them compare their ideas with Nick's. How does thinking about their own worries help them better understand Nick and his feelings?

2 Read *Frindle*, pp. 30–33

BEFORE READING Have students recall what has happened in the selection so far. Remind them to look for details that reveal the character traits of both Nick and Mrs. Granger as they read the remainder of *Frindle.*

CRITICAL THINKING Have students read pp. 30–33 independently. Encourage them to think critically. For example, ask:

- Do you think Nick's plan to get Mrs. Granger off-topic was a good plan? Why or why not? What do you think might have been a better strategy for Nick to use so that he would be more comfortable in his first day of class with Mrs. Granger?

AFTER READING Have students complete the Strategy Response Log activity (p. 32). Then encourage them to read the entire novel *Frindle,* another novel by Andrew Clements, or another novel about issues in elementary school. Students can create a character web and a plot chart based on their continued reading.

DAY 3

Audio CD AudioText

Group Time

AudioText

Strategic Intervention

ROUTINE

1 Practice Retelling

REVIEW STORY ELEMENTS Help students identify the main characters and setting of *Frindle*. Then guide them in using the Retelling Cards to list story events in sequence. Prompt students to include important details.

RETELL Using the Retelling Cards, have students work in pairs to retell *Frindle*. Monitor retelling and prompt students as needed. For example, ask:

- Tell me what this story is about in a few sentences.
- What is the author tying to tell us or teach us?
- Has anything like this ever happened to you?

If students struggle, model a fluent retelling.

2 Read "Punctuation Takes a Vacation"

BEFORE READING Read the genre information on p. 36. Point out that a fantasy may contain characters that could be real, such as students in a classroom, but that a fantasy contains things that could never happen in real life. As we read "Punctuation Takes a Vacation," think about the things that seem real. Think about the ideas in the story that could never happen in real life.

Read the rest of the panel on p. 36. Have students look for details in the title and illustrations that would help them predict that this story is a fantasy.

DURING READING Have students read along with you while tracking the print or do a choral reading of the selection. Students may need to discuss the text feature on p. 39, the postcards. Point out that these postcards are not merely "illustrations," but an important part of the story.

AFTER READING Have students share their reactions to the selection. Then guide them through the Reading Across Texts and Writing Across Texts activities, prompting if necessary.

- Do you think the students feel the same about Mr. Wright as they do about Mrs. Granger? What does this tell you about each teacher?
- What details about Mr. Wright and Mrs. Granger do you think are most important to include in your drawings? Why do you think these are the most important details?

Monitor Progress

Word and Story Reading

If...	then...
If... students have difficulty reading multisyllabic words in the selection,	**then...** have them look for and read meaningful parts in the words or have them chunk words with no recognizable parts.
If... students have difficulty reading along with the group,	**then...** have them follow along as they listen to the AudioText.

Advanced

ROUTINE

DAY 4

1 Read "Punctuation Takes a Vacation"

CREATIVE THINKING Have students read pp. 36–41 independently. Encourage them to think creatively. For example, ask:

- What would it be like to read and write if we had no punctuation marks?
- How would this story be different if it were a piece of nonfiction text about how to use punctuation?

AFTER READING Have students meet with you to discuss the selection and Reading Across Texts. Have students do Writing Across Texts independently.

2 Extend Genre Study

RESEARCH Have students locate additional fantasy stories. Invite them to contribute to a class fantasy list. They can write stories they recommend on index cards to share in a class library. Cards should include titles, plot summaries, main characters, and what makes this fantasy a "must read"!

WRITE Have students rewrite part of *Frindle* as if it were a fantasy. They can share their work with classmates and compare and contrast their fantasies with the original story.

AudioText

Group Time

Strategic Intervention

ROUTINE

1 Reread for Fluency

MODEL Tell students that good readers use expression when they read aloud. They think about the characters and how they would sound when they speak. Draw students' attention to the first paragraph on p. 3 of the Leveled Reader *The Spelling Bee*. Ask how a teacher would sound when asking a student to be quiet in class. Read Mr. Harper's words in a sing-song, sweet voice. Then read them with a tone that is a little more to-the-point and stern. Ask students which reading made the most sense with the words. Then read p. 6 in a monotone voice word-by-word. Have students tell you which model is better. Discuss how paying attention to the emotion of the speakers as you read makes them more realistic.

PRACTICE Have individuals silently reread passages from *The Spelling Bee*. Encourage students to self-correct. Then have partners reread passages aloud. For optimal fluency, they should reread three or four times. Students in this group are assessed in Weeks 2 and 4.

PearsonSuccessNet.com

2 Retell Leveled Reader *The Spelling Bee*

Model how to skim to find the main points of the plot to retell a story. Model with pp. 3–5. Then ask students to retell *The Spelling Bee*, focusing on the main points of the plot. Prompt them as needed.

- What problems does Kate have in class?
- How does Mr. Harper help Kate?
- Who else helps Kate?
- What does Kate accomplish at the end of the story? How does she feel about it?

Monitor Progress

Fluency

If...	then...
If... students have difficulty reading fluently,	**then...** provide additional fluency practice by pairing nonfluent readers with fluent ones.

For alternate Leveled Reader lesson plans that teach **Plot and Character,** **Prior Knowledge,** and **Lesson Vocabulary,** see pp. LR1–LR9.

On-Level

ROUTINE

1 Reread for Fluency

MODEL Tell students that good oral readers use expression when they read. Expression helps bring a character to life—the character seems like a real person. When students read, they should pay attention to characters' feelings and emotions and show them in their voices. Read aloud p. 5, showing emotion in your tone of voice. Ask students to identify how each character feels based on your oral reading.

PRACTICE Have individuals silently reread passages from *Learning from Ms. Liang.* Remind them to use expression as they read. Then have partners reread passages aloud. For optimal fluency, students should reread three or four times. As students read, monitor fluency and provide corrective feedback. Students in this group are assessed in Week 3.

2 Retell Leveled Reader *Learning from Ms. Liang*

Have students skim for major events in the plot as they retell the story. Prompt as needed.

- Where does this story take place?
- Who are the characters in this story?
- What are the characters like?
- Why do you think the author wrote this story?

Advanced

ROUTINE

1 Reread for Fluency

PRACTICE Have students silently reread passages from the Leveled Reader *This Is the Way We Go to School.* Then have them reread aloud with a partner or individually. As students read, monitor fluency and provide corrective feedback. If students read fluently on the first reading, they do not need to reread three to four times. Assess the fluency of students in this group using p. 41a.

2 Revisit Leveled Reader *This Is the Way We Go to School*

RETELL Have students retell the Leveled Reader *This Is the Way We Go to School.*

EDUCATION LAWS Have students share the community or state laws they learned about and how reasonable or restrictive they are. Ask students how they would change the laws to make them better.

Group Time

DAY 1

Strategic Intervention

ROUTINE

1 Build Background

REINFORCE CONCEPTS Display the Challenges in Nature Concept Web. This week's concept is *challenges in nature*. Different kinds of weather can be challenging. Some people study challenging weather. Discuss the meaning of each word on the web, using the definitions on p. 42l and the Concept Vocabulary routine on p. DI•1.

CONNECT TO READING This week you will read about challenges in nature. You will read a tall tale about weather and nonfiction pieces about severe weather and people who study it. What kinds of challenges in nature have you heard about, read about, or experienced? *Answers will vary. Students may describe severe weather they have experienced or natural disasters they have seen on the news, such as hurricanes or tsunamis.*

2 Read Leveled Reader *Storm Danger!*

BEFORE READING Using the Picture Walk routine on p. DI•1, guide students through the text focusing on key concepts and vocabulary. Ask questions such as:

p. 3 This page shows lightning. What do you know about lightning? What damage can lightning do?

p. 4 This photograph shows damage caused by a storm. What kind of damage can storms cause?

pp. 10–11 These photographs show the results of a flash flood. What do you think causes a flash flood? Why would this be dangerous?

DURING READING Read pp. 3–5 aloud while students track the print. Do a choral reading of pp. 6–9. If students are capable, have them read and discuss the remainder of the book with a partner. Ask: What are some different kinds of severe weather? What things can you do to stay safe during severe weather?

AFTER READING Encourage pairs of students to discuss the different types of storms and why they are dangerous. We read *Storm Danger!* to learn the facts about several types of severe storms. Knowing facts about storms will help us realize what parts of *Thunder Rose* are greatly exaggerated fiction.

PearsonSuccessNet.com

Monitor Progress

Selection Reading and Comprehension

If... students have difficulty reading the selection with a partner,	**then...** have them follow along as they listen to the Online Leveled Reader Audio.
If... students have trouble remembering how to stay safe during severe weather,	**then...** reread pp. 9, 11, 13, 15, and 17 and help students summarize the bulleted lists of tips.

For alternate Leveled Reader lesson plans that teach **Cause and Effect, Monitor and Fix Up,** and **Lesson Vocabulary,** see pp. LR10–LR18.

On-Level

ROUTINE

DAY 1

1 Build Background

DEVELOP VOCABULARY Write the word *terror* and ask students to define it in their own words. *(Terror is great fear.)* Invite students to pantomime fear. They can show a facial expression associated with fear or a situation that would make them fearful. Repeat this activity with the words *furious* and *destruction* and other words from the Leveled Reader *The Challenges of Storm Chasing*. Use the Concept Vocabulary routine on p. DI • 1 as needed.

2 Read Leveled Reader *The Challenges of Storm Chasing*

BEFORE READING Have students create a KWL chart about tornadoes. In the K column, they can write what they already know about tornadoes. In the W column, they can write questions they want to learn. As they read, they can note what they learn in the L column.

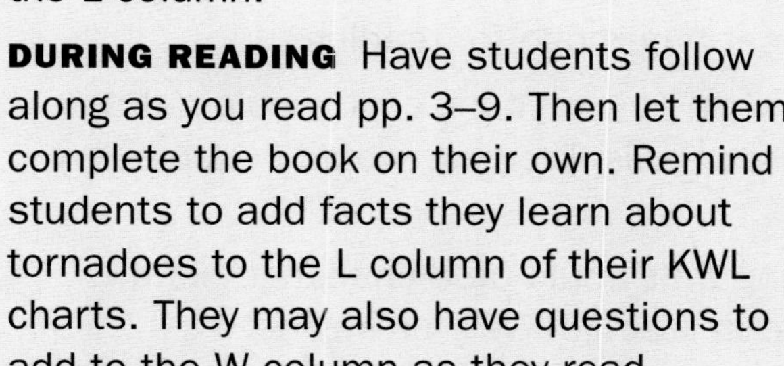

DURING READING Have students follow along as you read pp. 3–9. Then let them complete the book on their own. Remind students to add facts they learn about tornadoes to the L column of their KWL charts. They may also have questions to add to the W column as they read.

AFTER READING Have students compare their KWL charts. Point out that knowing facts about tornadoes might help them figure out why tomorrow's selection *Thunder Rose* is a piece of fiction.

Advanced

ROUTINE

DAY 1

1 Read Leveled Reader *Forecasting the Weather*

BEFORE READING Recall the Read Aloud "Night of the Twisters." What do you think it would be like to experience a tornado? *(Answers will vary.)* Today you will read about methods that meteorologists use to forecast weather events such as tornadoes.

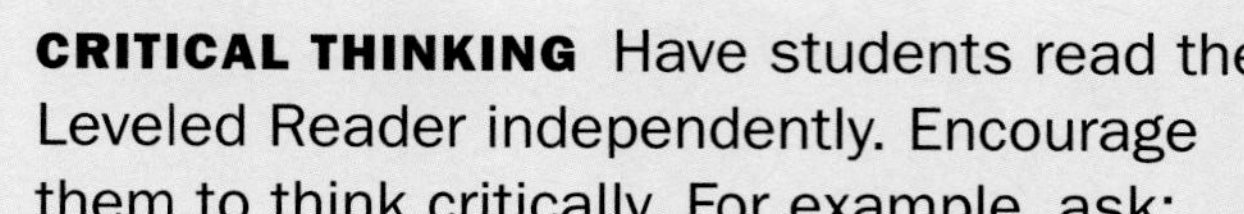

CRITICAL THINKING Have students read the Leveled Reader independently. Encourage them to think critically. For example, ask:

- Why would we not have weather without the sun?
- How has weather forecasting changed? What do you think are the most important tools that have been developed for weather watching?
- What do you think would be the most exciting part of being a meteorologist? What would be the most challenging part of the job?

AFTER READING Have students review the selection to find five or more unfamiliar words and determine their meanings. Then ask them to write a brief definition for each in their own words and create an illustration. Have students meet with you to discuss the selection and share their definitions. Compile their work in a student dictionary.

2 Independent Extension Activity

NOW TRY THIS Assign "Now Try This" on pp. 22–23 of *Forecasting the Weather* for students to work on throughout the week.

Group Time

DAY 2

Strategic Intervention

ROUTINE

1 Word Study/Phonics

LESSON VOCABULARY Use p. 44b to review the meanings of *branded, constructed, daintily, devastation, lullaby, pitch, resourceful, thieving,* and *veins*. Have individuals practice reading the words from word cards.

DECODING MULTISYLLABIC WORDS Write *stampeding,* saying the word as you write it. Then model how to decode a base word with an ending. First I look for meaningful parts. If I see a part I know, such as *-ed* or *-ing,* then I look for a base word. I say the parts of the word: *stampede ing*. Then I read the word: *stampeding*.

Use the Multisyllabic Word routine on p. DI • 1 to help students read these other words from *Thunder Rose: thoughtful, obliged, commendable, twisty,* and *whirling*. Be sure students understand the meanings of words such as *obliged* and *commendable*.

Use *Strategies for Word Analysis,* Lesson 2, with students who have difficulty mastering word analysis and need practice with decodable text.

Audio CD AudioText

2 Read *Thunder Rose,* pp. 46–55

BEFORE READING *Storm Danger!* was a book of facts that described different types of dangerous storms and gave tips for staying safe in each one. This selection is a tall tale about a girl who can do things no person can really do.

Using the Picture Walk routine on p. DI • 1, guide students through the text, asking questions such as those listed below. Then read the question on p. 46. Together, set a purpose for reading.

p. 50 What is Rose doing that an actual young child would not be able to do? *(Rose is carrying four pails. The pails would be too heavy for a real young girl to carry.)*

pp. 58–59 What is Rose doing that would be a challenge? Is this something that could be done in real life? Why or why not?

DURING READING Follow the Guiding Comprehension routine on pp. 48–55. Have students read along with you while tracking the print or do a choral reading of the selection. Stop every two pages to ask what has happened so far. Prompt as necessary.

- How does Rose's family know she is different from other children?
- What does Rose do to help her family when she is five years old? What does she do when she is eight and nine?

AFTER READING What has happened in the selection so far? What do you think will happen next? Reread passages as needed.

Monitor Progress

Word and Story Reading

If...	then...
If... students have difficulty reading multisyllabic words in the selection,	**then...** have them look for and read meaningful parts in the words or have them chunk words with no recognizable parts.
If... students need practice reading words fluently,	**then...** use the Fluent Word Reading Routine on the DI tab.
If... students have difficulty reading along with the group,	**then...** have them follow along as they listen to the AudioText.

Advanced

ROUTINE

DAY 2

1 Extend Vocabulary

CONTEXT CLUES Choose and read a sentence or passage containing a difficult word, such as this passage from p. 8 of *Forecasting the Weather:* "The ancient Greek philosopher Aristotle wrote a book to describe weather phenomena, or unusual events." What does the word *phenomena* mean? *(unusual, or strange, events)* How did you determine the word's meaning? *(I used the context, or the words around the word. The sentence says "or unusual events" between commas, which means that "unusual events" and "phenomena" mean the same thing.)* Discuss why context clues are helpful, and remind students to use the strategy as they read *Thunder Rose.*

2 Read *Thunder Rose,* pp. 46–55

BEFORE READING In *Forecasting the Weather,* you read about the challenges meteorologists face when they try to predict the weather. Today's selection tells about challenges faced by a larger-than-life character, Thunder Rose. As you read, look for details about weather that are realistic. Look for details that show this selection is a tall tale, or a humorous, exaggerated story.

Have students record what they know about tall tales in their Strategy Response Logs (p. 46).

CREATIVE THINKING Have students read pp. 46–55 independently. Encourage them to think creatively. For example, ask:

- What exaggerations do you find in this story? Think of three other exaggerations that could describe Rose and her actions.

AFTER READING Have partners discuss the selection and share their Strategy Response Log entries. Have them list what makes *Thunder Rose* a tall tale and compare the traits of the story with their original lists (p. 55). Then have students think of other exaggerated statements about Rose. Students can create a poem about Rose in which each line is an exaggeration of the character. Have students meet with you to discuss the selection and their poems.

Audio CD AudioText

Group Time

DAY 3

Strategic Intervention

ROUTINE

1 Reinforce Comprehension

SKILL CAUSE AND EFFECT Have students tell what an effect is. *(something that happens)* Ask students what a cause is. *(something that makes the event happen)* If necessary, review the meaning and provide a model. An effect is something that happens. A cause makes it happen. If you drop a book, that's a cause. The effect is a loud noise. Read students the following statements. Ask them to identify the causes and effects in each one. Rose's parents loved her *(cause)* so they sang her a lullaby. *(effect)* Because Rose wanted a big drink *(cause),* she lifted a whole cow to get a drink. *(effect)* Rose's mom praised her. *(cause)* Rose blushed. *(effect)*

Audio CD AudioText

2 Read *Thunder Rose,* pp. 56–63

BEFORE READING Have students retell what happened in the selection so far. Ask: What problems did you have understanding when you were reading? What did you do when you realized that you were having a problem understanding the story? Reread pp. 52–53. Model how to monitor as you read and fix up when you no longer understand what you read. In the second paragraph, I read that Rose did a commendable job of staking the fence without a bit of help. I was confused, because I didn't know what *commendable* means. I read on about Rose building a skyscraper all by herself. The author is describing Rose's accomplishments, or great things that she does. *Commendable* must mean something good. If someone does something commendable, it means that people should praise it or think highly of it. Remind students to monitor their own understanding as they read. When they have trouble understanding something, they should stop and use a fix-up strategy to try to understand what they are reading. **STRATEGY Monitor and Fix Up**

DURING READING Follow the Guiding Comprehension routine on pp. 56–63. Have students read along with you while tracking print or do a choral reading. Stop every page or two to ask students what has happened so far. Prompt as necessary

- What word would you use to describe Rose in this part of the story?
- What was the main problem in the story? How was the problem solved?

AFTER READING Describe the challenges that Rose faces in this story. Tell what she does to meet these challenges. Reread with students for comprehension as needed. Tell them that tomorrow they will read "Measuring Tornadoes," a piece of expository nonfiction that explains how scientists measure the strength of tornadoes.

Monitor Progress

Word and Story Reading

If... students have difficulty reading multisyllabic words in the selection,	**then...** have them look for and read meaningful parts in the words or have them chunk words with no recognizable parts.
If... students have difficulty reading along with the group,	**then...** have them follow along as they listen to the AudioText.

Advanced

ROUTINE

DAY 3

1 Extend Comprehension

SKILL CAUSE AND EFFECT Have students identify three cause-and-effect relationships in the story. Have them write sentences about the causes and effects using a clue word or phrase, such as *so, because,* and *as a result.*

STRATEGY MONITOR AND FIX UP Invite students to identify where they had trouble understanding a word or idea as they read the story. Encourage them to explain what they did when they encountered this difficult part. Did they reread? read on? look for a clue in the text? think about what they already knew about the topic? ask for help?

2 Read *Thunder Rose,* pp. 56–63

BEFORE READING Have students recall what has happened in the selection so far. Remind them to look for causes and effects as they read the remainder of *Thunder Rose*.

CREATIVE THINKING Have students read pp. 56–63 independently. Encourage them to think creatively. For example, ask:

- Think of another way that Rose could have solved the problem in the story. Do you think the author chose the best way for Rose to solve the problem? Explain why or why not.

AFTER READING Have students complete the Strategy Response Log activity (p. 62). Then have them find and read a famous tall tale. They can create a two-column chart to record causes and effects in the tall tale. Students might also list exaggerations they find to "prove" that this story is a tall tale. Have students meet with you to discuss the story.

Audio CD AudioText

Group Time

DAY 4

Strategic Intervention

ROUTINE

1 Practice Retelling

REVIEW STORY ELEMENTS Help students identify the main character and setting of *Thunder Rose*. Then guide them in using the Retelling Cards to list story events in sequence. Prompt students to include important details.

RETELL Using the Retelling Cards, have students work in pairs to retell *Thunder Rose*. Monitor retelling and prompt students as needed. For example, ask:

- What is the main character in this story like?
- What is the problem in this story?
- How was the problem solved?

If students struggle, model a fluent retelling.

2 Read "Measuring Tornadoes"

BEFORE READING Read the genre information on p. 66. Point out that expository nonfiction contains facts about a topic. This piece of expository nonfiction gives facts about tornadoes. Facts are pieces of information that could be proved true or false.

Read the rest of the panel on p. 66. Point out that a chart gives information in a format that is easy to understand. Model reading the title and headings on the chart to show students the types of information they will find. Ask a question to lead students to use the chart, such as: Which classification of tornado has wind speeds of 113–157 miles per hour? *(F-2)* How many tornadoes are classified as incredible? *(1 in 100)*

DURING READING Have students read along with you while tracking the print or do a choral reading of the selection. Students may need to discuss the chart on p. 67. Prompt them with leading questions as needed.

AFTER READING Have students share their reactions to the selection. Then guide them through the Reading Across Texts and Writing Across Texts activities, prompting if necessary.

- Look at the features of the tornadoes in the picture on p. 60. What items do you see in the picture that show you the strength of the tornado?
- What damage can a storm of that magnitude do? Reread the description in the chart before you write about the damage.

AudioText

Monitor Progress

Word and Selection Reading

If... students have difficulty reading multisyllabic words in the selection,	**then...** have them look for and read meaningful parts in the words or have them chunk words with no recognizable parts.
If... students have difficulty reading along with the group,	**then...** have them follow along as they listen to the AudioText.

Advanced

ROUTINE

DAY 4

1 Read "Measuring Tornadoes"

CRITICAL/CREATIVE THINKING Have students read pp. 66–67 independently. Encourage them to think critically. For example, ask:

- Why do you think it was important for Theodore Fujita to invent this classification scale? Why is the classification scale useful to scientists?
- If you were watching a weather report, why might you want to know the strength of a tornado that is coming to your community? How would knowing its strength affect what you would do to prepare?

AFTER READING Have students meet with you to discuss the selection and Reading Across Texts. Have students do Writing Across Texts independently.

AudioText

2 Extend Genre Study

RESEARCH Have students locate newspaper or magazine articles about tornadoes. Encourage them to link the information in the articles to the Fujita scale. Students can write brief summaries or make copies of articles and place them on a bulletin board with the Fujita ratings. Students will be able to see the damage done by actual tornadoes according to their scale readings.

WRITE Have students conduct and write an interview that draws on the information in the article. The person being interviewed should have witnessed a tornado of a particular strength. Questions could focus on what the witness saw and heard during the storm.

Group Time

DAY 5

PearsonSuccessNet.com

Strategic Intervention

ROUTINE

1 Reread for Fluency

MODEL Tell students that good readers think about their tone of voice when they read aloud. Their voices rise and fall as they read sentences—the voice falls when coming to the end of a statement and rises when coming to the end of a question. The reader pauses at a comma and makes a longer pause at a period. Read aloud pp. 3–4 of *Storm Danger!* Emphasize such features as the rise at the end of the question on p. 3, the enthusiasm conveyed by the exclamation point at the end of p. 3, and the pauses at the commas in the sentences on p. 4.

PRACTICE Have students silently reread passages from *Storm Danger!* Encourage students to self-correct. Then have partners reread passages aloud. For optimal fluency, they should reread three or four times. Assess the fluency of students in this group using p. 67a.

2 Retell Leveled Reader *Storm Danger!*

Model how to skim the book, retelling as you skim. Model with pp. 3–5. Then ask students to retell *Storm Danger!,* focusing on one type of storm at a time. Prompt them as needed.

- What type of storm is it?
- What happens during this type of storm?
- How can you stay safe during this type of storm?

Monitor Progress

Fluency

If... students have difficulty reading fluently,	**then...** provide additional fluency practice by pairing nonfluent readers with fluent ones.

For alternate Leveled Reader lesson plans that teach **Cause and Effect, Monitor and Fix Up,** and **Lesson Vocabulary,** see pp. LR10–LR18.

On-Level

ROUTINE

1 Reread for Fluency

MODEL Read aloud p. 3 of the Leveled Reader *The Challenges of Storm Chasing.* Emphasize pausing at periods and commas, with the longer pauses at ends of sentences. Have students note the long, dramatic pause at the colon in the last sentence on the page. Discuss how paying attention to the tone of voice creates a natural rhythm in the reading.

PRACTICE Have students silently reread passages from *The Challenges of Storm Chasing*. Remind them to consider the tone of voice as they read Then have partners reread passages aloud. For optimal fluency, students should reread three or four times. As students read, monitor fluency and provide corrective feedback. Students in this group are assessed in Week 3.

2 Retell Leveled Reader *The Challenges of Storm Chasing*

Have students skim and use the photographs as they retell the important points in the selection. Prompt as needed.

- What was this section mostly about?
- What did you learn from reading this selection?
- Why do you think the author wrote this book?

Advanced

ROUTINE

1 Reread for Fluency

PRACTICE Have students silently reread passages from the Leveled Reader *Forecasting the Weather*. Then have them reread aloud with a partner or individually. As students read, monitor fluency and provide corrective feedback. If students read fluently on the first reading, they do not need to reread three to four times. Students in this group were assessed in Week 1.

2 Revisit Leveled Reader *Forecasting the Weather*

RETELL Have students retell the Leveled Reader *Forecasting the Weather.*

NOW TRY THIS Have students share their weather forecasts. Discuss with them what sources they used to compile their work. Are their forecasts accurate? Why or why not?

Group Time

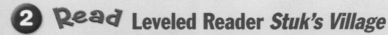

Strategic Intervention

ROUTINE

DAY 1

1 Build Background

REINFORCE CONCEPTS Display the Survival Concept Web. This week's concept is *survival.* People need different kinds of skills and tools to survive in certain surroundings. Discuss the meaning of each word on the web, using the definitions on p. 68l and the Concept Vocabulary routine on p. DI • 1.

CONNECT TO READING This week you will read about characters who face different challenges in order to survive in their surroundings. What kinds of things do you need to survive? How do you get those items? *(food, shelter, water, and clothing; from my family; from my community)*

PearsonSuccessNet.com

2 Read Leveled Reader *Stuk's Village*

BEFORE READING Using the Picture Walk routine on p. DI • 1, guide students through the text focusing on key concepts and vocabulary. Ask questions such as:

p. 3 This page shows Stuk's home. What kind of home is it? What do you think it would be like to live in this kind of home?

pp. 4–5 These illustrations have captions. Listen to the captions as I read them. What do the captions tell you about living in Stuk's village? *(A lot of work goes into making the canoes. The villagers tie the wood together instead of using nails or similar tools.)*

p. 7 This illustration shows something that people need to survive. What is it? How do the villagers get what they need? *(People need food to survive. The villagers use nets to fish.)*

DURING READING Read pp. 3–5 aloud while students track the print. Do a choral reading of pp. 6–9. If students are capable, have them read and discuss the remainder of the book with a partner. Ask: What is life like in Stuk's Village? How is it different from your life?

AFTER READING Encourage pairs of students to discuss what Stuk and the villagers do in order to survive in their environment. *Stuk's Village* tells what people who live in a certain place do to survive. Understanding how people meet the challenges of their surroundings is an idea we will also think about as we read *Island of the Blue Dolphins.*

Monitor Progress

Selection Reading and Comprehension

If...	then...
If... students have difficulty reading the selection with a partner,	**then...** have them follow along as they listen to the Online Leveled Reader Audio.
If... students have trouble understanding the setting of the story,	**then...** reread pp. 3 and 4 and lead students in visualizing important details about the setting.

For alternate Leveled Reader lesson plans that teach **Theme and Setting,** **Visualize,** and **Lesson Vocabulary,** see pp. LR19–LR27.

DAY 1 Island of the Blue Dolphins

On-Level

ROUTINE

1 Build Background

DEVELOP VOCABULARY Write the word *quartz* and ask students what they know about quartz. *(Quartz is a type of mineral.)* Quartz is a hard mineral that is usually found as glass-like crystals. It is used in the making of watches, jewelry, and some electronic equipment. Invite students to describe and tell what they know about *adobe* and other words from the Leveled Reader *Toby's Vacation.* Use the Concept Vocabulary routine on p. DI·1 as needed.

2 Read Leveled Reader *Toby's Vacation*

BEFORE READING Have students draw T-charts to record facts about Santa Cruz Island and about San Clemente Island. As you read, list on your chart the types of wildlife found on the islands, the size and location of the islands, and how endangered species on the islands manage to survive.

DURING READING Have students follow along as you read pp. 3–9. Then let them complete the book on their own. Remind students to add facts to their T-charts as they read.

AFTER READING Have students compare their T-charts. Point out that exploring the wildlife and environments of islands will help them visualize the setting of *Island of the Blue Dolphins* and understand what life is like there.

Advanced

ROUTINE

DAY 1

1 Read Leveled Reader *Harvesting Medicine on the Hill*

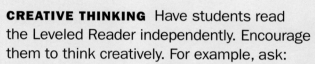

BEFORE READING Recall the Read Aloud "The Sign of the Beaver." What do the characters in this selection do to survive in the wilderness? *(They catch fish, cook it, and eat it.)* Today you will read a story about characters who find plants that they can use for medicine. This helps them survive.

CREATIVE THINKING Have students read the Leveled Reader independently. Encourage them to think creatively. For example, ask:

- What problem was Red Hawk most worried about? How would you have felt if you were Red Hawk? How would you have solved the problem?
- How did the different plants help solve the Chumash's health problems?
- How do you think this selection connects to events in the world today? What happens when cultures "meet"?

AFTER READING Have students review the selection to find five or more unfamiliar words and determine their meanings. Then ask them to write statements that include the words to show they know what the words mean. Have students meet with you to discuss the selection and share their statements and questions.

2 Independent Extension Activity

MEDICINES FROM NATURE Have students read "Medicines from Nature" on p. 24. Then invite them to research other medicines or medical treatments that can be found in nature. Ask them to create a display to share their findings.

Group Time

DAY 2

Strategic Intervention

ROUTINE

1 Word Study/Phonics

LESSON VOCABULARY Use p. 70b to review the meanings of *gnawed, headland, kelp, lair, ravine, shellfish,* and *sinew.* Have individuals practice reading the words from word cards.

DECODING MULTISYLLABIC WORDS Write *sheltered,* saying the word as you write it. Then model how to use chunking to decode the word. First I take off the ending *-ed.* I see a chunk at the beginning of the word: *shel.* I see the next part: *ter.* I say the chunks slowly: *shel ter.* I know the word *shelter.* Then I add the ending *-ed.* I say the parts fast to make a whole word: *sheltered.* Is it a real word? Yes.

Use the Multisyllabic Word routine on p. DI • 1 to help students read these other words from *Island of the Blue Dolphins: brackish, sandspit, hollow,* and *utensils.* Be sure students understand the meanings of words such as *brackish* and *sandspit.*

Use Strategies for Word Analysis, Lesson 3, with students who have difficulty mastering word analysis and need practice with decodable text.

Audio CD AudioText

2 Read *Island of the Blue Dolphins,* pp. 72–79

BEFORE READING *Stuk's Village* described life in an American Indian village. This selection tells about an American Indian girl who lives on an island and what she needs to do to meet the challenge of surviving on the island.

Using the Picture Walk routine on p. DI • 1, guide students through the text, asking questions such as those listed below. Then read the question on p. 73. Together, set a purpose for reading.

p. 74 Describe the environment in the picture. What do you think might be challenging about living in this place?

pp. 77, 79, and 80 What kinds of tools does Karana use? How do you think she got them? How do you think those tools help her survive?

DURING READING Follow the Guiding Comprehension routine on pp. 74–79. Have students read along with you while tracking the print or do a choral reading of the selection. Stop every two pages to ask what has happened so far. Prompt as necessary.

- Why does Karana live all alone?
- Karana has to face many challenges to survive on the island. What are the challenges? How does Karana meet them?

AFTER READING What has happened in the selection so far? What do you think will happen next? Reread passages with students for comprehension as needed.

Monitor Progress

Word and Story Reading

If...	then...
If... students have difficulty reading multisyllabic words in the selection,	**then...** have them look for and read meaningful parts in the words or have them chunk words with no recognizable parts.
If... students need practice reading words fluently,	**then...** use the Fluent Word Reading Routine on the DI tab.
If... students have difficulty reading along with the group,	**then...** have them follow along as they listen to the AudioText.

Advanced

ROUTINE

DAY 2

1 Extend Vocabulary

DICTIONARY/GLOSSARY Choose and read a sentence or passage containing a difficult word, such as this passage from p. 4 of *Harvesting Medicine on the Hill*: "Gnarled oaks spot the golden yellow hills beneath you, all the way down to where the ocean crashes against the shore." I'm not sure what the word *gnarled* means. I look at the sentences before and after the sentence, and there aren't many clues in the story. An oak tree could be tall, dying, and leaf-filled. Any of those words would make sense in the sentence. I can guess what the word means, and then I will use a dictionary to check my meaning. *Gnarled* means "knotted and twisted." That description of an oak tree makes sense. Discuss why it is helpful sometimes to use a dictionary or glossary to find or check a word's meaning, and remind students to use the strategy as they read *Island of the Blue Dolphins.*

ISLAND of the BLUE DOLPHINS
by Scott O'Dell illustrated by E. B. Lewis
How will Karana meet the physical challenges that face her?

Audio CD AudioText

2 Read *Island of the Blue Dolphins,* pp. 72–79

BEFORE READING In *Harvesting Medicine on the Hill,* you read about the challenges of battling diseases that come from a new culture and how people met those challenges. Today's selection tells about challenges faced by someone who lives alone on an island. As you read, look for details about the challenges the character faces and how she meets those challenges.

Have students visualize the island setting and predict what it will be like to live there in their Strategy Response Logs (p. 72).

CREATIVE THINKING Have students read pp. 72–79 independently. Encourage them to think creatively. For example, ask:

- What problems does Karana work to solve first? Would you have handled her problems differently? In what ways?

AFTER READING Have partners discuss the selection and share their Strategy Response Log entries. Have them tell how their predictions did or did not match what actually happened in the story (p. 79). Then have students make a list of images that describe Karana's island—what would they see, hear, smell, feel, and taste there? They can compile their images into a poem about the island.

Group Time

DAY 3

Audio CD AudioText

Strategic Intervention

ROUTINE

1 Reinforce Comprehension

SKILL THEME AND SETTING Have students explain the meaning of the word *theme* in a story. *(what the author wants you to remember after you read—a lesson)* Ask students what a setting is. *(where and when a story takes place)* If necessary, review the meanings and provide a model. The setting is the time and place of a story. The setting of this story is an island off the coast of California. The time is from 1835 to 1853.

Write the words *Island of the Blue Dolphins: Setting* in a circle on the board. Have students supply details to create a web that tells about the setting of the selection.

2 Read *Island of the Blue Dolphins,* pp. 80–83

BEFORE READING Have students retell what happened in the selection so far. Ask: What could you picture in your mind as you read the story? How did picturing the setting of the story in your mind help you understand it better? Reread p. 75. Model how to visualize as you read. As I read, I pictured the clear sky with the clouds in the distance. I pictured the headland, a piece of land that juts out into the ocean. I also thought about the wild dogs. I could hear them barking and whining. I pictured the ravine and could hear the water rushing down the ravine in the springtime as I felt the warm air and the sun shining on my skin. Remind students to visualize as they read. How does visualizing help them understand the setting? **STRATEGY Visualize**

DURING READING Follow the Guiding Comprehension routine on pp. 80–83. Have students read along with you while tracking the print or do a choral reading. Stop every page or two to ask students what has happened so far. Prompt as necessary

- What does Karana do to solve her problem about shelter?
- How does Karana get food?
- How would you describe Karana?

AFTER READING Describe the challenges that Karana faces in this story. Tell what she does to meet these challenges. Reread with students for comprehension as needed. Tell them that tomorrow they will read "Seven Survival Questions," an interview that explains what to do to survive when you're lost.

Monitor Progress

Word and Story Reading

If... students have difficulty reading multisyllabic words in the selection,	**then...** have them look for and read meaningful parts in the words or have them chunk words with no recognizable parts.
If... students have difficulty reading along with the group,	**then...** have them follow along as they listen to the AudioText.

Advanced

ROUTINE

DAY 3

1 Extend Comprehension

SKILL THEME AND SETTING Have students identify the setting of the story. Remind them that a theme is a big idea or statement of what the author might want them to remember after they have read.

STRATEGY VISUALIZE Invite students to visualize the possible location of Karana's shelter and why she rejected it. Students can close their eyes as you read p. 77. Invite them to recall the details they visualized that really "brought this island to life" for them.

2 Read *Island of the Blue Dolphins,* pp. 80–83

BEFORE READING Have students recall what has happened in the selection so far. Remind them to think about the setting and a possible theme as they read the remainder of *Island of the Blue Dolphins.*

CRITICAL THINKING Have students read pp. 80–83 independently. Encourage them to think critically. For example, ask:

- What do you think of Karana? What words would you use to describe her? Do you think she took the right approach to solve her problems? Why or why not?

AFTER READING Have students complete the Strategy Response Log activity (p. 82). Have students meet with you to discuss the selections. Then have them research the homes of various American Indians. They might want to consider how homes vary according to the environment in which they are found.

ISLAND of the BLUE DOLPHINS
How will Karana meet the physical challenges that face her?

Audio CD AudioText

Group Time

DAY 4

AudioText

Monitor Progress

Word and Selection Reading

If... students have difficulty reading multisyllabic words in the selection,	**then...** have them look for and read meaningful parts in the words or have them chunk words with no recognizable parts.
If... students have difficulty reading along with the group,	**then...** have them follow along as they listen to the AudioText.

Strategic Intervention

ROUTINE

1 Practice Retelling

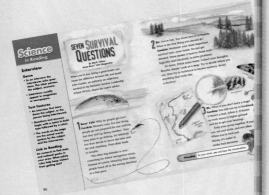

REVIEW STORY ELEMENTS Help students identify the main character and setting of *Island of the Blue Dolphins.* Then guide them in using the Retelling Cards to list story events in sequence. Prompt students to include important details.

RETELL Using the Retelling Cards, have students work in pairs to retell *Island of the Blue Dolphins.* Monitor retelling and prompt students as needed. For example, ask:

- Where and when does this story take place?
- What is the character in this story like?
- What is the author trying to tell us or teach us?

If students struggle, model a fluent retelling.

2 Read "Seven Survival Questions"

BEFORE READING Read the genre information on p. 86. Point out that an interview is like a dialogue between the interviewer and the subject of the interview. An interviewer asks questions, and the subject answers them. As we read "Seven Survival Questions," pay attention to the question-and-answer format. As you read, think about who is speaking.

Read the rest of the panel on p. 86. Preview the text with students, explaining that *BL* stands for *Boys' Life,* the magazine that published the interview. Preview the bulleted lists on p. 89. Explain that the bulleted lists summarize information in an easy-to-read format.

DURING READING Have students read along with you while tracking the print or do a choral reading of the selection. To help students understand the text structure, you may want to model with a page or two, having a student read the part of the interviewer while you answer the questions.

AFTER READING Have students share their reactions to the selection. Then guide them through the Reading Across Texts and Writing Across Texts activities, prompting if necessary.

- What needs did Karana meet first? How would meeting her needs fit into her lists of "dos" and "don'ts"?
- How will you decide which of the tips are most important to Karana's survival?

Advanced

ROUTINE

DAY 4

1 Read "Seven Survival Questions"

CRITICAL THINKING Have students read pp. 86–89 independently. Encourage them to think critically. For example, ask:

- What did you learn about survival that you didn't know before?
- Which of these survival tips do you think is most important to follow? Why do you think so?

AFTER READING Have students meet with you to discuss the selection and Reading Across Texts. Have students do Writing Across Texts independently.

2 Extend Genre Study

RESEARCH Have students locate additional articles about wilderness survival. Encourage them to find a story about a survivor. What did the survivor do to meet the challenges of his or her environment? Which of the tips in the article did this person follow to ensure survival?

WRITE Have students think of questions to ask a classmate about meeting challenges, whether those challenges were outdoors, in school, or in some other area. Once students write questions, allow them to pair up and interview each other. They can write the questions and answers in the form of a brief informational article.

Audio CD AudioText

Group Time

DAY 5

Strategic Intervention

ROUTINE

1 Reread for Fluency

MODEL Tell students that good readers vary their pitch when they read. Pitch is how high or low your voice sounds. When we read dialogue, we might change our voices to match the character. If something is very important, we might change the pitch of our voice to match the importance of the information. Read aloud p. 6 of the Leveled Reader *Stuk's Village* for students. Emphasize the short sentence *Everybody helps,* explaining that this is an important idea to emphasize, so you change the pitch of your voice as you read.

PRACTICE Have individuals silently reread passages from *Stuk's Village.* Encourage students to self-correct. Then have partners reread passages aloud. For optimal fluency, they should reread three or four times. Students in this group are assessed in Weeks 2 and 4.

2 Retell Leveled Reader *Stuk's Village*

Model how to skim to find the main points of the plot to retell a story. Model with pp. 3–5. Then ask students to retell *Stuk's Village,* focusing on the main points of the plot. Prompt them as needed.

- Where and when does this story take place?
- Who are the characters in the story? What are they like?
- What is the problem in the story? How was it solved?

PearsonSuccessNet.com

Monitor Progress

Fluency

If... students have difficulty reading fluently,	**then...** provide additional fluency practice by pairing nonfluent readers with fluent ones.

For alternate Leveled Reader lesson plans that teach **Theme and Setting, Visualize,** and **Lesson Vocabulary,** see pp. LR19–LR27.

On-Level

ROUTINE

DAY 5

1 Reread for Fluency

MODEL Tell students that good oral readers think about pitch, or tone of voice, when they read. They read dialogue and important parts of the story with different pitches in their voices. Model with pp. 3–4 of *Toby's Vacation.* Change pitch with the sentence that ends with the exclamation point on p. 3. Change pitch when reading the dialogue on p. 4.

PRACTICE Have students reread passages from *Toby's Vacation* individually or with a partner. Remind them to think about pitch as they read. How should it change to read dialogue? For optimal fluency, students should reread three or four times. As students read, monitor fluency and provide corrective feedback. Assess the fluency of students in this group using p. 89a.

2 Retell Leveled Reader *Toby's Vacation*

Have students skim for major events in the plot as they retell the story. Prompt as needed.

- When and where does this story take place?
- What is Toby like?
- What is the author tying to tell us or teach us?

Advanced

ROUTINE

DAY 5

1 Reread for Fluency

PPRACTICE Have students silently reread passages from the Leveled Reader *Harvesting Medicine on the Hill.* Then have them reread aloud with a partner or individually. As students read, monitor fluency and provide corrective feedback. If students read fluently on the first reading, they do not need to reread three to four times. Students in this group were assessed in Week 1.

2 Revisit Leveled Reader *Harvesting Medicine on the Hill*

RETELL Have students retell the Leveled Reader *Harvesting Medicine on the Hill.*

MEDICINES FROM NATURE Have students share what they found out about medicines found in nature. Encourage them to share their findings in displays that can be shared with the class. Were students surprised by how many cures could be found in natural settings?

Group Time

Strategic Intervention

ROUTINE

1 Build Background

REINFORCE CONCEPTS Display the Personal Challenges Concept Web. This week's concept is *personal challenges.* The selections focus on athletes. At different periods in history, female athletes and African American athletes faced discrimination. Discuss the meaning of each word on the web, using the definitions on p. 90l and the Concept Vocabulary routine on p. DI • 1.

CONNECT TO READING This week you will read about real people who overcame great personal challenges to succeed at what they liked to do best. What characteristics do people need to face difficult challenges? *(People need strength, bravery, the ability to stick to something and see it through, and so on.)*

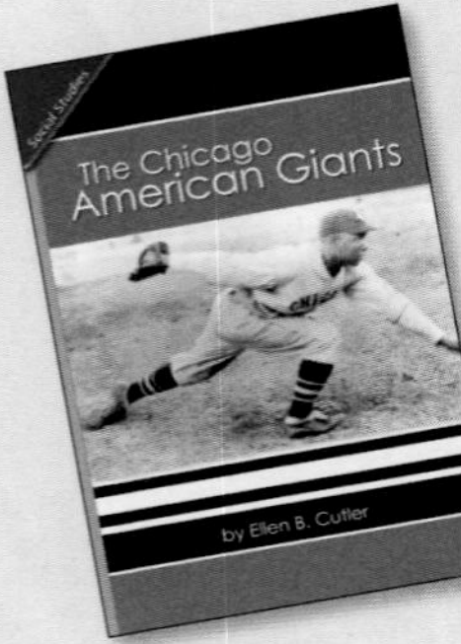

PearsonSuccessNet.com

2 Read Leveled Reader *The Chicago American Giants*

BEFORE READING Using the Picture Walk routine on p. DI • 1, guide students through the text focusing on key concepts and vocabulary. Ask questions such as:

pp. 4–5 What do you notice about the people playing baseball and most of the spectators? *(They are African American.)* What do you notice about the number of people in the stands? What does this tell you about the game? *(There are not many people in the stands. The game or the players must not have been very popular.)*

p. 9 This plaque shows Rube Foster. This is an actual plaque in the Baseball Hall of Fame. Let's read it to find out Rube Foster's accomplishments.

p. 16 How is this photograph different from the other photos in the selection? *(This is the first photo that shows a white player with an African American player.)* Let's read the caption to find out more.

DURING READING Read pp. 3–5 aloud, while students track the print. Do a choral reading of pp. 6–9. If students are capable, have them read and discuss the remainder of the book with a partner. Ask: What was life like for African American baseball players before 1947? Why did they have to form their own teams?

AFTER READING Have pairs of students discuss the personal challenges that the African American baseball players faced. *The Chicago American Giants* describes the challenges of African American baseball players and the league that they formed to play their favorite sport. You will be reading about another African American player, Satchel Paige, and what made him a great athlete.

Monitor Progress

Selection Reading and Comprehension

If... students have difficulty reading the selection with a partner,	**then...** have them follow along as they listen to the Online Leveled Reader Audio.
If... students have trouble following the sequence of events in the selection,	**then...** go to the time line on pp. 18–19 to review the major events in the selection.

For alternate Leveled Reader lesson plans that teach **Sequence, Ask Questions,** and **Lesson Vocabulary,** see pp. LR28–LR36.

On-Level

ROUTINE

1 Build Background

DEVELOP VOCABULARY Write the word *courage* on the board and ask students to name a synonym for *courage,* or a word that means the same or about the same thing. *(bravery)* Then ask students to name an antonym for the word. *(fear)* Invite students to give synonyms and antonyms for *exclude, dainty, excel,* and other words from the Leveled Reader *Famous Women Athletes.* Use the Concept Vocabulary routine on p. DI•1 as needed.

2 Read Leveled Reader *Famous Women Athletes*

BEFORE READING Have students create a web with the words *women athletes* at the center. This book tells about many women who were athletes. As you read, list the women on the web. Around each woman's name, add details such as the sport the woman played and words that would describe her.

DURING READING Have students follow along as you read pp. 3–9. Then let them complete the book on their own. Remind students to add names, sports, and characteristics to their webs as they read.

AFTER READING Have students compare their webs. Draw attention to the personal characteristics that helped these women meet challenges. Encourage students to look for these same types of personal characteristics that describe Satchel Paige as they read tomorrow's selection *Satchel Paige.*

Advanced

ROUTINE

1 Read Leveled Reader *African American Athletes*

BEFORE READING Recall the Read Aloud "Teammates." What challenge did Jackie Robinson face? How did Pee Wee Reese help him? *(Jackie Robinson was the first African American player in major league baseball. When he was enduring taunts and threats, a white player, Pee Wee Reese, supported him.)* Today you will read a selection about African American players in baseball and in other sports.

CRITICAL THINKING Have students read the Leveled Reader independently. Encourage them to think critically. For example, ask:

- What do you find most inspiring about the athletes in this book?
- Do you think that African American athletes still face discrimination today? Why or why not?
- Which of these athletes do you think overcame the greatest personal challenges? Explain why you think so.

AFTER READING Have students review the selection to find five or more unfamiliar words and determine their meanings. Then ask them use the words in "newspaper headlines" about athletes in this book and their accomplishments. Have students meet with you to discuss the selection and share their headlines.

2 Independent Extension Activity

NOW TRY THIS Assign "Now Try This" on pp. 22–23 of *African American Athletes* for students to work on throughout the week.

Group Time

Strategic Intervention

ROUTINE

DAY 2

1 Word Study/Phonics

LESSON VOCABULARY Use p. 92b to review the meanings of *confidence, fastball, mocking, outfield, unique, weakness,* and *windup.* Have individuals practice reading the words from word cards.

DECODING MULTISYLLABIC WORDS Write *hesitation,* saying the word as you write it. Then model how to decode a base word with an ending. First I look for meaningful parts. If I see a part I know, like the suffix *-ion* or *-tion,* then I look for the base word. The base word is *hesitate.* I know the word *hesitate* means "to pause." I say the parts of the word: *hes i ta tion.* Then I read the word: *hesitation.*

Use the Multisyllabic Word routine on p. DI•1 to help students read these other words from *Satchel Paige: havoc, paycheck, teammates, rickety, powerful,* and *exhaled.* Be sure students understand the meanings of words such as *rickety* and *exhaled.*

Use *Strategies for Word Analysis*, Lesson 4, with students who have difficulty mastering word analysis and need practice with decodable text.

Audio CD AudioText

2 Read *Satchel Paige,* pp. 94–103

BEFORE READING *The Chicago American Giants* gives information about African American baseball players who played in special leagues because they could not play in the major leagues. This selection tells about an African American baseball player, Satchel Paige. Using the Picture Walk routine on p. DI•1, guide students through the text, asking questions such as those listed below. Then read the question on p. 95. Together, set a purpose for reading.

pp. 97–99 Look at the setting in these pictures. How are the pictures similar to the photographs in *The Chicago American Giants?*

p. 107 How does the crowd feel about Satchel Paige? How can you tell? *(The crowd and the players admire him. The team is lined up watching him. The crowd is cheering and trying to shake his hand.*

DURING READING Follow the Guiding Comprehension routine on pp. 96–103. Have students read along with you while tracking the print or do a choral reading of the selection. Stop every two pages to ask what students have learned so far. Prompt as necessary.

- How would you describe Satchel Paige?
- What major events have happened so far in Paige's life and career?

AFTER READING What have you learned so far? What do you think you will learn about tomorrow? Reread passages with students for comprehension as needed.

Monitor Progress

Word and Story Reading

If...	then...
If... students have difficulty reading multisyllabic words in the selection,	**then...** have them look for and read meaningful parts in the words or have them chunk words with no recognizable parts.
If... students need practice reading words fluently,	**then...** use the Fluent Word Reading Routine on the DI tab.
If... students have difficulty reading along with the group,	**then...** have them follow along as they listen to the AudioText.

Advanced

ROUTINE

DAY 2

1 Extend Vocabulary

CONTEXT CLUES Choose and read a sentence or passage containing a difficult word, such as this passage from p. 3 of *African American Athletes:* "Even while they're struggling through adversity, the greatest athletes must find a way of masking their weaknesses from their opponents." I'm not sure what the word *adversity* means. I look at the sentence to find clues to the meaning of the word. I see the word *struggling*—adversity is something that you need to struggle against. The author goes on to say that people under adversity find a way of masking weakness. *Adversity* must mean "a difficult or challenging situation." Point out that context clues aren't always found in the same sentence as the unknown word—sometimes the context clues occur in the sentence before or after the sentence with the unknown word. Remind students to use this strategy as they read *Satchel Paige*.

Audio CD AudioText

2 Read *Satchel Paige,* pp. 94–103

BEFORE READING In *African American Athletes,* you read about the challenges faced by many African American athletes throughout history. Today's selection gives more details about the life of Satchel Paige and the personal characteristics that allowed him to meet his challenges. As you read, look for details about his challenges and about his personal traits.

Have students write two questions about Satchel Paige and his life and record them in their Strategy Response Logs (p. 94).

CRITICAL THINKING Have students read pp. 94–103 independently. Encourage them to think critically. For example, ask:

- What did you read about African American athletes in the book yesterday? How does that information connect to what you are reading about Satchel Paige in this selection?

AFTER READING Have partners discuss the selection and share their Strategy Response Log entries. Have them tell whether they can answer the questions they posed. Ask what new question they would like to ask (p. 103). Then have students write a brief character sketch of Satchel Paige, describing his most striking qualities.

Group Time

DAY 3

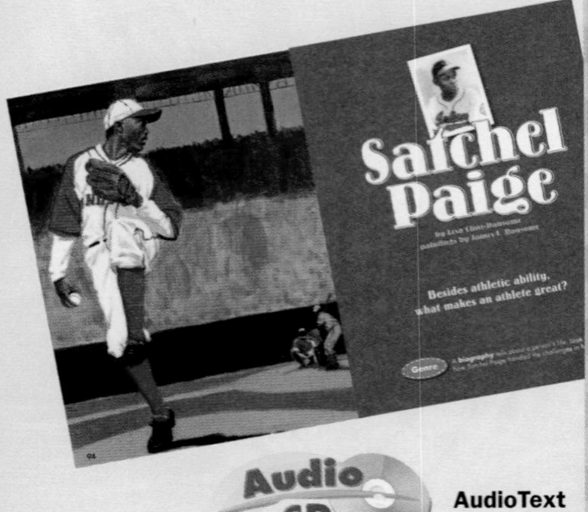

Audio CD AudioText

Strategic Intervention

ROUTINE

1 Reinforce Comprehension

SKILL SEQUENCE Have students explain the meaning of *sequence. (The sequence is the order in which things happen.)* If necessary, review the idea of sequence and provide a model. The sequence is the order in which things happen. If I make a sandwich, for example, I put peanut butter on the bread slices first. Next, I put jelly on the bread. Then I put the pieces of bread together to make a sandwich. You can look for clues to figure out sequence, such as words like *first* and *later,* and dates.

Write events from *Satchel Paige* on the board. Have students put the events in order. They can retell the events and insert clue words, such as *first, then,* and *next.*

Satchel develops a unique style of pitching.
Satchel gets called up to the Negro Baseball League.
Satchel decides to become a baseball player.
Satchel moves from one team to another.

2 Read *Satchel Paige,* pp. 104–107

BEFORE READING Have students retell what happened in the selection so far. Ask: What questions did you have before you read? Were you able to find the answers to your questions? How did asking questions help you set a purpose for your reading? Reread the last paragraph of p. 101. Then model asking questions about your read. After I read this paragraph, I wondered what it would be like to travel on an old bus. I wondered if the bus ever broke down and left the players stranded, unable to play. I wondered how Satchel and the other players felt about all the traveling they had to do. I read on to see if my questions were answered. Remind students to ask questions as they read. How does asking questions help them set a purpose for reading? **STRATEGY Ask Questions**

DURING READING Follow the Guiding Comprehension routine on pp. 104–107. Have students read along with you while tracking the print or do a choral reading. Stop every page or two to ask students about the selection. Prompt as necessary.

- Describe the meeting between Satchel's team and Josh Gibson's team.
- What personal traits helped Satchel Paige meet personal challenges?

AFTER READING Describe Satchel Paige's personal challenges. Tell what he does to meet these challenges. Reread with students as needed. Tell them that tomorrow they will read "The Girls of Summer," a selection that tells about a baseball league for female players.

Monitor Progress

Word and Selection Reading

If... students have difficulty reading multisyllabic words in the selection,	**then...** have them look for and read meaningful parts in the words or have them chunk words with no recognizable parts.
If... students have difficulty reading along with the group,	**then...** have them follow along as they listen to the AudioText.

Advanced

ROUTINE

DAY 3

1 Extend Comprehension

SKILL SEQUENCE Have students identify the main events of the selection and put them in correct time order. They might place the events on a time line or other graphic organizer.

STRATEGY ASK QUESTIONS Invite students to write questions they have about Satchel Paige and about the Negro Baseball League. How might they find the answers to these questions? Tell students that reading the remainder of *Satchel Paige* may answer some of their questions but that they may have to use reference sources to answer some of their questions.

Audio CD AudioText

2 Read *Satchel Paige*, pp. 104–107

BEFORE READING Have students recall what has happened in the selection so far. Remind them to think about the sequence of events and ask themselves questions as they read the remainder of *Satchel Paige.*

CRITICAL THINKING Have students read pp. 104–107 independently. Encourage them to think critically. For example, ask:

- What do you think of Josh Gibson and Satchel Paige's "meeting"? How did the actions of the two men show what kind of people they were?
- Would you have liked to see this baseball game? What was important about it?
- What do you think it would have been like to be a baseball fan during this period of history? How would you feel about segregated leagues?

AFTER READING Have students complete the Strategy Response Log activity (p. 106). Have them meet with you to discuss the selection. Then have them create a Hall of Fame plaque or a baseball card for either Satchel Paige or Josh Gibson.

Group Time

DAY 4

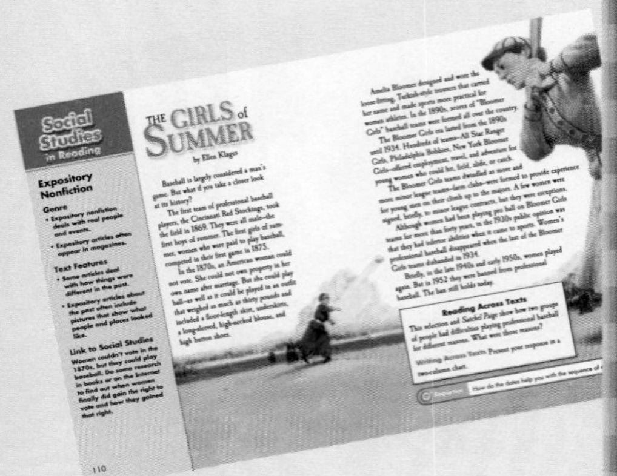

AudioText

Strategic Intervention

ROUTINE

1 Practice Retelling

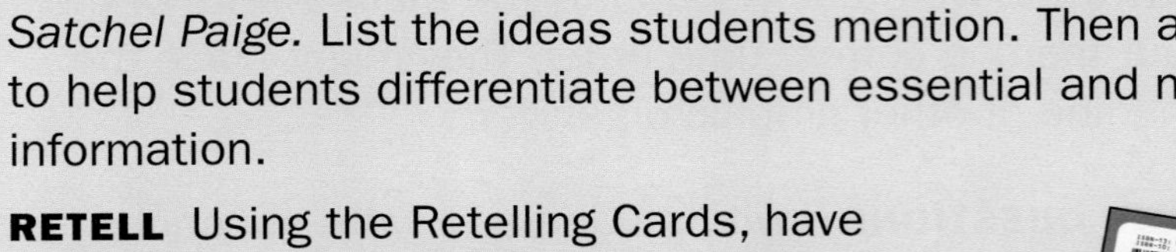

REVIEW MAIN IDEAS Help students identify the main ideas in *Satchel Paige.* List the ideas students mention. Then ask questions to help students differentiate between essential and nonessential information.

RETELL Using the Retelling Cards, have students work with partners to retell the important ideas. Show partners how to summarize in as few words as possible. Monitor retelling and prompt students as needed. For example, ask:

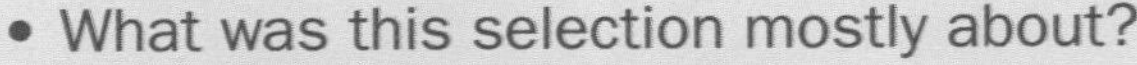
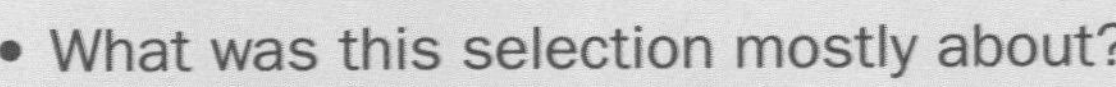

- What was this selection mostly about?
- What did you learn from reading this selection?

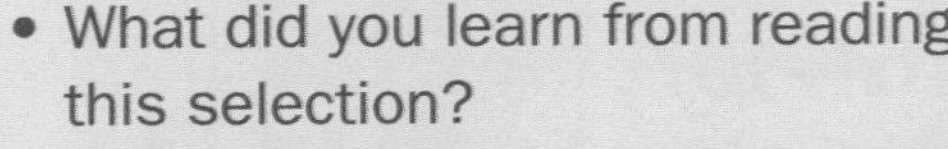

- What was the author trying to tell us?

If students struggle, model a fluent retelling.

2 Read "The Girls of Summer"

BEFORE READING Read the genre information on p. 110. Recall the Read Aloud "Teammates" and the selection *Satchel Paige.* Remind students that all of these selections are nonfiction, or selections about real people and events. As we read "The Girls of Summer," look for facts about women who played baseball in the past.

Read the rest of the panel on p. 110. Lead students to look closely at the illustration. Ask them what the illustration tells them about what it was like to play baseball in the past. Students might notice the women's uniforms and talk about how difficult it would be to play baseball in a skirt!

DURING READING Have students read along with you while tracking the print or do a choral reading of the selection. As you read, stop to talk about details that show how challenging it must have been for women to play baseball long ago.

AFTER READING Have students share their reactions to the selection. Then guide them through the Reading Across Texts and Writing Across Texts activities, prompting if necessary.

- Why was it difficult for Satchel Paige to play baseball? Why was it difficult for women? How were their challenges the same? How were they different?
- What will you title your chart? How will you be sure to include enough details about Satchel Paige and women baseball players?

Monitor Progress

Word and Selection Reading

If... students have difficulty reading multisyllabic words in the selection,	**then...** have them look for and read meaningful parts in the words or have them chunk words with no recognizable parts.
If... students have difficulty reading along with the group,	**then...** have them follow along as they listen to the AudioText.

Advanced

ROUTINE

1 Read "The Girls of Summer"

CRITICAL THINKING Have students read pp. 110–111 independently. Encourage them to think critically. For example, ask:

- Why do you think that women wanted to play baseball when it was so difficult for them to do so?
- Do you think that women's baseball helped change public opinion about the role of women and about what rights women should and should not have? Explain.

AFTER READING Have students meet with you to discuss the selection and Reading Across Texts. Have students do Writing Across Texts independently.

AudioText

2 Extend Genre Study

RESEARCH Have students use online or print resources to find out more about the women's baseball leagues. Encourage them to ask questions to guide their research, such as "Were there any famous female players? How much money did the female players make? What did their friends and families think of them for playing baseball?"

WRITE Have students use information they found to write a short expository piece that might have appeared in a 1940s sports magazine. Be sure the writing includes facts that would help a reader understand the challenges that women faced as they played baseball.

Group Time

Strategic Intervention

ROUTINE

DAY 5

1 Reread for Fluency

MODEL Tell students that good readers pay attention to phrasing when they read. If words are between commas, for example, you would pause before and after the phrase, reading the entire phrase together. Prepositional phrases and other types of phrases would also be read together, without pausing between the words in the phrase. Read p. 5 aloud for students. Point out the various prepositional phrases, showing how you string those words together to make meaningful phrases.

PRACTICE Have students reread passages from *The Chicago American Giants* with a partner or individually. For optimal fluency, they should reread three or four times. Assess the fluency of students in this group using p. 111a.

2 Retell Leveled Reader *The Chicago American Giants*

Model how to retell by looking at important details in the photographs. Model with pp. 3–5. Then ask students to retell *The Chicago American Giants*. You might have them focus on retelling one page at a time. Prompt them as needed.

- What was this page mostly about?
- What did you learn from reading this selection?
- What do you think the author is trying to tell us?

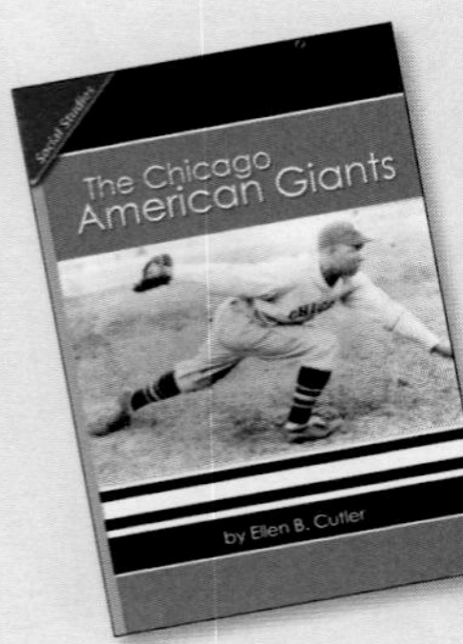

PearsonSuccessNet.com

Monitor Progress

Fluency

If... students have difficulty reading fluently,	**then...** provide additional fluency practice by pairing nonfluent readers with fluent ones.

For alternate Leveled Reader lesson plans that teach **Sequence, Ask Questions,** and **Lesson Vocabulary,** see pp. LR28–LR36.

On-Level

ROUTINE

1 Reread for Fluency

MODEL Tell students that good oral readers use phrasing when they read. They think about phrases that would make sense together, such as all the words in a prepositional phrase or all the words in a clause. Model with p. 3 of *Famous Women Athletes.* First read with proper phrasing, such as "In the 1800s," "held in 1896," "By the beginning of the 1900s," and "At those Olympic Games." Then read the same page interrupting the phrases with pauses: "In the (pause) 1800s"; "By the beginning of (pause) the 1900s"; "At those (pause) Olympic Games." Discuss the difference in the way the readings sound and how the first reading helps with understanding.

PRACTICE Have students reread passages from *Famous Women Athletes* with a partner or individually. Remind them to think about phrasing when they read. For optimal fluency, students should reread three or four times. As students read, monitor fluency and provide corrective feedback. Students in this group were assessed in Week 3.

2 Retell Leveled Reader *Famous Women Athletes*

Have students skim as they retell the main ideas in *Famous Women Athletes.* Prompt as needed.

- What was the section mostly about?
- What personal characteristics of women athletes helped them meet challenges?
- What do you think the author is trying to teach us?

Advanced

ROUTINE

1 Reread for Fluency

PRACTICE Have students reread passages from the Leveled Reader *African American Athletes* with a partner or individually. As students read, monitor fluency and provide corrective feedback. If students read fluently on the first reading, they do not need to reread three to four times. Students in this group were assessed in Week 1.

2 Revisit Leveled Reader *African American Athletes*

RETELL Have students retell the Leveled Reader *African American Athletes.*

NOW TRY THIS Have students share their interviews with Jackie Robinson. They may want to "perform" their interviews live, with one student taking on the role of Jackie Robinson while the other takes on the role of reporter. Be sure that students focus on the challenges that Jackie Robinson faced and how he met those challenges.

Group Time

Strategic Intervention

ROUTINE

1 Build Background

REINFORCE CONCEPTS Display the Life in a New Country Concept Web. This week's concept is *life in a new country.* The selections focus on the experiences of immigrants, or people who move from one country to another. Discuss the meaning of each word on the web, using the definitions on p. 112l and the Concept Vocabulary routine on p. DI•1.

CONNECT TO READING This week you will read about people who moved from one country to another. What challenges do you think people would encounter when they move to a new country? How might they meet these challenges?

PearsonSuccessNet.com

2 Read Leveled Reader *Immigrant Children in New York City*

BEFORE READING Using the Picture Walk routine on p. DI•1, guide students through the text focusing on key concepts and vocabulary. Ask questions such as:

p. 3 What do you notice about the street in the photograph? What are the people doing? What do you think it would be like to live there?

pp. 6–7 Look at the photographs. Describe what the inside of the rich New Yorker's home might look like. Describe what the inside of the immigrant's home might look like. Why would it be more challenging to live in the immigrant's home?

pp. 8–9 This photograph shows the working conditions of the immigrants. What must it have been like to work in these conditions? *(The immigrants were packed closely together in a place with poor lighting. It looks like an uncomfortable place to work.)*

DURING READING Read pp. 3–5 aloud, while students track the print. Do a choral reading of pp. 6–9. If students are capable, have them read and discuss the remainder of the book with a partner. Ask: What was life like for immigrant children during the early 1900s in New York City? Look for details that tell what their lives were like and the ways in which people tried to help them.

AFTER READING Encourage pairs of students to discuss the challenges faced by the immigrants in New York City. *Immigrant Children in New York City* describes what it was like for people to come to New York City from other countries and what made life challenging for the newcomers. Tomorrow you will read about a sixteen-year-old boy trying to make a new life for himself in New York City.

Monitor Progress

Selection Reading and Comprehension

If... students have difficulty reading the selection with a partner,	**then...** have them follow along as they listen to the Online Leveled Reader Audio.
If... students have trouble understanding difficulties that immigrant children faced in New York City in the early 1800s,	**then...** reread pp. 6–8 and discuss the desire for education versus the need to work.

For alternate Leveled Reader lesson plans that teach **Cause and Effect,** **Summarize,** and **Lesson Vocabulary,** see pp. LR37–LR45.

On-Level

ROUTINE

1 Build Background

DEVELOP VOCABULARY Write the word *immigration* on the board and ask students to define it in their own words. *(Immigration is coming to a new country to live.)* Why might people become immigrants? *(They might want to find a new job or live in a better place.)* Invite students to discuss words such as *advised, newcomer, peddler,* and other words from the Leveled Reader *A Nation of Many Colors.* Use the Concept Vocabulary routine on p. DI•1 as needed.

2 Read Leveled Reader *A Nation of Many Colors*

BEFORE READING Have students create a three-column chart. This book tells about three different ethnic groups in the United States: Hispanic Americans, African Americans, and Jewish Americans. As you read, list details about each group in a column on the chart. Include the customs, cultural products, languages, and values of each group.

DURING READING Have students follow along as you read pp. 3–8. Then let them complete the book on their own. Remind students to add details to each column of the chart as they read.

AFTER READING Have students compare their charts. Have students compare and contrast information about the various groups in the United States. Encourage students to discuss the personal characteristics of these groups as they became part of the United States. Invite students to consider these personal characteristics as they read *Shutting Out the Sky.*

Advanced

ROUTINE

1 Read Leveled Reader *The Land of Opportunity*

BEFORE READING Recall the Read Aloud "Journey to Ellis Island." What challenges did the immigrants introduced in "Journey to Ellis Island" face when they first arrived? *(They had to carry all their belongings up a huge flight of stairs. They had to wait in a crowded room that was hot and noisy.)*

Today you will read a selection about the journey that many immigrants made to the United States. Some of these immigrants landed at New York City and were processed at Ellis Island.

CRITICAL THINKING Have students read the Leveled Reader independently. Encourage them to think critically. For example, ask:

- What do you think was the most difficult part of the journey for immigrants?
- Do you think the journey was worth all the hardships? Why or why not?

AFTER READING Have students review the selection to find five or more unfamiliar words and determine their meanings. Then ask them to use the words in statements or questions about immigrants to the United States. Have students meet with you to discuss the selection and share their statements and questions.

2 Independent Extension Activity

NOW TRY THIS Assign "Now Try This" on pp. 22–23 of *The Land of Opportunity* for students to work on throughout the week.

Group Time

DAY 2

Strategic Intervention

ROUTINE

1 Word Study/Phonics

LESSON VOCABULARY Use p. 114b to review the meanings of *advice, advised, circumstances, elbow, hustled, immigrants, luxury, newcomer,* and *peddler.* Have individuals practice with word cards.

DECODING MULTISYLLABIC WORDS Write *awkwardly*, saying the word as you write it. Then model how to decode a word with a suffix. This is a three-syllable word formed from the base word *awkward* and the suffix *-ly*. First I cover the suffix and read the base word: *awkward.* Then I blend the base word and the suffix to read the whole word *awkwardly*. The suffix *-ly* means "in a way." So *awkwardly* means "in an awkward way."

Use the Multisyllabic Word routine on p. DI•1 to help students read these other words from *Shutting Out the Sky: scribbled, stranger, nervous, miserable, business,* and *earnings.* Be sure students understand the meanings of words such as *nervous* and *miserable*.

Use *Strategies for Word Analysis*, Lesson 5, with students who have difficulty mastering word analysis and need practice with decodable text.

Audio CD AudioText

2 Read *Shutting Out the Sky,* pp. 116–123

BEFORE READING *Immigrant Children in New York City* gave information about what it was like for immigrants who made new lives in New York. This selection tells about one immigrant in New York who becomes a peddler to make a living in his new country.

Using the Picture Walk routine on p. DI•1, guide students through the text, asking questions such as those listed below. Then read the question on p. 117. Together, set a purpose for reading.

pp. 116–117 What do you see in the photograph? Yes, a man is looking across the river at a large city. Do you suppose he is an immigrant looking at his new home? How do you suppose he feels?

p. 118 Which of these images shows the idea of hope in a new life? Which shows that life in New York was difficult for immigrants?

DURING READING Follow the Guiding Comprehension routine on pp. 118–123. Have students read along with you while tracking the print or do a choral reading of the selection. Stop every two pages to ask what students have learned so far. Prompt as necessary.

- What have you learned about Marcus Ravage?
- Why did Marcus Ravage come to the United States?

AFTER READING What have you learned so far? What do you think you will learn about tomorrow? Reread passages as needed.

Monitor Progress

Word and Story Reading

If... students have difficulty reading multisyllabic words in the selection,	**then...** have them look for and read meaningful parts in the words or have them chunk words with no recognizable parts.
If... students need practice reading words fluently,	**then...** use the Fluent Word Reading Routine on the DI tab.
If... students have difficulty reading along with the group,	**then...** have them follow along as they listen to the AudioText.

Advanced

ROUTINE

1 Extend Vocabulary

CONTEXT CLUES Choose and read a sentence or passage containing a difficult word, such as this passage from p. 4 of *The Land of Opportunity:* "Immigrants left their home countries for all kinds of reasons. Some left because they were afraid that their government would imprison them or discriminate against them for their religious beliefs." I'm not sure what the word *discriminate* means. I look at the sentence to find clues to the meaning of the word. The author says that immigrants were afraid that their governments would imprison them or discriminate against them. The author goes on to say that the immigrants would be discriminated against for their religious beliefs. How would you use these clues to figure out the meaning of the word *discriminate?* Point out that context clues aren't always found in the same sentence as the unknown word—sometimes the context clue occurs in the sentence before or after the sentence with the unknown word. If needed, share the meaning. *Discriminate* means "to judge or treat unfairly because of a person's beliefs." Remind students to use this strategy as they read *Shutting Out the Sky.*

DAY 2

AudioText

2 Read *Shutting Out the Sky,* pp. 116–123

BEFORE READING In *The Land of Opportunity,* you read about the challenges faced by different groups of people who started new lives in the United States. Today's selection gives more details about the life of one immigrant in New York City. As you read, look for details about his challenges and what he did to meet those challenges.

Have students write their predictions about the selection in their Strategy Response Logs (p. 116).

CREATIVE THINKING Have students read pp. 116–123 independently. Encourage them to think creatively. For example, say:

- Put yourself in Marcus's place. What things would you have done the same as Marcus? What things would you have done differently?

AFTER READING Have partners discuss the selection and share their Strategy Response Log entries. Have them tell whether their predictions were accurate. Have them write new predictions (p.123). Have them write a letter from Marcus to his family back home. Meet with students to discuss the selection and their letters.

Shutting Out the Sky

Group Time

DAY 3

Audio CD AudioText

Strategic Intervention

ROUTINE

1 Reinforce Comprehension

SKILL CAUSE AND EFFECT Ask students to explain the difference between a cause and an effect. *(An effect is something that happens. A cause makes that effect happen.)* If necessary, provide a model. If it rains and I am outside, I get wet. The cause is the rain. The effect is that I get wet. When reading, sometimes there are clue words for causes and effects, such as *because, so,* and *as a result.*

Write causes and effects from the selection on the board. Have students identify the causes and effects.

Marcus didn't bring his coat *(cause)* **so he was cold.** *(effect)*
The family had seven members *(cause)* **so their apartment was crowded.** *(effect)*
Because Marcus was new to America, *(cause)* **there were many things about the country he didn't understand.** *(effect)*

2 Read *Shutting Out the Sky,* pp. 124–127

BEFORE READING Have students retell what happened in the selection so far. Ask: What has happened in the selection so far? Think about the most important ideas. Then say: A summary is a telling of the most important ideas. When you tell a friend about a movie you saw, you don't tell every detail, just the most important ones. Those important ideas are a summary. Model creating a summary by naming the most important events so far in *Shutting Out the Sky.* Remind students to think about the most important details as they read and include those details in a summary. **STRATEGY Summarize**

DURING READING Follow the Guiding Comprehension routine on pp. 124–127. Have students read along with you while tracking print or do a choral reading. Stop every page or two to ask students about the selection. Prompt as necessary.

- What challenges did Mrs. Segal present to Marcus?
- What did Mrs. Segal want Marcus to do?
- Who gave Marcus good advice?

AFTER READING Describe the challenges Marcus faced in his new country. Tell what he did to meet these challenges. Reread with students for comprehension as needed. Tell them that tomorrow they will read "The Immigrant Experience," a selection with an e-mail message and online resources about immigration.

Monitor Progress

Word and Selection Reading

If... students have difficulty reading multisyllabic words in the selection,	**then...** have them look for and read meaningful parts in the words or have them chunk words with no recognizable parts.
If... students have difficulty reading along with the group,	**then...** have them follow along as they listen to the AudioText.

Advanced

ROUTINE

DAY 3

1 Extend Comprehension

SKILL CAUSE AND EFFECT Have students create a two-column chart with the headings *cause* and *effect*. They can place *causes* and *effects* from the selection in the appropriate places in the graphic organizer.

STRATEGY SUMMARIZE Invite students to summarize the first sections of the selection. As students summarize, ask them if they have included the most important pieces of information in their summaries.

2 Read *Shutting Out the Sky*, pp. 124–127

BEFORE READING Have students recall what has happened in the selection so far. Remind them to think about causes and effects and the most important ideas as they read the remainder of *Shutting Out the Sky.*

CRITICAL THINKING Have students read pp. 124–127 independently. Encourage them to think critically. For example, ask:

- What things does Marcus find so amazing about the United States? Why do you think the author focused on these details in the selection?
- What was difficult about Marcus's job as a peddler? What other job choices were possible for immigrants?
- Marcus ends up being very successful in his new country. What qualities does Marcus have that predict his success in the future?

AFTER READING Have students complete the Strategy Response Log activity (p. 126). Then have them create an advertisement for Marcus's peddling business. The advertisement could include a challenge or goal that Marcus has for his business. Meet with students to discuss the selection and their advertisements

Audio CD AudioText

Group Time

DAY 4

AudioText

Strategic Intervention

ROUTINE

1 Practice Retelling

REVIEW MAIN IDEAS Help students identify the main ideas in *Shutting Out the Sky.* List the ideas students mention. Then ask questions to help students differentiate between essential and nonessential information.

RETELL Using the Retelling Cards, have students work with partners to retell the important ideas. Show partners how to summarize in as few words as possible. Monitor retelling and prompt students as needed. For example, ask:

- What was this selection mostly about?
- What did you learn from reading this selection?
- What was the author trying to tell us?

If students struggle, model a fluent retelling.

2 Read "The Immigrant Experience"

BEFORE READING Read the genre information on p. 130. Point out that an e-mail is a way to get information from someone. Ask students what they know about e-mails. As we read "The Immigrant Experience," think about the way that the writer of the e-mail researches to find important information.

Read the rest of the panel on p. 130. Lead students to examine the e-mail to identify important parts, such as the address box and the message.

DURING READING Have students read along with you while tracking the print or do a choral reading of the selection. As you read, discuss the idea that the message sounds like a friendly letter but that it contains only the most important information that the researcher needs.

AFTER READING Have students share their reactions to the selection. Then guide them through the Reading Across Texts and Writing Across Texts activities, prompting if necessary.

- Use a Venn diagram to compare and contrast the experiences of the two immigrants.
- What details from your Venn diagram do you think are most important to include in your paragraph? Be sure your paragraph's beginning sentence tells what you're writing about.

Monitor Progress

Word and Selection Reading

If... students have difficulty reading multisyllabic words in the selection,	**then...** have them look for and read meaningful parts in the words or have them chunk words with no recognizable parts.
If... students have difficulty reading along with the group,	**then...** have them follow along as they listen to the AudioText.

Advanced

ROUTINE

1 Read "The Immigrant Experience"

CRITICAL THINKING Have students read pp. 130–133 independently. Encourage them to think critically. For example, ask:

- Do you think the Internet is a good source to use for research? Explain why or why not.
- Why do you think Rachel found the article so surprising? What did you find surprising about the article?

AFTER READING Have students meet with you to discuss, the selection and Reading Across Texts. Have students do Writing Across Texts independently.

2 Extend Genre Study

RESEARCH Have students use online or print resources to find out more about immigrants today. Discuss with students that not all Internet sources are accurate. Help them recognize sources that are acceptable, such as sites hosted by the government or universities.

WRITE Have students use information they found to write a short expository piece that could appear in a Web site about immigration. Be sure the writing includes facts that would help a reader understand the challenges that people face when they move to a new country.

DAY 4

Audio CD AudioText

Group Time

Strategic Intervention

DAY 5

ROUTINE

1 Reread for Fluency

MODEL Tell students that good readers pause at appropriate places when they read. They pause at periods and commas, and they also pause to emphasize important words and feelings. Read aloud p. 3 of the Leveled Reader *Immigrant Children in New York*. Emphasize the pauses at the end of each sentence. Have students note that the pauses make the selection seem dramatic and help the reader picture the scene more clearly.

PRACTICE Have students silently reread passages from *Immigrant Children in New York City*. Then have partners reread passages aloud. For optimal fluency, they should reread three or four times. Assess any students you have not yet checked during this unit.

2 Retell Leveled Reader *Immigrant Children in New York City*

Model how to retell by skimming for important details and looking at boldfaced words. Model with pp. 3–5. Then ask students to retell *Immigrant Children in New York City.* You might have them focus on retelling one page at a time. Prompt them as needed.

- What was this page or section mostly about?
- What did you learn about immigrant children and the people trying to help them?
- What do you think the author is trying to tell us about the challenges of moving to a new home?

PearsonSuccessNet.com

Monitor Progress

Fluency

If... students have difficulty reading fluently,	**then...** provide additional fluency practice by pairing nonfluent readers with fluent ones.

For alternate Leveled Reader lesson plans that teach **Cause and Effect, Summarize,** and **Lesson Vocabulary,** see pp. LR37–LR45.

On-Level

ROUTINE

1 Reread for Fluency

MODEL Tell students that good oral readers pause when they read. They pause at periods, commas, and places where they want to add emphasis to the reading. Model with p. 6 of *A Nation of Many Colors*. Be sure to pause at periods and commas. Discuss with students the idea that natural language contains pauses. How does pausing make the reading sound more like "real" speech?

PRACTICE Have students reread passages from *A Nation of Many Colors* with a partner or individually. Remind them to think about appropriate places to pause. Pauses should be comfortable. For optimal fluency, they should reread three or four times. As students read, monitor fluency and provide corrective feedback. Assess any students you have not yet checked during this unit.

2 Retell Leveled Reader *A Nation of Many Colors*

Have students skim as they retell the main ideas in *A Nation of Many Colors.* Prompt as needed.

- What was this section mostly about?
- How are the groups of people in the book similar? How are they different?
- What message do you think the author is trying to teach about the melting pot of the United States?

Advanced

ROUTINE

1 Reread for Fluency

PRACTICE Have students reread passages from the Leveled Reader *The Land of Opportunity* with a partner or individually. As As students read, monitor fluency and provide corrective feedback. If students read fluently on the first reading, they do not need to reread three to four times. Assess any students you have not yet checked during this unit.

2 Revisit Leveled Reader *The Land of Opportunity*

RETELL Have students retell the Leveled Reader *The Land of Opportunity.*

NOW TRY THIS Have students complete their immigration projects. You may wish to review their work to see whether they need more ideas. Then, as they share their projects, students can compare their work to the details in the selections. Discuss the challenges of immigration that students included in their projects.

Characters

Understanding characters helps readers comprehend a story and make good predictions about what will happen next. Use this routine to help students understand characters.

1 REVIEW CHARACTER TRAITS

Remind students that readers learn about characters by thinking about what they do, say, and think and how they interact with other characters. Readers infer character traits by thinking about these clues and their own experiences.

2 TEACH CHARACTER DEVELOPMENT

Explain that events in a story often cause a character to change in a significant way, such as in attitudes or beliefs. Students should read to see if this happens to the main character.

3 MODEL INFERRING TRAITS

Provide an example from a story you have read. Model inferring character traits from the character's words and actions. Point out how and why the character changes. Compare characters with each other and with real people.

4 APPLY TO A SELECTION

Read with students a story in which there are well-developed characters. Have students draw conclusions about character traits from clues in the story and their own experiences.

5 USE A GRAPHIC ORGANIZER

Have students record clues about a character in a web. They can record details about what the character said and did and how characters interacted.

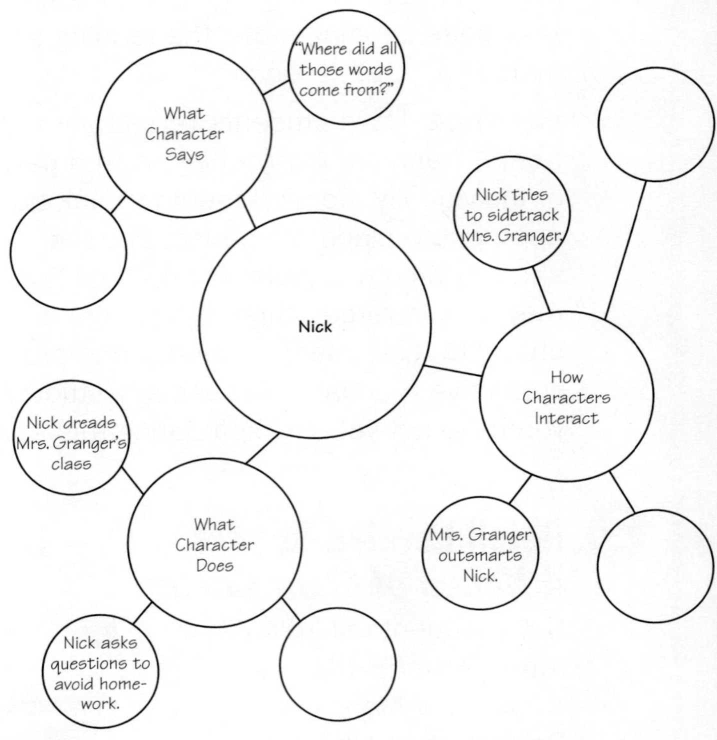

▲ **Graphic Organizer** 16

Research on Characters

"In life and in books, children can sense differences in human beings and are capable of recognizing and responding to well-developed characters. Even in the simplest stories it is possible to find characters that verify truths about human nature."

Rebecca J. Lukens,
A Critical Handbook of Children's Literature

Lukens, Rebecca J. *A Critical Handbook of Children's Literature.* Pearson Education, 2003, p. 94.

Cause and Effect

Students who are able to connect what happens in a selection to the reason why it happens can better understand what they read. In fiction, this skill will help them figure out why characters do what they do. In nonfiction, it will give them a better grasp of factual information. Use the following routine to teach cause and effect.

1 DEMONSTRATE CAUSE AND EFFECT

Remind students that an effect is what happens. A cause is why it happened. Demonstrate by turning out the lights. Ask:

What is the effect? (It is dark.)

What is the cause? (You turned off the lights.)

2 IDENTIFY CAUSE AND EFFECT

Write this sentence on the board: *Because it is raining, I took my umbrella to school.* Explain that sometimes a sentence has a clue word such as *because, so,* or *since* that signals a cause-and-effect relationship. Have volunteers circle the cause *(it is raining)* and the effect *(I took my umbrella)* and underline the clue word *(because).*

3 APPLY TO A SELECTION

Read with students a story that has causes and effects. Several causes can lead to one effect: Sunshine and water make flowers grow. One cause can lead to several effects: Leaving a bike in the hallway can cause someone to trip and break an arm.

4 RECORD CAUSES AND EFFECTS

Have students use a cause-effect chart to record the causes and effects in the selection.

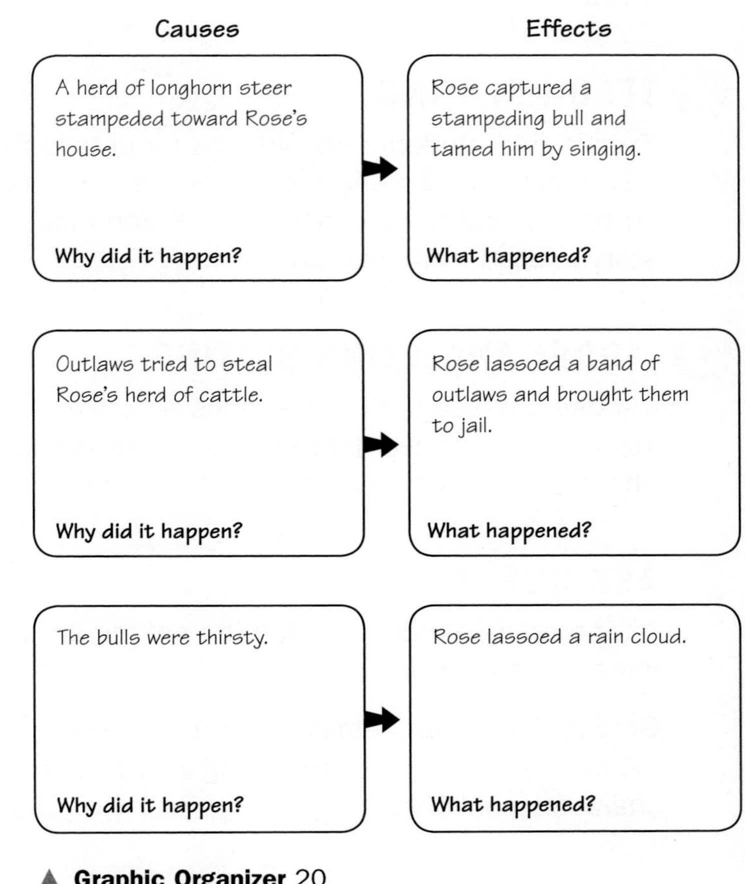

Causes
Effects
A herd of longhorn steer stampeded toward Rose's house.
Why did it happen?
Rose captured a stampeding bull and tamed him by singing.
What happened?
Outlaws tried to steal Rose's herd of cattle.
Why did it happen?
Rose lassoed a band of outlaws and brought them to jail.
What happened?
The bulls were thirsty.
Why did it happen?
Rose lassoed a rain cloud.
What happened?

▲ **Graphic Organizer** 20

Research on Cause and Effect

"A great deal of our thought process has to do with cause and effect. To be fully fluent thinkers, children need to learn the logic of cause and effect."

Stanley Greenspan and Serena Weider,
Learning to Think Abstractly

Greenspan, Stanley, and Serena Weider. "Learning to Think Abstractly." *Scholastic Early Childhood Today* (May/June 1998).

Setting

When students can describe the setting of a story and analyze its effects on characters and plot, they better understand the story. Use this routine to teach setting.

1 DEFINE SETTING

Explain that setting is the time and place in which a story occurs. It may be general (a city in the future) or it may be specific (the *Titanic* in April, 1912).

2 TEACH SETTING

Explain that students should look for details that help them visualize the setting. Sometimes the setting affects the characters, plot, and mood of a story in significant ways.

3 MODEL ANALYZING SETTING

Choose a passage that describes a setting from a story students have not read. Model analyzing the effects of the setting on characters and plot.

4 ASK QUESTIONS

After reading a story in which the setting is integral, ask questions:

Grades 3–4: *What details help you visualize the setting? How does the setting influence a character's actions?*

Grades 5–6: *How does the setting affect the outcome of the story? In what ways does the setting set the mood? How would the story be different if it were set in a different time or place?*

5 USE A GRAPHIC ORGANIZER

Have students fill in a web with details that help them visualize the setting of a story. Tell them to look for sensory details that describe the sights, sounds, textures, tastes, and smells of the setting.

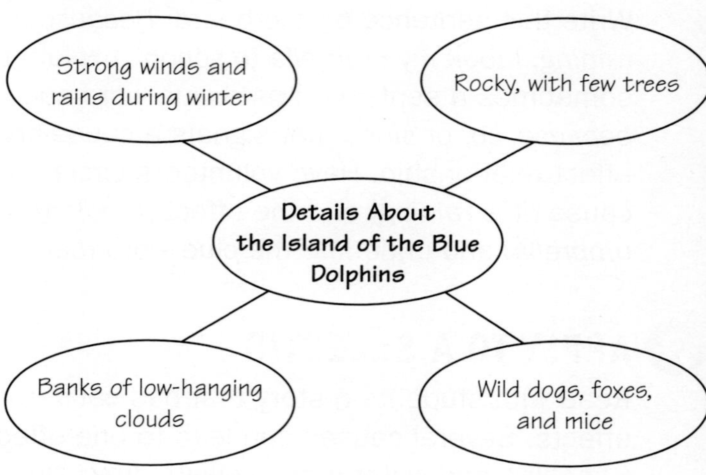

▲ **Graphic Organizer** 15

Research on Setting

"When reading narrative, good readers attend closely to the setting and characters."

Nell K. Duke and P. David Pearson,
"Effective Practices for Developing Reading Comprehension"

Duke, Nell K., and Pearson, P. David. "Effective Practices for Developing Reading Comprehension," In *What Research Has to Say About Reading Instruction,* edited by Alan E. Farstrup and S. Jay Samuels. Third Edition. International Reading Association, 2002, p. 206.

Sequence

Keeping track of the sequence of events helps students understand what they read. Use this routine to help students develop sequence skills.

1 DISCUSS SEQUENCE

Tell students it is important to keep track of the sequence, or order, of events to understand some stories and articles. Discuss a story recently read in which the sequence of events was crucial to a correct understanding of the story.

2 TEACH CLUE WORDS

Write clue words on the board that can signal sequence, such as *first, next, then,* and *finally.* Explain that these words show the order in which things happen. Also teach that dates and times of the day also signal sequence.

3 SEQUENCE SENTENCE STRIPS

Write a clear sequence of events on sentence strips. Partners can work together to place the strips in the correct order. They can retell the events, inserting clue words to show the sequence.

4 RECORD A SEQUENCE ON A CHART

- After reading a story, students can work in pairs to create story sequence charts to show the order of events.
- For a nonfiction selection, partners can create time lines to show the chronological sequence of events.

Title
Satchel Paige
Characters
Leroy "Satchel" Paige, Josh Gibson
Setting
United States, 1923 – 1942
Events

1. In 1923 at the age of 19, Satchel Paige became a semipro pitcher.
2. Satchel moved up to the Negro major leagues in 1924.
3. Satchel gets married in 1946.
4. Satchel struck out Josh Gibson, the best hitter in the league, at the 1942 Negro World Series.

▲ **Graphic Organizer** 9

Research on Sequence

"Classes that read widely will encounter all sorts of ways authors play with time; recognizing flashbacks and attending to words and phrases denoting the passage of time or the sequential order of events are crucial to comprehension."

Sharon Kane,
"Teaching Skills Within Meaningful Contexts"

Kane, Sharon. "Teaching Skills Within Meaningful Contexts." *The Reading Teacher,* vol. 52, no. 2 (October 1998), pp. 182–184.

Cause and Effect

Students who are able to connect what happens in a selection to the reason why it happens can better understand what they read. In fiction, this skill will help them figure out why characters do what they do. In nonfiction, it will give them a better grasp of factual information. Use the following routine to teach cause and effect.

1 DEMONSTRATE CAUSE AND EFFECT

Remind students that an effect is what happens. A cause is why it happened. Demonstrate by turning out the lights. Ask:

What is the effect? (It is dark.)

What is the cause? (You turned off the lights.)

2 IDENTIFY CAUSE AND EFFECT

Write this sentence on the board: *Because it is raining, I took my umbrella to school.* Explain that sometimes a sentence has a clue word such as *because, so,* or *since* that signals a cause-and-effect relationship. Have volunteers circle the cause *(it is raining)* and the effect *(I took my umbrella)* and underline the clue word *(because).*

3 APPLY TO A SELECTION

Read with students a story that has causes and effects. Several causes can lead to one effect: Sunshine and water make flowers grow. One cause can lead to several effects: Leaving a bike in the hallway can cause someone to trip and break an arm.

4 RECORD CAUSES AND EFFECTS

Have students use a cause-effect chart to record the causes and effects in the selection.

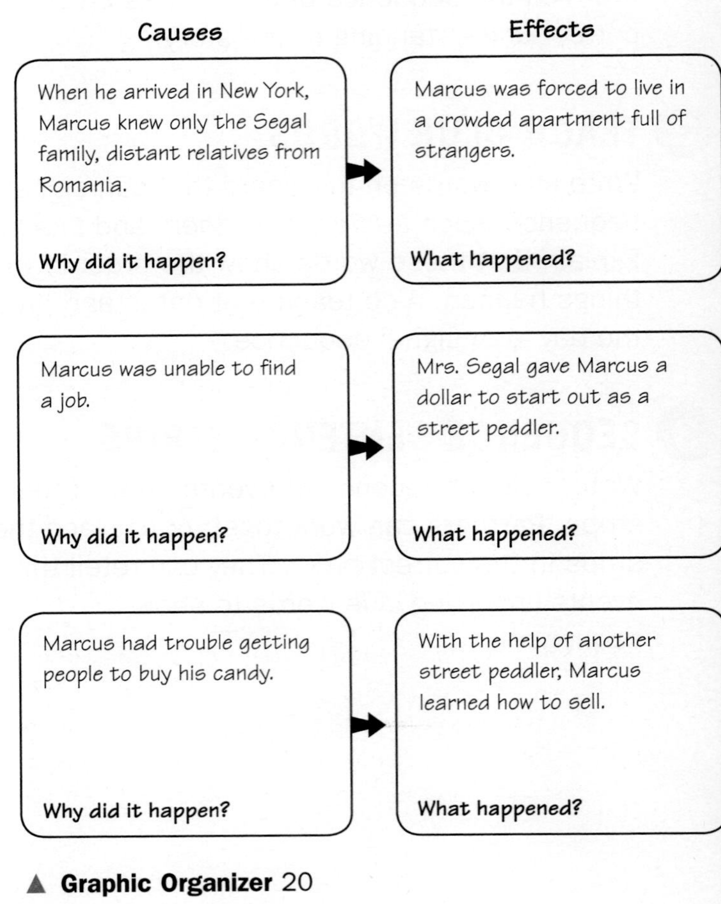

Causes
Effects
When he arrived in New York, Marcus knew only the Segal family, distant relatives from Romania.
Why did it happen?
Marcus was forced to live in a crowded apartment full of strangers.
What happened?
Marcus was unable to find a job.
Why did it happen?
Mrs. Segal gave Marcus a dollar to start out as a street peddler.
What happened?
Marcus had trouble getting people to buy his candy.
Why did it happen?
With the help of another street peddler, Marcus learned how to sell.
What happened?

▲ **Graphic Organizer** 20

Research on Cause and Effect

"A great deal of our thought process has to do with cause and effect. To be fully fluent thinkers, children need to learn the logic of cause and effect."

Stanley Greenspan and Serena Weider,
Learning to Think Abstractly

Greenspan, Stanley, and Serena Weider. "Learning to Think Abstractly." *Scholastic Early Childhood Today* (May/June 1998).

Providing students with reading materials they can and want to read is an important step toward developing fluent readers. A running record allows you to determine each student's instructional and independent reading level. Information on how to take a running record is provided on pp. DI•59–DI•60.

Instructional Reading Level

Only approximately 1 in 10 words will be difficult when reading a selection from the Student Edition for students who are at grade level. (A typical fifth-grader reads approximately 120–140 words correct per minute.)

- Students reading at grade level should read regularly from the Student Edition and On-Level Leveled Readers, with teacher support as suggested in the Teacher's Editions.
- Students reading below grade level can read the Strategic Intervention Leveled Readers. Instructional plans can be found in the Teacher's Edition and the Leveled Reader Teaching Guide.
- Students who are reading above grade level can read the Advanced Leveled Readers. Instructional plans can be found in the Teacher's Edition and the Leveled Reader Teaching Guide.

Independent Reading Level

Students should read regularly in independent-level texts in which no more than approximately 1 in 20 words is difficult for the reader. Other factors that make a book easy to read include the student's interest in the topic, the amount of text on a page, how well illustrations support meaning, and the complexity and familiarity of the concepts. Suggested books for self-selected reading are provided for each lesson on p. TR14 in this Teacher's Edition.

Guide students in learning how to self-select books at their independent reading level. As you talk about a book with students, discuss the challenging concepts in it, list new words students find in sampling the book, and ask students about their familiarity with the topic. A blackline master to help students evaluate books for independent reading is provided on p. DI•58.

Self-Selected/Independent Reading

While oral reading allows you to assess students' reading level and fluency, independent reading is of crucial importance to students' futures as readers and learners. Students need to develop their ability to read independently for increasing amounts of time.

- Schedule a regular time for sustained independent reading in your classroom. During the year, gradually increase the amount of time devoted to independent reading.
- Encourage students to track the amount of time they read independently and the number of pages they read in a given amount of time. Tracking will help motivate them to gradually increase their duration and speed. Blackline masters for tracking independent reading are provided on pp. DI•58 and TR15.

Name ______________________________

Choosing a Book for Independent Reading

When choosing a book, story, or article for independent reading, consider these questions:

_____ 1. Do I know something about this topic?

_____ 2. Am I interested in this topic?

_____ 3. Do I like reading this kind of book (fiction, fantasy, biography, or whatever)?

_____ 4. Have I read other things by this author? Do I like this author?

If you say "yes" to at least one of the questions above, continue:

_____ 5. In reading the first page, was only about 1 of every 20 words hard?

If you say "yes," continue:

_____ 6. Does the number of words on a page look about right to me?

If you say "yes," the book or article is probably at the right level for you.

Silent Reading

Record the date, the title of the book or article you read, the amount of time you spent reading, and the number of pages you read during that time.

Date	Title	Minutes	Pages

Taking a Running Record

A running record is an assessment of a student's oral reading accuracy and oral reading fluency. Reading accuracy is based on the number of words read correctly. Reading fluency is based on the reading rate (the number of words correct per minute) and the degree to which a student reads with a "natural flow."

How to Measure Reading Accuracy

1. Choose a grade-level text of about 80 to 120 words that is unfamiliar to the student.
2. Make a copy of the text for yourself. Make a copy for the student or have the student read aloud from a book.
3. Give the student the text and have the student read aloud. (You may wish to record the student's reading for later evaluation.)
4. On your copy of the text, mark any miscues or errors the student makes while reading. See the running record sample on page DI • 60, which shows how to identify and mark miscues.
5. Count the total number of words in the text and the total number of errors made by the student. Note: If a student makes the same error more than once, such as mispronouncing the same word multiple times, count it as one error. Self-corrections do not count as actual errors. Use the following formula to calculate the percentage score, or accuracy rate:

$$\frac{\text{Total Number of Words} - \text{Total Number of Errors}}{\text{Total Number of Words}} \times 100 = \text{percentage score}$$

Interpreting the Results

- A student who reads **95–100%** of the words correctly is reading at an **independent level** and may need more challenging text.
- A student who reads **90–94%** of the words correctly is reading at an **instructional level** and will likely benefit from guided instruction.
- A student who reads **89%** or fewer of the words correctly is reading at a **frustrational level** and may benefit most from targeted instruction with lower-level texts and intervention.

How to Measure Reading Rate (WCPM)

1. Follow Steps 1–3 above.
2. Note the exact times when the student begins and finishes reading.
3. Use the following formula to calculate the number of words correct per minute (WCPM):

$$\frac{\text{Total Number of Words Read Correctly}}{\text{Total Number of Seconds}} \times 60 = \text{words correct per minute}$$

Interpreting the Results

An appropriate reading rate for a fifth-grader is 120–140 (WCPM).

Running Record Sample

Running Record Sample

Did you know that every day in cities across the United States, students like you are helping others?

Each year in Louisiana, a young student and her younger brother have gone around collecting stuffed animals for children who live in a homeless shelter.

In New York City, seventy-six students from Harlem teamed up with four Olympic athletes to transform a run-down park into a playground featuring a daffodil garden.

And each year in Indiana, a young student has gone around collecting hundreds of bundles of baby clothes and other baby items. In the fall she delivers them to a home for mothers who are having tough times.

—From *Using Special Talents*
On-Level Reader 5.2.1

Symbols

Accurate Reading
The student reads a word correctly.

Hesitation
The student hesitates over a word, and the teacher provides the word. Wait several seconds before telling the student what the word is.

Insertion
The student inserts words or parts of words that are not in the text.

Omission
The student omits words or word parts.

Substitution
The student substitutes words or parts of words for the words in the text.

Self-Correction
The student reads a word incorrectly but then corrects the error. Do not count self-corrections as actual errors. However, noting self-corrections will help you identify words the student finds difficult.

Mispronunciation/Misreading
The student pronounces or reads a word incorrectly.

Running Record Results
Total Number of Words: **107**
Number of Errors: **5**

Reading Time: **51 seconds**

Reading Accuracy
$\frac{107 - 5}{107} \times 100 = 95.327 = 95\%$

Accuracy Percentage Score: **95%**

Reading Rate—WCPM
$\frac{102}{51} \times 60 = 120$ = 120 words correct per minute

Reading Rate: **120 WCPM**

Teacher Resources

Table of Contents

TEACHER NOTES

Unit 1	Vocabulary Words		Spelling Words			
Frindle	acquainted assignment essential expanded	guaranteed procedures reputation worshipped	**Short vowel VCCV, VCV** distance method anger problem butter petals	 enjoy perhaps figure channel admire comedy	 husband tissue mustard shuttle advance drummer	 regular denim
Thunder Rose	branded constructed daintily devastation lullaby	pitch resourceful thieving veins	**Long vowel VCV** fever broken climate hotel basic vocal	 native silent labor spider label icon	 agent motive vital acorn item aroma	 legal solo
Island of the Blue Dolphins	gnawed headland kelp lair	ravine shellfish sinew	**Long vowel digraphs** coast feast speech wheat Spain paint	 arrow needle charcoal praise faint maintain	 crease groan breeze willow appeal bowling	 complain sneeze
Satchel Paige	confidence fastball mocking outfield	unique weakness windup	**Adding *-ed, -ing*** supplied supplying denied denying decided deciding	 included including admitted admitting occurred occurring	 qualified qualifying identified identifying delayed delaying	 satisfied satisfying
Shutting Out the Sky	advice advised circumstanc-es elbow hustled	immigrants luxury newcomer peddler	**Contractions** they're you've weren't needn't there'd they've mustn't	 what'll doesn't hadn't could've would've should've might've	 wouldn't who've shouldn't who'd this'll couldn't	

Unit 2	Vocabulary Words	Spelling Words
Inside Out	caterpillar, cocoon, disrespect, emerge, migrant, sketched, unscrewed	**Digraphs *th, sh, ch, ph*** shovel, southern, northern, chapter, hyphen, chosen, establish, although, challenge, approach, astonish, python, shatter, ethnic, shiver, pharmacy, charity, china, attach, ostrich
Passage to Freedom	agreement, cable, diplomat, issue, refugees, representa-tives, superiors, visa	**Irregular plurals** staffs, ourselves, pants, scissors, loaves, volcanoes, chiefs, buffaloes, flamingos, beliefs, echoes, shelves, quizzes, sheriffs, dominoes, thieves, measles, avocados, chefs, pianos
The Ch'i-lin Purse	astonished, behavior, benefactor, distribution, gratitude, procession, recommend, sacred, traditions	**Vowel sounds with *r*** snore, tornado, spare, appear, career, square, report, prepare, pioneer, chair, beware, smear, repair, sword, ignore, order, engineer, resort, volunteer, declare
Jane Goodall's 10 Ways to Help Save Wildlife	conservation, contribute, enthusiastic, environment, investigation	**Final Syllables *-en, -an, -el, -le, -il*** example, level, human, quarrel, scramble, evil, oxygen, wooden, double, travel, cancel, chuckle, fossil, toboggan, veteran, chisel, suburban, single, sudden, beagle
The Midnight Ride of Paul Revere	fate, fearless, glimmer, lingers, magnified, somber, steed	**Final Syllables *-er, -ar, -or*** danger, wander, tractor, dollar, harbor, eager, eraser, surrender, solar, sticker, locker, helicopter, pillar, refrigerator, caterpillar, rumor, glimmer, linger, sensor, alligator

WORD LIST

Unit 3	Vocabulary Words	Spelling Words
Wings for the King	admiringly, permit, scoundrel, subject, worthless	**Schwas** jewel, kingdom, gasoline, factory, garage, tropical, pajamas, estimate, tomorrow, humidity, Chicago, bulletin, carnival, illustrate, elegant, census, terrific, celebrate, operate, celery
Leonardo's Horse	achieved, architect, bronze, cannon, depressed, fashioned, midst, philosopher, rival	**Compound words** waterproof, teaspoon, grasshopper, homesick, barefoot, courthouse, earthquake, rowboat, scrapbook, countryside, lightweight, fishhook, spotlight, blindfold, whirlpool, tablespoon, greenhouse, postcard, humming-bird, thumbtack
The Dinosaurs of Waterhouse Hawkins	erected, foundations, mold, occasion, proportion, tidied, workshop	**Consonant sounds /j/, /ks/, /sk/, and /s/** excuse, scene, muscle, explore, pledge, journal, science, schedule, gigantic, scheme, Japan, excellent, exclaim, fascinate, ginger, scholar, scent, dodge, smudge, schooner
Mahalia Jackson	appreciate, barber, choir, released, religious, slavery, teenager	**One consonant or two** address, college, mirror, recess, committee, collect, Mississippi, immediate, command, appreciate, announce, possess, Tennessee, gallop, opponent, barricade, broccoli, accomplish, allowance, zucchini
Special Effects in Film and Television	background, landscape, miniature, prehistoric, reassembled	**Prefixes *un-, de-, dis*** uncover, defrost, uncomfortable, discourage, disadvantage, unfortunate, unfamiliar, disability, discomfort, deodorant, unemployed, deflate, disbelief, unpredict-able, disapprove, disappoint, unpleasant, dehydrated, disqualify, undecided

Unit 4	Vocabulary Words	Spelling Words
Weslandia	blunders civilization complex envy fleeing inspired rustling strategy	**Words from many cultures** khaki hula banana ballet waltz tomato vanilla canyon yogurt banquet macaroni polka cobra koala barbecue safari buffet stampede karate kiosk
Stretching Ourselves: Kids With Cerebral Palsy	abdomen artificial gait handicapped therapist wheelchair	**Prefixes *over-, under-, sub-, super-, out-*** overlook underline subway subset supermarket outlet underground overboard undercurrent superstar overtime supersonic submarine undercover overcast outfield output supernatural subdivision subhead
Exploding Ants: Amazing Facts About How Animals Adapt	critical enables mucus scarce specialize sterile	**Homophones** cent sent scent threw through weather whether their there they're chili chilly tide tied pale pail aloud allowed course coarse
The Stormi Giovanni Club	cavities combination demonstrates episode profile strict	**Suffixes *-ible, -able*** sensible washable available agreeable fashionable valuable flexible reasonable favorable breakable convertible forgettable laughable sociable allowable divisible hospitable reversible respon-sible tolerable
The Gymnast	bluish cartwheels gymnastics hesitation limelight skidded somersault throbbing wincing	**Negative prefixes** invisible illiterate irregular irresistible impossible informal illegal impatient independent incorrect inactive imperfect impolite immature illogical indefinite imperfect immobile irrespon-sible inexpensive

Unit 5	Vocabulary Words	Spelling Words
The Three-Century Woman	eerie, intersection, pondered, severe, spectacles, withered	**Multisyllabic words**: elementary, vehicle, miniature, probability, definition, substitute, variety, literature, elevator, Pennsylvania, ravioli, cafeteria, mosaic, tuxedo, meteorite, fascination, cylinder, intermediate, centennial, curiosity
The Unsinkable Wreck of the R.M.S. *Titanic*	cramped, debris, interior, ooze, robotic, sediment, sonar	**Unusual spellings**: league, sergeant, yacht, doubt, fatigue, debt, blood, vague, anxious, foreign, bargain, condemn, intrigue, villain, cantaloupe, flood, depot, cordial, subtle, disguise
Talk with an Astronaut	accomplish-ments, focus, gravity, monitors, role, specific	**Greek word parts**: geology, thermometer, astronaut, atmosphere, biology, thermal, disaster, meteorology, technology, hemisphere, zoology, sociology, biosphere, thermos, asterisk, thermostat, astronomy, spherical, ecology, mythology
Journey to the Center of the Earth	armor, encases, extinct, hideous, plunged, serpent	**Latin roots**: project, audience, decade, territory, auditorium, terrier, decimal, injection, December, reject, eject, terrace, audit, decimeter, audition, audible, decathlon, terrarium, dejected, terrain
Ghost Towns of the American West	economic, independence, overrun, scrawled, vacant	**Related words**: politics, political, major, majority, equal, equation, sign, signature, arrive, arrival, inspire, inspiration, human, humanity, clean, cleanse, resign, resignation, unite, unity

Unit 6	Vocabulary Words		Spelling Words			
At the Beach	algae concealed driftwood hammocks	lamented sea urchins sternly tweezers	**Suffixes** ***-ous, -sion, -ion, -ation*** famous invention election furious imagination education	nervous explanation various decision relaxation conversation	tension humorous exhibition attraction invasion creation	occupation destination
The Mystery of Saint Matthew Island	bleached carcasses decay parasites	scrawny starvation suspicions tundra	**Final Syllable** ***-ant, -ent, -ance, -ence*** important experience ignorant entrance difference instance	absence appearance intelligent evidence pollutant clearance	confidence conference insurance ambulance hesitant consistent	excellence persistent
King Midas and the Golden Touch	adorn cleanse lifeless	precious realm spoonful	**Words with** ***ei*** **and** ***ie*** brief believe receive leisure piece relief	seize ceiling field neither apiece receipt	yield deceive achieve grief niece protein	shield conceited
The *Hindenburg*	criticizing cruised drenching	era explosion hydrogen	**Compound words** ice cream a lot keyboard fairy tale horseshoe piggy bank	textbook guidelines newspaper space shut- tle hay fever	dead end password teenager skateboard everything barbed wire	cartwheel root beer fingerprint
Sweet Music in Harlem	bass clarinet fidgety forgetful jammed nighttime secondhand		**Easily confused words** quiet quite finely finally except accept	than then since sense affect effect	from form later latter adapt adopt	medal metal

Grade 4 Vocabulary

Use this list of fourth grade tested vocabulary words for review and leveled activities.

A
aboard
affords
amazed
amphibians
ancestors
ancient
anticipation
appeared
aquarium
astronauts
atlas
aviator
avoided
awkward

B
bargain
bawling
bewildered
biologist
bluff
boarding school
bow
brilliant
brisk
bustling

C
canopy
capable
capsule
cargo
celestial
chant
chorus
cockpit
colonel
conducted
Constitution
continent
convergence
cord
coward
coyote
cradle
crime
crumbled
curiosity

D
dangle
dappled
daring
depart
destruction
dignified
dismay
docks
dolphins
dormitory
draft
drag
dudes
duke
dungeon

E
elegant
enchanted
endurance
escape
etched
exhibit
expected

F
fascinated
favor
flex
flexible
forbidding
forecasts
fouled
fragrant
frost
furiously

G
generations
genius
glacier
gleamed
glider
glimpses
glint
glorious
grand
granite
grizzly

H
hangars
hatch
heaves
homeland
hoop
horizon
howling
humble

I
icebergs
immense
impressive
inland

J
jersey

L
lagoon
lassoed
link
lizard
longed
loomed
lunar
lurking

M
magician
majesty
manual
marveled
massive
mechanical
memorial
migrating
minister
miracle
module
monument

N
naturalist
navigation
noble
numerous

O
offended
outspoken

P
palettes
parlor
payroll
peasant
peculiar
politics
pollen
pollinate
porridge
positive
prairie
preserve
prideful
pulpit
pulses

Q
quaint
quarantine
quivered

R
recalls
reference
reptiles
reseats
resemblance
reservation
responsibility
rille
rim
riverbed
roundup
rudder
ruins
rumbling
runt

S
salamander
scan
scent
scholars
sculptures
seeker
selecting
shatter
shielding
shimmering
shrieked
slithered
slopes
society
solemnly
solo
species
speechless
spurs
staggered
stalled
stern
still
stumped
summoning
surface
surge
swatted

T
taunted
temple
terraced
terror
thickets
timid
torrent
towering
trench
triumph
tropical
trudged

U
unbelievable
uncover

V
vain
vanished
vehicle

W
wharf
wilderness
wondrous

Y
yearned

Grade 6 Vocabulary

Use this list of sixth grade tested vocabulary words for leveled activities.

A
absurd
abundant
access
accustomed
aggressive
aliens
apparently
application
architecture
artifacts
astronomers
authority

B
barge
basin
beacon
behalf
benefits
bondage
burden

C
campaigns
candidate
captive
caravans
characteristic
charities
collapse
collide
combustion
commissioned
compact
companionship
comrades
confidently
conformed
conquer
converts
corridors
corrode
counselor
customary

D
dean
decline
decrees
delirious
democracy
densest
destination
destiny
detect
devise
dingy
diploma
disgraced
dismounted
distressed
dramatic
dubiously

E
earthen
eaves
efficiency
emphasized
empire
encounter
engulfed
enraged
enrich
equator
erosion
eternity
evaporates
existence
expanse
expedition
exploit
exported
extract

F
fixtures
flimsy
flourish
foreigners
formal
former
fragile
frantic
frustration
fulfill

G
galaxy
generated
groping

H
hatchet
hoard
homesteaders
hospitable
hovers

I
ideal
identity
ignite
immortal
imprinted
incident
industrial
insulated
invaders
isolation

L
lance
legacy
leisure
lunging
lush

M
maintenance
manuscripts
materialize
medieval
menacing
migration
misfortune
moisture
molten
momentous
mongrel
mythology

N
navigator
negotiate
nub

O
obedient
observatory
obstacle
opera
ordeal
ore

P
painstaking
particles
patron
percentage
permission
persisted
physical
pleas
poisonous
prejudice
presence
prey
primitive
privileged
proclaimed
progress
promoted
provisions

Q
quests
quill

R
receded
recital
recycled
refrain
registered
reigned
reject
relish
renewed
renowned
repay
reproduce
resound
retreat
revolting
romping
rowdy
rural

S
sanctuaries
secretive
settlement
sluggish
slung
smoldered
specimens
speckled
squire
stiffened
stimulating
stunned
subscribe
sufficient
surplus
survive

T
technology
tolerated
toll
torment
transmitted
traversed
treacherous
treaded
tropics

U
unaccompanied
unison
universal
urban

V
ventured
verify
version
vigorously
volcanic

W
waft
waning
wilt

Legibility

When handwriting is legible, letters, words and numbers can be read easily. Handwriting that is not legible can cause problems for the reader and make communication difficult. Legibility can be improved if students are able to identify what is causing legibility problems in their handwriting. Focus instruction on the following five elements of legible handwriting.

Size

Letters need to be a consistent size. Students should focus on three things related to size: letters that reach to the top line, letters that reach halfway between the top and bottom line, and letters that extend below the bottom line. Writing letters the correct size can improve legibility. Often the letters that sit halfway between the top and bottom line cause the most problems. When students are writing on notebook paper, there is no middle line to help them size letters such as *m, a, i*, and *r* correctly. If students are having trouble, have them draw middle lines on their notebook paper.

Shape

Some of the most common handwriting problems are caused by forming letters incorrectly. These are the most common types of handwriting problems:

- round letters such as *a*, *o*, and *g* are not closed
- looped letters such as *i*, *e*, and *b* have no loops
- letters such as *i*, *t*, and *d* have loops that shouldn't be there

Have students examine one another's writing to indicate which words are hard to read, and then discuss which letters aren't formed correctly. They can then practice those particular letters.

Spacing

Letters within words should be evenly spaced. Too much or too little space can make writing difficult to read. A consistent amount of space should also be used between words in a sentence and between sentences. Suggest that students use the tip of their pencil to check the spacing between words and the width of their pencil to check the spacing between sentences.

Slant

Correct writing slant can be to the right or to the left, or there may be no slant at all. Slant becomes a legibility problem when letters are slanted in different directions. Suggest that students use a ruler to draw lines to determine if their slant is consistent.

Smoothness

Written letters should be produced with a line weight that is not too dark and not too light. The line should be smooth without any shaky or jagged edges. If students' writing is too dark, they are pressing too hard. If the writing is too light, they are not pressing hard enough. Usually shaky or jagged lines occur if students are unsure of how to form letters or if they are trying to draw letters rather than using a flowing motion.

D'Nealian™ Cursive Alphabet

a b c d e f g
h i j k l m n
o p q r s t u
v w x y z

A B C D E F G
H I J K L M N
O P Q R S T U
V W X Y Z . , ' ?

1 2 3 4 5 6
7 8 9 10

D'Nealian™ Alphabet

a b c d e f g h i
j k l m n o p q r s t
u v w x y z

A B C D E F G
H I J K L M N O
P Q R S T U V
W X Y Z . , ' ?

1 2 3 4 5 6
7 8 9 10

Manuscript Alphabet

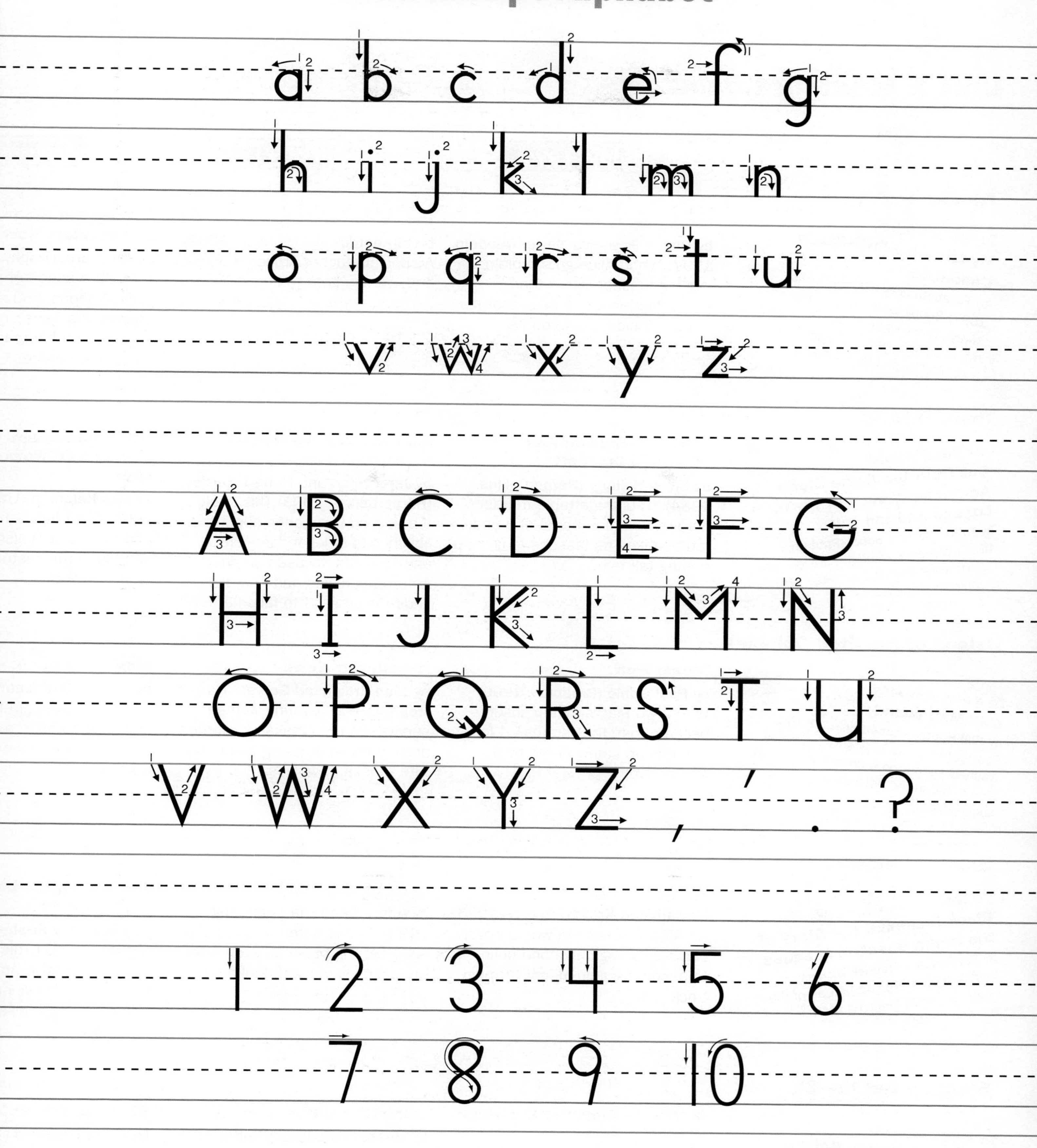

Unit 1 *Meeting Challenges*

	Below-Level	On-Level	Advanced
Frindle *To Read Aloud!* **My Life As a Fifth-Grade Comedian** **by Elizabeth Levy (HarperCollins, 1997)** Bobby learns that a joke isn't always funny when he is faced with the possibility of being transferred to a school for problem children.	**The Agony of Alice** **by Phyllis Reynolds Naylor (Aladdin, 1997)** When Alice gets a plain-looking teacher rather than a glamorous one, she sees that it's "what's inside" that counts.	**The Year of Miss Agnes** **by Kirkpatrick Hill (Aladdin, 2002)** A special teacher arrives in Alaska and, as she gets to know the students, transforms their lives.	**Nothing But the Truth: A Documentary Novel** **by Avi (HarperTrophy, 1993)** Through a series of memos, conversations, and newspaper articles, it's the story of how a boy at odds with his teacher becomes a national debate.
Thunder Rose *To Read Aloud!* **Cut From the Same Cloth: American Women of Myth, Legend and Tall Tale** **by Robert D. San Souci (Putnam, 1993)** Women's strength, bravery, and humor are presented in these geographically arranged tales.	**Sally Ann Thunder Ann Whirlwind Crockett** **by Steve Kellogg (HarperCollins, 1984)** An unforgettable frontier heroine wrestles bears and uses rattlesnakes as lassoes in this rip-roaring tall tale.	**Hippolita and the Curse of the Amazons** **by Jane Yolen and Robert Harris (HarperCollins, 2003)** This book, the second in a series about the childhoods of legendary heroes and heroines, focuses on an Amazon princess and how she finds the courage to face her fears.	**Into a New Country: Eight Remarkable Women of the West** **by Liza Ketchum (Little Brown, 2000)** Eight independent women and their accomplishments are profiled in this history of the American West.
Island of the Blue Dolphins *To Read Aloud!* **Wild Man Island** **by Will Hobbs (HarperCollins, 2002)** Fourteen-year-old Andy survives being washed ashore on a deserted Alaskan island and in the process gains self-knowledge.	**Dream Wolf** **by Paul Goble (Bradbury, 1990)** When two Plains Indian children become lost, they are cared for and guided safely home by a friendly wolf.	**Julie of the Wolves** **by Jean Craighead George (Harper Trophy, 1972)** A young woman survives in the Alaskan wilderness and forms an amazing friendship with a pack of wolves.	**Sing Down the Moon** **by Scott O'Dell (Laurel Leaf, 1997)** A young Navajo girl faces many challenges and is eventually forced onto a reservation with her tribe.
Satchel Paige *To Read Aloud!* **Black Diamond: The Story of the Negro Baseball Leagues** **by Patricia and Fredrick McKissack (Scholastic, 1998)** The heroes of the Negro Baseball Leagues are honored in this fine history.	**Wilma Unlimited** **by Kathleen Krull (Harcourt, 1996)** An African American woman overcame crippling childhood polio to become a gold-medal Olympic track star.	**Hang Tough, Paul Mather** **by Alfred Slote (HarperTrophy, 1993)** Paul is determined to continue playing baseball even after he is diagnosed with leukemia.	**Jim Thorpe, The Legend Remembered** **by Rosemary Kissinger Updyke (Pelican, 1997)** This book tells about the Native American Olympic-medal winner known as one of the best all-around athletes in history.
Shutting Out the Sky *To Read Aloud!* **Hope in My Heart: Sofia's Immigrant Diary** **by Kathryn Lasky (Turtleback Books, 2003)** Through diary entries, nine-year-old Sofia tells the story of her family leaving Italy in 1903 and their new life in America.	**Coming to America: The Story of Immigration** **by Betsy Maestro (Scholastic, 1996)** This picture book tells how some immigrant groups have faced challenges and contributed to American culture.	**Immigrant Kids** **by Russell Freedman (Puffin, 1995)** The lives of young urban immigrants at home, school, work, and play at the turn of the century are explored though photos and personal recollections.	**97 Orchard Street, New York** **by Linda Granfield (Tundra, 2001)** In text and with archival photos, this book tells the story of four immigrant families, including details of everyday life, their joys, and their struggles.

See also *Assessment Handbook*, p. 119

Unit 1 Reading Log

Name ____________________

Dates Read	Title and Author	What is it about?	How would you rate it?	Explain your rating.
From ________ to ________			Great 5 4 3 2 1 Awful	
From ________ to ________			Great 5 4 3 2 1 Awful	
From ________ to ________			Great 5 4 3 2 1 Awful	
From ________ to ________			Great 5 4 3 2 1 Awful	
From ________ to ________			Great 5 4 3 2 1 Awful	

See also *Assessment Handbook*, p. 111

Unit 1 Narrative Retelling Chart

Selection Title ____________________ **Name** ____________________ **Date** __________

Retelling Criteria/Teacher Prompt	**Teacher-Aided Response**	**Student-Generated Response**	**Rubric Score** (Circle one.)
Connections Has anything like this happened to you? How does this story remind you of other stories?			4 3 2 1
Author's Purpose Why do you think the author wrote this story? What was the author trying to tell us?			4 3 2 1
Characters Describe ________ (character's name) at the beginning and end of the story.			4 3 2 1
Setting Where and when did the story happen?			4 3 2 1
Plot Tell me what the story was about in a few sentences.			4 3 2 1

Summative Retelling Score 4 3 2 1

Comments ____________________

See also *Assessment Handbook*, p. 112

Unit 1 Expository Retelling Chart

Selection Title ________________________ **Name** ____________________ **Date** ________

Retelling Criteria/Teacher Prompt	**Teacher-Aided Response**	**Student-Generated Response**	**Rubric Score** (Circle one.)
Connections Did this selection make you think about something else you have read? What did you learn about as you read this selection?			4 3 2 1
Author's Purpose Why do you think the author wrote this selection?			4 3 2 1
Topic What was the selection mostly about?			4 3 2 1
Important Ideas What is important for me to know about ________ (topic)?			4 3 2 1
Conclusions What did you learn from reading this selection?			4 3 2 1

Summative Retelling Score 4 3 2 1

Comments ____

____

____

Reading

Concepts of Print and Print Awareness	Pre-K	K	1	2	3	4	5	6
Develop awareness that print represents spoken language and conveys and preserves meaning	•	•	•					
Recognize familiar books by their covers; hold book right side up	•	•						
Identify parts of a book and their functions (front cover, title page/title, back cover, page numbers)	•	•	•					
Understand the concepts of letter, word, sentence, paragraph, and story	•	•	•					
Track print (front to back of book, top to bottom of page, left to right on line, sweep back left for next line)	•	•	•					
Match spoken to printed words	•	•	•					
Know capital and lowercase letter names and match them	•	• T	•					
Know the order of the alphabet	•	•	•					
Recognize first name in print	•	•	•					
Recognize the uses of capitalization and punctuation		•	•					
Value print as a means of gaining information	•	•	•					

Phonological and Phonemic Awareness	Pre-K	K	1	2	3	4	5	6
Phonological Awareness								
Recognize and produce rhyming words	•	•	•					
Track and count each word in a spoken sentence and each syllable in a spoken word	•	•	•					
Segment and blend syllables in spoken words			•					
Segment and blend onset and rime in one-syllable words		•	•					
Recognize and produce words beginning with the same sound	•	•	•					
Identify beginning, middle, and/or ending sounds that are the same or different	•	•	•					
Understand that spoken words are made of sequences of sounds	•	•	•					
Phonemic Awareness								
Identify the position of sounds in words		•	•					
Identify and isolate initial, final, and medial sounds in spoken words	•	•	•					
Blend sounds orally to make words or syllables		•	•					
Segment a word or syllable into sounds; count phonemes in spoken words or syllables		•	•					
Manipulate sounds in words (add, delete, and/or substitute phonemes)	•	•	•					

Phonics and Decoding	Pre-K	K	1	2	3	4	5	6
Phonics								
Understand and apply the ***alphabetic principle*** that spoken words are composed of sounds that are represented by letters	•	•	•					
Know letter-sound relationships	•	• T	• T	• T				
Blend sounds of letters to decode		•	• T	• T	• T			
Consonants, consonant blends, and consonant digraphs		•	• T	• T	• T			
Short, long, and r-controlled vowels; vowel digraphs; diphthongs; common vowel patterns			• T	• T	• T			
Phonograms/word families		•	•	•	•			
Word Structure								
Decode words with common word parts		•	• T	• T	• T	•	•	•
Base words and inflected endings			• T	• T	•	•	•	•
Contractions and compound words			• T	• T	• T	•	•	•
Suffixes and prefixes			• T	• T	• T	•	•	•
Greek and Latin roots						•	•	•
Blend syllables to decode words			• T	• T	• T	•	•	•
Decoding Strategies								
Blending strategy: Apply knowledge of letter-sound relationships to decode unfamiliar words		•	•	•	•			
Apply knowledge of word structure to decode unfamiliar words		•	•	•	•	•	•	•
Use context and syntax along with letter-sound relationships and word structure to decode		•	•	•	•	•	•	•
Self-correct			•	•	•	•	•	•

Fluency	Pre-K	K	1	2	3	4	5	6
Read aloud fluently with accuracy, comprehension, appropriate pace/rate; with expression/intonation (prosody); with attention to punctuation and appropriate phrasing			• T	• T	• T	• T	• T	• T
Practice fluency in a variety of ways, including choral reading, partner/paired reading, Readers' Theater, repeated oral reading, and tape-assisted reading		•	•	•	•	•	•	•

• instructional opportunity   **T** tested in standardized test forr

ork toward appropriate fluency goals by the end of each grade			• T	• T	• T	• T	• T	• T
ad regularly in independent-level material			•	•	•	•	•	•
ad silently for increasing periods of time			•	•	•	•	•	•

ocabulary (Oral and Written)	**Pre-K**	**K**	**1**	**2**	**3**	**4**	**5**	**6**
ord Recognition								
cognize regular and irregular high-frequency words	•	•	• T	• T				
cognize and understand selection vocabulary		•	•	• T	•	•	•	•
derstand content-area vocabulary and specialized, technical, or topical words			•	•	•	•	•	•
ord Learning Strategies								
velop vocabulary through direct instruction, concrete experiences, reading, listening to text read aloud	•	•	•	•	•	•	•	•
e knowledge of word structure to figure out meanings of words			•	• T	• T	• T	• T	• T
e context clues for meanings of unfamiliar words, multiple-meaning words, homonyms, homographs			•	• T	• T	• T	• T	• T
e grade-appropriate reference sources to learn word meanings	•	•	•	•	• T	• T	• T	• T
e picture clues to help determine word meanings	•	•	•	•	•			
e new words in a variety of contexts	•	•	•	•	•	•	•	•
amine word usage and effectiveness		•	•	•	•	•	•	•
eate and use graphic organizers to group, study, and retain vocabulary			•	•	•	•	•	•
xtend Concepts and Word Knowledge								
ademic language	•	•	•	•	•	•	•	•
assify and categorize	•	•	•	•	•	•	•	•
tonyms and synonyms			•	• T	• T	• T	• T	• T
mographs, homonyms, and homophones				•	• T	• T	• T	• T
ultiple-meaning words			•	•	• T	• T	• T	• T
lated words and derivations					•	•	•	•
alogies					•		•	
nnotation/denotation						•	•	•
gurative language and idioms			•	•	•	•	•	•
escriptive words (location, size, color, shape, number, ideas, feelings)	•	•	•	•	•	•	•	•
gh-utility words (shapes, colors, question words, position/directional words, and so on)	•	•	•	•				
ne and order words	•	•	•	•	•	•	•	•
ansition words						•	•	•
ord origins: Etymologies/word histories; words from other languages, regions, or cultures					•	•	•	•
ortened forms: abbreviations, acronyms, clipped words			•	•	•	•	• T	

ext Comprehension	**Pre-K**	**K**	**1**	**2**	**3**	**4**	**5**	**6**
omprehension Strategies								
eview the text and formulate questions	•	•	•	•	•	•	•	•
et and monitor purpose for reading and listening	•	•	•	•	•	•	•	•
tivate and use prior knowledge	•	•	•	•	•	•	•	•
ake predictions	•	•	•	•	•	•	•	•
onitor comprehension and use fix-up strategies to resolve difficulties in meaning: adjust reading rate, read and read on, seek help from reference sources and/or other people, skim and scan, summarize, e text features			•	•	•	•	•	•
eate and use graphic and semantic organizers		•	•	•	•	•	•	•
swer questions (text explicit, text implicit, scriptal), including *who, what, when, where, why, what if, how*	•	•	•	•	•	•	•	•
Look back in text for answers			•	•	•	•	•	•
Answer test-like questions			•	•	•	•	•	•
enerate clarifying questions, including *who, what, where, when, how, why,* and *what if*	•	•	•	•	•	•	•	•
ecognize text structure: story and informational (cause/effect, chronological, compare/contrast, scription, problem/solution, propostion/support)	•	•	•	•	•	•	•	•
ummarize text		•	•	•	•	•	•	•
Recall and retell stories	•	•	•	•	•	•	•	•
Identify and retell important/main ideas (nonfiction)	•	•	•	•	•	•	•	•
Identify and retell new information			•	•	•	•	•	•
sualize; use mental imagery		•	•	•	•	•	•	•
se strategies flexibly and in combination			•	•	•	•	•	•

Comprehension Skills								
Author's purpose			• T	• T	• T	• T	• T	• T
Author's viewpoint/bias/perspective					•	•	•	• T
Categorize and classify	•	•	•	•				
Cause and effect		•	• T	• T	• T	• T	• T	• T
Compare and contrast		•	• T	• T	• T	• T	• T	• T
Details and facts		•	•	•	•	•	•	•
Draw conclusions		•	• T	• T	• T	• T	• T	• T
Fact and opinion				• T	• T	• T	• T	• T
Follow directions/steps in a process	•	•	•	•	•	•	•	•
Generalize					• T	• T	• T	• T
Graphic sources		•	•	•	•	• T	• T	• T
Main idea and supporting details		• T	• T	• T	• T	• T	• T	• T
Paraphrase			•	•	•	•	•	•
Persuasive devices and propaganda				•	•	•	•	•
Realism/fantasy		•	• T	• T	• T	•	•	•
Sequence of events		• T	• T	• T	• T	• T	• T	• T
Higher Order Thinking Skills								
Analyze				•	•	•	•	•
Describe and connect the essential ideas, arguments, and perspectives of a text			•	•	•	•	•	•
Draw inferences, conclusions, or generalizations, support them with textual evidence and prior knowledge		•	•	•	•	•	•	•
Evaluate and critique ideas and text			•	•	•	•	•	•
Hypothesize						•	•	•
Make judgments about ideas and text			•	•	•	•	•	•
Organize and synthesize ideas and information			•			•	•	•

Literary Analysis, Response, & Appreciation	Pre-K	K	1	2	3	4	5	6
Genre and Its Characteristics								
Recognize characteristics of a variety of genre	•	•	•	•	•	•	•	•
Distinguish fiction from nonfiction		•	•	•	•	•	•	•
Identify characteristics of literary texts, including drama, fantasy, traditional tales		•	•	•	•	•	•	•
Identify characteristics of nonfiction texts, including biography, interviews, newspaper articles		•	•	•	•	•	•	•
Identify characteristics of poetry and song, including nursery rhymes, limericks, blank verse	•	•	•	•	•	•	•	•
Literary Elements and Story Structure								
Character	•	• T	• T	• T	• T	• T	• T	•
Recognize and describe traits, actions, feelings, and motives of characters		•	•	•	•	•	•	•
Analyze characters' relationships, changes, and points of view		•	•	•	•	•	•	•
Analyze characters' conflicts				•		•	•	•
Plot and plot structure	•	• T	• T	• T	• T	• T	• T	•
Beginning, middle, end	•	•	•	•	•			
Goal and outcome or problem and solution/resolution		•	•	•	•	•	•	•
Rising action, climax, and falling action/denouement; setbacks						•	•	•
Setting	•	• T	• T	• T	• T	• T	•	•
Relate setting to problem/solution						•	•	•
Explain ways setting contributes to mood						•	•	•
Theme		•	• T	• T	•	•	•	•
Use Literary Elements and Story Structure	•	•	•	•	•	•	•	•
Analyze and evaluate author's use of setting, plot, character				•	•	•	•	•
Identify similarities and differences of characters, events, and settings within or across selections/cultures		•	•	•	•	•	•	•
Literary Devices								
Allusion								•
Dialect						•	•	•
Dialogue and narration	•	•	•	•	•	•	•	•
Exaggeration/hyperbole					•	•	•	•
Figurative language: idiom, jargon, metaphor, simile, slang			•	•	•	•	•	•

• instructional opportunity   **T** tested in standardized test for

shback						•	•	•
eshadowing							•	•
mal and informal language				•	•	•	•	•
nor					•	•	•	•
gery and sensory words			•	•	•	•	•	•
od				•	•		•	•
sonification				•	•	•	•	•
nt of view (first person, third person, omniscient)					•	•	•	•
s and word play				•	•	•	•	•
nd devices and poetic elements	•	•	•	•	•	•	•	•
literation, assonance, onomatopoeia	•	•	•	•	•	•	•	•
hyme, rhythm, repetition, and cadence	•	•	•	•	•	•	•	•
ord choice				•	•	•	•	•
nbolism				•	•	•	•	•
e							•	•
thor's and Illustrator's Craft								
tinguish the roles of author and illustrator		•	•	•				
ognize/analyze author's and illustrator's craft or style			•	•	•	•	•	•
erary Response								
ollect, talk, and write about books	•	•	•	•	•	•	•	•
ect on reading and respond (through talk, movement, art, and so on)	•	•	•	•	•	•	•	•
sk and answer questions about text	•	•	•	•	•	•	•	•
rite about what is read	•	•	•	•	•	•	•	•
se evidence from the text to support opinions, interpretations, or conclusions		•	•	•	•	•	•	•
upport ideas through reference to other texts and personal knowledge				•	•	•	•	•
ocate materials on related topic, theme, or idea				•	•	•	•	•
enerate alternative endings to plots and identify the reason for, and the impact of, the alternatives	•	•	•	•	•	•	•	•
thesize and extend the literary experience through creative responses	•	•	•	•	•	•	•	•
ke connections: text to self, text to text, text to world	•	•	•	•	•	•	•	•
uate and critique the quality of the literary experience				•	•	•	•	•
er observations, react, speculate in response to text				•	•	•	•	•
erary Appreciation/Motivation								
w an interest in books and reading; engage voluntarily in social interaction about books	•	•	•	•	•	•	•	•
ose text by drawing on personal interests, relying on knowledge of authors and genres, estimating text culty, and using recommendations of others	•	•	•	•	•	•	•	•
d a variety of grade-level appropriate narrative and expository texts		•	•	•	•	•	•	•
d from a wide variety of genres for a variety of purposes	•	•	•	•	•	•	•	•
d independently			•	•	•	•	•	•
ablish familiarity with a topic			•	•	•	•	•	•
tural Awareness								
elop attitudes and abilities to interact with diverse groups and cultures	•	•	•	•	•	•	•	•
nect experiences and ideas with those from a variety of languages, cultures, customs, perspectives	•	•	•	•	•	•	•	•
erstand how attitudes and values in a culture or during a period in time affect the writing from that ure or time period						•	•	•
npare language and oral traditions (family stories) that reflect customs, regions, and cultures		•	•	•	•	•	•	•
ognize themes that cross cultures and bind them together in their common humanness						•	•	•

nguage Arts

riting	**Pre-K**	**K**	**1**	**2**	**3**	**4**	**5**	**6**
ncepts of Print for Writing								
elop gross and fine motor skills and hand/eye coordination	•	•	•					
t own name and other important words	•	•	•					
te using pictures, some letters, and transitional spelling to convey meaning	•	•	•					
tate messages or stories for others to write	•	•	•					

Create own written texts for others to read; write left to right on a line and top to bottom on a page	•	•	•					
Participate in shared and interactive writing	•	•	•					
Traits of Writing								
Focus/Ideas								
Maintain focus and sharpen ideas		•	•	•	•	•	•	•
Use sensory details and concrete examples; elaborate		•	•	•	•	•	•	•
Delete extraneous information			•	•	•	•	•	•
Rearrange words and sentences to improve meaning and focus				•	•	•	•	•
Use strategies, such as tone, style, consistent point of view, to achieve a sense of completeness						•	•	•
Organization/Paragraphs								
Use graphic organizers to group ideas		•	•	•	•	•	•	•
Write coherent paragraphs that develop a central idea			•	•	•	•	•	•
Use transitions to connect sentences and paragraphs			•	•	•	•	•	•
Select an organizational structure based on purpose, audience, length						•	•	•
Organize ideas in a logical progression, such as chronological order or by order of importance		•	•	•	•	•	•	•
Write introductory, supporting, and concluding paragraphs					•	•	•	•
Write a multi-paragraph paper				•	•	•	•	•
Voice								
Develop personal, identifiable voice and an individual tone/style			•	•	•	•	•	•
Maintain consistent voice and point of view						•	•	•
Use voice appropriate to audience, message, and purpose						•	•	•
Word Choice								
Use clear, precise, appropriate language		•	•	•	•	•	•	•
Use figurative language and vivid words				•	•	•	•	•
Select effective vocabulary using word walls, dictionary, or thesaurus		•	•	•	•	•	•	•
Sentences								
Combine, elaborate, and vary sentences		•	•	•	•	•	•	•
Write topic sentence, supporting sentences with facts and details, and concluding sentence			•	•	•	•	•	•
Use correct word order				•	•	•	•	•
Use parallel structure in a sentence							•	•
Conventions								
Use correct spelling and grammar; capitalize and punctuate correctly		•	•	•	•	•	•	•
Correct sentence fragments and run-ons					•	•	•	•
Use correct paragraph indention				•	•	•	•	•
The Writing Process								
Prewrite using various strategies	•	•	•	•	•	•	•	•
Develop first drafts of single- and multiple-paragraph compositions		•	•	•	•	•	•	•
Revise drafts for varied purposes, including to clarify and to achieve purpose, sense of audience, precise word choice, vivid images, and elaboration		•	•	•	•	•	•	•
Edit and proofread for correct spelling, grammar, usage, and mechanics		•	•	•	•	•	•	•
Publish own work	•	•	•	•	•	•	•	•
Types of Writing								
Narrative writing (such as personal narratives, stories, biographies, autobiographies)	•	•	• T	• T	• T	• T	• T	• T
Expository writing (such as essays, directions, explanations, news stories, research reports, summaries)		•	• T	• T	• T	• T	• T	• T
Descriptive writing (such as labels, captions, lists, plays, poems, response logs, songs)	•	•	• T	• T	• T	• T	• T	• T
Persuasive writing (such as ads, editorials, essays, letters to the editor, opinions, posters)		•	• T	• T	• T	• T	• T	• T
Writing Habits and Practices								
Write on a daily basis	•	•	•	•	•	•	•	•
Use writing as a tool for learning and self-discovery				•	•	•	•	•
Write independently for extended periods of time			•	•	•	•	•	•

ENGLISH LANGUAGE CONVENTIONS in WRITING and SPEAKING	**Pre-K**	**K**	**1**	**2**	**3**	**4**	**5**	**6**
Grammar and Usage in Speaking and Writing								
Sentences								
Types (declarative, interrogative, exclamatory, imperative)	•	•	• T	• T	• T	• T	• T	• T
Structure (simple, compound, complex, compound-complex)	•	•	•	•	•	• T	• T	• T

• instructional opportunity **T** tested in standardized test form

Parts (subjects/predicates: complete, simple, compound; phrases; clauses)				• T	•	• T	• T	• T
Fragments and run-on sentences		•	•	•	•	•	•	•
Combine sentences, elaborate			•	•	•	•	•	•
rts of speech: nouns, verbs and verb tenses, adjectives, adverbs, pronouns and antecedents, njunctions, prepositions, interjections		•	• T	• T	• T	• T	• T	• T
age								
Subject-verb agreement		•	• T	•	•	• T	• T	• T
Pronoun agreement/referents			• T	•	•	• T	• T	• T
Misplaced modifiers						•	• T	• T
Misused words					•	•	•	• T
Negatives; avoid double negatives					•	•	•	•
echanics in Writing								
pitalization (first word in sentence, proper nouns and adjectives, pronoun *I*, titles, and so on)	•	•	• T	• T	• T	• T	• T	• T
nctuation (apostrophe, comma, period, question mark, exclamation mark, quotation marks, and so on)		•	• T	• T	• T	• T	• T	• T

pelling	**Pre-K**	**K**	**1**	**2**	**3**	**4**	**5**	**6**
ell independently by using pre-phonetic knowledge, knowledge of letter names, sound-letter knowledge	•	•	•	•	•	•	•	•
e sound-letter knowledge to spell	•	•	•	•	•	•	•	•
Consonants: single, double, blends, digraphs, silent letters, and unusual consonant spellings		•	•	•	•	•	•	•
Vowels: short, long, *r*-controlled, digraphs, diphthongs, less common vowel patterns, schwa		•	•	•	•	•	•	•
e knowledge of word structure to spell			•	•	•	•	•	•
Base words and affixes (inflections, prefixes, suffixes), possessives, contractions and compound words			•	•	•	•	•	•
Greek and Latin roots, syllable patterns, multisyllabic words			•	•	•	•	•	•
ell high-frequency, irregular words		•	•	•	•	•	•	•
ell frequently misspelled words correctly, including homophones or homonyms			•	•	•	•	•	•
e meaning relationships to spell					•	•	•	•

andwriting	**Pre-K**	**K**	**1**	**2**	**3**	**4**	**5**	**6**
ain increasing control of penmanship, including pencil grip, paper position, posture, stroke	•	•	•	•				
ite legibly, with control over letter size and form; letter slant; and letter, word, and sentence spacing		•	•	•	•	•	•	•
ite lowercase and capital letters	•	•	•	•				
Manuscript	•	•	•	•	•	•	•	•
Cursive				•	•	•	•	•
ite numerals	•	•	•					

istening and Speaking	**Pre-K**	**K**	**1**	**2**	**3**	**4**	**5**	**6**
stening Skills and Strategies								
sten to a variety of presentations attentively and politely	•	•	•	•	•	•	•	•
elf-monitor comprehension while listening, using a variety of skills and strategies	•	•	•	•	•	•	•	•
sten for a purpose								
For enjoyment and appreciation	•	•	•	•	•	•	•	•
To expand vocabulary and concepts	•	•	•	•	•	•	•	•
To obtain information and ideas	•	•	•	•	•	•	•	•
To follow oral directions	•	•	•	•	•	•	•	•
To answer questions and solve problems	•	•	•	•	•	•	•	•
To participate in group discussions	•	•	•	•	•	•	•	•
To identify and analyze the musical elements of literary language	•	•	•	•	•	•	•	•
To gain knowledge of one's own culture, the culture of others, and the common elements of cultures	•	•	•	•	•	•	•	•
ecognize formal and informal language			•	•	•	•	•	•
sten critically to distinguish fact from opinion and to analyze and evaluate ideas, information, experiences		•		•	•	•	•	•
aluate a speaker's delivery				•	•	•	•	•
terpret a speaker's purpose, perspective, persuasive techniques, verbal and nonverbal messages, and e of rhetorical devices					•	•	•	•
peaking Skills and Strategies								
eak clearly, accurately, and fluently, using appropriate delivery for a variety of audiences, and purposes	•	•	•	•	•	•	•	•
e proper intonation, volume, pitch, modulation, and phrasing		•	•	•	•	•	•	•
eak with a command of standard English conventions	•	•	•	•	•	•	•	•
e appropriate language for formal and informal settings	•	•	•	•	•	•	•	•

Speak for a purpose								
To ask and answer questions	•	•	•	•	•	•	•	•
To give directions and instructions	•	•	•	•	•	•	•	•
To retell, paraphrase, or explain information		•	•	•	•	•	•	•
To communicate needs and share ideas and experiences	•	•	•	•	•	•	•	•
To participate in conversations and discussions	•	•	•	•	•	•	•	•
To express an opinion	•	•	•	•	•	•	•	•
To deliver dramatic recitations, interpretations, or performances	•	•	•	•	•	•	•	•
To deliver presentations or oral reports (narrative, descriptive, persuasive, and informational)	•	•	•	•	•	•	•	•
Stay on topic	•	•	•	•	•	•		•
Use appropriate verbal and nonverbal elements (such as facial expression, gestures, eye contact, posture)	•	•	•	•	•	•	•	•
Identify and/or demonstrate methods to manage or overcome communication anxiety						•	•	•

Viewing/Media	Pre-K	K	1	2	3	4	5	6
Interact with and respond to a variety of print and non-print media for a range of purposes	•	•	•	•	•	•	•	•
Compare and contrast print, visual, and electronic media					•	•	•	•
Analyze and evaluate media			•	•	•	•	•	•
Recognize purpose, bias, propaganda, and persuasive techniques in media messages			•	•	•	•	•	•

Research and Study Skills

Understand and Use Graphic Sources	Pre-K	K	1	2	3	4	5	6
Advertisement			•	•	•	•	•	•
Chart/table	•	•	•	•	•	•	•	•
Diagram/scale drawing			•	•	•	•	•	•
Graph (bar, circle, line, picture)		•	•	•	•	•	•	•
Illustration, photograph, caption, label	•	•	•	•	•	•	•	•
Map/globe	•	•	•	•	•	•	•	•
Order form/application						•	•	•
Poster/announcement	•	•	•	•	•	•	•	
Schedule						•	•	•
Sign	•	•	•	•		•		
Time line				•	•	•	•	•

Understand and Use Reference Sources	Pre-K	K	1	2	3	4	5	6
Know and use parts of a book to locate information	•	•	•	•	•	•	•	•
Use alphabetical order			•	•	•	•		
Understand purpose, structure, and organization of reference sources (print, electronic, media, Internet)	•	•	•	•	•	•	•	•
Almanac						•	•	•
Atlas		•		•	•	•	•	•
Card catalog/library database				•	•	•	•	•
Dictionary/glossary		•	•	•	• T	• T	• T	• T
Encyclopedia			•	•	•	•	•	•
Magazine/periodical				•	•	•	•	•
Newspaper and Newsletter			•	•	•	•	•	•
Readers' Guide to Periodical Literature						•	•	•
Technology (computer and non-computer electronic media)		•	•	•	•	•	•	•
Thesaurus				•	•	•	•	•

Study Skills and Strategies	Pre-K	K	1	2	3	4	5	6
Adjust reading rate			•	•	•	•	•	•
Clarify directions	•	•	•	•	•	•	•	•
Outline				•	•	•	•	•
Skim and scan			•	•	•	•	•	•
SQP3R						•	•	•
Summarize		•	•	•	•	•	•	•
Take notes, paraphrase, and synthesize			•	•	•	•	•	•
Use graphic and semantic organizers to organize information		•	•	•	•	•	•	•

• instructional opportunity **T** tested in standardized test for

est-Taking Skills and Strategies	Pre-K	K	1	2	3	4	5	6
derstand the question, the vocabulary of tests, and key words			•	•	•	•	•	•
swer the question; use information from the text (stated or inferred)		•	•	•	•	•	•	•
ite across texts				•	•	•	•	•
mplete the sentence				•	•	•	•	•

echnology/New Literacies	Pre-K	K	1	2	3	4	5	6
on-Computer Electronic Media								
dio tapes/CDs, video tapes/DVDs	•	•	•	•	•	•	•	
n, television, and radio		•	•	•	•	•	•	•
mputer Programs and Services: Basic Operations and Concepts								
e accurate computer terminology	•	•	•	•	•	•	•	•
eate, name, locate, open, save, delete, and organize files		•	•	•	•	•	•	•
e input and output devices (such as mouse, keyboard, monitor, printer, touch screen)	•	•	•	•	•	•	•	•
e basic keyboarding skills		•	•	•	•	•	•	•
sponsible Use of Technology Systems and Software								
rk cooperatively and collaboratively with others; follow acceptable use policies	•	•	•	•	•	•	•	•
cognize hazards of Internet searches			•	•	•	•	•	•
spect intellectual property					•	•	•	•
formation and Communication Technologies: Information Acquisition								
e electronic web (non-linear) navigation, online resources, databases, keyword searches			•	•	•	•	•	•
e visual and non-textual features of online resources	•	•	•	•	•	•	•	•
ernet inquiry			•	•	•	•	•	•
dentify questions			•	•	•	•	•	•
ocate, select, and collect information			•	•	•	•	•	•
nalyze information			•	•	•	•	•	•
Evaluate electronic information sources for accuracy, relevance, bias				•	•	•	•	•
Understand bias/subjectivity of electronic content (about this site, author search, date created)					•	•	•	•
ynthesize information					•	•	•	•
ommunicate findings				•	•	•	•	•
e fix-up strategies (such as clicking *Back, Forward,* or *Undo;* redoing a search; trimming the URL)			•	•	•	•	•	•
mmunication								
llaborate, publish, present, and interact with others		•	•	•	•	•	•	•
e online resources (e-mail, bulletin boards, newsgroups)			•	•	•	•	•	•
e a variety of multimedia formats			•	•	•	•	•	•
oblem Solving								
lect the appropriate software for the task	•	•	•	•	•	•	•	•
e technology resources for solving problems and making informed decisions			•	•	•	•	•	•
termine when technology is useful				•	•	•	•	•

e Research Process	Pre-K	K	1	2	3	4	5	6
oose and narrow the topic; frame and revise questions for inquiry		•	•	•	•	•	•	•
oose and evaluate appropriate reference sources			•	•	•	•	•	•
cate and collect information	•	•	•	•	•	•	•	•
ke notes/record findings				•	•	•	•	•
mbine and compare information				•	•	•	•	•
aluate, interpret, and draw conclusions about key information		•	•	•	•	•	•	•
mmarize information		•	•	•	•	•	•	•
ake an outline				•	•	•	•	•
ganize content systematically		•	•	•	•	•	•	•
mmunicate information		•	•	•	•	•	•	•
Write and present a report			•	•	•	•	•	•
Include citations						•	•	•
Respect intellectual property/plagiarism						•	•	•
Select and organize visual aids		•	•	•	•	•	•	•

A

G

H

I

J

K

L

S

T

Teacher's Edition

Text

KWL Strategy: The KWL Interactive Reading Strategy was developed and is used by permission of Donna Ogle, National-Louis University, Evanston, Illinois, co-author of *Reading Today and Tomorrow*, Holt, Rinehart & Winston Publishers, 1988. (See also *The Reading Teacher*, February 1986, pp. 564–570.)

Page 18m: From *Understood Betsy* by Dorothy Canfield Fisher. Copyright 1916, 1917, 1944, 1945 by Meredith Corporation. Reprinted by permission of Henry Holt and Company, LLC.

Page 42m: From *Night of the Twisters* by Ivy Ruckman. Copyright © 1984 by Ivy Ruckman. Used by permission of HarperCollins Publishers.

Page 68m: From *The Sign of the Beaver* by Elizabeth George Speare. Copyright © 1983 by Elizabeth George Speare. Reprinted by permission of Houghton Mifflin Company. All rights reserved.

Page 90m: From *Teammates* by Peter Golenbock. Copyright © 1990 by Golenbock Communications. Reprinted by permission of Harcourt, Inc.

Page 112m: From "The Final Hurdle," *Journey to Ellis Island* by Carol Bierman. Text © 1998 by Carol Bierman. Jacket, Design, and Compilation © 1998. The Madison Press Limited. A Hyperion/ Madison Press Book. Reprinted by permission of Harcourt, Inc.

Artists

Greg Newbold: cover, page i

Photographs

Every effort has been made to secure permission and provide appropriate credit for photographic marerial. The publisher deeply regrets any omission and pledges to correct errors called to its attention in subsequent editions.

Unless otherwise acknowledged, all photographs are the property of Scott Foresman, a division of Pearson Education.

Photo locators denoted as follows: Top (T), Center (C), Bottom (B), Left (L), Right (R), Background (Bkgd)

42M Getty Images; 111L Brand X Pictures/Getty Images; 160J Digital Wisdom, Inc.; 228I Getty Images; 288M Getty Images; 315L Getty Images; 316M Getty Images; 388K Brand X Pictures; 392M Getty Images; 412M (T) © Comstock Inc. (Bkgd) GettyImages; 436M ©Dover Publications; 457L Getty Images; 476K Getty Images; 484M ©Image Source Limited; 512M Getty Images; 535L ©Royalty-Free/Corbis; 536M Hemera Technologies; 560M Getty Images; 634M Brand X Pictures; 654M Getty Images; 674M ©Dover Publications; 762M Brand X Pictures

TEACHER NOTES

TEACHER NOTES

TEACHER NOTES

TEACHER NOTES

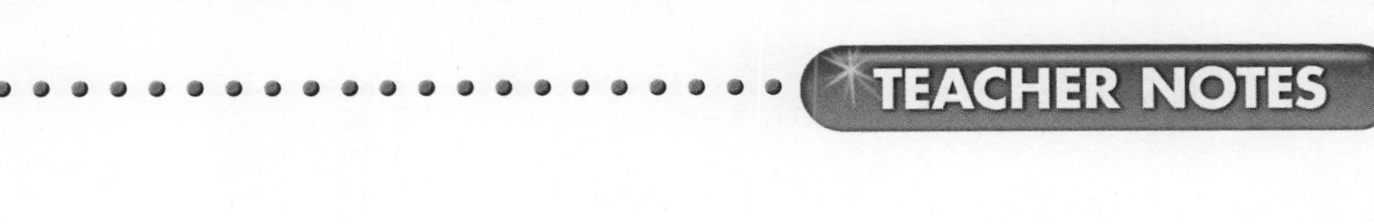
TEACHER NOTES